A COMPANION TO RELIGIOUS STUDIES AND THEOLOGY

Edited by
Helen K. Bond,
Seth Kunin
and
Francesca Aran Murphy

EDINBURGH UNIVERSITY PRESS

This book is dedicated to the memory of
Professor James Thrower, who taught
Religious Studies at Aberdeen University
from 1969 until his death in 1999.

'A good man is hard to find'
(FLANNERY O'CONNOR)

Editorial material and organisation © Helen K. Bond, Seth D. Kunin and Francesca Aran Murphy, 2003. Copyright in the chapters is retained by the individual contributors.

Edinburgh University Press Ltd
22 George Square, Edinburgh

Typeset in Sabon and Gill Sans by
Pioneer Associates, Perthshire, and
printed and bound in Great Britain by
The Cromwell Press, Trowbridge, Wiltshire

A CIP record for this book is available from the British Library

ISBN 0 7486 1456 7 (hardback)
ISBN 0 7486 1457 5 (paperback)

The right of Helen K. Bond, Seth D. Kunin, Francesca Aran Murphy and the contributors to be identified as authors of this work has been asserted in accordance with the Copyright, Designs and Patents Act 1988.

Contents

Contents

Notes on the Contributors

Ken Aitken is a lecturer in the Hebrew Bible, Department of Divinity and Religious Studies, University of Aberdeen. His publications include *Proverbs* (1986) and numerous articles on the Hebrew Bible.

Helen K. Bond has been a lecturer in the New Testament, Language, Literature and Theology at the University of Edinburgh since 2000 and previously lectured at the University of Aberdeen and Northern College, Manchester. She is author of *Pontius Pilate in History and Interpretation* (1998) and is currently completing a book on the Jewish High Priest Caiaphas.

Derek Cross, CO graduated from St John's College, Annapolis, Maryland, the 'Great Books School'. He is a Father of the Oratory of St Philip Neri in Toronto, where he teaches Philosophy at St Philip's Seminary and is chaplain to the students of Mary Mother of God School. He has taught Philosophy at the Catholic University of America, Howard University and Gannon University. He was Research Associate at the American Enterprise Institute for Public Policy Research. He served as Research Assistant to the Distinguished Scholar in Residence at SRI International's Strategic Studies Center. He was Managing Editor of *The Review of Metaphysics* and *Comparative Strategy*. He has been Book Review Editor of *Crisis* and a member of the editorial board of *Interpretation*. He is presently on the editorial board of *The Chesterton Review*. He served as the American organiser of the first 'Centesimus Annus and the Free Society' institute at the Dominican House of Studies in Krakow and is a lecturer at the summer institute 'Tertio Millennio and the Free Society' in Bratislava. He has written for numerous journals including *First Things*, *Crisis*, *Religion and Liberty* and the *Review of Metaphysics*, and contributed chapters to *Awakening from Nihilism* (Derek Cross and Brian Anderson, eds, 1995), *Christianity and Economics in the Post-Cold War Era* (Herbert Schlossberg and Ronald A. Sider, eds, 1994) and *The Fourth Annual Aquinas Symposium*.

Douglas J. Davies is now Professor in the Study of Religion at Durham University. He studied at the Universities of Durham and Oxford, was Professor of Religious Studies at Nottingham University and also holds an honorary degree from the University of Uppsala. His background in both anthropology and theology has led to many studies that seek to show how beliefs relate to ritual and other forms of religious activity in such different contexts as cremation and burial, in Mormonism, in rural parish life and the life of the clergy in the Church of England. His major books include *Meaning and Salvation in Religious Studies* (1984), *Death, Ritual and Belief* (1997 and 2002), *The Mormon Culture of Salvation* (2000), and *Anthropology and Theology* (2002).

Paul Ellingworth is a former translation consultant with the United Bible Societies and Honorary Professor of New Testament, University of Aberdeen. He is the author of the New International Greek New Testament commentary on Hebrews (1993), and of several volumes in the United Bible Societies' Translators' Handbook series.

Hugh Goddard is Reader in Islamic Theology in the University of Nottingham, where he has taught since 1984. He studied Oriental Studies (Islamic History) at Oxford, and Theology (Christian–Muslim Relations) at Birmingham, and he has also studied in Amman and Cairo. He is the author of *Christians and Muslims: From Double Standards to Mutual Understanding* (1995), *Muslim Perceptions of Christianity* (1996) and *A History of Christian–Muslim Relations* (2000).

Seth D. Kunin is Head of the School of Divinity, Religious Studies and Philosophy at the University of Aberdeen. He studied Anthropology at Columbia University. He subsequently received an MA in Jewish Philosophy from the Jewish Theological Seminary of America. His doctoral research at the University of Cambridge examined biblical and rabbinic myths from a structuralist perspective. Dr Kunin has written several books and articles applying structuralist theory to many aspects of Israelite and Jewish culture; these include *The Logic of Incest: A Structuralist Analysis of Biblical Myth and God's Place in the World* (1995). Dr Kunin's current research is on the Crypto-Jews of New Mexico.

Martin A. Mills is a lecturer in the Anthropology of Religion in the Department of Divinity and Religious Studies, University of Aberdeen.

He has also taught Anthropology in the School of African and Asian Studies at the University of Sussex. He is the author of *Identity, Ritual and State in Tibetan Buddhism: the Foundations of Religious Authority in the Gelukpa Order* (2002) and has contributed numerous articles on Buddhism to journals of anthropology and of religious studies.

Francesca Aran Murphy is Reader in Systematic Theology in the Department of Divinity and Religious Studies, University of Aberdeen. She is the author of *Christ the Form of Beauty: A Study in Literature and Theology* (1995) and *The Comedy of Revelation: Paradise Lost and Regained in Christian Scripture* (2000). She has translated Rocco Buttiglione's *The Thought of Karol Wojtyla: The Man Who Became John Paul II* (1997) and edited the *Political Memoirs* of Aurel Kolnai (1999). She has just completed a book about Etienne Gilson and is currently translating *The Threshold of Beauty: Towards a Theological Aesthetic* by Bruno Forte.

F. Michael Perko is a member of the Society of Jesus, a Roman Catholic religious order. He holds a PhD from Stanford University. He is presently Professor of Education and in History at Loyola University of Chicago, and directs the university's Center for the Advanced Study of Christianity and Culture. Additionally, he has served as Scholar in Residence at the Ecumenical Institute for Theological Research (Jerusalem), Visiting Scholar at Heythrop College of the University of London, and Senior Fellow at the Institute for the Advanced Study of Religion at the University of Chicago. The author, co-author or editor of six books and monographs – as well as over a hundred articles, book chapters and papers – he has also served as Contributing Editor to the British journal of Christianity and international affairs, *The Month*. His research interests focus on religious and cultural history, and he has written extensively on religion, society and international affairs.

Henry R. Sefton was ordained as a minister in the Church of Scotland in 1957. He taught Church History at the University of Aberdeen from 1972 to 1992 and was Senior Lecturer and Master of Christ's College from 1982 to 1992. He was most recently Co-ordinator of Christian Studies for the University of Aberdeen's Continuing Education department, where he authored a number of workbooks and taught several courses. His study *John Knox: An Account of his Spirituality* appeared in the Devotional Library Series of St Andrew Press in 1993.

John Swinton is Senior Lecturer in Practical Theology at the University of Aberdeen, Scotland. He has published widely within the field. His books include *Building a Church for Strangers* (1999), *From Bedlam to Shalom: Towards a Practical Theology of Human Nature, Inter-Relationships* *and Mental Health Care* (2000), *Resurrecting the Person: Friendship and the Care of People with Mental Health Problems* (2000) and *Spirituality in Mental Health Care: Rediscovering a 'Forgotten Dimension'* (2001). He currently edits the UK's leading journal of practical theology, *Contact: The Interdisciplinary Journal of Pastoral Studies*, and sits on the editoral board of *The Scottish Journal of Health Care Chaplaincy*, *The Wayne Oates Journal* and *The Journal of Religion, Disability and Health*. Dr Swinton is an office-bearer of the International Academy of Practical Theology.

Matthew Wood completed his doctoral dissertation at the University of Nottingham in 1999. Based on ethnographic fieldwork of an alternative religious network in the UK, it develops a new sociological account of authority and organisation for phenomena that are usually classed as 'New Age'. A book based on this work will be published in 2003, provisionally entitled *Possession, Power and the New Age: Ambiguities of Authority in the Modern World*. Currently Research Officer and Visiting Lecturer in Anthropology at the School of Sociology and Social Policy, University of Surrey, Roehampton, he is researching the effects of globalisation on black majority Methodist congregations in London.

Acknowledgements

The editors would like to thank all the contributors for their industry, inventiveness and solidarity. We are grateful to Kathleen Brebner, secretary to the Department of Theology and Religious Studies at Aberdeen University, for her patience and calm; and to our editors at Edinburgh University Press, Nicola Carr and Eddie Clark. Thanks to John Bond for his map-drawing.

The fictional characters who appear in the 'Systematic Theology' and the 'Philosophy of Religion' chapters – Father Jack, Josh, Betsy, Joan V., Father Reginald, the Professor, Anthony, Lara, Cathy, Fred, Greg, Jamaal, Philip, Bob and Rosie – bear no relation to any real person, living or dead.

Introduction

Many text books cover either Religious Studies or Theology. This book is unique in bringing you two related – yet very different – academic subjects in a single volume. We've designed the material with first-year undergraduates or the general reader in mind. Whatever your interest in religion – whether you are interested in Islam, Buddhism or Christian theology – we hope that you will find this volume useful and stimulating.

Part I is devoted to Religious Studies. But how do we study religions, particularly those that are not our own? The first Section, 'Theories of Religion', explores a number of diverse approaches. Chapter One looks at some significant thinkers of the past who took what are broadly called theological approaches to the study of religion. These people mostly accept that there is some type of essential religious experience that underlies the origin and continuation of religion. Many of the most significant studies seek to understand and describe the nature of this fundamental experience. A significant feature of these approaches is that they try to describe or discuss religion through the eyes of a believer. Chapter Two introduces what are known as psychological and phenomenological approaches to religion. Psychological approaches move the focus from an external transcendental other to the individual and the individual's psyche, suggesting that religion reflects a process that primarily occurs within the individual's unconscious. Although the phenomenological tradition emphasises the study of religions, it is ultimately concerned with religion as such – that is, the essence of religion and its history, rather than specific religions. Although these approaches are significantly different, they share an emphasis on the individual and individual experience, and seek to understand religion rather than religions.

The third chapter introduces anthropological and sociological approaches. What distinguishes these approaches from the ones in earlier chapters is that anthropologists and sociologists are not primarily interested in an essential phenomenon, 'religion', that can be examined outside of a particular ethnographic context. They focus instead on specific religions in specific ethnographic locations. The chapter moves from theories that are essentially ethnocentric, or Euro-centric, to approaches that are able to encompass a wider range of ethnographic phenomena. The chapter concludes by raising an issue that is a recurring theme throughout Section One: is there such a thing as a universal definition of religion?

Section One does not attempt to cover every theory of religion. Rather, these three chapters explore the development of ideas and lay the foundation for future study of theories of religion. In order to preserve this line of argument, we only examine theories that try to explain the nature of the institution and practice of religion as a whole, rather than theories that examine parts of religion, such as secularisation, or what types of personalities are attracted to different forms of religion.

The second section, 'Case Studies', returns to this theme. It analyses religions from the perspective of different approaches to Religious Studies. Its opening chapter, on anthropological theories and indigenous traditions, examines religious practice not in relation to an overarching definition but in terms of specific practices in specific cultural settings. Most of the remaining chapters present short surveys of 'world religions', including Christianity. We have chosen to include Christianity, in spite of it being the focus of much of Part II, in order to show how, like all other religions, Christianity can be understood from the perspectives of religious studies.

Chapters Six and Seven in the 'Case Studies' section pick up themes relating to developments within American and European religions today. We examine the developments within new religious movements and the New Age and suggest that new models for understanding how people use religion today need to be constructed. In the final chapter we look at general trends within religions as they face the challenges of modernity.

Part II covers subjects you encounter if you study 'Theology'. Theology (which means 'talk about God') is a broad term and covers a range of subsidiary disciplines. The first section in this part looks at 'Biblical Studies'. The Bible contains texts which are 2,000–2,500 years old. They were written (in Greek or Hebrew) in an alien world with an unfamiliar worldview, and cover a variety of genres: history, poetry, letters, books of wisdom and apocalyptic speculation. Different ways of reading the Bible are presented in the opening chapter but most biblical critics see their task as drawing out the original meaning of these texts. To do this, they make use of linguistics, ancient history, literature, philosophy, sociology and – when all else fails – imagination. The aim is to allow the biblical text to speak from its own historical and literary context. The interpreter tries to transport themselves back into the ancient world and to understand what these texts meant when they were first written. It is left for the theologians to formulate doctrinal systems and to draw out contemporary meanings.

Part II also contains sections on 'Practical Theology', 'Systematic Theology' and 'Philosophy of Religion'. As you read through these sections you may well be struck by the fact that all these disciplines are studied from inside the Christian faith. Every word written by the giants of Christian theology, from Augustine, through Martin Luther and John Wesley to Hans Urs von Balthasar, is an expression of their passionate engagement in Christianity. At one time it was hoped that, if only Christian theologians could detach themselves a bit from their religiosity, they could find a shared meeting place with students of non-Christian religions. But today, very few young and active thinkers use Religious Studies as a jumping-off place for inter-religious dialogue. This does not mean that inter-religious dialogue is dead. But inter-religious meeting is no longer initiated by divesting oneself of one's own religious commitment. The meeting between religions is now best exemplified by the Ribat es Salam (the 'Bond of Peace') in Algeria, where Christians and Muslims join together in common prayer. Here Muslims and Christians meet *as* Muslims and Christians.

Systematic Theology and Philosophy of Religion are creative disciplines that can be pursued in a variety of ways. In the interests of exposing you to as many different ways of 'doing' Theology as possible, some of the chapters in these two sections present themselves, even visually, a little differently from the rest of this part. Here we have followed in the footsteps of books like *Sophie's World* and the dialogue conclusion to Daniel Migliore's *Faith Seeking Understanding*. The 'Systematic Theology' section opens with a historical overview of Christianity, followed by a descriptive chapter on Christology. The next three chapters are presented as a dialogue between nine Theology students as they make their way through three courses in Systematics: 'Bases', 'Spirit, Creeds and Church', and 'Revelation and the Trinity'. Each character faithfully represents a single viewpoint within Systematics, such as liberation theology or narrative theology. The interactive form could be useful material for your own dialogues in Theology seminars. Maybe you can identify with some characters and not with others. We hope that this will make for lively and fun reading, and help you to engage with rather abstract subjects. The 'Philosophy of Religion' section is composed of letters between a priest and three inquirers. You might like to think of these chapters as computer games! The section on 'Practical Theology' is a straightforward and engaging treatment of the subject matter.

We wanted to make the contents of this book as diverse as the actual exploration of religion and theology in our times. Rather than presenting an artificial similarity of approaches to Religious Studies and Theology, we have tried to give you the same scope of opinion as you will encounter in the news, or in a library, in cyberspace, and in real life. Every serious student of Theology needs to know what cutting-edge researchers in Religious Studies are saying about their field; and, in relation to Christianity, every Religious Studies student needs to consult the articulate indigenous practitioners – that is, the theologians. We hope the two parts will provide enough information for you to see the differences between 'Religious Studies' and 'Theology', and to help you discover where your own particular interests lie. The plurality of approaches in this book is reflected in the writers' styles. For instance, some writers retain the Christian timelines, denoted by the expressions BC and AD; others use BCE and CE.

This book should also be a springboard into more reading. If you want help on what the authors think are the crucial books in their field, you will find that in the 'Further reading' section at the end of each chapter. The 'Further reading' sections contain the texts you should be using to cover the topic. In addition to that, every single book mentioned or referred to in this volume is listed at the very end of the book, in the 'Selected Bibliography' section. 'Further reading' sections are for immediate use; the 'Selected Bibliography' is for reference.

PART I

RELIGIOUS STUDIES

Section One: THEORIES OF RELIGION

CHAPTER ONE

The Theology of Religion

Douglas J. Davies

- ❑ Introduction
- ❑ Biblical background
- ❑ Catholic perspectives
- ❑ Protestant perspectives
- ❑ Scholarly visions
- ❑ Contemporary perspectives
- ❑ Conclusion: Personal experience and encounter
- ❑ Further reading
- ❑ Questions

Introduction

The theology of religions helps theologians interpret religion in much the same way as sociological or psychological theories help social scientists understand religion. One difference, however, is that it also often serves to relate a theologian's own religious tradition to the many 'other' religions in the world. This dual purpose adds a degree of complexity to the theology of religion precisely because it involves a kind of self-reflection or self-analysis within the overall task. In this chapter we show some of the ways in which Christianity has sought to understand the relationship between itself and the religious life of other people.

Biblical background

Christianity identifies its roots in the ancient historical tradition of the

Jews, one that is represented today by Judaism. At the very outset Christianity has to explain to itself the separate nature of Judaism, especially as an ongoing way of life of millions. The Christian Bible, with its subdivision into the Old and New Testaments, already provides the beginning of an explanation, for the very names 'Old' and 'New' Testaments stand for the difference between an old and new 'testament' or 'covenant' relationship between God and humanity. This 'Old' Testament is not, of course, 'Old' as far as Jews are concerned. Within Judaism the books of the Hebrew Scriptures, with sections dealing with divine laws, the history of kings and prophets and with wisdom writings including Psalms and Proverbs, all speak of a living and dynamic relationship between God and God's chosen people of Israel. In this chapter we will specifically use these names of the 'Old' and 'New' Testaments as a constant reminder of their specifically Christian value and significance, for while Christians accept this material they also interpret it as a preparation for the coming of Jesus of Nazareth as the Messiah or Christ. Christ, God's specially chosen and appointed one, began a new period of divine activity by establishing a new 'chosen' people that was not restricted to the Jews but was open to everyone.

From the Old Testament Christians find one prompt on how other religions may be viewed through the idea of idols and idolatry. Many groups are described as worshipping false gods, gods that are nothing but artefacts. The new Testament offers brief glimpses of how some early Christians looked at other religions of their day, as with Paul at Athens. There he is portrayed as giving an address to those with philosophical and religious interests and refers to the various shrines present in the city. He talks of God as the Creator of all and as having made all people with the capacity to 'seek God in the hope that they might feel after him and find him' (Acts 17: 27). The true God, he says, transcends all shrines and yet is profoundly close to all people. In a much less liberal spirit, however, the Letter to the Romans describes God as showing divine truth to people through the creation only to have it rejected (Romans 1: 20). Even so, Paul seems prepared to accept that human nature along with its own sense of conscience can result in human action that accords with the principles of the divine law as understood by the Jews (Romans 2: 14–16).

For some centuries afterwards, the young Christian church continued to reflect on its origin and its difference from other religions. St Ephrem, for example, a renowned fourth-century Syrian, compared Moses and Paul on the question of why Moses's eyes radiated divine glory while Paul was struck blind when encountering God's presence. Ephrem answers that 'even though the eyes of Moses were physical, like those of Paul, his interior eyes were Christian' (1994: 308). Here a Christian reads a 'Christian' status back into the ancient Jewish stories while he also shows the contrast between Jew and Christian grounded in the eye of faith. Earlier still, Origen (186–255) draws attention to the mysteries of the Egyptians, Persians, Syrians and Indians and 'to all those who have a literature and a mythology' (1869: 410). The fact of early Christian life is that believers had often come from other groups and were well aware of other schemes of religious rites and belief.

Community base

Sociologically speaking, the earliest Christians were both converts and communitarian, they followed Jesus and were committed to a community that enshrined his values. For those of them who were Jews, as well as for those who might have adhered to other forms of religious activity involving Greek or Roman religion, life had changed. They now belonged to a community whose message was grounded in a changed view of the world brought about by what they saw as the resurrection from the dead of someone in whom God was especially present and whose life was animated by a divine power they called the Holy Spirit. This background and double dynamism of resurrection and spirit ensured that other groups could not be given the same level of authenticity. These earliest Christians had not simply wandered into a group from some neutral religious world; for the disciples-turned-apostles, their Jewish identity had undergone a significant transformation, and a similar sense of change was anticipated from non-Jews who became Christian. This meant that what we might call their theology of religion was grounded in a distinction between lesser and greater points of divine revelation and divine action.

Catholic perspectives

More than a thousand years later Catholic Christians would still be engaged with such issues, albeit as a result of a wider experience of the world. In the fifteenth century the Catholic Nicholas of Cusa (1400–64) wrote *De Pace Fidei*, an account of peace between different kinds of faith, while Francis Xavier (1506–52), for example, was a highly influential Spanish missionary who travelled very extensively from India to Japan. He sought to understand the problems that Orientals had in understanding Christianity and sought, to a degree, to relate Christian teaching to them – as when Japanese converts worried about the fate of their ancestors who died before receiving the Christian Gospel and the ministrations of the church. Francis, along with his friend Ignatius Loyola, was amongst the very first members of the new order of the Jesuits. Ignatius had been influential in retaining Francis within the Catholic Church after a period in which he had shown considerable interest in emergent Protestantism while a student at Paris. For Francis, then, the issue of religious adherence with the possibility of conversion from one position to another was something of a reality in his presenting of the Catholic faith to people of non-Christian religions. While Francis had responded to a call from the King of Portugal to serve as a missionary in the extensive Portuguese empire, he also went beyond it and, as such, stands as a point of transition between the medieval world of religion as part of the power of empires and the modern world in which missionary work would come to stand alone as a venture of faith-inspired groups.

Reorientations

This was also the period of Martin Luther (1483–1546), who initiated what came to be called the Reformation, an example of Troeltsch's protest against churchly compromise. For the next three hundred years much Christian energy went into an internal warfare of doctrine. Theology of religion was, if anything, an obsessive theology of the truth of one's own part of Christendom and a denial of the other. When Catholic or Protestant countries, in their imperial power, conquered other lands they sought to make its inhabitants denominational Christians and even when Christian mission movements emerged and flourished in the eighteenth and nineteenth centuries more effort went into fostering one form of faith than in considering others. Exclusivity tended to predominate.

However, a major change in attitude towards the theology of religions emerged within the Roman Catholic Church in the 1960s through the Second Vatican Council. John Oesterreicher in his official introduction and commentary on the 'Declaration of the Relationship of the Church to Non-Christian Religions' emphasises the particular significance of this document amongst all the products of Vatican II. 'For the first time in history', he pronounces, 'a Council acknowledges the search for the absolute by other men and by whole races and peoples, and honours the truth and holiness in other religions as the work of the one living God' (1969: 1). What is tellingly important is that this document developed from a specific concern of Pope John XXIII to have a considered Church statement on the status and significance of the Jews. One powerful theological motivation to come to terms with Judaism was derived from a theological anti-Semitism that some levelled against Catholicism, not least in connection with politics and Nazism. This concern with Judaism then extended to other major religions, not least to Islam with a statement that the 'God of Islam is the one living and true, merciful and almighty God' (Anawati 1969: 151).

R. C. Zaehner, an influential Catholic historian of religion to whom we will return later, rapidly drew attention to these Vatican II documents in his Gifford Lectures of 1967–69, arguing that the Catholic Church, under the impetus of Pope John XXIII, had 'come to reaffirm what the early Church had always understood, namely, that all truth, wherever we find it, must proceed from God' (1970: 12). Zaehner drew attention to the Council's affirmation that the Catholic Church rejected nothing 'which is true and holy in other religions' and to the fact that each world religion was given some attention in that Council's deliberations. While he does draw attention to what is not said, he notes that 'the age of anathemas seems to have passed away' (1970: 14).

This Council drew attention to the distinction between two forms of divine engagement with humanity that, from the medieval period, had distinguished between general and special knowledge of God, a distinction that bears some resemblance to the additional idea of general and special revelation. The general picture is rooted in God as creator, with humanity depending upon its conscience and natural ability to see evidence of divine handwork in the world itself. The revealed position emphasises the bible, Christ and the development of Christian doctrine as media through which humanity gains a vision of God that would never be gained through human reflection left unaided.

Human and divine quests

One of the most important parts of the study of religion from the perspective of Christian theology asks: just what is it we are doing? For example, the Catholic theologian Karl Rahner (1904–84) stressed the way in which humans seek out knowledge by engaging with the world around them and, in a sense, entering into that world. But since that world is God's world and full of divine grace, as people genuinely give themselves to it so they are, in a sense, giving themselves to God. Their search for knowledge is a search for God, whether they know it or not. This led to the idea of 'anonymous Christians' and provided a positive value, amongst other things, for the way in which Christians could view non-Christian religions. But here, of course, another problem emerged because, although it may sound generous and kind on the part of Christians to see non-Christians as 'anonymous Christians', and while this may help Christians construct one sensible theology of religions, it may not appeal to non-Christians. They may think that they are having a Christian identity thrust upon them that they do not wish to claim for themselves. This approach is reflected, for example, in the Roman Catholic view associated with the Second Vatican Council of the 1960s. The Protestant theologian George Lindbeck, however, is one of those who adopt a negative view of this idea. Indeed, he goes so far as to describe it as 'a nonsense' and the approach associated with it as 'thoroughly unreal' (1984: 62). While Lindbeck's perspective is powerful in itself, it overlooks the significance of the change of mind in Catholic perspectives.

The 'anonymous Christian' idea says as much about Catholic willingness to shift in its orientation to the world at large as it does about the devotees of other religions.

From a social scientific perspective all doctrines, and most especially doctrines of salvation, can be expected to reflect the institution that propounds them. The case of the Roman Catholic Church is no exception. This Church holds firmly to a belief in its divinely granted authority, with its leadership expressing in a distinctive way the power of Christ and its sacraments affording the prime means of salvation. This sense of authority and power can, of course, be wielded in different ways. In a stark authoritarian mode of exclusivism it can damn believers of other religions but with an inclusive spirit it can, equally, adopt a very positive attitude to them. This latter approach was the case with the Second Vatican Council and it can also be seen in the clearest possible way in Dhavamony's account both of that Council and in his own Catholic analysis of world religions. Although it may not be convincing to all readers, Dhavamony speaks of the way in which those of good intention in non-Christian religions can 'somehow be inserted into the mystery of the Cross in a mysterious way, known only to God alone' (2001: 137). His study is important, covers considerable ground within the theology of religion for both Catholic and some Protestant sources and should be regarded as a major text in this field. As far as the Council was concerned, a key feature concerns the grace of God that works secretly in the hearts and religious endeavours of non-Christians. In other words, a key concept, that of grace, is deemed to be fundamental whether operating within the explicit and visible church or in other contexts.

Protestant perspectives

Protestant thought has also emphasised grace but, especially at its origin, its main view of other religions was as a corruption of the true knowledge of God. Context can never be ignored when analysing theology and it is instructive to see that John Calvin, as one of the first systematisers of Protestant theology, devoted chapters ten to twelve of the first book in his *Institutes of the Christian Religion* to idolatry. It is perfectly clear that his prime agenda was to oppose Catholic forms of worship and popular piety in relation to statues and depictions of holy persons and events. Calvin is keen to note that both 'sculpture and painting are gifts of God' but he is not persuaded that most minds are able to employ them appropriately, so great is human degradation (Book 1. chap. XII). This is a good example of how Christianity's internal theology of religion preoccupied Europe in the sixteenth and seventeenth centuries.

Much more recently Karl Barth (1886–1968) reflected a similar concern but in response to the liberal theologians of the nineteenth century, marking a renewed kind of orthodoxy. In the last resort, Barth sets God and God's ways beyond human comprehension in order to stress divine grace in the saving work of Christ as God's word spoken to humanity. Religion at large was as negative a reality as was all human endeavour. In his magisterial study *Church Dogmatics* he argues, for example, that 'religion is unbelief. It is the one great concern of Godless man. In religion man bolts and bars himself against revelation by providing a substitute' (1.2.299). Barth basically sets true religion in the Protestant tradition in which the individual gains a sense of being addressed by the word of God through sermons, Scripture and the person of Christ. This sets non-Christian religions and even some sorts of Christian traditions far from the real truthfulness of things.

History of religions and theology of religion

One important aspect of the theology of religion concerns the status of the material theologians need when learning about other religions and setting out upon their analysis of how those religions relate to the message of Christianity. In particular, there is the question of the presuppositions of the academic disciplines furnishing much of that information, in particular the history, anthropology and sociology of religions. Wolfhart Pannenberg, a German Protestant theologian, even thinks there is a need for a theology of the history of religions, and his work on this topic is particularly valuable (1971: 65–118).

Formal questions about the theology of religion were of particular concern to several earlier Protestant theologians. Ernst Troeltsch (1865–1923) helped foster these debates by arguing that one should understand religious beliefs very much within the cultural context of their origin and development. In *The Social Teachings of the Christian Churches* (1931) he described hundreds of Christian groups, setting them in their historical contexts and showing how they manifested different aspects of Christian faith. Troeltsch benefited from Max Weber's sociology of religion and classified religious activity in terms of church, sect and mysticism and laid a foundation for later sociologists of religion. Troeltsch was convinced that Christianity existed on the ground in a complex process of compromise and protest. The Gospel's incisive message lost its edge when a church-type organisation accommodated the demands of the world but sect groups then tended to arise in protest at the compromise and with a demand for a renewed purity of commitment – and that protest often came from relatively disadvantaged people. In one sense Troeltsch presents us with a kind of theology of Christian religion except that it is not abstract and philosophical but much more grounded in a description of actual historical events.

Troeltsch was influential on Paul Tillich (1886–1965), a Protestant theologian who stressed the existential aspects of life and faith as developed in, for example, his *Christianity and the Encounter of World Religions* (1963). He argued that 'Religion is the state of being grasped by an ultimate concern, a concern which qualifies all other concerns as preliminary and which itself contains the answer to the question of the meaning of our life.' Here the sense of an ultimate concern can be applied to a wide variety of human experiences drawn from a wide variety of religions and does not work on an exclusive basis, as his *Systematic Theology* also shows (1964: 118–72). Tillich gave full weight to the importance of culture, along with politics and art, as the dynamic environment within which human values take varied symbolic forms. Terence Thomas's *Paul Tillich and World Religions* shows the various influences upon Tillich, especially through contact with leaders of other faiths, particularly Buddhism. Such friendly encounters were the diametrical opposite of, for example, the Crusades, which Tillich saw as the outcome of culture contact between Christian and Muslim and as the first major occasion when a developed form of Christianity was prompted into a judgement on another religion to an almost fundamentalist degree.

Doctrinal guidelines

From quite a different theological direction and under totally different cultural circumstances H. H. Farmer, Professor of Divinity at Cambridge University, delivered his Gifford Lectures at the University of Glasgow in 1950, later published as *Revelation and Religion*. There he sought an interpretation of religion at large 'from the standpoint of the Incarnation' (1954: viii). In pursuing his theological goal he makes much use of psychological ideas about personality that were increasingly common in the 1940s and 1950s, especially of the need for the integration of the self. Similarly, he draws from social anthropology to comment on 'primitive religion'. Still, despite these additional resources, his focus remains solidly theological but with a strong emphasis upon the philosophy of religion and with an eye to the issue of religious experience. His presuppositions are that there has ever been a 'divine initiative and activity in making a personal approach and revelation to men' not only in Christianity but 'within the whole religious history of mankind' (1954: 84). He speaks of the divine self-disclosure 'pressing in upon the human spirit'. He then explores a series of types of religion in which this encounter has taken place. His account of primitive religion and polytheism is, perhaps, the last theological study to depend upon anthropological perspectives that were already becoming obsolete. As lectures delivered in 1950, the book marks a kind of watershed in the twentieth-century study of anthropology as an influence upon theology.

Similarly, it shows the influence of scholars like the psychologist William James and the phenomenologist van der Leeuw as Farmer sets out to construct different types of religiosity, each showing a different impact and reception of deity upon humanity. These include the types of absolute dependence, ideal values, introversion, obligation, withdrawal and fulfilment. Despite his intention to ground his work in the Incarnation, this study remains far more philosophical than theological and shows the profound mark of philosophical theology upon British considerations of deity. Still, Farmer's conviction of the interplay between deity and humanity, one that could lead to rejection and a decrease in spiritual awareness just as it could to an increase of unity of purpose and fulfilment, is useful as a prelude to the more sophisticated yet complementary approach of John Bowker.

Scholarly visions

John Bowker, an Anglican priest and academic, whose *Oxford Dictionary of World Religions* (1997) is a major contribution to the study of religion, has also added significantly to the theology of religions in his two studies *The Sense of God* (1973) and *The Religious Imagination and the Sense of God* (1978). Bowker sees religions as a kind of communication system in which humans, within their cultures, are set in some form of interaction with the underlying reality of the universe. There is, as it were, a feedback system between, in more traditional terms, deity and humanity. That relationship is complex and involves the fact that people cannot think just whatever they wish to think, for we all exist under certain constraints of existence. He draws from anthropology and psychology as much as from theology and literature to press his vision of humanity and its engagement with its destiny in the God of the universe.

R. C. Zaehner (1913–74) held an influential professorship at Oxford University in Eastern Religions and Ethics and had been a convert to Roman Catholicism when aged 23. His views on theology were often negative, for he thought that theologians often get caught up on commenting on other scholars' work until they were far removed from the power of religious experience itself. He was, similarly, very critical of people who wanted to see easy comparisons amongst world religions. His extensive studies of religions brought him to the conclusion not that all religions were, somehow, 'the same' but that 'there is in man a craving for an incarnate God strong enough to force its way into the most unpromising religious systems' (1970: 443). As with most Christian thinkers his work, too, is inspired by what he saw as a 'centre of coherence' that 'can only be Christ' (1970: 16). In broad terms,

Zaehner's relative emphasis upon the human desire to relate to such a figure echoes Bowker's upon the pressure from the divine source that impinges upon human religions. Each seems to deal with the total universe within which religious experience senses or longs to sense the divine presence even though particular cultural contexts may hinder that encounter and fruitful relation. For Zaehner, any purely theological or philosophical approach to other religions will fail if it wishes to seek some kind of concord because of some real doctrinal differences existing between them. He even speaks of Christianity being 'plagued by theology' from the beginning, always trying to define the indefinable, while for Zaehner, as for Max Müller before him, experience told far more than did immeasurable systematising.

John Hick, Presbyterian theologian and philosopher of religion, has written with a keen awareness of the differences between religions and especially of the ways in which they sometimes seem to contradict each other over what are, apparently, basic truths. His theology of religion is one that sets such philosophical issues within the long term and framed by the serious dialogue of religion with religion. It is no accident that he edited one important book entitled *Truth and Dialogue* (1974) in which key scholars of the 1960s and 1970s came together in a conference to explore relationships between world religions fully conscious of conflicting truth claims. His own contribution was entitled 'Dialogue into Truth' and reflects his commitment to the power of mutual discussion in bringing people to see the point of other people's commitment and even to reformulations of belief to reflect the views of others. So, for example, he suggests that Christian ideas of life after death, whether in intermediary states or in heaven, could be equated with Indian notions of transmigration of souls as long as the major emphasis was placed upon survival rather than its precise mode. All that was needed was a kind of exploratory philosophical turn of the imagination. It is, of course, doubtful whether many ordinary believers are concerned with such mental exercises or would even want to embrace the apparently strange beliefs of other traditions. Hick saw very clearly the problems inherent in relating apparently conflicting beliefs and conceded that, at that point, he could not see the way ahead and had to admit a degree both of doubt and hope. His example is important, though, for its stress on philosophical issues underlying theological reflection and on traditional forms of argument that have given integrity to Christian doctrine in the past. He exposes, as it were, the bare bones of Christian thinking to see how those foundational structures might resemble or relate to the foundational elements of other religions. Hick is, of course, mindful of the fact that such theological anatomy is not the first love of ordinary believers who may be personally fond of the more familiar surface features of their religion and suspicious of the alien form of others. Still, his hope was that persons from different religions might 'dialogue into truth' and that a 'fuller grasp of truth' would help transcend 'our present conflicting doctrines' (1974: 155).

One way in which Christians might organise that dialogue about their scheme of faith, whether amongst Christians of differing outlooks or with persons from other religions, was taken up by George Lindbeck in his important book *The Nature of Doctrine* (1984). There he argued for what he called a 'cultural linguistic' approach to religions and their doctrine. A religion is like a language within which many things made sense and a Christian theology of religion will approach other religions as being similar worlds of meaning. The process of dialogue then becomes, in part, an exercise in developing a competence in seeing how other people construct their religious worldview.

An influential Canadian scholar of Islam and of the history of religion, Wilfred Cantwell Smith (1916–2000), provided a different kind of perspective upon the theology of religion in his influential book *The Meaning and End of Religion*, which drew a telling distinction between 'faith' and 'cumulative tradition'. By 'faith' he referred to the personal experience of individuals and by 'cumulative tradition' to the whole framework of their religion, including its history, architecture, sacred texts, doctrine and worship. He wisely drew attention to the way in which two people of different religions often miss the point when discussing together because it is easy for one of them to speak out of his or her own 'faith' experience when criticising what is not the 'faith' experience but the cumulative tradition of the other person. For anything like genuine communication to take place 'faith' must speak to 'faith'. Likewise, it is possible for both to discuss their cumulative traditions and, within those traditions, it will not be difficult to find some point of contact just as it is easy to find disreputable periods in the history of all religions. He argued that 'religion' was too broad a word to embrace both the intimate and dynamic domain of personal experience and all the historical and cultural aspects of a tradition as well.

Experience and insight

Cantwell Smith is significant because his perspective raises the issue of sympathetic understanding between religions within the theology of religion. Just how an individual or group approaches people of a different faith is profoundly important. Is it from a position of assured superiority or, perhaps, simply with the desire to convert the other? Might it emerge from a genuine desire to understand how others think and, perhaps, to see if new light can be brought to bear upon one's own faith? It benefits everyone if some degree of self-understanding, along with a grasp of why one is setting out to engage with others can precede the venture. This is not to say that a person's attitude will not change in the process of relating to people of other traditions, such natural changes are to be expected. Indeed, the very notion of humility is of some benefit over this issue. One of the most significant developments in human thought since the middle of the nineteenth century has been a growing sense of the power of historical and cultural contexts over human thought and self-understanding. To know that one's thinking and self-understanding is ever framed by time, place and culture is knowledge that can impact upon people in different ways. For some of an existentialist philo-sophical stance, it can be a depressing thought, almost triggering a sense of impotence of the self under such social forces. For others, it can evoke a sense of humility and strength at being part of a communal venture in living.

Two well-known Christian theologians who have developed an inter-est in the shared aspects of religion across religious divides are Rudolph Otto (1869–1937), especially his *Idea of the Holy*, and Friedrich Heiler (1892–1967) in his study *Prayer*. Otto's study analyses the experience of 'the holy' or what he called the 'numinous', while Heiler devoted himself to a study of prayer and experiences associate with it in differ-ent religions. These typify one major thrust in the theology of religion, that which emphasises human experience of the divine and tends to assume a unity amongst religious persons, whatever their religion of origin. Others prefer not to stress the commonality of contemporary experience but to trace the development of ideas from the past.

Salvation history and salvation's future

Religious traditions, not least Christianity, often stress history in this way, not least because they draw a great deal of their power and author-ity from the past. This is especially the case when Christians believe that God is intimately involved in the past, as is indicated by the theological term 'salvation history'. Originating as the German notion of *Heilsgeschichte*, 'salvation history' has come to describe God's saving action in relation to humanity. Some discuss it in a way that is best inter-preted as mythical, as they construct a broad doctrinal picture of the history of Israel leading into the Incarnation and the life of Jesus, all to be viewed by faith and grasped by faith as something not open to detailed historical analysis. Others speak more practically of the history of Christian events and their saving potential. Despite many criticisms, the term retains some use as a means of connecting Judaism with Christianity and the subsequent history of churches. What is even more interesting relates to the future. If, in terms of belief and doctrine, there has been a salvation history is there a salvation future? If there is, how does it relate to other religions? Are other religions part of Christian salvation history in its ongoing future? So, although originating strictly as a means of describing past events in the history of Israel and of Christianity and investing them with divine significance, it also lies open to wider interpretation. For one basic question in the theology of religion is whether, and how, the many religions of the world reflect something of a divine engagement. Why are they there? What is their future? How do they relate to Christianity? Do they, for example, offer the possibility of adding new dimensions to Christianity itself? This is part of the openness implied in Panikkar's position described later in this chapter.

Missionary theology and practice

An open attitude to other religions is quite different from the theology of religions that tended to motivate traditional missionary work. Christian theology of other religions has long tended to view them as inadequate vehicles of salvation. One liturgical expression of such theology is found in the Church of England's 1662 *Book of Common Prayer* and one of its special prayers for Good Friday. This is an extremely telling prayer as far as salvation history is concerned, not least because it was written a century and more before the idea of salvation history was constructed. The prayer asks God to 'have mercy upon all Jews, Turks, Infidels and Heretics' and to 'take from them all ignorance and hardness of heart and contempt of thy Word'. It then asks God 'so to fetch them home . . . that they may be saved among the remnant of the true Israelites and be made one fold under one shepherd, Jesus Christ our Lord'. Here a Christian view sees itself as the centre of salvation, albeit one that has emerged from Judaism to become the 'true Israelites'. It then asks that remaining Jews, along with Muslims – the Turks and Infidels of the prayer – accept Christian teaching symbolised here by God's 'Word'. This theology of religions is exclusivist and centripetal, it wants to draw others into itself to ensure their salvation. A similar prayer for Good Friday in the Roman Catholic Church had, in fact, been changed by Pope John XXIII so as to pray for the Jews and not, as hitherto, for the 'unbelieving Jews' (Oesterreicher 1969: 5), the change reflecting a much less judgmental attitude.

The Anglican prayer might, from another angle, be thought odd in that the Church of England in its origin was not a missionary church whose prayers for others would lead to their evangelisation, though the Society for Promoting Christian Knowledge (SPCK) was founded in 1698. Still, it was not until the very late eighteenth and early nineteenth centuries that missionary societies were organised to bring about the conversion of people in non-Christian societies. This is a most important feature of Christian history. Peter van Rooden has argued that Christianity itself underwent a significant change during this period and became, for the first time, a missionary religion (1996: 65–87). Some Christians would immediately reject this idea because they have been brought up to think, for example, about St Paul's missionary journeys, as they came to be called by later Christians, and they give an impression of missionary work. But van Rooden's argument is that in the nineteenth century several streams of Protestantism in Europe came to think of Christianity in a new way, and a new form of modern Western Christianity emerges. It comes to operate in the private world in such a way as to transform the social world. It comes to imagine the world as a potential community of faith and, for the first time in history, the 'modern mass organisation run by a professional staff' emerged as missionary societies (van Rooden 1996: 78). Here we can see the earliest instances of globalisation taking shape. These missionaries have a desire to bring a particular 'product' – the Christian gospel – into the lives of people everywhere.

It is important to stress the existence of these missionary societies in connection with the theology of religions because religious ideas do not exist simply in some abstract way but are usually related to some concrete practice. Just as doctrine is expressed in sacraments, so theology of religion came to be expressed through missionary societies such as the London Missionary Society of 1795 or the British and Foreign Bible Society of 1804. These and subsequent groups were not an arm of government but expressed a new form of self-identity among Christians acting together motivated by a theology that not only conferred a deep sense of identity upon individual Christians but impelled them to bring the same to others. The foundation for these ideas lay in the belief that salvation was to be gained through hearing and receiving the message of the death of Christ for the sins of humanity and that a new form of life could then be lived in relationship with others belonging to a distinctive community. The centrality of Christ for Christian mission and also for the theology of religions would long continue, almost irrespective of the particular way in which it would be applied. One of the clearest examples is in the work of J. N. Farquhar (1861–1929), a student of Max Müller, and a missionary to India. His influential book *The Crown of Hinduism* (1913) refers to Christ viewed as the one who alone could bring fulfilment to all the highest ideals of Hinduism.

Farquhar knew India; Albert Schweitzer (1875–1965) did not. But Schweitzer must be included here, not only because he wrote about Indian religious thought or because he admitted having no experience of practical Indian religion, but because he demonstrated a Christian commitment grounded in an ethical ideal (Seaver 1955: 301). Amongst the greatest intellectuals and practical Christians of any generation, he made immense contributions to biblical studies, the history of civilisation and to music. As an individual he demonstrated that will to live and to cause others to flourish that lay firmly beneath his Christian faith. Schweitzer felt impelled to gain some understanding of world religions, especially Hinduism, and to engage in a critique of them. Astonishingly, perhaps, for so great a thinker, he comes to the conclusion that each rational faith must choose between being 'an ethical religion or...a religion that explains the world', and he sees Christianity as the ethical option with ethics involving a combination of a sense of the immediacy of God and the necessity of living for the benefit of one's neighbour (1923: 73).

When in his prime as a celebrated Western intellectual he felt called to become a medical missionary in Africa, trained for this and pursued his work there. The debts he incurred were often paid by giving organ recitals in Europe. One was given in Holland and the story is told of a peasant who was asked why he had come to the concert. He replied that he had come to listen to the man who had done something while everyone else only talked. Schweitzer's was a mind set, from childhood, upon the pursuit of truth, of the underlying insights that alone could motivate human action. Basic questions about the religions of the world came to occupy his thought for ethical reasons and under the double distinction between 'world and life negation' on the one hand and 'world and life affirmation' on the other. When evaluating Indian religions he described the situation as 'warfare between giants', the giants of negation and affirmation (1951: 250).

In terms of the theology of religions, Schweitzer judges them according to their ethical consequences. This is of profound importance for him because he experienced something of an intellectual and emotional conversion on the topic of ethics. Ethics is, itself, the theory of moral action and explores reasons for morality. For Schweitzer, this had been a particular problem and the answer to it came in a canoe amidst a herd of hippopotamuses. The story is almost like that of some novel but he tells it as the stark truth. As an account, it perfectly reflects some psychological theories that bracket together moments of discovery and of conversion. He had become 'exhausted and disheartened' when trying to come to the heart of ethical issues and 'could not grasp it' (1933: 185). Then, on a difficult African boat trip, he was covering sheets of paper with disconnected ideas when, 'at sunset' as they were 'making their way through a herd of hippopotamuses, there flashed through my mind, unforeseen and unsought, the phrase, "Reverence for Life"'. He speaks of the iron door yielding and the path becoming clear. This becomes his clarion call as the ethical basis for life and the judgement to be used of religions. In 1919, for example, he was invited to Sweden to give a lecture at the great university town of Uppsala, and as he worked out some of the implications of the idea of reverence for life he tells us that he 'was so moved that' he 'found it difficult to speak' (1933: 218). The worldview that emerges from 'reverence for life' is what he calls 'ethical mysticism', a perspective that increasingly motivated his life.

Schweitzer represents the final phase of Western intellectual Christianity heroically engaging with the unchristian masses. It is a stance much criticised by some who see it as a patronising Western imperialism. Be that as it may, from the mid-twentieth century a different style of theology of religions began to emerge through broad movements of indigenous or contextual theology, as well as from narrative and liberation theology. These reflected local rather than exported forms of Christian thought. A book such as C. S. Song's *Third Eye Theology* explores ways in which Christian theology comes to itself within a variety of Asian contexts. It shows, for example, the inadequacies of Tillich's engagement with Buddhism or Schweitzer's with Hinduism and, more substantially, it demonstrates how the rich diversity of humanity can engage with Christianity to yield its own grasp of the faith. At that point a theology of religion becomes part of a theology of self-identity for a community.

Ancestor salvation

The context of ancestor worship affords a good example of the kind of critical issues Christianity encounters with potential converts from non-Christian religions. Ancestors have played a powerful part in the lives of many peoples, especially those of tradition-focused societies, being viewed as still influential upon the living and able to bless or curse their endeavours. Funeral rites and many other commemorative rites have bound the ancestors together with the living in an overall community. It is not surprising, then, that the ancestors could prove either a strong barrier to the acceptance of a new creed or, possibly, a bridge to its acceptance. The potential barrier emerged, for example, with the Japanese in the case of the early missionary work of Francis Xavier, mentioned above. How could living Japanese become Catholic if that meant separating themselves from their highly influential and deeply respected ancestors? One answer lay in the Christian view that God had implanted a sense of the moral law within all people (Romans 2: 14–15) and, in that sense, they had had the opportunity to engage with divine commandments in their own day, albeit under a different religious frame.

When the Pope decreed that ancestor worship was forbidden in 1704 it brought very negative consequences for the Catholic Church in China. Rites associated with the dead can also, of course, be part of the commemoration of the dead and, in many churches, that has a positive part to play in the liturgical life of the community (Song 1980: 150–7). Prayers for the dead and the Christian idea of the Communion of Saints could help deal with the understandable commitment the living often show to their dead. An even more direct and immediate answer was provided by nineteenth-century Mormon missionaries when, for example, they encountered New Zealand Maoris. The Maori also held their ancestors in deep respect and, partly because of this, they found a certain attraction in the Latter-day Saint belief that rituals performed by descendants could give their ancestors an opportunity to become Latter-day Saints in the afterlife.

God, religion and cultures

From these individual accounts of particular theologians we pass to a more abstract but significant question of the Christian theology of religions and one that is, in a sense, potentially destructive. It asks how God might be either beneficially revealed or have the revelation frustrated by human cultures. This is a most difficult question involving, as it does, a kind of logical juggling act. If Christianity is God's self-revelation, how can it frustrate God's revelation? Equally, since each human culture is very specific to itself, if divine revelation comes through one specific culture, it would seem proper to ask if there might not be some aspect of God that could not be expressed very well in that cultural form. One might ask, for example, whether divine grace is best expressed through a culture heavily grounded in a sense of strict reciprocal relations. If, that is, a culture sees justice in terms of an eye for an eye or fair wages for fair work, then how can that culture truly be a means for expressing the notion of grace as a divine generosity not limited by rules of equal reciprocity? It might only be able to express it as a contradiction of ordinary rules.

One might, however, decide that as Christianity, for example, spreads throughout the diverse cultures of the world it is able to shine through the different coloured 'glass' of each culture. Different languages make some ideas easier to express than others, different temperaments allow Christian values to come to expression in different ways. And, besides that, the very fact that people from quite different cultures come to Christian faith expresses, quite practically, its claim to be universal. When, say, a small group of British, African and Chinese Christians gather together, the very fact of their difference announces the message of God's emergent world of influence. The character and habit born in each culture allows Christian virtues to be displayed in subtly different ways. There is a wonder and a beauty in that. It is a kind of beauty born of cultural diversity and it challenges any strict uniformity bred by extreme control over inwardly focused sect-like churches. In biblical terms, the Acts of the Apostles in its account of what has loosely been called the Council of Jerusalem in Acts 15 gives a minor degree of freedom to non-Jewish converts to Christianity whilst still feeling the pull of traditional Jewish ways of being religious. There is an ongoing debate in Acts as to whether converts to Christianity ought to be circumcised, as were all Jews, or whether they need not be so given the mark of the covenant. The very fact that the weight of opinion came to fall on the belief that it was the inward presence of the Holy Spirit and not an outward bodily mark that counted before God allowed for a major breakthrough in early Christian expansion. For the Spirit might be appropriated in differing cultural ways, even though the Spirit's presence might transform aspects of culture in distinctive ways. In other words, the Christian theology of religions does well to be open to a dynamic sense of the future and to surprises that may emerge in it.

Experience and knowledge

The whole issue of experience is of deep significance within the theology of religion, being at one and the same time, both profoundly helpful and yet problematic. This dichotomy merits some explanation. Experience is a helpful feature for theologians when they interpret it as a sign of divine presence within people. By its very nature experience is open to a wide variety of interpretation and theologians can bring to it a wide variety of explanation. They can easily read into other people's experience the theological significance given to their own experience. To those who have an inclusive and open attitude to world religions, experience is the common foundation that demonstrates that God makes the divine presence felt at will. Experience can, by contrast, also be a hindrance for those with an exclusivist attitude and who would either wish to rule out experience as a basis for comparing cases of divine presence or who might even interpret experience as the outcome of evil influences.

Still, it is of considerable interest that some theologians are capable of writing extensive volumes of theology without hardly ever discussing experience as such. For them, it seems as though theology is all about doctrine and the historical development of doctrine. Theologies of Christian religion are often pursued either by ignoring experience or by assuming its importance in some implicit way, as though experience can simply be taken for granted. It is equally interesting, however, that the fact of experience becomes increasingly less easy to ignore when approaching non-Christian religions, most especially the religions of the East. This is largely because Eastern religions have tended to develop theories about experience as part of their meditative practices. In most Hindu, Buddhist and Sikh practice, part of the goal of life is to become free from the ties that bind human consciousness and affections to the material world; because some form of meditative practice is basic to that goal, it is inevitable that descriptions of types or levels of experience or of levels of consciousness should become built into explicit accounts of the religious life. Experience is part of the very process of change as the self shifts from its materialistic focus to higher centres of concern. Christianity, by contrast, has tended to stress the power of divine acts in saving mankind through Jesus Christ. It is almost as though the basic acts of salvation lie outside the individual. Of course, the individual is expected to appropriate and relate to the saving acts of God, and here worship and prayer along with, for example, experiences of religious conversion and rebirth do play an important part. But the experience itself is not the saving act.

Mystics and charismatics

One field in which a Christian theology of religion does pay particular attention to experience both within its own territory and also in other religions is that of mysticism. Mysticism describes a variety of experiences sharing a family resemblance in a powerful sense of oneness with the ultimate source of life, of timeless insight into the real nature of things and an awareness of the purposefulness of life itself. Although it is a radically individual experience, it does not take the form of loneliness. In the Christian tradition, itself dotted with mystics, this experience often takes the form of a love union with deity. Christian theologians tend to have something of an ambivalent attitude towards mysticism because it is experience that can claim a kind of immediate knowledge of God that can lead those experiencing it to sit lightly to the dogmatic theology of any particular church. Protestant theologians such as Emil Brunner and Reinhold Niebuhr have located mysticism closer to some form of Greek paganism than to authentic Christianity. While mystics have existed throughout Christian history, it is interesting that in the first half of the twentieth century, after a generation of critical scholarship had undermined much biblical certainty, numerous authors devoted themselves to describing and advocating mysticism as a prime feature in Christianity and a potential bridge of connectedness with other religions, as with W. R. Inge's *Christian Mysticism* (1899), Rufus Jones's *Studies in Mystical Religion* (1909) and Evelyn Underhill's *Mysticism* (1911).

If mysticism was the witness to mysterious domains of a God–humanity interaction at the opening of the twentieth century, charismatic religion marked it at its close. The emergence of charismatic renewal movements that made their presence very firmly felt between the 1970s and the 1990s within most mainstream Christian denominations demanded the rise of a theology to explain it and to help it take form. Here we see the need for a theology of Christian religious activity more than of other religions. Although the Pentecostal denomination had emerged at the outset of the twentieth century, with its own doctrinal emphasis on the presence of the Holy Spirit as demonstrated in various gifts such as speaking in tongues or gaining visions or engaging in healing, the mainstream denominations were rather taken by surprise when many of these features upsurged in their more traditional ranks. It is interesting, for example, to note that the 1958 edition of the *Oxford Dictionary of the Christian Church* had no entry on the Charismatic movement. This would become an impossible omission for any such reference book after the 1970s. The case of the charismatic movement is instructive for the theology of religion, for it shows how a theological interpretation of a phenomenon often follows after its appearance, marking once more the priority of experience. This is another potential pitfall for some theologians, for while they are happy to agree, for example, that the emergence of the doctrine of the Holy Trinity was a Christian reflection upon experiencing the various persons of the Trinity, they are not always so content to see such a 'subsequent form of interpretation' for religious phenomena they may regard as marginal to traditional religion. But the truth is that theological interpretation often, indeed usually, follows on after experience and does not precede it. With time, however, any church seeks to use its pre-existing doctrinal scheme not only to interpret but also to control new developments. If a focus on Christ controlled the theology of religions at the end of the nineteenth century, and continues to the present, it has been increasingly complemented by an emphasis upon the Spirit.

Contemporary perspectives

Having dealt rather separately with Catholic, Protestant and broad academic approaches to the theology of religions over a wide canvas, we now conclude with an engagement of a contemporary Anglican theologian, Rowan Williams, and with the important work of Raimundo Panikkar, a twentieth-century Roman Catholic theologian with extensive knowledge and experience of Indian religious life and practice. Pannikkar's *The Unknown Christ of Hinduism* (1968) explored ways in which Christ is a discernible presence within practically any religion, an expression of the important notion of non-Christians being 'anonymous Christians'. He also stressed the importance of the Christian doctrine of the Holy Trinity, a key foundation of Christian doctrine and a central feature of orthodox belief. Panikkar's later work emphasised this doctrine to argue that the dynamic nature of God is encountered in the complex world of humanity and of religions. The Christian is always working from a Christian encounter of this active Trinity in a way of life he calls 'Christianness'.

This perspective appealed a great deal to Rowan Williams, scholar, archbishop and one of the most influential of twenty-first-century British theologians. He was attracted by the fact that Panikkar did not slide into exclusivism, nor turn everything into inclusivism, nor yet frame everything in some higher design or 'meta-theory' (2000: 170). These negatives can best be presented in what sociologists often call ideal types, brief summaries of the essential features of a given phenomenon.

Exclusivism regards Christianity as the only way of explaining the true nature of God and as the only way of salvation for humanity. It stresses Christian uniqueness, leaving no way open for any positive evaluation of other religions. If it seeks to explain their presence in the world at all, it does so as strictly human ways of trying to understand the meaning of life. In other words, it accepts that Christianity is a divinely inspired venture and that all others are merely human. One way in which this has often been expressed is in the contrast between God seeking after mankind in Christianity and humanity seeking after God in other religions. At its most extreme, this outlook describes non-Christian religions as a kind of deceit perpetrated by the Devil, who thereby leads people away from the true God of Christianity.

Inclusivism, on the other hand, assumes that all religions are the same as far as their underlying nature is concerned. Broadly speaking, it seeks to explain the origin of the world and of humanity, have some explanation for the failures of human nature and for the evils that befall people in life and, finally, to advance some plan to deal with these flaws. This plan outlines a way of salvation, enlightenment or release that normally involves an ethical way of living alongside forms of devotion and worship directed towards a transcendent focus. People interested in inter-faith dialogue often adopt some version of this inclusivism because it gives to all concerned a degree of common ground as they pursue their overall goal of seeking to understand the religions of others in the light of their own faith. This, then, is a kind of pluralism, an outlook that accepts the variability of human religion as people seek to engage with the complex ultimate reality of deity. A slightly different form of this inclusivist outlook concerns Panikkar's reference to a 'meta-theory' adopted by some pluralists. Williams describes such people as trying to locate 'all traditions on a single map and relating to their concrete life' (2000: 170). The 'meta-theory' is an explanation of different views. As an explanation it works on a different basis from each religious explanation of things and is a 'higher order' or 'meta' account of things.

A third way, and it is the one Williams admires in Panikkar, takes a different view. It does not work by exclusivist or inclusivist principles, nor does it adopt that rather superior attitude that thinks it possible to map out what all religions are doing. In other words, it does not stand above and in judgement of other views. Instead it works from within one tradition, in this case a Christian one, and can be described in terms of a 'Christianness' grounded in a sense of confidence. For Panikkar, this confidence is not rootless but works out from the 'christic fact', from the historical case of Jesus as the Christ and of what he did in the world and of what God continues to do through him. The key to this outlook is to see it as dynamic. It concerns the power or dynamism of God as something that is ongoing and not only present today but also as a causal impact on tomorrow. In other words, the Christian, or any other religious devotee, cannot predict the future and cannot ensure the outcome of any sort of inter-faith activity. That is why, for example, Williams decries the 'meta-theory' view of religions. That view thinks in terms of having religions and their activities under control. For it can be a feature of intellectual life to hold on to theories that seem to explain trends of human thought, and ironically this is sometimes more often the case in the humanities than in the sciences.

Williams's preference follows Panikkar into a kind of collaboration, a working together to see what will happen as people pursue their interest in religions, both in their own and in those of others. In other words, because God is ever dynamically active and at work and because humanity can enter into that activity there is no knowing what may happen. Here doctrine gives pride of place to life as it is lived. Christians may be influenced by the 'christic fact' and direct their understanding in relation to God's actions in Christ but that does not predict any particular outcome in the here and now.

Conclusion: Personal experience and encounter

The importance of personal experience cannot be ignored as far as the theology of religions is concerned. Books are, of course, of great help in outlining the history, doctrine and practice of different traditions, and they can also describe the life experiences of others, but ultimately it is important for individuals to experience something of other traditions and their meaning to persons holding those faiths. Even one visit to a place of worship of another religion can teach what a book may never achieve. The great Lutheran archbishop and Swedish Professor of Uppsala Nathan Söderblom (1866–1931) strongly argued the case that understanding of other religions extended from the experience of one's own. His 1931 Gifford Lectures, *The Living God*, is an extremely good example of the influence of the disciplines of the anthropology and the history of religions upon Christian theological thought of more liberal Protestants. He offers, though without the label, a theology of religion that is grounded in extensive scholarly knowledge and wide practical experience framed by a deep personal piety. In some respects he echoes William Robertson Smith (1846–94), the Aberdeen theologian who pioneered the anthropology of religion and whose *Religion of the Semites* can be read as a kind of theology of ancient or primitive religion that was influential over the turn of the nineteenth century. It sought an understanding of the place of community experience and the presence of deity at what were reckoned to be earlier stages of religious development.

Christian theology is very interesting as far as this realm of experience is concerned and it is worth noting how some of the scholars we have mentioned have, themselves, been affected by personal contact with believers from other religions and with aspects of the actual practice of other ways of believing. In terms of some of the scholars we have already mentioned, Panikkar was brought up with Hinduism alongside his Christianity and, though originating from Spain, had a Hindu father. As a young Catholic priest, Panikkar went to work in India. Bede Griffiths (1907–93) went to India as a middle-aged Christian monk and devoted himself to understanding and experiencing how utterly dependent human beings are upon God. He gained considerable respect amongst Hindus, though, as is often the case when serious thinkers express themselves in ways that diverge from the normal tradition, he was not, perhaps, fully appreciated by his own Catholic Church. Both Paul Tillich and John Hick, amongst many others, have been influenced in their philosophical and theological thoughts by actual encounters with individuals of other religions. It has also been argued that it was such contact with Jews that prompted Pope John XXIII to initiate studies of Judaism that would result in major changes in Catholic attitudes to other religions at large, as discussed above. Tillich certainly advocates 'actual participation' as 'the only authentic way' to understanding the spiritual life of other religions (1964: 151).

 ## Further reading

Anawati, Georges C. (1969), 'Excursus on Islam', in *Commentary on the Documents of Vatican II*, ed. Hebert Vorgrimler, New York: Herder and Herder.

Bowker, John (1973), *The Sense of God*, Oxford: Oxford University Press.

Bowker, John (1978), *The Religious Imagination and the Sense of God*, Oxford: Oxford University Press.

Bowker, John (1997), *The Oxford Dictionary of World Religions*, Oxford: Oxford University Press.

Dhavamony, Mariasusai (2001), *Christian Theology of Religions*, 2nd edn, Bern and Oxford: Peter Lang.

Ephrem (1994), *St Ephrem the Syrian: Selected Prose Works*, Kathleen McVey (ed), Washington, DC: Catholic University of America Press.

Farmer, H. H. (1954), *Revelation and Religion*, London: Nisbet and Co.

Farquhar, J. N. (1913), *The Crown of Hinduism*, Oxford: Oxford University Press.

Hick, John (1974), *Truth and Dialogue*, London: Sheldon Press.

Lindbeck, George (1984), *The Nature of Doctrine: Religion and Theology in a Postliberal Age*, London: SPCK.

Oesterreicher, John M. (1969), 'Declaration on the Relationship of the Church to

Non-Christian Religions', in *Commentary on the Documents of Vatican II*, ed. Hebert Vorgrimler, New York: Herder and Herder.

Origen (1869), *Ante-Nicene Christian Library*, ed. A. Roberts and J. Donaldson, Edinburgh: T. and T. Clark.

Pannenberg, Wolfhart (1971), *Basic Questions in Theology*, vol. 2, London: SCM Press.

Panikkar, Raimundo (1968), *The Unknown Christ of Hinduism*, London: Darton, Longman and Todd.

Schweitzer, Albert (1923), *Christianity and the Religions of the World*, London: Allen and Unwin.

Schweitzer, Albert (1933), *Albert Schweitzer: My Life and Thought*, London: Allen and Unwin.

Schweitzer, Albert (1951), *Indian Thought and Its Development*, London: Adam and Charles Black.

Seaver, George (1955), *Albert Schweitzer: The Man and His Mind*, London: Adam and Charles Black.

Song, C. S. (1980), *Third Eye Theology*, London: Lutterworth Press.

Thomas, Terence (1999), *Paul Tillich and World Religions*, Cardiff: Cardiff Academic Press.

Tillich, Paul (1961), *Christianity and the Encounter of World Religions*, New York: Columbia University Press.

Tillich, Paul (1964), *Systematic Theology*, vol. 3, London: Nisbet.

Williams, Rowan (2000), *On Christian Theology*, Oxford: Blackwell.

Zaehner, R. C. (1970), *Concordant Discord: The Interdependence of Faiths*, Oxford: Clarendon Press.

Questions

1. Do you agree with Cantwell Smith that the time has come to drop the use of the word 'religion' as too broad to make any real sense?

2. Does Albert Schweitzer's idea of 'reverence for life' provide a useful basis for dealing with the contemporary human concern for ecology?

3. Do you think that all religions are really about the same underlying reality or not?

4. Is it better to work with people of different faiths on practical projects rather than spend time discussing these religions? Or is practical work a way of avoiding the most important issues?

Psychological and Phenomenological Theories of Religion

Seth D. Kunin

- ❏ Introduction
- ❏ William James: Making what is necessary easy
- ❏ Sigmund Freud: Sex, murder and illusion
- ❏ Carl Gustav Jung: The collective unconscious
- ❏ Joseph Campbell: The mythologist as hero
- ❏ The phenomenology of religion and the birth of the study of religion
- ❏ Mircea Eliade: The myth of the eternal return
- ❏ Ninian Smart: The dimensions of religion
- ❏ Conclusion
- ❏ Further reading
- ❏ Questions

Introduction

In this chapter we will introduce two important approaches to the study of religion. Although there are significant differences between these approaches both on the wider level, between the psychological and the phenomenological, and among the various thinkers within a specific approach, there are also common threads which link them. Some of these threads link the approaches as a whole – as with, for example, the emphasis on the individual and individual experience, though some thinkers see this as relating to a transcendental other, while their opponents see it as purely a psychological experience. Other threads link particular thinkers – thus Jung, Campbell and Eliade are linked through both the concept of the sacred and through their perception that religion rests on an unconscious collective and universal basis. Most of these thinkers, with the exception of Freud, also see religion as essentially a positive phenomenon, with Jung and Eliade seeing it a necessary source of enlightenment and growth.

This chapter focuses specifically on some of the early exemplars of these approaches, particularly in respect of psychology. This is due to two main reasons. First, we are primarily concerned here with examining theories or definitions of religion as a whole. Many more recent theories in psychology focus on aspects of religion or on aspects of the personality of those people within religious structures. While these areas are of great interest, they fall outside the purview of this short survey. Second, we hope this book will provide a basis for further study and thought, so rather than examining every theory we are highlighting some of the more interesting and significant theories as a platform from which the student can address the discipline of religious studies and the other interrelated disciplines discussed.

William James (1842–1910): Making what is necessary easy

> As there seems to be no one elementary religious emotion, but only a common store house of emotions on which religious objects may draw, so there might conceivably prove to be no one specific and essential kind of religious object and no one specific and essential kind of religious act.
>
> Religion ... shall mean for us the feelings, acts and experiences of individual men in their solitude, so far as they apprehend themselves to stand in relation to whatever they may consider the divine.
>
> William James, *The Varieties of Religious Experience.* (1982: 28, 31)

Like many of his predecessors, William James developed a theory of religion which had its roots in individual experience. This experience, which is psychological and subjective, becomes the basis for religion as a phenomena and religion as a social institution. Unlike Otto or Schleiermacher, who traced the experiential origin of religion to a specific faculty or to an interaction between a faculty and an external other, James discusses religion as arising from a broad range of human experiences that are analogous to experiences in other realms. Religious emotions are the same as other emotions; what makes them religious is that their object is religious.

James's definition of religion is also more encompassing than many other discussions in respect of the object of religion. His discussion suggests that there is not necessarily one specific type of religious object which is essential to all forms of religion. Thus, his definition focuses on the characterisation of the individual or group, emphasising that the religious object is 'whatever they may consider divine'. His definition also opens the possibility of including a wide range of activities as religion, arguing that there is no act that is essentially religious and that possibly any act (and thus perhaps any institution), depending on how it is perceived, can be a religious act.

Although James's theory does not depend on the existence of an external other, he does not deny that a common feature of religious experience, that of being 'subject to external control', has a basis in experiential reality. He does, however, suggest that this experience derives from a psychological root, the subconscious, rather than an external object. Although the experienced other is internal rather than external, the experience of otherness and subjectivity is, in a sense, real. James argues that the subconscious is experienced as an objective other and that the sense of being controlled is due to the fact that we are indeed controlled by our own higher faculties. He argues further that the experience of union with the divine is also real, in that it actually is a union of the self. Unlike Jung, however, this union and its explanation stays on the psychological level rather than moving to the mystical.

James was a major figure in the developing philosophical school of Pragmatism, and this approach had a clear influence on his understanding of religion. He viewed religion as both essentially functional and positive. Religion, in part, has the role of making aspects of our life or experience which are intolerable, tolerable. It enables individuals to accept and do what is needed, to perform the sacrifices and surrenders upon which survival depends. Thus, James suggests that 'religion ... makes easy and felicitous what in any case is necessary'. Upon the same philosophical foundations James also distinguishes between religions that are healthy-minded and those that are not; religion in a positive sense is optimistic and formative as opposed to emphasising the presence of evil. He does, however, recognise that the 'morbid-minded' approach to religion covers a wider range of experience than does the 'health-minded' form and therefore in some ways it is a more comprehensive philosophy of experience.

In spite of his validation of a wide range of religious emotions and objects, James contends that there is a commonality to individual religious experience, that is, the mystical experience. He argues that mystical states are defined by four categories: ineffability – that they defy expression; noetic quality – mystical states are states of knowledge and authority; transiency – they cannot be sustained; and passivity – the will is in abeyance. His further discussion of specific cases also brings out the quality of unity or the overarching sense of oneness. Even if these experiences are grounded in actuality of the self and the subconscious, his emphasis on them suggests that religion is an essentially unitary phenomenon.

Critique

There are many positive aspects of James's discussion. His analysis allows us to discuss religion without positing a supernatural other and provides a basis of discussion on a testable, that is, the nature of human psychology. James also, at least in terms of the first part of his exposition, allows us to address a wide range of divergent phenomena based on a common function rather than a specific source or object. His analysis, in this respect, foreshadows some of the more broadly functionalist theories developed by anthropologists.

There are, however, some specific problems with this approach. The most significant of these also holds true for the other psychological approaches, that is, it bases its discussion of religion on individual experience rather than the social or institutional level. Although experience would provide a sufficient explanation for individual belief, it does not provide a valid explanation for the persistence of religion as an institution and the participation of a wide range of individuals who do not report such experiences. If the institutional aspect of religion is secondary, arising as a means of domesticating the religious experience, or perhaps as a platform for the creation of future religious experience, then the explanation does not deal with the complexity and multiplicity of objects and practices which are found both within specific religious structures and among various religions. On a wider level, James's theory discounts the meaning and role of the most significant aspects of religion, the institutional, which are the most common way that individuals experience religion – religious experience is most often that of the institution rather than of a supernatural or subconscious god.

James's approach to religion as emerging from the individual suffers from an even more serious problem; it assumes that the religious experience is in some sense essential and specifically individual, with each person as an abstract entity. As Marx points out in respect of Feuerbach's theory of religion, which also emerges from the individual, 'religious sentiment' or in this case religious experience is a social product, it is shaped by and emerges from a particular society, and therefore from a particular institution rather than the reverse.

Although James's theory opens the possibility for a variety of religious objects and practices, and thus the huge variability found in religions around the world, his emphasis on one form of mystical experience limits the application of this model. If religious objects and practices are variable, then it is logical that religious experiences would be equally variable. A good example of this variability is found in regard to mystical union, an important aspect of James's theory. Although this is an aspect of many mystical systems, there are systems, such as Judaism, in which mystical union never takes place. Other religious systems may betray no aspect of mystical experience and thus would seemingly fall outside of James's discussion.

Sigmund Freud (1856–1939): Sex, murder and illusion

Sigmund Freud's analysis of religion has been influential both in respect of psychology and a wide range of other disciplines that study the history and function of religion for the individual and society. His analysis can be divided into two main areas: his evaluation of religion as an illusion, which is developed in *The Future of an Illusion* (1961), and his discussions of the origins and nature of religion and ritual, developed in *Totem and Taboo* (1950).

The Future of an Illusion

Although there are significant differences in the discussion of the nature of religion found in these sources, as they focus on different aspects of the phenomena, there are some fundamental propositions that underlie both expositions. Perhaps the most important of these is the analogy between individual experience and societal experience, individual psychological development and societal development. In both texts Freud suggests that religion is analogous to the fantasies or illusions of young children, particularly in regard to their perception – both positive and negative – of their fathers. Thus, for example, in *The Future of an Illusion* he argues that religion and the concept of God is analogous to a baby's perception of the world and, most importantly, of its father. The baby perceives that it lives in a world that it cannot control and which is potentially uncontrollable. The baby creates out of its father an all-powerful being which reduces the anxiety created by the uncontrollable universe. In a similar way, humanity projects the image of the father, God, as an all-powerful being who controls the universe and thereby reduces the sense of helplessness.

The theory of recapitulation

This argument is then taken a step further. On a simple level, the illusions of childhood are related to the exaggerated fantasies and illusions of the neurotic – in both cases these are individual rather than essentially societal experiences. Thus, for example, the Oedipus complex, the desire of a boy to kill his father and sleep with his mother, is found in boys and, if not resolved, becomes in exaggerated forms the basis of adult neuroses. Freud suggests that while these complexes are essentially individual in modern Western society, they played a social role in earlier societies. Thus, the Oedipus story is a public myth in ancient Greek society but is the stuff of dreams within our own society. Freud considers myths as the actual recapitulation of events that are the basis for the creation of the human institution of religion. In effect, he makes an analogy between the child, the neurotic and the 'primitive'.

This analogy rests on a concept that was influential in biology and extended to theories of cultural evolution, the theory of recapitulation, or ontogeny recapitulates phylogeny. This theory suggests that the individual member of a species will undergo in its own development a shortened recapitulation or repetition of all of the stages of its species' evolutionary past. In biology it was argued that the foetus goes through all of the past stages from fish to modern human being, and in culture it was suggested that the child goes through all stages of cultural evolution. Thus, the child's experience of the Oedipus complex is in part a recapitulation of a stage in cultural evolution – a stage contemporary cultural evolutionists believed some societies retained. This concept allows Freud to work on two levels. He can examine the processes as essentially individual, and therefore examine their individual dynamics, but also examine them as social processes, justifying his consistent analogy between the individual and the communal.

Cultural evolution

As suggested, one of the theoretical principles which underlies Freud's discussion of religion is the acceptance of a unilinear model of cultural evolution, that all human societies are progressing, albeit at different speeds, along a single line of development. This model sees Western European culture as the highest form, with all other cultures being further down the line of development. Freud's use of this model reflects many of the contemporary theorists, particularly Frazer, and Tylor, and underlies the concept of recapitulation. It also underlies Freud's belief that science would ultimately replace religion as the basis of human action.

The Future of an Illusion focuses on the role religion plays in human society, and although it also touches on the origins of religion as an institution, most of that discussion is found in *Totem and Taboo*. One of the significant themes developed is the concept of illusion. Freud argues that an illusion is not necessarily an error, rather it is a belief which is held because one wishes it were so rather than resting on any other form of evidence. As indicated above, he argues that religion develops in order to give meaning to an apparently meaningless universe, to make us feel less helpless. The significant feature of this argument is that, whatever its benefits to society, religion rests on deception, made no better because it is essentially self-deception.

Freud does suggest that religion plays a partially positive role in society; that it provides a basis for law and societal order. God in this model plays a similar societal role to the father in shaping or expressing the super ego. In spite of this, he argues that even if the results are useful – as, for example, the law against killing is useful – the reasons for the development of that law have little to do with practicality or the rational ordering of social relations, as ultimately their basis is in illusion and deception.

The conclusion of *The Future of an Illusion* returns to the evolutionary aspects of the recapitulation model. He argues that culture can mature out of its need for religion. Although religion does currently play an important role in shaping people's behaviours, this role can be taken over by science. In an argument reminiscent of James Frazer, he suggests that the religious stage of cultural development can and will be replaced by the scientific. His ultimate judgement of religion is found in the conclusion, where he argues that there is no domain of human affairs which cannot properly be explained by science, thus at the final stage of human maturity or development there is no need or place for religion.

Totem and Taboo

Prehistoric man, in the various stages of his development, is known to us through the inanimate monuments and implements which he has left behind, through the information about his art, his religion, and his attitude towards life which has come down to us either directly or by way of tradition handed down in legends, myths and fairy tales, and through the relics of his mode of thought which survive in our own manners and customs. But apart from this, in a certain sense he is still our contemporary. There are men still living who, as we believe, stand very near to primitive man, far nearer than we do, and whom we therefore regard as his direct heirs and representatives. Such is our view of those whom we describe as savages or half savages; and their mental life must have

> particular interest for us if we are right in seeing in it a well-preserved
> picture of an early stage of our own development.
>
>   If that supposition is correct, a comparison between the psychology
> of primitive peoples, as is taught by social anthropology, and the psy-
> chology of neurotics, as has been revealed by psycho-analysis, will be
> bound to show numerous points of agreement and will throw new light
> on familiar facts in both sciences.
>
> Sigmund Freud, *Totem and Taboo* (1950: 1)

Totem and Taboo presents a comprehensive analysis of the origins and
evolutionary development of religion. The book builds on the evolutionary theories of Frazer and Tylor and presents detailed arguments
supporting Freud's understanding of recapitulation. Indeed, these concepts are highlighted in the opening section of the first essay, 'The
Horror of Incest' (see the above text box). The book also extends the
analogy of religion with neurosis through the comparison of the nature
and origin of religious rituals with those created by neurotics.

Murder, incest and the primal horde

One of the most innovative and controversial aspects of the book is
Freud's discussion of the origins of totemism, and in effect both religion
and society. Freud speculates that human beings originally lived in primal
hordes. These groups were made up of a senior male, his wives and their
sons. The main feature of this grouping was that the senior male, or the
father, had sole sexual access to the women. At some point the sons
group together, slaughter and eat the father, and have sex with the
'mothers'. This leads to a sense of guilt because the sons both loved and
hated their father, which expresses itself in the creation of social norms,
for example, the prohibitions against incest and killing. Rituals and religion are created around the father figure, who initially is resurrected in
the form of a totemic animal. All religions are developments from this
original act of violence and the guilt created by it.

The Oedipus complex

Freud presents this primal event as a manifestation of the Oedipus
complex – the young men kill their fathers and have sex with their
mothers. Thus, the narrative is illustrative of the concept of recapitulation: among early human societies the Oedipus scenario was actually

experienced, today it is recapitulated in young children who psychologically experience the Oedipus complex. Individuals who were psychologically unable to handle their Oedipal feelings as children may become neurotic adults with continuing Oedipus complexes. Similarly, children and neurotics, like early man, create rituals and religious practices as a means of expressing the psychological energy and the guilt created by that expression.

Critique

Although Freud suggests some interesting lines of thought regarding religion, there are some significant problematic assumptions and lines of argument. One of the most significant of these underlies the persistent theory of cultural evolution and recapitulation. Both of these theories have been challenged and demonstrated to be ethnographically unsupportable. The theory of cultural evolution, which Freud inherited, was unilinear; it assumed that all cultures go through a single progressive path of development. Ethnographic evidence suggests that there is no single path of development; each society develops in its own way based on choices it makes and elements that it borrows or rejects from other societies. Thus, there is no useful analogy with other living societies and our own past. The theory of cultural evolution as expressed by Freud is also questionable because it is essentially ethnocentric, assuming a culturally superior position from which other cultures or values can be qualitatively assessed and ranked.

If unilinear cultural evolution is open to challenge, then cultural recapitulation is equally problematic – if it exists at all it would need to be culture specific rather than universal. The basis of cultural recapitulation is also challengeable because no mechanism is described which would lead children to experience the stages through which the society developed.

The main argument of *Totem and Taboo* is equally problematic. If Freud is suggesting that the primal horde is a historic reality rather than a construction or model of the past, and he seems to so suggest, then his speculation has no ethnographic or evidential support. The theory also relies on some form of transmission of this original event via both culture and the individual – thus, in part, suggesting genetic transmission. A modern understanding of genetic transmission does not support the transmission of acquired traits, so there would be no way for the experiences to be genetically passed down. Freud's model would require that this event was experienced by the ancestors of every modern human but discoveries about the geographic spread of early man, who existed long before the development of totemism, would make such a common experience highly unlikely.

Freud's analysis also rests on a sleight of hand through which individual experiences and psychological states are assumed to be analogous to social constructs, as in the analogy between religion and neurosis. Freud, however, does not present any compelling evidence that would link up these very different phenomena, and his theory almost suggests that society has a mind with an unconscious, as does the individual – but the location and nature of such a mind poses many possibly insurmountable theoretical problems.

The Oedipus complex, the psychological state central to Freud's argument, is also problematic. Freud's analysis assumes that this complex is common to all human individuals and societies. This assumption is challengeable on several levels. Even if it is accepted that it is found in the society from which Freud had actual empirical data, this does not allow us to assume that it is found in other differently organised societies either geographically or historically distinct from our own. Ethnographic data from other societies suggests that the Oedipus complex is specific to cultures which have certain forms of familial or social organisation. Thus, for example, in societies with matrilineal patterns of descent, in which the father plays a weak role (other than his procreative role), complexes other than the Oedipus complex will develop. This suggests that psychological complexes and religion, if it is indeed related to them, are at least in part shaped by their particular cultural context and do not reflect universal human psychological states.

Carl Gustav Jung (1875–1961): The collective unconscious

In speaking of religion I must make clear from the start what I mean by that term. Religion, as the Latin word denotes, is a careful and scrupulous observation of what Rudolf Otto aptly termed the *numinosum*, that is a dynamic agency or effect not caused by an arbitrary act of will. On the contrary, it seizes and controls the human subject, who is always rather its victim than its creator. The *numinosum* – whatever its cause may be – is an experience of the subject independent of his will. At all events . . . this experience is being due to a cause external to the individual.

Carl Gustav Jung, 'Psychology and Religion' (1969: 7)

Unlike Freud's essentially negative conception of religion, Jung saw religion as emerging from an essentially positive and nurturing aspect of the psyche. To an extent, his writings suggest that underlying the creation of religion as an institution is a form of religious experience that is not worlds apart from that discussed by Otto. He sometimes appears to suggest that religious experience, a sense of absolute unity, comes from outside the individual and has significance both to the individual and society. The experience which he describes in this context owes much to contemporary ideas about Eastern religions. This aspect of Jung's approach is taken up by several of his followers, particularly Joseph Campbell.

The collective unconscious

The most significant element of Jung's theory of religion is the collective unconscious. Jung distinguished between the personal unconscious (similar to that of Freud) and the collective unconscious, which is much more foundational and is universal rather than individual. Jung describes that as the repository of the 'whole spiritual heritage of mankind's evolution'. The collective unconscious somehow stands outside and is shared by all human beings, with each individual and community drawing on it and contributing to it. The collective unconscious particularly includes the non-rational aspects of human experience, a non-rational aspect that is essential to individual growth and at its heart is the basis of religion. The fact that all human beings share this common source of religious inspiration and experience underlies what Jung perceives as the commonalities that are shared by all human religions.

The archetypes

The collective unconscious contains objects that Jung refers to as archetypes. These are the stuff of which religion, myth and dreams are made. The most significant of these is the self. This archetype is sometimes presented as the objective basis of God and is seen as an objective psychic reality. Other archetypes relate to other aspects of human personality and development. These archetypes include the wise old man, the divine child, or acts like slaying a dragon. Due to his understanding of the collective unconscious, these figures represent to Jung internal psychic realities as well as external collective realities. It is for this reason that he posits a close relationship between myths, dreams and fantasies – all are shaped by the interaction between the inner and outer unconscious. A key feature of Jung's argument is that these archetypal figures will be found as the basis of all religious and mythological systems, as well as being common to the dreams of people from all parts of the world. Thus Jungian analysis, like that of Freud, though starting from a very different point, argues for a common basis of religion and a common basis of interpretation for all religions – both arise from the unconscious, in Freud's case the individual unconscious and in Jung's the collective unconscious. The key distinction between the two is their assessment of the status of religion: for Freud it emerges from a negative assessment of the unconscious, analogous to neurosis, and for Jung it reflects a positive valuation of the collective unconscious as a source of growth.

Recapitulating recapitulation

Like Freud, Jung deploys the concept of recapitulation. This is developed most clearly in his analysis of mythology. Jung suggests, influenced perhaps by Lévy-Bruhl, that the 'primitive' lives in a world perceived purely through the unconscious. Thus, he thinks and lives in a way that is qualitatively distinct from individuals in 'modern' Western societies. Jung suggests that in 'primitive' man the various aspects of the mind are not differentiated: 'the primitive does not think consciously, but rather . . . thoughts appear' (1969: 153). Actions and thoughts are not based on conscious volition; they are rooted in the unconscious. He argues further that 'primitive man' cannot tell the difference between dreams and experiences.

Jung then extends this discussion to encompass both the dream in 'modern' individuals and more specifically the child in Western society. Like Freud, Jung suggests that childhood experience and perceptions are qualitatively different from those of the adult and are directly analogous to those of 'primitive man'. On occasion Jung also extends the metaphor to include aspects of neurosis; this, however, is not a significant aspect of his argument due to his positive valuation of the collective unconscious.

Herein also lies a key difference between his understanding of recapitulation and his respective valuing of religion and modernity. Although Jung does see 'primitive' thought as essentially childlike, it has relative positive value due to its association with the collective unconscious. Modernity, in direct opposition to Freud's essentially positive valuation, is relatively negative because it attempts to ignore the collective unconscious. Religion, as a reflection of religious experience and an affirmation of it, is a possible cure to the problems created by modernity. Thus, for Jung religion is essentially positive, as a link to the collective unconscious, while for Freud it is negative for precisely the same reason.

Critique

Jung's theory raises many of the same issues as that of Freud as well as several unique to it. We have already examined some of the issues related to cultural evolution and the theory of recapitulation that is derived from it. These critiques are relevant to both Jung and Freud. In addition, Jung's assumption that 'primitive thought' is qualitatively distinct from 'modern thought' is not born out by ethnographic analysis. All the evidence suggests that although different communities develop their own forms of rationality, there is no essential qualitative distinction; no human society lives or thinks purely in the realm of the unconscious. In all societies individuals and groups seem to function both on the conscious and unconscious levels in much the same way.

The two major building blocks of Jung's theory, the collective unconscious and the archetypes, are also open to some very serious challenges. The collective unconscious is problematic both from a logical and ethnographic perspective. If such a collective phenomenon exists we need to ask where it is located, inside all human beings or outside all human beings? If it is inside it would need to be genetic but, as suggested above regarding Freud, there is no genetic mechanism for the passing down of acquired traits, therefore no mechanism for developing the content of or inheriting the collective unconscious, unless it was relatively fixed from the very roots of human evolution and its content developed solely on the basis of chance mutation. Both of these possibilities seem highly unlikely. If there is no internal genetic basis then it must derive from an external source, either related to the community or standing outside all communities. If it derived from each specific community there would be no basis for the universality, which is an essential attribute of Jung's theory. If it stands outside human communities then it becomes essentially a mystical phenomenon, which is not demonstrable or explicable in scientific terms. Thus, there seems to be no possible location for the collective unconscious to exist, unless it becomes a relative collective unconscious (and thus no longer universal) maintained and sustained by specific cultures through the process of enculturation. As suggested, Jung views the collective unconscious as universal and thus rests his theory on a mystical or spiritual rather than scientifically demonstrable entity.

The archetypes, due to their close connection with the collective unconscious, are equally problematic. If we put aside their basis in a mystical entity, they are questionable on the grounds of both their apparent simplicity and with regard to ethnographic observability. Many of the archetypes, particularly those that appear to have wide application, are so broad as to be found in almost any mythological or narrative text. Although Jung might argue that this apparent broadness is due to the archetypes' pervasive presence, in many cases the very breadth limits their value in telling us anything about the individuals or communities who created the narratives. Other of these common archetypes are so closely linked with human biological functions that they do not require a concept of an external collective unconscious to explain them, and even if we accept their relative universality this does not imply that they are interpreted or understood similarly in the culture or communities in which they are found. Where the archetypes are more specific, as in the interpretation of particular objects or colours, these interpretations can be seen to be culture specific rather than having any universal compass. It might be true that specific cultures create complex symbolic entities, or archetypes, which are shared by members of that particular culture. These entities, however, do not owe their origin or power to any form of collective unconscious standing outside the particular community in that time and place, nor do they have any necessary extension beyond that community.

Joseph Campbell (1904–87): The mythologist as hero

> When the imagery (in dreams or madness)...stems from the Collective, the signals cannot be decoded in this way. They will be of the order, rather, of myth; in many cases even identical with the imagery of which the visionary or dreamer will never have heard... They will thus be actually presentations of *the archetypes of mythology* in a relation of significance to some context of contemporary life, and consequently will be decipherable only by comparison with the patterns, motifs, and semantology of mythology in general.
>
> Joseph Campbell, *Myths, Dreams and Religion* (1970: 171)

Joseph Campbell's analysis of myth and religion owes much to the work of Jung and, if anything, emphasises the problematic aspects of Jung's theories. Campbell, even more than Jung, emphasises the mystical, unifying aspects of Eastern religion as the underlying basis of all religious systems. This is emphasised in his most important book, *The Hero with a Thousand Faces* (1972), in which he suggests that the individual reading the book is, in effect, the hero going an a journey of self-discovery which concludes with becoming aware of the unity at the centre of the self.

This journey or pilgrimage in turn becomes the basis of the archetypes that Campbell emphasises in his analysis; they cluster around the progress of the narrative and are understood as reflecting stages of the individual's journey to self-awareness. Like Jung, Campbell's archetypes are so broad and self-evident that it would be almost impossible to tell any story without them. On this basis, Campbell takes a huge range of mythological narratives totally out of their cultural contexts and argues that they are all essentially describing the same psychological event.

The phenomenology of religion and the birth of the study of religion

> Phenomenology does not try to compare the religions with one another as large units, but it takes out of their historical setting the similar facts and phenomena which it encounters in different religions, brings them together, and studies them in groups. The corresponding data, which are sometimes nearly identical, bring us almost automatically to comparative study. The purpose of such study is to become acquainted with the religious thought, idea or need which underlies the group of corresponding data. Its purpose is not to determine their greater or lesser religious value. Certainly, it tries to determine their religious value, but this is the value that they had for the believers themselves, and this has never been relative, but is always absolute. The comparative consideration of corresponding data often gives a deeper and more accurate insight than the consideration of each datum by itself, for considered as a group, the data shed light on one another. Phenomenology tries to gain an over-all view of the ideas and motives which are of decisive importance in all of History of Religion.
>
> W. Brede Kristensen, *The Meaning of Religion: Lectures in the phenomenology of religion* (1971: 2)

The phenomenological approach to religion tends to examine religion outside of its cultural context, being interested in what religion is rather than what religion does. The discussions of religion that it presents tend to (or claim to) be descriptive and classificatory rather than analytical. The phenomenologist is interested in describing the observable aspects of religion with the ultimate goal of determining religion or religious form and structure. Some phenomenologists have been satisfied with the descriptive elements of the approach, others have attempted to synthesise the descriptive and typological approaches and move to the level of

essences – this is particularly true of the work of Mircea Eliade discussed below. To a degree, this search for essences moves towards a
more classical form of phenomenology which seeks to understand the
nature, structure and essence of the/an experience itself.

One of the significant aspects of phenomenology is its rejection of
theory. It argues that religion needs to be examined on its own terms,
not on the basis of theories constructed outside of it, often to examine
other aspects of culture. This point is specifically made by C. J. Bleeker
(1898–1983), who suggests that religion can only be understood by
approaches that are specifically designed for it. On this basis, many
phenomenologists and other scholars of religion reject a wide range of
sociological or psychological approaches, as they are often examining
both religion and a wider range of cultural constructs, as well as examining religion in relation to culture rather than as a separable construct
of a broad idea of human consciousness. The assumption sometimes
appears to be that their analysis is atheoretical and thereby an objective
description capable of being understood by believer and phenomenologist alike.

Although many phenomenologists argued that to be properly understood religion had to be looked at from the viewpoint of the believers,
their emphasis on classification and morphology militated against this
internal or emic approach. Thus, many of these analyses take small segments of religious symbols or practices out of their institutional, cultural,
geographic and chronological settings and group them with other apparently similar phenomena – often ignoring the profound differences that
would be clearly seen in the contextualised object. The morphology
takes no account of the believers' understanding or practice in respect of
the particular religious object.

For many phenomenologists, particular religions are of interest but
they are not the primary goal of the analysis. The goal of the analysis is
to understand religion rather than religions. This goal assumes that there
is a general phenomenon, religion that stands in some sense outside of
any of its particular manifestations, and that by looking at comparable
decontextualised fragments of a wide range of religious phenomena one
can build up the structure and essence of religion.

W. Brede Kristensen's (1867–1953) discussion of the basis of phenomenology raises some additional issues that are worth examining. In
his discussion of the essence of religion he takes up Otto's concept of the
holy. Unlike Otto, however, he does not use the concept itself as the
starting point; rather he suggests that we should start with the believer.
He separates holiness from any particular object but continues to argue
that 'holiness is the most essential element in reality itself' (1971). Thus,
in spite of its move to the believer, the basis of his discussion still retains
this essentialist aspect.

In his discussion of cultural or institutional evolution he makes a similar move. In general he marshals some very strong arguments against concepts of evolution in respect of cultural forms. He suggests that there are many different paths and no one path or one religion can be seen as the pinnacle of evolutionary development from which all other forms can be judged. This position, however, is not a move towards cultural relativism. Although it begins to collapse concepts of higher or lower, as does his perception that the 'holy' can only be internally defined and thus not evaluated in a qualitative sense, the key feature which brings his analysis together and gives it an essentialist basis is that the holy experienced in all these different traditions is one and the same rather than specific to each tradition. And while the perception might be that the nature of this absolute is determined from the data, it seems likely that consciously or unconsciously the data which is brought together and the notion of the holy derived from it is culturally conditioned by the context of the observer. This approach can be seen as an external and possibly ethnocentric view of the cultural and religious elements being dissected.

Mircea Eliade (1907–86): The myth of the eternal return

> We shall see that, as the rite always consists in the repetition of an archetypal action performed *in illo tempore* (before 'history' began) by ancestors or by Gods, man is trying, by means of the hierophany, to give 'being' to his most ordinary and insignificant acts. By its repetition, the act coincides with its archetype, and time is abolished. We are witnessing, so to speak, the same act that was performed *in illo tempore*, at the dawn of the universe.
>
> Mircea Eliade, *Patterns in Comparative Religion* (1958: 32)

Mircea Eliade is one of the most influential of the figures who arose from within the phenomenological approach. His approach shares many of the features described above while also making some overtures to the psychological approaches discussed in the beginning of this chapter. Although Eliade's approach to religion is not essentially psychological – it falls in the school of religious phenomenology – it has many similarities to that of Jung, both in respect of its understanding of the basis of religion as arising from an actual external other, which is described in terms heavily influenced by Eastern thought, and in its analysis of symbolism, which sees most symbols has having a collective or universal basis.

One of the key features of Eliade's thought is that religion can only be properly understood as religion. Religion is ultimately irreducible and rests on a universal spiritual intuition or experience. On this basis, Eliade is able to decontextualise the phenomena which he studies and to draw examples from a wide range of sources – at times from all corners of the world and from the Neolithic to the present.

Much of Eliade's work is in determining the morphology of religion as an essential and abstract subject. This is done by what purports to be comparative analysis – seeking to create a comparative typology of religious symbols. Eliade examines a number of symbolic complexes and in doing so often appears to be suggesting that at some deep level the specific symbols have the same meaning wherever they are found. Thus, in *Patterns in Comparative Religion* he examines a wide range of symbolic complexes, including agriculture, sacred places, the moon and the sun. In each discussion each of the complexes is analysed as, in effect, an archetype with a common and universal meaning. The analysis is supported by examples from a wide range of religions wrenched totally out of their ethnographic contexts.

His analysis of religion shares with Durkheim's a distinction between the sacred and the profane. The sacred includes a wide range of objects, the key common feature of which is that they are all 'hierophanies', a locus of the sacred in which the object 'ceases to be itself' though its material form is unchanged. The hierophany allows the believer to look beyond the profane material world and connect to an unchanging transcendent reality. The concept of hierophany also includes a historical element. Each hierophany is located in a particular historical moment; in some cases it is limited to that moment, in others it has a more universal basis. Eliade implies that there is a dialectical aspect to the development of hierophanies and thus some aspect of progress and teleology – an element which is emphasised by the usage of 'supreme mystery' for the incarnation of Christ in the world.

The fundamental element that underlies all of these strands is the view that there are patterns or structures that underlie religion and the religious experience. As suggested above, rather than examining or focusing on the structures of particular religions, Eliade seeks to determine the repetitive patterns that underlie all religions. These patterns can then be analysed and ultimately integrated into the dialectical concept of the sacred, which becomes a feature of consciousness in terms which bring to mind both Otto and Jung. Like Jung, Eliade also sees his task as one of enlightenment: through understanding the morphology and nature of this dialectical pattern human beings can be led to experience and grow with this mode of consciousness.

Critique

Eliade's analysis poses problems at almost every level, all of which ultimately rest on his view that religion is irreducible and thus can be examined out side of its cultural context. This type of claim for the status of religion can only be based on a conception which sees religion as arising from something either essential to the human consciousness or as something which derives from an external source, for example, 'the holy'. If religion arises from human consciousness alone, then this should and needs to be demonstrated on the basis of detailed analysis of particular religions and only then of detailed and contextualised comparisons. If it arises from some external other, then we move out of the sphere of analysis to one of theology, where the discussion is based on a preconceived belief. Eliade consistently argues in favour of this theological approach and so his work should be seen as a theologically motivated exercise rather than one which is based on social scientific principles, whether those of phenomenology or of the mainstream social scientific disciplines.

Based on this concept of the universality of the religious experience, Eliade consistently draws on material from a wide range of sources to back up his arguments. For example, in a discussion of the 'Moon and its Mystique' he cites myths from Mexico, New Zealand, American Indians, Eskimos, the Greeks and the Celts. In other discussions he introduces Neolithic art as well. In no case are these examples contextualised or discussed in detail. The similarities he highlights are often not intrinsic to the myth or object in the way it is used and understood in its ethnographic context, and in the case of the Neolithic material – which has no verbal explanation – it is impossible to assume that it has the meaning he applies. Ethnographic analysis demonstrates that symbols do not have an intrinsic meaning. Their meaning arises from the culture or community that interacts with them and uses them.

When particular symbols are examined in detail they often can be demonstrated to work in very different ways than suggested by Eliade. In *The Myth of the Eternal Return* and elsewhere he makes sweeping statements about the role of the temple in all societies. One example he introduces is that of the Temple in Jerusalem. When this temple is examined in the context of the Israelite understanding, Eliade's arguments seem to relate little to its symbolic and cultural role. It seems likely that when other symbols are similarly closely examined in their own cultural contexts, they too will significantly diverge from Eliade's analysis.

As already suggested, there is a strong theological basis to Eliade's discussions. This theology is problematic (from a social scientific perspective) on two levels. We have already touched on the problem of demonstration – it is impossible to prove the existence of a transcendent other or sacred – and thus his analysis rests on belief. On a second level, his theological approach often seems to have an underlying concept of evolution or progress, a fact suggested by his understanding of the dialectical development of the hierophany. At times this evolutionary basis seems to move into a more Christian theological position, as suggested in the phrase 'supreme Incarnation of the Word in Christ' (1958: 26). This theological bias is also clearly demonstrated in the conclusion of *The Myth of the Eternal Return*, in which he suggests 'that Christianity is the "religion" of modern man, of the man who simultaneously discovered personal freedom and continuous time' (1971: 161). This approach does not seem consistent with an objective analysis of religions and can only arise from an almost Hegelian approach that is really interested only in the history of religion rather than that of religions.

Ninian Smart: The dimensions of religion

Ninian Smart picks up some of the less problematic aspects of phenomenology and develops them into a descriptive model of religion. Like the phenomenologists, he is looking for patterns in religion. He descerns these patterns in a set of eight different dimensions that are found, he argues, to a lesser or greater extent in all religions. In doing this he is attempting to focus on an internal view while also recognising, in contradistinction, that external models belonging to other academic disciplines will also address important, if different, aspects of religion. A significant aspect of his argument is an attempt to move away from searching for essences or defining particular aspects as essential. He also properly emphasises pluralism both within and among religious traditions.

Smart suggests that religions are composed of eight dimensions (in earlier developments of this theory he suggested six). The first dimension is the 'practical and ritual dimension'. This dimension includes the full range of religious practices and rituals, from highly elaborate liturgies to the meditative practices of the Buddhist. The second dimension is the 'experiential and emotional'. This dimension emphasises that all religions include an affective element. This can be a highly defuse experience, like fellow feeling, or a more exuberant experience like an ecstatic trance. The third dimension is the narrative or mythic. This dimension expresses the idea that all religions not only express themselves through dogma or ritual, they also have a narrative element, a story of how and why things are the way they are, or how the religion itself developed. He adds that this dimension is often closely related to the ritual dimension. Alongside the narrative are norms and values expressed in the fourth and fifth dimensions: the 'doctrinal and philosophical dimensions' and the 'ethical and legal dimensions'. The remaining three dimensions relate directly to the setting and practice of the religion: the 'social and institutional' dimension emphasises, as have most of the more developed theories, the essentially social and communal character of religions; the 'political' level indicates the roles of power, authority and hierarchy; and the 'material' dimension suggests that all religions use or articulate ideas and values in the form of material objects, for example, architecture (Smart 1971: 15–25 and 1973: 43).

Smart's discussion raises several additional areas of interest. His model does not include any specific content: each of the seven areas could be filled with a wide range of different forms and variations, thus the model usefully presents a very open-ended tool of analysis. As he suggests, the model can encompass a range of modern ideological worldviews; for example, Marxism, which in models that include specific content, as in the requirement that there be god or gods, would be excluded from the discussion of religion. Smart also suggests that the dimensions should not be examined singly, as often done in more classical phenomenology, but should be examined in relation to each other. On these bases Smart's theory is a clear advance from phenomenology.

Critique

Although Smart's approach to religion avoids most of the problems associated with phenomenology, there are two main problematic areas. The first area relates to the nature and selection of the seven dimensions of religion. The second regards the nature of the approach as a whole: is it description or analysis?

Although Smart is very careful to indicate that the seven areas will be found in differing amounts and qualities in different religious traditions, it is unclear why these seven areas are chosen to be diagnostic of particular phenomena. It seems that there must be a pre-existing definition of what religion is, based on a Western understanding, which underlies the selection of the different elements. It would seem to be equally possible to construct a definition of religion that would only include some of the elements, or indeed include other elements, such as worldview. On the basis of this issue, it is also difficult to see why this should be considered an internal model, as the content of the model is based on a pre-existing understanding of religion and its dimensions, not one which arises from the particular ethnographic context.

In addition, although Smart does suggest that the dimensions should be analysed in relation to each other as a complex set of interactions, he follows the phenomenologist in seeing religion as essential and separable from its cultural context. He does not follow the route suggested by Weber in looking at religion in relation to all other social phenomena. If religion is thus embedded in the particular institutions and elements highlighted by the seven dimensions, can it be better understood as part of a specific cultural complex rather than as phenomena which stand independent of each other and of culture?

The second problematic area relates to the nature of his discussion as a whole. Although some of his discussion suggests that it is analytical – and, as indicated above, it rests on an, albeit unstated, theoretical foundation – the discussion of the dimensions and their application suggests that the method is primarily one of description. While description is useful to highlight the characteristics of a particular system and may facilitate comparison with other related systems, it does not replace the need for analysis; analysis would allow the understanding of the function of the system and how and why it works within its particular context. It would also allow more useful comparison, examining why religions or ideologies do different things and develop in different ways.

This last point is also relevant in regard to the application of his model to areas not normally considered religion. The case of political idealogies raises some questions and these are compounded when the theory can be applied to football or other similar phenomena. If the theory had a stronger analytical element it could be used to explain (rather than describe) why these phenomena were similar, and also highlight and evaluate the areas of difference.

Conclusion

In this chapter we have touched on a wide range of approaches to the study of religion. Although there are many differences between the approaches, as in Freud's suspicion of religion and most of the other thinkers' appreciation of it, all of these approaches share a common basis in the individual experience. This basis is most clearly seen in the psychological, but is also found in the phenomenological, approach, as demonstrated in the latter's retention of an *a priori* experience of the holy as the basis of religion. Due to this foundation in individual experience, all of these theories need to distinguish between the essence of religion, which is individual, and the institutional structures of religion. The institutional level is thus, by definition, secondary. In some cases the institutional level becomes the object of suspicion, in other cases it is seen as a platform that can enable religious experience. All of these approaches ignore the fact that, for most people, it is the institution they experience and that whether or not the institution has its root in some religious experience, that experience is very remote from the current adherents. One might almost see these arguments as examples of the genetic fallacy. A second problem which is common to all these approaches arises from their essentialist understanding of religion. If religion has an essential and universal core, then all religions ultimately have the same basis or root. This allows the different scholars to pull examples out of their cultural context to demonstrate this common root or essence. To a great extent it seems as if they accept *a priori* this common essence and then seek to demonstrate it rather than working from the evidence itself and seeing where it might lead.

Despite these and other specific problems, there are several positive aspects developed in many of these approaches. Many of them begin to move away from the racial connection to cultural evolution, seeing all human beings as having the same brains and ways of thinking. On another level, the psychological approaches also introduce the irrational or arational into the discussion of religion. And, although we might challenge the universal application or mystical elements of their analyses, psychological approaches are useful at a culture specific level in understanding some aspects of how and why religions work. The psychological approaches also introduce a functional basis for religion at both the individual and societal level, and this emphasis is taken up in many of the sociological and anthropological theories discussed in the next chapter. Additionally, many of the phenomenological thinkers, at least in principle, emphasise the importance of understanding the internal perspective – what the believers think about their beliefs and ways of believing.

 Further reading

Eliade, Mircea (1958), *Patterns in Comparative Religion*, London: Sheed and Ward. Eliade has been one of the most influential thinkers about religion in the twentieth century. This book provides both a good introduction to his approach and an extended example of it in practice.

Freud, Sigmund (1950), *Totem and Taboo*, New York: Norton. This book, along with *The Future of an Illusion* (1961), present a good introduction to Freud's understanding of religion. *Totem and Taboo*, in particular, reveals both the strong points and weaknesses of his very influential arguments.

Kristensen, W. Brede (1971), *The Meaning of Religion*, The Hague: Martinus Nijhoff. This book provides a very good entry point to phenomenology in its general introduction. The remainder of the book provides a very clear example of the practice of phenomenology.

Loewental, Kate (2000), *The Psychology of Religion: A Short Introduction*, Oxford: One World. This volume provides a good introduction to the psychological study of religion. In moves well beyond the discussion of Freud and Jung included here, also examining psychological approaches to different constituent elements of religion, for example, experience and belief.

Spilka, Bernard and Daniel N. McIntosh (eds) (1997), *The Psychology of Religion*, Oxford: Westview. This volume focuses on the different theoretical perspectives within the psychological approach to religion. Its chapters are written by some of the most creative thinkers in the field and it develops some of the more recent ideas not covered here.

? Questions

1. What is the effect of the concept of recapitulation on the psychological theories of Freud and Jung?

2. If religion arises from individual psychology or experience, how can it be related to the essentially social aspects of religion?

3. Consider the similarities and differences between the work of Jung, Otto, Lévy-Bruhl and Eliade.

4. Does Smart's model resolve the inherent problems in the phenomenological approach to religion?

CHAPTER THREE

Anthropological and Sociological Theories of Religion

Seth D. Kunin

Introduction

This chapter examines some of the significant anthropological and sociological theories of religion. It focuses specifically on theorists who developed comprehensive approaches to religion rather than those who examined specific aspects of religion or religious experience. Several of these more specific approaches are discussed in Section Two's first chapter on indigenous traditions.

One of the aspects which will become increasingly clear as this chapter progresses is the relationship of the theories developed here to those of the phenomenologists and, more significantly, the psychologists. For example, most theorists writing in the latter half of the twentieth century had, at least in part, to address the unconscious aspects of social phenomena and in many cases to place the affective aspects of religion to the fore.

One of the most significant themes suggested by the theories discussed is the rejection of ethnocentric models. This development is seen in the move away from unilinear evolutionary models. These models almost invariably view the development of culture and religion in a teleological sense, with Western Europe or America being the pinnacle from which all other cultures are judged. These approaches have been challenged both in respect of ethnographic evidence and by increasingly relativist models that deny a basis from which both quality and evolution can be judged. Similarly, most modern theories of religion aim to be comprehensive in respect of all religious systems. Rather than suggesting a clear difference between 'primitive' and 'modern' culture, they suggest that religious systems from all cultures, both 'world' and 'indigenous', should be analysed using the same methodologies, models and theories.

The theories in this chapter should be read in a developmental sense. Each theory builds on its predecessors, both rejecting and developing ideas. The theories examined in the final sections draw on many of the themes developed by the earlier approaches and represent an introduction to the theories used today by academics working on the anthropological and sociological approaches to religion.

Evolutionary theories of religion: From simplicity to complexity

Darwin's theory of evolution by natural selection was highly influential not only in relation to the study of biology but also on a broader level to research on human culture. Scholars on both sides of the Atlantic developed theories of religion closely associated with evolutionary theories of culture. Although different theorists selected different aspects of culture or religion to emphasise, all of the evolutionary theories shared significant common features: unilinear development, the notion of progress, and the analogy between 'primitive' societies and early forms of societal development.

Unilinear development

The theories of cultural evolution diverged from biological evolution in assuming that there was one path through which all cultures would develop. At the bottom of this path were the simplest forms of societies, perhaps hunters and gatherers, and at the top was either England or the United States, depending on the location of the theorist. Different markers were used to determine the place of a particular society. Some theorists, for example Herbert Spencer (1820–1903), used complexity, the more complex societies being more advanced evolutionarily than the less complex. Other thinkers, for example Louis Henry Morgan (1818–81), used technology or other aspects of material life. Whichever marker was chosen, Western culture was always the peak from which all other cultural forms were judged.

The theorists faced the problem of explaining why different societies evolved at different speeds; if all human societies had existed for the same amount of time, why were there still hunting and gathering societies? They answered these questions in two ways. Some scholars mixed biological evolution with cultural evolution, providing a racist argument for the different pace of development. Other scholars, arguing for the genetic unity of humanity, explained the differences in geographic terms; different geographies, for example the cold of the ice age, were seen as forcing the pace of cultural development. In spite of the rate of development, all societies would ultimately develop along the single path of evolution, culminating in a form equivalent to that of the Western European.

Notion of progress

Although classic Darwinian thought does not imply progress, evolution can be seen as change rather than progress: all of the models of cultural evolution assumed that each level of evolutionary development was qualitatively better than that which it followed. The model assumed a teleological evolution that led to the form of society, religion and culture found in Western Europe. This concept had profound effects on the relationship between various colonial powers, both European and American, and their subjected populations. It justified a paternalistic attitude and both ignorance and destruction of indigenous practices, beliefs and values.

Ancient–primitive analogy

The evolutionary theorists attempted to demonstrate their theories on the basis of modern non-Western societies. They argued that, due to the differentials in pace in cultural evolution, societies existing today (that is, in their own time) were equivalent to forms of our own society of thousands and hundreds of thousands of years ago. On this basis they could demonstrate how society developed by looking at these different forms. Each society could be placed on the ladder of development and explain aspects of our own development. As suggested below, the only way of supporting this analogy is to assume that each society progressively invents all the elements of its cultural repertoire, allowing the significant elements that define each stage of development to appear when historically necessary. If this is not the case, then it is impossible to see any single line of development or any analogy between currently existing societies and our own past.

The primary proof that was introduced to demonstrate the analogy between contemporary 'primitive' societies and our own past was the concept of 'a survival'. A survival was an element that is found in a 'more advanced' society that no longer serves a purpose, yet has been retained for non-functional reasons. An example in our society might be the bow and arrow, which once had a practical function but now is only retained for sport. In religion, the soul might be considered a survival from an early stage in which all things were thought to have souls.

Religion and evolution

The first requisite in a systematic study of the religions of the lower races is to lay down a rudimentary definition of religion. By requiring in this definition the belief in a supreme deity or of judgment after death, the adoration of idols or the practice of sacrifice, or other partially diffused doctrines or rites, no doubt many tribes may be excluded from the category of religious. But such narrow definition has the fault of identifying religion with particular developments than with the deeper motive that underlies them. It seems best to fall back at once on this essential source, and simply to claim, as a minimum definition of Religion, the belief in Spiritual Beings.

Edward B. Tylor, *Primitive Culture* (1871: 383)

Alongside the other aspects of society, religion was also understood to develop along a unilinear path. Edward Tylor (1832–1912), one of the earliest anthropologists, developed an evolutionary theory of religion that sought to explain both the origins and the development of religion. He argued that religion could be understood as a product of reason and that all human beings had the same capacity for thought.

Tylor defined religion as the 'belief in Spiritual Beings', suggesting that to make it more specific, for example including belief in a supreme

being, would exclude many groups which should be included. He identified animism as the most fundamental of human beliefs. He suggested
that animism was the original human belief system and was still the
religious system of 'tribes very low in the scale of humanity' (1871: 383).
Tylor argues that animism can be divided into two dogmas: the existence
of souls that continue to exist after death and the existence of spiritual
beings who control the material world.

Tylor posited a model for the origin of these concepts and their
subsequent development into other 'higher' forms of religion. At a basic
level, he argued that animism originates in the concept of the soul.
Human beings faced with the problem of death, and the vision of the
self in dreams developed the concept of soul to explain both issues.
The phantom seen in dreams was understood to be the soul, which
could exist separate from the body and on death remained in existence
absolutely separated from the body. The concept of soul was also
extended to other animals and to inanimate objects, for example plants
and trees. To a degree, Tylor seems to be suggesting the inability to
distinguish between subject and object, everything is subjectified. As
religion continued to evolve, the souls associated with material objects
began to be seen as controlling powers and ultimately as gods who
unified more aspects of the material world, becoming the belief system
defined as polytheism. At religion's highest level, nature, in relation to
developing models of social organisation, is unified in the 'highest'
concept, monotheism.

Tylor makes an interesting distinction between religion and magic.
He suggests, as does Frazer (see below), that magic is essentially a rational activity with a clear logic and structure. It arises from an attempt to
explain causality and, like science, it is based, at least in part, on observation. Unlike science, however, which has a correct understanding of
causality, magic makes the mistake of assuming that causality is related
to analogy or similarity – that is, 'like things affect like things'. Thus
understood, magic is poor science. It attempts to explain why things
happen in an impersonal way but does so improperly; religion, on the
other hand, deals with a different sphere of understanding, a subjective
personified universe.

Critique

Models of cultural evolution, particularly unilinear evolution, are
problematic on many levels. At their most basic they are founded on a
false analogy with biological evolution. Biological evolution is based on
chance mutation and is passed on through the genes. Social processes of
development and transmission are not analogous to genetic processes.
Although biological evolution does imply change, it does not imply
qualitative progress – organisms adapt to fit new ecological situations,

those that do so more effectively survive better than those that do not. Evolution therefore has no necessary direction, the evolution of humanity was based on chance rather than design, and if some of the prior forms that led to humanity still existed their future evolution might lead to something very different than *Homo sapiens sapiens*. Evolutionary movement has no necessary direction or teleology: a change is not progressive, it is merely a fortuitous change which by chance allowed the organism to survive. Thus, the very analogy breaks down. As cultural evolutionary models imply that all cultural evolution follows a single path leading to a single end – what is perceived of as the most advanced form – there is no basis in biological evolution and no cultural necessity that this type of cultural teleology should exist. Nor does evolution necessarily move towards complexity – at times, simplicity might be more adaptive – thus Spencer's evolutionary arguments are equally problematic in respect of universal, biological and cultural development.

If biological evolution is rejected as a basis for cultural evolution, there seems little basis for a unilinear model. If there is not inherent impetus to develop in a particular way, and there seems no logical source for such impetus, then it is much more likely that there will be many paths of development rather than a single path. Although it is possible that there might be a small range of paths, it seems probable that there are almost as many paths as there are cultures. The development or history of a particular culture should also not be seen in 'progressive' evolutionary terms. Although clearly all cultures change over time, these changes are not progressive, moving from a worse to a better state; rather they are just changes from one state to another. Religion as a component of culture will also develop in different ways and directions depending on its particular cultural context, and thus there are as many paths of religious development as there are of cultural development.

If unilinear evolution is challengeable, then the observational basis of the entire set of cultural evolutionary theories is equally challengeable. The cultural evolutionists use cultures existing in their own time as exemplars of past historical development; but if there is no single line of development, then these other societies bear no necessary resemblance, except perhaps in relation to specific elements out of context, to our own past. Even if one element seems to be found in both, it does not imply that the other configuration of elements will be the same. Non-unilinear development allows no analogy between societies existing today and those of the past. The only way we can understand the development of our own institutions is to look at their specific development through history and archaeology.

The cultural evolutionary models ignore two other important points: time and diffusion. They ignore the fact that all societies existing today have, along their specific paths of development, existed for the same amount of time – they have all had the same time to change and develop in different directions. They also ignore the fact that no society exists in a vacuum and that no society invents all of the cultural elements which it employs. All human societies exist in relation to other societies; each society will invent certain elements of its cultural repertoire and borrow some elements from its neighbours. Thus, there can be no single path of cultural evolution because different societies will invent and borrow different things depending on cultural investment and values. If we look at our own cultural repertoire we will find elements, which were invented, in our own societies along with elements from Africa, China or almost any other part of the globe. Unilinear cultural evolution improperly over-emphasises human inventiveness and ignores the fact that each culture is a composite, a fact that can be equally seen in any religion.

Finally, unilinear evolution is inherently ethnocentric. Each of the theories selected an element which the theorist considered to be significant, based on their perception of self, and assumed that the element is the decisive factor in development. Thus, Spencer chose complexity (assuming the British society was the most complex), while other thinkers emphasised technology. There seems no logical reason why either of these or other similar elements should be a general measure of development, as different societies have different values, choose different paths of change and in their own self-perception choose different measures of development.

James Frazer (1854–1951): Magic, religion and science

James Frazer's reputation underwent a wide shift in valuation during the course of the twentieth century. Anthropologists in the early part of the century, for example Malinowski, praised his work and saw it as a significant building block in the development of anthropology as an academic discipline. As the century progressed, however, most critics became increasingly scathing about the value of his work. Today, his classic work *The Golden Bough* (1922) is little more than a curiosity or a step in intellectual history, with little or no value as either a source of data or analysis. Nonetheless, in its time Frazer's work was highly influential and it was relied on by scholars studying religion from many academic perspectives.

Like Tylor and the other evolutionists, Frazer develops an evolutionary model in relation to his understanding of religion. Within this model, evolutionary developments occur not only within religion but also on a wider scale; religion is seen as part of a progressive development from magic to science, the intermediate phase between these two alternative sources of knowledge.

Magic

Frazer's understanding of magic is closer to Tylor's than to the more individually oriented practices discussed by Durkheim (see below). Like Tylor, Frazer saw magic as essentially rational. It was an attempt, albeit a failed one, to explain causality based on essentially impersonal forces. The main difference between Tylor and Frazer in respect of magic was that Frazer saw it as the first stage of evolutionary development, while Tylor saw it as an essentially separate phenomenon.

Frazer also presented a more systematic analysis of magic than had Tylor. He suggested that magic was based on two interrelated laws: the law of similarity and the law of contagion. The law of similarity is based on the principle that 'like produces like'. For example, action in relation to one object will produce a similar result in a similar object (usually the second object is more significant than the first). The law of contagion suggests that objects which have a relation to each other, or which have once been connected, retain that connection even after they have been divided. This principle is seen in the common practice of using a person's hair or fingernails to cause some effect in that person. The magician uses these laws in an impersonal way, there are no spiritual personages involved, much in the same way that modern science understands the use of technology. The difference between magic and science is that magic is based on a misunderstanding of causality and nature; it is an attempt to use reason but one founded on error.

If magic is thus next of kin to science, we still have to enquire how it stands related to religion. But the view we take of that relation will necessarily be coloured by the idea that we have formed of religion itself; hence a writer may reasonably be expected to define his conception of religion before he proceeds to investigate its relation to magic ... By religion, then, I understand a propitiation or conciliation to powers superior to man which are believed to direct and control the course of nature and human life. Thus defined religion consists of two elements, a theoretical and a practical namely a belief in powers higher than man and an attempt to propitiate or please them. Of the two, belief clearly comes first, since we must believe in the existence of a divine being before we can attempt to please him.

James Frazer, *The Golden Bough* (1922: 65–6)

Religion

Religion is the next stage in societal development, and although in some senses it is seen as a progressive move from magic, Frazer also sees it as a temporary abandonment of using reason or observation. Religion takes the place of magic when it is no longer perceived that the world is governed by laws and, equally, that magic does not work to manipulate these laws or forces. With the rejection of law that accompanies the demise of magic, law is replaced by personal capricious forces – that is, supernatural beings. These beings or gods were believed be able to be propitiated and conciliated. He argued that religion consisted of two elements: the theoretical and the practical. The theoretical was the belief that the world was controlled by 'higher powers' that acted on the basis of caprice and will; the practical were those elements designed to conciliate or propitiate these powers – rituals and other practices associated with religion.

Science

As society further evolves, Frazer suggests that religion is overtaken by science. The scientific mode of thought emerges due to the intellectual problems associated with the belief in supernatural forces. One might discern in the evolution of religion a move to increasingly impersonal forces that, by the time of the rise of science, render religion a belief system increasingly untenable and unnecessary. Science, in a certain respect, is a return to aspects of the magical understanding of the universe; like magic, it believes that the world is governed by immutable, impersonal laws. The primary distinction of science is that it bases its understanding of the universe on precise observation and experiment, the scientific method, and thus presents a more correct understanding of causality. The process of evolution, however, might not end with science. Frazer suggests that 'as science has supplanted its predecessors, so it may here after be itself superseded' (1922: 932).

Critique

Frazer's work has been criticised on a number of different levels. We have already highlighted some of the problems with unilinear evolutionary approaches; these problems are also inherent in Frazer's studies. Frazer's clear dislike of religion and preference for the scientific method underpins much of his evolutionary concepts and his depiction of the phenomena analysed.

A more devastating criticism relates to the nature of Frazer's methods and material. Like many of his predecessors and scholars from the related discipline of phenomenology, Frazer makes no attempt to contextualise the material which he discusses. His argument marshals examples from a wide range of cultural sources with very little attention to cultural context or the ways in which the elements fit into a broader cultural model. Additionally, the sources from which Frazer draws his ethnography are often very poor – missionaries, travellers' tales, reconstructions of myths, as well as more academic studies. Very often the material he used included a high degree of ethnocentrism and misunderstandings of the societies described, and so was poorly suited to the development of any type of useful analytical construct.

An additional problem with Frazer's theories were that they were based on his attempt to reconstruct the development of ways of thinking – based on his own ways of thinking. Rather than drawing his conclusions from the data, he used the data to demonstrate his conclusions. Thus, he thought, on the basis of his logical reconstruction, that the first way of thinking was based on magical, impersonal laws. Also based on his attempt to logically map development, he then proceeded to religion and ultimately to science. Moreover, he chose ethnocentric material to illustrate this progression. If he had closely examined the ethnographic data that was increasingly available, he would have realised that his generalisations about the presence of particular ways of thinking in particular forms of society actually bore little resemblance to the ethnography.

Karl Marx (1818–83): Religion and materialism

Karl Marx's materialist analysis of economics, politics and religion was one of the most influential models of the twentieth century. This model shaped, to some degree, political structures and influenced most academic disciplines. Although most people are aware of Marx's statement that religion is the opiate of the people, his views of religion were much more complex and perhaps somewhat self-contradictory.

Marx and cultural evolution

Like many of their contemporaries, Marx and his collaborator Engels accept an evolutionary model for the development of culture. Much of this model is similar to that developed by Tylor. In Marx's thought the process of evolution is both unilinear and dialectical. Religion, like other aspects of society, goes through a process of evolution closely tied to economic and societal structure. In *The German Ideology*, Marx and Engels suggest that at least one form of religion, 'natural religion', emerges as an attitude towards nature. This attitude and the practices associated with it are interrelated with the 'form of society' from which the individual emerges. As forms of society evolve so natural religion will evolve. There is some debate whether the 'natural religion' forms the basis of modern forms of religion.

Historical materialism

In order to understand Marx's most important discussions of religion we need to touch on his concept of materialism. Marx suggests that much of what we see as culture should be understood as epiphenomenal or superstructure. For example, politics and religion are secondary phenomena and in order to properly understand society one has to examine the primary structure – that is, economics. Marx argues that the economic structure of society is that from which all other aspects develop. Religion and politics serve to justify or hide the exploitative economic base of society. Although Marx's theory is materialist, it is not based on a distinction between the material and mind – rather mind and therefore ideas are understood as part of the material.

Religion therefore cannot be examined in its own terms as a separate and essential phenomenon, as it is in phenomenology, but rather must be examined in the context of its economic structure. On this basis Marx suggests that religion is a means of justifying and thereby validating the exploitative patterns that are inherent in class society. In part, Marx sees religion as a form of ideology. Ideology is shaped by the ideas and values of the ruling class, those involved in economic exploitation, and thus religion reflects and supports those patterns of exploitation.

Religion and alienation

Marx posits that religion is also closely related to a second aspect of class society: alienation. In part, religion arises as a reflection of the existence of alienation in society. Religion reflects the fact of exploitation and is, in essence, a protest against it. At this level, religion is partially positive; Marx, however, argues that since religion is a reflection of alienation, in a society where exploitation (and therefore alienation) did not exist religion would not be necessary.

Whether religion arises from alienation or serves as a justifying ideology for alienation, Marx views it as essentially false. It is a form of consciousness that prevents the working class from perceiving their actual nature, and thus prevents them from acting to transform their exploited condition. Religion as false consciousness, in as much as it creates happiness, creates illusory happiness; for Marx, true happiness can only come about through a revolutionary transformation of the economic structures which would do away with class, exploitation and alienation and thus remove the need for the illusions created by religion.

Critique

Marx's theory can be challenged on two levels: its evolutionary basis and its apparent materialist reductionism. As suggested above, he uses a unilinear evolutionary model inherited from Tylor. Marx's use of this model can be challenged on much the same grounds as were the evolutionists that preceded him. Marx also takes the model further and projects evolutionary developments of society into the future. At times he can appear to have an almost deterministic basis to his theory of societal development, though some aspects of agency are introduced as part of the motor of revolutionary transformation.

If the deterministic and unilinear evolutionary aspects are removed from his overall theory, it still retains some important insights into the development of society and religion. It emphasises that society and religion are the creations of human beings as groups and therefore need to be understood as social phenomena. It provides a method of studying and evaluating the role of economic structures and exploitation in the development of religious ideas. It also provides a mechanism for the transformation of religion and society, even if these are not deterministic or understood in unilinear evolutionary terms.

Marxist analysis has been criticised for being reductionist, for reducing all other phenomena to the material. As already suggested above, his materialism is not simplistic – it recognises that mind is part of the material – but it does consider all other social phenomena epiphenomenal. Economic structure and related patterns of exploitation and ideology do play a significant role in shaping social institutions, particularly religion; however, many aspects of religion and other similar phenomena are more complex and relate to a wider range of human individual and social experience than can explained solely by recourse to these elements.

Marxist analysis of religion may be challenged on one additional level: it discusses religion in essentially negative terms, as an ideological tool for the ruling class. Religion expresses their values and supports their power and validates their patterns of exploitation. While this is true of much of the mainstream institutional forms of religion, it does not take fully into account religion's role as a form of protest. For example, Islamism can be understood as a protest movement against totalitarian states and, even more importantly, as a means of protesting against and challenging Western imperialist neo-colonialism. Similarly, liberation theology can be understood as a left-wing protest against right-wing, American-supported totalitarian states. Although this does give religion a role not directly predicted in classical Marxism, these movements do arise from the extreme end of alienation, which is in part reflected in religion. Equally, although these movements are a form of protest, and do challenge right-wing or neo-colonialist powers, they are not truly revolutionary, as they do not want to fully transform the economic structure or the nature of capital. Thus, they can be seen as a means by which the capitalist structure attempts to maintain itself.

Cultural materialism – cow lovers and pig-haters

Materialist interpretations of culture and religion were highly influential in the development of anthropology in the twentieth century. Marvin Harris was one of materialism's most eloquent exponents. In a popular book, *Cows, Pigs, Wars and Witches* (1975), as well as in other sources, he explores some of the more enigmatic aspects of religion using a materialist analytical approach. His analysis reveals some of the strengths and weaknesses of cultural materialism.

The first two chapters of the book examine why Hindus venerate the cow and Jews (and Muslims) abhor the pig. In both cases the analyses focus on the material value or role of the animal to the specific society. In the case of the cow, Harris argues that as a source of food (meat) the cow would effectively be a poor investment. It would produce relatively few calories for a much greater investment in grain. A more efficient use of the cow is to provide dung, a resource, which enables agricultural production sufficient to support India's huge population. This population could never have been supported if the cow was used for food. Thus, the cow was considered sacred and inedible.

Similarly, the pig was hated by the Israelites because it was not only economically problematic but was in direct competition with human beings for food and water. The pig, he suggests, is inefficient in the desert, as it needs a lot of water; using his arguments, we might also suggest that it also produces less calories than are necessary to support it. Unlike the cow, which in the Israelite context could graze on the desert grass and did not need much water, the pig produces nothing of value; therefore, while the cow is considered to be edible and sacrificable, the pig is abhorred. Thus, the Israelites' abhorrence developed from these economic factors.

The version of cultural materialism developed in these arguments is much less nuanced than that presented in classical Marxist analysis. While it suggests reasons why particular objects were chosen to be venerated or forbidden, it examines these elements out of the context of other symbols or cultural constructs. The pig, for example, is only one part of a much wider system of food rules. It needs to be explained as part of a system rather than merely on its own. It may be emblematic of the system but it is not the system. On another level, this type of analysis mistakes the suppositional origin of a practice for its continuation. Economic explanations which relate to the desert seem to have little value in explaining why Jews and Muslims in Western countries continue to abhor the pig. Thus, in order to understand religious practices we need to speculate about origins and likewise to examine how and why they continue to be used when those origins are no longer directly relevant.

Max Weber (1864–1920): The Protestant ethic and the spirit of capitalism

Along with Emile Durkheim, Max Weber has been one of the most influential thinkers on religion both within and beyond his own discipline of sociology. In his own terms, he was interested in the relationship between the economic ethic and religion – both world religions and, more narrowly, Protestantism. His analysis, however, was broader than merely focusing on the economic; he also discusses the interrelationship between social structure and religion.

In analysing religion, Weber, like Marx, focused on religion as a feature of social life. He argued that individuals are shaped by the groups of which they are part, and their ideas as well as their actions must be seen in the context of this social arena. The groups on which he focused are similar to the classes in Marxist analysis and, as in Marxist analysis, these status groups are seen as in conflict with each other. These status groups are the basis of shared values and worldview. Although worldview, and therefore religion, had a basis in the material or economic aspect of these groups, Weber also argued that it contained an ideal component. In this sense, Weber can be understood as bringing together in social analysis both the material economic base and the ideal or spiritual base.

Although the social aspect and the role of status groups are significant aspects of Weber's analysis, he also laid a very strong emphasis on the individual. A basic aspect of his sociological method was the need to study human action in relation to the subjective beliefs of the actors. This aspect was also a significant part of his discussion of religion. He suggests that the continuation of beliefs and institutions has as a significant component the beliefs of the individual social actors in relation to those conventional beliefs and institutions. Unlike Durkheim, Weber suggests that culture is ultimately vested in the individuals rather than in some external collective construct.

Although Weber understood the role that religion had as a conservative force, maintaining and validating particular forms of stratification, he also saw religion as a motor for change in society. Protestantism, for example, was not merely the child of capitalism but was one of a complex set of processes which enabled the very development of capitalism. The two phenomena, Protestantism and capitalism, are intertwined but not in the simplistic way suggested by historical materialism.

In *The Protestant Ethic and the Spirit of Capitalism* (1958) Weber examines both capitalism and Protestantism in order to determine their relation one to the other. He suggests that each of these phenomena has an underlying ethos and that these are interrelated. Weber sees rational capitalism as being a recent phenomena – in analysing it, he focuses on its ethos, its way of thinking. This ethos – to accumulate more capital and not disperse it – is found at all levels and is the basis of the work ethic of both the capitalists and the workers. It is the basis of the capitalists' desire to accumulate more and more and the workers' desire to work harder to earn as much as possible. Protestantism expresses a similar ethos, the emphasis on increased worldly activity and the associated self-denial or asceticism. In the Protestant concept of calling, Weber also identified the capitalist notion of vocation in the workplace. In drawing together the ethos of capitalism and that of Protestantism, Weber is not claiming that Protestantism was a necessary or sufficient cause for capitalism, rather he is suggesting that it was one among many causal factors which enable the successful development of capitalism as an economic and social institution by giving individuals an ethos which enabled them to work within a capitalist framework.

Weber's work on religion also focused on the dynamic processes within religion. Charisma was one of the most important of these. Charisma is understood to be related to Durkheim's concept of the sacred and is a dynamic force of personality which sets persons or objects off from the routine. Weber saw charisma as essentially a social process which arose between an individual and a group, and which tended to challenge traditional norms and values. As such, charisma was one side of a pendulum of change and transformation within religions. The other side of the pendulum swing was the progressive bureaucratisation of charisma, which began with the death of the charismatic figure. Religions attempt to retain the charismatic aspect but not in uncontrollable form; rather they create different forms of institutionalised or bureaucratised charisma that retain aspects of the sacred without challenging the system.

Critique

Like the other figures mentioned thus far, Weber included elements of evolutionary theory in his analysis. Essentially, he saw religions as progressing towards increased rationalisation. There is, however, no clear qualitative aspect to his discussion. He does seem to suggest at times that religion is a sacrifice of intellect, though one, if based on 'unconditional devotion', which was morally distinct from intellectual hypocrisy.

Weber has also been criticised in respect of specific details of his analysis, especially for his over-emphasis on the role and shape of Protestantism. If we put aside issues particular to that analysis, Weber's discussion has much to offer – principally in bridging the gap between material and ideal. Weber opens the analysis of the relation of religion and the economic but allows us to see that historic transformations are complex, with the mental playing a significant role along with the material.

Joachim Wach (1898–1955) picks up many aspects of Weber's

approach, particularly Weber's comparative discussions. Wach also adds some aspects of Otto's concept of the holy into his more broadly sociological analysis. In a philosophical or theological sense, he emphasised the unifying aspect and saw religion as the foundation for the other human faculties, moving the holy from being a separate faculty to a position of structure with the other faculties being superstructure. Wach emphasises the need to examine the interrelationship between religion and other aspects of culture, with the ultimate goal of understanding the nature of the religious experience, which, he suggests, in contradistinction to Otto, is a highly diverse phenomenon.

Lucien Lévy-Bruhl (1857–1939): Primitive thought

Lévy-Bruhl is one of the most controversial figures in early twentieth-century anthropology due to his qualitative distinction between the 'primitive' and 'modern' ways of thinking. Lévy-Bruhl draws on the work of Durkheim, focusing on the ways in which thinking is shaped by the collective representations of society. In analysing these collective representations, however, he suggests that the ways of thinking that are found in 'native' thought are qualitatively different from those of modern society. Unlike modern thought, which is based on the individual use of rationality, 'native' thought was essentially collective and non-rational. He uses the term pre-logical to describe 'primitive' modes of thought.

Lévy-Bruhl's description of 'native' thought is very similar to that of Jung. Like Jung, he suggests that the world is not perceived through reason but rather through emotion. It is a highly subjective view of nature, in which nature is personified and subjectified. This is not to imply that individuals in these societies were ignorant of their surroundings but, in spite of their practical knowledge, much of their experience and understanding was essentially mystical. Like Jung, he also suggests that individuals in these societies viewed the products of dreams and visions as similar or identical to their sensual experience of the world.

Among the differences which distinguish the mentality of primitive communities from our own, there is one which has attracted the attention of many of those who have observed such peoples under the most favourable conditions – that is, before their ideas have been modified by prolonged association with white races. These observers have maintained that primitives manifest a decided distaste for reasoning, for what logicians call the 'discursive operations of thought'; at the same time they have remarked that this distaste did not arise out of any radical incapability or any inherent defect in their understanding, but was rather to be accounted for by their general methods of thought...

Then we shall no longer define the mental activity of primitives beforehand as a rudimentary form of our own, and consider it childish and almost pathological. On the contrary, it will appear to be normal under the conditions in which it is employed, to be both complex and developed in its own way. By ceasing to connect it with a type which is not its own, and trying to determine its functioning solely according to the manifestations peculiar to it, we may hope that our description and analysis of it will not misrepresent its nature.

Lucien Lévy-Bruhl, *Primitive Mentality* (1923: 21, 33)

Lévy-Bruhl suggests that 'primitive thought' is characterised by ways of thinking that have similarities to the two laws which Frazer sees as underlying magic. One of the most significant characteristics of pre-logical thinking is 'participation'. By participation he meant a thought process which saw both objects and their symbolic referents as being in some sense identical. Lévy-Bruhl also argued that 'primitive thought' was not concerned with contradictions and thus justified the term 'pre-logical'. He contended that this form of mystical and subjectivised thinking, which sees gods and spirits throughout the natural world, is the basis of religion.

Critique

There are several obvious problems with Lévy-Bruhl's theory. The most commonly cited is ethnographic. As many ethnographers have pointed out, although individuals in other societies might have more limited technical or scientific knowledge than that found in our Western indus-trialised society, much of any human being's life, like ours, is guided by a logical and practical approach to experience. Individuals in all soci-eties generally experience the world not in a mystical way but through practical reason. As Malinowski suggests, individuals only turn towards more mystical or magical solutions when the practical or logical is in some way insufficient. Other anthropologists, particularly Evans-Pritchard, have suggested that although ways of thinking in other societies may be different from ours, this is not due to a different mode of thought; their systems do include logic, albeit a different logic than our Western, culturally accepted understanding.

The theory, however, is also inherently illogical. It suggests that there is an absolute qualitative distinction between 'primitive' and 'modern' ways of thinking. If this is so, how does one move from one to the other? If it is gradual, then the difference is not as absolute as suggested. If it is non-gradual, it is difficult to see how and why the transition would be effected. On another level, the theory also does not account for mystical thinking in modern industrialised cultures – as it does not account for logical thinking in pre-modern cultures.

Emile Durkheim (1858–1917): The society as God

> We can now understand how the totemic principle, and more general-ly every religious force, is external to the things it inhabits, for the notion is not composed of the impression the thing produces directly on our minds and senses. Religious force is the feeling the collectivity inspires in its members, but projected outside and objectified by the minds that feel it. It becomes objectified by being anchored in an object which then becomes sacred, but any object can play this role. In princi-ple, none is predestined by its nature to the exclusion of others, any more than others are precluded. It all depends on the circumstances that cause the feeling generating religious ideas to alight here or there and is not implicated in its intrinsic features, it is added to them. The world of the religious is not a particular aspect of empirical nature: it is superimposed.
>
> Emile Durkheim, *The Elementary Forms of the Religious Life* (2001: 174)

Emile Durkheim is in many respects one of the most influential figures in the development of both sociology and anthropology, particularly regarding their approaches to the study of religion. Durkheim's seminal work, *The Elementary Forms of the Religious Life*, first published in 1912, attempts to establish the basic forms and causes that underlie all forms of religion. His interest was not to determine whether religion was true or false; rather he was concerned with the role religion played in society to answer basic needs. These needs, he argued, were no less true in modern forms of religion than in the simpler or less complex forms.

Although, as discussed below, Durkheim does retain an evolutionary aspect to his approach to religion and society, his analysis does not establish a qualitative distinction between simple and complex forms. He states: 'these religions (simple forms) are no less respectable than others. They respond to the same needs, they play the same role, they depend on the same causes.' He thus examines the simpler forms because their very simplicity allows a clearer exposition and analysis of the needs, roles and causes upon which all religions depend.

Mechanical and organic solidarity

Durkheim's analysis of simple and complex forms of society and there-fore religion rested on a broad distinction between two types of society: societies based on mechanical solidarity and those based on organic solidarity. Although there is an evolutionary relationship between the two categories, in Durkheim's usage the two are used for description and analysis and are not essentially historical.

Mechanical solidarity is found in societies where communities are not divided in terms of labour or access to material needs. In essence, it is solidarity based on similarity. Because the life experiences of the individuals are essentially the same, their beliefs and understanding of the world will also be essentially the same. The collective values of soci-eties with mechanical solidarity will be maintained by sanctions.

Organic solidarity is found in societies which have more complex patterns of organisation and a high degree of division of labour. Solida-rity is not based on similarity; rather it is based on interdependence. Durkheim introduces the organic aspect to emphasise that this form of solidarity is like that of a living organism. Each part of the organism plays a different role, yet is interdependent with the other parts or organs to survive. Durkheim suggests that the sanctions for maintaining values in societies organised by organic solidarity will be restitutive.

Durkheim also suggests that there is a direct relationship between the scope of religious representations and the move towards societal com-plexity. As society becomes more complex, religion plays a progressively smaller role. In the least complex societies, religion plays a pervasive role – in effect, religion and society are the same. As societies progress, the particular functions in other cultural areas – economic, political, and the like – slowly separate out from religion.

Religion as a social fact

Durkheim also emphasises that the sociological study of religion is not directly concerned with the individual; rather its goal is to analyse what Durkheim calls social facts. Social facts are those phenomena which are the province of sociology (or anthropology), as opposed to other sciences. They are ways of thinking and acting which arise outside of the individual and which control him or her. Their source is society rather than the individual. This concept is the foundation for understanding that much of our experience in and of society and religion is socially constructed. It further emphasises that to understand religion properly one must look first to society and then to the individual.

The collective understanding of religion stated above is clearly artic- ulated in Durkheim's definition of religion: a unified set of beliefs and practices relative to sacred things, that is to say, things set apart and forbidden; beliefs and practices which unite one single moral community; all those that adhere to them. The definition brings out the two main elements of Durkheim's analysis: that religion is about the sacred, or the distinction between the sacred and the profane, and that religion as a social phenomenon serves as a means of uniting a specific social group.

The sacred and the profane

Durkheim argues that the distinction between sacred and profane is found in all religions and is the fundamental characteristic of religious thought. In making this distinction, Durkheim is not marking any par- ticular object or action as sacred or profane; rather any object can be so marked. The significant feature is that this distinction be made and the two realms be maintained and kept distinct one from the other.

Each set of collective representations relating to this distinction is held by a group and translated by that group into institutions and collective actions – that is, rituals. The group element is as fundamental to religion as is the concept of the sacred; Durkheim suggests that, in fact, the two elements are inseparable aspects of the definition and highlights this definition by distinguishing religion from magic. Although belief in magic maybe very common or indeed universal, the beliefs and practices associated with it are essentially individual and do not lead to the main- tenance or construction of group identity.

Religion and the group

The dualistic model that underlies Durkheim's conception of religion may be associated with the function of religion in creating or maintain- ing group identity. This aspect is seen most clearly in his argument that religion arises neither from a mistaken understanding of natural phe- nomenon, nor from the idea of the soul expanded into animism, but rather as best expressed in totemism, in which the totemic animal is nothing more than a self-representation of the clan, that is, the group itself. God and religion are the embodiment of the society and thus participation in religion becomes a means of validating and unifying the social group. If religion, the sacred, is the representation of the group itself and serves to unify it, it must do so in opposition to the other, those who are not in the group. Thus, the profane represents the rejected other and its existence serves to validate and maintain the importance of the sacred, the group itself.

Ritual and effervescence

Given Durkheim's emphasis on the group and group identity, it is not surprising that religious ritual should play an important role in his analysis; there are few more significant aspects of religion in respect of group cohesion. For Durkheim, the role of ritual was the reaffirmation of the collective affirmations of religion, and therefore the identity of the collective itself. Individuals need a locus whereby they can validate their connection to society. Religious ritual serves this need by creating experiences in which the individual feels part of something greater than himself or herself. It creates an atmosphere of heightened enthusiasm or effervescence in which the individual loses the sense of individuality and feels united with God and thereby the group. This aspect of Durkheim's argument highlights the essentially functionalist aspect of his argument: ritual and religion ultimately serve the societal function of creating and maintaining social solidarity.

Critique

Although Durkheim's theories, particularly his development of a functionalist analysis of society, were highly influential, there are some specific issues which arise from it which need to be addressed. These issues include the evolutionary aspects of his model, the over-emphasis on religion in mechanical solidarity, the de-emphasis on the individual and the location of social facts.

As suggested above, although Durkheim does not over-emphasise the evolutionary aspect of his model, it is found in several strands of his discussion. It is most clearly found in the distinction between mechanical and organic solidarity, an analytical distinction which suggests a historic relation between the two, and a qualitative distinction in terms of complexity. Perhaps more seriously, the evolutionary argument also underpins his use of totemism as the elementary form which underlies religious forms; this suggests that societies which practice totemism today are analogous with the societies out of which more complex forms of religion developed. He does, however, minimise the progressional aspects of this in his arguments, which suggest that religion performs the same functions at whichever societal level it is found.

Durkheim also argues that in societies based on mechanical solidarity, religion and society are one and the same. As Brian Morris (1987) points out, if all elements are effectively one, than any one of those elements can be given priority. Thus, one could argue that society was originally entirely economic or political on the same basis as Durkheim is arguing that it is religious.

Evans-Pritchard, in *Theories of Primitive Religion* (1965), usefully criticises Durkheim's theory on a number of levels. He highlights the problems found in theories that seek to discover the origin of religion. He suggests that any such arguments are by definition conjectural, and even go beyond legitimate conjecture. He challenges the assumption, which he suggests is taken up by Radcliffe Brown (see below), that religious entities conform to social structure and are in effect no more than society, suggesting that the reasoning behind this is no more than plausible, and often in contradiction to the ethnographic evidence.

Although Durkheim's emphasis on society and the social construction of the individual is a very important building block in the understanding of religion and society, it does, perhaps to too great an extent, devalue the importance of the individual as a mediator for social facts. Social facts do shape the individual but he or she equally shapes them through the practice of the social facts. Shared conceptions are shared not because they exist in some collective consciousness outside of the individual but because they are instantiated in each individual through that individual's use of them.

Religion is partially a social phenomenon but it also is an individual experience and functions on levels not directly related to the group. Many scholars have highlighted the fact that this individual aspect undermined the distinction between religion and magic. The distinction is further challenged by many ethnographic observations which emphasise that magic is often a means of defining self in opposition to other or a means of redressing issues within a group and thus, at some levels, is indistinguishable from Durkheim's concept of religion.

The Functionalists: Society as organism

Durkheim was especially influential on the development of both anthropological and sociological theories of society and religion. This influence can be clearly seen in the functionalists we are discussing here. All of these theorists examined religion as essentially social, as part of a system which could be understood by an organic metaphor in which each part or institution had some role or function which was necessary in maintaining the whole society. Although some functionalists emphasised the individual and others the social level, all of them shared the view that these functions were interrelated and served both individual and social purposes.

A. R. Radcliffe Brown (1881–1955) was one of the significant figures in anthropological functionalism. His analysis focused on social structures and societal functions rather than the individual and individual functions and needs. Rather than attempting to determine the origin of particular practices, Radcliffe Brown sought to discover their social function. Using the organic metaphor, he saw culture as essentially adaptive, with each part working in relation to other parts to serve some role in the functioning of the community as a whole.

In his analysis of religion he specifically argues against the assessment of the truth of a particular construct as a search for origins; rather he suggests that religion as a part of society has a social function and this social function should be the focus of analysis. Radcliffe Brown suggests that the social function of religion relates to maintenance of the orderly conduct of social life. In this analysis he emphasises that rituals and beliefs must be looked at together but ultimately it is the rituals that most strongly work to regulate social behaviour. Due to this emphasis on social control, Radcliffe Brown suggests that there is a close correspondence between religion and the particular type of social organisation in which it is found.

Bronislaw Malinowski moves functionalism in a slightly different direction, focusing on the individual and individual needs rather than social structure. Like Radcliffe Brown, he advocated an essentially organic model, in which all parts serve a function and are interrelated one with the other. His analysis of function started with the individual's basic needs and worked from there to broader societal functions. Broadly stated, he suggests that culture rests on the fulfilment of three areas of individual need: basic needs (for example, sexual or nutritional), instrumental needs (as in social control) and integrative needs (such as worldview).

Within this context Malinowski suggests that religion arises from individuals' biological needs; it is not essentially speculative or reflective, rather it arises from the 'tragedies of human life'. Death becomes for Malinowski the key element in the basis of religion. Religion functions to resolve the psychological need arising in relation to death by giving an individual the hope of some form of immortality. On a broader level, religion can be seen in relation to the psychological crisis created by any form of upheaval, especially emotional upheaval, which threatens both the individual and society. Religion is therefore essentially positive, serving and resolving the mental conflicts which arise out of individual and social existence (and potential non-existence).

Malinowski follows some of his predecessors in distinguishing between magic, religion and science. This distinction, however, is not essentially evolutionary; rather Malinowski sees each of these as modes of thought that exist in all forms of society. Malinowski clearly challenges Lévy-Bruhl's assertion that 'primitive mentality was pre-logical'. He argues that empirical knowledge or science is found in every society and is essential to human survival, and for any type of planning or work within society. Magic, however, is also a mode of thinking characteristic to all societies. Magic is a specific area of thinking which is narrower than religion. It relates to those areas of practical activity that are prone to accidents, in which uncontrollable natural events play a part, and where human activity is not sufficient to guarantee results. Magic provides a means of gaining a sense of security in realms in which security is not possible through science; it is essentially practical whereas religion is moved to the sphere of integrative needs.

Many of Malinowski's ideas were taken up in the work of Talcott Parsons, who also focused on the resolution of frustration as a key aspect of his understanding of the function of religion and magic. He defines religion as beliefs, practices and institutions that relate to those areas of human experience that are not understandable or controllable. These elements are brought together in a conceptual system which includes the supernatural and situates individuals in a system of meaning and value with respect to their own lives and that of society. This definition includes the basic concept of the function of religion as establishing for the individual and society a sense of value and order. It also emphasises, as did Malinowski, the psychological problem of frustration and the need for society to develop institutions to resolve it. Parsons moves beyond Malinowski's arguments by bringing together magic and religion into one category, thus resolving some of the problems inherent in Malinowski's analysis. Parsons also emphasises in a similar way to Weber the problem of meaning as a significant feature of his definition, an issue that is taken up again in both Spiro's and Geertz's definitions discussed below.

E. E. Evans-Pritchard emerges from the anthropological functionalist tradition, advancing some of its perspectives and challenging others. In *Theories of Primitive Religion* (1965) he clearly rejects the possibility of determining the origin of religion, seeing all such attempts as speculative. He also argues that the truth of particular religious ideas is not theoretically relevant, emphasising the impossibility of proving or disproving the existence of spiritual beings (or of god). The anthropological study of religion is about sociological facts that are observable and empirical, rather than questions that are either theological or ontological. Ultimately, the role of the anthropological study of religions is to 'determine their meaning and social significance' (1965: 17).

He suggests that in order to understand religion, or for that matter any social phenomena, one must examine it in the context of its relation to other cultural elements; rather than looking at religion as a belief system on its own, it must be analysed as part of a larger system of thought. Thus, religion must be examined in relation to social structure and other 'social facts', for example the ethical or economic. The point that he is emphasising is that religion is part of a coherent system, all parts of which must be examined one in relation to the others – no part of the system is reducible to any other. Regarding this coherent system of thought, Evans-Pritchard particularly emphasised that although it might be based on a different system of logic, internally it is as consistent and comprehensive as Western models of thinking.

In *Witchcraft, Oracles and Magic Among the Azande* (1976), Evans-Prichard presents a system of thought which is based on a logic very different from our own. When any event happened – for example, a granary falling on a person and killing him – the Azande attempted to resolve two questions: one was how did the granary fall, answered in a scientific way – that is, termites ate it – and the other was why did it happen, always answered in terms of magic. Thus, at one level the magical ideas functioned to explain why things happen. The concepts of magic, however, also functioned in relation to social structure; witchcraft was a means of bringing social tensions to the surface and resolving them. The concepts also related to political structure, reinforcing patterns of hierarchy, as witchcraft accusations could never be made against someone from a higher social status. This example touches on the coherent logic of the system; it emphasises that a particular cultural concept needs to be examined in relation to other social facts and it demonstrates a functionalist aspect of Evans-Pritchard's approach.

Critique

Functionalist theories of religion move away from those that focus on a particular essence or on the evolutionary development of culture, and therefore open a more useful discussion relevant to a broader range of anthropological or sociological analysis. Nonetheless, they contain many problematic aspects, some of which they share with the approaches discussed thus far and some more uniquely their own.

Functionalism is often seen as a form of reductionism. In the case of Malinowski, individual needs become the sole basis of culture. Similarly, in the case of Radcliffe Brown, societal needs, particularly those of social control and maintenance of social structure, become the significant motivators for all cultural artefacts. Although the elements under discussion clearly do play a significant role in shaping cultural forms, just as the Marxist emphasis on economics is an essential feature, none of these elements is a sufficient explanation for all cultural beliefs, forms or practices. Many different factors come into play and no one factor seems to be the structural basis upon which all other elements are developed.

Another serious problem with functionalist analyses of culture is that they are ahistorical. They present culture and elements of culture in an almost static or timeless form. The organic model emphasises continuity and leaves little room for the types of transformations that are seen in most, if not all, cultures. In order not to fall into the trap of cultural evolution, the functionalists tend to ignore discussions of transformation and in doing so seem to deny diachronic development within the societies that they analysed. A second aspect created by ignoring transformation is the absence of awareness of conflict within society – conflict may be present and resolved but it is not usually portrayed as a transformative or creative force.

An additional problem is one of argumentation. Many functionalist analyses seem to present a circular form of argument. Function is both the explanation of the ritual and the cause of the ritual. Such an argument undermines both its explanation of function and, more seriously, its explanation of origins – it does not advance the argument, merely uses the object to explain itself.

Although Evans-Pritchard's ethnographic and theoretical discussions are open to some of these challenges, in several respects he begins a development of theory which addresses these issues. Thus, although there is occasionally some degree of circularity and reductionism, his more relational analysis defies simple reductionism. He is also particularly aware and critical of the static, ahistorical aspect of functionalist theory, emphasising the need to take the history of a set of institutions into account as part of a proper ethnographic study.

An intellectualist interlude: Religion as communication and structure

One aspect of Radcliffe Brown's and Evans-Pritchard's approaches, which we have thus far omitted, is the structuralist aspect of their discussions of religion and social structure. The type of structuralism, which these thinkers introduced, focused on the patterns of thinking or relating symbols found in specific cultural constructs. Radcliffe Brown, for example, examined legends of the Andaman Islanders and demonstrated that underlying the narratives the symbols were arraigned in a triadic pattern shaped around the sea, land and tops of trees. Evans-Pritchard discerned a dualistic order to the symbols of the Nuer, associating them with spirit and earth. The structural order of symbols was associated with the structural order of society. This approach to narrative and other aspects of religion developed in the latter half of the twentieth century into the school of French structuralism advocated particularly by Claude Lévi-Strauss.

Along with Lévi-Strauss, Mary Douglas and Edmund Leach have been central to the development of a more sophisticated form of structuralist analysis which examined religious symbols, for example myth and ritual, in order to discover the underlying structural principles; in effect, to determine what these objects indicated about the way that a particular society thought, and ultimately how human beings think.

Structuralism is based on a concept of underlying structure, an unconscious and abstract structuring pattern that ultimately derives from biological structures in the brain. Underlying structure is seen as the pattern, which is used unconsciously, to create or think all aspects of culture. Thus, structuralist theory would suggest that the same logical structures would be exemplified in myth or theology and social structure as suggested by Radcliffe Brown and Evans-Pritchard, as well as in the perceptions of self and the natural world.

Lévi-Strauss emphasises the communicative aspect of myth. He argues that myth is a means of communicating underlying structural ways of thinking. Religion, in his analysis becomes a cultural sphere similar to other cultural spheres, emerging from and communicating underlying structural patterns. Unlike Leach, Douglas, Radcliffe Brown and Evans-Pritchard, Lévi-Strauss does not see structure merely in relation to or emerging from social structure; rather, as suggested above, social structure and religion share the same structural pattern because they both emerge from underlying structure.

Edmund Leach's analysis of myth and ritual both develops aspects of French structuralism, as in his analysis of biblical myths, and addresses the issue of symbols and communication. Leach distinguishes between ritual, which is symbolic behaviour, and behaviour that arises out of an actual emotional state. Thus, mourning practices in many cultures are conventional rather than reflecting individual or real psychological states. Leach suggests that myth and ritual are about communication rather than affective experience. At different points Leach focuses on different forms of communication but his primary argument is that the structure of myth and ritual communicates social structure.

Mary Douglas develops the symbolic and cognitive aspects of structuralist analysis in her discussion of Israelite food rules. She convincingly demonstrates that the food rules properly understood emphasise both the nature and status of categories – pure and impure, edible and not edible, sacrificable and not sacrificable – and the problems which arise when these categories are infringed or challenged. She also demonstrates that these ways of categorising and the attitude towards infringement are not absolutes, and that different cultures have different ways of structuring and relating their categories.

In a slightly different context, Mary Douglas examines the relationship between social control and bodily control. This discussion raises important issues about the role of embodied symbols in shaping experience. Her analysis suggests that not only are social control and bodily control structured in a similar way, there is in fact a direct relationship between the two. Douglas suggests that the degree of control of the individual by society is directly related to the degree of control of the body by the individual. Her analysis is particularly significant with respect to religion, as it forms a basis for explaining the nature of different types of religious experiences, suggesting that the nature and valuation of religious experience is related to both the control of the symbolic system and of the individuals and their bodies. Her theory suggests that the weaker the control of the body and the symbolic system, the greater the freedom and loss of control which will characterise the religious experience.

Melford E. Spiro: Oedipus and God the father

In 'Religion: Problems of Definition and Explanation' (1968), Melford Spiro presents a clearly articulated discussion of issues relating to the definition of religion and his own synthesis of Freudian theory with anthropology. The article first examines different forms of definitions, challenging the form of definition that seeks to define the essence of the object of study. Spiro argues that this type of definition, which he calls 'real definitions', are 'necessarily vague and almost always non-empirical' (1968: 89). Real definitions also, and perhaps most importantly, are almost always narrow; this narrowness can be seen as both limiting the application of the definition and essentially ethnocentric. When the attempt is made to broaden these definitions, the result is to make them increasingly vague and thus useless as analytical tools.

He also addresses the second category of definitions, functionalist explanations, pointing out the fact that functionalist definitions are similar to real definitions, merely replacing the defining essential element with a defining essential function. He adds further that the significant problem with functionalist definitions is that they are usually too broad to be useful – if religion serves to create social order or solidarity, then so too does football or socialism.

The need for definitions

In spite of this problem, he argues that we cannot do without definitions. If we are to know what to study, particularly if we are engaged in comparative study, we need to have a prior definition. In order to keep our definition free of unconscious bias, it must be clear, explicit and articulated. The definition must move away from the essentialist aspects and form the basis of a testable hypothesis. The working definition will include specific elements chosen by the researcher, not to encapsulate the essence of religion but as a means of developing a working hypothesis that can be tested through empirical research.

Spiro suggests that in developing this type of working definition a significant feature must be that it can be applied to a wide range of cultures; he, however, also suggests that it need not be universal. He argues that its absence in specific cultures, far from being a problem, actually can serve to raise important questions about the nature of the phenomena under analysis.

An additional element in constructing the definition is that it be acceptable within one's cultural framework: the definition should not go against the basic understanding and acceptance of the people hearing it. On the basis of this principle he argues that it would be counter-intuitive for a definition of religion not to include supernatural beings and he in fact makes this a core variable that should be found in any definition.

Spiro suggests a working definition of religion: 'an institution consisting of culturally patterned interaction with culturally postulated superhuman beings' (1968: 96). This definition provides a means of distinguishing religion from other similar cultural institutions, for example Marxist ideological systems. It also emphasises that religion is essentially a social phenomena, a point which is important in respect of the psychological and therefore potentially individual aspect of his approach. It also introduces two additional aspects of religion. As a system of 'culturally patterned interaction', Spiro emphasises that religion includes both a value system to pattern this interaction and a ritual system, a forum for the performance of this interaction. The definition also emphasises that religion is a belief system, indeed a particular kind of belief system, one that is based on the postulated existence of the supernatural.

Once the definition of religion is established, Spiro suggests that anthropological analysis must account for the existence of the phenomena so defined. He argues, like Evans-Pritchard and the functionalists, that this discussion should not be about origins, as these will never be testable and they do not account for why a particular phenomenon persists. His analysis of the existence and persistence of religion rests on both causal and functionalist explanations.

On the causal level, he addresses the basis for the acceptance of the truth of a particular religion by its adherents. He argues that, as a social phenomenon, religion is learned through the process of enculturation. The perception of religion as 'true', however, is not purely based on a learned perception but rather has its roots in the individual's psychological experience. Spiro argues that Freud's model, in which the child projects their image of their father into a supernatural figure, is the basis on which the perception of religion as true rests. He adds, in distinction to Freud, that since relations with the father or parent are different in different ethnographic contexts, the nature of the supernatural projections will also differ.

His analysis of the practice of religion moves into the territory of functionalism, albeit a functionalism shaped by his Freudian approach. He suggests that all practices persist because they fill a need; these needs are more sophisticated but not dissimilar to those suggested by Malinowski. He divides these needs into societal and individual, and focuses primarily on the individual needs. An important aspect of his discussion is the suggestion that needs do not have to be recognised and/or intended. Previous anthropologists had already made the distinction between latent and manifest function – that is, functions of which we are aware and those of which we are unaware. Due to his Freudian perspective, Spiro adds into the discussion functions which are intended unconsciously but which are not recognised consciously.

Spiro highlights three areas of need that are served by religion: cognitive, substantive and expressive. The cognitive function refers to religion's role in explaining how and why things happen. The role is served when there are either no alternative methods of explanation or no explanations are available. The second area of function, the substantive, is the fulfilment of the actual desires associated with the particular religious act. For example, desire for rain might be the substantive function of a rain dance. The expressive function arises more directly from Spiro's Freudian approach. This area of function is the one that allows individuals and communities to express desires and feelings that could not positively be expressed through other means. The expression of violence, which is found in sacrifice, would be a positive means of expressing this negative emotion.

Critique

Spiro's analysis has many positive aspects. One of the most important of these is the transformation of the psychological analysis from one of origins to one of persistence. Spiro explains both what religion does and, more importantly, why people continue to use it. His selection of functions also has two positive elements: it recognises both individual and communal levels of function and it also emphasises that religious practices and symbols are about both communication and emotion.

There are, however, alongside some of the issues already suggested in relation to functionalist and Freudian analysis, two additional problematic areas. The first problem with his discussion is found in respect of his definition. In spite of his claim that the definition is ostensive rather than essential, its provisional status is undeveloped. The discussion that follows the definition does not seem to test it and seems to be clearly based on an acceptance of the essential character of the definition.

This leads us back to the content of the definition. Spiro chooses to emphasise the supernatural content of religion. He bases this on two stated and one unstated (but perhaps most decisive) arguments. The two stated arguments are that most, if not all, religions include concepts of the supernatural and that a definition of religion that did not include the supernatural would be counter-intuitive. The first of these is problematic because it can only derive from a pre-existing definition of religion used to determine whether the supernatural element is present. The second argument is essentially ethnocentric – what is counter-intuitive is based on a particular culture's perception, usually of what it considers important or significant, and should not be the basis of an academic definition. The unstated argument is the Freudian theory that underlies his approach. If religion's persistence is ultimately tied to a projection of a parent or parents on reality, then religions would need to have a personified supernatural to fulfil this prescription. This argument is inherently circular and thus cannot be or should not be the basis of definition.

Peter Berger: The social construction of religion

Peter Berger and Thomas Luckman in a classic book, *The Social Construction of Reality* (1991), developed aspects of Durkheim's and Weber's analyses of the relationship between religion and society and the individual and society. The thesis focuses on the fact that our perception of reality, our understanding of cosmos, is socially constructed, and religion is the projection of society upon the world around us – in effect, the creation of cosmos. It has subsequently been refined and developed by Berger in *The Sacred Canopy: Elements of a Sociological Theory of Religion* (1967).

In *The Sacred Canopy* Berger develops this argument by analysing the relationship of the individual to society, the role of religion in the creation of cosmos and its role in legitimising and maintaining cosmos. He suggests that the individual and society are in a dialectical relationship. Although society is a human creation and thus the act of human beings, it acts upon its creators. This is particularly true of the individual who emerges from society and is a product of society. Society is defined as the part of culture that organises human beings' social relationships. Culture is the broader set of human creativity, which includes all things produced by human beings, including their understanding and perception of the world. Thus, culture can be said to be the humanly created world which, due to the lack of an instinctual relationship with the world, allows us to function and act within it. Although culture is a human creation – like society, it is objectified – it is perceived of possessing a reality separate from its creators and acting upon them. As the concluding act of the dialectical process, the objectified culture must be internalised, creating a unity between the subjective individual consciousness and the objective – reshaping the individual in relation to the cultural understanding of cosmos. Aspects of this argument, and Berger's suggestion that the socially constructed world is essentially a structuring or ordering process, have clear links with Lévi-Strauss.

Religion is part of the process of world-making; it is the process of world-making that uses the sacred as its mode of expression. The sacred is 'a quality of mysterious and awesome power' (Berger 1967: 25). This quality may be associated with a wide range of objects, individuals or institutions; it may also be perceived in an understanding of supernatural objects or beings. As in Durkheim, the sacred is defined in opposition to the profane and, perhaps more importantly, chaos, the opposite of order. The religious or sacred perception of cosmos is particularly powerful because it both stands over and against the human being but also directly addresses him or her. Religion, like other processes of world-making, is a process of projection or externalisation. Ultimately, it projects the human on cosmos and thereby actually creates cosmos. The order that it externalises, however, is not individual but arises from the social, and thus religion becomes the externalisation of society.

> It can thus be said that religion has played a strategic part in the human enterprise of world-building. Religion implies the farthest reach of man's self-externalisation, of his infusion of reality with his own meanings. Religion implies that human order is projected into the totality of being. Put differently, religion is the audacious attempt to conceive of the entire universe as being humanly significant.
>
> Peter Berger, *The Sacred Canopy* (1967: 27–8)

Berger also examines a second aspect of religion, that of validation or legitimisation. He points out that all such social constructions are unstable. Thus, processes within culture need to anchor the elements of social order and validate them as 'real' or perhaps in other terms as sacred or natural. Religion, as the ultimate externalisation of social order into the realm of the sacred or the mysterious, is one of the most powerful methods of legitimisation. In effect, religion validates society or social institutions by showing that they are structured in the same way as is ultimate reality, that is, the sacred. As Berger suggests, this validation is based on an inherent relationship between the microcosm, society, and the macrocosm, the sacred cosmos.

Critique

Berger's approach to religion brings together different strands from Durkheim, Weber, Lévi-Strauss and others, particularly within the sociological tradition. It also shares elements, particularly its concept of cosmos, with the approach developed by Geertz discussed at the conclusion of this chapter. Although there are many significant and persuasive elements to his argument, particularly the emphasis on the social construction of reality and the dialectical relationship between the individual and culture/society, there are also a few areas which are problematic.

Brian Morris in *Anthropological Studies of Religion* suggests that Berger over-emphasises the nature of the symbolic universe constructed by religion, that is, the world-making role of religion. He argues that although this form of extensive symbolic universe is found in many cultures, there are also certain ethnographic examples in which only minimal symbolic universes are constructed. The limited nature of conscious order or structure may also be seen among the Dorze, who, according to Sperber, have only minimal conscious articulation or interpretation of symbols.

A second point relates to the societal emphasis of Berger's arguments. Although society and culture are central in the creation and perception of social universes, it seems likely that religion also serves some individual needs not directly related to social structure. Some of these needs are highlighted by both Geertz (below) and Spiro. As Spiro suggests, religion can serve to validate social structure but its persistence requires that it also serve needs recognised or not of the individual – particularly in a world that Berger recognises is increasingly secular.

Clifford Geertz: Religion as a symbolic complex

In 'Religion as a Cultural System', Clifford Geertz develops one of the most influential recent discussions of religion. Although Geertz shares some elements with the intellectualist tradition, particularly the emphasis on religion as a communicative system, the development of this aspect in relation to other cultural elements also has linkages to Weber, as does his discussion of religion and ideology. His model also introduces aspects that are related to the Durkheimian model, as in his discussion of moods, which is in some respects similar to Durkheim's discussion of effervescence. The key aspect, however, which sets Geertz's approach apart is its emphasis on religion and other aspects of cultures as systems of symbols.

Definition of religion

These elements are particularly clear in Geertz's definition of religion.

> Religion is: (1) a system of symbols which acts to (2) establish powerful, pervasive, and longlasting moods and motivations in men by (3) formulating conceptions of a general order of existence and (4) clothing these conceptions with such an aura of factuality that (5) the moods and motivations seem uniquely realistic.
>
> Clifford Geertz, *The Interpretation of Cultures* (1973: 90)

The primary feature of the definition is the emphasis on religion as a system of symbols. Geertz suggests that the term should be used for anything, for example an object or an act, which carries a conception. The conception can be as narrow as the relationship between a number of objects and the idea of the number, to the wide range of ideas or meanings associated with the cross. It should be emphasised that these conceptions and their related symbols are cultural constructs and as such lie outside of the individual and are specific to particular cultures.

Symbols as models of and models for

Geertz extends the discussion of symbols to complexes of symbols that partially work on the analogy with genes; symbolic complexes replace genetic instinctual models by providing cultural blueprints or models for shaping action. This leads Geertz to distinguish between two types of symbolic complexes: 'models of' and 'models for'. These should be seen as ideal types in a Weberian sense – that is, a useful analytical distinction but one that is not usually found in an absolute or ideal sense. All symbols are both models of and models for. Models of are meant to describe pre-existing systems, as for example the model of evolution is meant to describe a process that occurred outside of the particular symbolic system. A model for is one that is used to shape systems outside of the symbolic realm. Thus, if a blueprint is used to build a house then it becomes a model for.

Models for are seen in many parts of the natural world, as well as in the human realm, thus the gene is a biological model for constructing all living organisms. Geertz suggests that models of are rare and possibly only found in the human realm. They create the possibility of bringing together, at least at a conceptual level, sets of elements that arise from totally different areas of human experience. The human ability to move between the two types of models is characteristic of human thought and the source of the power of symbolic systems.

Moods and motivations

Within religious systems two responses arise: moods and motivations. Moods are short-term emotional or experiential responses to the particular religious symbolic constructs. They are similar to a fog that shapes all aspects of the experience within it but vanishes as soon as one moves outside of it. The emotions encapsulated in these moods can vary in several ways; they can have different degrees of intensity or cover the full gamut of emotional response. Moods are powerful or meaningful because when within them they shape one's experience and perception of reality.

Motivations are the long-term religious constructs. Although the term ethos includes some of the motivations that can arise, they can be both more specific and less specific. They can engender a specific action or a long-lasting attitude, as in the passivity against adversity that might be a characteristic of certain forms of Buddhism. A key feature of motivations is that they are goal-oriented, while moods are existential. Both moods and motivations are important though secondary aspects of Geertz's model: moods ultimately validate the religious symbolic construct by demonstrating that the construct is patterned in the same way as experiences; and motivations shape action by making it conform to that religious symbolic pattern. Thus, moods and motivations represent the two interrelated uses of symbols, moods being models of and motivations being symbols for.

Conceptions of a general order

One of the problems in defining religion in a non-essentialist way is that it often becomes such a broad category that a wide range of diverse activities or systems can be included within its purview. Geertz attempts to limit the definition by arguing that the symbolic system must also relate to 'conceptions of a general order of existence'. At one level this can be seen as a model of reality in which, with differing degrees of subtlety or development, the world or universe was made in some sense meaningful or understandable. Thus, sport is similar to religion in respect of moods and motivations but usually fails to fit the category because most of its fans do not use it to explain or give meaning to their reality as a whole.

Geertz suggests that within these 'conceptions of a general order of existence' three areas threaten the coherence of the system and thus must be addressed. The first is the problem of explanation. This refers to the need that human beings have to explain the processes that occur in their experiential universe. This need echoes the work of early anthropologists like Tylor and Frazer and would also include the work of Evans-Pritchard on the Azande. The second need is the problem of suffering: why bad things happen to good people. Geertz emphasises that the problem for religious systems is how to make suffering bearable or understandable. Finally, there is the problem of evil. This problem relates to the apparent difficulty or impossibility of explaining the existence of evil. Each of these areas is significant because they challenge the symbolic resources of the religious system and thus force the system to address them and to deny that they are in fact problems.

Auras of factuality

The aura of factuality that validates and thus upholds the religious symbolic complex is particularly engendered in religious ritual. The ritual brings together the three areas: moods/religious experience, motivations/ethos and conceptions of a general order/worldview. In doing so, it emphasises the relationship between the symbols of and the symbols for. The ritual allows the congruence between social order and spiritual reality to be demonstrated and, in doing so, simultaneously validates both the social order and the worldview. The congruence and validation of the two realms also allows the denial of those areas that challenge the system and thus completes the symbolic circle.

Uniquely realistic

The final aspect of Geertz's argument relates to the relationship between religion and the social system in which it is found and the relationship between the religious and common-sense worldviews. Geertz suggests that although religion has a relation to social system, it is not the simple or direct relationship between religion and social structure that is suggested by Berger. He mirrors Weber in suggesting that rather than merely being a projection of social structure, religion, like other cultural constructs, also shapes society.

He also suggests that as it is impossible for people to remain within the religious worldview at all times, the relationship between the common sense worldview and the religious worldview needs to be addressed. If the symbolic circle discussed above is maintained, then the religious worldview is privileged by being experienced as uniquely real. It thereby becomes the unique factor in correcting, completing and shaping the common-sense worldview.

Critique

Talal Asad has critiqued Geertz's understanding of religion in *Genealogies of Religion*. We will touch here on several aspects of his arguments. Asad begins by suggesting that it is impossible to develop a universal definition of religion. This is due to the fact that religion is a historically conditioned institution and that any definition is also the product of a particular historical location. He suggests that, at least in part, definitions of religion arise from both the imposition of Christian categories and the particular Christian concern about defining particular categories. Thus, Geertz's analysis, like all the other discussions included above, would fall foul of this critique.

His second criticism challenges Geertz's understanding of symbols. He argues that although Geertz distinguishes between the symbol and the conception it represents, in much of his argument this distinction is not maintained and the conception becomes equated with the symbol. He also suggests that this confusion makes it difficult to analyse the social production of symbols and the processes that give certain symbols or symbolic complexes authority. Asad's arguments emphasise the need to see symbols not as carriers of meaning essential unto themselves but as carriers of meaning contextualised within a particular social setting.

His third criticism raises the role of religious symbols in creating a distinctive set of responses. Geertz's argument seems to suggest that the moods and motivations can be decontextualised and seen in direct relation to a specific and unique set of religious symbols. Asad suggests that we can neither predict the moods and motivations that will arise from a symbolic construct, nor can we limit the moods and motivations to that specific construct. As in his previous criticism, we need to see the dispositions within the broader social and individual context.

Asad also takes up similar themes in addressing issues of truth and ideology. He suggests that Geertz's arguments ignore the political or power aspects of the creation of truth. It is not only symbols which create a sense of truth but the full range of historically contextualised political and religious sanctions which enforce acceptance of and conformity with the socially accepted truths.

A final issue that might be raised in respect of Geertz's discussion is one that it shares with some phenomenological discussions. In focusing on religious process in a somewhat decontextualised way, which is also seen for example in his discussion in *Islam Observed*, Geertz seems to suggest that religion's symbolic systems can be examined without ethnographic context. As indicated in all of Asad's criticisms, this approach ignores the fact that religion is shaped by its context and associated worldviews as much as it shapes them. Particular religious experiences and beliefs are related to systems of power and hegemony and the individual biography and experiences within these hegemonic structures and therefore must be historically and culturally contextualised.

Conclusion

In this chapter we have examined the development of theories of religion within the social scientific disciplines of anthropology and sociology. If we consider these theories in the light of Asad's critique of Geertz and theories of religion in general, it becomes clear that these theories arise in particular political and social contexts and reflect the interests and power relations of those social contexts. This is clearly true of the evolutionary theories that were closely implicated in late nineteenth- and early twentieth-century colonialism. It is also true, at a more subtle level, of those theories developed after the colonial period.

If we followed Asad's argument to its logical conclusion, we should put aside any attempt to define religion and, at a broader level, to attempt any form of definition in respect of any aspect of culture or indeed the concept of culture itself. While Asad poses a needed critique of definitions and the process of establishing definitions, and specifically the role of power and power interests, these issues can become part of the reflexive critique of theory, or perhaps the dialectic in theory rather than denying the possibility of theoretical discussion. Without some type of broadly based theory no cross-cultural comparative discussion can take place.

The developments within theory discussed in this chapter suggest some elements that might usefully provide the basis for this dialectical theory of religion. First, it should include a concept of internal development and transformation without a concept of progress or evolution. Second, it would need to avoid a simplistic form of reductionism, while still allowing for religion as a social phenomenon to arise from a similar set of human cultural responses; these might include responses to issues of ontology, biology and/or environment, as well as economic and social structure. The definition, however, would need to be open to an almost infinite range of responses to these issues. Third, although the social sciences are concerned with religion as a social construct, relating to issues that arise from human beings' interrelations with each other and the socially constructed environment in which they live, analysis of religion must take seriously the internal perceptions and understandings of reality. The theory must also balance the societal aspects of religion with the roles it plays for individuals. Finally, it must be aware of the relationship of religion to its specific cultural context, specifically in terms of power and power structures and the relationship of the theorist and his or her analysis to a related set of power and power structures.

Further reading

Capps, Walter H. (1995), *Religious Studies*, Minneapolis: Fortress Press. This book presents a comprehensive discussion of all of the theories of religion from all of the major disciplines. Although its discussions are relatively short, they consistently highlight the significant aspects of the thinkers and approaches.

Fenn, Richard K. (2001), *The Blackwell Companion to Sociology of Religion*, Oxford: Blackwell. This volume brings together chapters by some of the most significant names in the sociology of religion today. It explores the development and critique of theory, the relation of religion to society and how sociological approaches relate to other disciplinary approaches.

Hamilton, Malcolm (1995), *The Sociology of Religion*, London: Routledge. This book provides a clear discussion of the major approaches to religion from the sociological perspective. It also introduces a wide range of comparative material to contextualise the theories.

Lambek, Michael (ed) (2002), *A Reader in the Anthropology of Religion*, Oxford: Blackwell. This volume includes abridged versions of many of the classic discussions of religion from an anthropological perspective. It includes essential ethnographic and theoretical material.

Lessa, W. A. and E. Z. Vogt (eds) (1979), Reader in Comparative Religion, New York: Harper and Row. This volume provides an essential collection of articles and extracts by some of the most significant anthropological thinkers on religion. Although some of the chapters are abridged, many are not.

Morris, Brian (1987), *Anthropological Studies of Religion*, Cambridge: Cambridge University Press. This book provides a detailed and critical analysis of the major anthropological theories. It also discusses many of the related theories from the cognate disciplines of psychology, sociology and phenomenology.

Questions

1. What problems arise when constructing a theory of religion that uses one's own religion as its foundation?

2. Explore the similarities and differences found in the theories of Lévy-Bruhl, Jung and Eliade.

3. Throughout much of the early discussion of religion distinctions were made between religion, magic and science. Are these distinctions useful or valid?

4. If functionalist definitions of religion are still essentialist, are they still useful in understanding religion?

5. Is Asad correct in arguing against the possibility of any encompassing definition of religion?

Section Two: CASE STUDIES

CHAPTER ONE

Indigenous Traditions and Anthropological Theory

Seth D. Kunin

- ❑ Introduction
- ❑ Ritual and the ritual process
- ❑ Religious experience
- ❑ Symbolism
- ❑ Mythology
- ❑ Conclusion
- ❑ Further reading
- ❑ Questions

Introduction

This chapter examines some aspects of indigenous religious traditions. This category is very broad and includes the majority of religions. Although they are discussed together, this category is one of great diversity and little can be said which unites all these traditions, save that they are not considered world religions. Thus, their definition is negative, what they are not, rather than positive, what they are.

In some quarters there have been attempts to find commonalities within this category, either to demonstrate a particular unity of a specific group of indigenous traditions or to demonstrate a qualitative distinction between indigenous traditions and 'world religions'. These attempts have usually been based on three different motivations: political, theological or evolutionary.

Political approaches

The political motivation attempts to create a sense of unity of indigenous peoples by stressing the commonalities of their cultures either at the local, national or global levels, usually in opposition to Western cultural imperialism. While one may agree with their political aspirations, very often the attempts to create a homogenised understanding of culture, for example a Native American or African culture, ignores the significant diversity found among Native American or African communities (both within and between 'cultures'). These approaches emphasise specific features usually out of context and in ways that would not be recognisable in the particular communities or cultures.

Theological approaches

The theological motivation moves outside of the realm that can be appropriately studied by the social scientific approaches to religion. It assumes that there is a common spiritual experience that is found in every culture. Thus, indigenous religions are shaped by this experience and are seen as preserving it in a pure, uncorrupted form. This approach would suggest that underlying all specific cultural forms, which in effect are accretions, is a common spiritual experience. The specific forms are unimportant, only the common spirituality is of significance. There are two major problems with this approach. First, it tends to ignore differences by arguing that they are of no significance. In doing this, it often emphasises elements of a tradition that may be important to the observer but of no importance to a member of the community being studied. Second, it posits an essential nature to religion that by its nature cannot be directly observed by social scientific methods. This essential nature is externally posited and then supported by elements taken out of cultural, geographic and temporal context.

Evolutionary models and the 'primal tradition'

The evolutionary approach, discussed in detail in the chapter on anthropological and sociological definitions, is often found underlying the other approaches and is the most problematic. This approach assumes that the indigenous traditions are in some sense comparable to earlier forms of our own cultural development. This is seen in the term 'primal religions', which is often used in religious studies to refer to these religious traditions. The term suggests that these religions are, in some sense, less developed. The term is used as a way of distinguishing these traditions on a qualitative basis from the so-called world religions. Definitions of primal religions tend to include some of the following elements: they are oral rather than written, they are 'this-worldly', religion tends to be co-extensive with culture, and they are the traditions from which the world religions developed.

The commonalities that are posited to the 'primal traditions' can only arise from an evolutionary and ethnocentric model. The model clearly sees the 'primal traditions' as being prior and in some sense similar or identical to the forms that were earlier stages of the 'world religions'. This evolutionary model allows theorists to emphasise the supposed commonalities and to use these traditions to explain how and why 'world religions' take the forms they do today. The model thus supposes a unilinear model of evolutionary development, which thereby justifies the existence of the common features of the 'primal religions' and the qualitative difference from the 'world religions'.

The model of unilinear cultural evolution that underlies these approaches has been demonstrated to be an inadequate analysis of culture since the early part of the twentieth century. It is an ethnocentric model that is an extension of Western imperialism into cultural analysis, using Western cultural forms – for example, literacy and thus scriptures

---

Although, following convention, I have headed this section 'the primal tradition' these peoples whom historians of religion regard as having a 'primal' outlook on the world represent a great diversity of cultural and religious adaptations scattered widely over time and space. However, whether found in the distant or recent past, and in whatever part of the globe, people living in small-scale, non-literate, and for the most part, tribal societies have a sufficient number of features in common for us to consider them as having a common worldview – a worldview which lies at the base of all known cultures and which has not entirely disappeared from the outlook of men and women in the Western world.

The greatest single difference, however, between modern Western men and women's way of looking at the world and the world seen through 'primal' eyes lies in the fact that whereas modern men and women see the world as impersonal, as an 'it' set over against them, in the primal apprehension of the world the world is experienced as personal, as a 'Thou' which confronts men and women as a living presence.

James Thrower, *Religion: The Classical Theories* (1999: 11–12)

– as a yardstick with which all other religious traditions are measured. Modern social sciences agree that there is no single path of development;

each culture develops according to its own trajectory and so no contemporary culture can be used to model our culture's past because, to a large degree, all cultures are unique and have their own paths of development.

The theory of primal religions also suggests that men and women living in the 'primal' worldview experience the world in a different way than modern Western men and women. The fundamental difference in experience is related to the subjectivisation of the experienced world: in the 'primal' traditions the world is seen as a personified subject while in the modern tradition it is treated as an object. This distinction harks back to similar distinctions by Lévy-Bruhl (see Chapter Three in the previous section, on Anthropological and Sociological Theories) and Jung (see Chapter Two in the previous section, on Psychological and Phenomenological Theories). Ethnographic analysis of a wide range of communities does not support this distinction. All human societies have a range of ways of appropriating the world, including the objective and subjective. No clear distinction or pattern can be determined on the basis assumed by the 'primal tradition' theorists.

'World religions' and 'indigenous religions'

An additional problem found in models that make a strong qualitative distinction between 'world' and 'indigenous' religions relates to the perception of internal consistency. The model suggests that there are many different 'indigenous' religions, each associated with and shaped by a specific cultural context, usually on a very local level. In opposition to this, it projects a view of the 'world' religions as transcending local cultural contexts and having a significant amount of internal consistency as well as an essential nature which is found regardless of the context. It is argued here that this model ignores the heterogeneous nature of the 'world' religions. They are, in fact, made up of a multitude of often diverse local traditions that are closely interrelated, like the 'indigenous' religions with their cultural context. In this sense, every local variation of the 'world' tradition is exactly analogous to the 'indigenous' religions. Although these variations are, to different extents, unified by literary or scriptural traditions or patterns of hierarchy or authority, the local aspect is nonetheless of particular significance because it is this aspect that allows the religion to respond to the specific needs of the local community and is shaped by the unique historical experience of that community.

Functionalist and culturist approaches to religion

The approach taken here rejects the essentialist concepts that underpin these three attempts to find broad commonalities within indigenous traditions that would distinguish them from the world religions. But, as indicated in the preceding chapters, it is essential to have some basis of defining the term religion in order to be able to classify a particular cultural phenomenon as religion or not. The definitions that underlie the material presented in this chapter have been termed culturist or functionalist. They attempt to examine what religion does rather than what religion is. Culturist definitions are, in one sense, still essentialist, as the function itself becomes the essential defining feature; a function can be specifically defined but still encompass a wide range of differing phenomena.

The function examined might work at the level of social structure, conscious or unconscious, or more broadly by examining phenomena that address similar existential questions, for example the problem of meaning or of evil. An essential aspect of a good culturist definition is that it does not seek to impose content. It looks at a wide range of phenomena used by different cultures to respond to similar problems or issues, emphasising that each cultural response will derive from that culture's unique trajectory of development. In this sense there is nothing specifically unique to indigenous traditions such that they could be positively defined in relation to world religions. Rather, all religions are defined in the same way, not by a particular aspect of content or by emerging from a single element of experience but as unique cultural responses to particular human and cultural experiences.

This chapter does not attempt to present a single definition of religion, nor does it seek to present a broad model of indigenous traditions. Instead, it seeks to explore some aspects of anthropological approaches to religion, based on culturist theories of religion, and to use examples from a wide variety of indigenous traditions as a means of exemplifying these theoretical constructs and questions. This approach will allow us to emphasise the great variety that is found among indigenous traditions and to argue that the same issues and theories that are used to analyse indigenous traditions could be similarly be used for any of the world religions.

Ritual and the ritual process

Ritual has been identified as a significant feature of religions from the earliest stages in the anthropological study of religion. Ritual as a category of action can be partially defined as culturally prescribed, patterned behaviour that contains both affective and communicative elements. Different theorists, as well as different cultural traditions, emphasise different aspects of this definition. In some contexts ritual is seen as a highly communicative phenomenon that is similar in content to language or, more specifically, mythology. What and how ritual communicates will be culture specific. In other cases, however, the internal view might emphasise the affective aspect of ritual, sometimes denying that ritual or particular rituals communicate anything on the conceptual or symbolic level. Dan Sperber examines the case of the Dorze in Ethiopia. He suggests that although Dorze rituals include material that might be considered by the ethnographer to be symbolic and thus communicative, from the perspective of the Dorze these elements are not interpreted and are only discussed in the context of how they are used. One could view these elements as communicating on an unconscious level, or examine how the rituals affect the individuals and communities who participate in them. One of the important features of ritual is that it involves some use of the body and, in doing so, whether communication or affect is emphasised, the practice of the ritual clearly has an impact on both, as both mind and body are involved in the actions.

Rites of passage

Although each culture or community will have its own sphere of ritual action, anthropologists have observed that rituals often have a patterned structure that might be termed the ritual process. In the classic work *Rites of Passage*, first published in 1909, Arnold van Gennep suggested that rituals relating to transformation – that is, rites of passage – had a common structure based on three stages: separation, liminal and incorporation. The three stages could be found within a single ritual or could be found within a cycle of interrelated rituals. The separation phase centres around practices that remove the individual from their previous status or social position. The liminal or threshold phase is that in which the transformation occurs. It is the in between stage where the individual has no status or is between statuses, often seen as being ambiguous or dangerous. The incorporation phase is that in which the individual is returned to society with their new status or role.

These three stages are found in rites of passage and other ritual processes in many societies; however, in some cases one of the stages might be either emphasised or de-emphasised. The model should therefore not be seen as prescriptive but rather as allowing rituals to be examined and raising important questions depending on the particular cultural configuration.

Communitas, or social antistructure. A relational quality of full unmediated communication, even communion, between definite and determinate identities, which arises spontaneously in all kinds of groups, situations, and circumstances ... It is a liminal phenomenon which combines the qualities of lowliness, sacredness, homogeneity, and comradeship. The distinction between structure and communitas is not the same as that between secular and sacred; communitas is an essential and generic human bond . . .

The bonds of communitas are undifferentiated, egalitarian, direct, extant, non-rational, existential, I–Thou (in Buber's sense). Communitas is spontaneous, immediate, concrete, not abstract. It is part of 'serious life'. It does not merge identities; it liberates them from conformity to general norms, though this is necessarily a transient condition if society is to continue to operate in an orderly fashion . . .

Victor Turner and Edith Turner,
Image and Pilgrimage in Christian Culture (1978: 250)

Victor Turner's analysis of the ritual process emphasises the liminal stage. He argues that the essential feature of the liminal stage is the experience of *communitas* – an experiential state in which boundaries between individuals are dissolved, status distinctions are removed and a sense of unity or community is created. To an extent he presents the liminal phase as standing in opposition to the hierarchical nature of society, suggesting that the higher the degree of hierarchy or structure, the greater the communitas or anti-structure. Turner extended the model of rites of passage to include pilgrimages, which he saw as the paradigmatic example of *communitas* and ritual, allowing individuals to move outside of the normal cultural structures and hierarchies.

Rites of passage among the BaMabuti of the Ituri Forest

Colin Turnbull presents a fascinating example of a rite of passage in *The Forest People*. In this ethnography he specifically focuses on the BaMabuti, a hunting and gathering people who live in the Ituri Forest of the Congo in Africa. The rites of passage are particularly interesting because they are found at the interface between the BaMabuti and the Bantu villagers who live and farm on the outskirts of the forest. Each of these communities has a different understanding of the same rite of passage depending on their own cultural understanding and the perceived function of the ritual.

The particular rite of passage in question is the nkumbi, or the initiation ceremony for boys. The nkumbi ceremony is a ritual controlled by the Bantu villagers and is seen by them as a rite that transforms a boy from childhood into adulthood; it is an essential ceremony, which culminates in circumcision. At times it may even be performed for a boy who has died prior to participating in the ritual, as the nkumbi is required for the person to be joined to the ancestors. The ritual transforms the child and also links him to his community, both to the ancestors of the past and to the present members and ultimately to the future life of the tribe. In relation to the BaMabuti, the Bantu villagers see the ceremony as creating a patron–client relationship with those BaMabuti who participate.

The BaMabuti see the ceremony very differently. They do not consider it as transformative: the boy will not become an adult until he has killed his first game and participates in the elima, the initiation ritual for girls. They undergo the ceremony for purely pragmatic reasons. Nkumbi is required to create a tie with a villager that can be essential for economic reasons, providing employment or resources that are not available in the forest.

The village nkumbi ritual includes all of the elements found in van Gennep's model. The separation phase is illustrated by the location of the ritual. The children are removed from their homes and communities and placed in a special encampment in which the main aspect of the rite occurs. The children's heads are shaved, symbolising the end of the previous stage of life. Both of these elements are common features of the separation phase in many societies. The liminal phase takes place in the special encampment. The time in the encampment is meant to be filled with taboo – the boys are restricted from eating certain foods and are subject to physical ordeals – and is meant to be a time of terror. The liminal phases culminates with the circumcision. The incorporation phase is found when the village boys return to the village as men, taking on the new status and responsibilities.

For the villagers the nkumbi functions as a rite of passage in the classic sense described by van Gennep. Perhaps, however, the aspect of *communitas* between the village children and the BaMabuti children might not be as strongly present as suggested by Turner's model. For the BaMabuti, the ritual clearly does not function as a rite of passage; it is merely a necessary stage in defining their relations with the villagers.

This difference is clearly seen in the description of the ritual that Turnbull observed. Turnbull discusses a particular example in which no village children were present and, due to the rule of the ritual, no villagers could be present during the nights. While the BaMabuti followed the restrictions and rules during the day when the village men were present, during the night they ridiculed the taboos and clearly indicated the lack of meaning of the ritual for them.

As suggested above, the BaMabuti had no specific rite of initiation for boys. A boy became an adult through killing game. This suggests that, unlike the villagers, who strongly emphasised liminality in the BaMabuti case there appears to be no liminal period: the boy is a child until he kills the game and becomes an adult, in effect, upon doing so. It seems likely that the lack of hierarchy and structure in BaMabuti society means there is less need for anti-structural elements and thus less need for liminality.

Maurice Bloch: Rebounding violence

Maurice Bloch brings together aspects of sacrifice and rites of passage, particularly focusing on the transformative aspect of violence. He suggests that violence in ritual can be a means of effecting symbolic death and thereby gaining access to spiritual power in a process that he calls rebounding violence.

A good example of this process can be seen in a rite of passage among the Orokaiva of New Guinea. The Orokaiva see human beings as being composed of two elements, a pig-like aspect and a spirit-like aspect. In order for children to gain the spirit aspect, they must die in regard to the pig aspect. Sacrifice, or symbolic death, in the initiation process allows the boys to come, at least for a time, in contact with death and thereby the spiritual realm.

Prior to the ritual, which occurs in the bush, where the children are seen as purely spirit, the pig element is their essential nature. The separation phase occurs when the children are chased or hunted as pigs into the forest, where they symbolically die as pigs. While in the bush, the liminal phase, the boys are subject to a wide range of rules forbidding them from washing, eating normal food or looking out of the initiation hut – they are told that they have become bird spirits of the dead. As in many rites of passage, they go through ordeals and are taught the things they need to know as initiated adults. When they return to their village they are no longer the hunted prey and have become instead the hunter of pigs. The essential aspect of the ritual is that upon their return they are transformed; through violence they have come into contact with the world of the spirits. Upon their return, however, they must re-enter the human, pig-like realm but in a transformed way. The transformation is symbolised in the role of hunter: they now hunt and eat pig rather than being purely pigs. Bloch emphasises that violence in ritual is essentially transformative, whether it occurs to a sacrificed animal or symbolically allows a contact with spiritual power, and the violence rebounds in a greater form giving power to the sacrificer or initiate.

Religious experience

Religious experience is closely related to issues of liminality and *communitas*. Anthropological research has demonstrated that these types of experiences are culturally constructed and closely interrelated to other aspects of social structure. The ritual process provides a common setting for religious experience and in many respects shapes the type of experiences that will occur. The liminal phase is particularly well-suited for the construction of religious experience, as it moves individuals and groups out of their normal social settings and relations, and *communitas* can be understood as one form of it. Clifford Geertz has pointed out that religious experience also serves a broader role as a means of validating and supporting worldview.

Although one might commonly see religious experience as referring to ecstatic experiences like trance or spirit possession, the term refers to a much wider range of phenomena. At one end of the scale, it might be the feeling of connection or community; at the other, it might be the loss of all bodily control in a case of spirit possession or trance. The type of experience found in a particular ritual or occasion is not spontaneous or haphazard but is closely related to cultural expectation and context.

Mary Douglas: the body and society

Mary Douglas in *Natural Symbols* (1986) suggests that there is a close relationship between the degree to which society controls the individual and the degree to which the individual controls their body. In relation to religious experiences, this suggests that in communities that exercise a high degree of control, both in respect of thought and action, the individual will not lose control of their body. Thus, religious experience will be highly controlled, the individual will remain in control of their body – limiting the experience to a pervasive mood or feeling – and the interpretation of the experience will stay within the acceptable understanding of that particular group. As the control of the group is lessened, the individual's control over their body will become weaker and allow more active forms of religious experience. In tandem with the lessening control over the body, the control over ideas also plays a significant role in shaping the experience; the weaker the control over interpretation, the more possibilities of experiences that include new sources of information.

Mary Douglas presents an interesting example of how three neighbouring societies in Africa – the Dinka, the Nuer and the Mandari – due to their different models of social control, have different patterns of religious experience and different ways of valuing that experience. The Dinka view spirit possession positively and in the context of ritual are willing to go into an uncontrolled state. This pattern of positive, active spirit possession is associated with a relatively weak societal control over actions and thought. Unlike the Nuer, who have a wide range of rules regulating these realms, the Dinka are less structured. Their society, as a whole, is only weakly structured and highly segmentary. Thus, as suggested by Douglas's theory, weak control of action and thought is associated with a high degree of positive spirit possession.

The Nuer have a more negative perception of spirit possession. It is divided into two categories, temporary and permanent. Temporary spirit possession is associated with illness. It is a condition that needs to be resolved and removed. Permanent spirit possession is found in the prophets who stand outside of Nuer society and are somewhat ambiguous. The Nuer view possession as dangerous and anomalous. This understanding of spirit possession is associated with a range of mechanisms of social control. These include taboos associated with cattle (both the Nuer and Dinka are pastoralists), as well as other regulations concerning purity and pollution. Douglas suggests that, alongside these aspects of social control, Nuer society is also somewhat more tightly structured, with clear ideas of bounded social units. Thus, the Nuer, with a higher degree of social control, also display a weaker aspect of religious experience than do the Dinka.

The Mandari are introduced by Douglas as an example of a society with a higher degree of social control than either the Nuer or the Dinka and thus an even weaker degree of spirit possession. Unlike the other two societies, whose patterns of leadership are relatively weak, the Mandari have a complex organisation of chiefdoms in which boundaries and allegiance are especially significant. Alongside this political structure, the Mandari also have very clearly articulated understandings of sin and offence. As suggested by Douglas's model, the high degree of social control is matched by an equally negative attitude towards spirit possession.

Christian religious experience

The model of religious experience presented here is also applicable to religious experience in various contexts within our own societies. Within the Christian context a number of different types of religious experiences can be identified: the sense of community or communion, speaking in tongues – either privately or publicly, being slain by the spirit, the Toronto Blessing, and prophecy. Each one of these kinds of experience can be associated with particular religious structures. Thus, in those contexts that are highly structured and hierarchical we would expect to find only the weaker types of religious experience, whereas in those contexts that are much less formally structured the more active forms of religious experience will be found. Similarly, where an inappropriate form of spirit possession intrudes it may be interpreted as negative, demonic possession rather than positive possession by the Holy Spirit.

I. M. Lewis: Religious experience and power

I. M. Lewis adds an additional dynamic element to the understanding of religious experience. He suggests that at times spirit possession is a means by which disempowered individuals can challenge the social structure, and at least for a time take a more activist role in society. A good example of this form of spirit possession is found in Islamic Somalia. In that society, there was a strong hierarchical distinction between men and women, with women generally being powerless. Marriage was precarious, polygamy was practised and was a source of tension between men and women. In this society, women were often thought to be possessed by malevolent demons called Sar. When possessed, women were able to make demands for food or luxuries and to use forms of language that were normally the preserve of men. The possession could only be resolved by feeding the demon and ultimately by hiring a woman shaman.

Several interesting aspects are found in this example. The possession, as suggested by Lewis, is associated with lack of power. It provides a means of temporarily challenging the system and empowering the women. Interestingly, Lewis suggests that the possession is often associated with the husband taking a new wife and so challenging the position of the original wife. It can therefore be seen as a release valve for tension implicit within the system. Although for many women the empowerment is temporary, for some it provides a means of gaining social power. The shaman, who must be a woman, gained her status by having been possessed and being cured.

In Christian Ethiopia, *zar* possession is not in fact a monopoly of the fair sex. The disease also affects and the cult equally embraces men of subordinate social status, particularly people of such marginal social categories as half-Sudanese Muslims and ex-slaves ... Membership of the local *zar* club and participation in its dramatic rituals offers these otherwise underprivileged persons some degree of emancipation from frustrating traditional confinements. Within these clubs, which may also function as savings societies and credit associations, members of a low-class minority group have the opportunity of striking up useful associations with people who, though Amhara, are handicapped in other ways. And, in keeping with what is happening on the wider Ethiopian scene, a new aspiration towards upward social mobility is evident in the increasingly exalted status of the status of the spirits which now possess people of humble origins.

I. M. Lewis, *Ecstatic Religion* (1989: 91)

Lewis also distinguishes between peripheral and central cults of spirit possession. The peripheral cults are those that challenge traditional values or roles within a society. As in the example from Somalia, these cults are found among the socially oppressed. They include both an aspect of protest against dominant structures and a means for temporarily relieving pressure within the social structure. Central cults of possession are those which support society and its norms and values. Very often the spirits found in peripheral cults are perceived as being demonic, from outside the culture, while those associated with central cults are often ancestors or spirits perceived of as being within the community. In central cults possession is used as a means for legitimising or maintaining patterns of hierarchy and authority.

Witchcraft and magic

Anthropological studies of witchcraft often address similar issues to those raised by Lewis regarding religious experience. Witchcraft is seen as a means of addressing areas of social tension or a means by which disempowered individuals can challenge political, economic or communal structures. Witchcraft is often also seen as part of models of explanation – that is, why certain events happen to specific individuals.

Evans-Pritchard: Witchcraft, oracles and magic

Evans-Pritchard's study of the Azande, who live in the southern Sudan in Africa, is one of the classic texts on witchcraft and illustrates many of the pertinent issues. Among the Azande, witchcraft was part of a more general understanding of causality. If a granary fell on a person sitting under it, two questions of causality might be addressed, the scientific and the moral. The scientific question is: how did the granary come to fall? The reason given might be that termites ate the wooden posts. This explanation, however, is not sufficient. The Azande also ask for the moral basis of the event: why did the granary fall at that moment, when a specific individual was sitting under it? The answer given to that question would be that a witch caused it to happen.

The Azande believe that any person can be a witch. Witchcraft derives from a black substance called *mangu*, which is found in the person's belly. A witch is born with this substance and does not need to be consciously aware of its presence. In general, witchcraft is understood to be an unconscious rather than conscious phenomenon. A key feature of Azande witchcraft accusations is that the accursed is always someone who is either within or close to the family; witchcraft is understood to work only at close distances. The *mangu* is also only activated by the witch having feelings that are considered to be inappropriate, for example anger or jealousy towards a co-wife in a polygamous marriage.

When the Azande believe that witchcraft has occurred they use a number of different oracles to determine the identity of the witch. The person addressing the oracle will mention those who he perceives as being sources of tension. After the witch has been identified, the *mangu* can be cooled and the attack ended.

In the case of the Azande, witchcraft serves as a means for bringing into the open areas of tension within the family or communal structure. It allows these tensions to be aired and, at least to some extent, resolved. Witchcraft also serves as a mechanism for social control. If any individual can be a witch, they do not know whether they have *mangu* inside of them, so they need to control their emotions in order not to heat up the *mangu* and thereby become an active witch.

John Middleton: Ghost invocation among the Lugbara

John Middleton presents an interesting variation on this theme among the Lugbara of East Africa. Among the Lugbara certain illnesses are attributed to ghosts. The invocation of the ghosts, which leads the ghosts to cause the illnesses, is not due to the negative force of witchcraft but rather the proper and positive indignation of lineage elders. The basis for ghost invocation is very clearly articulated. When an individual infringes on the rights of the elder or the lineage, ghosts may be invoked against the person. The invocation is done in connection with a lineage or family shrine that represents the identity and unity of the lineage or family. Although individuals claim to have consciously invoked their ghosts, it is often unclear whether this is necessarily conscious; more usually the claim is associated with feelings connected to infringement on an elder's prerogatives.

Like the Azande, the Lugbara have a system of oracles to determine the cause of illness. The answer given by the oracle is shaped by the elder asking the questions, who will use his knowledge of tensions within the lineage structure to identify who has invoked the ghost and why it was done. In this example, the act of invocation is positive yet, like the witchcraft accusation among the Azande, it serves to bring into the open areas of tension and to offer a temporary resolution to them. The accusation can also highlight future points of segmentation within the lineage.

Navaho witchcraft

Clyde Kluckhohn presents an analysis of witchcraft among the Navaho, a semi-nomadic pastoralist Native American tribe in the American south-west. Among the Navaho, witchcraft serves as a mechanism for expressing aggression and hostility in a socially acceptable way. In the normal course of events, expression of these emotions is not permitted. If, however, they are expressed in the form of an accusation of witchcraft, this is seen as an acceptable way for expressing the strains within the close communities. He also suggests that it is a way of harmlessly displacing these feeling of aggression and thus preventing violence or other more active expressions of anger.

Witchcraft accusations also serve as a means of social control on a broader societal level. Where individuals seem to have more success than others, either in terms of power (spiritual or political) or resources, they may be accused of witchcraft. Thus, at least in part, witchcraft might keep individuals from standing out and encourage them to share what they have. Kluckhohn suggests that this aspect might be in part connected with a conflict in cultural norm, between acquisitive American capitalism and the norms of sharing and community that were traditional to the Navaho. The use of accusations might therefore also reflect and be a means of addressing this area of conflict and tension.

Nor does witchcraft belief merely channelize antagonisms between one individual and another. The feuds between different extended family groups (which perhaps often actually rest primarily upon a realistic conflict over land or water resources) are frequently given a formulation in witchcraft terms. For instance, one group had complained to the Indian agent of the drinking and fighting of some of their neighbors; these retaliated by threatening to kill an old man of the accusing group as a witch.

Witchcraft belief also permits a limited amount of direct verbal expression of aggression against relatives. Guarded gossip about a tyrannical maternal uncle is a useful safety valve! On several occasions I have had a Navaho in a communicative mood say to me, 'Yes, my maternal uncle is a big singer, all right. But some people say he is a witch too.' Such gossip about close relatives is relatively rare, but cases of direct accusation against affinal relatives are not infrequent.

Clyde Kluckhohn, *Navaho Witchcraft* (1967: 99)

Witchcraft and spirit possession can also be a means for establishing or defining self. The location of the witch can be a means of challenging and maintaining internal structures or, if the witch is from outside the group, it can be a means of strengthening group identity in opposition to the other. Among the Navaho, witchcraft accusations are often a means of defining and strengthening the local group. Historically, due to Navaho semi-nomadism and greatly dispersed population, members of clans that lived in distant parts were often accused of being witches, allowing the blame or explanation for misfortune to be placed outside of one's immediate family, lineage and clan. The definition of the other as witch also strengthened the local boundaries and sense of self.

Keith Thomas: Witchcraft and the English Reformation

Keith Thomas discusses witchcraft in England using similar models of explanation to those presented above. He suggests that witchcraft served a dual function as an explanatory model for evil and as a means of expressing points of tension in English society. He notes that the major period for witchcraft accusations and executions was during the six-teenth century. Thomas suggests that this rise in witchcraft was due to economic changes in the structure of society. Simplistically, one might see it as the move away from communitarian values to an increasingly individualist emphasis on capitalist modes of private property. Those individuals who were accused of being witches, and who perhaps saw themselves as witches, were the members of society who had been cared for by the community and were now increasingly disenfranchised. Like the cases described above, the rise in witchcraft mirrored a rise in con-tradiction within the social structure and therefore a rise in tension that needed to be expressed and alleviated.

The use of the term witchcraft raises interesting questions in relation to the theoretical argument made here, which assumes that all religious constructs should, in principle, be amenable to analysis using the same theoretical models. Although we do find religious constructs within our own society who call themselves witches, these constructs do not fit the model in two respects. First, they seem to be religions that use the term witch to identify a practitioner, rather than an individual within a tradition who consciously or unconsciously, or even more usually via accusation, specifically answers the ethical question of evil or reveals points of tension or transformation within social structure. Second, as these practitioners are part of their own social and religious constructs they do not form a part of the primary religion's understanding of evil or of society in general. There might be witchcraft in the technical sense in both Wicca and other traditions in Western societies but it is not found in those individuals who call themselves witches.

Although many of the forms of religion touched on in this chapter are found in a wide range of societies, assuming that each specific element will be found is a misunderstanding of the analytical perspective. We are specifically not assuming that all religions will be composed of exactly the same elements, rather we are suggesting that the method used for analysing the elements that are found will be based on the presupposi-tion that religions are human constructs related to particular cultural contexts and working in some way in relation to those contexts. Thus, it should not be surprising that witchcraft is not found in all societies and it is likely that in societies that do not have this element other structures will help to resolve or work on the issues and problems that witchcraft helps to present or resolve. The distinction between societies is not one of evolution or progress from witchcraft to religion or science but rather one of societal emphasis or choice – different religions will use different structures, sometimes to deal with identical problems but more often the differences will arise because even the problems or issues are not the same.

Symbolism

Definition of symbols

One of the most significant features of all religious systems, and culture in general is the use of symbols. Symbols are best understood if they are distinguished from signs. A sign has a one-to-one correspondence with the object that it signifies. For example, a stop sign means stop and must be clear and unequivocal. A symbol, however, has a more complex relationship with what it signifies. Rather than being one-to-one, it is multivocal; it evokes or brings together a complex set of diverse elements. A good example might be the crucifix, which will evoke a range of ideas, some shared and some individual. A symbol often evokes concepts, feelings and memories. As suggested, these elements will in part be shared by a community – that is, public – and in part be specific to the individual – that is, private. In some cases either the public aspect of the symbol or the private aspect will predominate; as it moves toward the private end it will communicate with fewer and fewer people, and as it moves towards the public end it will evoke a smaller range of individual memories and feelings. Symbols are particularly useful within religious structures as they allow the communication to work on many levels at the same time, communicating both concepts and, perhaps even more importantly, emotions.

Are symbols universal?

Symbols, like all cultural artefacts, are specific to the culture that creates or uses them. This is in part due to the lack of any necessary association between the symbol and what it symbolises. Each community, in a complex interrelationship between individuals and the group, selects those areas that it finds meaningful and the symbols that will evoke those areas. Thus, the study of specific symbols can only be done in relation to the specific community from which those symbols arise.

The process of creating and using symbols can properly be analysed cross-culturally, specific symbols cannot be so analysed.

There are, however, some symbols that arise out our common experience of the world as human beings, for example the relationship between mother and son, or the sexual aspects of the phallus. Some have interpreted this common experience as a basis for universal interpretation of at least these basic symbols. Sometimes this universal interpretation is seen as almost biologically determined, arising out of the unconscious, a common feature of all human beings. Although we would strongly support the biological unity of humanity, it does not follow that the content of the unconscious must be universal. Ethnographic evidence suggests that the unconscious is shaped by our cultural experience, particularly in relation to family structures and cultural understandings of the nature of personality. Thus, despite the fact that variations of the elements, motherhood or the phallus, are found in many societies, as symbols their associations and meanings are still culturally determined. Specific societies may use precisely the same element to mean very different things.

Symbols and the body

One of the most powerful areas in which symbols operate is in connection with the body. Symbols associated with aspects of the body, such as hair, or taken into the body, such as food or drink, are particularly able to mobilise the affective possibilities of symbolic communication. Different parts of the body may also be given different symbolic valuation. Thus, in some societies different parts of the body may be acceptably seen in public and others may not. For example, among the Mehinacu in South America, men usually did not cover their genitals – they did, however, wear a belt around their waists. Removal of the belt was understood as nakedness, rather than revealing one's sexual organs. Different ways of using the body can also have symbolic meaning specific to different cultures or communities. A good example of this is found in the use of hair as a means of communicating different aspects of status.

Judith Okely: the Rom and the Gorgio

In *The Traveller-Gypsies,* Judith Okely analyses the way that the Rom in the UK use food and eating as one aspect of a larger pattern of purity and boundary maintenance. The Rom make a strong distinction between pure and impure, which, in part, is associated with the opposition between the inner and outer body. The inner body is seen as pure while the outer body is impure. The outer body, in part, symbolises the public aspect of the Rom's relation with the wider society, whom they call

Gorgios. The inner body thus represents the secret communal and individual identity of the Rom. On another level the outer body, the impure, represents Gorgio society and the inner body, the pure, represents the Rom. Much of the Rom's practices in connection with eating, camping and categorisation of the world is shaped by the need to keep these two realms separate and distinct.

The emphasis on ritual purity brings out a common area of misunderstanding between Rom and Gorgio society. The Rom distinguish between two types of dirt. *Chikli* refers to harmless dirt, that is, normal dust or grime, which Gorgio society would usually interpret as dirt. *Mochadi* refers to the arena of ritual impurity. The Rom are generally not concerned with *Chikli* and are considered dirty by the Gorgio. The Gorgio are likewise not concerned with *Mochadi* and are considered impure by the Rom. The Rom consider a hospital to be particularly impure because the two realms are mixed in it almost by definition.

This symbolism is particularly evident regarding food and its preparation. Due to the nature of Rom society, most food must be procured from the wider society. In order to minimise the possible contamination of the food by the outer body, only specific categories of food are obtained. These foods tend to be pre-packaged and thus protected from

The Gorgios' [non-Rom] failure to make this distinction between inner and outer body is not seen by the Gypsies as merely accidental, but a means of drawing positive ethnic boundaries. A Gypsy is partly defined or defines him or herself by an adherence to these rituals of cleanliness. A Gypsy woman said: 'He's a *real* Gypsy. You wouldn't find him washing his hands in the same bowl as he washes his cup.' A Gypsy man said: 'If you look at a Gypsy trailer, you won't find a sink, that's what Gorgios use.' These ritual beliefs have historical continuity. *The Journal of the Gypsy Lore Society* (1910: 156) recorded how a Gorgio charity invited Gypsies to a local hall for a 'high tea'. Before the giant meatpie was brought in, the local baker wrapped it in a blanket to keep it 'piping hot'. The blanket, associated with the outer body, would thus have contaminated the food. One Gypsy informed the others. Consequently no Gypsies would eat the pie, except for an old man who took one taste to spare the Gorgio's feelings. From then on he was nicknamed 'Blanket Pie'.

Judith Okely, *The Traveller-Gypsies* (1983: 83)

contamination, which can even come from a person's shadow. Although food produced in factories is also prone to impurity, the distance between preparation and consumption, and perhaps the impersonal nature of the process, seems to minimise the perception of impurity.

Food preparation is another area that must be protected from impurity. This is particularly seen in a separation of bowls used for food preparation and those used for washing the body. If a bowl has been used for the latter, it can never be used for food. Even proximity can cause impurity. Okely describes a case in which a fork was placed near a bar of soap and thus made impure. Damaged crockery is considered prone to carry impurity and is also thrown away.

These food rules and body symbolism are part of a more general model that shapes the way the Rom understand animals, geography and, as suggested, their own ethnic identity in relationship to the wider Gorgio identity. It allows them to validate their minority ethnicity and worldview through the definition of the other as impure.

Food rules are used by many other societies as a means of defining self. In many cases, as in that of the Rom, this definition is done through opposing self to other and thereby creating a strong boundary between the two. A particularly well-developed example of this is found in the Jewish system of food rules. Although the Jewish system is built on a different understanding of purity than that of the Rom, it nonetheless forms part of a broader system of categorising the world and creating different levels of boundaries. Other societies that use food rules in similar ways include Islam and the Church of Latter-day Saints (Mormons).

Mythology

Myth is found in some form in every religious system as a means articulating symbols and communicating ways of being and understanding. Although some approaches use the term as a way of distinguishing Western society from other traditions both past and present, perhaps creating an opposition between myth and history or between myth and science, many modern anthropological approaches suggest that myth is connected with making sense of the world rather than with a specific strategy for doing this. Broadly speaking, myth can be defined as the ways in which human beings construct models for understanding their world and their place in it. Myth can use a historic model or a fictional model; it can also use a scientific model of understanding or one that relies purely on imagination. This definition emphasises a high level of abstraction, focusing on the aspect of worldview; it also, however, includes many other levels simultaneously. Myth works on the conscious level of explaining or justifying institutions or practices and emerges in interrelation with them. It also works on the unconscious level of shaping and validating patterns of thinking and categorising our understanding of the world.

Sally Falk Moore in 'Descent and Symbolic Filiation' examines the prevalence of incest, particularly brother–sister incest, in many mythological systems. Her analysis focuses on Lévi-Strauss's argument that mythology serves, in part, to resolve or overcome contradiction. She touches on two other theories that account for the presence of this motif: the psychological and the historical.

The psychological argument suggests that the common occurrence of incest is due to an expression of Oedipal desires, which are, according to this model, universal. In this interpretation brother–sister incest is a displacement of the desire for mother–son incest. One significant problem with this interpretation is that it only accounts for the presence of incest, it does not account for the fact that specific types of incest, mother–son, father–daughter, brother–sister, correlate with specific types of social structure. Thus, although incest may draw part of its power from Oedipal desires, it is also likely that it plays some role in relation to social structure. Moore argues that, at a societal level, unconscious desires may be expressed but only if they serve a purpose in relation to social structure.

The historical argument contends that where myths include patterns that are different from those of the society telling the myth, those patterns reflect previous ways of behaving, either the specific action or other related patterns of behaviour. The incestuous practices in myth are therefore sometimes seen as reflecting the fact that they were actually practised at some earlier stage of societal development or used to support a particular type of matrilineal land inheritance, with incest being a way that men could wrest control of land from their sisters. Related arguments are used to demonstrate the existence of matriarchal societies at some earlier point in human history. Moore suggests that this way of treating myths is an overly literalist approach and, more significantly, that it is probable that myths serve to validate current behaviour rather than to present images of the past.

Moore suggests that these myths serve to resolve a paradox arising within certain societies that have two common elements. The first is exogamy, a rule requiring that individuals marry outside of a particular group. The second is a creation myth that posits a single creation – and thereby the possibility that the original pair were brother and sister. The contradiction is between the original act of incest, which is implied by common descent, and the requirement of exogamy and its associated rules against incest. An additional aspect of the contradiction is the paradoxical relationship between the specifically delineated kinship group and the rest of humanity. The myth resolves these contradictions by emphasising the unity of humanity, and by suggesting that all marriages contain an element of incest. The myth thereby justifies exogamy as an acceptable means of recapitulating the original act. Since different societies have different models of descent – through the male line, the female line or both lines – different forms of incest are used to relate to these different patterns of descent. Moore's model is thus able to explain both the role of mythological incest and the correlation of specific forms of incest with the contemporary social structures in which the myths are used.

As suggested above, Moore argues that one of the significant indicators of the social function of mythological incest is that particular forms of incest are found in relation to particular models of social structure. This is specifically the case regarding societies with either patrilineal or matrilineal modes of descent. In patrilineal societies, the mother comes from a different lineage or descent group than her husband and son, who are in the same lineage or descent group. In matrilineal systems, the father and his children are part of different descent groups, while mother and her children, male and female, are part of the same matrilineage. Moore points out that in patrilineal systems mythological incest is often in the form of mother–son, while in matrilineal systems it is between father and daughter. In both cases the sexual act brings together both issues – the sexual act is simultaneously incestuous and exogamous – and so justifies both the understanding of creation and the need for or possibility of exogamy.

The Dogon of the Sudan in Africa are a good illustration of Moore's arguments. Theirs is a patrilineal and patrilocal society, where descent and residence are through the male line. They also have a rule against marrying within the patrilineal group and a preference for marrying one's mother's brother's daughter. The Dogon also specifically associate their marriage patterns with their creation myth.

The Dogon creation myth saw the original creation as being a twin set of placentas each containing a male being, each male associated with a female spiritual principle. One of the male spiritual beings was born too early and separated from his female half. He ultimately attempted to procreate with his placenta, symbolically his mother, but in order to bring creation back into order the proper twins were brought back together and humanity was born.

The Dogon myth clearly includes mother–son incest, the form that Moore associates with patrilineal society. In Dogon society, a boy is allowed to take liberties with his mother's brother's property to the extent of having sex with his mother's brother's wife; these elements are symbolically the mother and thus recapitulate the original incestuous act. The circle is complete with marriage to the mother's brother's daughter, who, being part of the same patrilineage as the mother, is symbolically also the mother. The myth provides a logical link between the two families through symbolic incest and common humanity and therefore justifies the rule of exogamy.

Interestingly, one could make a similar argument in relation to endogamous societies, that is societies that have a requirement to marry inside one's own group. Here the paradox is somewhat different. Common creation and therefore common descent suggest that all human beings are related and therefore possible marriage partners; endogamy, however, limits marriage partners to a very narrow group. In this type of case, mythological incest can be used not to emphasise common humanity but rather to create models of marrying as closely as possible. This type of resolution is found in Genesis, in which all of the ancestors of Israel, a society with a preference for endogamy, have either actual or symbolic incestuous marriages.

Conclusion

In this chapter we have touched on some of the themes anthropologists have analysed regarding religion. The themes were chosen to reflect different theoretical approaches to this study and to bring out different issues, particularly the role of affect and communication as significant features of all religious constructs. The particular 'indigenous' religions chosen for this discussion are not meant to be taken as either diagnostic or characteristic; rather they were chosen because they were appropriate to illustrate the particular theoretical point being discussed.

One of the key points this chapter hopes to emphasise is the diversity found within and between all religious traditions. The analyses discussed here suggest that religion is closely interrelated with other aspects of specific cultures and that all religions will be shaped by and address issues of significance to individuals within those cultures or communities. This issue is evidently true of the 'indigenous' religions, as they are usually associated with a specific community, but it is also demonstrably true of the 'world' religions, which, although containing elements that are shared by all or most adherents, are also and most importantly shaped by the particular contexts in which the religions finds themselves.

This chapter has also argued against approaches which see religion or religious institutions as deriving from an essentialist core standing outside its particular instantiations – there is no one thing which can be called 'religion'. Although most, if not all, religions share certain institutional forms or the use of myth and symbol, this does not mean that these elements will serve an identical purpose or mean the same thing whatever the context. In different cultural contexts these elements will be practised and gain meaning in relationship to their particular context. If these elements share any commonality, it derives from the fact that they are socially constructed by human communities.

We need to be wary of making our definitions of religions over-deterministic. If religions are highly contextualised, and ultimately derive from individual and communal practise, then what religion is will also be specific and contextualised to a specific community. The definition needs to focus on what religion does in particular contexts rather than what religion is. In analysing religion we need to take a pragmatic attitude that focuses on the community rather than the abstract theory. Rather than defining religion by what we do or do not do, we need a broad definition that encompasses a wide range of social situations and allows us to address or ask interesting questions both of the culture being studied and of ourselves.

 ## Further reading

Bowie, Fiona (2000), *The Anthropology of Religion*, Oxford: Blackwell. This book provides a useful introduction to most aspects of the anthropology of religion. Although it is mostly in the form of expanded lecture notes, it provides direction towards the significant texts and theories.

Lambek, Michael (2002), *A Reader in the Anthropology of Religion*, Oxford: Blackwell. This volume includes abridged versions of many of the classic discussions of religion from an anthropological perspective. It includes essential ethnographic and theoretical material.

Lessa, W. A. and E. Z. Vogt (eds) (1979), *Reader in Comparative Religion*, New York: Harper and Row. This volume provides an essential collection of articles and extracts by some of the most significant anthropological thinkers on religion. Although some of the chapters are abridged, many are not.

Turnbull, Colin (1993), *The Forest People*, London: Pimlico. This ethnography of the BaMabuti of the Ituri Forest is very approachable and evocatively written. It provides a good introduction to ethnography and touches on many of the issues discussed in this file.

Questions

1. Explore the relationship between the theories about rites of passage and Bloch's theory of rebounding violence.

2. Is religious ritual about communication or experience/feeling?

3. Is there any value to using the terms 'primal religion' or 'world religion'?

4. In what ways can Christian charismatic experiences be understood using models of religious experience?

Judaism

Seth D. Kunin

Introduction: Judaism and Judaisms

From its origins in the ancient Near East, Judaism has spread to most parts of the globe. In most cases, the gradual dispersion of the Jewish people has come about through the creation of trading networks and the establishment of small communities around these networks of commerce. In other cases, the spread has been due to attempts to escape from different forms of persecution and anti-Semitism and at times from expulsion due to religious, political or economic reasons. Although in some discussions of Jewish history the emphasis has been on the periods of persecution, the Jewish experience in diaspora has included both positive, outward-looking periods and negative periods marked by persecution and an inward focus.

Today the Jewish people number some thirteen million worldwide.

Although the majority of the Jewish community is found in the United States, approximately six million, this is a recent development. Prior to World War II, the majority of the Jewish community found its home in Eastern Europe – much of this community, and its distinctive Jewish cultures, was destroyed by the Nazis during the Holocaust. Only a small remnant of these once vibrant communities remains in the countries of Eastern Europe. For example, 500,000 Jews continue to live in Russia, 400,000 in the Ukraine and 8,000 in Poland. The same pattern is true of other countries in continental Europe: 600,000 Jews continue to live in France and some 60,000 in Germany. Although many of these countries had different histories after the Holocaust, for example the dominance of Marxist ideologies in Eastern Europe until the last decade of the twentieth century, the cumulative effect of persecution and histories of anti-Semitism has led to communities that are generally demoralised and inward-looking. The United Kingdom, however, was not affected by the Nazi policies of genocide and in spite of some traces of genteel anti-Semitism has been generally positive and supportive of its Jewish inhabitants. Accordingly, its Jewish community remains reasonably strong and confident.

The United States and Israel

The Jewish community today revolves around two main centres of population, culture and creativity. As mentioned above, the United States has the largest Jewish community and is also a significant player in the ongoing development of Jewish culture and religion: two of the modern forms of Judaism, Conservative and Reconstructionist, have their origins in the United States, and although Reform Judaism is found in Europe and originally emerged from Germany in the nineteenth century, much of its continuing strength and creativity has its centre in American Jewry. The State of Israel is as equally significant a centre as the United States. Its Jewish population numbers approximately five million and is the second-largest Jewish community worldwide. Much of world Jewry looks to Israel as a source of both culture and identity; indeed, for many Jews, Zionism or the support of the State of Israel is the most significant feature of Jewish identity. Israel has also been a catalyst for many Jews in thinking about the ethics of power. During the last several decades of the twentieth century and the first decade of the present century, Israel has been engaged in an almost constant battle with its Palestinian neighbours, primarily in areas occupied by Israel since 1967. This conflict has polarised the Jewish community. Although the majority of the community has supported Israel's actions, a significant minority has re-examined this default support of Israel and raised issues about the tension between Israel's actions and the ethics that arise from both Judaism and modern liberal values.

Diaspora

Due to its history of diaspora, the Jewish community has perforce interacted with many different cultures and traditions. In each country in which it has resided, the Jewish community has learned from its neighbours and taken on a wide range of different cultural forms and distinctive ways of living. These cultural elements have significantly often included language. Thus, the Jews who lived in Spain developed a distinctive form of Judeo-Spanish, while the Jews who lived in Germany developed Yiddish, a language that is primarily made up of an early form of German with some Hebrew elements. These distinctive languages have themselves never remained static. As they were carried from country to country, new words and concepts have been incorporated into them. This pattern is not only true of language. It is also found in dress, eating habits and ritual and religious life. At the level of culture, it is therefore impossible to speak of one Jewish culture – there are as many Jewish cultures as there are distinctive Jewish communities.

The development of distinctive Jewish cultures has been a continuous process affecting all aspects of Jewish life. These divergences have been recognised by the Jewish legal tradition from its earliest sources, engendering an awareness that different communities will develop their own customs and that these customs may vary from community to community and in different historical contexts. On a broad level, the differences are enshrined in the traditional division between the Ashkenazic and Sephardic communities. Ashkenazic Jews are those descended from Jewish communities in Germany and northern Europe. Sephardic Jews are descended from Jews from Spain, with the spread of Sephardic Jewry primarily occurring after 1492 with the expulsion of the Jews from Spain. Between these two broad divisions there are clear differences in both language – there are several differences in the pronunciation of Hebrew – and in details of Jewish law. The distinctions are highlighted in the Shulhan Arukh (see below), the major code of Jewish law that lists the different practices and laws relating to these communities. The diversity is also found within these two groupings. For example, the Sephardic community includes a wide range of different communities from around the Mediterranean, many of whom had no direct connection with the Spanish community. Within these smaller communities there are very often unique forms of language usage, as well as customs and practices that are widely divergent from other Jewish communities.

Religious diversity

Throughout its history Judaism has allowed and even encouraged religious diversity at the level of the individual community. Prior to the destruction of the Second Temple in the year 70 CE, there appears to have been a wide range of 'Judaisms', each with its own practices and its own legal traditions. Perhaps the only unifying elements were a shared respect for those texts that became the Torah and a sense of genealogical connection. Since the destruction of the Temple, and with the increased importance of the diaspora, Jewish law has been allowed to develop at the level of the community; in general, there have not been strong hierarchical institutions with the authority to determine the law for the entire community (or even substantial parts of the community). Rabbis at the local level were given the authority to make determinations of Jewish law and so practice, until the modern period, was characterised by heterogeneity rather than homogeneity. The legal system and process of determining the law remained consistent but particular decisions were tailored to local needs and local understandings.

In the modern period – that is, since the middle of the nineteenth century – Judaism has divided more consciously into different and sometimes competing movements. Although it is true that this process can be seen in the separation of the Hasidic movement in the eighteenth century, it only becomes a conscious process in the nineteenth, with the foundation of the Reform movement. Since that time, different Jewish movements have been established with differing theologies and, perhaps more importantly, differing attitudes towards Jewish law. Thus, today the diversity which was always present in Judaism has been formalised in the major competing movements, each of which claims to be an authentic form of Judaism – and in some cases, particularly the various Orthodox or Ultra-Orthodox movements, denies authenticity to forms other than themselves. In some countries there is, from either an external or an internal view, a default form of Judaism. In the United Kingdom, for example, Orthodox Judaism is the category to which Jews, particularly those with no formal communal connection, will claim affiliation. Equally, due to the office of the Chief Rabbi (actually the Chief Rabbi of the major Orthodox movement), Orthodoxy is also externally perceived as the established form of Judaism. In the United States, although the communities are all roughly equal in size, Reform Judaism is often seen as the default form.

This chapter on Judaism therefore does not actually examine Judaism in some ideal sense separate from its diversity both historical and contemporary. Rather it examines and emphasises this diversity, seeing all forms as being authentic representations of Judaism. To an extent, the emphasis here is on 'Judaisms' rather than Judaism.

Historical roots and models

Although there is great diversity within Judaism, most Jewish traditions share a common sense of history and perhaps of time. It is this shared experience, and understanding of past, present and future, that is often seen as one of the key elements holding Judaism together. Equally, the separation of Judaism and Christianity can be seen as a division in the understanding of the future. Christians believed that the Messiah had come; Jews believed and continue to believe that the Messiah or Messianic age is yet to come.

The Jewish understanding of history is shaped by a number of sometimes incompatible models, each of which gives meaning and value to the experience of both particular communities and often the community as a whole. Two of the most significant models have their roots in the biblical text: the covenant and exodus.

Covenant

The covenant model underlies the Jewish understanding of the experience of history. This model is based on a biblical concept of an agreement or relationship established between God and the Israelites, and

> And when Abram was ninety years old and nine, the Lord appeared to Abram, and said unto him: 'I am God Almighty; walk before Me, and be thou whole-hearted. And I will make My covenant between Me and thee, and will multiply thee exceedingly.' And Abram fell on his face; and God talked with him saying: 'As for Me, behold, My covenant is with thee, and thou shalt be the father of a multitude of nations. Neither shall thy name any more be called Abram, but thy name shall be Abraham; for the father of a multitude of nations have I made thee, and kings shall come out of thee. And I will establish My covenant between Me and thee and thy seed after thee throughout their generations for an everlasting covenant, to be a God unto thee and to thy seed after thee. And I will give unto thee, and to thy seed after thee, the land of thy sojournings, all the land of Canaan, for an everlasting possession; and I will be their God.'
>
> Genesis 17: 1–8

subsequently with the Jewish people. The covenants, although primarily found in Genesis, culminate in the covenant between God and Israel at Mount Sinai. The idea of covenant has implications both for the understanding of God and of Israel. In respect of God, it suggests that God has obligation to Israel over time and it is this understanding that underlies the Jewish notion of salvation history. History and events have meaning because God acts through history to realise God's side of the covenant with Israel. Similarly, the covenant underlies the Jewish concept of obligation and therefore the entire system of Jewish law. Israel, at Sinai, is understood to have freely chosen to accept God's law for itself and for its descendants.

The covenant plays itself out in the biblical notion of reward and punishment: Israel is rewarded, as per God's responsibility, if it fulfils its side of the covenant and punished if it fails to fulfil it. This understanding, with some modifications, underlies Israel's view of history and events chronicled in the biblical text and continued to play a role in the understanding of history until the twentieth century. Some thinkers had challenged the concept of reward and punishment prior to the Holocaust. In the decades following the Holocaust, however, the idea that the covenant was expressed by the Jews' experience of history – and therefore that the Holocaust was an act of God and a punishment of the Jewish community – was considered by most theologians to be no longer a viable model. Increasingly, the personal omniscient God of the covenant has been replaced by a more limited God who allows human beings free will, and the view that history is an outcome of free will rather than God's will.

Exodus

The exodus model has its roots in the narrative found in Exodus and culminating in Joshua and Judges with the conquest of the land. This model is intrinsically bound up with the covenant model, as the justification for the redemptive aspect of the exodus lies in the covenant. This model has two key aspects: a period of punishment or exile followed by a redemptive act by God returning Israel/the Jews to their land. The version of the narrative found in Exodus (although there are three versions of it found in Genesis, that is Genesis 12: 10, 20, 26) is the most elaborated version and through including the covenant at Sinai (in effect, the basis for both the punishment and the redemptive act) becomes the paradigmatic version of the model.

The exodus model is perhaps most clearly articulated in modern Judaism through its interpolation in Zionist ideology. Zionism, or the political movement which advocates for and supports the State of Israel, has developed a model of history that uses the exodus model as a way of interpreting all aspects of Jewish history. Jewish existence, historical and cultural, is interpreted as falling into two categories, that of exile and that of being in the land. The two categories are qualitatively evaluated as negative and positive respectively. Exile, or Egypt, is a negative category in which the Jewish people are living in an artificial condition and are prone to persecution and cultural inactivity. The land of Israel – or the State of Israel – is seen as redemptive space and in every positive respect the opposite of existence in exile.

The Holocaust has, in part, become an aspect of this model. It is interpreted as the paradigmatic experience of exile. Thus, it is the culmination of a long line of similar experiences that have framed Jewish experience since the end of the Jewish Commonwealth. The foundation of the State of Israel is seen as the redemptive end of exile and therefore the proper and divinely sanctioned response to the Holocaust.

Peoplehood

There is, however, an additional myth that is perhaps even more significant in shaping Jewish identity and linking the diverse Jewish communities together – the myth of genealogy. One of the most consistent and continuous themes in Jewish sources, from the biblical text until today, is the concept of genealogical unity. The early chapters of Genesis establish a model of peoplehood that is dependant on descent from a common ancestor. Abraham is portrayed as the ancestor of the Jewish people, with the line continuing through Isaac, Jacob, Jacob's twelve sons and then their descendants, who become the twelve tribes of Israel. Thus, Judaism and Jewish identity are not seen as being the adherence to a particular set of beliefs, or even acceptance of a notion of divine law, but as being part of a common people. Accordingly, diversity in cultural form or religious practice does not challenge the ideal of Jewish unity provided that the model of genetic unity is maintained.

The genealogical model used for the last two thousand years by the Jewish community as a whole is built on matrilineal descent. If one's mother is a Jew then one is a Jew oneself. The religion or national origin of the father is not relevant in the definition of the child's identity. Until the late twentieth century, this definition of Jewishness was shared by all groups within the Jewish community and provided at least a notional aspect of unity. In recent years, however, this model has begun to be challenged. The Reform movement in the United States and the Liberal movement in the UK have challenged the unilineal descent model. In principle, they have moved to a non-descent model in which identity is related to the way a child is raised rather than some genetic quality. To an extent, they are re-examining the meaning of Jewishness – changing it from a national or genetic identity and transforming it to fit modern definitions of religion within a Western intellectual context (with religion limited to the sphere of belief and ethics).

Halakhah – Jewish law

One of the fundamental differences between Judaism and Christianity rests on the different understandings and emphasis on law (action) and belief (dogma) within the two religious traditions. Broadly speaking,

most Christian traditions, with the possible exception of Roman Catholicism, derive their unity from shared dogma. Identity is defined and to
an extent determined by a shared and authoritative form of belief. On
the basis of this, action becomes the domain of individual choice and is
considered of less significance or importance. In Judaism, however,
shared identity derives from a shared understanding of action rather
than shared belief. This difference of emphasis has allowed Judaism to
include a very wide range of beliefs, many of which seem mutually
contradictory, and yet still retain, at least historically, a sense of unity.

The School of Hillel and the School of Shamai argued for three years,
one saying the law is according to our position and the other say the law
is according to our position. A heavenly voice came forth and said both
of them (the words of Hillel and Shamai) are the words of the living
God.

Babylonian Talmud, Eruvin 13b

One way of understanding the relationship between the conceptualisation of both thought and action is the concept of religious relativism.
An underlying theme of all rabbinic discussions and debates is the
concept of plurality of truths. Many rabbinic texts dealing with either
matters of practice or belief list many different and possibly mutually
exclusive statements without the need to fix or determine which statement is the accepted version. The structure of the texts implies that all
of the interpretations are valid provided that they arise from a dialogue
with the Torah or the text being interpreted. Other texts suggest that
even absolutely opposing views can be seen as equally the word of God.
In the sphere of belief, this concept of mutually exclusive plural truths is
continued with no attempt to determine which truths are authoritative.
In the sphere of action, however, there is an attempt to establish which
law is binding and it remains clear that, in spite of the need to have a
common understanding of correct action, the rejected laws are still considered to be in some sense true and equally the product of revelation.

Despite this essential role of creating a unifying basis for Judaism,
Halakhah properly understood has not created a homogeneous community all acting in the same way based on a single authority; rather the
decisions of Jewish law have been vested in the hands of communities
and rabbis and thus diversity has been the norm. The unifying feature
of the Halakhah is not found in a particular text or a particular set of

decisions but in the process by which generations of rabbis have interpreted and decided questions of Jewish law. In a sense, each set of decisions is provisional, bound to a particular time and place, while the system or process is relatively fixed and pervasive.

Midrash

The process by which Jewish law has been determined has developed for slightly more than the last two thousand years. It initially centred on different methods of interpreting the biblical text, particularly the Torah (the first five books of the Hebrew Bible). These interpretations are called Midrash, a term which comes from the Hebrew root meaning to search, delve, or to interpret. Early Midrashic texts preserve some of the discussions and debates of the early sages (rabbinic figures) as they sought to find meanings in the biblical text for their own times. The structure of these texts suggests that it was the process of interpretation and the debates, rather than the specific decisions, that were important.

As Jewish law developed from these early roots, it seems to have followed two interrelated paths. On the one hand, it continued the path established by the Midrashic method, focusing on argumentation and with decisions being secondary to the process by which they were come to. On the other hand, there also developed a counter trend that emphasised the decision rather than the process. This second trend is, in many respects, similar to Hellenistic understandings of law.

These two approaches are found in the development of the Jewish legal tradition and often follow one after the other. The earliest approach, prior to 220 CE, was characterised by the former path, with the emphasis on discussion and debate. These discussions were for the most part not written down but were preserved orally and only began to be transcribed towards the end of the period. Some of these discussions can be found in the early collections of Midrash Halakhah, legal Midrash.

Mishnah

In the period beginning the third century CE, culminating in approximately 220 CE, we see the other process at work. The Mishnah, compiled by Judah HaNasi is written in the form of a clear and concise code of law. It is based on Midrash Halakhah but removes all or most of the discussion and usually presents a clear statement of the law. The principle for determining the law is stated in Mishnah Eduyot 1.5, which indicates that the law follows the majority of the sages. It also suggests that minority positions are not forgotten, as they can be the sources of future decisions by later rabbis.

The structure of the Mishnah is also based on a different model than previous Midrashic discussions. Whereas texts of Midrash are tied directly to the biblical text – they are ordered by the biblical verses they interpret – the Mishnah is divided into thematic sections. The overall text is divided into six sections: Seeds (agricultural laws), Feasts (laws concerning religious festivals), Women (marriage and other related issues), Damages (civil and criminal laws), Hallowed Things (laws concerning the Temple) and Cleanness (laws concerning ritual purity). Each of these sections is further subdivided into thematically related sections. It should be noted that Jewish law not only deals with areas that we consider to be the preserve of religion today but also with all other areas of life, including civil and criminal law.

Moses received the Torah from Sinai and committed it to Joshua, and Joshua to the elders, and the elders to the prophets; and the prophets committed it to the men of the Great Assembly. They said three things: be deliberate in judgment, raise up many disciples, and build a fence to protect the Torah.

Simon the Just was of the last of the Great Assembly. He used to say: The world is upheld by three things: by the Torah, by work (or the service of the Temple) and by acts of loving-kindness.

Mishnah, Avot 1–2

Talmud

After the Mishnah was completed, the pendulum swung back to the opposite path. The two versions of the Talmud, the Jerusalem Talmud (completed in the fifth century) and the Babylonian Talmud (completed in the eighth century), are based on the Mishnah. They, however, expand it in several directions. First, they attempt to reconstruct all the arguments, debates and proof texts that were removed to create the concise form of the Mishnah. Second, they add in case law and extend the application of the law to areas that were not stated in the Mishnah. Third, they introduce new issues that were not raised in the Mishnah. Both Talmuds are highly complex texts that, unlike the Mishnah, make little or no attempt to be concise and clearly state the final decision. The Talmuds emphasise process rather than a specific set of contingent decisions.

Due to the contingencies of history, the Babylonian Talmud became the authoritative legal text for the entire Jewish community. This was due in part to the text's structure, which allowed for open-ended interpretation and application, and perhaps even more importantly to the location of the academies that produced it. These academies were based in the heart of the growing Islamic empire and so derived their authority from cultural, political and economic centrality.

After the completion of the Babylonian Talmud, two complementary directions of Jewish law developed: the codification process and the responsa. Almost immediately upon its completion, rabbinic leaders began the process of trying to concisely and clearly present the decisions reached by the Talmud. Initially, these attempts at codification focused on specific areas but eventually they culminated in a set of codes that were intended by their authors to be both final and comprehensive. Two of the most significant of these were the Mishne Torah by Moses Maimonides (1135–1204) and the Shulhan Arukh by Joseph Caro (1488–1575). In both these cases the texts are written in clear and concise Hebrew with no discussion or debate.

The codes

The ultimate fate of the two texts is indicative of the trends already highlighted. Although Maimonides was recognised as one of the pre-eminent legal scholars of his age, the Mishne Torah never achieved the highest authoritative status. Almost immediately upon its publication, other scholars questioned his decisions and, even more importantly, the way in which the decisions were reached. As Maimonides did not include any discussions of these issues, his text was considered to be somewhat problematic. They also highlighted the fact that Maimonides did not allow for minority opinions and that he suggested that his text made study of the Talmud unnecessary. The rabbinic attitude towards the Shulhan Arukh, however, was much more positive and it has achieved the status of the primary arbiter of Jewish law, particularly for the Orthodox community. The difference in treatment is due to three different elements. First, the Shulhan Arukh did not stand alone as a concise code without argumentation: it rested on the foundation of a much larger work by Caro, the Bet Yoseph, which included all of the argumentation upon which Caro's decisions were based. Second, the Shulhan Arukh was written in a period of crisis and insecurity just after the expulsion of the Jewish community from Spain in 1492. It is likely that the text provided a source of security and clarity when the community as a whole was in ferment. Third, Rabbi Moses Isserlis (d. 1572) added a set of glosses to the original text, making it applicable to the Ashkenazic as well as the Sephardic community. In spite of its general acceptance as the primary code of Jewish law, the text has continued to develop with the addition of commentaries and discussions, which are usually published with it.

The responsa

Alongside this trend towards codification is a complementary trend that emphasises discussion and debate – the responsa literature. This literature was based on the process of local communities seeking legal decisions and advice from well-known and authoritative figures. Letters, *she'elot* – literally, questions – would be written asking specific questions of law. The authorities would respond with *tishuvot* – literally, answers – which would present an argument and an answer to the question. Although the specific *tishuvah* (answer) was binding on the specific community, other sages could answer the same or similar question in different ways, which in turn would be binding upon the community to whom they were sent. Thus, the responsa literature preserves and emphasises both the argumentative process and the diversity within the community at large. In the modern Jewish community, the responsa literature continues to be a force for diversity and flexibility alongside the more conservative trends that arise from a fixed code of law.

Philosophy

Although the biblical text and many rabbinic texts reveal an awareness of philosophical issues, for example the nature of God or the question of whether the world was created or eternal, neither biblical nor rabbinic texts can be considered to be philosophical texts. They do not present a coherent and systematic analysis of the questions. Nonetheless, these texts, particularly the Torah, provide a foundation for philosophical discussion and debate. In some cases, the text establishes the normative view. For example, most rabbis and Jewish philosophers (until the modern period) interpreted Genesis chapter 1 as a statement of *creatio ex nihilo* (creation from nothing), which was the normative understanding of creation. In other cases, the biblical text required extensive interpretation. Thus, all of the anthropomorphic texts needed to be reinterpreted to fit into philosophers' understandings of God, who was understood to be absolutely incorporeal and beyond description.

Hellenism

Jewish philosophy emerges, as does Islamic philosophy, from encounters with Hellenistic thought and culture. The initial encounter with Hellenism occurred after the conquest of Judea and most of the Near East by Alexander the Great in the third century BCE. The influence of Hellenistic ideas is found in some of the later biblical texts, as well as influencing the development of theologies within rabbinic material. As suggested, this influence did not lead to the development of systematic philosophies within these texts but it did shape the questions that were asked and, to some extent, the way they were answered.

The significant development of a more systematic form of Jewish philosophy is found in the work of Philo of Alexandria (20 BC–50 CE), who attempted to rethink Judaism and Jewish texts through Platonic

And the Lord said to Abraham, 'Depart from thy land, and from thy kindred, and from thy father's house . . .

That he means by Abraham's country the body, and by his kindred the outward senses, and by his father's house uttered speech, we have now shown. But the command, 'Depart from them,' is not like or equivalent to, Be separated from them according to your essence, since that would be the injunction of one who was pronouncing sentence of death. But it is the same as saying, Be alienated from them in your mind, allowing none of them to cling to you, standing above them all; they are your subjects, use them not as your rulers . . .

Philo, *On the Migration of Abraham*, II.7–8

philosophy. Philo's work can be divided into three types: exegesis, historical and philosophical. The philosophical – and particularly the exegetical aspect – are features that are found in many Jewish philosophers, particularly those who are attempting to re-understand Judaism in the light of a particular philosophical approach. Exegetical analysis allows the philosopher to re-read and re-understand the text, and in effect to transform it (at least in the philosopher's eyes) into an esoteric philosophical text. Philo used the method of allegorical analysis, characteristic of the Alexandrian school, to discover the philosophical meanings that were hidden within the Biblical text.

Philo's philosophical system, developed in both the exegetical and philosophical texts, was essentially Platonic. As with the other Platonisms developing at the same time, there was a strong mystical element, with a focus on the soul's ascent from the world of matter, which was seen as imperfect, back to its divine source. The concept of ascent was predicated on a hierarchical understanding of the universe, with the material component being merely an imperfect image of the ideal realm of the intelligibles – that is, the logos – which in turn was an image of God. Although Philo developed an important philosophical reading of Judaism, he does not appear to have had significant influence on medieval Jewish philosophy, which arose in response to a second encounter with Hellenism via the Islamic world.

Philosophy in the Islamic world

From the ninth century CE, theological and philosophical schools flourished in the Islamic world. This was due, at least in part, to the rediscovery of Hellenistic ideas and the attempt to reconcile these philosophical ideas with Islam and revelation. Jewish scholars struggled with many of the same questions: some used philosophical argumentation as a means for demonstrating or proving truths already known via revelation and tradition, while others attempted to create comprehensive philosophical systems in which revelation was a secondary source of knowledge.

One of the best examples of the theological model is found in the work of Saadia Gaon (882–942). His *Book of Belief and Opinions* was directly influenced by the Mutazalite school of Islamic theology or Kalam. Saadia does not attempt to develop a coherent and systematic philosophy; rather he uses philosophical argumentation to defend beliefs that were established by revelation. This does not mean, however, that he was defending a literalist interpretation of the biblical text. Like the Mutazilites, his starting point was a strong emphasis on the absolute unity of God and the denial of anthropomorphism and attributes in regard to God. Thus, while he strongly defends creation from nothing – using texts from the Bible as part of his argumentation – when he discuss God's essence, he uses a non-literal reading of the Bible to allow him to move away from anthropomorphism and attributes.

Moses Maimonides (1135–1204 CE) was the most systematic and significant of the medieval Jewish philosophers. Maimonides attempted to develop a synthesis between Aristotelian thought and Judaism. The result of this synthesis is found in *The Guide for the Perplexed*. Unlike Saadia, Maimonides was not using philosophical argumentation to prove revelation but was presenting it as an independent source of knowledge that was complementary, if not superior, to revelation. Maimonides' philosophy is much more thorough than that of Saadia. Thus, as a result of his philosophical argumentation, in which he argues that nothing positive can be said of God, he concludes with a much more transcendent and incomprehensible understanding of God than that found in almost any other Jewish philosophical text.

Although variations on Aristotelian philosophy are the primary approaches taken by medieval Jewish philosophers, some philosophers, notably Ibn Gabirol (c. 1021–c. 1057 CE) and Ibn Paquda (twelfth century CE), were heavily influenced by Neo-Platonism. Unlike the Aristotelian model, which emphasised the separation between the finite and the infinite, Neo-Platonism used an emanation model. It argued that all existence ultimately flowed from God – defined as absolute existence. Neo-Platonic philosophies often included an almost mystical aspect in the ascent of the soul back to its source. In many respects, the contemporary developments in Jewish mysticism reflect very similar ideas about the relationship between God and the universe.

The Enlightenment

The next flowering of Jewish philosophy occurred during the Enlightenment. To a great extent it was interrelated with the increased access of Jews to Western European culture and, eventually, to academic institutions. One of the great early philosophers of the Enlightenment, Spinoza (1632–77) emerged from the Jewish community of Amsterdam. Although his philosophy in many respects moved away from the general trajectory of Jewish thought, particularly in respect of his monistic view of existence, Spinoza provides a link between the philosophers of Spain and the Islamic world, particularly Maimonides, and the emerging philosophers of the Jewish Enlightenment. One can particularly see influences in the political aspects of the philosophy of Moses Mendelssohn.

And even today, no wiser advice than this can be given to the House of Jacob. Adapt yourselves to the morals and the constitution of the land to which you have been removed; but hold fast to the religion of your father's too. Bear both burdens as well as you can! It is true that, on the one hand, the burden of civil life is made heavier for you on account of the religion to which you remain faithful, and, on the other hand, the climate and the times make the observance of your religious laws in some respects more irksome than they are. Nevertheless, persevere; remain unflinching at the post which Providence has assigned to you, and endure everything that happens to you as your lawgiver foretold long ago.

Moses Mendelssohn, *Jerusalem* (1983)

Moses Mendelssohn (1729–96) can be seen as representing a key stage in the participation of Jews in the Enlightenment. Mendelssohn developed a philosophy of Judaism that both reflected its Enlightenment context, with clear influences of Locke, Leibniz, Hobbes and Spinoza, and attempted to rethink Judaism to fit into the new philosophical and cultural context. His philosophical arguments were addressed to both the gentile and the Jewish communities, and can be seen in part as an argument for the inclusion of Jews and Judaism into the Enlightenment enterprise. Mendelssohn's work initiated the process in which Judaism began to reassess itself in the light of modernity – a process that continues to underlie the work of Jewish philosophers.

One of Mendelssohn's most significant philosophical works is *Jerusalem or, On Religious Power and Judaism. Jerusalem* presents a two-sided interrelated argument. It seeks to argue against the role of the state in compelling a particular religious system and thus allows for religious systems to be both multiple and, more importantly, individual. He then argues that Judaism is a religion of reason, fitting into the broader discussions of religion that were an important aspect of Enlightenment philosophical debates. Both arguments together validate the acceptance of both Judaism and Jews into the European polities. A second aspect of

---

To man the world is twofold, in accordance with his twofold attitude.

The attitude of man is twofold, in accordance with the twofold nature of the primary words which he speaks.

The primary words are not isolated words, but combined words.

The one primary word is the combination *I-Thou*.

The other primary word is the combination *I-It*; wherein, without a change in the primary word, one of the words *He* and *She* can replace *It*.

Hence the *I* of man is also twofold.

For the *I* of the primary word *I-Thou* is a different *I* from that of the primary word *I-It* . . .

The extended lines of relations meet in the eternal *Thou*.

Every particular *Thou* is a glimpse through to the eternal *Thou*; by means of every particular *Thou* the primary word addresses the eternal *Thou*. Through this mediation of the *Thou* of all beings fulfilment, and non-fulfilment, of relations comes to them: the inborn *Thou* is realised in each relation and consumated in none. It is consumated only in the direct relation with the *Thou* that by its nature cannot become *It*.

Martin Buber, *I and Thou* (1958: 3, 75)

---

his argument is significant for the development of the reforming or modernising trends within Judaism. In situating his understanding of Judaism within the Enlightenment concept of a religion of reason, Mendelssohn made a distinction between the moral and ethical aspects that are the heart of the religion – as they can be derived by reason alone – and the revealed aspects, which are secondary and particular. Although Mendelssohn did not himself take the path of reform, this distinction within Judaism of the essential ethical elements and the revealed law provides a philosophical justification for the later reformers in their attempts to weaken the authority of the law.

Modern Jewish philosophy

In the subsequent centuries Jewish philosophers have continued to re-examine aspects of Judaism in the light of modernity. Like Mendelssohn, they attempted to synthesize Judaism with a current philosophical system. In the nineteenth century, philosophers such as Nachman Krochmal (1785–1840) and Samuel Hirsch (1815–89) used Hegelian ideas to shape their philosophical systems. Other philosophers, particularly Hermann Cohen (1842–1918), worked from a Neo-Kantian perspective. Although Cohen began to explore the Jewish implications of his philosophical system only towards the end of his life, his system provided a strong philosophical basis for the ethical imperative already present in the Reform movement. The concept of God as an idea, in the Kantian sense, also laid the foundations for some of the more interesting Jewish theologies of the twentieth century.

Jewish philosophy in the twentieth century can be divided into two categories: those philosophers with their roots in the early twentieth century, who do not essentially respond to the Holocaust, and those philosophers whose work primarily responds to the Holocaust. The former group includes Franz Rosenzweig (1886–1929), whose work introduces a move away from Kantianism to a more grounded existential approach to Judaism, and Martin Buber (1878–1965), who in his ground-breaking work *I and Thou* extended the existentialist rethinking of Judaism and centred it on the direct relationship between the individual (the I) and God (the Eternal Thou). Although Abraham Joshua Heschel (1907–72) builds on the existentialist model, his roots in Hasidic mysticism (see below) lead him to a more traditional experientialist approach to Judaism. Mordechai Kaplan (1881–1983) developed an understanding that drew from sociology, particularly Durkheim, as much as it did from philosophers, particularly Dewey. In *Judaism as a Civilization* Kaplan argues for a non-supernatural understanding of God and a cultural understanding of Judaism – that is, as a civilisation like other civilisations. In spite of his emphasis on naturalism, his work presses the notion of progress and development as one of the key laws or processes in the universe. Despite the Holocaust and its challenge to ideas of progress, Kaplan's work continued to emphasise the potentiality of humanity and the almost inexorable move towards a better world.

Three intellectual pillars of Progressive Judaism: Leo Baeck, philosophical and moral leader of the German Reform community; Lily Montagu, a founder of the British Progressive Movement; and Martin Buber, a revolutionary philosopher whose work underpins much of modern progressive thought. Leo Baeck College

A naturalistic conception of religion does not commit us to the choice of either adopting the traditional belief in the chosenness of Israel or dissociating altogether the manifestation of Divinity from the life of peoples or nations in general, least of all the Jewish People. On the contrary, *complete dissociation of Divinity* from peoplehood or nationhood is incompatable with any kind of religion, just as the assumption of *exclusive chosenness* is incompatable with naturalist religion. The truth is that every people in the world, insofar as it shows signs of seeking to achieve human perfection instead of power to domineer, experiences the revelation of divinity and has found its own true vocation.

Mordechai Kaplan, *Judaism Without Supernaturalism* (1958: 28)

In the years after the Holocaust most Jewish philosophers attempted to try to understand key aspects of Judaism in the light of the tragic events. Emile Fackenheim focuses on the uniqueness of the Holocaust in history and argues that the only positive response to it is one of survival, suggesting that the Holocaust revealed a new commandment, the 614th: Jews must survive in order not to hand Hitler a posthumous victory. Other philosophers focused more specifically on the nature of God and the Jewish people. One of the starkest positions is that taken by Richard Rubenstein in *After Auschwitz*. He argues for a need to transform most of the key aspects of Jewish self-understanding, suggesting that after the Holocaust one can no longer speak of chosenness. Equally, one cannot speak of a God who acts in history nor can one use classic models of theodicy. He emphasises this position by speaking of the 'death of God'. Other philosophers have tried to find mediating positions. Some seeking to find a meaningful existence of God despite the Holocaust, speak of a limited or self-limiting God – which allows both human freedom as well as human evil. Others, trying to find meaning above and beyond mere survival, have looked to mysticism and notions of *tikkun olam*, repairing the world. Perhaps it is still too soon after the events for a normative response to the Holocaust to develop.

Mysticism

Mysticism, an approach to the transcendent through the medium of experience, has been a part of Judaism from its origins in the biblical period. Thus, many biblical texts either record ecstatic experiences of the divine, as in 1 Samuel 10: 9–13, or prophetic utterances that appear to be similar to visions and experiences of mystics at later dates, for example Ezekiel 1. The biblical mystical experiences, particularly those found in the prophetic texts, are usually considered to be prophecy rather than mysticism. This distinction, however, is more to do with establishing the nature of authority – prophecy is authoritative, mysticism is not – than it is defining real categories.

The distinction between prophecy and mysticism becomes most relevant by the rabbinic period, at which point the rabbis were developing new models of authority. Authority was no longer seen to be derived from literal communication or experience of God but rather through the process of engagement with God's word. The concept of revelation was transformed from direct experiential revelation to indirect textual revelation. The authority of both formed the interrelated oral and written Torahs. Mysticism became a separate and esoteric form of Jewish religious experience and was not seen as an authoritative source of knowledge.

Merkavah mysticism

Merkavah mysticism (chariot mysticism) emerged during the early rabbinic period – some texts suggest that major Rabbis were engaged in both legal (halachic) disputation and mystical experimentation. This form of mysticism focused on two primary areas: maaseh merkavah (literally, work of the chariot) and maaseh bereshit (literally, work of creation). The first of these includes mystical speculations on the nature of God and the heavenly realm. It used the text of Ezekiel as a catalyst for mystical experience and speculation. Experience of the chariot or *merkavah*, first described in Ezekiel, is the ultimate goal. The texts describe the journey of the mystic through the seven heavens until he experiences a vision of the glory of God. Despite this experiential emphasis, merkavah mysticism maintained a strong notion of the absolute transcendence of God. Maaseh bereshit focused on the esoteric aspects of the process of creation. In *Sefer Yitzirah* (The Book of Creation), a late text that arises from this tradition, we find a complex depiction of creation in which God uses numbers and letters to create the spiritual and material worlds. Some texts suggest that this form of speculation was understood to have a practical aspect, with mystics able to create through the manipulation of numbers, letters and divine names.

Classic kabbalah

It is in the twelfth and thirteenth centuries that we find the roots of the kabbalah, the classical Jewish mystical tradition. This tradition emerged from the creative ferment of Provence – heavily influenced by the Cathars – and the philosophical speculations, particularly Neo-Platonism, of Spain and the Islamic world. The *Zohar* (The Book of Splendour) written by Moses DeLeon towards the end of the thirteenth century is the most influential kabbalistic text. In this highly complex text, the author develops and expands mystical concepts about God that link the finite with the infinite. One of the significant theological innovations of the classical kabbalah was the concept of *sefirot*, vessels of divine power that were emanated from within the infinite aspect of the divine. These vessels were identified with the different attributes of God and were

> One, is the source of the sea. A current comes forth from it making a revolution which is *yod*. The source is one, and the current makes two. Then the vast basin known as the sea is formed, and it is like a channel dug into the earth. It is filled by the waters issuing from the source, and the sea is the third thing. This vast basin is divided up into seven channels,

resembling that number of long tubes, and the waters go from the sea into the seven channels. Together, the source, the current, the sea, and the seven channels make the number ten. If the Creator who made these tubes should choose to break them, then the waters would return to their source, and only broken vessels would remain dry, without water.

In this same way the Cause of causes has derived the ten aspects of His Being which are known as the sefirot, and named Keter [crown] the Source, which is a never-to-be-exhausted fountain of light, wherefrom He designates Himself 'eyn sof, the Infinite. Neither shape nor form has he, and no vessel exists to contain him. This is referred to in the words: 'Refrain from searching after the things that are too hard for thee, and refrain from seeking for the thing which is hidden from thee'.

Moses DeLeon, Zohar (II: 42a–43b) (Blumental 1978: 130)

the aspects of the divine encountered by mystics in their mystical experiences. The concept of *sefirot* preserved the unknowable, infinite aspect of the divine, while also allowing aspects of the divine that could encounter and be encountered by the finite.

A second innovation was the concept of *tikkun*. In the *Zohar tikkun* – literally, repairing – became a dynamic process between humanity and God. The text describes a process in which divine energy flows down to the material world and is refocused and sent back to the divine. Due to sin and other esoteric causes, blockages could appear in the flow within God. *Tikkun* was the process by which human beings could refocus the energy and repair the blockages within God. Thus, the *Zohar* provides a means by which the infinite can reach down to the finite and the finite, in effect, respond and reach for the infinite.

Lurianic kabbalah

The expulsion of the Jews from Spain in 1492 had a significant effect on all aspects of Judaism and a particularly strong influence on the development of mystical ideas. These transformations centred on the town of Safed in northern Galilee and on the personality of Isaac Luria (1534–72). The mysticism that developed emphasised the catastrophic in humanity, history and most importantly within God himself. It emphasised exile and a much more activist and transformative role for mystics and mystical speculation.

One of the primary themes of Lurianic kabbalah is the concept of

Shevirat HaKelim – the breaking of the vessels. This concept introduced the notion of catastrophe into God's very essence. The mystics describe a cosmic spiritual catastrophe in which, in the midst of emanating the *sephirot*, the lower seven vessels of God's power shatter and spread sparks of divine light throughout the lower worlds. The lowest *sephirah* is separated and exiled from the rest of God. These mystical speculations take the human experience of history and re-understand God in their own light. They see the human experience of catastrophe, expulsion and exile as mirroring a process within the divine.

The Lurianic mystics also re-understood the concept of *tikkun*. *Tikkun* became the fundamental role of Israel in relation to God and the world. It was seen as the process through which the catastrophic events of the breaking of the vessels was reversed and through which both human and divine redemption was achieved. *Tikkun* was associated with the performance of *mitzvoth* – commandments – with the right intention, that is the intention of raising the sparks back up to God and ending the exile of the *sephirah* of Malkut (the lowest *sephirah*, which also represented Israel).

These concepts were closely tied to ideas of messianism. The concept of *tikkun* and the end of exile was associated with an activist process whereby the coming of the Messiah could be hastened. In the following centuries a number of individuals influenced by these ideas claimed to be the Messiah – bringing about the end of the process of *tikkun* and the beginning of the final redemption. One of the most significant of these false messiahs, Shabbatai Tsvi (1626–76), had great influence on a large segment of Jewry and added a new dimension to *tikkun*, arguing that evil acts which were done with the right intention were important in bringing about the final stages of redemption. A more inward form of Lurianic kabbalah also led to the development of Hasidism, which in part was a response to the excesses and dangers posed by the ideas of Shabbatai Tsvi. Hasidism attempted, not always successfully, to see the process of *tikkun* and redemption as an internal spiritual process, allowing mystical practices to be practised at a popular level and to reduce the element of messianic speculation and activism.

The Jewish life

Alongside the cognitive aspects of Jewish traditions, practice or the living of a Jewish life is perhaps even more significant in shaping Jewish identity. Although all three of the areas – halakhah, philosophy and mysticism – shape all forms of modern Judaism, it is the instantiations of halakhah in lived experience which is the significant defining factor of each of the major Jewish movements.

Jewish practice is divided into two primary realms, the synagogue and the home. Both of these places can be considered to be sacred space and each, at least in part, is seen as a replacement for the Jerusalem Temple. The type of sacred space exemplified by these locations is significant: it is based on the presence of people living or acting in a certain way, rather than some intrinsic quality of space. Jewish action creates both sacred time and sacred space.

Jewish ritual action can be divided into two cycles, that of the year and of life. Each one of these cycles is punctuated by significant moments through which the individual and the community can define themselves in relation to God, and particularly in relation to the covenant. These cycles also bring together the two ritual domains, the home and synagogue, with elements of practice in both sacred spaces; by doing this, they emphasise the intrinsic connection between the family, centred on the home, and the community, centred on the synagogue.

Rites of passage

The Jewish life cycle, like many other cultural systems, is divided by a number of rituals that allow individuals to move from one socially defined status to another. Anthropological theory, beginning with the work of Arnold van Gennep, has viewed rites of passage or transition as being divided into three stages: separation, liminal and reincorporation (see previous chapter). The separation phase is characterised by rituals that remove the individuals from their prior status, sometimes including a change of clothing or cutting of hair. The liminal phase is that in which the transformation actually occurs, an in between status in which the individual is of no status and therefore able to move between statuses. Liminal rituals often include elements of danger and ambiguity. The final stage, reincorporation, is that in which the individual is returned to society with their new status. One of the significant features of the anthropological analysis of rites of passage is that participants in the cultures studied see them as effective, as causing the change to occur.

Within the Jewish life cycle there are a number of events that seem to fit into this classification. These events, like classical rites of passage, punctuate the particularly dangerous moments of life – birth, adulthood, marriage and death. It is suggested here that although these life cycle events are similar to those analysed in the anthropological literature, they are significantly different in three respects. First, the events do not include a significant aspect of transformation; the change of status is usually one of definition rather than transformation. Second, there is no significant liminality in the rituals; this is closely related to the lack of transformation and thus the lack of ambiguity. Finally, the rites of passage are demonstrative rather than effective; the rite of passage does not cause the transformation, it merely celebrates or demonstrates it.

Brit Milah

Brit Milah, the Covenant of Circumcision, is the first rite of passage that occurs for all Jewish boys. The significant feature of this ritual is the act of circumcision. Brit Milah is performed on the eighth day after the boy's birth. In Orthodox communities, the ritual is usually performed in the home by a *mohel*, a man trained to perform the operation. In non-Orthodox communities, a doctor who is also certified as a *mohel* often performs the ritual in a hospital. The circumcision, although a significant symbolic act, is not an effective act. It does not transform the boy into a Jew (the boy is born a Jew) but symbolises the covenant with God. A child who could not be circumcised, for example a child with haemophilia, would still be a Jew and within the covenant with God. Thus, Brit Milah should be seen as a demonstrative act rather than a transformative act. The significant liturgical aspect of the ceremony is the statement by the father (or parents) that he/they are responsible for raising the child within the covenant. This begins a period in which the parents are responsible for the acts of the child and culminates in the Bar or Bat Mitzvah, at which the child becomes an adult and responsible for himself or herself.

Although in Orthodox communities there is traditionally no similar ritual for girls, many non-Orthodox communities have begun to explore new rituals celebrating the birth of a daughter. These ceremonies range

> The *mitzvah* of *berit mila* [sic] is rather straightforward, and can be fulfilled in a matter of minutes. However, as with most Jewish rituals, a multiplicity of customs, developed in different times and places, has transformed the enactment of this *mitzvah* from a simple perfunctory ceremony into a celebration of major significance. These customs include: various naming traditions; special clothing worn by the infant; particular foods served at the *se-udat mitzvah*; and the singing of special songs. This phenomenon of creating customs specific to a particular community continues today. In recent years, especially among Reform Jews, there has been growing concern not just with the obligatory, technical aspects of the *mitzvah* but with its personal significance as well. In this context, the aesthetics of the *berit mila* ceremony become very important: poetry, music and the sharing of personal statements enhance the simple traditional ceremony and make it a memorable event.
>
> Lewis Barth (ed.), *Berit Mila, in the Reform Context* (1990: 16)

from covenantal ceremonies in the home, which may mirror liturgical elements from the Brit Milah, to naming ceremonies in the synagogue. Like the Brit Milah, these rituals are not transformative but they celebrate the birth of the child and emphasise parental responsibility towards both the child and God.

Bar and Bat Mitzvah

Like Brit Milah the Bar or Bat Mitzvah – Son or Daughter of the Commandments – is a covenantal ceremony. It marks the change in responsibility from that of a child, in which the parents are responsible, to that of an adult, in which the individual is responsible. This ceremony occurs when the child is thirteen years old. Although the Orthodox community has not traditionally had a ceremony for girls, a less significant ritual has been added in some Orthodox congregations to mark a girl's transition to womanhood. This ritual is often performed at the age of twelve. It is sometimes called Bat Hayil, Daughter of Valour, a reference to Proverbs. Among non-Orthodox communities the Bat Mitzvah ceremony, which is equivalent to that performed by the boys, has been added; it is usually performed at thirteen years of age as well.

The actual ceremonial part of the Bar/Bat Mitzvah has undergone many changes. In some synagogues, it includes a recitation of blessings connected to the reading of the Torah and reading the weekly section from the Prophets or the Haftarah. In other communities, the boy or girl might lead a significant part of the service. Whatever form it takes, the Bar or Bat Mitzvah has the same symbolic value. It publicly represents the child taking upon him or herself the responsibilities of an adult Jew. This transformation is represented in the traditional practice by the father publicly relinquishing his responsibility.

The Bar and Bat Mitzvah, like Brit Milah, are not in and of themselves transformative ceremonies. The boy or girl becomes a responsible adult whether or not they perform the ritual and the ceremonies celebrate the event rather than causing it. It is a public demonstration of the child's new responsibility and his or her obligation to be part of the covenant with God. In line with this non-transformative aspect, there is no significant liminality within the ceremony; the transformation, if such there is, occurs immediately upon the boy or girl achieving the appropriate age.

Kabbalat Torah and Confirmation

Although traditionally the Bar Mitzvah marks the move into adulthood, in the American Reform movement and the British Liberal movement an additional ritual marking adulthood has been added. This ceremony is variously called Kabbalat Torah – receiving the Torah – or Confirmation.

Unlike the other rites of passage, this is a group ritual. It is usually performed when young men and women achieve the age of sixteen. The ritual may take place on the festival of Shavuot, which commemorates the receiving of the Torah on Mount Sinai by Moses and the Israelites. The group will usually lead most, if not all, of the Shavuot evening service.

Interestingly, this new religious practice can be seen to have some aspects of liminality and transformation. The ritual itself is seen as the culmination of at least a year of education, which is required in order to participate. During this time, the group may be seen to have a liminal and ambiguous status, neither children nor adults. Unlike Bar or Bat Mitzvah, the individual does not automatically become confirmed – though there does not seem to be any impediment to participation by individuals who are not confirmed. The aspect of transformation is specifically found in the British Liberal movement. In some communities, children are not allowed to lead services until after Kabbalat Torah. It is not unlikely that these liminal aspects have become part of these Liberal and Reform practices due to the greater influence of Western cultural models, which include a strong aspect of liminality.

Huppah

The term *huppah* comes from the marriage canopy under which Jewish marriages are performed and has become one of the terms used for Jewish marriages. Marriage in Judaism is not seen as a sacrament but rather as a contractual arrangement between the groom and bride. It establishes their mutual obligations to each other and affirms their obligation to raise a family within the covenant with God.

The contractual aspect of the marriage is encapsulated in the *ketubah*, the marriage contract, which is given by the groom to the bride. This document, which historically was a protection of the bride's rights introduced by the rabbis at a time when the bride/wife had no legal protection, sets out the groom's obligations both during the marriage and upon divorce. In non-Orthodox communities, the *ketubah* often also includes the wife's obligations to the husband. It also often includes the wife's right to divorce her husband, a right which traditionally was only given to the husband. Thus, one of the significant features of the *ketubah* is that it recognises the possibility of divorce and the need for the woman's rights to be protected. The inclusion of divorce within the context of marriage has implications regarding the level of transformation within the rite of passage. If transformation were emphasised, then the possibility of divorce – in effect, a move back to a previous state – would be minimised or prohibited. The inclusion of divorce supports the argument that little or no transformation is present.

The marriage ceremony itself is divided into two sections, historically two separate ceremonies. The first part, *kiddushin*, was a betrothal ceremony. It includes a blessing over wine and the giving of a ring to the bride by the groom. In non-Orthodox ceremonies there is a reciprocal exchange of rings. The second part, *nisuin*, was the marriage ceremony. The central aspect of this part of the service is the reading of the seven blessings of marriage. Both of these parts are performed under the *huppah* and are separated by a reading of the *ketubah*. The ceremony concludes with the breaking of a glass, which symbolises the destruction of the Temple and the inclusion of sadness even at a joyful event.

Intermarriage is one of the issues that arose in the twentieth century and threatens to divide the Jewish community. As suggested above, genealogy or peoplehood is one of the primary Jewish models of self. This model rests on the idea that all Jews are related to each other and that this genetic tie, at least for the last 2,000 years, has passed down through the matrilineal line. Thus, the definition of a Jew is a person with a Jewish mother. Exogamy challenges this model because it allows the possibility of breaking this genetic tie. The children of a non-Jewish mother would technically not be Jewish (at least according to the Orthodox and Conservative understanding of Jewish identity). This issue has become increasingly problematic in many parts of the Jewish community due to fears for the survival of Judaism after the Holocaust.

The movements have taken different stands in relation to this question. The Orthodox and Conservative movements, and the British Reform movement, continue to follow the traditional genealogical model: they reject intermarriage (even between a Jewish woman and a non-Jewish man) and their rabbis will not perform intermarriages. The British Reform movement will generally welcome intermarried couples but children of a non-Jewish mother will be asked to convert to Judaism. The British Liberal and the American Reform movements are developing a new understanding of Jewish identity that no longer relies as strongly on the peoplehood model. Many of their rabbis will perform intermarriages and take a positive attitude towards the couples and their children. If the children are raised as Jews, these movements consider them to be Jews regardless of which parent was Jewish. Ultimately, this division in practice may lead to Jews of different movements being unwilling to marry each other, as they will have incompatible ways of establishing Jewish identity.

Death and mourning

Unlike many rites of passage surrounding death in which both the dead person and the mourners are transformed, Jewish rituals surrounding death are not transformative. In respect of the person who has died, the ritual acknowledges both the life – particularly in a eulogy – and the fact of death. Regarding the mourners, the rituals provide a space and context for mourning.

After a death the body is ritually cleaned and prepared by members of the community. The funeral should take place as soon after the death as possible. Judaism has always venerated the body and believes that even after death it should be treated with great respect; in light of this, most Jewish communities are against both post-mortems and cremation, though cremation is increasingly practised in non-Orthodox communities, particularly in the United Kingdom.

Following the funeral, Jewish tradition prescribes a three-stage mourning process. The first seven days after the funeral are called Shivah, coming from the Hebrew word for seven. During this period the mourners are meant to stay at home and abstain from a range of practices, which include shaving, cutting of hair and sexual intercourse. It is also customary to hold religious services at the home of the mourners, which are attended by other members of their community. This is followed by a thirty-day period, the Sheloshim, in which the restrictions are somewhat relaxed: for example, the mourners return to some aspects of communal activity but still refrain from activities like parties or other joyous events. Children of the person who has died will then have an additional period of mourning culminating at twelve months after the funeral. Each one of these periods allows the individuals to progress through the stages of mourning and eventually return to full participation in communal life. Many communities also close the mourning process with a gravestone-setting. This usually occurs between eleven and twelve months after the funeral.

The yearly cycle

The Jewish year, like the Jewish life, is punctuated by ritual events that bring together the home and the synagogue, the family and the community. The year is divided in several different ways: the weekly cycle of Shabbatot; the celebrations surrounding the Jewish New Year – Rosh HaShanah and Yom Kippor; the three harvest or pilgrimage festivals, Pesach, Shavuot and Sukkot; and a range of minor festivals and commemorations. Like the life cycle events, these rituals focus on the covenantal relationship between Israel (the people) and God, and through associations both historical and redemptive bring together an understanding of the Jewish experience of past, present and future.

Shabbat

Although Shabbat occurs each week, from Friday evening until Saturday evening, it is the most important of all Jewish festivals. It brings together most of the religiously significant symbolic complexes. Shabbat is most directly associated with the last day of creation, the day on which God is said to have rested. It is also liturgically connected with the exodus from Egypt. Thus, it is directly tied to the symbolic complexes of creation and redemption. It is also strongly connected to the complex of revelation, with the reading of the Torah, a re-enactment of revelation, being the heart of the main Shabbat service. Shabbat is also connected to ideas of the future redemption and the coming of the Messiah or the Messianic age. Mystical understandings of the Shabbat see it as a moment out of time in which believers taste the world to come.

The Shabbat is structured around three services: Kabbalat Shabbat on Friday night, the Shabbat morning service, and Havdalah on Saturday evening. Although Kabbalat Shabbat refers in part to a joyful service in the synagogue in which many songs are sung to welcome in the Shabbat, it is primarily a celebration in the home. Traditionally, there would be a festive meal on Friday night in which the family would gather together to welcome the Shabbat. The lighting of two candles and the blessing

---

What is the Sabbath? A reminder of every man's royalty; an abolition of the distinction between master and slave, rich and poor, success and failure. To celebrate the Sabbath is to experience one's ultimate independence of civilization and society, of achievement and anxiety. The Sabbath is an embodiment of the belief that all men are equal and that the equality of men means the nobility of men. The greatest sin of man is to forget that he is a prince.

The Sabbath is an assurance that the spirit is greater than the universe, that beyond the good is the holy. The universe was created in six days, but the climax of creation was the seventh day. Things that come into being in the six days are good, but the seventh day is holy. The Sabbath is holiness in time.

What is the Sabbath? The presence of eternity, a moment of majesty, the radience of joy. The soul is enhanced, time is a delight, and inwardness is the supreme reward. Indignation is felt to be a desecration of the day, and strife the suicide of one's additional soul. Man does not stand alone, he lives in the presence of the day.

Rabbi Jules Harlow (ed.), *Siddur Sim Shalom: A Prayerbook for Shabbat, Festivals, and Weekdays* (Conservative), (1985: 869)

---

and drinking of a glass of wine would welcome the Shabbat. In many Reform communities today, much of the home and family aspect of Jewish celebrations has moved to the temple (Reform congregations, particularly in the United States, tend to call their houses of worship temples rather than synagogues). Thus, many of the practices once based on the home, like the lighting of Shabbat candles, have now moved to the temple and become a communal rather than a family-oriented act.

The Shacharit or Saturday Morning Service is the most important of the Shabbat services. The central part of the service is the weekly reading from the Torah. The Torah is divided into weekly portions, which are read throughout the year. In Orthodox and many Conservative congregations, the entire Torah will be read consecutively during the course of the year. In Reform congregations, the rabbi or leader of the service may select a section of the weekly Torah portion that he or she considers to be relevant to the community. The reading of the Torah in effect re-enacts the moment of revelation at Sinai, bringing together past and present. It should be seen as a reaffirmation of the covenant with God. It is not coincidental that in both Orthodox and non-Orthodox congregations, Bar and Bat Mitzvah is very often celebrated in the Shabbat Morning Service, as it too is essentially a covenantal celebration. The Shabbat Morning Service is specifically a communal event, with its main elements requiring a *minyan* (ten men, or both men and women in non-Orthodox communities), which is seen as the requisite number for a communal event.

The closing ritual of Shabbat is the Havdalah Service. Havdalah is the service that marks the separation between the Shabbat and the rest of the week. The service uses many of the symbols found earlier in other Shabbat rituals, for example candles and wine, but re-articulates them to emphasise the spiritual distinction between the type of time represented by the Shabbat and that represented by the weekdays. Although the Havdalah ritual makes a strong distinction between the two, it also allows the possibility that some of the light, some of the spirituality represented by the Shabbat, can permeate the rest of time as well.

One other aspect of Shabbat that needs to be mentioned is the general character of the day as a whole. Shabbat, as stated in the Ten Commandments, is a day of rest. In traditional communities, work is not permitted on the Shabbat, including the lighting of a fire or driving a car. The types of work that are forbidden are those that can be logically tied to the thirty-nine types of work needed to build the tabernacle in the wilderness. Non-Orthodox Jews understand this commandment in different ways. In general, the Conservative movement attempts to follow the commandment not to work, though it also recognises the needs of people in the modern world, particularly regarding the use of cars to get to the synagogue. The Reform movements leave the definition of work to individuals and generally are much more permissive regarding what people can or cannot do. Most Reform Jews emphasise the need to make Shabbat a joyful day, rather than stringently focusing on what is allowed by Jewish law.

The Jewish New Year

Although Rosh HaShanah is often called the Jewish New Year, it is only the beginning of a ritual cycle culminating in Yom Kippor, the Day of Atonement. This New Year cycle is, in one sense, the beginning of the Jewish year, since it celebrates the creation of the universe and is the time at which the numeration of the year changes – the Jewish year is calculated from the time that the world was believed to be created. In another sense, however, the 'new' is not the beginning of the year: Rosh HaShanah is the first day of the seventh month in the year, with the first month of the year falling in the spring. The Mishnah records that there were four new years, each commemorating a different element, some in respect of nature, like Tu Bishvat, the New Year of the Trees, and others cultural, such as the New Year which celebrates the anniversary of a king's ascension to the throne (Rosh HaShanah 1.1). Thus, Rosh HaShanah might be seen not as the beginning of the year in respect of natural cycles or political cycles – which occur in the spring or at different times in the year – but rather as the beginning of a new spiritual year.

The New Year cycle of Rosh HaShanah and Yom Kippor is collectively called the Days of Awe. Rosh HaShanah introduces a period of spiritual self-examination and judgement. Traditionally, it was seen as the day upon which God began the process of judging all creation – Rosh HaShanah was also called Yom HaDin the Day of Judgement. One of the primary symbols of the Holyday is the *Shofar*, the ram's horn. The evocative sound made by the blowing of the *Shofar* is symbolically connected with the sacrifice of Isaac, reminding God of Abraham's willingness to give his son to him. It is also meant to wake the congregants up to their need to examine their past deeds and prepare for repentance.

The days between Rosh HaShanah and Yom Kippor are collectively known as the ten days of repentance. During this period, Jews are meant to consider their lives over the past year and to seek forgiveness from those whom they have hurt. This process includes those things that stand in the way of their relations with other people and those that stand in the way of their relationship with God. Jewish tradition states that anyone who truly tries to repent will be forgiven by God.

Yom Kippor, the Day of Atonement, is the culmination of this process. It is the day upon which God is believed to forgive all those who repent. It is the most solemn and formal of all Jewish religious events. Yom Kippor is a day when Jews fast, neither eating or drinking, from sundown to sundown Like all Jewish Holydays, Yom Kippor begins in the evening and concludes on the following evening. As suggested by the name, Yom Kippor is the occasion upon which the Jews as individuals and community are made one with each other and God.

> If a man said, 'I will sin and repent, and sin again and repent,' he will be given no chance to repent. [If he said,] 'I will sin and the Day of Atonement will effect atonement,' then the Day of Atonement effects no atonement. For transgressions that are between man and God the Day of Atonement effects atonement, but for transgressions that are between a man and his fellow the Day of Atonement effects atonement only if he has appeased his fellow.
>
> Mishnah, Yoma 8.9

The pilgrimage festivals

Pesach, Shavuot and Sukkot are the three pilgrimage festivals. In the period up to 70 CE (the destruction of the Temple in Jerusalem), Israelites were obligated to journey to Jerusalem for each of these festivals. During the biblical period, the primary aspect of these celebrations was sacrifice in the Temple; after the destruction the rituals were transferred to both the synagogue and the home. Each of these festivals brings together at least three different domains: the agricultural cycle, history and Messianic expectations.

Pesach, or Passover, is the most popular of the pilgrimage festivals. The major focus of celebration is the Passover Seder, a special ritualised meal that is performed on the first two nights of the eight-day festival. (According to biblical law, Pesach was celebrated for seven days. Today, outside of Israel, traditional Jews add on an additional day to most festivals. Thus, Pesach is celebrated for eight rather than seven days. Reform and Liberal Jews do not add the extra day to the festivals.) During the Seder, different foods are eaten that symbolise the experiences of the Israelites during slavery and the eventual exodus from Egypt. The key aspect of the celebration is not one of memory but to actually relive and become part of the events recounted in the text. The festival is also connected with the harvest of winter wheat and the birth of lambs. In addition to the rituals, which take place in the home, there are also synagogue services on each of the days of the festival.

Shavuot, or the feast of weeks, occurs forty-nine days after the second day of Passover. Shavuot is celebrated for one or two days. It commemorates the receiving of the Torah on Mount Sinai and is connected with the barley harvest. Unlike Passover, there is no particular ritual in the home. The primary ritual is a service in the synagogue, which includes a reading of the Book of Ruth. In Progressive and Reform congregations, Kabbalat Torah and Confirmation is often performed on Shavuot. These services symbolise the acceptance of the Torah by the young adults and Shavuot more broadly symbolises the reaffirmation or the reacceptance of the Torah by all Jews. Shavuot also has a Messianic or mystical aspect, which is found in an all-night ritual called Tikkun Le'yel Shavuot. In this ritual, sections of significant texts are studied. It looks forward to the ultimate perfection of creation in the Messianic age.

Sukkot, or Tabernacles, is connected to the forty years of wandering in the wilderness. One of the major elements of the celebration is the Sukkah, or booth a temporary hut, which is traditionally built by every family. Over the eight days of the festival, meals are eaten in the Sukkah. It symbolises both the journey of the past and the journey Jews are still on today, again looking forward to the eventual coming of the Messiah or Messianic age. Like the other pilgrimage festivals, Sukkot is also connected to the agricultural cycle, celebrating the autumn harvest. In the biblical and early rabbinic periods, Sukkot was one of the most popular festivals: it was called heHag, the Festival. At the conclusion of Sukkot, Jews celebrate the Simchat Torah, Rejoicing in the Torah. During this celebration, the end and the beginning of the Torah is read, symbolising the end and beginning of the cycle of reading the Torah.

Minor festivals

In addition to the major festivals mentioned above, there are a number of minor festivals that celebrate particular historical events and times in the year. These festivals include some of the most popular festivals, for example Hanukah and Purim. Hanukah is celebrated in the late autumn or early winter. It is connected with the victory of the Jews, led by the Macabees, against the forces of the Syrian Greeks. The name – meaning rededication – refers to the re-dedication of the Temple. Hanukah is celebrated for eight days and is also called the Festival of Lights, due to the fact that candles are lit on each of the nights. Purim commemorates the events chronicled in the Book of Esther, and the reading of that text is the central part of the festival service. It is a bittersweet festival that reminds Jews of both salvation and the possibility of persecution. Other minor festivals or commemorations include Tu Bishvat, the New Year of the Trees, and Tisha B'Av, the commemoration of the destruction of the Temples (and other tragic events in Jewish history). Recently two additional events have been added into the Jewish calendar: Yom HaAzmaut (Israel Independence Day) and Yom HaShoah (Holocaust Memorial Day).

Modern Jewish movements

All modern movements are shaped by the different elements examined in the previous sections: that is, Halakhah, philosophy, mysticism and practice. In addition to the different combinations of these elements, these movements are also shaped by a response to aspects of modernity, either in the form of a strong acceptance or different levels of rejection. Although there are many significant differences in practice and form, due to limitations of space we highlight some aspects of the historical development of the movements and their attitude to the four areas. The different roles of women will be used to exemplify some of these issues, especially in regarding practice and the related aspect of Halakhah.

Reform

The Reform movement had its origins in Germany in the first quarter of the nineteenth century, the first synagogue being established in Hamburg in 1817. Many of the early developments in the movement were attempts to make traditional Judaism more approachable to the increasingly assimilated Jewish community and, more importantly, more acceptable to the wider Christian community. It was only in its later stages that the Reform movement began to develop a more distinctive theology and especially a different attitude towards Halakhah.

The Reform movement, unlike other traditional forms of Judaism, emphasises cognitive or theological aspects of religion as opposed to practice. Practice is seen as secondary, as a means for supporting a particular understanding of or relationship to the divine. Thus, as it developed the movement put aside those aspects of tradition that were seen as being out of step with a modern way of thinking or understanding of theology. In making these changes, the movement generally did not seek to work within the traditional legal system, rather it made the changes that it believed were demanded by modernity.

Modern Reform practice is shaped by a response to modernity more than a response to tradition. This is seen particularly in respect of the changed role of women. From its roots in the nineteenth century, the movement began a process of equalisation of the roles of men and women, a process that accelerated in the twentieth century, particularly in the 1960s and 1970s. The primary impetuses for these changes were the developing women's movement and the increased equality women achieved in Western European and American society, rather than any development within Jewish tradition. The changes established by the movement include men and women sitting together during services; greater participation in the organisation and running of communities; equalisation in participation and roles within ritual; and finally, the acceptance of women as rabbis. All of these changes were made without recourse to the process of Halakhah and were instead validated by an understanding of the demands of both morality and modernity.

The Reform movement has also emphasised aspects of both Jewish philosophy and mysticism. In the period between the mid-nineteenth century and the latter half of the twentieth century, the movement emphasised the rational aspects of the Jewish tradition. It traced a thread between figures like Maimonides and Hermann Cohen, emphasising Judaism as a religion of reason. In this respect, Reform could be seen as a child of the enlightenment, readily accepting nineteenth-century notions of positivism. These ideas not only shaped theological understandings of God and human nature, they also shaped liturgy and practice. Many aspects of liturgy were significantly transformed, with a removal of the poetic and metaphorical, a move from particularism to universalism, and a strong emphasis on a transcendent concept of ethical monotheism – if religion was about anything, it was about ethics and morality.

Towards the end of the twentieth century, however, there was a significant shift in Reform thinking. Rather than emphasising the rational aspects, it now seeks to emphasise the spiritual and the mystical. This change is found in liturgy, most overtly with the inclusion of mystical texts and themes but also more subtly in a shift to a more individual and particularist form of liturgy with an emphasis on experience and an immanent understanding of the divine. It is also found in regard to practice, with a return to a more experiential and emotional and thus less cognitive form of religious practice. This shift in emphasis is similar to that which is occurring more widely in Western culture with the rise of New Age religious forms.

Orthodox

Although the Orthodox movement sees itself as a continuation of traditional Judaism, as a self-conscious movement it owes its origins to the beginnings of the Reform movement. In many respects, it should be seen as a response against the changes instituted by Reform, while also being shaped by many of the same forces. Orthodoxy, however, is not monolithic: over the past one hundred and fifty years it has been pulled in a number of directions. One the one hand, Modern Orthodoxy, descending from Samson Raphael Hersch (1808–88), seeks to find some accommodation with modernity, accepting those aspects that do not come into conflict with Jewish law. On the other hand, Ultra-Orthodoxy, descending from Moses Sofer (1763–1839), rejects modernity and seeks to isolate Judaism from any external influence. Although both these forms of Judaism lead to very different forms of living, both are based on a common understanding of Jewish law. They see it as God-given and unchanging. They look to the Shulhan Arukh and seek to minimise any change. Unlike Reform, where authority is vested in the individual, in all forms of Orthodoxy authority is vested in the rabbi and the recognised legal authorities.

Although there are some differences between the Modern Orthodox and Ultra-Orthodox attitudes towards women, particularly in respect of women's activities in secular society, for example employment and education, in the ritual context both of these groupings continue to restrict women's roles. Men and women are separated in the synagogue, with women restricted to a gallery or sometimes behind some type of curtain or wall. In many communities, the synagogue is almost the exclusive property of the men, with women functioning almost entirely in the home. Women are not allowed to have any public ritual role (particularly when men are present) and are similarly not allowed to function in any public position of ritual authority. Women within these communities see their spiritual fulfilment as coming from the private sphere of the home and family rather than the public sphere of the synagogue. Today, many women within the Modern Orthodox community, due in part to their roles in secular life, are seeking to expand their ritual life outside the home. Many of them attend synagogue on a regular basis and in some communities are seeking to establish women's services where they can fulfil public ritual roles – but this change has not become the normative position in Modern Orthodoxy and is not found in Ultra-Orthodoxy.

Unlike Reform, all forms of Orthodoxy emphasise practice and Halakhah as opposed to philosophy and mysticism. Practice is established by tradition and communal authorities, and is the foundation of identity. Mysticism and philosophy are left to the individual. In general, Modern Orthodoxy places little emphasis on mysticism and within Ultra-Orthodoxy mysticism is left to an esoteric elite. The only exception to this is the Hasidic movement, which is discussed separately below. Although modern philosophy has had some influence on Modern Orthodoxy, in general it has not substantially transformed theology, which is still roughly within rabbinic formulations with some influence from thinkers like Maimonides. The only area that has led to some rethinking is that of theodicy, particularly in response to the Holocaust. Most of the creative thinking in this area, however, has been done outside of the Orthodox traditions.

Conservative

Conservative Judaism has attempted to find a middle road between Orthodox and Reform. It both tries to accept modernity and transformation while also maintaining the importance of Jewish law. These two themes were encapsulated in the two foundational concepts established by Solomon Schechter, one of the pivotal figures of the movement – that is, 'Catholic Israel' and 'positive historical Judaism'. Catholic Israel is the conservative force, recognising that Judaism can only change at a rate acceptable to its constituency. Positive historical Judaism is a concept that recognises that Judaism, like all cultures and traditions, has undergone a continuous process of change. It validates this change and accepts that change will continue to occur to meet changes in the community's experiences of the world.

Although Conservative Judaism accepts that Judaism changes over time, it argues that this change needs to be done through a legal process. Unlike Reform, it believes that change should not occur merely because of modern values or fads but that Jewish law has a trajectory of development and that change must fit into that trajectory. Nonetheless, during its history Conservative Judaism has made significant changes in Jewish law, often moving in a similar direction to Reform, albeit at a slower and Halakhicly defended pace. Authority in Conservative Judaism is vested neither in the individual nor in the rabbi; rather it is vested in the community in the form of a committee of legal experts, the Committee of Law and Standards. This committee deliberates over changes and, through a process of Halakhic argumentation, establishes the law for the movement as a whole.

It is Conservative Judaism that most directly confronts the challenge to integrate tradition with modernity. By retaining most of the tradition while yet being hospitable to the valuable aspects of modernity, it articulates a vital, meaningful vision of Judaism for our day. Difficult as this task is, there is comfort in the observation of out Sages that *lefum tzaara agra*, according to the pain involved is the reward (Avot 5:24).

The twentieth century, the most eventful in Jewish history, has made this task especially important. The establishment of the State of Israel, the horror of the Holocaust, and the extraordinary growth and creativity of the North American Jewish community all demand new synthesis and applications of the new and old in both thought and action ... the Conservative community has its own distinctive views of many of these issues, one which is coherent and yet pluralistic, thoughtful and yet oriented to action, traditional and yet responsive to the present.

Emet Ve-Emunah: Statement of Principles of Conservative Judaism (Commission on the Philosophy of Conservative Judaism 1990)

The process used by Conservative Judaism for establishing practice is clearly seen in its attitude to the role of women. During the twentieth century, women progressively achieved ritual equality with men. Although on the surface the change is similar to that of the Reform movement, each change was only enacted after Halakhic discussion and debate. Only those changes that could be justified by Jewish law were accepted. Thus, at the culmination of the process the movement decided that women could be as equally ritually obligated as could men and that, although women could be rabbis, they could not function as witness in a religious context, as that aspect was unambiguously prohibited by the Halakhah.

Conservative Judaism emphasises both practice and theology. Its thinkers have generally been accepting of modernity and, like the Reform movement, its philosophers have been influenced by the philosophical trends of the nineteenth and twentieth centuries. It has always included a wide range of theological perspectives, at times including rabbis who denied the existence of a supernatural God and others who took a traditional view of a personal, acting, supernatural God. Although the Conservative movement has generally been similar to Reform in its acceptance of more rational approaches to God, from the mid-twentieth century it was already exploring the more mystical or experiential approaches advocated by Abraham Joshua Heschel. In recent years, it has increasingly been exploring the more spiritual aspects of Judaism, responding to the same forces that are transforming Reform theology.

Reconstructionist

Reconstructionist Judaism is the most radical form of Judaism as a religion. It was an offshoot of Conservative Judaism and, at least at its beginnings, was very similar in respect of practice. The movement was founded by Mordecai Kaplan (1881–1983), who for most of his career worked within the Conservative movement, teaching at the Jewish Theological Seminary in New York. Kaplan's primary innovations were in two areas: theology and community. Most importantly, he argued for a Judaism without supernaturalism, emphasising that Judaism was a civilisation rather than merely a religion. He also emphasised the communal aspect of Judaism, taking Schechter's concept of Catholic Israel and seeing it as the essential motivating force of Jewish history, particularly in the processes of transformation and innovation.

Reconstructionist Judaism shares with Reform a positive attitude towards modernity. This attitude has shaped the movement's liturgy and its attitude towards women. Like Reform, liturgy is significantly transformed to respond to modern ideas and values; thus, all particularist elements have been removed. Similarly, the movement has always emphasised the equality of the sexes and perhaps has been the most open to active involvement at all levels by women.

Although the Reconstructionist movement was most radical in its rejection of supernaturalism, this acceptance of progress and positivist values has not remained a cornerstone of the movement. In a similar pattern to that found in all other movements, subsequent developments have seen a return to exploring mysticism and the spiritual. Perhaps because of its radical origins, it has been more willing to explore some of the more extreme alternatives in these areas. Today, each

Reconstructionist community (and perhaps sub-groups within each community) has moved in many alternative directions, with little clear consistency. The movement has never succeeded in drawing a large constituency, though many of the areas that it has explored have influenced Conservative and Reform thinkers.

Hasidism

The Hasidic community is one of the most distinctive branches of Judaism today. Hasidic Jews wear very characteristic forms of dress and live in tightly knit communities. Although Hasidism shares many similarities with some of the more extreme forms of Ultra-Orthodoxy, it is also highly unique in terms of its theology and, more significantly, in its communal organisation.

Hasidism originated in the eighteenth century as a challenge to the established authorities and practices of Eastern European Judaism. In its origins it was a revolutionary mystical movement that moved away from traditional forms. Although it maintained its mystical focus, it quickly returned to the established forms of traditional Judaism. Today, Hasidism (like Ultra-Orthodoxy) gains much of its identity through its opposition to all forms of modernity – though some of its groups are willing to take advantage of modern technology to spread its values and ideals. In respect of theology, it is its mystical emphasis that makes Hasidism unique. This focus has, at times of crisis, taken a Messianic form and the movement can be understood as an activist form of mysticism seeking to transform the individual and ultimately the world. The primary difference between Hasidism and other forms of Judaism is found in its unique pattern of social organisation. The Hasidic movement is divided into a large number of small groups, which are tightly organised around charismatic leaders called Rebbes or Tzadikim. Originally these leaders gained their positions through their own personal charisma; today they gain the position and charisma through inheritance. In all other Jewish communities, leadership is vested in rabbis, who gain their position through education and employment. The relationship with the Rebbe is also unique; it is very personal, with the Rebbe being seen as a conduit between the Hasid and God. Each Rebbe has his own court (in a regal rather than legal sense) and Hasidim who are associated with that court from generation to generation. Each community is shaped by the personality of its Rebbes, both in terms of practice and theology.

Conclusion: Judaism in the twenty-first century

Although it is likely that the different movements mentioned above will continue into the twenty-first century, Judaism like other modern religions is being pulled in at least two different directions: towards the individual and individual spirituality, and towards more authoritarian and traditional patterns of individual and communal structures. Whereas all forms of Judaism in the nineteenth and twentieth centuries, with the exception of Hasidism, emphasised rationality and ethics, Judaism today emphasises spirituality and individual need.

On the one hand, many Jews within the less traditional branches are engaging in spiritual shopping, moving outside of the traditional communal structures and looking to different sources of meaning and value. These sources often arise from the mystical traditions of Judaism, repackaging the ideas to fit modern individualism. There is an associate move to create new patterns of spirituality, often presented in the form of healing, spiritual and physical. Initially, this move took the form of breaking down synagogues into small units based on families and like-minded individuals; today, it is increasingly individualistic and non-communal. Those synagogues which are most successful are those which emphasis mysticism and individual religious enthusiasm.

On the other hand, many Jews are rejecting the forms of Judaism that have made accommodations with modernity. Increasingly, individuals within the Modern Orthodox Jewish community are moving towards more authoritarian Ultra-Orthodox forms of practice – seeking, perhaps, to move away from the difficulties of individual choice and responsibility. This move towards authority has also affected the other less traditional branches. There is a movement of individuals to Ultra-Orthodoxy, called *baale tishuvah*, and within the movements there are calls for clearer patterns of authority and structure.

As Judaism continues to struggle with assimilation and secularism and to create patterns of continuity, it is probable that the less traditional movements will continue to move away from concepts of universalism and increasingly focus on particularism and individual spirituality. More traditional forms, needing to move away from a discredited modernity, will continue to move back to more authoritarian forms, seeking to define themselves in opposition rather than in relation to modernity.

 ## Further reading

Borowitz, Eugene B. (1983), *Choices in Modern Jewish Thought*, New York: Behrman House. This book examines the full range of modern Jewish theological and philosophical thought. Although Borowitz presents a 'partisan guide', it nonetheless provides a good introduction to the thinkers.

De Lange, Nicholas (2000), *An Introduction to Judaism*, Oxford: Oxford University Press. Although there are many good short introductions to

Judaism, this volume is both comprehensive and clearly written. In includes a wide range of material for reference and stimulating (and some times controversial) analyses.

Gillman, Neil (1993), *Conservative Judaism*, New York: Behrman House. This book provides a clear and comprehensive discussion of Conservative Judaism, including both historical and theological discussion.

Rayner, John and Bernard Hooker (1978), *Judaism for Today*, London: ULPS. This book introduces many of the significant aspects of Liberal Jewish thought. It is also relevant to the understanding of American Reform theology.

Sacks, Jonathan (1990), *Tradition in an Untraditional Age*, London: Vallentine Mitchell. This book, written by the Chief Rabbi of the Orthodox community in the United Kingdom, presents an analysis of Orthodox responses to modernity. It also explores some Orthodox responses to thinkers in the Reform movement.

Scholem, Gershom (1954), *Major Trends in Jewish Mysticism*, New York: Schocken. A classic discussion of all forms of Jewish mysticism written by one of the greatest scholars in the field.

Seltzer, Robert (1980), *Jewish People, Jewish Thought*, New York: Macmillan. This is the best one-volume history of Judaism. The book covers Jewish history from its roots until the twentieth century. It also includes insightful analyses of Jewish thought in the contexts of historical discussions.

Sirat, Colette (1985), *A History of Jewish Philosophy in the Middle Ages*, Cambridge: Cambridge University Press. This volume covers all the major schools of medieval Jewish philosophy from the ninth to the fifteenth century. It provides a sufficient degree of discussion and analysis to give the reader a clear introduction to the specific thinkers and the development of Jewish thought in the period covered.

Werblowsky, R. J. Zwi and Geoffrey Wigoder (eds) (1997), *The Oxford Dictionary of the Jewish Religion*, Oxford: Oxford University Press. This one-volume dictionary provides a useful resource for reference on all aspects of Jewish religion.

Questions

1. In what way is history essential in understanding Judaism?

2. Is it meaningful to speak of a Jewish tradition?

3. Given that Jewish philosophy and mysticism ask many of the same questions, what are the significant areas of difference and similarity in their answers? Are they more similar today than they were in the Middle Ages?

4. Is there a fundamental foundation upon which all of the different forms of Judaism are built?

5. Explore the similarities and differences in the way that Judaism and other religions use myths or models to explain their experience in history and the world in which they live.

Christianity

Douglas J. Davies

Introduction

Historically speaking, Christianity has been the most successful of all world religions, spreading far beyond its point of origin, developing new forms of itself in many different cultures and collecting many millions of members over a period of two thousand years. This is different from Zoroastrianism, Judaism, Hinduism and Sikhism, which very largely remained the religions of distinctive ethnic groups, even when following them into new parts of the world, as with Jews in New York or Sikhs in Canada. More like Buddhism, and especially like Islam, Christianity came to appeal to people in societies quite different from its original source. Over time, Christian cultures emerged within many of those societies and this new religion came to function rather as the ethnic traditions of Judaism or Sikhism. For nearly two thousand years, the shared and written history of the Western world came to be divided by the life of Jesus into the eras before him (BC, before Christ) and after him (AD, the year of our Lord or *anno domini* in Latin). Only towards the end of the twentieth century did it become fashionable to use the

161

abbreviations BCE (before the common era) or CE (common era) to refer in a less explicit way to this great division of time.

An ancient root

In origin, Christianity was an outgrowth and a transformation of Judaism, so much so that the Christian religion makes absolutely no sense at all apart from Judaism. This is most clearly seen in the figure of Jesus when he is described as Jesus Christ. For 'Christ' comes from a Greek word that, in turn, translates the Hebrew for Messiah, and the Messiah was the specially anointed one who was to be the messenger of the God of Israel. To describe Jesus as Christ, or Messiah, only makes sense against the history and culture of Israel, a people with a monotheistic religion worshipping the one and only God, who periodically sent prophets to announce the divine will and commandments to humanity, promising a future world of divine reign centred on a chosen and obedient people.

Messiah and deity

Earliest Christianity emerged from the Jewish-influenced belief that God had appointed Jesus to be the Messiah, one who would deliver God's people from injustice and bring about a society grounded in justice and righteousness. All that made sense within the historical tradition of Judaism. But, and this is the important point of change, this Messiah figure was believed by the earliest Christians (being mostly Jews) to have died and to have been raised again to life. Despite the fact that he had been tried by Roman authorities on criminal charges and had been subject to the capital punishment of crucifixion, his death was interpreted through Jewish beliefs combining the ritual sacrifices of animals and the suffering of a divine servant for the removal of sin. His resurrection was seen to validate his sacrificial death and showed that God had, indeed, specially chosen him to bring salvation.

Expanding community and leadership

But to whom had Jesus brought salvation? That was the prime question. Obviously, he was bringing salvation to God's people, the Jews. The earliest believers were sure of that and read their own sacred scriptures as pointing to Jesus as the Messiah. This made them see themselves as living at a special time. Some even thought that Jesus, having been resurrected, would soon come again on the clouds of heaven and transform the earth and human society, bringing about a complete renewal of things. These early Jewish Christians had a deep sense of change, of divine promises being fulfilled in their own days amongst the immediate group of Jesus's disciples and amongst other Jews who had accepted the message of Jesus as the Messiah. But then something unusual and unexpected happened. Some Gentiles – as non-Jews were called – also experienced something of their new sense of life and accepted that Jesus was the focus of God's activity. In other words, the early Christian group was developing as a community of believers that had started with Jews and, fairly rapidly, came to include Gentiles.

At more or less the same time the traditional Jewish establishment was turning against these Jewish Christians and making them stand alone. A new and distinctive identity was emerging, the identity of 'Christian'. Many people, both women and men, seemed to join; many were poor but some were rich; some might be slaves or had been slaves whilst others had been in substantial social positions. Membership was, quite specifically, open to both sexes and not – for example, as in Mithraism – only to men. In particular, Christians did not have to come from any particular family, clan or race-like group but could come from anywhere into this new community defined in terms of Jesus. It was even described as a kind of extension of his identity, as the 'body of Christ'. Of particular importance in early Christianity was the part played by individual leaders who took the message and their experience of Jesus and forged a new religion. Indeed, when thinking of Christianity it is as important to focus on key leaders as to think of doctrinal systems of thought. In practice, these individual leaders have constructed new avenues of thought, leaving their own imprint upon the cumulative development of the faith. Two of the earliest and most significant were Paul and Peter.

Paul

Paul, though not actually one of the very first group of Jesus's disciples, nevertheless came to be amongst the first to theorise about this new community. He described it as being this 'body of Christ', as though the community was a form of Jesus. Entry into this body-like community was not by birthright, as in Judaism, where the circumcision of baby boys at eight days old formally admitted them to the congregation of God's elect people on the basis that their mother was a Jew. Birth to a Jewish mother and circumcision at the hands of a male complemented each other to produce a member of the chosen race that entered a covenant with God. Entry into the Christian community was different. It was accomplished when God acted upon those who heard the message about Jesus and empowered them with a spiritual inspiration. The Holy Spirit, as this power was called, was an experience of the individual shared with the group. The sense of the presence of the Holy Spirit might be manifest in speaking in tongues but also related to an awareness of community or of a fellowship of believers, as well as of the power of God. Early Christians took baptism from the Jewish practice of initiating converts and made it central to their own way of life; in a sense, the Jewish idea of birth and circumcision was paralleled by the Christian view of spiritual rebirth and baptism.

Paul had himself experienced a power which he not only interpreted as supernatural but which he believed to have been an actual encounter with the resurrected Jesus of Nazareth. Underlying Paul's conversion and the experiences of the earliest group of disciples fairly soon after Jesus's death and what they called his resurrection was an awareness of a power or dynamic force that they called the Holy Spirit. Even the records of the appearances of Jesus to his disciples after his resurrection did not transform them into dynamic members of a new community. Indeed, the opposite is the case, for they are described as rather timid, hiding from the Jewish authorities who seemed set against them. But they did shortly come to a sense of power, one that made them speak publicly about their new understanding of life focused on Jesus as God's chosen representative, who saved people from their sin and its potential consequences, and on the Holy Spirit, whose influence seems to have generated the new community of brothers and sisters. One strong undercurrent of this scheme of things was a belief both that death had been conquered and that a sense of newness of life could be experienced as a member of this new community. So it was, for example, that Paul, as one of the major theorists of the new religion, contrasted their old life with their new life and saw the new as a spirit-empowered form of existence. Christians were to live 'in the Spirit' as members of the 'body of Christ'.

Paul was not the only one trying to make sense of what he had experienced himself and of this new community of which he felt himself to be a part. Indeed, his whole identity seemed to have changed and he reflects on this as he wrote numerous letters to small groups of these early Christians. He had been formally trained as a Jewish thinker and was now having to think again. And much the same lies behind the letters and gospels – those specially written accounts of the life of Jesus – as they ponder aspects of Jewish religion and interpret them in the light of new community realities.

Peter

Peter is the other major Christian leader who, more as an ordinary Jew and not a devoted scholar of the law as was Paul, also underwent something of a powerful experience that changed his own understanding of what the new movement was like. Peter had, of course, been one of the close disciples of Jesus and had not had an easy time in trying to work out just what Jesus was teaching. It was only after the resurrection and the experience of power in the new, Spirit-led community that Peter really grasped the fact that this community was genuinely open to all. His traditional Jewish commitment to specific food rules had, as one would expect, helped reinforce the idea of God's chosen people of Israel, to which he belonged. His dream or vision, described in the Acts of the Apostles, involved a fundamental conflict between tradition and the new revelation in Jesus. Peter has a dream-vision in which a large sail comes down from heaven filled with animals that were ritually unclean for a Jew. At the same time a divine voice tells him to kill and eat them. Here is a classic example of conflict between custom and divine innovation. As this happens, Peter receives an invitation to take the Christian message to Gentiles – that is, to non-Jews. He does so and, as a result, grasps the fact that Christianity is open for all.

Dissonance

This example of a form of dissonance within an individual's religious life offers, perhaps, an early example of what some have described as cognitive dissonance, an experience in which a person's firm expectation encounters quite a different outcome and prompts either a sense of hopelessness or else some recharged effort in a new direction. Peter the Jew had followed Jesus the Jewish Rabbi and believed him to be the Christ who would deliver God's people Israel from all their trials. What had happened was that while the contemporary Jewish religious establishment had rejected this option, some Gentiles had accepted the belief that something dramatic had come about through Jesus's death and also through what many believed to be his resurrection from the dead. Certainly Peter seems to have been impelled forward through his new grasp of the situation he found himself in. At the same time, Paul had also come to see that the Gentile world would be a prime arena in which the divine spirit would now become active. So, while Peter's dream-vision is seldom spoken of as his conversion, it is not far removed from the transformed outlook associated with Paul's celebrated conversion on the road to Damascus (described below).

Change and growth

It soon became apparent to Peter and Paul that Jesus was not, for example, coming back on the clouds of heaven. It looked as though Christianity was in for a long future and that needed to be understood. And all the time Christian communities were growing and the societies within which they existed were changing too: the Roman Empire covered the Mediterranean world and much of Europe, extending out from that great sea to the colder waters of northern Europe, reaching into the north of England. So political circumstances would soon make their own mark on the growing Christian group. Roman Emperors set themselves against the Christians, who seemed to owe their primary allegiance to a heavenly leader and neither to Caesar nor to Judaism, a religion that Rome had, at times, allowed to continue with its own traditions. But the time came, in AD 70, when Rome turned even more violent and destroyed Jerusalem's great Jewish Temple and, as time went on, hunted down Christians in a series of persecutions that began to make martyrs of these brothers and sisters in faith. Just as Jesus had had his physical body crucified, so now these members of his metaphorical 'body' were being crucified or otherwise killed.

But, as the phrase has it, 'the blood of the martyrs is the seed of the Church' and Christianity was not destroyed but strengthened. Then, most remarkably, the Emperor Constantine became a Christian. In a short space of time Christianity was made the official religion of the Roman Empire. This was significant because the Roman Empire had always had some form of religious activity at its heart, often the worship of the emperor conceived of as a deity. Indeed, emperors were often viewed as divine after their deaths. Now a new kind of 'God' lay at the heart of this powerful system of human organisation. In some respects, an element of the old Roman system of apotheosis – a term that refers to the making of a god out of a human being – now came to frame the identity of Jesus.

If the earliest Christians had had to think about just who Jesus was they now thought even harder. If they had to ponder the identity of the man from the village of Nazareth in the light of their own experiences of forgiveness of sins, a power of the Spirit that seemed to come from God and was in some way associated with Jesus, and the strength of the new community that was some kind of community of Christ in which the Spirit made its power felt, now they had to think again. Through a series of special conferences, often organised under the weight of influence of the Roman Empire that was now 'Christian', a picture emerged of Jesus as a divine being. Because Christianity had emerged out of Judaism, this was no easy argument. Jews had held that God was one and Jews were certainly not polytheists. He was the one and only God who ruled over all things. He might speak through prophets and be approached through priests and even rule through kings but he could not be identified with any of them.

But now we find Christians speaking of Jesus in much the same way that Jews had spoken of God. In fact, they developed a doctrine called the doctrine of the Holy Trinity. This asserted that God was really and actually one, a belief firmly emphasising the long-standing Jewish view of monotheism, but it then went on to argue that this single deity was to be understood as being internally threefold. Accordingly, Christians were to regard God in terms of being Father, Son and Holy Spirit. Each of these was seen as vital to do justice to Christian experience. Here we see the power of experience to forge doctrine and this was an important development within early Christianity. There had been a variety of opinions in the world of the Jews and of their Mediterranean neighbours concerning divine or supernatural agents, not least over different kinds of angels and intermediary figures that spanned the gap reckoned to exist between humanity and God. But now a doctrine – that of the Holy Trinity – was taking firm shape and it would influence Christianity for the next millennium.

A Holy Trinity

This doctrine asserted that God is Three in One and One in Three. The Jewish origins of Christianity were reflected in the idea of God as one, while the Jewish Christian experience of Jesus and of the power of the Spirit that had been felt as the new community took shape yielded the notion that Jesus was also divine and so was the Spirit. Three forms of experience from ancient Israel and from the new Israel came together to mark the identity of the Christian community. Essential to this scheme was the belief that the divide between God and humanity had been bridged forever. The bonding between God's nature and human nature had become inseparably eternal in the person of Jesus. He it was, argued succeeding generations of Christians, who had both a human and a divine nature within his one being. The significance of this cannot be exaggerated. Traditionally speaking, God was different from humanity, God belonged to a different order of things; but in Jesus, these two orders found a mutual relationship. One of the Creeds (statements of belief) of the early church councils argued that Jesus was 'of one substance with the Father'. This was a kind of philosophical shorthand for saying that the real essence or nature of God was also the real essence or nature of Jesus. This was a real breakthrough because, in traditional terms, God was 'of a difference substance' from that of humanity: God was the creator and humanity was created. So to argue that Jesus, a man, born of a woman, flesh of her flesh, should be 'of one substance with the Father' – that is, with God – was a dramatic and powerful statement. Throughout Christianity's first four hundred or so years, many church leaders (often bishops) debated this and other key issues in the developing religion. Augustine of Hippo (354–430) discussed the nature of the Trinity and also argued the power of divine grace in human life over and above human effort as advocated by Pelagianism. Augustine's collection of books called *The City of God* is one important collection of Christian thought. Many arguments ended in a statement of true doctrine against heresy, with heretics being excommunicated. The ascetic form of monastic life adopted by monks allowed time for such debate and for the writing of history and observation of the world, as with the Venerable Bede (673–735) in the North of England at

Jarrow. Still, the doctrine of the divinity of Jesus remained crucial and would come to serve as a kind of keynote, a distinctive feature of later Christian thought, of what was called Incarnational and sacramental thought.

Incarnation

The Incarnation was the doctrine that God had 'become' human in Jesus. And this should not be interpreted as some kind of spirit coming to indwell a body. It was not like the older Greek idea of the human as a combination of a body and a spirit. The Christian doctrine of the Incarnation wanted to argue that Jesus of Nazareth really was human and really was divine in his very identity as one person. It did not matter how difficult this would be to interpret in any philosophical, psychological or biological way, it was a conviction of faith. And it was a conviction with consequences. For if God had taken on the human condition in the physical identity of Jesus, then it meant that God had a positive attitude towards physical matter itself. Matter, the material of this world, could now be viewed as a potential channel for a divine expression. Although we think about this expression in ritual later in this chapter, it is important to highlight here the power of this idea of God's involvement with the world. In contemporary society, many Christians speak of the world by using terms such as sacramental theology or incarnational theology. These terms describe the belief that God and the world are not strangers to each other but that God is committed to material reality and to events in the world at large. Although these terms have their origin both in the specific rituals called sacraments and in the doctrine of the Incarnation, they try to push these rites and doctrine into ever-wider fields of significance.

Sacraments

Historically speaking, by the twelfth century Catholic traditions identified seven sacraments: baptism, confirmation, Eucharist, penance, unction, ordination and marriage. Through the sixteenth century Reformation, however, most Protestants and Anglicans eliminated most of these to claim only baptism and the eucharist as sacraments. More recently still, groups such as the Quakers and the Salvation Army do not use sacraments at all.

Differences between Christian churches are instructive because they both reflect and help construct different views of the world. The more sacramental a church, the more it depends upon specialist priests and adopts distinctive rituals to access God under their control. There is a big difference, for example, between a conservative Catholic position that believes the church has the power to excommunicate someone and, technically speaking, to place them outside the arena of salvation and a group like the Quakers that embraces individuals not even claiming explicit Christian convictions. It may be that the nineteenth century witnessed the high-tide of sacramentalism in this controlling sense, both in Catholic and, for example, in Anglican thought because, from the mid-twentieth century, especially after the Roman Catholic Second Vatican Council of the 1960s, the high profile of priesthood control increasingly softened to draw out the importance of all Christian members of churches and their duties and responsibilities in the world. But, at the same time, theologians began to stress certain outcomes both of the idea of a sacramental outlook on life and of the Incarnation. So it was that a general view developed, one we can identify as sacramental and Incarnational, and this used a very wide-angled lens to view the world as a place where God was active and involved well beyond the narrow confines of church-based rituals or any strict doctrine of God becoming human in Jesus of Nazareth. One consequence of this was that many forms of art – painting, sculpture and dance, as well as architecture, drama, film and literature – came to be viewed as means of engaging with the divine.

While, in some respects, this is very far removed from the classic development of sacramental thought associated with the name of Thomas Aquinas (1225–74) in the thirteenth century, such cultural resources would probably not have been possible without it. Thomas argued the doctrine of transubstantiation. He worked with philosophical terms that described anything in terms of its 'substance' and 'accidents', meaning by 'substance' the essence or real 'inner' nature of a thing and by 'accidents' the appearance of that thing to human senses. In those terms, he described the Mass or Eucharist as a rite in which the accidents of bread and wine remained the same – bread still looked and tasted like bread and so on – but the substance changed and became the very substance of the body of Christ. Likewise, with the wine and the very blood of Christ. So, under the form of the accidents of bread and wine, the believer actually received the body and blood of Christ. So it was that this idea came to be called the doctrine of transubstantiation, meaning the change of the substance from one to another. As a doctrine, it was accepted at the Lateran Council of 1215 and more formally defined at the Council of Trent in 1551.

For someone to appreciate and accept this belief involves an almost inevitable sense of wonder and worshipful response to the rite in which the miracle of transformation took place. So it was that the rite of the Mass developed in ways that ensured that only a properly ordained priest could perform the rite and he needed to prepare himself to do so. The ritual itself involved confession of sin and the cultivation of a proper attitude or intention. The moment of the miraculous transformation was identified with the words 'this is my body' and 'this is my blood' when said by the priest in the prayer of consecration. A bell might be rung at this time and priest and people might bow or kneel to acknowledge the coming of the Lord in this special way. They then spoke of Christ's 'real presence' amongst his people. The priest, and later the people too, would eat the bread and drink the wine with a sense of devotion and with practices that aimed to ensure that no bread was dropped or wasted nor any wine spilt. Often this meant the priest would place the bread, in the form of a specially prepared wafer, onto the tongue of the faithful recipient while an attendant held a container to catch any fragments.

Other rituals grew up around the Mass, which had come to be the core rite of Catholic Christianity, as with Confession, Benediction and acts of devotion to the sacred heart of Jesus. Confession in private to a priest helped prepare people to receive the body and blood of Christ at the Mass, and was emphasised from the thirteenth century; it was also associated with the idea of the 'seal of the confessional' or the fact that priests must never disclose what they are told in confession. Benediction is a rite in which the consecrated bread or host is placed in a special container, called a monstrance, that allows the host to be seen at the centre of some design such as sun's rays extending outward. The priest held this aloft for the people to see and blessed them. He would often employ a special cloth to hold the monstrance, thus further stressing the holiness of the object that held the very body of Christ. Separate Benediction services decreased towards the close of the twentieth century or often became part of an evening Mass. The Mass itself also underwent change, especially since, after Vatican II in the 1960s, the rite that had been performed in Latin throughout the Catholic world now came to be said in local languages. A new attitude emerged that meant, for example, that the majority of ordinary worshippers now received the wine as well as the bread, which had not always been the case. This symbolised the doctrinal emphasis upon all Catholics as being the people of God without singling out priests as some extra-special group. What this brief sketch of the Eucharist shows is how ideas of holiness, of where and how God and humanity might best meet, as well as of doctrines of priesthood and of the people of God, change over time.

Churches and power

Doctrine alone tells but a small part of Christianity's history, for politics and secular power have often played their part in the development of religion. Christianity first came to power in a political sense when the Emperor Constantine, after a vision of the cross before the battle of the Milvian Bridge in 312, assigned a positive status to what was still very much a minority religious tradition, and one not generally accepted by others of Roman aristocratic standing. His new capital city of

Constantinople (now Turkey's Istanbul) served as a focus for the development of that style of Christian worship described as Orthodox (or often as Eastern Orthodox).

This alliance between political rulers and Christianity was to be repeated many times over the next two thousand years, with numerous consequences for Christian social values and ethics. Russia, for example, became a Christian domain in 988 after one of its princes converted to Orthodoxy and brought his people with him. It was, then, only for a period of just under seventy or so years under Communism in the twentieth century, that the Russian Orthodox Church did not hold sway in that country. The early twenty-first century is witnessing a resurgence of Orthodoxy (as of other forms of religion) in Russia, with that church in particular being eager to maintain an official position over and against other churches, especially those of Protestant origin.

In the Crusades of the twelfth and thirteenth centuries, believers formally adopted the sign of the cross (hence their name) to regain Christian sites in the Holy Land from Muslim hands. This was a major example of how religious attitudes affected military action and also shows the place of sacred sites within Christian consciousness. Nearly a thousand years later the same geographical area was, once more, on a Western religious agenda when, after World War I and following the Peace Treaty of Versailles, Britain was granted a Mandate for Palestine, following the collapse of the Turkish Ottoman Empire. It was decided by the British Government that the country should provide 'a national home for the Jewish people' but on the understanding that 'nothing shall be done which may prejudice the civil and religious rights of existing non-Jewish communities'. This Balfour Declaration of 1917, called after Lord Balfour, Foreign Secretary in Lloyd George's Cabinet, was influenced, some think, by Christian ideals and the cultural influence of the Bible in Britain. Others would emphasise the political reasons why Britain wanted its own influence in that part of the eastern Mediterranean. The British decided that Jerusalem would be the capital and took possession in December 1917 when General Allenby famously entered the ancient city on foot. Its first High Commissioner, from Britain, was a Jew, Sir Herbert Samuel. In May 1921 the first clash occurred between Jews and Arabs. A White Paper of May 1939 rescinded the spirit of the Balfour Declaration but was never fully implemented. Much trouble over Jewish illegal immigration led to the partition of the land into two in 1947 and the Law of Return was formalised by the new state in 1950. All this hints at how biblical history, theology and belief may come to interfuse with political decision-making. Not least does it bring us back to the Bible as a deep source of reflection in human endeavours and to the moment in history when the Bible made its first and earlier major impact upon world history at the Reformation.

The Bible and Reformation

One of the most dramatic of all changes in the history of Christianity came in what has been called the Reformation in the sixteenth century. Many streams fed into this wave of religious activity: intellectual concerns over human knowledge and a revival of interest in ancient texts and languages ran alongside political concerns and the use and abuse of religious power. Martin Luther (1483–1546), a German monk and focus of the Reformation, offers another case of Christian leaders who changed the world. His concern was with salvation as a personal experience and the way it fitted into church and social life, all under the teaching of the Bible. For him, the Bible had come alive as it taught him anew that God had acted to save men and women in the death of Jesus. Faith in this divine effort was the means of entering into a new grasp of life and a new knowledge of God. No longer could the demands of a human religious institution, the Church, be the sole foundation for authority and the means of salvation. Faith alone counted and it was rooted in God's grace. Grace cut across any human attempt at merit-making as a means of gaining salvation. Certainly the practice of indulgences was to be abolished; indulgences involved purchasing a kind of certificate from the Catholic Church that could guarantee release from penalties for sin that people suffered after death. Indulgences serve almost as a shorthand or symbol of what the Reformation was about – that salvation came from God through Christ and not from any church source, it was freely given and not earned by merit. The Reformation also opposed the use of relics (parts of the dead bodies of saints and other holy people) kept in churches that became places of pilgrimage for many people, as for example with St Cuthbert at Durham Cathedral. This often made pilgrimage churches very rich and powerful.

The Reformation opposed such practices and tried to set the Bible as the basic guide for faith and authority in Christian life and worship. Many countries now translated it into their own languages and encouraged ordinary people to read it. This was a dramatic move. The Latin Bible had been the domain of priests and scholars. Ordinary believers might hear it read but had no idea of what it said or meant. The rise of a priestly caste had reinforced the division between religious expert and the rest. Celibacy had also been required of the clergy and by about the eleventh century was a rule. This meant that all married people led a kind of second-class Christian life. The Reformation changed all this. The ordinary man and woman could read for themselves and act accordingly. To be married was no problem and Christian leaders need not follow celibacy. It was as though the life of the monastery now shifted to the home. The Jewish society out of which Christianity was born had been strongly focused on the family and Jewish leaders were expected to be married; now, after a thousand years, the Protestant religion named after its protest against the Roman form of Christianity emerged from the Reformation favouring marriage and family and would do so into the twenty-first century.

The Reformation had not been the first occasion for protest within Christianity but to date it has been the most enduring. Late in the second century, for example, the Montanists preached that the world would soon end with the new Jerusalem descending to earth and advocated a strict ascetic form of life alongside an experience of the Holy Spirit. These followers of Montanus drew a sharp distinction between their own Spirit-filled members and the more earthly members of the wider church. Many another group in later generations has reflected this emotional commitment to the early zeal of Christianity with a marked division between its members and all the rest. The Reformation, however, paralleled developments in national politics and the establishment of nation states in Europe in a complex weaving together of political and religious factors. These combined factors ensured that the Reformation had a lasting effect in the growth of Lutheranism, especially in Germany and parts of Scandinavia, of Reformed Churches in Holland and France and of Anglicanism in England. The subsequent missionary activities of all these churches led to an exporting of the reformed traditions into all parts of the world.

The Reformation highlights the importance of the Bible and its power as a source of religious material. The fact that the Bible exists has many consequences, most especially that it provides a reference point and a potential source of authority for many kinds of people. The existence of this book has caused millions of other books to be written. The universities of Europe, especially during the period of the Reformation, gained a new sense of responsibility in discussing just what the Bible was and what it had to say about life. Textual study of ancient cultures made issues of history and historical understanding of prime importance. Many other disciplines had to pay attention to the Bible and to the religion created around it. All in all, the history of Christianity is the history of the relationship between a community and a text.

Analysis

Against this briefest sketch of Christian history, we can now think of how to analyse Christianity and although we could do so in many different ways, we will take six major trends, dynamic sources that have, at various times and places, exerted transforming forces on this religion. These are Christianity's (i) fostering of individuals, (ii) creation of community, (iii) conquest of death, (iv) missionary drive and salvation, (v) elaboration of worship and (vi) complexity of organisation. These creative tendencies are always present, ready to exert themselves and affect the way the religion was developing.

Fostering of individuals

Christianity began with the single individual, Jesus of Nazareth, who probably belonged to a respectable family that might, in modern terms, be described as self-employed. They would probably have been moderately well-off and not an impoverished family in the image fostered by the Christmas story of Jesus being born in a stable. He gathered a group of disciples around him and taught a particular attitude towards God, within the context of his own Jewish culture and religious tradition. His emphasis was upon sincerity of heart in loving a God who was aware of individuals and who prized the inner conviction of people over and above any outward display of religious activity. Following a long Jewish tradition, Jesus taught the importance of justice and concern for one's fellow human beings also over and above formal religious tradition. In all this, the individual remains of prime importance. Certain of the twelve disciples then stand out as people with their own convictions, needs and doubts, and after Jesus's death several of these come into positions of leadership in a growing community of people who believe that Jesus had been raised from the dead and brought them a new sense of their own significance and worth, not least because their sins had been forgiven.

Then, alongside the disciples Peter and James, for example, there emerges the figure of Paul. He had been a much better educated man and, after a period in which he persecuted the earliest Christians because he believed them to be following a false belief, he had a kind of conversion experience in which he believed the risen Christ encountered him while he was on the road to Damascus in pursuit of Christians and now charged him to become a preacher of the message he was attacking. In the Acts of the Apostles this man now changes his name from Saul to Paul and becomes a key figure in arguing that Jesus was, in fact, the awaited Messiah who had come into the world to save people from sin and to create a group of people who should live life in a new way. At first, Paul thought that the resurrected Jesus would come again soon in a dramatic way and set up the Kingdom of God on earth. As time passed, he realised this was not going to happen and that Christians should commit themselves to a dedicated way of life on earth prior to a final resurrection that would mark the end of time as we knew it. Then, God would resurrect dead believers just as God has resurrected Jesus. With their new spiritual bodies, they would exist in God's perfect world of the future. This idea of resurrection was not new, for many Jews, including those called the Pharisees, held to it at the time of Christ; but Paul's emphasis on the resurrection gave it a new impetus by linking it closely with the central figure of Jesus and with the new community of believers that was a powerful experience in the life of the Christian group.

Time and again in subsequent Christian history, specific individuals emerge as leaders, reformers, thinkers and martyrs, each possessed of a new sense of their own self-identity as believers and feeling impelled to assist others in the Christian community to new levels of religious thought and action. In this way, the community becomes renewed over time. The Reformation has been viewed by many as a period that added significance to human individuality and prompted people to take responsibility for their own actions in life. The sociologist Max Weber in *The Protestant Ethic and the Spirit of Capitalism* in 1904 described how religious ideas influence action. Here, Protestant individuals develop a sense of responsibility before God and while knowing full well that salvation comes from God and can never be earned, still seek some way of establishing the fact of their salvation. Given the Protestant form of the doctrine of predestination – the idea that God has divided the world into two groups, one to be saved and one damned – they seek some way of assuring themselves that they are in the saved group. While in one sense they can never be sure of this, since God alone knows who lies in which category, they work at the problem indirectly. On the assumption that God blesses his people, they see their own economic flourishing as a sign of divine favour and of their membership amongst those elected to eternal life. Luther's idea of a person's 'calling' in life had taken the idea of 'vocation' to apply to anyone's profession and not simply to that of priests, monks and nuns. People needed to be faithful in their calling and this, combined with the need to know of one's salvation, led to some engaging in economic activity in careful ways that did not squander any profit but re-invested it in further financial ventures. So it was that capitalism came to be related to a Protestant worldview and to a perspective upon individualism.

Creation of community

Still, at heart, Christianity remained communal and, through the Reformation, reaffirmed the importance of the congregation of believers. The first Christian communities had been absolutely fundamental both to the success and to the meaning of Christianity, just as periods of renewal and reformation in subsequent centuries were vital for Christianity's life. It is important, however, not to take the idea of community too much for granted. Early Christianity was a constructed community rather than a naturally occurring society. It was composed of believers in Jesus as the Christ and their sense of focus on him also resulted in strong networks of relationships amongst each other, leading them to think of themselves as spiritual brothers and sisters. This community of faith came to be as significant as any community of birthright, as is reflected in one of the sayings of Jesus that anyone who loved their parents more than they loved him was not worthy to be his follower.

So it was that this community, bound together by mutual ties of brotherhood and sisterhood and by devotion to Christ as Master, was composed both of men and women, Jews and Gentiles, richer and poorer people. Some were slaves, some had been slaves and some were more highly placed in society. Unlike the secret societies of the first century, the church was not available only to men or to people of a certain social standing. In fact, its very mixed nature was thought to reflect God's acceptance of all sorts of people. Indeed, the biggest issue of all for the Jews who were the first and closest followers of Jesus was the highly problematic idea that God wished to have direct dealings not only with the Jews as his specially chosen people but with non-Jews, or Gentiles, too. God's covenant relationship with Israel was now undergoing expansion and it demanded expanded imaginations on the part of his disciples to appreciate what was happening. This was not simply because Gentiles would now come to stand alongside Jews in a single community, for it always been possible for Gentiles to convert and become associated with Jews, but was because the believing Jews themselves had a change to undergo. The Acts of the Apostles is the key text in which this double realisation of the acceptance of the Gentiles and the reorientation of Jews is set out.

And this occurred when Judaism itself received the body-blow of the destruction of the Temple at Jerusalem at the hands of the Romans. The Epistle to the Hebrews is one New Testament document that can be read as a Jewish Christian reflection on Jesus interpreted as the real high priest who conducted the business of sacrifice both in his death on the cross and by his presence in the heavenly realms beyond this earth. Christian Jews were encouraged to see that they need not be tied to any earthly temple or to the sacrifice of animals because all that might be achieved through them had been brought to an even greater conclusion in Jesus. Sociologically speaking, this Christian community possessed two great strengths: it was not tied to any single place of ritual but was free to be worldwide; and it provided an alternative family-like network of fellow believers as a support group in a world that often lacked such encouragement. And all this was happening in the Mediterranean world where business and commerce involved some people in a great degree of travel and exchanges with many others of different societies. From Jerusalem down to Egypt, along the North African coast, across to Spain and up to Ireland and Britain then over to mainland Europe, throughout much of this region the Roman Empire had its roads and channels of communication that merchants and others could use to their mutual advantage. Into this mobile society Christian individuals ventured and benefited from the communities of faith established here and there throughout the Roman Empire. The power of this Christian community can be summarised in the three ideas of faith, hope and love (I Corinthians 13: 13): faith expressed something of their sense of knowing Jesus, hope their anticipation of the future, and love the quality of relationships in which everything else was embraced.

Conquest of death

As welcome and powerful as a community can be to persons who lack social support or much status in life, the new context gains a great deal if it is driven by some idea or belief that brings energy to the relationships formed. What was this driving force? For the earliest Jewish Christians a great deal of power lay in the belief that Jesus was the Messiah, the one promised by God. Doubtless some hoped that this specially anointed one would help the Jews to be freed from the oppression of foreign military control. Others might have hoped that God would soon transform the world in some miraculous way. But irrespective of whether the early believers were drawn from Jewish or Pagan backgrounds, there was one aspect of life that could speak to them and to any others in a shared and common way – and that concerned death.

Death has long been a driving force in religions as they have sought to bring meaning to life and to the fact that it seems to end in death. Indeed, it is possible to see death-conquest as a major feature in defining world religions. And, almost always, the interest that religions have in death has contained a very definite moral dimension. As social beings, humans are almost inevitably concerned with how people live in relation to the rules of their societies. Christianity was a powerful movement because it brought together three significant factors in a way that magnified each of them: one was the power of the new community as a group of people, another was the figure of Jesus as a divine focus of action, and the third was the sense of the conquest of death. In terms of the interlinked nature of these elements, we have a community of people whose identity is rooted in the life, death and resurrection of Jesus. Social support, forgiveness of sin and a sense of overcoming the great enemy of humanity was all combined in one way of life.

Missionary drive and salvation

Some religions survive and grow on the basis of the newborn children of members. These birthright religions, such as Hinduism, Judaism, Sikhism, Jainism, Zoroastrianism and the numerous local 'primal' religions, are strongly associated with particular geographical parts of the world. They become so-called world religions only in the sense that adherents sometimes migrate and form communities across the world. Through rules of marriage, they often ensure that people stay within the boundaries of the community, boundaries that are often reinforced through various codes of dress, behaviour and diet. Conversion religions, by contrast, are typified by missionary activity and seek to bring people from many societies into their membership, especially in Christianity and Islam, though also with Buddhism to a lesser extent.

Max Müller, in the context of a lecture delivered at Westminster Abbey on 3 December 1873, drew a distinction between Non-Missionary and Missionary religions. His key point concerning the Missionary 'cluster of religions' is that 'however they may differ from each other... they share in common ... faith in themselves, they all have life and vigour, they want to convince, they mean to conquer.' (1880: 255) Müller closely identifies early Buddhism and its missionary spirit with what he sees as a 'new thought... in the history of the whole world. The recognition of a duty to preach the truth to every man, woman, and child.' (1880: 257) This idea of announcing a new truth is of crucial significance for conversion in world religions because it introduces a process of conceptual transcendence in which pre-existing ideas are asserted to be inadequate and another set of ideas is offered as a replacement. Cultural contact, especially when related to missionary endeavour, often involves such competition between explanatory schemes and one of them often comes to be relegated to an inferior status.

Elaboration of worship

Christianity's origins in Judaism deeply influence its style and mode of worship in a combination of congregational and individual forms of religious expression. Christianity reflected elements both of the synagogue and the home. Much early worship took place either in people's homes or else, for example, in the space afforded by catacombs. Within these contexts, people prayed, sang songs and heard talks about the faith. One element that came to be increasingly developed with time was a rite in which they ate bread and drank wine as a form of memorial meal, with its focus on Jesus. This rehearsed the fact that he had held a form of the Jewish Passover meal with his disciples at the very period when he was to be betrayed by one of them, days before he was killed through crucifixion.

In worship, believers turned their human attention towards God, expressing their own human inadequacy and sin whilst also proclaiming divine qualities of mercy and forgiveness expressed in salvation and rejoicing in God's power as source of the universe expressed in creation. Worship has been of enormous significance in the rise and development of Christianity for several crucial reasons. As a group activity, it has helped unite believers into strong communities, as well as affording individuals a deep sense of personal identity. In many parts of the world, local identity has become intimately aligned with Christianity or with particular denominational forms of the religion. This has had both positive and negative effects, especially when faith and patriotism have fused in forms of defensive and offensive nationalism. In quite a different way, worship was a means of taking formal doctrine and some quite abstract ideas and making them accessible to the ordinary lives of believers through hymns, songs and through the sermons and talks included within acts of worship. Music became particularly important in allowing local cultural traditions to serve as the vehicle for incoming religious ideas and in fostering change over time. Even though many Christian missions, especially in the nineteenth century, tended to export their hymns and music along with other forms of cultural habit such as dress, many Christian groups came to realise the importance of indigenous expressions of faith and fostered these, especially from the mid-twentieth century.

The imagination

Christian art, music, poetry, hymns and architecture have all sprung from the inspiration of biblical images and of church practices that have developed in close liaison with them. In many parts of the world, churches are found which not only point believers, as it were, beyond themselves to God but also bring the excitement and the sense of truth into the visual world of art and architecture. Christian architecture has marked eras of significant social involvement with religion, just as the musical compositions of over a thousand years have increasingly left an inheritance of insight into the mystery of the world, of human life and of God. It is particularly important to stress these buildings and sounds because, for the great majority of Christians throughout the ages, this is the way they have engaged with Christian belief. Formal doctrine has usually been the domain of priests and theologians even though they have sought to use illustrations from particular societies to express something of the nature of God.

Complexity of organisation

Through such cultural adaptation, as well as internal developments of Christian groups, many churches, especially the very large denominations, provided a great variety of opportunity for different kinds of people to feel at home within their boundaries.

Religion of religions: Adaptability traditions

One reason why Christianity survived and flourished in an expanding and changing world lay in its adaptability. Not being tied to a particular priestly caste, geographic area or any particular building, it had a certain freedom of movement. Wherever people met people and were able to associate in worship focused on Jesus, a church could exist. Even in the New Testament itself there is strong evidence of a variety of Christian traditions existing from the beginning. The style of spirituality present in the gospels of Matthew, Mark and Luke differs to a degree but certainly presents a different picture from that of John's gospel. If to this we add the outlooks present in the Epistle to the Hebrews or of Revelation, the last book of the Christian Bible, we can see that Christianity had a considerable pool of potential orientations from which to draw during its subsequent history.

In England at the beginning of the twenty-first century, for example, Christianity exists as a state church in the Church of England, as Roman Catholicism and as various kinds of Protestantism, such as the Baptists and Methodists. Additionally, there are distinctive groups such as the Quakers and the Salvation Army. Then there are numerous forms of the religion that are disputed by the dominant denominations, such as the Jehovah's Witnesses, Mormons, Christian Scientists and Scientologists. Within the major denominations are found other forms of difference, with some emphasising tradition, while others change for new situations, including the Charismatic movement stressing the powerful presence of the Holy Spirit, Liberal theology offering new interpretations of belief and, for example, Celtic Christianity seeking a sensitive awareness of God's presence in nature and blessings upon personal life. Yet other groups advocate the power of faith to promote health and wealth or see religion as a means of understanding and furthering particular views of human sexuality.

All this became possible because Christianity came to possess a kind of critical mass of believers during its first three hundred or so years of existence. This allowed traditions to grow and develop alongside each other. One major stream emphasised a style of leadership focused on a bishop, the central Christian leader in each major Mediterranean town or city. The bishop, surrounded by his presbyters or priests and deacons, formed one kind of hierarchical pattern of organisation. It gained much of its power from the fact that it controlled the key rituals of baptism and the regular eucharistic meal ritual, which together provided the boundary of Christian identity. But this was no static organisation and many challenges to doctrine and to church organisation within numerous forms of Christianity emerged with time. Two different ways of interpreting these developments are offered, first by a sociological classification of groups and, second, by an approach from the history of religions.

Church, sect, denomination, cult

One way of making sense of these many forms of church organisation was suggested by Ernst Troeltsch (1865–1923). This German historian of religion argued in his *Social Teachings of the Christian Churches* in 1912 that Christianity existed as a kind of interplay of two forces: one tended to compromise the faith in relation to its own cultural pressures while another rose up to protest against that accommodation and to establish the pure commitment of faith once more. Here we have the basis for his distinction between 'church' and 'sect', which together had channelled Christianity from its earliest times. He also realised that there were some who fitted neither of those types of response but who were more 'mystical'. Later scholars have developed these ideas, especially in seeing sects as protest movements, close-knit groups of people viewing themselves as brothers and sisters in Christ and set to follow a pure form of Christianity devoid of compromise. Sects often demand loyalty and proof of commitment and have the power to exclude those who do not show an exclusive commitment.

Bryan Wilson showed how Christian sects could be classified in terms of the way they viewed evil and sought to overcome it, as is the case with Conversionist sects that describe the human heart as evil and in need of salvation through a new birth brought about by the Holy Spirit. Many evangelical groups are of this kind. Revolutionist groups, by contrast, see the whole political organisation of the world as evil and think that salvation lies in a divine intervention to judge the world and condemn evil. God alone can do this, as is argued by the Jehovah's Witnesses. Reformist sects also believe the world is evil but think that men and women can work in collaboration with God to bring about its trans-formation – groups such as Moral Rearmament and, to a degree, the Mormons follow this line. Thaumaturgical or wonder-working sects take some specific behaviour or ritual as a focus and trial of faith, as in snake-handling groups or some faith-healers. Utopian sects tend to withdraw from contact with others to establish their own communities of faith, as with the Amish and Hutterites.

Richard Niebuhr, an American theologian, in his *The Social Sources of Denominationalism* in 1929 described how denominations, unlike sects, tended to reflect a degree of compromise between the world-acceptance of the church and world-rejection of the sect. Denominations often reflected a variety of group interests, as is the case with the many American denominations that continued the cultural practices of the countries from which people migrated to the USA. This was especially important in the late nineteenth and early twentieth centuries. From his theological perspective, Niebuhr felt that these community interests could easily become introverted and serve as a denial of that openness of Christianity to all people that we described above. He also saw the problem that sects had when the first generation of eager converts has to cope with the new inborn generations. This suggested that, to a degree, sects became churches once they had to educate their own children. While there is some truth to this, it is also the case that many sects have means of bringing about personal conviction and conversion in their inborn children and thereby maintain the sense of urgency and dedication in the overall membership.

In the latter part of the twentieth century it became popular to describe certain religious movements as cults, a word with very strong negative connotations. Cults are often felt to be dangerous because they separate converts from their families, make people prisoners within the group and engage in some form of brainwashing that takes away people's own sense of judgement and control. These negative accusations are seldom true but they do reflect a degree of fear felt by people in relation to freedom of choice and the maintenance of family and social order. Some countries will not even allow leaders of some religious movements to visit them lest this kind of cult activity be fostered.

History of religions: Temple and meeting place

The second form of analysis, drawn from Harold Turner's 1979 study *From Temple to Meeting House*, took up the idea of early Christianity and its relatively informal gatherings, as opposed to the much more established Jewish focus on the Temple at Jerusalem, and made the distinction between the temple and meeting house. In doing this, Turner was establishing what sociologists often call ideal types, shorthand descriptions of the essential features of some phenomenon. He chose two as a means of embracing the history of Christian gathering, the temple and the meeting house. The temple he described by the Latin phrase *domus dei*, the house of God, a place thought of as somewhere for the deity to dwell. Individuals might visit it and priests conduct their business there in relation to the abiding presence of God. In the Temple at Jerusalem, God was conceived of as, in some special way, dwelling in the holy of holies, a secret and inner place that only the high priest could enter at appropriate times and in special ways. The people who visited the Temple might come to its outer courts but not to the holiest centre. By extension from this, Turner sees some of the great churches of Christianity as functioning rather like this Temple, in that they have specially holy areas set apart for the priests and for particularly holy objects that symbolise God's near presence.

Conclusion

To describe buildings is one thing: to attempt to describe the religious outlook of individuals is quite another. In this chapter we have dealt with explicit theology and theologians but, within Christianity's broad reach, a kind of theology of religion has also developed through the historical and comparative study of religion exemplified in Ninian Smart's many books. He, along with many others, showed that it is largely for academic reasons that we make distinctions between, for example, the economic, political, domestic, religious and leisure aspects of life even though, in practice, these factors merge into each other as people live their lives and societies take their path through history. No single word summarises this process of individual and communal life within society influenced by the internal aspects of creativity and strife and by the external factors of world events derived from other societies and from the natural world. Suffice it to say that religion is an extremely complex phenomenon whose kaleidoscopic variety of forms in different peoples demands more than any one theology of religion.

Further reading

Bowker, John (1987), *Licensed Insanities*, London: Darton, Longman and Todd.
Davies, Douglas J. (2002), *Death, Ritual and Belief*, 2nd ed., London: Continuum.
Grant, G. M. (1896), *Religions of the World*, London: A. and C. Black.
Huxley, T. H. (1889), 'Agnosticism', *The Nineteenth Century*, CXLIV, February.
Jordan, L. H. (1905), *Comparative Religion*, Edinburgh, T. and T. Clark.
Müller, Max (1880), *Chips from a German Workshop*, London: Longmans, Green and Co.
Müller, Max (1898), *Natural Religion*, London: Longmans, Green and Co.
Niebuhr, H. Richard (1929), *The Social Sources of Denominationalism*, New York: Harper and Row.
Smart, Ninian (1979), *The Phenomenon of Christianity*, London: Collins.
Turner, H. W. (1979), *From Temple to Meeting House: The Phenomenology and Theology of Places of Worship*, The Hague: Mouton.

Questions

1. How important do you think the conquest of death is when trying to construct a definition of a world religion?

2. What advantages and problems do you see in talking about Peter's 'conversion' in the way we do here?

3. How do you see the Christian idea of the Holy Trinity in terms of the monotheism of Judaism and Islam?

4. Max Weber stressed the relationship between belief (or idea) and action in religions. What examples can you give of that connection? Is it the same kind of link as that between doctrine and ethics?

Islam

Hugh Goddard

Introduction

Uniquely among the major religious traditions of the world, Islam derives its name not from a human teacher or a people or a geographical part of the world but rather from its central theological concept, as the meaning of the Arabic word 'islam' is simply 'submission', submission to God or, to use the Arabic word for God, Allah. The Arabic word 'muslim' is then simply someone who practises this submission, so that from the point of view of grammar, 'muslim' is technically the active participle of 'islam'. In the proper Islamic understanding, 'submission' is understood not passively, in the sense of resignation, or even fatalism, but rather actively, in the sense of 'making to submit', so that Allah, the Creator and Judge of the Universe, is to have everything on earth brought into submission to Him, a task which is the central vocation of the Muslim community as it seeks to practise Islam.

Having said that, Islam, like almost every other religious tradition, has developed and evolved over the centuries so that emphases have varied in different generations, and differences and variations in the expression of Islam have grown up in different areas of the Islamic world. The central theme of Islamic teaching and practice throughout, however, has consistently been that of submission to Allah.

The main language of Islam is Arabic, and many Islamic names and technical terms are also therefore originally Arabic ones. Since Arabic is a language with its own distinct alphabet, there are a number of Arabic sounds and letters which have no direct equivalent in the Roman/Latin alphabet used in most Western languages. The majority of the distinctive Arabic letters do at least have a close equivalent in the Roman alphabet, so that Arabic has two letters which are closely related to each of the Roman letters d, h, s, t and z, which makes it difficult to make clear which of the two Arabic letters is being referred to when translating Arabic names into Roman letters. There are two Arabic letters, however, that have no equivalent in the Roman alphabet and these are usually represented as follows: the Arabic letter 'hamza' becomes ' (Roman apostrophe, or single closing quotation mark), which is pronounced rather like a hyphen, or a short pause, while the Arabic letter 'ain' becomes ' (Roman single opening quotation mark). This is one of the most difficult Arabic letters for non-Arabic speakers to pronounce, with most language text books resorting to explaining it as 'a constriction of the throat' or 'a strangled sound'. For our purposes, it is simply important to remember that two different Arabic letters are represented by these two signs and that they should not be confused.

Origins

The geographical origins of the Muslim community lie in Arabia, until recently a relatively remote and inaccessible region of the world as a result of its inhospitable climate. Arabia was never conquered by any of the great empires of the ancient world and although in the Christian era some of its border regions began to be influenced by the neighbouring powers, the (Zoroastrian) Sassanian Persian Empire to the East and the (Christian) Byzantine Empire to the West, its heartlands remained comparatively isolated.

As regards its social organisation, Arabia before the establishment of Islam was essentially a tribal society, with each tribe taking its name from its mythical ancestor and providing the essentials of mutual support for its members. Some tribes were nomadic, moving around with their flocks, while others were settled in the various oasis towns of the area. Some tribes and some oasis settlements had an extensive involvement in the network of trade routes which criss-crossed Arabia for the purpose of transporting high-value luxury goods such as spices, perfumes and incense from the southern regions of Arabia (known today as the Yemen) to the Fertile Crescent to the north.

It was in one of the oasis towns on the western side of Arabia, Mecca, that the key proclaimer of the message of Islam, Muhammad, was born, somewhere around 570 CE.

Key dates in the career of Muhammad

c. 570	Born in Mecca
610	Call to be a prophet
622	Hijra (migration) from Mecca to Yathrib/Medina
632	Death

Brought up as an orphan as a result of the death of his father before he was born, and of his mother when he was aged about six, Muhammad himself became a merchant. According to the early Islamic accounts of his life, it was through his participation in trading expeditions that he visited neighbouring countries such as Syria and had a number of encounters with both Jews and Christians, the former of whom were present in Arabia in significant numbers but the latter of whom were rather fewer and far between. A consequence of all of this was that he seems to have developed some unease with both the social and spiritual condition of his home town, which led him to develop the habit of going out of the city occasionally in order to meditate in a nearby cave. There, in 610, he had some kind of climactic spiritual experience that he initially interpreted as being a sign of madness but that he later came to understand as being some kind of call or commissioning from Allah to be a prophet.

> *Muhammad's call to prophethood*
>
> Recite: In the name of your Lord who created,
> created humanity from a blood-clot.
> Recite: And your Lord is the Most Generous,
> Who taught by the Pen,
> Taught humanity that he knew not.
>
> Qur'an 96: 1–5

Prior to the time of Muhammad, Arabia had been a fundamentally polytheistic society, with the population worshipping many gods and goddesses, including both physical objects on earth and in the heavens and various personifications of deities. Partly under Jewish and Christian influence, and partly as a result of quite independent development, however, a belief had grown up in some areas that there was either a supreme god, Allah, or indeed that Allah was the only God, and after his dramatic spiritual experience Muhammad became convinced that it was Allah who had called him to prophethood.

Muhammad therefore began to proclaim the message he understood to have been given to him by Allah, in Mecca. The fundamental elements of the message were monotheism – that there is only one God – and the ethical consequences of that belief, namely to cease exploitation of the poor and vulnerable members of society, such as widows and orphans. Some Meccans accepted the message and joined Muhammad's community, while others were antagonistic. At first, Muhammad experienced no more than heckling and ostracism but this gradually developed into more active opposition, even persecution. In 622, with seventy of his followers, Muhammad abandoned his home town in order to migrate to the neighbouring town of Yathrib, to which he had been invited in order to mediate in a dispute between the different tribes of the town.

In Yathrib, Muhammad was able to graduate from being a prophet in the sense of being the bearer of a religious message to being a prophet in the sense of a statesman, someone like Moses in the Hebrew Scriptures, who led a political community and was able to use all the resources of that community to bring about the acceptance of his message. After his migration, armed conflict broke out with the Meccans, and there were several battles between the Muslims and the Meccans, with the honours at first being roughly even but with the latter eventually gaining the upper hand. In 630, after a series of diplomatic negotiations, Muhammad re-entered Mecca as its ruler. He died two years later but by then most of Arabia had come to accept his rule, and the previously fractured tribal society of Arabia was thus, for the first time ever, united under one ruler.

The Opening Chapter of the Qur'an
(in Arabic, the Fatiha)

In the Name of God, the Merciful, the Compassionate.

Praise belongs to God, the Lord of all Being,
The All-merciful, the all-Compassionate,
The Master of the Day of Doom.

You only we serve; to you alone we pray for succour.
Guide us in the straight path,
The path of those whom you have blessed,
Not of those against whom you are wrathful,
Nor of those who are astray.

Qur'an 1: 1–9

Throughout this twenty-two year period, Muhammad had continued to receive messages which he understood to be revelations from God. These revelations were memorised by his followers, or sometimes written down by them, and after his death they were collected together and compiled into the text of the Qur'an, which literally means 'recitation', the record of all that Muhammad was commanded by God to recite. Once transferred from an oral medium to a written one, these messages became the scripture of Islam, consisting of some 120,000 words, or roughly the same length as the Christian New Testament.

At the heart of Muhammad's message as contained within the Qur'an was a rigorous insistence on worshipping only the one true God, Allah, concerning whom much detail was provided in the different revelations.

Some Qur'anic teaching about God
(the so-called 'Throne' verse)

God
There is no god but He,
The Living, the Everlasting.

> Slumber seizes Him not, nor sleep;
> To Him belongs
> All that is in the heavens and the earth.
> Who is there that shall intercede with Him
> Save by His leave?
> He knows what lies before them
> And what is after them,
> And they comprehend not anything of His knowledge
> Save such as He wills.
> His Throne comprises the heavens and earth;
> The preserving of them oppresses Him not;
> He is the All-high, the All-glorious.
>
> Qur'an 2: 255

God is described in the Qur'an as both the Creator, that is the origi-nator of all that exists, and the Judge, the end point of all that exists, and it is for this reason that how human beings behave is a matter of vital significance. All created beings are described as being accountable to God and it is in the light of this fact that humans are called upon to repent. The Qur'an has thus been aptly described as being a supreme example of prophecy, calling as it does for its hearers and readers to believe in one God and behave appropriately to that belief.

Core beliefs

On the basis of the teaching of the Qur'an as a whole, traditional under-standings of Islam have often suggested that there are five main core beliefs, on the basis of summaries found in verses such as the following:

> *A Qur'anic summary of Muslim belief*
>
> O believers, believe in God and His Messenger
> And the Book He has sent down on His Messenger
> And the Book which He sent down before.

Whoso disbelieves in God and His angels
And His Books, and His Messengers,
And the Last Day, has surely gone astray into far error.

Qur'an 4: 136

Clearly the core beliefs referred to in the first, positive, half of the verse (God, His Messenger (that is, Muhammad), the Book sent down on Muhammad (that is, the Qur'an), and the Book sent down before (usually understood as the scriptures sent down on such earlier prophets as Moses and Jesus)) are slightly different from those referred to in the second, negative, half (God, His angels, His Books, His Messengers and the Last Day), but if the lists in the two halves of the verse are combined into one, this presents the following scheme of the core beliefs of Islam:

Five core Muslim beliefs

God
Angels
Messengers (especially Muhammad)
Books (especially the Qur'an)
The Last Day

Muslims are thus called upon to be monotheists, to believe in and worship only one God; to believe in angels, spiritual rather than physical beings, created by God, and some good and some evil; to believe in messengers sent by God at different times and in different places to preach the same basic prophetic message of ethical monotheism, with Muhammad as the final messenger; to believe in books, the scriptures given to at least some of the prophets to record their messages, again with the Qur'an as the final book; and to believe in the Last Day, the day of judgement, when all created beings will be compelled to give account of themselves to God.

Very importantly, this faith that Muhammad proclaimed was not presented as being a new faith; rather it was presented as being a restoration of an earlier monotheistic faith, as practised by Abraham and others, that had subsequently been corrupted by distortions. In particular, according to the Qur'an, both the Jews and the Christians, who claimed to be the true descendants of Abraham, had introduced deviations: the Jews had claimed that they alone were God's chosen people and the Christians had lapsed from a true monotheism by adopting certain metaphysical ideas from the Greeks and teaching that Jesus Christ was an incarnation of God, God in human form, which, according to the Qur'an, could only be a diminution of monotheism. The message of Muhammad was not therefore, according to the Qur'an, a new one but rather the restoration of an earlier one: Abraham, Muhammad proclaimed, was a Muslim, someone who submitted to God, and his faith was to be restored in the faith of Islam.

The early history of the community

After the unexpected death of Muhammad – although he had been ill, there was no indication that the illness was life-threatening – the Muslim community selected leading figures from within its ranks to serve as successors to Muhammad as leader of the community. None of these ever laid claim to have succeeded to Muhammad's prophetic status, as it was generally believed that he was the last or 'seal' of the prophets, but they did bear the responsibilities of administrative and political leadership, being described either as *khalifa* (compare the English word caliph, literally meaning successor), or as *amir al-mu'minin* (literally 'commander of the faithful'), indicating respectively their governmental and military roles. Four caliphs were almost universally accepted by the Muslim community as being both politically legitimate and exemplary in their personal conduct, and these together are usually referred to as the 'rightly-guided caliphs'.

The four 'rightly-guided caliphs'

Abu Bakr	632–634
'Umar	634–644
'Uthman	644–656
'Ali	656–661

It was also during this period that the Muslim community had to adjust not only to the ending of revelation and the voice of prophecy but also to the personal absence of Muhammad. One way in which this process was made easier was by members of the community recalling and then compiling records of their recollections of Muhammad's own sayings (as distinct from the revelations of the Qur'an) and example, together with the sayings and practice of the other members of the early Muslim community, where appropriate. These recollections took the form of hadiths (literally sayings), and a great number of these hadiths quickly entered into circulation.

An example of a hadith

'A'isha [one of Muhammad's wives] reported that Harith ibn Hisham [one of Muhammad's early companions] asked the Messenger of Allah: 'O Messenger of Allah! How does revelation come to you?' The Messenger of Allah said: 'Sometimes it comes to me like the ringing of a bell and that is the hardest on me, and then he departs from me and I retain in memory what he says; and sometimes the Angel comes to me in the likeness of a man and speaks to me and I retain in memory what he says.'

'A'isha said: 'And I saw him when revelation came down upon him on a severely cold day, then it departed from him and his forehead dripped with sweat.'

From the Hadith collection of al-Bukhari

Since the human memory is not infallible, and some early Muslims were not immune from the temptation to make up hadiths to suit their own particular purposes, it was not long before problems began to arise concerning hadiths which contradicted each other or were dismissed as fraudulent by other members of the community. Methods were quickly evolved to address these problems, however, usually involving careful study of the genealogies or 'chains of transmission' of particular sayings and the character of the individuals named in those genealogies. By the ninth century, however, a considerable amount of effort had been devoted to the assessment and classification of the many hadiths in circulation, and the result was the production of approved collections of true or reliable hadiths. Six such collections were compiled during the ninth century and for the majority of Muslims these provide a supplementary source of guidance to that contained in the Qur'an, which is known as the Hadith, or Tradition.

The six collectors of Hadith (Tradition)

al-Bukhari	d. 870
Muslim	d. 875
Abu Da'ud	d. 888
al-Nasa'i	d. 915
al-Tirmidhi	d. 892
Ibn Maja	d. 896

In addition to their use as the building blocks of the Hadith, hadiths also formed the basis of two other important types of early Islamic literature, the sira or biography of the Prophet, and tafsir, literally explanation or commentary on the Qur'an. The first of these is important because the Qur'an itself provides very little detail about the life of Muhammad, consisting as it does of the messages he proclaimed and thus hardly focusing on the messenger at all. So for the biography of the prophet the Muslim community relies on the accounts given in the form of hadiths by his earliest companions, and then collected together and systematised by early Muslims such as Ibn Ishaq (d. 767). The second, tafsir, is then important because however authoritative the Qur'an was taken to be as the record of God's revelations to Muhammad, there was not always complete agreement as to what it meant. So here the opinions of the early Muslims, who were sometimes able to record what Muhammad had said that the words meant, or otherwise to put forward the interpretations of particularly pious or learned Muslims, again formed the building blocks for the most influential commentaries on the Qur'an.

Tafsir (Qur'an interpretation):
Five important commentators on the Qur'an

al-Tabari	d. 923
al-Zamakhshari	d. 1143
Fakhr al-din Razi	d. 1209
al-Baydawi	d. 1286
al-Suyuti	d. 1505

While this process of the collecting and compilation of the Hadith was unfolding, the political development of the Muslim community had been proceeding at a rapid pace too. The four 'rightly-guided caliphs' succeeded in holding the young community of Muslims together and indeed it was not long before they succeeded in enlarging the extent of the area under their political control. Large areas of the Middle East previously under Byzantine Christian rule and Sassanian Persian rule were conquered, including Palestine, Syria, Iraq, Egypt and Iran, but it is important to keep in mind that, at first, no attempt was made to convert the conquered peoples to the faith of Islam. As long as they were prepared to accept Islamic rule, they were allowed to retain their ancestral faith and so, initially at least, the expansion of the early Muslim state did not involve large numbers of people joining the Muslim religious community.

The Islamic conquests

636	Syria
637	Iraq
641	Egypt
642	Iran
667	expansion into Central Asia
670	North Africa
711	Spain
713	expansion into Indus Valley
732	battle of Tours (furthest expansion into Europe)

The rule of the fourth 'rightly-guided caliph', 'Ali, was not universally accepted as legitimate and during his five-year rule a civil war broke out concerning the question of succession to the position of caliph. The victor in this conflict, Mu'awiya, succeeded in establishing a dynasty and the institution of the caliphate remained within his Umayyad family for the best part of a century, until 750. Mu'awiya also moved the capital of the Islamic state from Yathrib, which had been Muhammad's political headquarters and where he had died, to Damascus, and this represented a significant shift in the centre of gravity of the Muslim state, from Arabia to the former Byzantine province of Syria. In 750, following an uprising against Umayyad rule, power was transferred to another dynasty, the 'Abbasid dynasty, who based their power partly on the fact that their ancestor, 'Abbas, was an uncle of Muhammad. The 'Abbasids also moved the capital of their state, this time to a new city, Baghdad, which they founded in Iraq, and again this shift brought about some significant changes in the organisation of the Islamic state, particularly since before the coming of Islam Iraq had been a part of the Sassanian Persian Empire, and so one consequence of the move to Baghdad was the increasing influence of Persian ideas and culture within the Islamic world.

Some significant Umayyad caliphs in Damascus (661–750)

Mu'awiya	661–680
'Abd al-Malik	685–705

Some significant 'Abbasid caliphs in Baghdad (750–1258)

Harun al-Rashid	786–808
al-Ma'mun	813–833

Acts of worship

Despite all these changes in both the size of the Islamic state and the development of its religious thought, a number of factors served to help to preserve the unity of the Islamic community. Most important amongst these were the five acts of worship, commonly known as the five pillars of Islam, which were common to almost all Muslims everywhere and which have remained basically unchanged in form throughout the whole of subsequent Muslim history.

The acts of worship in Islam
(or the five 'pillars' of Islam)

1. The declaration of faith (shahada)
2. Prayer (salat)
3. Charity (zakat)
4. Fasting (sawm) in the month of Ramadan
5. Pilgrimage (hajj) to Mecca

The first of these is the shahada, or declaration of faith, which is a simple creed consisting of two statements only: that there is only one God and that Muhammad is the messenger of God. The full wording in Arabic is *ashhadu an la ilaha illa allah, wa ashhadu anna muhammadan rasul allah*, which literally means 'I declare that there is no god except God, and I declare that Muhammad is the messenger of God.'

As regards the origin of this declaration, the gist of each of the two phrases is found separately, and repeated often, in the Qur'an but the precise wording of the declaration is based upon the Hadith. The importance of the shahada cannot be exaggerated, as it is a key element in the education of Muslim children, providing as it does a succinct summary of the two central elements of Muslim belief, and it is often used in public worship. Additionally, the saying of the shahada three times with genuine intent in the presence of two witnesses is sufficient to make someone a member of the Muslim community, so it is a crucial element in the process of conversion to Islam.

The second act of worship is salat – prayer, or literally 'bowing down' – which a Muslim should ideally perform five times daily, at dawn, noon (that is, the literal middle of the day, halfway between sunrise and sunset), mid afternoon, sunset and dusk, facing towards Mecca and using a series of words and bodily actions which express both physically and mentally the submission of the Muslim to Allah. In the Muslim world, a public summons to prayer is broadcast from mosques in the form of the adhan, or 'call to prayer', but today modern technology can also help Muslims recall when it is time to pray, wherever they are, through the use of text messages which can be received on mobile phones.

The words of the adhan (call to prayer)

God is most great.
I declare that there is no god except God.
I declare that Muhammad is the messenger of God.
Come to prayer.
Come to salvation/success (falah).*
God is most great.
There is no god except God.

*In the dawn prayer, the phrase 'Prayer is better than sleep' is inserted at this point.

As regards the precise form of salat, physical ablution or washing of the parts of the body which are exposed to the air (face, hands and feet) is performed as a preparation, both physical and symbolic, for prayer, and then the prayer ritual, which usually last around ten minutes, is performed. The words used consist of a series of phrases expressing praise to God, including the Fatiha (opening chapter) of the Qur'an, and seeking God's forgiveness and blessing both upon the individual Muslim and on the Muslim community as a whole. The action is essentially one of prostration before God, so that Muslims' foreheads physically touch the ground in order to express their islam to God. Words and actions thus combine as a demonstration of the principles of the faith.

The third act of worship, zakat – charity or the giving of alms but literally meaning 'purification' – involves the Muslim in the giving of a proportion on his or her wealth, usually 2.5 per cent, as an act of charity for the benefit of the poor and the less fortunate. It is significant that in Islam the calculation of how much should be given in zakat is based not upon income but on the entirety of a person's material possessions. If taken seriously, this clearly has significant implications for the rich, as well as having a considerable effect as regards the redistribution of wealth within society as a whole.

The fourth act of worship, sawm, involves the Muslim in fasting, abstaining from both food and drink between dawn and sunset during one month of the Muslim calendar, the month of Ramadan. Ramadan is the ninth month of the Muslim calendar, which is a lunar calendar consisting of twelve months of either twenty-eight or twenty-nine days; this makes the Muslim year some ten or eleven days shorter than the more widely used solar calendar, and has the effect that Ramadan does not fall at the same time of year in the Western (or Common Era) calendar.

According to the Hadith, Ramadan was chosen by Muhammad as the month of fasting for the community because the first revelation of the Qur'an (96: 1–5) was received on the night of 27th Ramadan. As regards the practice of fasting today, if Ramadan falls in the summer in hot parts of the world, such as the Middle East, it is not hard to see how onerous a requirement sawm is, but it is also demanding in more temperate climates, since here, even if temperatures are cooler, the period of time between dawn and sunset is much longer, so that for Muslims living in countries such as Britain the period of fasting if Ramadan falls in June may be as long as twenty hours.

Prayer times in London					
	Dawn	Noon	Mid-afternoon	Sunset	Dusk
21 June	02.31	13.02	17.25	21.21	23.33
21 December	06.36	11.59	13.37	15.53	17.21

The last of the acts of worship is then the obligation upon all Muslims who are physically and financially able to make the hajj, or pilgrimage, to Mecca once in their lifetime. Currently, over two million Muslims per year undertake the hajj, which takes place in the twelfth month of the Muslim calendar and comes to its climax on the tenth day of that month. In Mecca, pilgrims participate in a series of rituals such as walking around the Ka'ba (the ancient shrine of the city and now the point towards which Muslims turn in their prayers each day); running from one hill to another near to the Ka'ba; processing to a mountain (Mount Arafat, just outside the city) in order to spend a day in meditation and prayer; throwing stones at some concrete pillars in the town of Mina; and, at the end of the hajj, slaughtering a sheep or goat as a sacrifice. These rituals in part bear historical significance, involving pilgrims in re-enacting either certain events in the career of Muhammad or certain stories told in the Qur'an concerning Abraham, and in part have a symbolic and spiritual significance, indicating such things as the determination to flee evil (the running and the stoning), preparation for the Day of Judgement (the standing at Mount Arafat), and the willingness to make sacrifices for God (the slaughter of the sheep or goat, which also commemorates Abraham's willingness to sacrifice his son – see Genesis 22).

All of these acts of worship are thus intended to facilitate and encourage the submission of the whole of life to God. As well as the fundamental declaration of faith, prayer five times each day, the giving of zakat perhaps once a month, fasting for a month each year and then the once-in-a-lifetime experience of the hajj are all intended to achieve this aim, and it is important to remember therefore that for pious Muslims worship is not restricted to these five acts; rather the whole of life is worship, including work and all the other details of personal and community life, and the acts of worship are intended to provide a framework within which the whole of life can be submitted to God.

The Muslim calendar also provides a framework for this and each year it contains two major festivals that provide the opportunity for celebration by the community as a whole. These are the 'id al-fitr (literally, Feast of the Breaking of the Fast), which takes place at the end of Ramadan, and the 'id al-adha (literally, Feast of the Sacrifice), which takes place at the climax of the hajj when, all over the Muslim world, Muslims join with the pilgrims in Mecca in sacrificing a sheep or a goat.

Theological debates

All of these duties served, and serve, to unite Muslims. Other factors, however, have contrived to produce a degree of diversity, and even divisions, within the Muslim community. In the early centuries of Islam, as the geographical size of the Islamic state increased and as at least some of its members encountered representatives of other religious traditions, a number of theological questions were fiercely debated and sometimes came close to dividing the Muslims.

The earliest of these debates centred on the question of the relationship between free will and predestination. Are human beings autonomous, in the sense that they can make their own independent choices on the basis of their free will, or are all human actions predestined by God? Support for both points of view could be found in the Qur'an, which on the one hand called on human beings to repent, suggesting that they had a choice of whether to do so or not, and yet on the other also described God as all-knowing, all-powerful and even 'the compeller', thus implying that, whatever their perceptions to the contrary, human beings' actions were actually brought about, predestined, by God. On this basis, different schools of thought grew up within the Muslim community, some emphasising those parts of the Qur'an that seemed to support the idea of free will and some stressing Qur'anic verses which suggested divine predestination. During the ninth century, a school of theologians known together as the Mu'tazila grew up and made attempts to systematise the message of the Qur'an using logic and reason, suggesting that the answer to this question must be that human beings possessed free will, for if they did not, God would be unjust: how could He predestine human beings to perform evil actions and then punish them for those actions?

Other Muslim thinkers, however, rejected the conclusions of the Mu'tazila, either preferring to lay their emphasis on other parts of the Qur'an that laid more stress on God's omnipotence and power, or rejecting the Mu'tazila's readiness to use rational criteria in argument. Some suggested that the Qur'anic text needed to be taken absolutely literally, 'without asking how', rather than being subjected to some external criterion such as reason. After lengthy debates, the main body of the Muslim community, influenced by one of its greatest theologians, al-Ash'ari, adopted a kind of middle way, suggesting that ultimately all human actions did indeed come from God, so that He can indeed be described as the author of all things, yet human beings nevertheless do acquire the responsibility for their actions along the way, so that they can justly be judged by God for what they have done.

Other significant theological questions hotly debated within the Muslim community concerned such things as the attributes of God and the status of the Qur'an. As regards the attributes, the central question was essentially 'what is God like?' The Qur'an, on the one hand, asserts the greatness and incomparability of God, in other words his transcendence; on the other hand, it also asserts his nearness to human beings and sometimes describes God in rather physical terms, so that He is stated to have hands, feet, eyes and ears.

Two Qur'anic statements about God

He is God, One,
God, the Everlasting Refuge,
Who has not begotten, and has not been begotten,
And equal to Him is not anyone.

Qur'an 112: 1–4

We indeed created humanity; and We know
what his soul whispers within him,
and We are nearer to him than the jugular vein.

Qur'an 50: 16

How were these verses to be understood? Is God in some way like human beings, or is this to succumb to the danger of anthropomorphism, making God in the image of humanity? The question was keenly debated, with some theologians such as the Mu'tazila suggesting that the Qur'anic references to God's hands and eyes should be understood metaphorically, so that God did not literally have attributes, and some of their opponents arguing that, on the contrary, the Qur'an needed to be understood absolutely literally – if the Qur'an says God has hands, then God has hands. Again, the main body of the community eventually adopted a mediating position, holding the view that God does have attributes but they are not like human attributes.

The status of the Qur'an was another hotly contested question: was the Qur'an created, coming into being in the lifetime of Muhammad as the revelations were given to him by God, or was it rather uncreated, pre-existent with God even before its being sent down to Muhammad? The Mu'tazila argued that the first point of view must be correct, since to suggest that the Qur'an might be uncreated was to run the risk of having two gods; the Qur'an must therefore, they argued, be subordinate to God, created by Him. But their opponents argued that this was to downplay the status and authority of the scripture. If it was uncreated, having always existed with God, it could not be argued with, as those seeking to suggest that it was created were trying to do. In the time of the caliph al-Ma'mun, between 813 and 833, the power of the state was deployed to enforce belief in the created Qur'an within the Muslim community but, as is usually the case with such inquisitorial methods, this proved counter-productive, and the main body of the Muslim community came to believe in the uncreated status of the Qur'an, with the proviso, formulated by al-Ash'ari, that this statement applied to the primordial or original Qur'an that existed in God's presence, rather than to the physical texts of the scripture which exist on earth.

Significant students of kalam (theology)

The Mu'tazila	ninth century
al-Ash'ari	d. 935
al-Maturidi	d. 941
Ibn Hazm	d. 1064
al-Ghazali	d. 1111
Ibn Taimiyya	d. 1328

Al-Ash'ari was thus perhaps the most influential theologian of medieval Islam, to the extent that later generations regarded him as having founded a school of Ash'ari kalam (theology); but his was not the only such school, and although it became the dominant one at the western end of the Islamic world, another, tracing its genealogy back to his near contemporary al-Maturidi, was more influential in Central Asia and in the eastern half of the Muslim world. Moreover, these two figures, authoritative as they came to be, did not solve all the theological issues confronted by the Muslim community and later theologians such as Ibn Hazm in Spain, al-Ghazali in Iraq and Iran, and Ibn Taimiyya in Syria each developed their own ideas, sometimes within the framework established by al-Ash'ari and al-Maturidi but sometimes very definitely in opposition.

The development of law

Theological debates were paralleled by developments in the field of law. In various regions of the Islamic state differences arose over questions of behaviour and conduct, partly as a result of the different legal frameworks which had existed in different provinces before the coming of Islam, and partly because of the different opinions of legal scholars and experts. This whole area was the subject matter of the Shari'a, literally meaning 'path' but usually used in a technical sense to refer to the whole tradition of Islamic law. The Shari'a, as the code of behaviour to be followed by all Muslims, was based first on the Qur'an and second on the Hadith, recording as it did the example of Muhammad and the earliest Muslims. This much was pretty universally agreed but beyond that there was not such a great degree of unanimity: how much authority could be given to the subsequent reasoning of Muslim scholars? What was to be done when they disagreed with each other, as they sometimes did, profoundly? And was there any role for the community as a whole in deciding on the appropriate patterns of behaviour?

Four significant thinkers concerning Shari'a (law)

Abu Hanifa	(Iraq)	d. 767
Malik ibn Anas	(Medina)	d. 796
al-Shafi'i	(Iraq and Egypt)	d. 820
Ahmad ibn Hanbal	(Iraq)	d. 855

Again, as on theological questions, vigorous debate took place and the result was that, for most Muslims, the opinions of legal experts were recognised as having some legitimacy but within closely defined limits, so that no overt rejection of the clear pronouncements of either the Qur'an of the Hadith was permissible; and where a consensus emerged, ideally of the Muslim community as a whole but in practice among the legal scholars themselves, then these agreed points did become binding on all Muslims. For most Muslims therefore the Shari'a came to be seen as having four foundations: the Qur'an, the Hadith, the ijma' (consensus) of the community and qiyas (analogy) – that is, arguing by analogy from the three other already-existing sources of guidance. Opportunity for the free use of reason was thus fairly tightly controlled.

The four foundations of the Shari'a
(Islamic Law)

1.   Qur'an
2.   Hadith (Tradition)
3.   Ijma' (consensus)
4.   Qiyas (analogy)

While these four foundations came to be accepted by the overwhelming majority of legal scholars, there were still differences among them concerning the relative weight that was to be ascribed. For this reason, different law schools grew up in different parts of the Islamic world, each with their own distinctive emphasis.

The four schools of Islamic law			
Madhab (school)	Founder	Region where dominant	Distinguishing feature
Hanafi	Abu Hanifa	Middle East and Indian subcontinent	Freer early use of reason
Maliki	Malik ibn Anas	North and West Africa	Stress on Hadith (tradition)
Shafi'i	al-Shafi'i	East Africa and South-East Asia	Stress on qiyas (analogy)
Hanbali	Ahmad ibn Hanbal	Sa'udi Arabia and Kuwait	First two foundations only

The most widespread school, the Hanafi, is the one that, in the early period to a great extent and in later periods to some extent, has allowed the greatest freedom of interpretation to the legal scholars and for this reason it has been the school favoured by many political leaders, allowing them more discretion in the legal field. The Maliki school, by contrast, lays much more emphasis on Hadith and particularly on the example of the earliest Muslim community in Medina, as recorded by the founder of the school, Malik ibn Anas. The Shafi'i school then tried to mediate between the two, producing its own synthesis by taking up the best features of both but seeking to moderate their more extreme features. The Hanbali school, in a sense the odd one out of the four in that it only recognises two sources of law, the Qur'an and the Hadith, as authoritative, is sometimes used as a vehicle of protest against the opinions of the other three schools.

The purpose of the Shari'a was to provide comprehensive guidance to the Muslim community for all areas of life and help Muslims to bring every area of life into submission to the will of God. Thus, not only matters of religious practice but also matters of personal status (such as marriage and inheritance) and matters of social, economic and political importance were all discussed and included within the sphere of the law. The stipulations of the Shari'a were not always implemented in practice, however, either by individual Muslims, who inevitably varied in their degree of piety, or in the Muslim community as a whole, where different Muslim societies and rulers also differed in the degree to which they were prepared to take the stipulations of the Shari'a seriously.

Philosophical discussion

Another matter of dispute in the early Muslim community was the admissability or otherwise of studying Greek philosophy and other non-Islamic subjects. For some Muslims, if the Qur'an was the word of God then it was the primary source of all human knowledge and the thoughts of philosophers and scientific investigators were of little, if any, value, particularly if they lived before the revelation of the Qur'an and were influenced by the ideas and practices of other religious traditions that may not even have been monotheistic. For other Muslims, however, there was great value in studying such thinkers; even if some of their ideas seemed to clash with Islamic teaching, that did not mean that the whole of their system of thought was invalidated.

Thus, in the ninth century, particularly in Baghdad, the capital of the Islamic state at that time, a movement grew up devoted to the translation, study and discussion of the works of Greek philosophy and science.

Al-Kindi on the study of Greek philosophy and science

We should not be ashamed to acknowledge truth and to assimilate it from whatever source if comes to us, even if it is brought to us by former generations and foreign peoples. For him who seeks the truth there is nothing of higher value than truth itself; it never cheapens or abases him who reaches for it, but enables and honours him.

From the Preface to his *Metaphysics* (Walzer 1962: 12)

The Islamic philosophers discussed many of the same themes as the theologians, including such questions as the attributes of God, but whereas theologians such as the Mu'tazila gave primary importance to the Qur'an and used reason in order to systematise the message of the scripture, the philosophers made use of the opinions of Greek philosophers, particularly Aristotle but also, at least in some areas, Plato, and they were inclined to give as much status and authority to these sources as to their distinctively Islamic ones. One of the key questions to which they had to devote much attention therefore was the relative weight and authority of reason and revelation.

Al-Kindi, often referred to as the 'father' of Islamic philosophy, sought to give equal weight to the two authorities, arguing that all truth was given by God even if philosophers and prophets attained their knowledge of it by different means.

Five of the great figures of Falsafa (Philosophy)

al-Kindi	d. 870
al-Razi	d. c. 925
al-Farabi	d. 950
Ibn Sina	d. 1037
Ibn Rushd	d. 1198

Some of his successors, however, seemed readier to give authority to the findings of reason and the conclusions of the Greek philosophers than to the statements of the Qur'an, with al-Razi in particular coming close to suggesting that prophecy was of little, if any, value and that it was the God-given gift of reason that was significant for coming to a perception of the truth. The later philosophers, however, generally drew back from this extreme, with both al-Farabi and Ibn Sina (known in the medieval West by the Latinised form of his name, Avicenna) suggesting that prophets and philosophers were complementary, the former indeed being philosophers of a special kind and superior to the philosophers either because of their imagination (al-Farabi) or their intellect (Ibn Sina). The other great medieval Islamic philosopher who is as often referred to by his Latinised name as by his Muslim one, Ibn Rushd, or Averroes, seems by contrast to reverse the order, suggesting that reason is primary but prophecy is necessary at least for some, who, for whatever reason, are not able to perceive the truth by the employment of their intellect.

Because of the readiness of at least some of the philosophers to accept the opinions of Aristotle in preference to the unambiguous statements of the Qur'an, concerning such as things as the origin of the universe

– eternally existent, as posited by Aristotle, as opposed to created by God, according to the Qur'an – or the nature of the afterlife – involving the soul, according to the philosophers, or also the body, as suggested in the Qur'an – falsafa became a matter of particular controversy in the medieval Islamic world; and when the great theologian al-Ghazali launched a savage attack on it, entitled simply 'The Incoherence of the Philosophers', he thereby did much to undermine the status of the subject, contributing to its decline in subsequent centuries in most of the Islamic world. The efforts of Ibn Rushd in Spain, through his riposte 'The Incoherence of the Incoherence', and of some later philosophical thinkers in Iran to refute al-Ghazali have generally not been particularly successful.

Sufi mysticism

Another trend that grew up early in Islamic history and is therefore in a way another sub-tradition of Islam, is Sufism. This Islamic mysticism, which began to develop a separate institutional form in the eighth century and became highly influential in later centuries, in certain times and places has been rather suspect for some Muslims because its origins lay, in part, in certain aspects of Christian mysticism, and certain of its practices have been seen by some as compromising the essential core teachings of Islam.

Some of the great figures of Tasawwuf (Sufism)	
Hasan al-Basri	d. 728
Rabi'a	d. 801
al-Muhasibi	d. 857
al-Junaid	d. 910
al-Hallaj	d. 922
'Abd al-Qadir al-Jilani	d. 1160
Ibn 'Arabi	d. 1240
Jalal al-din Rumi	d. 1273

The Sufis developed their mystical ideas on the basis of the spiritual teachings of the Qur'an, which, with their stress on the Day of Judgement when all secrets will be revealed, clearly laid great emphasis on inner motivation and purity. Sufism was thus, in a sense, islam of the heart, complementing the Shari'a, whose emphasis was on providing guidance for the outward actions both of individual Muslims and the Muslim community as a whole. In addition, one particular experience of Muhammad – according to Chapter 17 of the Qur'an, he experienced some kind of miraculous Night Journey either into the presence of God or to Jerusalem (or both) – served as a specific precedent for the idea of a spiritual journey (or tariqa) towards God. As well as this, some Sufis were influenced by some of the other-worldly ideals of some of the Christian monks whom Muslims encountered in the Syrian desert after the conquests, and there are thus external as well as internal influences upon the development of Sufism.

Muhammad's 'Night Journey'

Glory be to Him, who carried His servant [Muhammad] by night,
from the Holy Mosque [Mecca] to the Further Mosque [Jerusalem]
the precincts of which We have blessed,
that We might show him some of Our signs [in the presence of God].
He is the All-hearing, the All-seeing.

Qur'an 17: 1

Sufis developed a whole system of doctrine and practice which was intended to make it possible for them to grow in their knowledge of God. This involved elaborate schemes of dhikr, mentioning the names of God, either individually or corporately. One particularly influential method of doing this was the recitation of the ninety-nine names of God, an idea based on listing some of the adjectives used to describe God in the Qur'an, memorising them, and then sometimes inducing a kind of trance-like state by the rhythmical repetition of the names, in combination with controlled breathing.

For some Sufis, the practice of dhikr was complementary with following the stipulations of the Shari'a. For others, however, Sufism became an alternative to or even a replacement of that requirement and it was this more extreme form of Sufism which became quite controversial at certain stages of Islamic history. When some of these more 'extreme' Sufis began to claim that they had experienced union with God, managing to extinguish their own personalities in the process, this was too much for the legal and theological authorities, for whom such ideas seemed to contradict the statements of the Qur'an about the otherness and transcendence of God, as well as running the risk of subverting their authority as scholars of Shari'a and kalam. A Sufi such as al-Hallaj was put to death by crucifixion, as a result of being found guilty of blasphemy for having declared 'I am the truth'. Not all Sufis followed this more extreme understanding of what it involved, however, and for many Sufism was simply a matter of seeking inward purification, particularly of their motivation.

One of the sayings of an early woman Sufi, Rabi'a (d. 801)

O my Lord, if I worship you from fear of Hell, burn me in Hell; if I worship you from hope of Paradise, exclude me thence; but if I worship you for your own sake, then withhold me not from your eternal beauty.

From the account of her life by al-'Attar (Smith 1972: 11)

The split between Sunni and Shi'i Muslims

Each of the areas which we have looked at so far as illustrations of diversity and even disagreement within the Muslim community – theological, legal, philosophical and mystical – has, without being devoid of passionate and even acrimonious debate and argument, not resulted in any explicit institutional division within the Muslim community. Put simply, despite the depths of their disagreements, Muslim theologians, legal scholars, philosophers and mystics would still normally be prepared to pray with each other, so that they did not establish their own separate mosques or communities.

The one area of debate and disagreement which did succeed in producing a formal division within the Islamic community, however, was that of politics, relating particularly to the understanding of the leadership of the Muslim community. As noted above, Muhammad himself united the role of religious teacher with that of political leader. When he died, the community selected from among its own number a succession of caliphs, successors to Muhammad as leader of the community. Within thirty years of Muhammad's death, however, civil war broke out over the question of who should be the leader of the Muslim community, and although the Umayyad and 'Abbasid dynasties gained the allegiance of the majority of Muslims, they did not gain the adherence of all. A significant minority of Muslims dissented on the question of leadership, arguing in particular that Muhammad's own family, his blood relatives, had a special claim to leadership, not only on account of their genealogy but also because of their special spiritual status and knowledge. They became known as Shi'i Muslims, members of the Shi'a (literally party) of 'Ali.

Muhammad had no sons and his nearest surviving male relative was 'Ali, who was both his cousin and his son-in-law, having married one of Muhammad's daughters, Fatima. Significantly, 'Ali was not chosen as leader of the community when Muhammad died. Later, however, a number of prominent Muslims began to promote his candidacy and civil war broke out in 656 when 'Ali was elected the fourth caliph under somewhat suspicious circumstances following the murder of his predecessor.

'Ali was defeated in the course of the civil war but his supporters continued to seek to elevate his descendants to the leadership of the Muslim community, on a number of occasions rebelling against the existing Umayyad and 'Abbasid caliphs. One particular rebellion had devastating consequences for the Muslim community as a whole when 'Ali's younger son, al-Husain, raised a revolt against the Umayyad caliph Yazid in 680. Yazid's response was to despatch an expedition to crush the rebellion, with the specific orders that al-Husain be arrested, but the leader of the expedition, for reasons that are not at all clear, took it upon himself to go further and executed and decapitated al-Husain at Karbala in Iraq. Given that disillusionment with the Umayyad dynasty was growing at the time, al-Husain therefore came to be regarded as a martyr, the innocent victim of a bloodthirsty tyrant, and for Shi'i Muslims he became the symbolic representative of the ideals of the early Muslim community abandoned by the Umayyads.

Shi'i Muslims therefore developed the view that, in order to be true to those ideals, the Muslim community needed to be ruled by a descendant of the prophet Muhammad, and this view found justification in Shi'i accounts of an incident towards the end of Muhammad's life where he designated 'Ali as his successor.

A Shi'i account of Muhammad's designation of 'Ali as his successor

He took 'Ali by the hand, raised it before the assembly, and said: 'Anyone who has me as his patron (or leader) now has 'Ali as his patron.
O God, befriend those who befriend him, and oppose those who oppose him.

From a Shi'i account by al-Majlisi (Williams 1994: 171)

Shi'is' conviction is thus that 'Ali and his descendants should have ruled the Islamic community as Imams (literally 'ones who stand before, or lead'). As in any genealogical system, however, disputes sometimes arise concerning which descendant is to succeed, and in the middle of the eighth century such a dispute arose among the Shi'a, with some choosing to follow the sixth Imam's elder son, Isma'il, and others choosing his second son, Musa. The followers of the former, known as the Isma'ilis, became more politically assertive, choosing the path of actively seeking to take over the caliphate, and for a time in the tenth century, under the leadership of the Fatimid dynasty, they came close to success; but within two hundred years the Fatimids had been overthrown and since then it has been the followers of Musa who have become the most influential group within the Shi'a.

Their resolution to the dilemma of how to bring about the rule of the Imam over the Muslim community was to evolve the belief that the twelfth Imam, Muhammad al-Mahdi, did not die but rather went into Occultation in 873. He will then emerge from hiding at the end of time in order to inaugurate the age of justice, as a kind of messianic figure, and on this basis this branch of the Shi'a, who are often referred to as the Twelvers, succeeded in legitimising their policy of not actively seeking to establish the rule of the Imam but rather waiting for the coming of the Imam.

The key event in the emergence of Twelver Shi'ism as the largest branch of Shi'i Islam was the decision by the Safavid dynasty in Iran, when it seized power there in 1501, to adopt Twelver Shi'ism as the official state religion of the country. It is for this reason that today Iran is the only region of the Muslim world in which Shi'i Islam is the dominant religion.

Significant dates in the history of Shi'ism

'Ali rules as fourth caliph	656–61
al-Husain martyred at Karbala	680
Muhammad al-Mahdi goes into Occultation	873
Fatimid dynasty seizes power in Cairo	969
Safavid dynasty seizes power in Iran	1501

The division between Sunni (the majority) and Shi'i Muslims is thus the deepest and most emotive split within the Muslim community, especially on the occasion each year when Shi'i Muslims re-enact, in the form of a kind of Passion-play, the events leading up to the death of al-Husain. This takes place each year on the anniversary of his death, 10th Muharram (the first month of the Muslim calendar), and is often the time when tension between the two communities runs highest. A further indication of the extent of the division between the two groups is that Sunni and Shi'i Muslims pray separately, in their own mosques, and although they share the Qur'an as scripture, they have their own distinctive collections of hadiths, their own legal traditions – with some modern Muslims suggesting that Shi'i law should be recognised as a fifth school of Islamic law – and their own traditions in the fields of theology and philosophy.

The arts and sciences

Generally speaking, the Islamic world has demonstrated considerable suspicion of many of the art forms which have been influential in other cultures. There is no tradition of sculpture in the Islamic world, essentially because of fear of idolatry, and Islamic teaching has normally prohibited the representation of living beings on the basis that it is God who gives life to these beings and it is not appropriate for created beings to attempt to imitate this process.

Islamic art has therefore taken different forms, focusing mainly on the representation of God's word in the form of calligraphy of the Qur'anic text, and on God's work in the design of creation in the form of decorative geometrical pattern. These two are often combined most effectively in the decoration of mosques as Muslim places of worship, whose design and decoration is intended to focus worshippers' minds on God's presence in His word. Some of the world's greatest architectural gems are examples of Islamic architecture, such as the Dome of the Rock in Jerusalem, the Great Mosque in Cordoba (Spain), the Suleymaniye mosque in Istanbul (Turkey), the mosque of Shah 'Abbas in Isfahan (Iran), or, perhaps most famous of all, the Taj Mahal in Agra (India), which is actually a tomb rather than a mosque. The modern era has also seen the construction of some fine new mosques, such as that built by King Hassan II of Morocco in Casablanca.

In the field of science too the Muslim world has made significant contributions to the growth of knowledge and understanding. In the field of medicine, the philosopher al-Razi (d. c. 925) was the first person to diagnose smallpox as a distinct disease, different from other less serious diseases with similar symptoms. The later philosopher Ibn Sina (Avicenna) (d. 1037) was also a great medical authority, whose medical encyclopaedia was translated into Latin and remained the main text book of the subject in Europe until the sixteenth century. In other scientific fields Muslim thinkers also made significant contributions. Just to take three examples, in medieval Baghdad scientists of the *bayt al-hikma* (literally 'house of wisdom', an institution founded in the ninth century and devoted to scientific research) calculated the earth's circumference on the basis of measuring its curvature; in the field of optics Ibn al-Haitham (d. 1039), in Cairo, was the first person to establish that light travelled to the human eye rather than the other way round, as the Greeks had thought, and he also calculated the height of the earth's atmosphere; and in astronomy, the world's first observatory was built in Iran by Nasir al-din Tusi (d. 1274).

Much of this scientific endeavour was inspired by religious concerns as well as intellectual curiosity for its own sake, since detailed observation of both the earth and heavens made it possible to be precise about such things as the direction and time of prayer. As with Islamic art, Islamic science therefore generally enjoyed a close relationship with the practice of the faith, rather than being an autonomous discipline or set of disciplines.

Early modern history

Many of the greatest achievements of Islamic art and science, however, were realised in the classical period of Islam, which corresponds roughly to what European historians usually call the Medieval period or the Middle Ages, in other words, between the periods of the ancient world and the modern world. This was the era of the Umayyad caliphs in Damascus and the 'Abbasid caliphs in Baghdad. This world, however, in a sense came to an end in 1258, when Baghdad was besieged and sacked by Mongol invaders from Central Asia. Most of the eastern half of the Muslim world was devastated by successive waves of Mongols and, in a sense, Muslim civilisation never recovered. The event is thus aptly compared with the fall of Rome to the Goths in the fifth century, in both its practical consequences and its symbolic significance.

The age of the 'Gunpowder Empires'

1453	Ottoman Turks capture Constantinople
1492	Spanish Christians capture Granada
1501	Establishment of Safavid dynasty in Persia
1529 & 1683	Ottoman Turks at gates of Vienna
1556–1605	Reign of the Moghul Emperor Akbar in India

It is true that by the early fifteenth century a measure of political stability had been restored, with the emergence of three great states that ruled over most of the world's Muslims, and a fair number of the world's Christians and Hindus as well. Moving from west to east, these were the Ottoman Empire, with its capital in Istanbul, ruling over what is today Turkey, most of the Arab world and considerable parts of south-eastern Europe and the area to the north of the Black Sea; the Safavid Empire, with its capital in Isfahan, ruling over what is today Iran, Afghanistan and large parts of Central Asia; and the Moghul Empire, based in Delhi and ruling over most of what is today India, Pakistan and Bangladesh. These states were militarily and politically powerful, and as we have seen they were also responsible for producing some of the world's greatest examples of Islamic architecture; but somehow they never succeeded in reproducing either the breadth or depth of the intellectual life of the classical period of Islam.

Reacting to the growth of European power

From the eighteenth century onwards, the position of these states began to be threatened by a new challenge – the growth of European power. At first, British, French, Dutch and Russian explorers and travellers began to criss-cross the Muslim world in search of knowledge and, in some cases, diplomatic or political advantage for their home countries. Not long afterwards, traders began to establish trading outposts in the port cities of the Muslim world; from these footholds the competing European powers then began to expand the areas of either their political influence or their direct political control.

The growth of Western power and influence

1757	British victory at the Battle of Plassey (India)
1774	Start of Russian expansion in Central Asia
1798	Napoleon invades Egypt
1830	French occupy Algeria
1882	British occupy Egypt
1907	Division of Iran into British and Russian spheres of influence
1917	Balfour Declaration on Palestine

By the heyday of this process, between the two World Wars of the twentieth century, the three great Muslim states of the early modern period had all been dismembered. Only three regions of the Muslim world had succeeded in preserving any kind of independence from European rule – Afghanistan, Turkey and Sa'udi Arabia – and even they had had to endure varying degrees of competition for influence by the different European powers.

The 'Islamic Revival'

By the middle of the twentieth century there was a widespread feeling of malaise in many parts of the Muslim world, based on the conviction that something had clearly gone wrong: the Muslim world, which had once been powerful, was now seen to be weak and considerable effort was devoted to trying to discern the reasons for this reversal of fortune. Some Muslim thinkers, often described as 'modernists', blamed the intellectual stagnation of the early modern period for the backwardness of the Muslim world; the solution was therefore to seek to emulate the progress of the part of the world which had not stood still, namely Europe, and to take over and benefit from European discoveries and achievements. Other Muslim thinkers, however, often described as 'traditionalists', put forward a different explanation: the Muslim world had become weak because it had ceased to take its Islamic faith and obligations seriously, and so the solution was to reverse that process and once again put Islam at the heart of the lives of both individuals and societies.

Some significant modern Muslim thinkers and leaders

Jamal al-din al-Afghani	(1839–97)	(revivalist thinker across the Muslim world)
Sayyid Ahmad Khan	(1817–98)	(modernist thinker in India)
Mustafa Kemal Ataturk	(d. 1938)	(secular leader of Turkey)
Ayatollah Khomeini	(d. 1989)	(Islamist leader of Iran)

Thus, in the nineteenth century a thinker such as Jamal al-din al-Afghani travelled widely across the whole of the Muslim world seeking to alert Muslims to what he perceived as the threat from the different European powers, especially the British, and calling upon Muslims to return to the pure practice of Islam, as exemplified by the earliest generation of Muslims. He suggested that the truest understanding of Islam was to be found in the Qur'an and the Hadith, and not the other two classical foundations of Islamic law, and the task for modern Muslims was to go back to the Qur'an and the Hadith. At the other end of the spectrum, however, Sayyid Ahmad Khan in India suggested that Europe was not so much a threat as an example Muslims needed to learn from, and the way forward was therefore to set aside many of the traditional details of Islamic faith and practice and concentrate on the essential theological and ethical teachings of the Qur'an.

In the twentieth century, the Muslim world saw governments adopt radically differing approaches to the understanding and practice of Islam. In Turkey, in the years after World War I, Mustafa Kemal enshrined secularism – the complete separation of religion and the state – as one of the fundamental principles of the Turkish republic. Subsequently, Turkey has joined NATO and would like to join the European Union. Over the past decades, by contrast, Iran has followed a diametrically opposite path, reacting strongly against any attempt to follow the Turkish path and adopting stridently anti-Western policies and rhetoric, as seen most dramatically in the Islamic Revolution of 1979 under the leadership of Ayatollah Khomeini.

In both of these countries, political and religious debates continue: some in Turkey would like to see at least some restoration of the role of Islam in the public life of the country, while some in Iran would like to adopt less stridently anti-Western policies and allow greater individual freedom to discuss and even dissent from traditional Islamic teachings. In other Muslim countries, similar debates go on between 'Islamists', those who would like to see a greater public recognition of Islam, and 'secularists', who would prefer the practice of Islam to be an essentially individual and private matter. In most Muslim societies there is thus a wide spectrum of opinion on most questions.

The growth of Islam in the West

Alongside all these significant developments in the Muslim world, a significant new development has been the growth of new Islamic communities in the West, both in Western Europe and in North America. These communities have grown up essentially as a result of economic causes, particularly the shortage of labour experienced by many Western economies in the years after World War II, which led to many Western governments actively seeking to recruit workers from their former colonies. As a result of this process, in the United Kingdom there is in 2002 a Muslim community of some 1.5 million people, making it the second-largest religious community in the country. The community is extremely diverse, including members from almost all regions of the Muslim world (and both Sunni and Shi'i Muslims), but roughly half come originally from what was British India (today's India, Pakistan and Bangladesh). The largest single element consists of those who came originally from Pakistan, who make up roughly a third of Britain's Muslims. Since most Muslim migration to the UK took place in the 1950s and 1960s, however, over a half of the Muslim community is now British-born.

Some significant landmarks in the growth of the British Muslim community

1890	First mosque built (in Woking, Surrey)
1944	Gift of land by King George VI for the construction of a mosque in Regent's Park, London
1985	First Muslim mayor elected (Muhammad Ajeeb in Bradford)
1997	First Muslim Member of Parliament elected (Muhammad Sarwar in Glasgow Govan)

In other Western countries, significant Muslim communities have also grown up over the past fifty years, with perhaps 1.75 million Muslims, mainly of Turkish origin, in Germany and over two million, mainly of North African origin, in France. In North America, the situation is slightly different in that the migration of Muslims to the region goes back to the nineteenth century, when significant numbers of people migrated to the New World from different parts of the Muslim world, but the result is that there are over three million Muslims in the United States today.

Conclusion

Islam has developed in significant ways over the centuries, just as it has spread geographically over the centuries. Today, the Muslim community is the second-largest religious community in the world, consisting of somewhere between 800 million and 1,200 million people, or between a sixth and a fifth of the population of the world. Muslims are present in all continents and most countries, whether as the overwhelming majority or as small minorities. And wherever there are Muslims communal prayers take place, serving to unite local communities and symbolise their membership of a universal Muslim community. Worship thus serves as a focus of Muslim unity, as well as enabling Muslims to centre their lives on God and submission to Him.

Debates and discussions also take place, however, and in conclusion brief reference will be made here to two debates occupying the attention of many Muslims in many different parts of the Muslim world today. The first centres on the social sphere and concerns the position of women in society. Here, the Qur'an itself seems at certain points to suggest different models, one of equality and one of subordination, and fierce debates rage about how the two models may be reconciled and which takes precedence in today's world.

Two verses of the Qur'an about the position of women

Men and women who have surrendered,
believing men and believing women,
obedient men and obedient women,
truthful men and truthful women,
enduring men and enduring women,
humble men and humble women,
men and women who give in charity,
men who fast and women who fast,
men and women who guard their private parts,
men and women who remember God often,
for them God has prepared forgiveness and a mighty wage.

Qur'an 33: 35

Men are the managers of the affairs of women
for that God has preferred
one of them over another, and they [men]
expend of their property [for women].
Righteous women are therefore obedient,
guarding their husbands' interests as God guards.
And those [women] you fear may be rebellious
admonish; banish them to their couches,
and beat them. If they then obey you,
look not for any way [of vengeance] against them;
God is All-high, All-great.

Qur'an 4: 34

The other area of considerable debate involves the political sphere and focuses on the desirability or otherwise of democracy. Here again, some Muslim thinkers and governments are broadly sympathetic towards democratic ideals, seeing them as perfectly compatible with Islamic teaching and therefore goals towards which Muslim communities should attempt to move, even if gradually. Other thinkers and governments, by contrast, see the principles of democracy as inherently contradictory to the teachings of Islam, since at the heart of democracy is the idea of 'the sovereignty of the people', while Islam is posited on the absolute and unique sovereignty of God; according to these thinkers, the two systems are inherently contradictory and democracy is seen as an enemy of Islam that Muslims should seek to resist rather than emulate.

Two modern judgements on democracy

[D]emocracy stands in contradiction with your belief . . . The Islam in which you believe . . . is utterly different from this dreadful system . . . There can be no reconciliation between Islam and democracy . . . because they contradict one another . . .

> Abu'l-A'la Maududi (1903–79) (from Pakistan),
> *Islam and Modern Civilization* (Tibi 1998: 187)

[D]emocracy is not a fond dream, but a necessity . . . There can be no stable regional political order in Islamic civilization without some measure of democratization.

> Bassam Tibi (from Syria), *The Challenge of*
> *Fundamentalism* (1998: 190; 197).

On these and other subjects debate within the Muslim community will no doubt continue but all within the framework of the shared convictions that there is only one God and that Muhammad is His messenger.

 ## Further reading

There are now a great many informative introductions to the Islamic Tradition from a number of different perspectives. Broadly speaking, some are historical in approach, beginning with the background to the emergence of the Islamic community in Arabia then looking at the origins of that community through the career of Muhammad and the message of the Qur'an. The elaboration of the different aspects of the tradition as it developed over the centuries and discussion of modern trends and issues in Islamic thought are included. Others are more phenomenological or existential in approach, seeking to focus more on the Islamic practices and to provide some insight into the meaning of Islam for Muslims. It is also instructive to compare presentations of Islam by 'outsiders' (non-Muslims) and those by 'insiders' (Muslims themselves).

Historical approaches

Esposito, J. L. (1998), *Islam: the Straight Path*, 3rd ed., Oxford: Oxford University Press.

Rahman, F. (1979), *Islam*, 2nd ed., Chicago: University of Chicago Press.

Rippin, A. (2001), *Muslims: Their Religious Beliefs and Practices*, 2nd ed., London: Routledge.

Waines, D. (1995), *An Introduction to Islam*, Cambridge: Cambridge University Press.

These are by 'outsiders' with the exception of Rahman, an 'insider'.

Phenomenological/existential approaches

Nasr, S. H. (2001), *Ideals and Realities of Islam*, Cambridge: The Islamic Texts Society.

Renard, J. (1996), *Seven Doors to Islam*, Berkeley and Los Angeles: University of California Press.

Schimmel, A. (1994), *Deciphering the Signs of God: A Phenomenological Approach to Islam*, New York: State University of New York Press.

Tayob, A. (1999), *Islam: A Short Introduction*, Oxford: Oneworld.

The first and last of these are by 'insiders', the second is by an 'outsider' and the third is by someone who, though born an 'outsider', has developed a sympathy and understanding very close to that of an 'insider'.

A number of English versions of the Qur'an are also available. The one I have normally used to quote from in this chapter is by A. J. Arberry, originally entitled *The Koran Interpreted* but now simply called *The Koran* (1964) published by Oxford University Press. Arberry's is the only English version which even attempts to capture the poetic quality of the language of the Qur'an, most of the rest simply attempting prose translations, but it has two disadvantages: first, its system of verse numbering is not the one generally used by Muslims, and second, it uses the now slightly archaic forms of 'thee' and 'thine'. Where I have quoted from the Qur'an I have therefore usually used Arberry's version but the verse numbers given are those of the more widely used Muslim system. I have also used 'you' and 'your', and generally substituted inclusive language ('humanity' for Arberry's 'Man').

A great deal of material about Islam is now also available on the Internet. Some of this is rather partisan, representing the opinion of particular schools of thought within Islam rather than the universally agreed principles of the faith, but a helpful guide to using and interpreting this material is G. Bunt, *Virtually Islamic: Computer-Mediated Communication and Cyber Islamic Environments* (2000), published by the University of Wales Press, which has a helpful supporting (and updating) website at www.virtuallyislamic.com. Another useful website devoted to the scholarly study of Islam and containing links to a large number of other sites is www.arches.uga.edu/~godlas, run by Dr Alan Godlas at the University of Georgia.

Questions

1. In the context of Arabia, how new was Muhammad's message, as recorded in the Qur'an?

2. How distinctive are Islam's core beliefs when compared with those of Judaism and Christianity?

3. 'We worship; therefore we are.' How accurately does this describe the central philosophy of Islamic worship?

4. What were the main areas of debate and difference of opinion that emerged in the classical Islamic period (– c. 1258)?

5. Which is the most important aspect of Islam for most Muslims – theology, law, philosophy or mysticism?

6. What are the main causes of the 'Islamic revival' of the past 200 years?

7. What do you think are the most important issues confronting Muslims living as minorities in the modern West?

CHAPTER FIVE

Hinduism and Buddhism

Martin A. Mills

Introduction

One of the great distinctions in the study of the world's great religious traditions can be found between those Abrahamic traditions born within the Middle East (Judaism, Christianity and Islam) and those traditions that came to fruition within South and East Asia (Hinduism, Buddhism, Sikhism, Confucianism). Whilst this distinction may ultimately be a dubious one, it is nonetheless helpful as a rubric for understanding religious difference. In this chapter, we will focus on two of the most important religions to have emerged within the Indian subcontinent – Hinduism and Buddhism. Of these two, Buddhism is perhaps more obviously a 'world religion', in that – like Christianity and Islam – the spread of its ideas (first throughout Asia and later to the West) was predicated on a universalism that made no theoretical distinction between race, ethnicity or gender. By comparison, Hinduism (like Judaism) has largely eschewed proselytisation and its spread on the world stage has primarily been through the movement of individuals and kin groups as a result of marriage, diaspora and economic mobility. Nonetheless, both Hinduism and Buddhism share a common religious history and conceptual vocabulary, most particularly in their guise as renouncer religions. To understand this common ground, however, the Western reader should approach with the understanding that certain issues cannot be effectively understood within a Christian-dominated Western framework for thinking about religiosity and morality. The most acute of these issues can be seen in three areas: the definition of 'religion' itself, the status of deities and the consequences of reincarnation.

Defining 'religion'

Conceptualising both Hinduism and Buddhism as 'religions' within the Abrahamic understanding of the term – irrevocably linked as it is to a central deity and a pronounced salvific and revelatory ethic – has always presented difficulties. In the case of Hinduism, its religious and ritual traditions are so diverse as to be almost impossible to encapsulate in any convenient set of doctrines or practices, whilst Buddhism has been argued by many – Buddhists and non-Buddhists alike – not to be a religion at all.

The status of deities

Unlike Christianity, for example, deities in Hindu and Buddhist life are not perceived to be wholly transcendent beings, cut off from humanity by a vast gulf of difference and necessarily representing the focus of all religious striving; rather they are often described as very much like humans, only more powerful. Indeed, Hindu and Buddhist traditions assert the capacity of divinity (or in the Buddhist tradition, Buddha-hood) to manifest itself in earthly forms and relationships: in Hindu and Buddhist kings; in 'God-men', gurus and incarnate lamas; and, in the more ordinary run of things, in gurus and husbands. In this sense, when a Hindu text says that a wife should see her husband as God, we must be careful not to assume that the meaning of divinity being evoked here is an Abrahamic one. Similarly, within the Buddhist traditions many deities are seen to exist and be appropriate objects of propitiation; they are, however, not seen as the source of spiritual salvation.

Reincarnation, suffering and morality

Almost all religious traditions assert the continuity of consciousness beyond death and the vast majority of them assert that the nature of reality beyond death is somehow determined by the moral nature of our actions in this life. At this point, however, the many paths diverge. Both Hinduism and Buddhism assert the reality of reincarnation: the belief that consciousness is reborn again and again, lifetime after lifetime, in either human, animal, divine or demonic form, and that this reincarnation has continued across thousands, possibly an infinite number, of lives. This is possibly one of the most marked distinctions between the Abrahamic religious traditions (where earthly life is singular and finite, followed by an endless heavenly or hellish afterlife) and the Indian ones. Within the Indian traditions, rebirth is seen to be determined by a process of *karmic* fruition, such that the nature of this life is determined by the moral actions of past lives. This moulds the nature of established morality in a variety of ways. For example, a person's 'moral biography' is seen as played out across a multiplicity of lifetimes, rather than beginning and ending with this one; thus, it is possible to conceive of present advantages and misfortunes in terms of (hypothetical) deeds committed in previous lives. By extension, the concept of moral innocence – even in the case of infants – makes little or no sense in a world where a one-day-old child is seen as having accumulated the moral weight of a thousand lives. Moreover, whilst the possibility of 'life after death' (in the sense of an eternal run of lives) may seem optimistic enough, for Indian thinkers it was uniquely negative: an endless trap of suffering and impermanent achievements. For this reason, whilst the Christian traditions may laud the possibilities of 'eternal life', the Indian renouncer movements sought an 'ending to rebirth', a renunciation of the becoming that inevitably leads to suffering. Both the Hindu and Buddhist renouncer traditions are emphatically 'other-worldly', rejecting the possibility of real happiness and fulfilment within the confines of this existence. Again, this transforms the nature of morality: for example, whilst Western morality (whether secular or otherwise) conceives of compassion largely in terms of this-worldly charity to the poor and sick, the Indian renouncer traditions assert that such acts, whilst momentarily useful, in no sense serve to reduce the sufferings of others at an ultimate level, which can only be achieved through renunciation of desire. Thus, for example, the Buddhist sees compassion (*karuna*, *metta*) primarily in terms of teaching the path to liberation from rebirth.

Hinduism

Hinduism is generally classed as one of the great 'world religions' of the modern era. Indeed, large Hindu populations can be found throughout the globe. Nonetheless, it very much takes the Indian subcontinent as its spiritual home in a far deeper way even than Islam's focus on the Arabian peninsula, and generally rejects the tendency to proselytisation found in Christianity, Islam and (to a lesser extent) Buddhism. With some 800 million adherents around the world, it has also been the cultural and religious fountainhead for several other religious traditions, most particularly Buddhism, Jainism and, in certain respects, Sikhism.

Today, Hindu communities and households are usually divided into the Vaishnava, Saiva and Shakta traditions, although these in no sense represent exclusive sectarian distinctions as do Sunni and Shi'i, Protestant and Catholic. Instead, they are interlacing traditions of worship that, while fully acceding to the validity of the other traditions, assert the centrality of their own. Neither Hinduism as a whole, nor its various traditions, has ever really come under the kind of centralised authority necessary to either rationalise its diversity, or generate a powerful sense of orthodoxy. It has, however, transformed again and again under the influence of different systems of rule and political ideology, whether the Islamic Moghul empires of the sixteenth to eighteenth centuries, Dutch and British colonial rule from the seventeenth to twentieth centuries, or – more recently – the rise of right-wing Hindu nationalist movements in post-independence India.

For the purposes of an introduction, however, it is possible to follow Srinivas' concept of 'Sanskritic' or 'All-India' Hinduism: those traditions and ideas that transcend regional differences and idiosyncrasies. This includes the worship of deities such as Vishnu and Shiva, the sacredness of certain rivers and pilgrimage sites, the sanctity of the cow, the ubiquity of the caste (*jati/varna*) system, the importance of the moral concepts of *dharma* and *karma*, and the popularity and influence of the two great epic poems, the Ramayana and the Mahabharata. Such an understanding of Hinduism is, of course, an abstraction and leaves out vast sections of the individual religious experience of almost every Hindu: ritual relations with particular local deities, the complex and subtle renouncer traditions, and the very differences of view that emerge out of the divisions inherent within the caste system. It can only therefore be the first step into this vast and diverse set of religious traditions.

'Hinduism' in history

Using the term 'Hinduism' in a historical context is always fraught with difficulty. There are, after all, two distinct histories to the term: first, the use of the word itself, and second, the complex and diverse civilisational traditions that it refers to. The word 'Hinduism' itself derives from the Sanskrit term *Sindhu*, originally meaning anyone resident within the Indus Valley area (in present-day Pakistan). Within the pre-colonial Indian subcontinent itself, evidence suggests that the term was used to designate the subjects and territories of any Saivite or Vaishnavite king that maintained the caste system, regardless of the 'majority religion' of those subjects and territories – it denoted, in other words, a certain kind of state power rather than religious identity. By the time the word entered into English (somewhere around the early seventeenth century), it was used to refer very broadly to any inhabitant of the Indian sub-continent south of the Indus River, of whatever religion. As British colonial influence in India expanded, 'Hinduism' – most particularly within the administrative and scholarly language of the British Empire – came to mean those adherents of the indigenous religion of India: in other words, a term that excluded certain religious communities, most particularly Muslims (depicted as having invaded India during the eleventh century, and who thus constituted an alien force of domination) and unified others, such as the Saivites and Vaishnavites (and occasionally Buddhists), under a single rubric. This final usage of 'Hinduism' is that employed by modern Hindu resurgence movements as a means to nationalist unification.

The second 'history' of the term refers to those relatively ancient genealogies of ritual, literary and ideological tradition that represent the forebears of what we presently identify as 'Hindu' tradition. Here, scholars are referring in particular to a relatively diffuse set of religious traditions that descend from the early Indian Vedic traditions. These date from c. 1500 BCE and were focused around the recitation of the Rig Vedas: devotional hymns to deities – such as the central creator god Indra, but also the deities Surya, Varuna and the fire-god Agni – as well as ascribed ritual practices linked to earlier traditions of *yoga* and *soma* sacrifice, aimed at the attainment of transcendental states of consciousness. By the end of the Vedic period, institutional religious prac-tice was predominantly organised around a priestly class of brahmans, who placed themselves even higher in the social ranking than the local kingly castes.

By the time of the Christian era, Hinduism had begun to centre on the worship of the deities Vishnu (the 'preserver') and Shiva ('the destroyer'). These two deities and their various consorts, children and manifesta-tions dominate Hinduism to this day. During the early first millennium

CE, developments in Hindu thought and practice were most substantially characterised by the development of bhakti, or devotional sects. Focused on a personal deity as the basis for extremely emotional forms of worship, bhakti cults renounced much of the Sanskrit-centred ritual of Vedism in favour of vernacular hymns (most often Tamil), speaking of an intense and personal love for a particular deity. Bhakti cults were extremely influential, spreading north from their early Tamil origins in the fourth century CE and increasingly rivalling and threatening other forms of worship (as well as Buddhism) by the end of the first millennium. This period also saw the rise to prominence of the worship of several deities associated with the retinues of Vishnu and Shiva, such as Ganesha (Shiva's elephant-headed son and patron deity of business and writing) and Vishnu's consort, Lakshmi – one of several goddesses whose emergence as objects of worship represented a marked departure from the male-dominated cosmology of the Vedas. It was not, however, until the fourth century CE that Durga (consort of Shiva and most controversial of Hindu deities) gained a firm foothold, and medieval times before the development of fully-fledged Shaktaism – the worship of the active, female principle.

The arrival of Muslim political and military domination in North India during the eleventh century caused substantial changes to Hindu practice. Whilst the majority of Muslim rulers maintained reasonable diplomatic relations with their Hindu subjects, some – such as the Firuz Tughluq (ruled 1351–88) – were strongly anti-Hindu and many Hindu temples (along with almost all forms of institutional Buddhism) were persecuted or simply destroyed. The withdrawal of royal patronage from Hindu institutions caused an increased emphasis on lay or household religious forms and led to the proliferation of diverse ritual traditions.

The eventual collapse of the Muslim-dominated Moghul empires would not occur until the early colonial period: in this sense, Hindu practices and institutions were, with the exception of the Nepalese kingships, dislocated from state power on the subcontinent from the eleventh century until the end of British colonial rule in 1947.

Hindu texts

Hinduism's oldest textual traditions are the Vedas. Revealed by the rishis (inpired sages), the Vedas are held to encapsulate an eternal religion, or dharma, that comes into being with the creation of every universe. The Vedic language is Sanskrit, regarded by both Hindus and many Buddhist schools as divine in origin, and the texts are thus – particularly when invoked in the form of mantras, which are seen to embody divine power, or *shakti* – seen as linking Man to the gods. In content terms, the Vedas include those hymns and rites that are a necessary part of Man's relationship with the gods and are essential parts of his responsibility to maintain the ritual order of the universe, which was seen as inextricably linked to the human social order: thus, rites for marriage, death, the ordering of the domestic household and the relations between the various castes are core sections.

Inspired by the early Vedas were the *dharma-sutras*, or 'manuals of *dharma*', containing extensive elaborations of the Vedic material on issues such as the many ritual obligations of daily life, as well as the various stages of life, dietary obligations, issues of law and punishment, and the obligations of kings. These short texts were, in turn, elaborated on within the more extensive *dharma-shastras*, the foremost of which was the Manu-smriti, which maintains a huge influence on Hindu understandings of law and morality to this day.

These commentarial texts on the Vedas were compiled during the early first millenium BCE and form the basis of much later Indian philosophy. They are distinct from the Vedas in several ways: they are far more philosophically and mystically inclined and they contain comparatively little ritual material. Moreover, they show a reduced emphasis on the propitiation of specific deities in favour of an increased elaboration of the concept of a central supreme being or reality (*Brahman*) and of the unity of the self (*atman*) with that being. The Upanishads also elaborate on the nature of reincarnation and the relationship between rebirth and morality.

During the first half of the first millenium BCE, the first of India's two great epic poems, the Mahabharata, was composed, nominally by the sage Vyasa. At 100,000 verses, certain versions of the Mahabharata are the longest pieces of epic poetry in existence. The story covers the complex and bloody dynastic struggles of the lineages of the two royal brothers Pandu and Dhartarastra, whose heirs battle for succession to the throne. Within this story, however, much of early Indian civilisation – its codes of morality and obligation, its rules of war and succession, its attitudes to love and marriage – is revealed, most poignantly in the struggles of the righteous but flawed king Yudhisthira, the love story of Nala and Damyanti and, most famously, the dialogue between Arjuna the archer and Lord Krishna on the eve of the final battle. This last piece forms the heart of the Mahabharata's most famous section, the Bhagavad-Gita, or Song of the Lord, in which Krishna gradually reveals himself as supreme lord of the universe.

The other epic text to arise during this period was the Ramayana, a lengthy tale of kingly succession and exile by the poet Valmiki. The poem centres on Rama, son of King Dasaratha and heir to the throne at Ayodhya, who is exiled on command of the king's stepmother. While Rama and his brother Laksmana are hunting in the forest to which they have been exiled, Rama's wife Sita is abducted by Ravana, the demon King of Sri Lanka. With the aid of the monkey general Hanuman, Rama kills Ravana and retrieves his wife, returning to Ayodhya in triumph. The people of Ayodhya, however, consider the virtuous Sita guilty of infidelity and eventually she is swallowed up by the earth goddess as a means of ending her tribulations and as a sign of her wifely purity. Like the Mahabharata, the Ramayana remains very much part of Hindu mythic consciousness and has been evoked in recent Hindu–Muslim conflicts as a focus for political identity (see box *The Ayodhya Conflict* later in this chapter).

By the middle of the first millenium CE, Sanskrit literature had begun to develop much of its present form. With the advent of the Puranas – closely linked in style and subject to the Mahabharata and Ramayana – ritual literature was clearly being organised around the worship of the deities Brahma, Vishnu and Shiva, although the single most popular and influential of the Puranas is the Bhagavata-Purana, with its extended treatment of the early life of Lord Krishna.

The Hindu conceptual world

Hinduism as a system of thought cannot easily be abstracted into a series of orthodox mnemonics, as can the Christian creeds. Nonetheless, certain ideas and practices have provided a shared vocabulary for thinking about, debating and legitimising religious thought and practice. Philosophically at least, central place goes to the linked concepts of *Brahman* and *dharma*. *Brahman*, when discussed in the early Brahmanical

> When [the *Brahman*] is related to such limiting conditions as the body and its organs, which are characterised by ignorance, it is called the individual embodied soul [*atman*]. When its limiting power is the power of eternal and unlimited knowledge, it is called the inner Ruler [*antarymin*] and Lord [*vara*]. The same soul [*atman*], being by nature transcendent, absolute and pure, can be called the immutable and supreme Self [*Brahman*]. Similarly, by this limiting, finite connection . . . the gods, different species, individuals, men, animals and so on, the Self assumes those names and forms.
>
> *Brahadaranyaka-Upanishad-Bhasya* by Sankara, 3.8.12. Cited in E. Lott (1980),
> *Vedantic Approaches to God*, London: Macmillan Press: 44.

texts, originally referred to the reality or power at the heart of all ritual practice that linked together the human and the divine. Later, within the writings of religious preceptors such as Shankara, of the non-dualist Vedanta school of thought (which came to be regarded during the nineteenth century as the core Hindu philosophical school), *Brahman* came to refer to the supreme reality and source of all things existent and non-existent, from which all other entities (including the gods) derive their existence or of which they are manifestations. To save confusion, it is important to note that it is distinct from the deity Brahma, the caste of brahmans and the set of texts known as the Brahmanas. *Brahman*, as a philosophical and mystical essence, is seen as both impersonal and personal: impersonal in the sense of an absolute and fundamentally neutral 'reality' at the heart of everything; personal in the sense that *Brahman* is also seen as the supreme reality of all persons (*atman*), integration with which is the aim of all religious striving. In this sense, *Brahman* is conceptualised as a different, deeper level of existence from cosmology in the sense of ranks of deities, or indeed a 'chosen' deity (*ishta devata*) to whom a Hindu has a personal sense of devotion. These latter – which are seen as magical manifestations (*maya*) of *Brahman* – include primarily Vishnu ('the protector and preserver'), Shiva ('the creator and destroyer') and Brahma ('the creator'). Vishnu is often associated with the preservation of the household, of kingly rule and of marriage, and is often worshipped through his manifestations (*avatar*) within the world, such as Rama and Krishna. Shiva, by contrast, is a far more ambiguous figure, encapsulating elements of both the saviour and the bringer of calamity, the powerful lover and the great ascetic, the protector and the avenger. Resident with his (equally powerful and double-sided) consort, Shakti, on the apex of Mount Kailasa deep within the Himalayas, Shiva has been the focus of extremely powerful ascetic traditions but also of the complex and ambiguous disciplines of tantra.

Relations with the gods

Central though *Brahman* may be to the philosophical underpinnings of Hindu thought, everyday religious life is dominated by relations with deities. Here, devotees of a particular *ishta devata* (personal deity) perform *puja* – devotional offerings to the god and its manifestations. This usually involves the offering of food, water, flowers and light to the deity, as well as the anointing of its form. This very physical act is encapsulated in the idea of *darshan*, the notion that a devotee's relationship with a god is very much a visual one: the devotee should be able to behold the

---

form of the deity, and the deity, through its statue or image, blesses through being able to 'see' the worshipper.

In this sense, deities are seen as immanent within statues and images, which are found in local temples, household and roadside shrines, on the dashboards of cars and rickshaws (most particularly in Kathmandu, where there are said to be 'more gods than people').

Within this kaleidoscope of refracted divine presence, however, certain places are seen to hold unique power. These sacred sites (*tirtha*) are the object of pilgrimage traditions (*yatra*) within all of the Hindu traditions. Pilgrimage sites are most usually the crossing-points of sacred rivers, travel to which is seen as a 'return' to the source of life and thus a purification in preparation for death (most noted here is Banares, where many Hindu pilgrims go to die), although they also mark the abodes of deities (such as mount Kailasa, the abode of Shiva in the Himalayas) and key sites within the great Indian epics (such as Ayodhya). Whilst many pilgrims go in search of spiritual boons, it is seen as equally feasible to search for worldly ones – children, wealth and success.

The interaction between these various deities can be seen in the creation myths surrounding Vishnu. Depicted as resting amongst the coils of Ananta, the eternal serpent, Vishnu slumbers on the cosmic ocean. With his awakening comes the beginning of the universe: from Vishnu's navel, a lotus appears bearing the deity Brahma, who creates the universe. Vishnu then maintains this fledgling universe until it is destroyed by Shiva. At this point, Brahma is enfolded back within the lotus and dissolves back into Vishnu, who drifts back to sleep until it is time for a new universe to form. Whilst this is clearly a traditional Vaishnavite depiction of the relationship between these gods (in the sense that it presents Vishnu as supreme), it also gives a sense of the balanced triumvirate of divine powers at the heart of Hinduism's extraordinarily rich cosmology and exemplifies much of the principle of differential responsibility – a social division of economic and moral labour – that organises Hindu social life. This can also be seen in Shakta, the worship of the goddess – a unification of all female deities into the single figure of Devi. Representing the female 'power' that lies at the heart of all divine forms, Shakta worship – which is as ambivalent as Shiva himself – thus cuts across established cosmological ranks. Whilst there may only be one single central 'reality' to the universe, it manifests itself in many forms and faces, to each of which is ascribed a partial reality and a distinct responsibility; or, in other words, a *dharma*.

Whilst *Brahman* may hold centre-stage in Hindu philosophical speculation, it is the concept of dharma that is most essential to its social and
moral organisation. Usually translated as 'religion' in the widest possible
sense, *dharma* implies a combination of the way things are as well as a
sense of the way things should be, with the latter deriving from the
former: thus, a cup holds water not simply because it is what I intend
it to do but because of the way it is made, because of the truth of its
nature – its dharma.

The elaboration of this concept – that things should ideally follow
their nature – has clear moral implications: for example, individuals
should not lie because to do so would be at odds with the truth of their
nature and actions. There is a sense therefore of the inherent 'truth' of
things that resides in their nature and that should be followed as the
basis for happiness and correct living. This truth is felt to naturally manifest itself as part of the unfolding of the universe, a principle illustrated
in Hindu literature, society and law: for example, in traditional Hindu
kingly law (and much epic poetry), a person could claim the right to
undergo a physical 'trial of truth', wherein the 'power of truth' (*satyagraha* – see box on Mahatma Gandhi later in the chapter) within their
legal declaration was seen to magically protect them from death, burning or drowning. More controversially, the notion of *dharma* was an
important support for the institution of caste, wherein people's birth
status was seen to determine much of their subsequent life. It was,
however, accepted that it could not represent all of a person's life. The
Manu-Smriti thus argues that an adult's life should accord foremost
with the demands of *dharma*, secondarily with the requirements of
artha (material well-being), and finally with the allurements of *kama*
(desire).

The place of dharma within Hindu life is therefore morally paramount:
it is, however, primarily manifest through action, a means of living life
(or orthopraxy) rather than a set of beliefs (orthodoxy). In particular,
the Manu-Smriti (amongst others) sets out detailed rules determining the
lives of 'twice-born' castes – those upper castes that received 'spiritual'
birth (in the form of initiation) as well as physical birth. For males, four
ideal stages of life – called *ashrams* ('resting places' or hermitages) – were
seen to follow initiation: life as a celibate student (*brahmacarya*), as a
householder (*grhastha*), as a forest-dwelling hermit (*vanaprastha*), and
finally as a wandering renouncer (*samnyasa*). By performing each of these
to the best of his ability, the ideal twice-born Hindu male discharges his
'three debts': by reciting the Vedas, he discharges his debts to the seers
(*rishis*) that revealed them; by tending the three sacred fires of the
household (into which offerings are made), he discharges his duties to
the gods; and by having sons who can perform his funeral rites, he
discharges his duties to the ancestors. Once these duties are fulfilled,
he may become a renouncer and seek liberation (*moksha*); should he

renounce the world without completing them, however, he will descend to hell. For females, by comparison, life comprised three stages: as an unmarried girl, as a wife and as a widow. In each situation, she is perceived as ideally dependent on those around her. Thus, the Manu-Smriti states:

> In childhood, she should be subject to her father,
> In youth to her husband,
> And when her husband is dead, to her sons.
> She should never enjoy independence.
>
> Manu-smriti 5: 148

Marked differences thus occur between the social status of men and women, and between those that are married and not married: whilst a widower is ideally an authoritative elder devoted to the pursuit of religion, a woman upon marriage passes from a state in which her capacity to produce children makes her a font of auspiciousness and female power (*sakti*) but as a widow she becomes dependent and deeply inauspicious. So deep is this transformation that certain Hindu castes have, at various historical points, practised *sati*, in which the widow joins her husband on the funeral pyre, thus apotheosising her status as a 'good wife' (this practice has been banned since the colonial period).

Reincarnation and caste

Whilst the early Vedas make little consistent reference to life after death, later Brahmanical developments asserted the existence of continual rebirth for all beings. Souls (or atman) were seen as trapped in a perpetual cycle of birth, suffering, death and birth again, called samsara ('circling'), driven by a combination of attachment to worldly things (which detracted from a consciousness of the true nature of *atman* and its unity with *Brahman*) and *karma* (or moral causation – different from *kama*, or desire). Such 'circling' was seen as deeply unsatisfactory, characterised by sufferings that were the 'fruits' of people's deluded moral actions, such that one experiences them again and again. Within Hinduism (and here it is distinct from, for example, Buddhism), *karma* was conceptualised in terms of a person's individual *dharma* and therefore exists relative to caste and social identity. Individuals, in other words, were seen as morally bound to perform the tasks that they were born to, an idea that lay at the very heart of the Hindu caste system and probably one of the most distinct – and at the same time controversial – aspects of the Hindu tradition.

The word 'caste' is a Spanish term, referring in the Indian context to the terms *varna* or *jati*. This refers to a model of the moral universe in which all socially recognised persons are divided into four varna, or 'colours': *brahmans* (priests – distinct from, but related to, the concept of *Brahman*), *kshatriya* (warriors), *vaishyas* (ordinary people) and *shudras* (servants). Here, the social identity and destiny of individuals (their social status, legal position, employment possibilities, marriage options and religious status) is determined by birth into a particular caste. All but the most limited social movement between castes is seen as opposed to that person's karmically determined dharma. Hindu tradition from earliest times has conceptualised and legitimated the hierarchies of the caste system in terms of an image of cosmic order derived from the Purusha Sukta, one of the later hymns of the Rig Veda, in which the various elements of humanity were described as being borne from the sacrificial dismemberment of Purusha, the cosmic man, by the gods. From the principal parts of Purusha's body, the social world was created, dividing people into separate varna: from his mouth sprung the priestly brahmans, destined to recite the Vedas and perform the rites that ensured the continuity of health, wealth and auspiciousness; from his shoulders, the kingly-warrior caste of the kshatriya, who ordered and defended society; from his hips, the vaishyas, farmers and traders who supported the other castes economically; and from his feet came the lowly shudras, born to serve the other three castes. Within the idealised vedic view of humanity, the different castes perform different functions, each supporting the continuity of a society whose structure was seen to be part of the legitimate, unchanging and interdependent cosmic order.

Interdependent as this vision of society may be, it was at the same time deeply hierarchical. In particular, it was organised around distinctions of ritual purity between the various castes that mirrored the body of the dismembered Purusha. Thus, just as the mouth (which receives food and ideally speaks religious truths) should be kept as the purest part of the body, so is the brahman caste most strongly associated with purity; conversely, just as the feet are the most likely to be polluted, so are the shudra caste seen as dharmically linked not simply with servitude but with impurity and occupations associated with it, such as sweepers and cleaners. Differential relations with purity also placed barriers between the various castes, since impurity is, almost by definition, contagious: theoretically at least, members of different castes should not eat together, share water or (with certain exceptions) inter-marry. As a result, shudras were traditionally excluded from the ranks of the 'twice-born' (*dvija*), whose right to receive initiation (*upanayana*) also entitled them to hear and recite the Vedas, a status marked by the wearing of the sacred red thread over one shoulder. At the same time, many families and communities within Hindu life were also classified as *avarna* – 'without varna' – and thus technically existed outside the social confines of the caste system. These were the 'untouchables' (widely known as *dalit*, or, in Mahatma Gandhi's later reformist term, *harijans* – 'children of God'), groups whose ritual status rendered them deeply polluting to members of the caste system, most particularly to the 'twice-born' castes: thus, for example, a brahman is instructed to bathe repeatedly for three days if an untouchable's shadow passes over him before he can eat safely with others of his caste. As a model, the varna code is very much an idealised legal fiction and in actuality the ethnographic structure of castes in Hindu life in India is vastly more complex: divided into hundreds of systems of jati, or 'species', the caste system in practice is often highly localised, idiosyncratic and often obscure even to Hindu outsiders in a particular area.

The very notion of jati has been under attack by reform-minded Indians and from dissenting religious traditions, such as the Buddhists. Reformers within the tradition, such as Mahatma Gandhi, have rarely demanded the total abolition of the caste system but have sought instead to improve the status of individual castes or caste groups. Despite limited success in dissolving caste barriers within urban areas of India, government moves in this direction still meet with entrenched resistance, such as the burning of untouchable university students in Delhi and Bombay. In different parts of India, certain caste groups have sought respectability within this system by 'upgrading' their caste position. An extremely successful example of this was the claim of the Rajputs that they were the kshatriyas, or nobles, of the second varna; to reinforce their claim, they invented a new lineage (Agnikula, the dynasty of Fire) to co-exist side by side with the Solar and Lunar lineages of ancient times. Similarly, untouchables have adopted caste habits of conduct and sought the status of shudra (or, more recently, converted to Islam and Buddhism) to escape from their pitiable social condition.

Attempts to comprehend the Indian caste system (which often spread beyond the boundaries of the specifically Hindu population, including, for example, much of India's long-standing Christian community) have pre-occupied Indian scholars for two hundred years. Since the dawn of the colonial period in India, colonial administrators, historians and anthropologists have sought to determine its religious, political or economic 'essence', a project driven more by the nature of the colonial project than any intrinsic intellectual or anthropological interest. British administrators in India, for example, were keen on social and legal reform in colonial India but maintained a policy of not interfering in indigenous religious institutions: if caste were found to be largely non-religious in essence, it could legitimately be reformed through colonial fiat. By contrast, Christian missionary organisations working under the aegis of British (and before it, Dutch) colonial rule argued that if caste were primarily a religious institution, then Indian Christians (whether indigenous or converted) should renounce any caste status. Either way, the Indian caste system has been an object of European reformist tendencies.

More recently, the caste system's similarity to forms of social segregation found elsewhere (such as racial distinctions in the United States, class divides in the United Kingdom, or more explicitly caste-like forms of social organisation in West Africa) has led to a plethora of comparative debates. Scholars such as Bailey have explained the Indian caste system in terms of a simple equation of caste and landed power. Marxist thinkers such as Menscher have, moreover, denounced the caste system as simply a religious gloss designed to unite the land-holding upper castes (whose comparative purity allows them to interact and marry without great difficulty) and divide the land-poor lower castes from one another through pollution restrictions (Menscher 1974).

Attractive though these arguments may be in many ways, they are in no sense final. The anthropologist Louis Dumont, in his iconically named book *Homo Hierarchicus*, has noted that whilst the relationship between high caste position and landholding status is generally true, the most substantial landholders (usually found within the aristocratic kshatriya castes) are not at the top of the caste system – the brahmans are. Moreover, no amount of wealth will render an untouchable pure and no amount of poverty render a brahman untouchable. Instead, Dumont argued that, unlike Western cultures (which are – in the sphere of values anyway – largely egalitarian), Indian society is fundamentally hierarchical, organised according to an understanding of social life that seeks always to distinguish between the pure and the impure (Dumont 1960), which itself tends to reorganise the distribution of wealth.

The world of renouncers

The ideas of the Vedic and Brahmanical traditions, whilst representing the cultural bedrock of householding life within Hinduism, should not so much be viewed as explicit doctrines as concepts around which debates and understandings formed. Throughout Hindu history, reform movements have questioned core elements of the Vedic worldview. However, whilst certain movements – such as the Buddhists – were so radical in their critique that they effectively became another religion, the vast majority of such questioning was far from heretical or even heterodox. Within the Mahabharata, for example, the tale is told of the virtuous king Yudisthira who, weary of a lifetime of war and blood feuds caused by his warlike cousin Dhuryadhana, goes in search of the god Indra's heaven in the Himalayas. Upon finally finding it, Yudisthira is shocked to discover it already inhabited by Dhuryadhana. Here, the god Dharma explains to him that, whilst Yudisthira has been virtuous and loyal to his friends, he did so at the expense of his dharma as a king; his cousin, however, by pursuing war and conquest, had fulfilled his dharma as a king and thus attained liberation. Whilst a mainstay of Hindu understandings of social obligation, the Mahabharata at the same time contains a subtle moral critique of Vedic understandings of dharma. That such concerns did not undermine Hinduism is largely a facet of its emphasis not on doctrine and matters philosophical but on the fulfilment of specific ritual duties. Nonetheless, the perceived moral insufficiency of the 'ordinary existence' of birth, death and rebirth led to the development of ideas that asserted the possibility of transcending the samsaric world of karma and caste. Such an escape (or 'liberation', *moksha*) was conceived of as possible within the many renouncer traditions that grew up within India.

The origins of the renouncer movements within Hinduism remain unclear: some argue that they emerged endogenously from the philosophically inclined Upanishad traditions; others that they emerged in response to the critiques of reform movements such as Buddhism and Jainism. Regardless of their origins, their broad features are well-defined: rejecting Vedic and Brahmanical authority as a source of illumination, and householder life as a means to spiritual fulfilment, the renouncer embarks on a quest for transcendent knowledge (*jñana*) through the practice of mental and physical disciplines (*yoga*), often combined with extreme asceticism (*tapas*). In particular, the training of mental attention to focus one-pointedly on objects of meditation was seen as an essential mechanism for the transformation of the mind: the eradication or 'uprooting' of greed and hatred, and the development of *jñana* and supernormal powers (*siddhi*). An important nuance of this spiritual path is its implicit downgrading of moral action (karma) as a means towards liberation; instead, the inner universe, or atman, becomes the focus of attention. In this regard, the Katha Upanishad (2.3: 10–11) likened the person as a whole to a chariot – the atman is the charioteer, the body the chariot itself and the senses are the horses. The renouncer, realising that only the atman is the source of happiness and fulfilment, restrains the senses in order that the body will do the atman's bidding; by comparison, the ordinary person mistakes the senses themselves for the source of fulfilment and is thus drawn ever onwards by them, a chariot out of control, the needs of the charioteer long since forsaken.

From the middle of the first millennium CE, certain renouncer traditions (most especially those associated with the worship of Shiva) began to incorporate a wide range of new ritual and yogic systems known as the tantras. Centred on the evocation and control of divine powers as a means to *jñana* and *siddhi* (supernormal powers), tantric traditions often contained substantial anti-nomial material: the performance of sexual yoga in cremation grounds, the evocation of ferocious deities and the ritual offering of meat, alcohol and impure substances such as semen and faeces to deities. Tantric practice declined substantially with the rise of Muslim control of North India and only continues to exist today within Tamil Nadu, Nepal and (subsequent to their adoption by certain schools of Mahayana Buddhism) within the Tibetan Buddhist traditions.

They did nonetheless have a profound influence on the Vaishnavite, Shaivite and Shakta movements.

The place of the renouncer within Hindu religious life received considerable attention during the second half of the twentieth century, largely from anthropologists seeking to understand the nature of both Hindu and Buddhist asceticism. In his influential text on hierarchy in Hindu society, Louis Dumont seminally asserted that the Indian renouncer is an 'individual out of the world' (1960: 267–86): upon entering the path leading to spiritual liberation, the renouncer performs his own funeral rites and by thus symbolically dying, transcends the world of caste. Dumont sought to distinguish the Indian renouncer from both the Western individual (who continues to exist within society) and the renouncer's caste-bound co-religionists (who, dependent on other castes for their religious identity, lack the individuality of the renouncer). Dumont's analysis is as provocative today as it was when it was penned in 1960. It is doubtful, however, whether it can encompass the full kaleidoscope of India's renouncer traditions: concepts of the 'renounced world', in particular, vary greatly from tradition to tradition. Most troubling of all, however, is the poverty of Dumont's choice of the Western-derived 'individual' as a bedrock for his discussion of religious traditions that do not simply seek to separate the person from 'the world' but rather to fully incorporate that world within the person.

Hinduism, colonialism and nationalism

The inheritance by the British of Muslim Moghul rule in India wrought great transformations upon the political and religious consciousness of Hindus, along with growing tensions between India's religious communities and the subsequent violent partition into India, Pakistan and Bangladesh in the months preceding independence in 1947. Many scholars have argued that the vehemence of the conflict, most particularly between Hindus and Muslims, derived from the peculiar changes that British rule brought to India. To understand this, we must understand something of the British administration of 'religion' in colonial India.

When the British government inherited India from the East India Company, they sought to rule through existing power elites and to act in a manner which left religious life undisturbed. This strategy was carried out through three policies. First, they endeavoured to govern existing social and caste groups within India through the religious and social codes that they gleaned from the Vedic texts and the writings of those they saw as the indigenous religious leaders (the brahmans). British rule therefore enshrined Brahmanical understandings of Indian life (including the caste system) as a means of almost universal governance for

Mahatma Gandhi (1869–1948)

No other single individual has had such a wide-ranging influence on modern Hinduism as Mohandas Gandhi (mahatma – 'great soul' – is an honorific given to him largely by his Western followers). Raised in a devout vaishna family in Gujarat, he studied law in London, from where he travelled to South Africa. Struck by the injustices of the apartheid system there, he began a lifelong campaign against what he perceived to be the hypocrisies of European colonial 'civilization'. Returning to India in 1915, he sought to realise the nationalist goal of independence, and a return to a truly 'Indian' India. As part of this, he eschewed British dress codes, wearing only homespun Indian cotton, and pursued a life of spartan asceticism. Gandhi rejected what he saw to be corrupt Western modes of political strategy, and advocated a form of passive non-violent resistance called *satyagraha* ('truth force'), in an endeavour to force the British hand into revealing its fundamental violence. His first major clash with the British came when, as a protest to the British-imposed Salt Tax, he marched to the Indian Ocean and picked up a handful of crystallised salt, thus flouting colonial law. He was arrested and began one of many jail terms. He also struggled to reform the caste system, which he felt had been corrupted, and to improve the status of untouchables, whom he dubbed *harijans* – 'Children of God'.

Much of Gandhi's political thought centred on the concept of truth (*satya*), which he saw as the dynamic that underlay Indian, as opposed to European, civilization (indeed, his autobiography is subtitled *The Story of My Experiments with Truth*). A wide reader, Gandhi's Hinduism was influenced by the Islam and Jainism of his native Gujarat, the Theosophical thought of late nineteenth-century Europe, as well as the growing Western scholarship on Hinduism (he first read the *Bhagavad-Gita* in English translation). Gandhi asserted a Hinduism that was both non-proselytising and at the same time profoundly inclusive, capable of holding all other religions within it. In this respect, the collapse of India into inter-religious division was a bitter disappointment to him. His protests against violent Hindu and Muslim nationalism were, in the end, his physical undoing: in 1948, he was assassinated in Delhi by a member of the militant Hindu movement, the RSS.

Hindus – a situation that had, in effect, never existed before. Second, colonial administrators, archaeologists and philologists (collectively known as 'orientalists') sought to unearth what they saw to be India's vast and lost philosophical and literary civilisation, a civilisation which dated from the time of the Vedas and which was deemed to be 'indigenous' to the Indian subcontinent. Apart from raising and unifying the political and religious consciousness of Hindus across India, this also implicitly portrayed the Muslim civilisation of the Moghuls as an alien force of foreign domination. Finally, as part of the endeavour to rule through the status quo, British officials instituted a series of All India Censuses, which sought to clarify the size of religious populations so as to more efficiently distribute colonial funds to religious groups and interests (mosque and temple maintenance and so forth) according to what percentage of the population they represented.

Combined together, these three policies of rule introduced a new concept to Hindu (and indeed Indian) religious and political life: the idea that rather than seeing 'other religious groups' in terms of specific individuals and families that one lived alongside, had as neighbours, employees or landlords, individuals were instead part of a much wider communal population of Hindus, Muslims, Sikhs or Buddhists competing for state largesse.

In time, these new modes of thinking about religious groups increasingly dominated Indian politics, as religious populations and their representatives began to compete. As the possibility of Indian independence from British rule and the introduction of secular self-governance from Delhi increased, political debate increasingly focused on the differential access to state power available to different religious groups. Muslims in Kashmir and many other Muslim-dominated northern states argued that they needed autonomy within a Hindu-dominated India, whilst Sikh communities in the Punjab asserted the wish for a Sikh homeland. In the last months of British India, Hindu, Muslim and Sikh populations threw the country into a state of civil war, forcing the British to announce the partition of the subcontinent into three sections: Hindu-dominated India and Muslim-dominated East and West Pakistan (the former of which is now Bangladesh). The announcement of the borders led to the desperate exodus of over 10 million people in either direction. During the chaotic and bloody months of partition, over a million people were slaughtered in mass killings, most of them Sikhs, who found themselves trapped between the two poles of communal identity.

Despite several wars between India and Pakistan, it is only since the 1980s that militant Hindu nationalism has gained real ground within pro-independence India. Within Hinduism, certain groups such as the Rashtriya Svayamsavek Sangh (RSS, a highly militaristic but ostensibly non-political volunteer association founded in 1925) , the Vishva Hindu Parishad (VHP, a brahmanically-dominated group founded in 1964 to give voice to Hindu religious leaders) and, more recently, the Baratiya Janata Party (BJP) have increasingly put forward the concept of *hindutva*, a Hindu national consciousness that seeks exclusive Hindu sovereignty within India. Often referred to as 'Hindu fundamentalism', the *hindutva*

> *The Ayodhya conflict*
>
> In 1992, Hindu protesters numbering in the hundreds of thousands destoyed the fifteenth-century Muslim mosque of Babar Masjid in the north Indian town of Ayodhya. The mosque had reputedly been built on the remains of an ancient temple dedicated to Rama, the mythical king at the centre of the *Ramayana* epic. Seeking to 'free Ram from his prison', the combined forces of the RSS, VHP and BJP converged on Ayodhya carrying bricks 'made from every Hindu village in Hindustan [India]' in order to rebuild Ram's temple on the rubble of the Masjid mosque. The Delhi-based government, at that time run by the secularist Congress (I) Party, attempted to halt the processions. Within days, the Masjid mosque lay in ruins, and over 2,000 people had been killed and 200,000 arrested in riots and clashes with police and army. At the time of writing, the temple to Rama has not yet been built, despite several attempts, and communal rioting centred on Ayodhya in 1995 and 2002.

movement is more accurately characterised as a fusion of a newly-organised Hindu religious identity and democratic nationalist exclusivism that is radically different from traditional Hinduism. Perhaps the clearest evidence of this difference lies in the response of the brahmanical VHP to recent attempts by Dalits in south India to convert to Islam or Buddhism as a means to ending their untouchable status. While traditional Hinduism would not have regarded untouchables as in any real sense 'Hindu' (because they were *avarna* – see above on the caste system), the VHP engaged on extensive campaigns selling Ganges water across South India to raise enough money to 'buy back' the Dalits to Hinduism. After all, without the untouchable castes, Hinduism in India would be in danger of dwindling into a 'minority religion'. Such movements derive directly from the modern political necessity to have a majority mandate. Whilst Hindu communities such as the ancient Vaishnavite renouncer sects have certainly engaged in religious conflict before, the militant communalistic movements of modern Hinduism – as with Islam and Buddhism – are very much the offspring of the modern, democratically structured nation state.

Buddhism

Of all the world's religions, Buddhism is probably the most universalistic, in the sense that its teachings are seen (in principle) to apply to all beings, of whatever nationality, status, sex, race, species (seen to apply to all conscious beings, not merely humans), and at whatever time (distinct from Islam and Christianity, where a theological distinction is made regarding whether a person lived before or after certain key revelations). It is perhaps this facet of Buddhism that has led to its extraordinary mobility across the modern world, and also to its often diffuse and malleable quality, adapting itself with extreme rapidity to particular social and cultural environments. Derived primarily from the teachings of Gautama Sakyamuni, Buddhism tends to avoid emphasising a central historical or divine figure, concentrating rather on a core dynamic between the universal existence of suffering and its solution in the attainment of *nirvana* or the status of Buddha ('Awakened One'). This 'awakening' – seen as open to all – derives from the practice of the Dharma-Vinaya, the teachings and discipline derived from Sakyamuni, which are depicted as the 'medicine' for the combined 'disease' of craving, ignorance and suffering. Whilst many lay Buddhist traditions (such as the Nichiren sects of Japan, or certain tantric schools in Tibet and Nepal) have grown up within Buddhism, its social organisation is most characteristically based on the lay support of monastic communities (or at least high religious virtuosi) called the *sangha*. Historically, this has produced two or more 'levels' to Buddhist religiosity: that pursued by the sangha; and that performed by laity, the latter being based on devotion to, and economic support of, the sangha. The Buddhist focus on the Buddha, the teachings (*dharma*) and the sangha is perhaps the most defining feature of the religious practice of the world's estimated 500 million Buddhists, encapsulated in the almost universal 'Refuge Prayer':

> Until the attainment of perfect enlightenment,
> I go for refuge to the Buddha,
> I go for refuge to the Dharma,
> I go for refuge to the Sangha.

The origins of Buddhism

As with 'Hinduism', 'Buddhism' is a term whose currency is relatively new, lacking any direct indigenous counterpart amongst the various schools of traditional Buddhist thought: instead, terms such as *marga* ('path') – implying a particular system of religious teachings and practice that does not, however, designate an exclusive religious population – are utilised. In this respect, Buddhism often goes hand in hand with other religious traditions. Nonetheless, in comparison with Hinduism, it is much easier to see Buddhism as a coherent set of traditions, nominally focused as it is on the teachings of a single founding figure, the historical Buddha (or 'Awakened One'), Gautama Sakyamuni.

Whilst the precise dates of the life of Sakyamuni – the so-called 'Sage of the Sakyas' and historical founder of Buddhism – are the subject of some scholarly debate, there is general agreement amongst Buddhists themselves that he was born as Siddhartha Gautama, the son of an aristocratic family, at Lumbini in north-east India, somewhere between 570 and 440 BCE. Destined to inherit a considerable kingdom and prophesied to become a *cakravartin* or 'World Conquering Emperor', Gautama grew increasingly dissatisfied with his cosseted courtly life. Eventually allowed to go forth into the kingdom he was to inherit, he is said to have witnessed the 'four great signs': an old man, a sick man, a corpse and a wandering mendicant. Distraught at the prospect that such suffering would inevitably befall not simply himself but all beings, Gautama defied his family by renouncing courtly and married life in search of the solution to the problem of human suffering. At the age of twenty-nine, he fled the palace and entered upon a rigorous six-year path of secluded meditation and yogic asceticism, much of which he practised with five ascetic companions. The Buddha-to-be (or *bodhisattva*) is said to have pushed himself further than all his companions, eating only a grain of rice a day for months on end and meditating long into each night. However, he became dissatisfied with the methods taught to him by his various teachers, and also with the extreme self-destructive austerities of the yogic life, which eventually brought him close to death. Gautama realised that the path to truth was not to be found in wholeheartedly embracing worldly life, nor in wholeheartedly rejecting it, but rather through the practice of a 'middle way' (*madhyamaka*) between these two extremes. Adopting this path, he entered into meditation under a tree in what is modern-day Bodhgaya, where his is said to have finally gained enlightenment. With this 'awakening' came knowledge of the causes of human suffering – the three 'fires' of ignorance, desire and hatred, which bind beings to constant rebirth and suffering in the world – and the means to their cessation, the 'snuffing out' (or *nirvana*) of the three fires, leading to an end of rebirth and suffering.

Eventually arising from his meditation seat, the Buddha sought disciples with whom to share his insight. Realising his previous teachers had passed away, he sought out his previous ascetic companions (who had rejected him for giving up austerity) and converted them to Buddhism through a series of discourses at the Deer Park at modern-day Sarnath. This discourse – which came to be known as the First Turning of the Wheel of Dharma – consisted primarily of the two central planks of Buddhist soteriology: the Four Noble Truths (see box) and the Eight-Fold Middle Way (the path to liberation that renounces both austerity and luxury). Having persuaded the five ascetics of the power and truth of his teachings, he ordained first one and later all of them to membership of a new Buddhist monastic order (or sangha) composed of monks (*bhikkus*) who had renounced household life and entered a life centred on the pursuit of *nirvana*.

The Four Noble Truths

The Truth of Suffering (*dukkha*): that all conditioned existence is characterised by dukkha, or unsatisfactoriness. This dukkha is located in the 'three signs of being': that all compounded phenomena are characterised by suffering, impermanence and an absence of self (*anatman*).

The Truth of Causes: that dukkha is caused by craving (either for or against things), based on ignorance.

The Truth of Cessation: that suffering or dissatisfaction can be ended when craving (in the form of attachment and hatred) and its cause, ignorance, is uprooted. This cessation of suffering is nirvana.

The Truth of Paths: that paths exist that lead towards the uprooting of ignorance and thus to an end of suffering. Central to these paths is the Eight-Fold Middle Way.

Statue of Buddha Sakyamuni, North-West India. By touching the earth with his left hand, whilst under the Bodhi tree, Sakyamuni is said to have called upon the Earth Goddess to witness his Enlightenment.
Martin A. Mills

The Buddha thus began a career of teaching and ordination that was to last for a further forty-five years. During this time, he built up a large community of wandering monks and nuns, supported by a wide network of lay-followers. As part of this, he constructed an extensive monastic code, designed to both maintain the integrity of the community and support individuals' path towards enlightenment.

Eventually, at the age of eighty, the Buddha died at Kusinaga following an extended bout of dysentery, thus passing into *paranirvana* (the state in which not only the desires of the mind but also the body upon which they feed departs from *samsara*). During his last day (described in the famous Mahaparanirvanasutta), the Buddha inquired three times of all the monks surrounding him whether there was anything further on which they needed clarification. Receiving no answer, he gave his final teaching and passed away.

The Buddha's final teaching

Behold now, bhikkus, I exhort you:
All compounded things are subject to decay.
Strive with diligence for perfection!

In the last months of his life, the Buddha very deliberately assigned no successor as leader of the sangha, instructing his closest companions that the teachings themselves – and in particular, the monastic code – should be their teacher. When pressed, he conceded that in cases of exceptional need, or where the teachings as laid down by him were insufficient to make a clear deliberation, all members of the sangha should congregate, debate and vote on the issue. Whilst all Buddhist monastic establishments have officers assigned to particular duties, this principle of democratic decision-making within the sangha has been maintained through to the present day.

The significance of the Buddha

Any introductory consideration of the life of Sakyamuni always runs the peculiar danger that the uninitiated reader will assume that Buddhism is somehow 'about' the Buddha, in the way that Christianity is 'about' Christ: that is, there is a danger of misinterpreting the Buddhist tradition as viewing Sakyamuni as a unique divine figure who is the focus of spiritual endeavour but whose status is effectively unattainable by anyone else. In actuality, Sakyamuni asserted the capacity of all people to achieve Buddhahood through their own efforts and rejected any over-emphasis on himself as an object of religious respect: what was seen as crucial instead was the possibility of Buddhahood and the capacity to achieve it through the dharma. Indeed, in the Samyutta Nikaya Sutra (III: 120) the Buddha is said to have chided a monk called Vakkali who displayed too much blind devotion to the Buddha as a teacher: 'Hush, Vakkali! What is there for you in seeking this vile, visible body? Vakkali, whoever sees Dharma, sees me; whoever sees me, sees Dharma.'

This emphasis on the Buddhist teachings, and on the Buddha as a pure manifestation of those teachings, threads through much Buddhist literature and iconography. Thus, whilst Buddhas are often depicted as god-like in their capacities (particularly within the Mahayana traditions), this should be read in context. As Peter Harvey has commented: 'While Christians see Jesus as God-become-man, then Buddhists see the Buddha as man-become-Dharma' (1990: 28). A more vexed question within the Buddhist context is the degree to which the Buddha might reasonably be propitiated with offerings and prayers, given his departure to *nirvana*. Some assert that such actions are merely empty ritual, born out of an emotional desire for deity. Others (in particular, within the Mahayana) assert that Buddhas are present within the world in some sense and, moreover, that prayers to the Buddha are beneficial even if 'not heard' because they plant beneficial karmic seeds in the mind of the worshipper.

The Dharma-Vinaya (teachings and discipline)

The precise form that the Buddha's teachings are held to have taken differs between the various Buddhist traditions. Within the Theravadan schools, the Buddhist doctrine is organised according to the so-called Tripitaka, or 'Three Baskets', of Buddhist doctrine.

The 'Three Baskets' of Buddhist doctrine

- The Suttapitaka ('basket of teachings'): accounts of those teachings ascribed to the Buddha;
- The Vinayapitaka ('basket of discipline'): the complete Buddhist monastic code applying to members of the sangha; and
- The Abhidhammapitaka ('basket of insights'): a collection of treatise on key issues on Buddhist thought, not directly ascribed to the Buddha but regarded as authoritative.

This combination of direct teaching by example, moral code and commentarial discussion of principles dominated much of Buddhist life. Indeed, the combination of teachings and moral code hides a deeper understanding within Buddhist thinking: each element was seen insufficient on its own as a means to the attainment of enlightenment.

The Eight-Fold Middle Way

Formulated as the key to transcending the twin cravings of desire and hatred through the avoidance of the extremes of indulgence and austerity, the eight central precepts covered the three areas of morality (*sila*), meditative concentration (*samadhi*) and wisdom (*prajña*):

Right View: Understanding the Four Noble Truths.

Right Resolve: A desire to renounce both desire and hatred.

Right Speech: Refraining from lying, abusive speech, divisive speech, and idle words and gossip.

Right Action: Refraining from sexual misconduct, stealing, or committing violent acts, especially killing.

Right Livelihood: Refraining from those professions that involve harming others or the relentless pursuit of gain, or promote superstition, intoxication, or confusion.

Right Effort: The diligent pursuit of truth and morality, and avoidance of indolence, indulgence in worldly concerns (both business and pleasure) and the rejection of spiritual responsibility.

Right Mindfulness: Careful and constant observation of the three kinds of activity: mental, verbal and physical.

Right Concentration: Regular practice of the four levels of meditative concentration (*jhyana*).

The foundation of the Buddha's message lay in his identification of the 'three marks' of all conditioned phenomena (such as one's own self, other people, tables, chairs, houses and so on): that they are impermanent (*anicca*); that their nature is unsatisfying (*dukkha*); and that they are 'no-self' (*anatman*). Sakyamuni taught that to engage with conditioned phenomena in a way that misconceives them as permanent, or as a source of satisfaction or happiness, or as though they had an intrinsic self or fundamental reality, is to cause oneself (and often others) suffering. Such a mistaken view of reality was not, however, merely a philosophical abstraction; rather it was an everyday, habitual emotional act that coloured our every waking and dreaming moment. It therefore required an enormous act of mental and emotional discipline to rein in such habitual tendencies, and a way of life and social environment conducive to such a radical 'turning around at the seat of consciousness'. Whilst the teachings were seen as leading towards enlightenment, the capacity to fully understand and internalise them required firm attention and a mind that was not constantly distracted by objects of desire and hatred – that is, a mind bound by firm discipline (encapsulated in the Buddhist monastic code and the Eight-Fold Middle Way) as part of a community of like-minded individuals. Conversely, whilst virtuous moral action could improve one's future prospects – by ensuring rebirth as an intelligent human being endowed with freedom and the capacity to study the dharma – karma itself (whether good or bad) merely continued the cycle of existence. It did not release an individual from samsara, which required actual insight into the nature of existence and suffering. It was for this reason that the Buddha referred to the path to enlightenment as a whole as Dharma-Vinaya.

The Dharma-Vinaya, as a system, centred on a combination of three basic aspects of spiritual endeavour: sila – moral discipline; samadhi, mental concentration in meditation; and prajña, or discriminating wisdom. In pragmatic terms, this involved the construction of communities that insulated individuals from the attractions and diversions of everyday life and yet allowed them to continue as viable social and economic entities: a monastic community centred on the transmission of the teaching, organised around the progressive disciplining of the mind and body, regulated by a comprehensive series of rules, but capable of being supported by a lay community.

Whilst certain areas (such as Japan) have increasingly sidelined monasticism within the popular Buddhist path, the place of a celibate ordained community remains at the heart of the Buddhist vision of liberation. Monasticism is organised around a two- or three-fold process of ordination, in which the candidate vows to abide by a series of 'training rules' (collectively known as the Vinaya) first as a novice and then as a semi- or fully-ordained monk. Traditionally, the monastic community focused on a central prayer hall, in which monks meet on most days as part of the ordinary running of the monastery. Monks are, however, only obliged to meet twice every lunar month – at the full and new moons – in order to recite the training rules and confess any breeches of discipline; and to observe the 'rainy season retreat', in which they refrain from leaving the monastery precincts during the summer months. As a whole, the Buddhist sangha contains no closed orders but specific groups of monks or individuals may go into closed retreat for periods of extended meditation (the most rigorous being the Tibetan 'three year, three month, three day' retreats).

The Buddhist sangha combines within it complementary principles of hierarchy and egalitarianism. Extremely respect-oriented, monks are obliged to show real deference to those who have received ordination before them (nuns of any level of experience and ordination, however, are obliged to show deference to all monks, regardless of status). This is particularly the case in situations where a more senior member of the sangha is one's teacher: within many Mahayana schools, for example, the student is encouraged to view their personal teacher as though they were themselves a Buddha. Simultaneously, Buddhist monasticism includes no vow of obedience such as that found within the Catholic Church, leading to a large degree of local autonomy; within monasteries themselves, moreover, important debates and internal problems are ultimately decided on by a vote amongst all ordained members, who, in this capacity, act as equals.

In these respects, Sakyamuni's legacy is as extraordinary one: despite considerable internal debate, Buddhist communities have, by and large, suffered none of the internecine conflict that has attended Christianity and Islam. His message has proved remarkably fruitful in terms of the sheer subtlety of its philosophical speculations and meditative disciplines. Last, and certainly not least, the Buddhist sangha has proved to be the single longest-surviving human institution in known history.

To what extent, however, did Sakyamuni's philosophy represent an innovation, a move away from, extant Hindu religiosity? Certainly, the Buddha was not alone in his call to world-renunciation: by the time of his birth, many renouncer traditions – called Śramana movements – had emerged to question the domination of the Brahmanical tradition and the Vedas (see Hinduism earlier in this chapter). Indeed, the Buddha's framing of the whole question of suffering in terms of the dynamic between sensory desire and karma, and as a movement from samsara to nirvana, was characteristic of the entire discursive environment of his day. What was distinctive about his teachings was his particular framing of the religious path within a peculiarly Buddhist conception of the person.

To begin with, the Buddha's conception of craving in terms of the three fires of attachment, hatred and, most importantly, ignorance – itself arguably a clever pun on the three sacrificial fires of the twice-born's household, echoing the Buddha's encouragement to 'go forth' from the household – drew a picture of the consciousness chained to suffering by a deeply habitual misconception about the way things exist and thus about the true basis for living life within the world. At the heart of this misconception lay the Buddha's primary divergence from existing Hindu speculation: his assertion of *anatman*, the absence of a deep abiding self, or *atman*. This rejection, later developed by the

Mahayana into the rejection of the true inherent existence of all phenomena, marked a radical step away from Upanishadic understandings of the world and of knowledge.

The doctrine of *anatman* implied a still further divergence from Hindu moral thought: since there was no *atman*, there was also no *Brahman* (with which it is seen as identical). This therefore constituted a rejection of the fundamental notion of dharma as an abiding reality, in terms of which moral life and *karma* were constructed (see Hinduism above). Indeed, within the *Aganna Sutra* the Buddha rejects the caste system as the basis for moral evaluation. Instead, he asserts suffering and its cause, craving, as the basis for any Buddhist understanding of morality: that personal moral discipline should be aimed at the uprooting of craving and that inter-personal morality should be solely conceived in terms of ending, or not causing, the suffering of others.

The canonicity of Buddhist teachings

Buddhism contains within it two contrasting tendencies as far as the notion of 'doctrine' is concerned: that of basing a determination of truth on one's own experience and that of respecting those who have gone before one on the spiritual path. In his teachings to the Kalama people on the nature of spiritual authority, the Buddha argued that following those before you simply because it was traditional to do so was like a line of blind men following one another off a cliff.

> Don't go by reports, by legends, by traditions, by scripture, by logical conjecture, by inference, by analogies, by agreement through pondering views, by probability, or by the thought, 'This contemplative is our teacher.' When you know for yourselves that, 'These qualities are skilful; these qualities are blameless; these qualities are praised by the wise; these qualities, when undertaken and carried out, lead to welfare and to happiness' – then you should enter and remain in them.
>
> Anguttara Nikaya III.65

Sakyamuni thus emphasised the necessity of testing particular insights for oneself, to see if they were practically useful in liberating one from suffering, rather than merely logical or authoritative. At the same time, the Buddha also praised those laity who showed respect for the Three

Jewels, and many subsequent Buddhist traditions (most particularly the Tibetan and Zen traditions) have argued that true liberation from suffering requires complete obedience to one's master – although, according to certain writers within the Tibetan tradition, such obedience should only come once the teacher himself has been fully tested, a process which may take up to twelve years!

This ambiguity has led to disagreements as to the canonicity of teachings. Often described as the Buddhist 'doctrine', the dharma refers to that corpus of teachings, either oral or written, that is accepted by particular groups of Buddhists as *buddhavasana*, 'the word of the Buddha'. What this means in practice is a point of disagreement amongst Buddhists themselves. Some, for example, argue that what counts as dharma is restricted to that material that can be reasonably related back to the actual teachings of Gautama Sakyamuni, the historical Buddha. Others argue that whatever is in line with the ethical and philosophical intentions of the Buddha constitutes dharma. Thus, the medieval Tibetan Buddhist scholar Geshe Tönpa put forward his own definition.

If it counteracts negative emotions, it is Dharma. If it doesn't, it is non-Dharma.

If it doesn't fit with worldly ways, it is Dharma. If it fits, it is non-Dharma.

If it fits with the scriptures and your instructions, it is Dharma. If it doesn't fit, it is non-Dharma.

If it leaves a positive imprint [on your mind], it is Dharma. If it leaves a negative imprint, it is non-Dharma.

Geshe Tönpa (Patrul Rinpoche 1994: 260)

There is therefore considerable disagreement within the Buddhist world as to what precisely constitutes 'authentic' dharma and many schools deny either the authenticity or the primacy of other teachings. However, a core body of conceptual material (most particularly the Buddha's 'First Turning of the Wheel of Dharma' at Sarnath, in which he outlined the Four Noble Truths and the Eight-Fold Middle Way) is accepted as part of the exoteric canon by all Buddhist schools.

Whilst canonical, the Four Noble Truths do not – as, for example, with the various Christian creeds, or the Islamic *shahadah* – represent an assertion of 'true belief' for Buddhists. They were instead analysed in the Buddhist scriptures as a means to understanding and curing the disease of suffering, in much the same way a doctor would: the examination of symptoms, the determination of causes, the identification of an antidote, and the administering of that antidote. As a result, once enlightenment is achieved, the Four Truths are rendered superfluous.

The development and spread of Buddhism

The death of the Buddha forced the sangha to decide on ways to continue to practise and propagate Sakyamuni's teachings. In particular, as Buddhism spread across India, it increasingly encountered cultures and conditions that required points of clarification in the Buddhist doctrine and monastic code. Soon after the paranirvana, therefore, the sangha convened the first great Buddhist Council at Rajagriha (around 486 BCE). Ananda, the Buddha's closest disciple, recited in full the Buddha's teachings as a series of *sutras* – records of discourses given by the Buddha – while the monk Upali recited the monastic code, or Vinaya. In the centuries following the Buddha's death, Buddhism spread with remarkable speed, following the trade routes of Asia in three principle directions: north, through modern-day Pakistan, Afghanistan and onwards to China, Korea and Japan; south, to Sri Lanka and Indonesia; and east, to Bangladesh, Burma, Thailand, Laos and Vietnam. Within three hundred years, Buddhist monks were to be found in almost all parts of South and Central Asia (with the major exception of Tibet).

During this time, the increasingly powerful position of the Buddhist sangha manifested itself in a variety of ways. First of all, there emerged the 'domestication' of the sangha, as monks shifted from their original wandering lifestyle to a more settled existence in Buddhist *viharas*, or resting houses. These, in turn, developed into the full-blown monastic establishments that characterised institutional Buddhism from the time of Christ onwards. Settled existence brought with it many changes: a regular income from a fixed population of nearby laity; a platform from which to provide ceremonial, teaching and pastoral duties, which gradually overtook the original eremitic asceticism of the monastic community; and increasing landownership by the sangha, as wealthy patrons donated large tracts of land to monastic establishments.

Political sponsorship increased too, particularly in the centuries following the conversion of the north-Indian emperor Asoka to Buddhism around 250 BCE. Asoka's patronage lent considerable weight to the notion of Buddhism not simply as an individual path towards liberation but as a broader system of social mores for laity and state.

The expansion of Buddhism, usually along the pre-existing trade routes of Asia, caused it to encounter new cultures and systems of rule and social organisation. This placed particular pressures on the constitution of the sangha and the interpretation of the Vinaya. This, in turn, led to the organisation of further Buddhist councils in India. The second council occurred some seventy years after the first, at Vaisali, where questions concerning ten points in the Vinaya were debated. In 250 BCE, Emperor Asoka convened a third council at Pataliputra in northern India, designed to encapsulate Buddhist thinking in one canonical format. Out of this council, the Tripitaka, or 'Three Baskets', was formed (see box on p. 247).

The first two hundred years following the Buddha's death thus saw several radical developments of Sakyamuni's vision: the creation of a settled monastic life, the production of a written canon and the development of substantial political power related to royal patronage. Moreover, the introduction of Buddhism into new cultures and social groups led to the proliferation of Buddhist schools from an early stage. Classically, Buddhists speak of eighteen principal schools of thought during this period, most of which have died away in the intervening centuries; the rest have been subsumed into the growing division of Buddhist thought into the twin movements of the Theravada and Mahayana that encompass modern Buddhism.

The rise of the Mahayana

During the period 100 BCE to 150 CE, Buddhist thinkers all across Asia began to develop existing Buddhist thought in a variety of key new ways. In particular, existing understandings of the nature of Buddhahood, the relatively rigid formulation of Buddhist philosophies of existence, and of the sangha's moral responsibilities in the world, came to be questioned. In the Indian context, this gave rise to the *bodhisattva-yana*, or 'path of the enlightenment hero', which concentrated not so much on the path of personal liberation from suffering, but on the attainment of enlightenment in order to save all beings from suffering. Ultimately, this new movement was to coalesce into the Mahayana, or 'Great Vehicle', of Buddhism, a set of schools profoundly different from the ancient and Theravada schools. In many respects this new thinking was more of a subtle shift of emphasis rather than an actual denial of the validity of the ancient schools, but the emergence of new bodies of Mahayana scripture – attributed to the Buddha but rejected by non-Mahayana schools – began to seal the difference, leading to a general bifurcation of the two forms of Buddhism into Mahayana and Theravada by around 500 CE.

Over the next thousand years, many Mahayana traditions also decreased their emphasis on enlightenment as the sole preserve of a monastic elite, with several traditions developing substantial lay traditions: indeed, in Tibet, certain schools argued that the necessity for engagement within the world by Buddhism's highest practitioners entitled certain married yogins to head large celibate monastic institutions.

Reality and the mind in Mahayana Buddhism

All [objects of knowledge] are within your own natures, yet your own natures are always pure. The sun and moon are always bright, but if they are covered by clouds, although above they are bright, below they are darkened, and the sun, moon, stars and planets cannot be seen properly. But if suddenly the wind of wisdom should blow and roll away the clouds and mists, all forms in the universe appear at once. The purity of the nature of the mind in this world is like the blue sky; wisdom is like the sun, knowledge like the moon. Although knowledge and wisdom are always clear, if you cling to external environments, the floating clouds of false thoughts will create a cover, and your own nature cannot become clear.

'Platform Sutra of the Sixth Zen Patriarch', H. Dumoulin (1994: 140)

In terms of the dharma (as opposed to the Vinaya), the Mahayana or the Theravada can be distinguished in three principal areas.

First of all, there are different understandings about the ultimate nature of phenomena. Whilst the Theravada, in line with other ancient schools of Buddhism, argue for the absence of a permanent self (*anatman* – no-self), Mahayana thinkers have endeavoured to push the boundaries of the anatman critique wider than was accepted within the ancient schools, arguing that all phenomena – including religious concepts such as nirvana and the Four Noble Truths – lack substantial existence. Certain Mahayana schools asserted that there was no distinction between subject and object, that all phenomena were of the nature of mind (*cittamatrin*, 'mind only'). This rejection of ultimate realities included a rejection of the ultimate reality even of Buddhist truths themselves, a pronounced anti-nomian tendency that can, in many respects, also account for the extraordinary religious and spiritual creativity of the Mahayana.

The next area of difference concerns understandings of the nature of Buddhahood. Whilst the Theravada generally see the Buddha as having departed to nirvana (and therefore as being unable to help ordinary beings), Mahayana thinkers have argued that such a distinction ignores the fundamentally compassionate nature of the Buddha's mission as a teacher, a compassion which they regard as an indivisible part of Buddhahood. This has led them to emphasise the *bodhisattva* – one heroically intent on enlightenment as a basis for relieving the sufferings of all beings – as the ultimate Buddhist figure.

The birth of new schools

68 CE	Arrival of Buddhism in China.
c.100	Life of Nagarjuna, founder of Madhyamaka (Middle Way) Schools of Mahayana Buddhism.
3rd C.	Expansion of Buddhism to South-East Asia.
4th C.	Asanga founds Yogacara School of Mahayana Buddhism. Early development of Vajrayana (tantric) Buddhism. Expansion of Buddhism to Korea.
5th C.	Founding of Nalanda Buddhist monastery. Chinese pilgrim Fa-hsien provides earliest account of Buddhist life in India. First evidence of emergence of Pure Land Buddhism in China. Sri Lankan Theravadin nuns introduce nuns' full ordination lineage to China.
520	Bodhidharma arrives in China from India.
6th C.	Buddhism enters Japan, to become state religion 50 years later (594).
650	Buddhism enters Tibet from China and Nepal. Chinese Pilgrim Hsuan-Tsang (602–64) visits India.
779	Founding at Samye of first Buddhist monastery in Tibet.
792	Great debate at Samye between Indian Mahayana and Chinese Ch'an Buddhism. Indian schools triumphant.
9th C.	Tendai School (founded by Saichō 767–822) and Shingon School (founded by Kukai 774–835) appear in Japan. Great Buddhist persecution in China (845).
11th C.	Atisha (982–1054) arrives in Tibet from India (1042). Marpa (1012–97) begins Kagyu Lineage of Tibetan Buddhism. The bhikkhu and bhikkhuni (monk and nun) communities at Anuradhapura, Sri Lanka, die out following invasions from South India. Sakya School of Tibetan Buddhism established. Revival of Theravada Buddhism in Sri Lanka and Burma.
12th C.	Theravada Buddhism established in Burma. Hönen (1133–1212) founded the Pure Land School of Japanese Buddhism. Eisai (1141–1215) founds the Rinzai Zen School of Japanese Buddhism.
12th C.	onwards: Muslim destruction of Buddhist centres in India.
13th C.	Dogen (1200–53) founds Soto Zen School of Japanese Buddhism. Shinran (1173–1263) founds True Pure Land School of Japanese Buddhism. Nichiren (1222–82) founds Nichiren school of Japanese Buddhism. Mongol conquest of Tibetan and China. Mongol court converted to Vajrayana Buddhism.
14th C.	Bu-ston establishes first definitive Tibetan Buddhist canon. Theravada Buddhism becomes state religion of northern Thailand.
15th C.	Tsongkhapa (1357–1419) founds Gelukpa school of Tibetan Buddhism.

Finally, there are differences in understanding the breadth of the Buddha's word. The Mahayana ascribe as canonical a far larger body of scripture than the contents of the older Tripitaka, arguing that certain of the Buddha's teachings remained hidden for several centuries because of their complex and esoteric nature. New revealed texts, most particularly the Prajñaparamita, or 'Perfection of Wisdom' sutras, which concentrate on the sophisticated but obscure epistemological arguments surrounding the concept of 'emptiness' (*sunyata*), began to appear between 100 BCE and 100 CE. The Theravada regard these texts as (at best) apocryphal but they constitute the heart of Mahayana philosophical and ethical thinking.

The distinction between the Theravada and Mahayana should not be interpreted as sectarian in the modern political sense. Whilst crucial (and often controversial) within Buddhist thought, differences in doctrine are not seen as fundamental to the constitution of the Buddhist sangha. Indeed, it was very common in early Buddhism for monks holding widely divergent philosophical and Buddhalogical views to live within the same monastic community (*nikaya*): what counted was that they shared the same orthopraxy, the code of behaviour that regulated monastic life. Whilst there are slightly different versions of this monastic code, or Vinaya, in general the Mahayana and Theravada concur on questions of monastic discipline: indeed, the Tibetan Buddhists (seen by many as completely divergent from the Theravada) maintain the Mulasarvastivadin monastic code of the ancient non-Mahayana schools.

Maturity and diversity

The rapid spread of Buddhism across Asia in the years after the Buddha's death came to an end at the beginning of the second millennium CE and was followed by a lengthy period of embedding and diversification. By this stage, Buddhism had effectively settled into a dual pattern of Theravada- and Mahayana-dominated countries.

The Theravada ('Doctrine of the Elders'), or 'Southern' tradition of Buddhism, has tended to predominate in South and South-East Asia, specifically Sri Lanka, Thailand, Myanmar (Burma), Cambodia and Laos. Centred strongly on an elite monastic tradition, the Theravada have often followed the ancient Indian tendency to divide religious personnel into community monasteries in village and urban centres (given over to teaching laity and providing ceremonial services) and 'forest-dwelling' hermitages (producing elite – and often politically powerful – religious virtuosi). As with all other Buddhist communities, both of these monastic groups are supported by networks of laity who provide food, land, labour, wealth and (most importantly!) new monks. Unlike in many Mahayana countries (such as Tibet), lifelong members of the sangha only represented a tiny proportion of Theravada Buddhists, although the monasteries often housed 'temporary monks', young men for whom a few months in a monastery was seen as an essential introduction to adult status.

The Theravada tradition maintained a strong conservative element, concentrating on the production of an elite monastic order designed to reproduce the word of the Buddha from one generation to the next; in this respect, Theravada has demonstrated a marked stability of form across the centuries, despite occasionally dying out in particular locations and being reborn through the importation of the lineage of ordination from elsewhere.

By contrast, Mahayana communities have historically tended to predominate in Central and Eastern Asia, most particularly in the countries surrounding China – Korea, Japan, Tibet and Mongolia. The tendency of the Mahayana to view Buddhist soteriology from a conceptual and soteriological standpoint, rather than sticking solely to a pre-existent framework, has led to a considerable proliferation of forms.

The Mahayana tradition has proved extremely fecund in many respects: in developing new systems of spiritual and ethical practice; in opening itself to the possibilities of advanced lay practice; and in adapting itself to surrounding cultures. It is therefore unsurprising that the most substantial innovations within Buddhist thought since Sakyamuni's time – the introduction of the Prajñaparamita literature and the development of Vajrayana, or tantric, Buddhism – were both Mahayana innovations.

From a philosophical perspective, the Mahayana has been dominated by two trains of thought: the Madhyamaka (or Middle Way School), which argues that the source of suffering lies in our ignorance of the manner in which deeply held concepts about the world are constructed; and the Yogacara (or Cittamatrin – 'Mind Only') traditions, which argued instead that all phenomena are 'mental' in nature and that suffering originates from our tendency to shatter a unified experience into a divided model of self-and-other. These two trains of thought – Yogacara and Madhyamaka – can be found throughout the Mahayana world, often within the same Buddhist community, and in many cases are taught simultaneously to monks. Cutting across this distinction, a variety of more concrete teaching and institutional traditions tend to be found in specific places. A few principal examples are set out below.

Ch'an (Zen) Buddhism
Centred in East Asia, Ch'an concentrates on the importance of meditation (zazen) as a means of liberation from *samsara*. The Zen schools are

probably most famous for their use of koan poetry – short riddles designed to shatter conceptual thought.

Pure Land Buddhism
Historically based in China and surrounding countries, this popular form of Buddhism emphasises faith in the salvific power of the Buddha Amitabha ('Boundless Light') and the possibility of being reborn in his Buddha Paradise as a result of the faithful and persistent recitation of his mantra.

Vajrayana ('Diamond Vehicle') Buddhism
Traditionally found in Tibet, Nepal and Mongolia, Vajrayana is a highly ritualised form of Mahayana that employs tantric modes of divine empowerment as a means to enlightenment.

None of these traditions represents a monolithic entity unto itself: both the Theravada and the Mahayana consist of a variety of different traditions emphasising different elements of Buddhist thinking and practice. There are, for example, four principal forms of Tibetan Buddhism – the Gelukpa, the Kagyu, the Sakya and the Nyingma – each of which represents a complex amalgamation of a variety of traditions, often borrowed from one another, with many monasteries continuing their own specific traditions of ritual and training.

The challenges of modernity

As with many traditions now classed as 'world religions' (including Islam, Christianity and Hinduism), nineteenth-century European colonialism had a substantial impact on Buddhism. The abeyance of Buddhism in India, the land of its birth, meant that it was left to European (and particularly British) explorers, archaeologists and colonial administrators to both rediscover and rewrite the story of early Buddhism through the uncovering of key sites, such as Bodhgaya, and the translation of Buddhist texts into German and English.

At the same time, colonial rule in regions such as Sri Lanka (with its attendant Christian-dominated schooling system) served to significantly remould what was perceived to be 'proper' Buddhism in the minds of the indigenous elite groups. Scholars such as Richard Gombrich had indeed spoken of the ascendancy of 'Protestant' forms of Buddhism, which stressed meditation, anti-ritualism and personal salvation, thus significantly shifting emphasis away from the traditional social and

Monks of the Gelukpa Order of Tibetan Buddhism: beginning as a novice as young as five years of age, a Tibetan monk progresses through several levels of vows of monastic discipline, usually as a lifelong vocation.
Martin A. Mills

ceremonial focus of Buddhism. Such individualised notions of Buddhism as a rational philosophy also became fashionable in European and American literary circles, leading to their adoption and further ideological reconstruction by movements such as the British Theosophical Society under Madame Blavatsky during the late nineteenth and early twentieth century. Many of these rewritten forms of Buddhism proved highly influential in many of the Buddhist nationalist movements of South-East Asia, most particularly Sri Lanka, where the propagation of 'scientifically-revised true Buddhism' became a principal cornerstone of the nationalist project of moulding the island as an independent Buddhist state.

In a different way, the rise of communism in the middle to late twentieth century presented considerable challenges to Buddhism's traditional place within Asian society. Communist movements in China, Cambodia, Vietnam, Korea and Mongolia succeeded in either drastically weakening or, in cases such as Cambodia and Tibet, effectively destroying Buddhism in those countries on a temporary basis. Whilst this position has eased substantially since the late 1970s (with the death of Mao and the end of the Vietnam War, amongst other factors), causing the rebirth of Buddhism in regions such as India and Mongolia, the traditional political and social influence of monastic Buddhism in Asia appears – for better or worse – to be very much a thing of the past.

Tibetan monks gradually creating a sand mandala – a representation of the divine palace, body, speech and mind of the tantric Buddha Yamantaka – one of the most distinctive ritual practices of Vajrayana Buddhism. Martin A. Mills

While interest in Theravada Buddhism remains roughly constant in Europe and America, and is often portrayed as the most 'true' form of Buddhism, the post-war years led to an upsurge in interest in Zen (particularly amongst the beat generation and its immediate cultural inheritors in the US) and Tibetan Buddhism (spurred, in particular, by the Tibetan diaspora that followed the Chinese invasion of Tibet in 1949, and the high public profile of key Tibetan lamas such as His Holiness the Fourteenth Dalai Lama since the late 1970s). Western interest has focused on a highly modernist interpretation of Buddhism: many writers and organisations (most obviously the Friends of the Western Buddhist Order) have sought to construct a specifically Western idiom for Buddhist thought, whilst playing down (and, in certain cases, editing out) many of the clear hierarchical, ritualistic and cosmological resonances of Buddhism's Asian forms.

Conclusion: Hinduism and Buddhism as religions

As we have seen, both Buddhism and Hinduism have undergone vast changes over their history and been the subject of a considerable number of highly politicised reform movements: the European colonial project to create a distinct 'Hinduism', urban middle-class endeavours in Sri Lanka to shed the ritual traditions of 'village' Buddhism in favour of individualist 'Protestant' forms centred on meditation and doctrine, and religious nationalist movements that have transformed both Hindu and Buddhist worlds. This means that students should be wary of uncritically assuming any substantive core to either tradition – especially when that core is conceived in terms of a series of rationalised practices or beliefs. Similarly, they should also avoid automatically assuming that such traditions are identifiable over time in an unproblematic way.

This issue is more than simply a historical one and goes to the heart of our understanding of religion as a concept. At the end of the nineteenth century, Edward Tylor famously defined religion as 'a belief in supernatural beings' (Tylor 1871). Though Tylor's discussion was clearly dominated by an Abrahamic emphasis on divinity (something largely rejected by subsequent writers on religion), Buddhism and Hinduism still raise vexing questions of categorisation.

In the Buddhist case, certain Buddhist tenets – the rejection of an ultimate creator god; the assertion that those gods that do exist also require liberation from suffering; and the apparently negative formulation of the notion of nirvana – have led some commentators (and quite a few Buddhists) to assert that Buddhism is not a religion at all but rather an ethical philosophy. This is not a universally accepted perspective. Many argue that Buddhist assertions of rebirth and karmic law, their institutionalisation of ethical soteriology in the form of monastic life and, indeed, the Buddha's own rejection of 'needless philosophising', mean that Buddhism can no more be treated as a philosophy (in the European Enlightenment sense of the term) than it can a religion.

The heart of the difficulty in discussing Buddhism as a religion per se lies in the assumption that any understanding of religion begins with a corpus of revealed truth about the world: that it begins with the truth of (for example) a central deity and works from there. By contrast, rather than being truth-centred, it is more helpful to look at Buddhism as problem-centred: that is, centred on the problem of suffering – or dukkha – the First Noble Truth. Solving that problem – rather than defining any particular set of truths as canonical – is the aim that structures much of Buddhist thought. This has led Buddhist teachings to contain within them several, often apparently conflicting, 'doctrines', each of which is to be evoked as the most 'skilful means' (in Sanskrit, *upaya kausalya*) to overcome suffering for a particular person at a particular stage in their spiritual career.

When discussing Hinduism, by comparison, the sheer diversity of the traditions encompassed by the term seems itself to defy categorisation. Many of the deities and supernatural figures encountered within Hindu traditions – Brahma, Vishnu, Shiva, Ganesha, Krishna – are only taken as central to religious practice by certain Hindu groups and not others, although all might accede in principle to their existence. Whilst this may seem to allow us to fall back to a position of asserting a certain 'general cosmology' as being the basis for religious identity, we are then faced with the problem that most of these deities are, awkwardly enough, believed to exist by most Buddhists, for whom they are an entirely peripheral component of religious practice!

Such conundrums have forced specialists in religious studies to follow one of three paths: first, to categorise Buddhism, and to a lesser extent Hinduism, as something other than a religion in the full sense of the word (or, more perjoratively, not a 'proper' religion); second, to assert that religion as we understand the concept covers a wide diversity of elements, only some of which apply to any one religion; and finally, to reject the concept of 'religion' itself as an analytical category that is in any sense meaningful beyond the confines of Christian doctrinal and polemical discussions. This remains an open debate; in all probability, all of these three approaches are insufficient.

Further reading

Hinduism

Dumont, L. (1960), *Homo Hierarchicus: The Caste System and Its Implications*, Chicago: University of Chicago Press.
Flood, G. (1996), *An Introduction to Hinduism*, Cambridge: Cambridge University Press.
Fuller, C. (1992), *The Camphor Flame: Popular Hinduism and Society in India*, Princeton: Princeton University Press.

Buddhism

Bechert, H. and R. Gombrich (eds.) (1991), *The World of Buddhism*, London: Thames and Hudson.
Harvey, P. (1990), *An Introduction to Buddhism: Teachings, History and Practices*, Cambridge: Cambridge University Press.
Williams, P. (2000), *Buddhist Thought: A Complete Introduction to the Indian Tradition*, London: Routledge.

Questions

1. What problems do Hinduism and Buddhism present for our understanding of the concept of 'religion'?

2. Hinduism and Buddhism seem to share many fundamental religious concepts, such as *moksha*, *karma* and *samsara*. To what extent do they also share a fundamental view of reality? Particular attention should be applied here to the views of Mahayana and Vedanta thinkers, and to the question of sel (*atman*).

3. What is meant by 'religious orthodoxy' within the Buddhist and Hindu traditions? Can we identify specific elements of those orthodoxies? What problems might attend such a project?

4. Both Hinduism and Buddhism emphasise the value of renouncing ordinary life as a means to attaining liberation. To what extent does this imply that they embody an 'anti-social' ethic?

5. What changes have modern history in general, and European colonisation in particular, had on indigenous understandings of religious identity? Be careful to distinguish between Hinduism and Buddhism.

CHAPTER SIX

New Religious Movements and the New Age

Matthew Wood

Introduction: The changing religious landscape

Studies of religion generally contend that since the 1970s there has been a change in the social landscape of the West, leading to religion becoming a private aspect of life. Although most people still profess a belief in God, the reference points by which such belief may be assessed have disappeared. However, whilst the last thirty years have seen the decline in mainstream church attendance steepen, there has been a quickening of the emergence and spread of new religious groups.

This can be illustrated by some results from the English Church Attendance Survey. The percentage of the population reported as attending a Christian church on an average Sunday dropped from 11.7 per cent in 1979 to 7.5 per cent in 1998 but over the same period members of new Christian groups, such as New Frontiers International and Ichthus Christian Fellowship, increased nearly fourfold. Likewise, many other new religions have become established and experienced growth in Britain. However, their presence may be reflected not so much in their memberships, which are relatively small, particularly in regard to the number of people who have ceased attending mainstream churches, but in their influence on people who have come into contact with one or other of their activities.

This situation has meant that theories of secularisation have been questioned. Although many sociologists still maintain the effect of secularisation to be, as Bryan Wilson wrote in the 1960s, 'the process whereby religious thinking, practice and institutions lose social significance' (1969: 14), the persistence of some religious beliefs and the creation of a plethora of new groups have meant that alternative theories have gained ground. Grace Davie, for example, writes of 'believing without belonging', describing Britons as believing in some sort of God whilst foregoing religious practice. By contrast, Steve Bruce defends the secularisation thesis by drawing attention to the marginal nature of religious beliefs for today's believers and to the small numbers who belong to the new religions.

This chapter will look at the new religious movements within the context of these changes to the religious landscape and the debates they have encouraged. In particular, it will locate within this situation those religious phenomena that have been called the New Age movement. To do this, it will take a sociological approach by focusing on authorities and organisations present within groups, enabling their comparison. To begin, some of the issues and literature about new religious movements and the New Age are presented.

New religious movements

'New religious movements' (NRMs) is the term used by sociologists typically to describe those new religions in the West originating since the 1970s that began to be characterised by mainstream society as groups attempting to gain conversions, or as holding unusual beliefs and lifestyles, or both. The range of groups covered by the term therefore has a tendency to be restricted to those which are Western, white-led, controversial and recently formed. The difficulties with these restrictions are discussed by George Chryssides, who concludes that NRMs lie outside mainstream religions and recruit from the culture in which they have arisen. However, this tends to exclude, for example, Opus Dei, a movement within the Roman Catholic Church, and Pentecostal groups, as well as pagan groups. This chapter questions the usefulness of the term 'NRMs', recognising that new religions are hardly an original feature of the 1970s in the West or elsewhere. To circumscribe them as such may be to limit analysis of the emergence of religions. However, good examples of work that treats new religions in a wider comparative perspective include Prince and Riches on the New Age and commune-based groups, such as Hare Krishna and the Hutterites, and Bryan Wilson on religious protest movements in the Third World.

The New Age

Religious networks that lie outside the traditions of churches, sects and NRMs in the West have come to be referred to as the New Age movement, a term applied to a great number of practices and beliefs since the 1980s. Academics, journalists, church spokespeople and even politicians have all contributed to building up a picture of a diffuse but widespread new social movement that has had an impact on the way many ordinary people think about and act towards their environments, both social and natural, and themselves.

The New Age is typically seen as a movement that has provided a religious approach to the counter-culture prevalent in the West since the 1970s but is to be distinguished from NRMs because of its less institutionalised, more diffuse, social nature. From this view, the New Age overlaps with sections of the human potential movement and the green and feminist movements, and is often described as taking the form of modern paganism. But the New Age is also believed by social commentators to encompass more mainstream aspects of society, such as some managerial skills and worker ethics within capitalism. The similarity between these apparently different facets of the New Age is its basis in individuals' empowerment and expression. Thus, the New Age is believed to be a form of religion that has arisen alongside society's increasing focus on choice and consumption informed by individuals themselves.

Authority and organisation

Sociological studies of religion have focused on two aspects of social power: the authorities that teach or influence people and the organisations in which these operate. Writing in 1913, Max Weber (1977: 295–301) distinguished between three types of religious authority: charismatic, traditional and routine. The first refers to contexts in which people are followed because they are deemed to display extraordinary qualities, the second to those in which norms exist which are deemed to have always been followed. The third refers to the routinisation of either charisma or tradition, or both, into a body of rules administered by officials – in other words, a bureaucracy.

It is primarily from this social psychological viewpoint that Weber developed an analysis of religious organisation, for example in his description of the way in which a congregation arises round a priesthood and is formed into a group with communal behaviour. The restrictions that surround local congregations were analysed by Weber to draw a distinction between churches and sects, the latter being marked by greater restrictions. Sectarian organisation, in contrast to churchly organisation, was characterised by the larger number of rules governing behaviour, especially personal behaviour, as well as the close-knit association between local congregations. Although this enabled the religious body as a whole to mark clear boundaries with other religious groups and with society in general, it also made sects prone to schism because they were less able to accommodate different doctrinal interpretations and rivalries of authority. The church/sect distinction and its development by other early sociologists of religion provided the basis for later discussions of the religious organisation of NRMs.

Varieties of new religious movements

Bryan Wilson, the foremost sociologist of sectarianism, eschews analysing sects in terms of the degree of their institutionalisation in order to free study of NRMs from the Christian context and Western basis of church/sect analysis. He characterises NRMs in terms of 'their offer of a proximate salvation; the implicit assault on spiritual élitism; their availability to a wider public; the accessibility of their techniques; the spiritual mobility that they facilitate; and their use of therapeutic claims' (1992: 210). From this view, NRMs are therefore more widely accessible than sects, offering an approach to salvation based more upon personal therapy that enables a greater degree of individual religious freedom. However, it is difficult to categorise in these terms all groups that have been treated as NRMs, some of which display sectarian qualities of authority and organisation.

Differences between NRMs are brought out by Roy Wallis's typology of their orientation to society, as world-affirming, world-rejecting and world-accommodating. The first type of NRM treats society and humans as essentially good but flawed in their present forms, therefore as not reaching their full potential. Wallis gives the Church of Scientology as an example because it arose from a fusion of scientific and psychotherapeutic ideas concerning self-development.

Scientology

Led by L. Ron Hubbard, Scientology spread outwards from the United States to establish centres that taught self-transformation through auditing, as well as promoting social welfare such as drug rehabilitation. According to Wallis, Hubbard had transformed himself into a charismatic leader

---

with a monopoly on the means of revelation by seizing control of publications and groups which taught the auditing technique of Dianetics, a movement of informal groups that he and others had established in the 1940s. Auditing was a psychotherapeutic technique that presented the mind as a computer that was mulfunctioning due to some keys being held down by engrams, locks that were created through habitual reactions to adverse situations. On the release of these locks, what is known as attaining clear, a human is able to express his or her real self as a thetan, an immortal godlike being with unlimited powers. Hubbard had created Scientology from Dianetics by standardising its practices and establishing a hierarchy of training.

Scientology does not demand that its members leave any other religion to which they belong, thus confirming Wilson's description of the spiritual openness of NRMs. However, the complexity of its teachings and the confrontational nature of auditing portrayed by sociologists such as Wallis and Harriet Whitehead, belies Wallis's characterisation of world-affirming movements as requiring ascription to no doctrine and as emphasising individual rather than collective actions.

Wallis's second type of NRM is world-rejecting, viewing society as irredeemably beyond salvation in its present form. By requiring the creation of a new world, they are characterised by an anti-materialist attitude. This is combined with the perception of a radical conversion, akin to being born again, upon being received into the movement, which is strongly authoritarian. One example is the Unification Church (UC), whose members are commonly known as Moonies.

The Unification Church

The Unification Church gained notoriety in the 1970s through accusations of brainwashing from some former members and relatives of members, although this has been thoroughly rebutted by sociologists. The lifestyle and hierarchy of the movement may require members to raise funds for the Church, to proselytise or to work in one of their businesses. Originating in Korea, the UC is Christian-based but has a new theology revealed by its leader Sun Myung Moon that talks of a new messiah, whom Moon's followers equate with himself, and that includes elements of traditional Korean religion, described by Chryssides as shamanic. It spread in the West when Moon moved to the United States in the early 1970s, where it has established, and been associated with, various business enterprises.

As with his world-affirming category, Wallis's world-rejecting category only characterises one of his main examples in part. In many respects, the UC does not display the anti-materialism and economic self-renunciation that he ascribes to it. Indeed, it is clear that the abandonment of considering what Wilson calls 'the extent to which they [religious movements] are institutionalized' (1975: 13) means that an important measure of the comparison between NRMs is lost. Scientology has much in common with the Unification Church in terms of authority and organisation, even in terms of their orientation to the world, so they can hardly be placed within different categories. Indeed, these movements appear to have much in common with sects as traditionally analysed.

Wallis treats his third category, world-accommodation, as less fixed than his other two, allowing for a broader spectrum of ideologies and acting as a conduit for the movement of groups between the extremes of world-affirming and world-rejecting ideologies. In this category, 'Religion . . . provides solace or stimulation to personal, interior life', enabling invigoration for life in the world but demanding few implications for how that life should be lived (1984: 35). Such movements do not seek to re-create society, either by redeeming it in terms of its essence or by abolishing it to create it anew, but allow their members to partake of society in a fresh way. One example is what Wallis calls neo-Pentecostal groups, Christian charismatic groups that emphasise the active experience of God working within individuals, displayed principally by glossolalia or speaking in tongues. These groups vary from independent churches or house groups to highly organised movements and are open to a range of ecumenical influences, such as by visiting evangelists. The wide variety of such groups again attests to the limitations of using a typology by which to describe NRMs, especially when social organisation does not feature strongly.

This discussion shows that the total life of NRMs needs to be considered; in other words, not only the leaders' lifestyles and doctrines but also those of the variety of followers, whether they be loose adherents or full-time inhabitants of a group's commune. It is only by looking at issues of authority and organisation that a more accurate picture emerges, one that is less prone to easy classification but that allows more meaningful comparison. These issues are crucial for our investigation into the New Age.

The scope of the New Age

The following description of the New Age can act as a starting point for its investigation: 'The New Age shows what "religion" looks like when it is organized in terms of what is taken to be the authority of the Self' (Heelas, 1996: 221).

The New Age Movement is commonly understood to be a form of

religion peculiar to contemporary Western society, distinguished from other forms of religion by the relative absence of social authority. There are no official bodies that represent New Agers at local, national or international levels or that say what is New Age and what is not. Nor are there texts or creeds that perform these functions. The question of authority therefore lies at the heart of most descriptions of the New Age. These pose the question, 'By what authority is the New Age organised?' The answer to this allows academic portrayals of the New Age to be scrutinised in terms of how well they describe authority and organisation in the groups to which they are addressed.

In contrast to well-organised religions such as churches, sects and new religious movements, many religious groups and networks in Europe and North America today appear to have weak leadership and social boundaries. Paul Heelas believes that each New Ager acts as his or her own authority. This means it is on the basis of their own experiences that New Agers decide which religious activities to practice or groups to join and for how long. It suggests that what they do is relatively unstructured by external authorities. New Agers, by this account, are not bound to those authorities described by Max Weber.

According to Heelas, the New Age has led to the emergence of a worldview that articulates this authority of people's selves. He calls this their lingua franca, or common language, of 'Self-spirituality' containing three main elements (1996: 18–20). First, people's lives are not working because they are hindered by beliefs such as self-doubt adopted during the course of becoming socialised to modern society, in particular through childhood. Second, people are spiritual gods but this is hidden because their lives are not working. Third, the only way people can realise their true godly nature is by releasing their socialisation through the practice of liberating techniques. It is the vast multiplicity of such techniques that gives the New Age its bewildering form, encompassing religious rituals from traditions across the world, psychotherapies and newly invented practices that typically draw from both. These techniques are seen as pathways to rediscovering the inner self and bringing it out into the external, physical world. This is believed to be a transforming experience that Heelas describes as a means for obtaining salvation – in other words, a new age. The Findhorn Foundation in Scotland provides an example of a centre in which these concerns can be articulated.

The Findhorn Foundation

The Findhorn Foundation is a community near Inverness that, since the 1960s, has acted as a centre for religious experimenters. Its aims and

---

social organisation have changed much over time, from the maintenance of a garden under the charismatic influence of its founders, Peter and Eileen Caddy, to a centre for human development under the direction of facilitators. At the present time, it has many commercial concerns, such as publishing, and is a place 'where around two hundred core members along with large numbers of peripherally connected paying "guests" uphold a highly successful lifestyle based around farming and education' (Prince and Riches, 2000: 268). The Experience Week provides an educational residential introduction to community life for visitors, structured through work placements and meditation.

Heelas uses the notion of 'Self-spirituality' to draw in a variety of groups and practices that he claims have a common orientation. Specifically, they form part of the broader area of 'self-religions', by which Heelas means groups which fuse religion with psychology to teach people that the self is divine in order that people may learn to live as gods. Heelas includes Scientology in this category but contends that the focus on the god within distinguishes self-religions from those NRMs that incorporate elements of psychology but teach that god is external, such as the International Society for Krishna Consciousness (ISKCON, popularly known as Hare Krishna) and Transcendental Meditation. However, there seems little to differentiate Heelas' description of the New Age from his earlier description of self-religions, except that the latter tends to be applied to groups marked by strong leaders and bureaucracies that became international organisations. Although it is not clear from Heelas' accounts whether self-religions are a part of the New Age or contrariwise, it does seem that the former are held to mark a transition from being counter-culturally opposed to mainstream society to being able to embrace elements of that such as capitalism, thus forming what he calls the prosperity wing of the New Age movement.

The notion of a common language or worldview to identify the New Age movement is found in other academic portrayals. Historian of religion Wouter Hanegraaff believes the New Age constitutes a movement because of a common worldview amongst people that criticises society on the basis of a secular adoption of the Western esoteric tradition. This tradition is Christian in origin and emphasises the unity of all things at a deep spiritual level and the evolutionary progression of all things toward spiritual perfection.

Likewise, J. Gordon Melton (1988: 35f) describes the 'transformative vision' arising out of a Western occult tradition but also views Eastern religions as important. The New Age movement emerged as this vision was proclaimed by exponents such as Baba Ram Dass, the American-born Richard Alpert who became the disciple of a Hindu guru in India and subsequently returned to the United States to proclaim transformation and to establish organisations teaching meditation in the 1970s. From such points, a set of networks grew and became ideologically or practically aligned together into a movement, this being facilitated by directories that told people what was going on, where and when. This interconnection of networks is emphasised in Michael York's account where the New Age is described as a decentralised movement built around a vision of transformation gained by practical experience. He pays attention to what he considers related feminist, 'Neo-pagan' and green movements, which, together with the New Age, make up a movement of movements.

Each of these accounts point to the problematic nature of describing practices, groups and networks that are bereft of the usual forms of authority and organisation to be found in mainstream or new religions. Steve Bruce describes them as cultic, a category used by sociologists to extend the church/sect dichotomy towards encompassing smaller, more local and less stable religions. Bruce divides New Age phenomena between client cults and audience cults. The former involve a relationship between an individual and someone offering a service, which may or may not be priced, as in a holistic healing therapy such as reikei, a term used to describe healing powers believed to be available to those who have been initiated to draw upon ki, the lifeforce that flows through the body. Audience cults involve the dissemination of material – whether spoken, recorded or printed – from a group or individual seeking an audience, as in workshops to learn about channelling. However, as the case of channelling shows, there are often no clear divisions between client and audience cults, nor do these encompass all the forms of organisation that are to be found in the networks.

Channelling

Channelling is the name given to the practice of spirit possession whereby a medium, or channeller, is believed to act as the physical presence for a spirit, typically to deliver speeches. In contrast to spiritualist groups, where the spirit is that of a deceased human, in channelling the spirit is of a highly evolved being such as an Ascended Master. When disseminated as printed material, the information given usually concerns cosmic events such as the evolution of humankind, placing this into a psychological framework. But at gatherings to hear spirits speak through channels, more intimate information may be provided. Channellers often speak to large audiences but may also form part of small study groups or one-to-one sessions. Although some channellers talk of a 'movement', there is little organisation between channellers. Further, those who listen to them rarely become adherents. It is more common for them to start channelling themselves, with messages that address their own, local religious involvement.

Bruce points out that it is very difficult to quantify how many people are involved in the New Age and research must focus instead on its influence. However, it seems more realistic to suspend judgement on whether a New Age movement really exists – and, if so, what its features and influence might be – until research has been carried out on the actual phenomena that are being described in so abstract a manner. Such research should involve detailed description of authority and organisation and it is this issue that is now considered here, both for the New Age and for NRMs.

Social contexts

Tensions and origins within society

Discussions of NRMs often focus on the tensions that exist between them and wider society. This is in part because study of NRMs arose out of the study of sects, which by Wilson's definition are protest movements against churches or society, but also because of the controversy some NRMs aroused in mainstream society. Although the number of these controversies may be rare compared to the number of NRMs and the people involved with them, the reciprocal relationship that exists between debates in the media and the sociology of religion mean that they have come to play an important part in the perception of these movements.

On the one hand, this controversy has been caused by accusations of practices deemed unsuitable for a religion to undertake in secular society. These accusations covered attempts to gain converts, for example The Family's use of offering sexual favours or 'flirty fishing', and attempts to keep converts by demanding the cessation of other social ties, especially with family. On the other hand, controversy has raged over NRMs that have seen the mass deaths of their members. Chryssides classifies these movements as 'suicide cults', although it is clear that in social organisation and doctrine each is akin to a different group of NRMs. The most extreme example involves the death of 919 members of The People's Temple in 1978. This Pentecostal group was led by Jim Jones in the United States to establish a community in the jungle in Guyana, South America, where their vision of a social gospel could be lived without interference from outside authorities. However, the authoritarian leadership that developed, which was ethnic white in contrast to the predominantly ethnic black membership, led to an investigation of the group that resulted in the response of a so-called mass suicide, despite the evidence that many members were shot by others.

These controversies have led to the establishment of institutions that monitor NRMs, often involving sociologists of religion. Some groups provide information on NRMs to any interested party, such as the Information Network on New Religious Movements (INFORM) founded by Eileen Barker in 1988 and funded by the British Home Office, the Church of England and other mainstream churches. By contrast, other groups have seized NRM members they believe have been brainwashed, in order to de-programme them. Some NRMs have reacted to these developments by themselves monitoring the so-called anti-cult organisations, for example the Church of Scientology's response to the Cult Awareness Network.

The ambiguous relationship between NRMs and wider society, in part reflected by Wallis's world-rejecting aspect, has often led to cases in the law courts. However, neither NRMs nor mainstream society are homogeneous and so these tensions are partial, not absolute. Although many commentators view the membership of NRMs as drawn from the disaffected youth of families who benefit most from society, this picture is misleading for two reasons. First, because of the constricted criteria of what constitutes a NRM, many black-led NRMs are overlooked, including those that arrive in the West through transnational migrations. Further, NRMs outside the West are also generally ignored, although there are some exceptions such as Clarke's study of Japanese new religions in Brazil.

The second reason concerns confusions over who is middle class. A discussion of this issue allows consideration of the origins of NRMs and the New Age. These are generally thought to have arisen from sectors of Western society that have benefited from the long economic boom that occurred after the Second World War and then grew dissatisfied with its materialist focus. The rise of political activism and alternative lifestyles amongst students and other young people in the 1960s, documented by Roszak's *The Making of a Counterculture* (1973), led to the search for new forms of authority that would encompass a spiritual component and this was found in the NRMs, particularly those from Eastern religious traditions.

Wallis, for example, characterises the participants of world-accommodating NRMs as the middle class and 'respectable' working class, those who are 'firmly integrated into the prevailing social order, who are not entirely unhappy with it, but who seek none the less some experimental reassurance of their general spiritual values' (1984: 37). More generally, Bruce writes 'the working-classes were absent from the new religions' and 'There are very few working-class New Agers' (1997: 183, 218). However, the collapse of many blue-collar sectors of employment since the 1970s and the rise of white-collar employment and managerial work, alongside expansions in higher education, has meant that traditional definitions of the working class and the middle class are largely obsolete. There is a lack of recognition of the working-class status of those involved in new religions, as discussed by Wood (2002) in relation to New Age movement studies, such that they are often interpreted as means by which people express their freedom rather than means by which people respond to their oppression.

New religions can better be seen as a response to the real difficulties faced by people in societies that are undergoing rapid changes, such as more widespread affluence and higher education. Whilst providing greater opportunities for the working class, these changes held opportunities for new risks and forms of oppression. The attraction of some NRMs to drug abusers and others disadvantaged by these social changes has been clearly documented, for example by studies of The People's Temple. Similarly, the spread of new religions at other times can be related to social changes. According to Geoffrey Nelson, the rise of Pentecostal and spiritualist groups from the 1840s, including amongst black slaves in the United States, was fuelled by disintegration of the social structure resulting from rapid industrialisation. Peter Worsley discusses how the so-called cargo cults of Melanesia in the twentieth century largely resulted from new patterns of labour engineered by colonisation. New religions, then, need to be related to social crises affecting all classes, not limited to one class or another on the basis of an account that does not consider the changes these classes are undergoing.

Non-formative and formative social organisation

The alignment of the study of the New Age Movement with study of NRMs suggests a need to focus on the realities of social organisation and authority for people involved in these religions. In particular, it is important to focus on these people's involvement with networks and multiple social authorities. This issue will be considered by looking at the sorts of phenomena commonly described as New Age, so that an assessment can be made of academic analyses based upon a view that authority in the New Age arises from the self.

It is clear that most accounts of the New Age underestimate the nature and extent of social authority that exists in the networks. During the Experience Week at the Findhorn Foundation in Scotland, Sutcliffe found that 'the notion of one's personal soteriological quest' formed a key motif such that the self becomes the prime source of authority (1995: 35). However, his rich ethnography shows how people's senses of self were socially constructed through group activities in what Sutcliffe himself calls 'a skilfully-executed process of re-education and peer-group confirmation' (ibid.). This occurred in many activities, such as instructions on attitudes to community work and times of group sharing, within a context which Prince and Riches describe as marked by 'hierarchical and authoritarian tendencies in the social organisation' (2000: 268).

Likewise, Heelas' focus on the authority of the self tends to ignore the strong leadership and social control that can exist in many of the groups he calls New Age and especially those he describes as self-religions. Kohn criticises Heelas' claim that groups such as these are marked by individual empowerment in terms of the self, arguing that the people involved learn techniques of self-transformation in contexts of external authoritarian control: 'where radical subjectivism is encouraged among followers, radical authority will be exerted by their leader' (1991: 136). In many groups, charismatic, traditional and bureaucratic authorities are to be found such that self-authority is marginal, illusory or simply of a different nature than that envisaged by academics.

Progress has been made in the sociological study of religion by describing how people's representations of self are socially constructed by external environments. Leaders, peers and texts all help to create a person's sense of self in the context of religious and non-religious groups and networks. The fact that a sense of self is constructed through social authorities should not lead to the conclusion that activities with weak authorities, as are often found in the so-called New Age networks, means that the self is a personal authority. Rather, it means that multiple social authorities, both religious and non-religious, have an effect on people and contribute in constructing a sense of self or, what is more likely, a number of senses of self.

There are many fallacies that result from the avoidance of these issues in New Age movement studies. First, by focusing on beliefs and world-views, the behaviour and social interaction of people is missed. Although a few prominent personalities and writers are held to have been influential in establishing the movement and attracting people to it, there is little discussion of the nature of the resulting networks or links between groups. Second, by focusing on texts, there follows a neglect of the way people use written materials. Third, this leads to too much emphasis on leaders and those who would seek to lead, rather than the majority which follow and seek to learn from others and who therefore appropriate materials in their own local contexts. Fourth, this ignores the fact that different people's understandings of words, phrases and beliefs cannot be assumed to be the same as one another or to be the same as an academic's understanding of them. Last, by focusing on descriptions of self, the social influences that construct them are theoretically circumvented. These fallacies suggest the need for a new conceptualisation of so-called New Age phenomena, one that may be fruitfully applied to NRMs as well. To do this, the concept of formativeness may be used.

The social authorities present in many religious networks are such that they do not act as formative for people's experiences. That is to say, most of the individuals involved do not have their beliefs and practices shaped into conformity with those who lead the groups to which they belong or with those authors they read. Rather, the religion of these individuals forms shifting patterns according to the multiple authorities with which they come into contact, both religious, such as channellers or healers, and secular, such as family and employment. People interested in particular authority figures are unlikely to follow them in formal ways or to adopt their paths of religious development. They are more likely to involve themselves in a loosely affiliated manner that maintains their social independence.

Because the so-called New Age phenomena are so loosely organised internally, whilst existing together in extensive networks, they have very little in common apart from the non-formative nature of their authority. By contrast, most NRMs maintain much greater social organisation leading to clearer boundaries between one religion and another. In such a situation, networking occurs mostly on the fringes of a religion, whilst those individuals drawn more deeply into the social organisation have their experiences formed by the prevailing social authorities. Sects and NRMs like the Unification Church are extreme examples of such formativeness; so-called cults and NRMs like Scientology are less so.

In this way, a spectrum ranging from formativeness to non-formativeness may be used to describe not only social authority and social organisation in a group but also the attitude adopted by those involved. A religious group may be located predominantly in one area of the spectrum, although there will nearly always be people involved who have a different attitude towards the religion than that expected by the leaders and most followers. This may be barely tolerated in tightly organised groups, whilst others of equally strong organisation, such as mainstream churches, may accept that a large number of those involved will commit themselves very little. Social phenomena with very little authority and organisation, coupled with very little commitment by those involved, can be described only as non-formative. It is in this manner that groups and networks involving most channellers, healers and others are more accurately named, rather than as New Age. These cannot even be described as a movement, since that description infers some more formative element than they provide, whether in terms of common doctrine, leadership or aims. In such a way, then, the formative–non-formative spectrum allows different NRMs to be distinguished from each other and to be distinguished from the mass of other new religious phenomena that exist in society.

Conclusion

This discussion of NRMs and the New Age has shown that they are best understood in terms of their social authority and organisation. By representing the reality of these for all those involved, different religious groups and practices may be compared one to another. This enables the limitations of focusing primarily on either doctrine or institutionalisation to be overcome because it allows a perspective that takes into account the variety of involvement to which religions are prone. The notion of formativeness was used to facilitate this perspective on authority and organisation, enabling non-formative religion to be formulated as a more accurate description of certain phenomena than that provided by the term New Age.

There are many more new religions and non-formative religions that are relevant to these issues than we have space to discuss in detail. The development of new religions outside the Western world has often received little attention, despite their increasing relevance due to transnational migrations. Religious syncretism, whereby different traditions are brought into contact to create new ones, is of particular interest in such a context. Likewise, the spread in the West of pagan traditions that exhibit a fierce tension between formative and non-formative elements is a topic there has not been room to discuss.

By providing an overview and flavour of new religions, this chapter has sought to indicate some of the reasons for their existence and persistence in terms of the social changes within societies. In relation to this, the spaces inhabited by new religions and the tensions by which they do so have been sketched so that a fuller social appreciation of them may be gained.

Further reading

New religious movements

Academic studies of NRMs fall within three categories: in-depth studies of one movement, comparative studies of several movements and edited volumes that scrutinise one aspect of religious life across many movements. Examples of all three are included in this selection.

Barker, Eileen (1984), *The Making of a Moonie: Brainwashing or Choice?*, Oxford: Blackwell. Barker's study of the Unification Church is an early excellent example of an in-depth study, focusing on the controversy that an NRM can cause.

Beckford, James (1985), *Cult Controversies: The Societal Response to New Religious Movements*, London and New York: Tavistock. A comparative study of reactions to NRMs by secular and religious organisations, and what NRMs have done to combat these criticisms.

Chryssides, George D. (1999), *Exploring New Religions*, London: Cassell. Provides the history and beliefs of a wide range of NRMs, categorised according to the religious traditions from which they emerged.

Wallis, Roy (1984), *The Elementary Forms of the New Religious Life*, London: Routledge and Kegan Paul. Establishes an influential typology by which to compare NRMs in terms of their attitude to wider society.

Wilson, Bryan and Jamie Cresswell (eds.) (1999), *New Religious Movements: Challenge and Response*, London: Routledge. Includes essays on a variety of aspects of NRMs, providing a good overview of academic lines of enquiry and including links with New Age studies.

New Age

Understanding of the New Age is hampered by the lack of empirical work, most being based on literature rather than detailed studies of groups or networks. This selection suggests a range of perspectives that may be compared to one another.

Heelas, Paul (1996), *The New Age Movement: The Celebration of the Self and the Sacralization of Modernity*, Oxford: Blackwell. The most influential and wide-ranging study of the New Age, focusing on the growth of self-spirituality in the West and its various manifestations.

Lewis, J. R. and J. Gordon Melton (eds.) (1992), *Perspectives on the New Age*, Albany: State University of New York Press. A range of essays from a largely American perspective that includes good discussions of channelling and the history of the New Age.

Prince, Ruth and David Riches (2000), *The New Age in Glastonbury: The Construction of Religious Movements*, Oxford: Berghahn Books. An ethnographic study of alternative religiosity in Glastonbury, focusing on people's representations of themselves and providing a comparison with alternative communities in other societies.

Sutcliffe, Steven and Marion Bowman (eds.) (2000), *Beyond New Age: Exploring Alternative Spirituality*, Edinburgh: Edinburgh University Press. Presents a range of interesting, often empirical, studies on the New Age, including healing, the London Festival for Mind-Body-Spirit and the Findhorn Foundation, as well as theoretical overviews of the subject.

Questions

1. What can the study of new religious movements and the New Age add to the secularisation debate?

2. What are the respective merits of different sociological classifications of new religious movements?

3. Explain the relevance of the privatisation of the self for studies of new religious movements and the New Age.

4. Describe how social authority may be both plural and contested in New Age networks.

5. To what extent have new religious movements been shaped by their tensions with wider society?

6. What can a focus on social class and 'race' tell us about the place of new religious movements and the New Age in wider society?

CHAPTER SEVEN

Recent Trends in Religion

F. Michael Perko, SJ

Introduction

One need only look at recent trends in religion worldwide to recognise its continuing vitality. Over 85 per cent of the world's population have some religious affiliation, a number that has grown in the last fifteen years. While religion largely is concerned with transcendence, it nonetheless operates within the context of the here and now. As a result, it both influences events in areas like education, culture, economics and politics, and is influenced by them. In a famous essay, 'Religion as a Cultural System', cultural anthropologist Clifford Geertz indicates that one feature of culture is its dynamism, its continual process of change and development. This is notably true of the culture of religion. While we might think of religious traditions as unchanging and unchangeable, they are always in flux. While such change may not be visible, it is always present. This is what allows religious groups to be a significant element of the societies in which they exist.

> Unlike genes and other nonsymbolic information sources, which are only models *for*, not models *of*, culture patterns have an intrinsic double aspect: they give meaning, that is, objective conceptual form, to social and psychological reality both by shaping themselves to it and by shaping it to themselves.
>
> Clifford Geertz, 'Religion as a Cultural System', in
> *The Interpretation of Cultures* (1973: 93)

Along with the continual change in religious groups, new groups are constantly coming into existence. Sometimes these split from existing religions; sometimes they remain as part of the original group as a kind of subgroup. In still other instances, the new religion springs up on its own. In all of these cases, the creation of the new faith provides adherents with elements that were previously unavailable to them.

In this chapter, we shall examine both of these kinds of religious change. In addition, we shall look at variations in the ways in which religions interact with each other, as well as shifts in their relationships with the wider world. The time frame, roughly, will be the last fifty years. While this may appear to be a long period of time, from the perspective of religious change and development it is really quite short, especially considering that a number of religions treated here are multiple thousands of years old.

Many important recent trends in religion do not move in a single direction. Rather, we can find examples of religious change that pull in different directions, situations in which the trend appears to be developing one way in a particular place and seems to be going in exactly the opposite direction in another. Religions always exist within a particular context and the directions that they take are related to that environment. When the contexts differ, so may religious developments.

Examples of trends that pull in opposite directions are seen in some of the most important religious developments since the 1950s. For example, the context of religion has become much more secular in recent years. We shall examine the whole notion of secularisation in more depth later but one of its most significant tenets is the insistence that the sacred and the ordinary be separated into different spheres of human life. Religion, it argues, ought to exist primarily in the private sphere, as a personal expression of belief, rather than in public life where it directly influences the way the society operates. As a result, secularisation tends to result in the marginalization of religion, of its being relegated to the sidelines of public life.

On the other hand, a number of current observers of religion world-wide see things moving in the opposite direction. Rather than becoming more secular, many societies are actually de-secularising, not returning to the ways in which religion and the broader world interacted before secularisation happened but creating strong new relationships.

Another instance of trends that appear to be pulling in opposite directions is the growing strength of exclusivity on the one hand, and certain kinds of religious expansiveness on the other. Here again, we can see evidence that leads us to argue for shifts in each of these directions in different religious contexts.

Perhaps the most obvious example of exclusivity's power is the rise of fundamentalism (examined in more depth later). Increasingly, the term has come to be applied to a variety of religious groups that have certain common ways of understanding the world and similar plans of action. Along with Christianity, Islam, Judaism and Hinduism all have fundamentalist manifestations. In various parts of the world, these seem to be growing, some at a startling rate.

While all of this is going on, however, there are also examples of religion becoming more expansive and liberal in its outlook. In Western Europe and North America, for example, the last half-century has witnessed a number of major organisations created to foster relationships among religious groups. One example of this is the set of relationships created by the Porvoo Declaration between a number of European churches, mainly Lutheran and Anglican in tradition.

A third instance of religious forces pulling in opposing directions is the development of traditional religious groups on the one hand, and the creation of new religious movements on the other. In each case, growth and decline can be seen. Since 1960, the number of Christians as a percentage of world population has grown. This is, however, largely accounted for by growth in the category 'other Christians', since Roman Catholic membership remained largely constant and Protestant and Anglican numbers lessened. Outside the Christian world, Islam has been the fastest-growing religion, with almost 20 per cent of the world's population at the end of the twentieth century. Hinduism, likewise, has experienced significant growth, while Judaism and Buddhism have declined.

Outside the world of traditional religion, new religious movements have also appeared during the last fifty to one hundred years. Some of these have grown rapidly to include memberships well into the millions. Many of these new movements are syncretic, encompassing elements of world religious tradition and aspects of primitive religion. Vodun and Santeria, for example, are Afro-Caribbean religions combining elements of Christianity with aspects of traditional African tribal religion. A variety of new Asian religious movements derive elements from Shintoism, Taoism and Buddhism.

At the same time, religious movements have arisen that are almost unique in their systems of belief and practice. Many of these are related to 'New Age' thought, a contemporary category of belief that emphasises various aspects of nature religion, spiritualism and self-reflective growth.

Along with these trends that pull in opposite directions are others that represent clear shifts in very particular directions. Here, two seem especially important.

A noteworthy phenomenon since the 1950s is what might be termed the 'greening' of religion. Sensitised by the growth of the ecological movement within the wider society, religious traditions have begun to articulate explicitly religious understandings of the relationship between human beings and the environment, and to develop policies from these reflections.

Changes in the understanding of the role of women in the world have been paralleled by increased attention to women's perspectives and issues in religion. Within the major world religions, increased attention has been paid to the development of theologies that articulate women's unique ways of seeing. In Judaism and Christianity, one of the most visible forms such concerns have taken has been the movement for the ordination of women to roles of ritual and educational leadership.

The trends summarised here in no sense represent all the significant happenings in the religious world from the mid-twentieth century onwards. It would be impossible to do that in a single chapter. They are, however, among the most important developments. With this brief overview in mind, let us begin to examine each of these directions in more detail.

Secularisation versus de-secularisation

The whole notion of secularisation can be traced to the Enlightenment. Its contemporary use, however, comes from the work of social scientists in the 1950s and 1960s. The idea is a relatively simple one: that the movement of a society from a traditional to a modern mode of organisation inevitably leads to the declining importance of religion. For many, this has been seen to be a good thing, since there has been a tendency to view religion as superstitious or backward.

People who believe that the world is becoming more secularised frequently point to Western Europe for evidence. In the Scandinavian countries and Great Britain, for example, fewer than 15 per cent of the population attend church on a weekly basis. Other countries, like France, Belgium and the Netherlands, have large populations who are either non-religious or identify with no particular religious group. Of all the countries of Western Europe, only in Ireland do more than half the population attend church at least weekly.

There appears to be some indication that Eastern Europe also is moving toward secularisation. In Poland, for example, the church functioned for a half-century as the embodiment of the Polish nation, a potent force of opposition to the communist state. With the fall of communism, the church's role as a counterweight ended. Since then, Polish Catholics have shown increasing pluralism in their interests and values. For example, consistent failure to support their church's teaching on abortion suggests that, like most Europeans, Polish Catholics are willing to pick and choose among church teachings. While Poland is likely a long way from the sort of secularisation that characterises French society, evidence suggests that it is moving in a more secular direction. These trends are even more dramatic in other Eastern European countries where the local church never exerted the power that Roman Catholicism did during the time of Polish partition and communist government.

A great deal of empirical evidence, then, suggests that the process of secularisation continues to exert a significant influence on the relationship between religion and the wider society, and indeed, upon religion itself. Even in places like Britain, where significant numbers of people still claim church membership, actual religious observance, especially through the state church, continues to wane. Both the forces of cultural marginalisation and the legacy of Enlightenment thought that simultaneously pushed religious groups toward rationalism and encouraged them to concentrate their efforts on people's private lives (rather than national public life) have helped to decrease the influence of religion.

What makes the picture murky is that the European model of secularisation seems not to apply in much of the rest of the world. In many places, the opposite seems to be happening. Societies that had moved in secular directions have begun to de-secularise, while others, like the United States, have never conformed to the European secularisation model.

To put it simply, experiments with secularized religion have generally failed: religious movements with beliefs and practices dripping with reactionary supernaturalism . . . have widely succeeded.

Peter L. Berger, 'The Desecularization of the World:
A Global Overview', in Peter L. Berger (ed.),
The Desecularization of the World (1999: 42)

Perhaps the most obvious example of de-secularisation is the rapid growth of fundamentalism. A brief survey of its growth points out how significant a dynamic de-secularisation has become during the last fifty years.

In the period following World War II, most of the newly independent nations of North Africa, the Middle East and South Asia, though religiously Muslim, were organised along modern secular lines. This was unsurprising, given that the individuals and groups that had fought colonial rule were committed to secular nationalism as a mode of political organisation. For example, the Baath, one of the largest pan-Arab parties, was created in the 1940s by a Christian and a Muslim with a philosophy of revolutionary nationalism, and was very politically powerful, especially in Syria and Iraq. In many other states, including Algeria, Egypt, Jordan and Lebanon, largely secular political structures were adopted.

By the end of the twentieth century, the scene had shifted dramatically. Afghanistan, Iran and Sudan had come under the control of fundamentalist regimes committed to creating officially Muslim states with legal codes based in sha'aria, orthodox Qur'anic religious law. In Egypt and Algeria, secular governments found their positions eroded by fundamentalist organisations like the Muslim Brotherhood. In Turkey and Pakistan, growing Islamic political power was checked only by military intervention. Although the Palestinian territories had no previous tradition of radical Islam, the end of the twentieth century witnessed growing fundamentalist Islamic power in that area, as did Indonesia, the world's largest Muslim nation.

Similar phenomena have occurred in Israel and India. In the former, founded in 1948 as an essentially secular state, ultra-conservative Jewish religious political parties have been highly successful both in achieving state support for their educational activities and pressing an expansionist political agenda with respect to the Palestinian territories. Growing Hindu fundamentalism also has come to play a significant role in challenging the secular political ideology of post-colonial India.

In other places, most notably the United States, secularisation seems never really to have occurred. Described by G. K. Chesterton as 'the nation with the soul of a church', it was in the twentieth century that American religious observance reached its peak. In 1776, only about 17 per cent of Americans belonged to some religious faith: during the twentieth century, however, American religious adherence ranged from 51 to 62 per cent of the population. In recent decades, the numbers have remained relatively fixed, with conservative evangelicalism on the rise and mainstream Protestantism in decline. Arguably, despite (or perhaps because of) the absence of an official state church, the United States has actually become more religious at the very time Western Europe has become more secular.

In still other instances, the rapid growth of conservative religious groups has discouraged secularisation, even though political structures remain essentially secular. One of the most striking examples has been the rise of evangelical Christianity in settings where it previously exercised minimal influence. In traditionally Catholic Latin America, evangelicals comprise about 30 per cent of the population and have produced two national presidents. In the Philippines, a recent president, Fidel Ramos, came from an evangelical background. The Faith Church, an evangelical group, is now the fourth-largest religious body in Hungary, after the Catholics, the Reformed and the Lutherans. One of the most interesting religious developments in present-day Taiwan has been the upswing in Buddhist evangelism, especially on the part of socially and politically engaged movements. Even in socialist China, with a significant record of religious oppression and persecution in the second half of the twentieth century, there has been an upsurge of interest in Buddhism; and while the Chinese government estimates its Christian population at around twenty million, some underground groups claim the actual number is over three times as large. All of these are examples of the growth of religious influence within a wide array of societies, arguing against the belief that secularisation is inevitable.

This pulling in opposite directions – increased secularisation in some places, while others are simultaneously becoming de-secularised – has had a number of implications. Much of the political tension in North Africa, the Middle East and South Asia, for example, is at least indirectly the result of competing interest groups, some of whom want their societies to become more secular while others are dedicated to limiting or ending secularisation. On a more global level, countries like those of Western Europe that have adopted a profoundly secular model of organisation find themselves in opposition to others, mostly in the Third World, for whom secularisation represents all that is wrong with Western life and culture.

Contraction versus expansiveness

Related to secularisation and de-secularisation, but somewhat different, is the whole tension between religious worldviews that emphasise a narrow or constricted way of understanding and those that tend to be more expansive. One direction taken by numerous groups of religious people in the last fifty years has been that of contraction. These groups, commonly labeled 'fundamentalist' no matter what their faith tradition, have moved in directions that have narrowed their religious perspectives.

Historians Martin Marty and Scott Appleby have identified a number of elements common to most fundamentalists. First of all, religion ought to scandalise: that is, it should not be rationalist. Rather, they insist that religion ought to be extraordinary and upset normal expectations. They also reach out for a set of basics that will define them as distinct from the rest of the religious world, keep them at a distance from those who believe otherwise, and define who is a part of God's kingdom. These definitions are usually the product of leaders invested with ultimate and unquestionable authority. They also emphasise doctrinal aspects that will help them to achieve power, even if these are not seen as critically important by the mainstream adherents of the religion. Jewish fundamentalists, for example, frequently place huge emphasis on conquering and subduing all the lands that were part of ancient Israel, an idea notably less important to most mainstream Jews.

While fundamentalists frequently claim as their objective the restoration of an earlier, purer form of religious belief, fundamentalist religion is not simply or even largely a return to traditional religion. Rather, elements of the tradition are re-ordered and given different emphases in order to preserve and enhance the group's identity in the context of a rapidly changing modern world. Usually, the goal is to change society rather than withdraw from it. Ultra-conservative though they are, fundamentalists often use the most advanced communications technology available to carry their message. Thus, the fundamentalist Islamic revolution in Iran was fueled by thousands of cassette tapes of sermons by the exiled Ayatollah Khomeini. Fundamentalists have no objection to certain aspects of modernity: instead, they react against perspectives that deny or marginalise their own understandings and activities.

> Fundamentalism is, in other words, a religious way of being that manifests itself as a strategy by which beleaguered believers attempt to preserve their distinctive identity as a people or group.
>
> Martin E. Marty and R. Scott Appleby,
> *The Glory and the Power* (1992: 34)

Test cases of the rise of fundamentalism can be seen in Christianity, Judaism and Islam. After Christian fundamentalism was born in the early years of the twentieth century in the United States, it went into a period of quiescence. Then, fuelled in part by the rise of feminism, youth protest against the Vietnam War and their parents' culture, and the United States Supreme Court's 1973 decision legalising abortion, it re-emerged as a significant part of the American social and political landscape. Fundamentalists created highly effective organisations to elect candidates to public office, promote sympathetic appointees to judicial and administrative positions and lobby for their particular concerns. Between 1965 and 1983, enrolment in independent Christian schools sponsored by fundamentalist groups rose some 600 per cent, while efforts were made to censor text books used in primary schools and ensure that 'creationism' was taught as an alternative to evolution. Fundamentalist women rose to challenge the basic tenets of feminism with an insistence that the Bible required traditional male and female social roles.

Over the space of a decade, fundamentalists were also able to take control of several Protestant denominations. Here, they reoriented denominational policy and purged seminaries of faculty whom they suspected of being heretical. While their direct influence in American political life has waned, fundamentalists nonetheless remain a potent force in the arena of public policy.

A second example is that of Jewish fundamentalists in Israel. While the majority of Israeli Jews are mostly secularised, a relatively small segment of the Israeli population is intense in its religious belief and observance in one of two ways. One group, rooted in the philosophy of Israel's first chief rabbi and his son, has adopted a brand of Zionism that sees the fulfilment of Israel's destiny as occurring only when the state returns to its ancient borders. Thus, settlement in the West Bank and Gaza is not only encouraged but demanded by God.

While these activists comprise only a small portion of the settlers in the Palestinian territories, their fanatical conviction gives them great power within the settler community. Seeing the Torah as trumping any law made by mortals, they oppose Arab sovereignty as well as attempts by the secular government to concede any additional territory to the Palestinians. Answering only to their own leadership and a highly distinctive interpretation of Jewish law, they appear prepared to use whatever means are necessary to further their religious agenda. Yigal Amir, who assassinated Israeli Prime Minister Yitzak Rabin in 1995, came from such a group and viewed the killing of the prime minister as the only way to thwart the imminent prospect of a Palestinian state on lands that had been part of biblical Israel.

What is the rule about this bad government ... Is it not the obligation of community leaders to warn the head of government and his ministers that if they keep pursuing the [Oslo II] agreement, after the terrible experience of stage one [Oslo I] in all of Judea and Samaria, they will be subject ... to the Halakhic ruling of *din moser*, as those who surrender Jewish life and property to gentiles?

Rabbis Dov Lior, Daniel Shilo and Eliezer Melamed, 'What is the Rule About this Bad Government?' in Dana Arieli-Horowitz (ed.), *Religion and the State in Israel, 1994–95* (1996: 120–3)

Very different from the activist settlers are ultra-orthodox Jews referred to as haredim, a word meaning 'quakers'. These highly religiously observant Israelis segregate themselves in towns or neighbourhoods made up of likeminded individuals. However, their isolation does not extend to an unwillingness to participate in the political process. Especially in recent years, many have mobilised in highly effective ways to ensure continued state funding of their extensive educational system and to insist upon the adoption of Jewish religious law as the principal legal code of the state. Thus, they have opposed the operation of public transit and the opening of restaurants and places of entertainment on the Sabbath – even though most Israelis do not keep rigorous Sabbath observance – because God's law ought to take precedence over the mere will of the majority. Although these groups have generally not held strong positions about the appropriate borders for the State of Israel, or concerning the solution of the 'Palestinian problem', in recent years some have become more conservative, exponents of the 'greater Israel' notion of the state and opposed to any concessions to the Palestinians.

The construction of Judaism made by these groups is not, strictly speaking, highly traditional. Instead, their understanding of scripture and Jewish law came into existence after, and as a response to, the Enlightenment. Their particular variety of Judaism was more text-oriented, legalistic and inward-looking than the earlier tradition. Charismatic leaders also became more prominent.

Though the activist settlers and ultra-orthodox separatists appear different, both exhibit classic profiles. Both have uniquely constructed ways of understanding the tradition that justify their own assumption of power to achieve their religious goals. Each has an array of charismatic leaders who both interpret the tradition and focus political mobilisation. Both see themselves as the only legitimate heirs of the tradition and construct tight boundaries between themselves and outsiders. Both have become adept at utilising modern means of public relations and communication to move their agendas forward.

Within Islam, fundamentalism has been present in Saudi Arabia since the eighteenth century. However, the present growth of fundamentalist movements is a product of the last two-thirds of the twentieth century. As the nations of the Middle East gained independence from European colonising powers, they were confronted with profound questions about their identity. Into the gap created by these societal changes stepped fundamentalist organisations like the Muslim Brotherhood, founded in Egypt in 1928. By the end of World War II, the Brotherhood had, in Egypt alone, half a million members and another half-million followers. However, it was not until the mid- and late twentieth century that a set of shifts occurred that brought fundamentalism to the fore throughout the Islamic world.

One element was alarm over the extent to which Western ideology and culture had come to dominate the Muslim world. Perhaps naively, civil leaders had presumed that they could pick and choose among the aspects of Western life. When this proved not to be the case, there began to be conservative counter-reactions.

Allied to this was the perceived failure of secular nationalism to create a strong, prosperous and unified Arab world. The inability of Middle Eastern states to prevent the formation and continued existence of the State of Israel has been viewed as a sign of Arab political and military weakness. Under Egyptian President Nasser, Egypt and Syria were formally united in 1958 into the United Arab Republic; the union broke apart three years later. The long tradition of secular nationalism among Palestinians has produced neither a nation nor economic progress. Similarly, the Jordanian economy has stagnated under Hashemite rule. Perhaps most dramatically, the participation of Arab nations on the Anglo-American side in the 1991 Gulf War revealed what knowledge-able observers already knew: that Muslim unity was an illusion. An end result was the discrediting of secular nationalism and the feeling on the part of many that conservative Islam offered the only possibility for ultimate equality with the West. The victory of Islamic fundamentalists over the Soviets and their client government in Afghanistan in 1992 only confirmed the hope that fundamentalist Islam could provide an answer.

> The failure of secular nationalist leadership and ideologies is also strongly associated in the Middle East context with repeated defeats by Israel . . . At the same time, alternative Marxist or socialist ideologies are seen as theoretically discredited . . . Given this political and ideological vacuum, fundamentalists were able to present their vision of an Islamic alterna-tive as the only viable . . . ideology for Muslims everywhere.
>
> Abdullahi A. An-Na'im, 'Political Islam', in Peter L. Berger (ed.),
> *The Desecularization of the World* (1999: 106)

The result of these forces was the adoption of sha'aria, Islamic reli-gious law, as the official legal code in several states, and fundamentalist pressure on others. Perhaps the most dramatic example of this was that of the puritanical Taliban government in Afghanistan. Sudan became an Islamic state in 1989, fuelling a continuing civil war between Muslim Arabs in the north and Christian and traditional religionists in the south. In Jordan, sha'aria forms part of civil law, and Muslim parties and reli-gious groups have significant power. In Libya and Syria, fundamentalist

Islamic groups now represent the most serious threats to the secular regimes, while in North Africa secular governments in Algeria, Tunisia and Morocco are under attack. The growing power of fundamentalist Islam is also becoming an issue in the world's largest Muslim state, Indonesia.

Like the other examples that we have seen, Muslim fundamentalism derives from a concentration on particular aspects of Islamic thought. One of these centres on Islamic societies as 'states of peace' and other political arrangements as 'states of war'. Since the Qur'an presents the caliph as the representative of God on earth, fundamentalists argue that the caliphate, which functionally ended over 700 years ago, is the ideal form of government. Thus, liberal democratic arrangements are to be rejected and Muslims are obliged to live in an Islamic state. In this, we can also see another feature common to fundamentalist thought, the desire on the one hand to oppose the prevailing culture and on the other to reshape the wider society according to fundamentalist belief.

These case studies of the recent rise of fundamentalism within the world's three major monotheistic religions point to the growing power of fundamentalism. They also demonstrate that, despite religious differences, fundamentalist movements have strikingly similar worldviews and ways of promoting their beliefs.

It is worth mentioning that, within Christianity, there has been comparable growth among less radical conservatives called evangelicals. Unlike fundamentalists, evangelicals mostly continue to serve as commentators on and critics of moral issues in society, rather than seeking to reconstruct society according to their own beliefs. In Latin America, approximately one person in ten is an evangelical, a total of 40 to 50 million people. In Africa and China, the estimates are for tens of millions. Worldwide, about 200 million people consider themselves to be evangelicals.

A few examples illustrate increasing evangelical strength. In historically Catholic Peru, nineteen Protestants were elected to Congress in 1990. In Chile, 20 per cent of the electorate belong to this sector of Christianity. The Assemblies of God, an evangelical denomination, alone account for 10 per cent of the population in Zimbabwe.

If some recent religious developments suggest that the religious movement in many societies is in the direction of contraction, others argue for movement toward expansiveness. This is to say that they are moving in a direction of greater inclusion, broader perspectives and a growing number of collaborative activities.

Numerically, mainline Christian groups coming from Protestant, Anglican and Catholic traditions have either decreased or remained stable since the 1970s, while Judaism has experienced a continuing decline. However, these denominations continue to exercise disproportionate influence in the societies of which they are a part, both because of their relatively high visibility and, in many instances, well-developed organisational structures.

Within Christianity, one way in which the expansive tendency is seen is in denominational mergers and inter-communion relationships. Several examples illustrate this tendency. In 1947, Anglicans, Methodists, Congregationalists, Presbyterians and Reformed united to form the Church of South India. This union has 3.8 million members and 14,000 congregations in 21 dioceses in India and Sri Lanka. The Evangelical Lutheran Church in America was created in 1988 by the merger of three North American Lutheran bodies, resulting in a membership in 1999 of 5.1 million.

A major breakthrough in inter-communion among churches was launched in Europe between 1989 and 1992 with the signing of the Porvoo Agreement by four Anglican Churches (the Church of England, Church of Ireland, Church in Wales and Scottish Episcopal Church) and eight Baltic and Nordic Lutheran groups (the Estonian Evangelical-Lutheran Church, the Evangelical-Lutheran Churches of Finland, Iceland, Latvia and Lithuania, and the Churches of Norway, Denmark and Sweden). Within the context of the 'new Europe', this created a communion of episcopal (having bishops) national churches stretching across northern Europe. A similar kind of inter-communion was created in North America by the agreement between the Evangelical Lutheran Church in America (the 'merged' church mentioned a little earlier) and the Episcopal church in 1997–8.

In the face of all the questions arising from our common mission today, our churches are called together to proclaim a duty of service to the wider world and to the societies in which they are set. Equally, they are called together to proclaim the Christian hope, arising from faith, which gives meaning in societies characterized by ambiguity.

Porvoo Common Declaration (1992)

Even without merging or entering into formal direct relationships, there have been numerous instances of increased ecumenical (among Christians) or interfaith (between Christians and other religious groups) activities since the 1950s. One of the most notable of these is the World Council of Churches. Founded in 1948 as an international fellowship of Christian Churches, the WCC now includes about 400 million Christians represented by more than 340 churches, denominations and fellowships in 120 countries and territories.

Comparable national bodies exist in many countries. The National Council of Churches of Christ in the United States of America is that country's leading agency for Christian ecumenical co-operation, with 36 Protestant, Anglican and Orthodox member denominations representing more than 50 million persons. Churches Together in Britain and Ireland (CTBI) represents 32 denominations, including the Roman Catholic Church in England and Wales, while the Action of Churches Together in Scotland (ACTS) has another nine members. Comparable groups are found both regionally and nationally throughout the world, virtually all of them created since the 1950s.

In addition, formal theological dialogues have been established between a number of religious groups, aimed at greater understanding. The Anglican–Roman Catholic International Commission (ARCIC), for example, met on numerous occasions from 1971 to 1981 and issued seven statements indicating areas of religious doctrine on which there was common agreement. A number of religious groups, including the Episcopal Church in the United States and the Roman Catholic Church, continue comparable dialogues.

Worthy of mention as well are communities in which members from different religious traditions work and live together. The Iona Community, on an island off the west coast of Scotland, was founded in 1938 as an ecumenical Christian community dedicated to working for social and political change, and for church renewal. At the time of writing, it has about 240 members. In 1965, the Corrymeela Community was established on the Antrim coast of Northern Ireland as an ecumenical community. Over the years, it has been involved in a wide range of religious and social programmes, with special attention to efforts at reconciliation in the context of the ongoing conflict in Northern Ireland.

Another aspect of such coming together is what sociologist Robert Wuthnow has termed the restructuring of religion. At the local level, especially in the United States among Christians, many individuals participate in activities across denominational lines that result in greater functional identification with their fellow participants than with other members of their own group who do not share in such activities. For example, Catholics, Presbyterians and Methodists who are part of an ecumenical prayer group tend to have more significant relationships with each other than they do with those who belong to their own churches but are not prayer-group members. Evidence suggests that individuals increasingly organise religiously in such functional ways, with less attention to the theological and cultural differences that have heretofore defined religious membership along strictly denominational lines, and that this is not unique to the American context.

> If religion has been restructured, this restructuring has been possible because religious organizations have had the resources with which to respond to the challenges set before them . . . The capacity to adapt has, in fact, been one of the impressive features of American religion.
>
> Robert Wuthnow, *The Restructuring of American Religion* (1988: 5)

Along with ecumenical expansiveness, the second half of the twentieth century witnessed a significant opening of relations between Christianity and other religious traditions. Arguably, the most notable of these inter-faith ventures was with Judaism. In 1927, the National Council of Christians and Jews (now the National Conference for Community and Justice) was founded in the United States to deal with religious prejudice over the first Catholic nominee for president, Al Smith. Over the years, it has sponsored a wide variety of activities in support of social justice for workers and people of colour, as well educational efforts to eliminate racial, ethnic and religious prejudice. Other organisations have been created in response to the Holocaust, including the International Council of Christians and Jews, an umbrella organisation of 36 national Jewish–Christian dialogue organisations worldwide. Organisations to foster Christian–Jewish dialogue exist in at least 30 countries, including states as varied as the United Kingdom and Uruguay.

Christian dialogue with religious traditions other than Judaism has also begun, though on a more modest scale. The International Council of Christians and Jews has begun to engage in the Abrahamic dialogue: the encounter among Jews, Christians and Muslims. These activities have also started at the local and national levels.

One of the most interesting recent attempts at inter-faith activity has been the Parliament of the World's Religions. In commemoration of the first major inter-faith conference ever held, a part of the Columbian Exposition in Chicago in 1893, a second Parliament of the World's Religions took place there in 1993. Some 6,500 people representing 250 religious traditions met for intensive seminars and dialogue. This event was so successful that another Parliament was held in South Africa six years later, and subsequent Parliaments are planned at five- or six-year intervals. These Parliaments provided the first forum in history that brought together a wide array of groups, including Asian and traditional indigenous religions.

Traditional mainstream versus 'new' religions

While not exactly a tension in the same sense as the previous two dichotomies, interesting developments have occurred both in traditional and 'new' religions. In this context, 'traditional' means those groups that have existed for more than a short period of time and are viewed by most observers as established entities. The term 'new' is used here to identify religious groups of two sorts. One is the case of groups that have come into existence in the last hundred years or so, either as off-spring of other groups or as entirely new creations – examples would be Asian religions like Soka Gakkai or Falun Gong, independent African churches and various forms of neo-paganism in northern Europe. The other is of religious groups whose origins are not entirely clear but that have become more prominent since the late twentieth century – a good example here would be Afro-Caribbean religions like Vodun (voodoo) or Santeria, which overlay a veneer of Christianity on deeper underlying tribal beliefs.

Among traditional world religions, most appear to be in a stable state. Roman Catholicism has been mostly stable, with a slight decline in the mid-1990s, while Eastern Orthodoxy has experienced a mild increase, as has Protestantism. Both Buddhism and Hinduism have also grown in numbers since the late twentieth century, so that the latter has become the world's third-largest religion. The greatest growth among the world religions, however, has been in Islam. As a result of continued conversions and the Third World's higher birth rates, Islam is the second-largest religion in the world, with somewhere around one in five persons numbered among its adherents.

Among Christians, there is evidence to suggest that what growth has occurred is on its right wing, among fundamentalists and evangelicals. This, taken with the growth of Hinduism and Islam, strongly implies that the world is becoming more conservative from a religious perspective.

Significant religious growth has also been seen among new religions, especially in Asia and Africa. Even when the new faiths have small numbers of adherents, they are worth considering as indicators of how people organise religiously in the contemporary world.

One of the most interesting phenomena in the European context is a reconfiguration of ancient religions. This is in groups that might be termed neo-pagan. These share common factors such as duotheistic or polytheistic belief, celebration of four main seasonal days of the year, conducting of rituals outdoors, concern for the environment and nature, and the absence of hierarchy. Probably the largest of these is Wicca, a collection of autonomous covens with worship centred on the goddess and her consort, the horned god, represented by the high priestess and high priest of the coven. One estimate places the number of Wiccans in the United States at about 750,000, making it the fifth-largest organised religion there, and at about 100,000 in the United Kingdom.

In the Nordic and Germanic countries, particular elements of ancient pagan tradition have been revived and embellished. Finnish pagan religion has its roots in shamanism, sharing many of its basic beliefs, which is unsurprising given Finland's geographical proximity to Siberian and Arctic people. Among Germanic peoples, Asatru adherents follow the Aesir sky gods (such as Odin, Friga, Thor and Baldur) and the Vanir earth gods (such as Frey and Freya). In at least one country, Iceland, the Germanic paganist revival has been significant enough for it to be recognised in 1973 as an official state religion along with Christianity.

East Asia especially has been fertile ground for new religious movements. Most of these are blends of Taoist, Confucian and Buddhist thought, together with some uniquely modern elements. A number of these groups have managed to attract large numbers of adherents over a relatively short time span.

One group, Chinese in origin, is the Hsien-T'ien Tao (Way of Former Heaven) sects. The basic doctrine of these is that the deity is a cosmic Mother who has given birth to the universe and humanity and now grieves that her children have lost their way. During two previous cosmic eras, only a small number returned to their Mother's side. Now, in the last era of the world, which will come to a catastrophic end, the Mother has intensified her efforts to bring her children back. For the most part, these groups have fewer than 20,000 members but several were quite strong in the earlier part of the twentieth century, with T'ien-te Sheng-chiao (Sacred Religion of the Celestial Virtue) having 3.67 million adherents in the late 1940s and Tao-yuan another 3 million in 1940. Both of these were founded at the beginning of the twentieth century.

Perhaps the most well-known new religion in China is Falun Gong. Indeed, there is some question whether it is a religion at all, or rather a set of mental and physical disciplines. Falun Gong incorporates principles drawn from Buddhism and Taoism, and combines these with exercise and body cultivation. The movement, founded by Li Hongzhi, was only made public in China in 1992, although he claims that the tradition is much older. Falun Gong has been severely persecuted by the authorities, who are well aware of the history of religious movements destabilising civil government in China. In spite of this, it has grown rapidly and, at the end of the twentieth century, claimed to have 70 million members in China and another 30 million in the rest of the world.

Japan also has been the seedbed of numerous such movements. Mahikari, founded by a Buddhist of the same name in 1959, is rooted in the founders' reception of a direct revelation from God Su. By the mid-1990s, it had gained between 350 and 400 thousand members. Rissho Kosei Kai, a Buddhist offshoot that emerged in 1938, was said to have nearly 5 million members by the early 1970s. Arguably, the most successful of the Japanese groups is Soka Gakkai. Originally formed in 1937, Soka Gakkai believes that humans can change themselves and, in changing, transform the surrounding world. This is accomplished by chanting the title of the Lotus Sutra, which results in an elevated mental and spiritual state. Soka Gakkai's pragmatic organisational structure and the simplicity and openness of its practices have contributed to its remarkable growth. The organisation claimed in 1970 to have over 16 million adherents but accurate estimates of present active membership place it at between 4 and 5 million.

Vietnam, too, has been host to a number of new religious movements. Hoa Hao was founded in 1939 by Huynh Phu So and is based on what the founder saw as a recovery of pure Buddhism mixed with elements of Confucianism and Taoism. Among other things, it emphasises home worship over the use of temples and pagodas. Having suffered repression under the French, the Vietnamese Diem regime and the communists, Hoa Hao has nonetheless continued to grow. With some 2 million members, it is considered one of the five most important religions in Vietnam. Even more prominent, however, is Cao Dai, a monotheistic religion that seeks to establish a basis for the unity of major world religions. For Cao Dai, all religions are one and simply have different names. Belief in reincarnation is the motive for followers to live moral lives, since the quality of one's rebirth depends on actions undertaken in the present life. Its hierarchy is based on that of the Catholic Church, with a pope, cardinals, bishops and archbishops. Established in 1925 by a native Vietnamese administrator working for the French, the movement has been staunchly anti-communist, a stance which has subjected it to persecution. However, it continues to grow and is estimated to have 7 to 8 million members in Vietnam, with another 30,000 in the United States, Europe and Australia. After Buddhism and Catholicism, it is the largest religious body in Vietnam.

Of those new religions that come from Asian roots, none has attracted more attention than the Holy Spirit Association for the Unification of World Christianity, also known as the Unification Church or Moonies, founded by the Rev. Sun Myung Moon in Korea in 1954. Moon began his religious career as a Presbyterian but was excommunicated in 1948. While Unification Church beliefs are recognisably rooted in Christianity, numerous elements in its theology differ radically from those of traditional Christianity. Among these are: an affair between Eve and the Archangel Lucifer; a spiritual rather than physical resurrection of Jesus; and the eventual arrival of a third Adam, who will complete the task left undone by Jesus of repairing the harm caused by Adam and Eve. While it is difficult to know total Unification Church membership, given inflated estimates by both friends and enemies, it is likely in the hundreds of thousands worldwide.

Africa has also been fertile ground for the spawning of new religious movements. Some of these have become powerful not only in Africa but also the Caribbean and South America, where many have African roots. Vodun (popularly called voodoo) can trace its roots to prehistoric times in West Africa. Its chief and lesser gods are derived from Yoruba tradition, while many of its hundreds of minor spirits come from other African traditions or the New World. Since both Catholicism and Vodun believe in a supreme being, an afterlife, and have a kind of ritual sacrifice, it was natural that elements of both religions would be combined, especially in the colonial world. The Loa, or Vodun spirits, resemble Catholic saints as intercessors and protectors, and frequently, in Latin America, bear the names of specific saints. It is estimated that over 60 million people worldwide practice Vodun, and it was formally recognised as Benin's official religion in 1996.

Similar to Vodun is Santeria (the Way of the Saints), which combines elements of Bantu, Yoruba and Catholic belief and practice. Concentrated in the Caribbean, Hispanic areas of the United States, South America, France and the Netherlands, it continues to grow. In the United States alone, estimates range from 500,000 to several million practitioners.

A number of other groups can be brought together under the general heading of 'African independent churches'. These tend to be offshoots of historic churches, frequently have a preoccupation with the Spirit, and seek to adapt traditional Western Christianity to indigenous beliefs and forms of worship. Many of these might also be called prophetic movements, since they are built on a strong leader, a prophet. The following examples are illustrative. One, the Christ Apostolic Church, began in 1933, grew rapidly and subsequently spread into Ghana. Another emerged in 1925 as a result of the activities of a charismatic leader and a young woman who had fallen into a trance during which she felt called to create a new church. The Cherubim and Seraphim Society, this new group, broke from Anglicanism in 1928. The largest denomination, the Church of the Lord (Aladura), was founded in 1930 by a Nigerian Anglican catechist and spread quickly into Ghana, Liberia and Sierra Leone. Eventually, branches were established in London and New York. The Legio Maria movement developed out of a Catholic lay spirituality group brought to Kenya by the 1930s. It developed its own theology emphasising the central role of Mary in Christian faith, and beliefs in the interaction between the world of spirits and human beings that differed from those of Catholicism. Having initially rejected what they saw as an over-emphasis on ordained clergy, this lay movement eventually developed its own hierarchy of a pope, cardinals, bishops and priests.

Numbers by themselves would make these churches important new additions to the African religious ecology. Aladura alone is estimated to have 1.1 million members, while the African independent churches as a whole have about 60 million adherents, with 1 to 5 million members added each year. One reason for their success has been their continued effort to create religious settings rooted in African tribal culture and in which individuals can feel comfortable.

In turbulent times, in times of great change, people head for the two extremes: fundamentalism and personal, spiritual experience . . . With no membership lists or even a coherent philosophy or dogma, it is difficult to define or measure the unorganized New Age movement. But in every major US and European city, thousands who seek insight and personal growth cluster around a metaphysical bookstore, a spiritual teacher, or an education center.

J. Naisbitt and P. Aburdene, *Megatrends 2000* (1990: 277–286)

Among the most difficult to categorise of the new religions are those that might be grouped under the heading of 'New Age'. These emerged in the United States in the 1960s and 1970s, spreading rapidly across North America and Europe. New Age beliefs and practices provided an alternative for those who were disenchanted with traditional Christianity on the one hand, and rejected secular humanism on the other. New Age has roots in Taoism, Hinduism, Gnosticism, Theosophy, Spiritualism and neo-paganism. Among New Age religious practices are the use of astrology, Tarot cards, fortune telling, alternative healing, drumming and chanting.

A look at two of the more organised New Age groups illustrates these characteristics. The Church of Scientology was founded in the mid-1950s in the United States. Rooted in the spiritual teachings of L. Ron Hubbard, who died in 1986, the church believes that individuals are Thetans, living souls. The human mind, in its reactive component, is psychically scarred by events in this and prior lives. In a process called 'auditing', individuals can remove the psychic scars and become 'clear'. A 'clear' individual, in turn, can see, hear and feel without access to normal senses. Rapidly growing throughout the world, the church claims to have 8 million members in over 120 countries.

The International Society for Krishna Consciousness (ISKCON) has its origins in Hinduism. However, it believes that Krishna is the supreme Lord over all deities, rather than the Hindu belief in Krishna as the eighth incarnation of the god Vishnu. Liberation from continual reincarnations is achieved by congregational chanting of God's names, which leads to

Krishna Consciousness. Jesus is viewed as a directly empowered representative of Krishna. Bhaktivedanta Swami Prabhupada came to the United States and organised ISKCON in 1965. With a head office in Los Angeles, ISKCON currently has a membership of over 1 million adherents throughout the world.

Other new directions

Several recent religious trends do not lend themselves to the 'opposite directions' way of analysis and deserve examination. These represent shifts in the religious world, in that they offer new emphases that have impacted directly and significantly on a wide variety of religious groups.

The first of these is what might be termed the 'greening' of religion. This involves a growing consciousness among religious groups and individuals of the importance of environmental concerns. Such consciousness frequently has been a part of the mainstream in many Asian religions but even though individuals like St Francis of Assisi in the Christian tradition held perspectives that emphasised the relations between humans and nature, it is only recently that Christianity as a whole has become more sensitised to the religious dimension of the relationship between people and the wider environment. Since the late twentieth century, the World Council of Churches has gradually made environmental concerns a more central part of its agenda, making explicit its growing work for 'Peace, Justice, and the Integrity of Creation' at the Vancouver Assembly of 1983. This phrase has become the WCC's rallying cry on environmental issues in numerous more specialised meetings.

When the ecological crisis is set within the broader context of *the search for peace* within society, we can understand better the importance of giving attention to what the earth and its atmosphere are telling us: namely, that there is an order in the universe which must be respected, and that the human person, endowed with the capability of choosing freely, has a grave responsibility to preserve this order for the well-being of future generations.

Pope John Paul II, 'Peace with God the Creator,
Peace with All of Creation' (1990)

The Roman Catholic Church has come to ecological issues somewhat later. The most definitive statement thus has been the Pope's message 'Peace with God, Peace with All of Creation', issued for the celebration of World Peace day in 1990. In this letter totally concerned with environmental issues, he develops a Catholic theology of the environment and offers suggestions – including environmental education, reflection on the lifestyles of modern society and internationally solidarity – as remedies for concerns.

The present Greek Orthodox patriarch, Bartholomew I, as been called the 'Green Patriarch' because of his outspoken concern about the environment. Like the Pope, he has insisted that human beings and the environment form 'a seamless garment of existence' and so 'it follows that to commit a crime against the natural world is a sin' (1997). Growing environmental concern is also seen in the creation of broadly based religious organisations to deal with ecological issues. A good example is the National Religious Partnership for the Environment founded in the United States in 1992 with mainline Protestant, Catholic, Evangelical, Orthodox and Jewish membership.

The 'greening' of religion has also been assisted by the growing number of religious groups, both neo-pagan and New Age, rooted in ancient paganism, traditional tribal spirituality and nature religion. For such communities, ties between human beings and the wider environment are integral elements of their belief.

A second new direction that ranges across an array of religious groups is growing feminism and sensitivity to women's issues. This concern has been expressed in a wide variety of different forms. Theologically, a major issue has been that of inclusivity of language, especially language related to God. Exclusively patriarchal language is generally rejected and many feminists believe that it is appropriate to think of God as both male and female. In addition, many women have tried to articulate their newly felt solidarity in a particular form of liberation thought called feminist theology. This especially emphasises mutuality and equality for women as integral aspects of a vital religious vision.

Spiritually, the new feminist emphasis places a premium on connection rather than dualism. Thus, distinctions between ordinary life and relationship with God or between the public and private spheres of human existence are felt to be unhelpful. In relationships, this new understanding emphasises mutuality and non-competitiveness over domination. An important element is the search for a spirituality that honours the body rather than subordinates it to the mind.

Within the political sphere, growing feminism frequently has centred on women's roles within religious communities, especially with respect to leadership. Within Christianity and Judaism, this has focused specifically on women's ordination. Numerous Protestant denominations had, by the 1960s, formally ordained women to ministerial roles. Within

Anglicanism, the first regular ordinations of women to the priesthood occurred in Hong Kong in 1971, with the Episcopal Church in the United States ordaining women in 1976 and the Church of England in 1992. At the time of writing, about 20 per cent of the clergy in the latter are women. Reformed Judaism first ordained women rabbis in 1972 and Conservative Judaism in 1985.

Several major religious denominations, however, have resisted women's ordination. The largest of these is the Roman Catholic Church, which has insisted in several statements from the 1980s on that the ordination of women to the priesthood is a theological impossibility. Similarly, Eastern Orthodoxy has refused to ordain women, although at least two respected theologians have argued that there are no intrinsic reasons to prevent this. Thus, while growing feminism has found expression in increased leadership roles for women in many religious groups, the issue of women's roles continues to be a topic of heated controversy.

Related to the issue of women's ordination is the broader question of the appropriate role of women in society. Here again, the place of a particular religious group on the liberal–conservative spectrum makes its influence felt. For conservative religious groups, the appropriate sphere of activity and influence for women is the family. Those who support this position frequently argue that such a stance does not imply inferiority or inequality but rather appropriate recognition of natural differences that are all part of God's plan. Liberal religious groups, on the other hand, support women's aspirations to take on whatever roles they choose within the family as well as within the larger professional and public world. They argue that religious tradition offers guidelines rather than absolute regulations about gender roles, and that even these must be interpreted.

As can be seen, growing feminist religious concern relates to this chapter's earlier examination of constrictive versus expansive religious understandings. Feminism can be seen as part of the broadening impulse in religion, a desire to make religious belief and practice open to a wider array of people. Not surprisingly, among groups that advocate a more narrowly defined understanding of religion, there is little support for, and frequently significant opposition to, changes that will bring women into the religious sphere in new ways. Indeed, in places like the United States, much of the disagreement between mainstream and fundamentalist religion has focused on the role of women both within the religious group and the wider society.

The final new direction that we shall consider is the growth of interest in spirituality since the last few decades of the twentieth century. Traditionally, spirituality has always been viewed within the framework of a specific religious group. Thus, there have been multiple spiritualities associated with various saints in Roman Catholicism, as well as different spiritual paths to be found within the context of particular interpretations of Buddhism, Islam and Judaism. In this sense, spirituality has been understood as the concrete set of beliefs and practices by which a person journeyed on a particular religious path. The connection between formal religious structures and spirituality, in this understanding, is integral.

The end of the twentieth century, however, has witnessed new ways of understanding and interpreting the term 'spirituality'. Frequently, spirituality is not only independent of any particular sect or religious group but exists completely outside the context of formal religion. Thus, someone can have a 'spirituality' without any explicit religious affiliation.

> Spirituality is very personal and usually involves a person's taking an holistic view of the world. It can include everything from our sense of awe at observing a special sunset or our emotional reaction to the denouement of a tragedy to our overwhelming response to organ music swelling and echoing through a cavernous building or our trance-like involvement in a well-loved ritual.
>
> Johanna H. Stuckey, *Feminist Spirituality* (1998: 6)

Arriving at an understanding of this new conceptualisation of spirituality is difficult, since its meaning has been transformed so completely. In fact, it can be argued that there is no longer any single definition that can be given to the term. Undeniably, however, spirituality in this sense represents a significant religious trend. One has only to look at the array of books on spirituality in most bookstores to realise how widespread the public interest is.

Many of these understandings of spirituality contain common elements. Someone interested in spirituality is seen as having concern with things beyond those of the material world. Spirituality, in this sense, is oriented towards the transcendent, that which lies beyond people's immediate day-to-day experience. It may involve refinement of thought and feeling, a kind of heightened aesthetic sense; it may have to do with things of the spirit, as contrasted with the body; some would describe it as attempting to find the 'source' of everything.

Another element frequently found in descriptions is what might be termed 'interiority' or the 'inner journey'. This implies a significant reflective component, the willingness to enter into rigorous introspection to arrive at self-awareness, and is contrasted with living life at a shallow level, never really coming into contact with one's 'true self' or the deeper realities and questions of human existence.

Allied to all this, in many instances, is the at least implicit notion of self-improvement. 'Spirituality exists to make me a better person,' one might say. In this sense, contemporary understandings of spirituality differ from many traditional definitions, since the goal now becomes focused on self rather than on God. Thus, much of contemporary spirituality tends to be very subjective, in contrast to traditional understandings in which well-defined spiritual paths are followed in order to arrive at specific goals.

These new forms of spirituality frequently both derive from and are tied to wider forces in the contemporary world. For many, especially in the West, traditional mainstream religion is viewed either negatively or with suspicion. Given the rapidity and stress of change in the modern world, however, many people feel a need to anchor themselves in something beyond their own immediate physical realities. Such new ways of viewing spirituality provide for this kind of security without demanding that practitioners belong to a particular religious organisation, with its attendant set of structures. The whole notion of the postmodern world, with its critique of scientific rationalism as the only legitimate way of knowing, has further encouraged interest in things not accessible by empirical examination.

Interest in nature, ecology and a holistic rather than component-oriented attitude towards oneself and the world have also been driving forces behind the new interest in spirituality. Here, the notion of 'connectedness' with the world of nature and a desire to see things as organic parts of a whole have become important elements.

In the West, beginning with Freud, understanding what makes human beings 'tick' has been possible without having to make reference to God or religion. This search for the 'inner self', seen in popular psychological and self-help literature, is also a component.

All these factors motivate the search for spirituality. For some, it takes the form of attention to aspects of New Age belief and practice, whether involving meditation or chanting, crystals or angels. Others take up practices like Hindu yoga, Jewish kabbalism and Sufi chanting without necessarily subscribing to the religions from which they originated. Still others develop highly individualised systems of belief and practice.

The success of spirituality literature is testified to by the continual stream of books published in this area. A preliminary search of the Internet for websites concerned with spirituality at the time of writing yields thousands of results, ranging from the spiritualities of Saints John of the Cross and Ignatius Loyola to the Institute for Astroenergetic Studies and the Society of Luminists. All of these bear witness to the deep and widespread interest exhibited by many in spirituality without necessarily being rooted in specific religious denominations or sects.

Conclusion

In the course of this chapter, we have examined a number of recent directions in the religious world. In several cases, various segments of society appear to be moving in opposite directions. Secularisation continues to be an ongoing phenomenon, especially Western Europe, but de-secularisation has also emerged as a strong force throughout the world, especially in the Middle East and South Asia.

Among religious groups themselves, some are moving in the direction I have called contraction. Rising fundamentalism among Christians, Jews and Muslims is perhaps the most obvious example of this sort of religious narrowing. At the same time, however, some groups are becoming more expansive, entering into closer relations with others by mergers and inter-communion agreements, as well as looser affiliations in co-operative organisations. In many instances, individuals increasingly are entering into common activities and relationships that cut across traditional lines.

The relative situations of traditional mainstream and 'new' religions have changed since the 1950s. For the most part, mainstream religions have been in a steady state, with the most rapid growths seen in Islam and Hinduism, as well as in the conservative sectors of other religious groups. The growth of new religions, however, frequently has been rapid and over a relatively short timespan. In Europe and North America, renewed interest in pagan and nature religion has been an area of development, as has New Age religion. Asia has given rise to numerous faiths that blend elements of traditional groups with new doctrines and membership of some of these numbers in the millions. In Africa and parts of the New World settled by Africans, faiths blending a Christian veneer with deeper tribal beliefs have continued to grow.

In some cases, religious trends appear headed in one dominant direction. One example is the 'greening' of religion. A wide variety of religious groups have become more sensitive to the ways in which environmental issues need to become elements in theological reflection, as well as social action. Individuals like the Pope and the Patriarch of Constantinople, as well as groups organised for ecological purposes, have moved this agenda forward.

Feminism, too, has become a significant issue within the religious world. Theologically, it has challenged understandings of God, human persons and the world of nature that some argue were implicitly rooted in male perspectives. Politically, it has striven to increase the level and scope of women's leadership. Here, the issue of women's ordination to ministerial roles has been a major focus. Socially, it has disputed traditional understandings of the role of women in the family and community, as well as exerting pressure for just economic treatment.

The widespread growth of interest in spirituality is also a recent and important shift. While traditional definitions of the term no longer seem to apply, spirituality generally appears to have to do with orientation towards something beyond oneself, as well as interior reflectiveness. Not necessarily tied to organised religion, it has become for many a centre path between materialism on the one hand and what are felt to be confining traditional religious structures on the other.

Taken together, what do all of these recent trends in religion have to teach us? Primarily, they provide evidence for the continued vitality of religion in the modern world. For any group, organisation, sect or denomination to be alive, it must be continually in the process of change. While core beliefs in traditional religions might very well not shift, perspectives, insights and interpretations are always in flux. Additionally, new movements continually appear in response to theological, social, cultural and political developments. While religion is grounded in the transcendent, it also needs to confront the issues of the world in which it finds itself, and be seen as meeting the needs of its adherents. Religious change and development such as we have examined in this chapter show us the degree to which faith communities, new and old alike, continue to do that, and to enrich their members and the wider human community as a result.

Further reading

Barrett, David B. (1968), *Schism and Renewal in Africa: An Analysis of Six Thousand Contemporary Religious Movements*, Nairobi: Oxford University Press.

Beckford, James A. (ed.) (1986), *New Religious Movements and Rapid Social Change*, London: Sage.

Berger, Peter L. (ed.) (1999), *The Desecularization of the World*, Grand Rapids, MI: Eerdmans.

Bradley, Ian C. (1990), *God is Green: Christianity and the Environment*, London: Darton, Longman and Todd.

Carr, Anne E. (1998), *Transforming Grace: Christian Tradition and Women's Experience*, San Francisco: Harper and Row.

Casanova, Jose (1994), *Public Religions in the Modern World*, Chicago: University of Chicago Press.

Davidson, Lawrence (1998), *Islamic Fundamentalism*, Westport, CT: Greenwood Press.

Hori, Ichiro (ed.) (1972), *Japanese Religion*, Tokyo: Kodansha International.

Lossky, Nicholas (ed.) (1991), *Dictionary of the Ecumenical Movement*, Geneva: WCC Publications.

Marty, Martin E. and R. Scott Appleby (1992), *The Glory and the Power: The Fundamentalist Challenge to the Modern World*, Boston: Beacon Press.

Stuckey, Johanna H. (1998), *Feminist Spirituality*, Toronto: York University.
Wuthnow, Robert (1998), *The Restructuring of American Religion*, Princeton, NJ: Princeton University Press.

? Questions

1. Indicate what arguments can be made for the view that the world is increasingly becoming more secular? What arguments can be made for desecularisation?

2. What are the major characteristics of fundamentalism? Compare and contrast its Christian, Jewish and Muslim manifestations.

3. In what ways have recent years witnessed trends toward unification and co-operation among religious groups?

4. Give examples of some 'new' religious movements. Why have such movements flourished in recent years?

5. What are some of the major features of feminist religion?

6. How do 'religion' and 'spirituality' differ? In what ways are they the same?

PART II

THEOLOGY

Section One: BIBLICAL STUDIES

CHAPTER ONE

Ways of Reading the Bible

Paul Ellingworth

Introduction

The title of this chapter illustrates the academic purpose of this Section: it is for students. But students (and their teachers) need to remind themselves from time to time that, even though the Bible remains the world's bestseller, regular Bible readers form a small proportion of the world's population, even of the world's Christian population. The parts of the world in which Christianity is growing the fastest are some of those which have a relatively low literacy rate. Particularly (but not only) in those countries, the Bible is widely communicated through non-print media, such as the internationally successful 'Jesus film' and audio cassette recordings. In developed and developing countries alike, many more people hear the Bible read in church than read it regularly for themselves. True, there are also many people who belong to informal Bible-reading groups, or who read the Bible systematically on their own, without being regular churchgoers. But it remains the case that Bible-reading is a minority occupation, a niche market.

Students of the Bible, who are likely to influence the ways in which others read it, should themselves consider and evaluate different ways of reading the Bible.

The authority of the Bible

Before we consider different ways of reading the Bible, the prior question arises: Why the Bible? What's special about it? The immediate answer is that virtually all Christians, since the New Testament writings were gathered together, have attributed to the Bible some kind of authority. This means, in very general terms, that the Bible is the basic book (or collection of books) for Christianity, the one to which one refers in order to know what Christianity is about.

Christians have interpreted the authority of the Bible in various ways. Some have found authority in each part, even each word, of the Old and New Testaments, in their original texts or even in a translation. Others have concentrated authority in the New Testament, or in the words attributed to Jesus, or in the 'Christ-event', using these as a thread to guide them through the rest of the Bible. Others, again, have found authority in the acts of God to which the Bible bears witness. Others have held that the Bible had authority for them because it was confirmed by their experience of life. Or, as R. Gnuse has put it, '[T]he [biblical] canon has authority because it contains the spiritual experiences of the earliest communities of faith and has inspired generations of Christians past and present.'

Random reading

First, there is the random way of reading the Bible: a way of reading the Bible that is totally without system. This way of reading (we cannot call it a method) may be applied to chapters, or even longer passages, but it is more commonly applied to individual texts. For some people, this presupposes that every part of the Bible is equally and in the same way the word of God, and that therefore, wherever you open it, you will hear God speaking to you. It also presupposes that the Holy Spirit guides readers to finding, and then understanding, the place at which their Bible will open.

This is not a way of reading the Bible which is generally taught in departments of Theology or Religious Studies. There are theological difficulties about it: the Bible is not a collection of magical texts, each of which can be used in isolation from its context. But before we dismiss completely this way of reading the Bible, we should recall that some great Christians have practised it at crucial moments in their lives.

Suddenly I heard a voice from some nearby house, a sort of sing-song repeated again and again, 'Take and read, take and read.' I arose, interpreting the incident as quite certainly a divine command to open my book of Scripture and read the passage at which I should open. I snatched it up, opened it and in silence read the passage upon which my eyes first fell: 'Not in rioting and drunkenness, not in chambering and impurities, not in contention and envy, but put ye on the Lord Jesus Christ and make not provision for the flesh in its concupiscences.' [Romans 13: 13.] I had no wish to read further, and no need.

Augustine, *Confessions* (book 8, chapter 12) (slightly abbreviated)

I think it was about five this morning, that I opened my Testament on those words, 'There are given unto us exceeding great and precious promises, even that ye should be partakers of the divine nature' (2 Peter 1: 4). Just as I went out, I opened it again on those words, 'Thou art not far from the kingdom of God.'

John Wesley, *Journal*, 24 May 1738 (1938: I, 472)

Devotional reading

Next, there is the devotional way of reading the Bible. In order to do justice to it, it is necessary to put this (and the rest of this chapter) in a wider context. This will involve a brief digression.

Any communication involves at least two people, a sender and a receptor. If the two people are close together in space, time and culture, for example a husband and wife in the same room, what the sender sends and what the receptor receives are likely to be almost exactly the same (though there can be misunderstandings even between husband and wife!). If the sender and the receptor are far apart in space, time and culture – if, for example, the sender is Isaiah in Jerusalem in the eighth century BCE and the receptor is a student in Scotland in the twenty-first century CE – the differences between what the sender sent and what the receptor receives are likely to be greater, and problems in understanding are more likely to arise. This is sometimes called the distinction between what the Bible said and what the Bible says.

Ways of reading the Bible may be roughly classified according to whether they concentrate mainly on what the sender sent or on what the receptor receives. The word 'mainly' is important. If a first-year student who does not yet know Hebrew is presented with the original text of Isaiah, without any translation or other receptor-oriented help, then communication will not take place. And communication is the name of the game.

Devotional reading of the Bible (to return from our digression) places most emphasis on the receptor and what the Bible is saying now to him or her. It is probably the most common way of reading the Bible, though probably also the least studied in departments of Theology and Religious Studies. Devotional readers are typically believers with a high respect for the Bible (though not necessarily any particular dogmatic view of its nature and authority) and an expectation that the Bible will have something to say to them by way of guidance and support for daily living. Such readers will have little or no interest in how, when, where, or even by whom the various books of the Bible were written, though they will probably accept traditional views on such questions. What matters is what the Bible has to say to them, here and now.

This is an essential dimension of reading the Bible. The Bible is not only a varied collection of historical documents. It is the book of a centuries-long, worldwide community of believers, first Jewish and later also Christian, whose life it has maintained and strengthened from generation to generation. At its best, devotional reading of the Bible may produce creative applications of the text of the highest value. Many such examples are to be found in hymns based on Old Testament texts. Isaac Watts's 'The heavens declare thy glory, Lord' is essentially a paraphrase of Psalm 19, but verse 4 takes off into a distinctively Christian application:

> Nor shall thy spreading gospel rest
>   Till through the world thy truth has run;
> Till Christ has all the nations blest,
>   That see the light or feel the sun.

Yet exclusive attention to devotional, receptor-oriented reading of the Bible can cause problems. Some parts of the Bible, such as several of the Psalms, are found by many believers to speak to them directly. You do not have to be an ancient herdsman in the Middle East to find support in a text such as 'The Lord is my shepherd' (Psalm 23: 1). The situation to which such a text relates is close to being a universal human condition.

But other parts of the Bible are so closely related to specific historical contexts that they cannot be simply transferred into a present-day situation. King David's dying instruction to his successor Solomon not to allow certain of his enemies to die of old age (1 Kings 2: 6, 9) could be dangerous if present-day readers applied it directly to their own relationships. More commonly, exclusively devotional reading of the Bible tends to become selective: certain texts speak directly to the believer and others do not, so the latter are left on one side. Again, devotional understandings of parts of the Bible tend to vary according to the reader's capacity, temperament or state of mind, so that in the last analysis there is no outside check on whether any particular reader's application of a text is in accordance with its original meaning.

Biblical criticism

At the opposite pole from these receptor-oriented ways of reading the Bible stand ways of investigation which aim to establish what the biblical texts said. They are therefore source-oriented and are collectively known as biblical criticism.

This phrase is easy to misunderstand. It does not imply criticising in the sense of passing judgement on the Bible, or even censuring it, but in the sense of 'the study and investigation of biblical writings that seeks to make discerning and discriminating judgments about these writings' (Achtemeier 1996: 141b).

The oldest distinction among types of biblical criticism is that between so-called 'lower' and 'higher' criticism – two more phrases easy to misunderstand. 'Lower' in this context does not mean 'inferior' and 'higher' does not mean 'superior'. 'Lower' means essentially 'basic, fundamental'; the kind of study which underlies any other scholarly reading of the Bible.

What used to be called 'lower criticism' is what is now more commonly called textual criticism. It involves establishing, as far as possible from the evidence now available, what was the original text of the Old and New Testament writings.

Textual criticism

All but a few small parts of the Old Testament was written in Hebrew, the rest in Aramaic, a related Semitic language. The New Testament (apart from a few words quoted in Hebrew or Aramaic) was written in normal first-century Greek, sometimes influenced by the Septuagint, the major Greek translation of the Old Testament.

The problems involved in establishing the original text of the Old and New Testaments are rather different. The oldest, almost complete, surviving manuscript of the Old Testament is (what is still called!) the Leningrad Codex of 1009 CE. It contains a standardised text developed by scribes called the Massoretes in the first few centuries of the Christian era. For certain books, notably Isaiah, the Dead Sea Scrolls include manuscripts about a thousand years older than the Leningrad Codex; otherwise, there are no witnesses independent of the Massoretic tradition. That tradition was maintained by generations of scribes with a very high degree of accuracy. But over such a long period, mistakes were inevitable; so translators and other scholars often have to refer to ancient translations of the Old Testament, and sometimes to make conjectures about what the original text might have been. For example, the New Revised Standard Version of Jeremiah 1–10 notes fifteen places where the Hebrew text is uncertain.

For the New Testament, too, a standard text eventually emerged, but fortunately we have a great number of manuscripts, the oldest from the second century CE, that in many places represent an older and better form of the text. For example, the United Bible Societies' Greek New Testament notes, in the text of the Letter to the Romans, 85 places where manuscripts differ sufficiently to affect the meaning. By careful comparison and evaluation of the evidence, it is usually possible to decide which reading (that is, which form of a text) is the most likely to be original – though, as in all such work with ancient documents, 100 per cent certainty can never be reached. In any case, the text of the New Testament is far better attested than that of other ancient writings, some of the most important of which survive only in a handful of manuscripts.

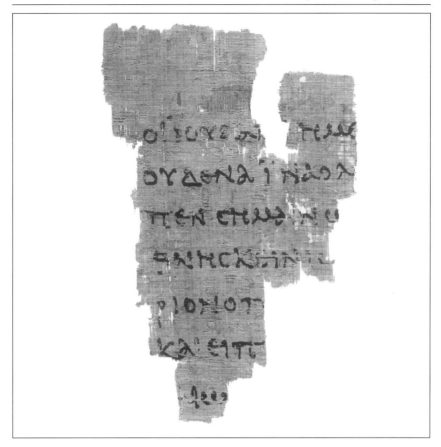

This tiny piece of papyrus, technically referred to as P52, is the earliest known fragment of the New Testament. It has John 18: 31–33 on one side and 18: 37–38 on the other. It was found in Egypt and probably dates from the early second century CE. Reproduced by courtesy of the Director and Librarian, the John Rylands University Library of Manchester.

'Higher criticism' involves 'the inquiry into the composition, date, and authenticity of the books of the Bible, from historical and literary considerations' (*Chambers English Dictionary*, under 'critic'). Its rise is usually dated from the second half of the eighteenth century. It is in this sense that a well-known series of commentaries is called 'The International Critical Commentary on the Holy Scriptures of the Old and New Testaments'. In the same sense, what is known as 'the historical-critical method' attempts to establish (again, as far as possible) the original circumstances in which the various biblical writings came into being.

Since those writings have been transmitted over so many centuries, it is not surprising that the rise of historical criticism entailed the questioning of many traditional views and caused controversies, some of which continue to the present day. For example: How much of the Old Testament is really history? Were the first five books of the Bible really all written by Moses? Is all the Book of Isaiah really by the prophet Isaiah of Jerusalem? Does the Book of Jonah have anything to do with the historical prophet of that name (2 Kings 14: 25)? What are the literary relationships between the four canonical gospels? How far do the sayings of Jesus in the gospels, and the apostles' speeches in Acts, represent exactly what was said? For whom were the gospels written? Which of the letters attributed to Paul were really written by him? What is the relation between John's gospel, the three letters of John and the Book of Revelation?

To raise such questions is not to pre-judge the answers to them: it is to opt for seeking the answers on the basis of evidence, rather than simply accepting the answers handed down by tradition (though tradition is part of the evidence). For example, the Letter to the Hebrews has been traditionally thought to be by Paul. In the Authorised Version, it is headed 'The Epistle of Paul the Apostle to the Hebrews'. Yet it is so different, in language and content, from other letters by Paul that virtually all scholars now agree that we do not know for certain who wrote it, though some speculation continues. Yet this (unusual!) scholarly agreement does not lead people to conclude that Hebrews should in future be thrown out of the Bible. Authorship and authority are two different things.

The historical-critical method has dominated biblical studies for well over a century and is not likely to disappear from the scene. It helps us to read the books of the Bible in their historical setting and thus to understand them better. In particular, it helps us to understand the setting of customs and practices which seem strange to us, in our very different time and culture. It brings us nearer to what the Bible said.

Yet it does not answer all our questions about the Bible. For some of them, available evidence is insufficient or totally lacking. What is more, in some cases even the historical question of what the Bible said may have several answers. For example, a psalm may begin as an individual believer's song of praise, or his or her cry to God for help. It may take on a different function and meaning when it is written down, handed on – perhaps for generations – and integrated into the worship of the Jerusalem Temple or teaching in the synagogues. A New Testament writer may re-read it in the light of faith in Jesus. All these strata of meaning may be part of what that part of the Bible said, even before we come to what Isaac Watts might have made of it.

There is an even bigger problem. To speak about and use the historical-critical method implies that we know what history is. We assemble and sift the evidence, and what we have left is historical fact, 'how it actually happened', as the nineteenth-century German historian Leopold von Ranke put it. That view of history is now generally seen as over-simplified. Just as in physics, observations are related to the viewpoint of the observer, so in history-writing the presuppositions of the historian can never be completely eliminated. In the same way, a source-oriented reading of the Bible can never completely eliminate the receptor; nor should it try to do so.

This principle can be illustrated from developments in the study of the first three (synoptic) gospels. Since the end of the nineteenth century this has largely concentrated on source criticism – that is, analysis of the sources believed to be used, especially by Matthew and Luke, in writing their gospels. Since the 1960s, however, it has been generally recognised that Matthew and Luke were not merely editors cutting and pasting materials they found in their sources. Like Mark and John, they were creative theologians with aims and convictions of their own. The study of the gospel writers' distinctive viewpoints is a major concern of redaction criticism, which builds on and co-operates with source criticism.

Redaction criticism also has its problems. Mark is generally believed to have been a source used by Matthew and Luke. When we compare Matthew and Luke with Mark, it is relatively easy to detect their special interests. To take a small but significant example, when Mark says 'their synagogue[s]' he means the synagogues of a particular town (Capernaum, 1: 23) or area (Galilee, 1: 39). When Matthew, more frequently (4: 23; 9: 35; 10: 9, 17; 13: 54; compare 23: 34), says 'their synagogue[s]' he usually means 'the synagogues of the Jews', suggesting the gradual distancing of Christians from Jews, a distancing which appears more strongly in John's distinctive use of the phrase 'the Jews'.

Where there is no source (such as Mark) available, the separation of tradition from redaction is more difficult. Probably Mark himself used sources, but since these are now lost, it is hard to tell how he may have adapted them. The same is still more true of John, whose adaptation of any source material is likely to have been more radical and more creative.

Where Matthew and Luke seem to be using a common source (known as Q), but differ from one another, the question arises: which of them (if either) is handing on the tradition without change and which is adapting it, and for what purpose? What did Jesus actually say: 'Be *perfect* . . . as your heavenly Father is perfect' (Matthew 5: 48), or 'Be merciful . . .' (Luke 6: 36)? 'If I drive out demons by the *Spirit* of God . . .' (Matthew 12: 28), or '. . . by the *finger* of God' (Luke 11: 20)? To even attempt an answer to such questions, it is necessary to build up from many pieces of evidence a general picture of the distinctive tendencies of each gospel writer. This is the essential aim of redaction criticism. To the extent to which it achieves that aim, it helps us, as we read the Bible, to hear different voices, or distinguish different strata, in what the Bible said.

Reader response criticism

The most recently explored way of reading the Bible is known as reader response criticism. This developed as a branch of general literary criticism, but it raises fundamental philosophical questions, particularly about the historical-critical method. It also appears in a large number of different forms, depending on whether the readers responding to the text are Marxist, liberation theologians, feminists, or something else. Feminist theologians, for example, may interpret such passages as 1 Corinthians 11: 2–16 and 14: 33b–35 either by claiming that Paul differentiates women from men without subordinating them, or by claiming that they are not by Paul, or by rejecting Paul more or less completely.

Our discussion so far has placed various ways of reading the Bible on a spectrum between mainly receptor-oriented and mainly source-oriented reading. Reader response criticism, as its name suggests, is more concerned with the receptor than the source, and therefore more with what the Bible says. But at a deeper level, it questions the whole distinction between source and receptor. It approaches the Bible as 'the book that reads me'.

To understand the origins of reader response criticism, it is necessary to go back to the French philosopher René Descartes (1596–1650). He is best known for a method of radical doubt which started from the position that one could be absolutely sure of only one thing, namely the thinking subject: 'I think, therefore I am'. The application of Descartes' thought in later generations thus tended to give priority to the subject, reducing everything else to the status of passive objects to be observed and analysed. This, according to reader response criticism (and much other current thinking), set Western philosophy off on a wrong track. Descartes' approach may have been useful, up to a point, in scientific research, but it proved a dead end as far as understanding personal being was concerned. What, according to some reader response critics, is required is something like what happens when we use our eyes. Each eye sees a slightly different picture, from a slightly different point of view, but somehow the brain integrates these two two-dimensional pictures into a single, three-dimensional image. Or one may think of the force of gravity. It does not operate in one direction only. All objects attract one another, though obviously with very different force: I do not attract the earth as much as the earth pulls me.

In the same way, what comes first in understanding the Bible is not the source and the receptor in isolation from one another but the relation between the two. Each time I read the Bible (or indeed, experience anything else), it has an effect of some kind on me; but at the same time I contribute something (though maybe not very much) to the continuing history of the Bible's influence or effect. What happens has been described by the German philosopher Hans-Georg Gadamer as a 'fusion of horizons' or areas of vision, much like the merging of what our two eyes see. This means that a reader's response to the Bible, and the message of the Bible itself, are inseparable from one another. Understanding involves a fusion of source and receptor.

The main problem with this line of thinking is obvious. It does not by itself address the question of truth, the question of the criteria by which one reader's response to the Bible may be judged to be more or less in agreement with the text than someone else's. As we know, some people's response to the Bible is highly eccentric – or at least seems so to most other people. '*It is* he that sitteth upon the circle of the earth' (Isaiah 40: 22, AV) has been taken to mean that the Bible always knew the earth was round. At the very least, reader response should not be understood in purely individualistic terms: for those who appreciate apostrophes, there should be a path from reader's response to readers' response.

Yet, at its best, and in conjunction with other ways of reading the Bible, reader response criticism can provide a valuable corrective to the assumption that only ecclesiastically or academically qualified people have the right to tell others what the Bible means. And for first-year students of Theology and Religious Studies, this should be an encouragement as they begin their work.

Which is the best English translation of the Bible?

This is best answered by another question: Best for what? At one end of the scale, there are extremely literal, word-for-word translations, often in very awkward English and sometimes printed in alternate lines with the Hebrew or Greek text. These are known as interlinear translations. They do not make for easy reading. For example, the translation listed at the end of this file under Kohlenberger begins Psalm 23: 'Yahweh one-being-shepherd-of-me nothing I-shall-lack.' Such translations are intended mainly for people beginning to learn Hebrew or Greek, though many teachers do not recommend them for this purpose.

At the other end of the scale, there are translations which aim to reproduce as exactly as possible the meaning of the text in simple and natural English. These are known as functional-equivalent (or dynamic-equivalent) translations: the best-known example in English is the Good News Bible (2nd ed. 1994). The Revised English Bible (1989) goes some way in the same direction but uses a more literary level of English.

Between the two extremes, there are translations which aim to preserve both the meaning and the structure of the Hebrew and Greek texts as far as this is possible without violating the standards of English grammar and style. The two best-known English Bible translations of this kind are the New Revised Standard Version (1989) and the New International Version (1979, New Testament revised as Today's New International Version, 2001). The NRSV's predecessor, the Revised Standard Version (1952), is rather more literal than the NRSV and for this reason is still sometimes used for study purposes.

 ## Further reading

All the dictionary articles listed below contain recommendations for additional reading. Some of them also deal with hermeneutics (the theory of understanding) particularly as applied to texts.

Achtemeier, Paul J. (gen. ed.) (1996), *HarperCollins Bible Dictionary*, 2nd ed., San Francisco: HarperSanFrancisco. Article 'Biblical Criticism', 141b–146a, by C. R. H[olladay] and W. [O.] W[alker].

Hayes, John H. (gen. ed.) (1999), *Dictionary of Biblical Interpretation*, 2 vols, Nashville, TN: Abingdon Press. Articles 'Authority of the Bible' by R. Gnuse, 1.87–91; 'Form Criticism, Old Testament' by M. J. Buss, 1.406a–413a; 'Form Criticism, New Testament' by K. Berger, 1.413a–417a; 'Reader-response Criticism' by E. V. McKnight, 2.370b–373b; 'Redaction Criticism, Hebrew Bible' by M. E. Biddle, 2.373b–376b; 'Redaction Criticism, New Testament' by J. R. Donahue, 2.376b–379b.

Kohlenberger, John R., III (1987), *The Interlinear NIV Hebrew–English Old Testament*, Grand Rapids, MI: Zondervan.

Osborne, G. R. (1993), 'Hermeneutics/Interpreting Paul', in Gerald F. Hawthorne, Ralph P. Martin and David G. Reid (eds), *Dictionary of Paul and his Letters*, Downers Grove, IL and Leicester: InterVarsity Press 1993, 388a–397b.

Osborne, G. R. (1997), 'Hermeneutics', in Ralph P. Martin and Peter H. Davids (eds), *Dictionary of the Later New Testament and Its Developments*, Downers Grove, IL and Leicester: InterVarsity Press 1997, 471a–484b.

Perrin, N. (1970), *What is Redaction Criticism?* London: SPCK.

More advanced

Porter, Stanley E. and David Tombs (eds) (1995), *Approaches to New Testament Study*, Sheffield: Sheffield Academic Press.

Questions

1. What do we mean by the 'authority' of the Bible?

2. What are the main ways of reading a biblical text taught in universities?

3. How does reader-response criticism differ from historically-orientated approaches?

4. Which Bible translation are you using? Do you know what are its strengths and weaknesses?

CHAPTER TWO

Introduction to the Hebrew Bible

Ken Aitken

Introduction

What is the Hebrew Bible and how should we study it? That is a question to which no simple answer can be given – in part because of the complex nature of the Hebrew Bible and the diverse character of its contents, and in part because the answer depends on the particular standpoint from which it is being studied at any given time, for example historical, literary, theological. By way of an answer, then, we will look at some of the major standpoints from which the Hebrew Bible is commonly studied and which you are likely to encounter in one form or another during the course of your undergraduate studies.

The Hebrew Bible as scripture

First and foremost, the Hebrew Bible is the canonical scripture of Judaism and – as the Old Testament – part of the canonical scriptures of Christianity. The term 'canon' comes from the Greek word *kanon* 'rod, ruler', and thence 'rule, standard, norm'. The term came to be used within Christianity of the official list of books accepted as authoritative scripture, providing the rule or standard for Christian faith and conduct. This usage goes back to the fourth century of the Christian era. Within Judaism, the corresponding term was 'the sacred writings' or – more graphically – 'books which defile the hands'.

The Hebrew canon

The canonical shape of the Hebrew Bible differs in certain respects from the Old Testament of the English Bible.

English Bible	Hebrew Bible
The Books of the Law Genesis–Deuteronomy	*The Torah* Genesis–Deuteronomy
The Historical Books Joshua–Kings Chronicles–Esther –	*The Prophets (Nevi'im)* Joshua–Kings (minus Ruth) – Isaiah–Malachi (minus Daniel)
The Poetical Books Job–Song of Solomon	*The Writings (Ketuvim)* Psalms, Job, Proverbs, Ruth, Song of Solomon, Ecclesiastes, Lamentations, Esther, Daniel, Ezra, Nehemiah, Chronicles
The Books of the Prophets Isaiah–Malachi	–

The most striking difference is that the Hebrew Bible has no division corresponding to the historical books. The books of Joshua, Judges, Samuel and Kings are classified among the Prophets. They were later distinguished from the more narrowly prophetic books of Isaiah onwards as the Former Prophets versus the Latter Prophets. The remaining historical books (Ruth, Chronicles, Ezra, Nehemiah and Esther) are found among the Writings.

The earliest reference to the tripartite division of the Hebrew Bible is found in the prologue to the Book of Ecclesiasticus (c. 132 BCE). It refers to 'the law and the prophets and the others that followed/and the rest of the books' (cf. Luke 24: 44). It is probable that the divisions were accepted as canonical in successive stages, beginning with the Torah around the time of Ezra (c. 400 BCE), the Prophets some time before the second century BCE, followed by the Writings. Though this last division was begun before the middle of the second century BCE (cf. Ecclesiasticus), it was not finalised until perhaps as late as the end of the second century of the Christian era, following debates in the rabbinical academies over the canonical status of a few of its books (for example, Ecclesiastes).

The Septuagint

Beginning with the Torah around the middle of the third century BCE, the Hebrew scriptures were translated into Greek for use among the Greek-speaking community of Jews in Alexandria. This translation came to be known as the Septuagint, which means 'Seventy' (hence, LXX), after the tradition that seventy-two scholars made the translation. What is interesting about the Septuagint is that it intermixes with the books of the Hebrew Bible the Apocryphal or Deutero-canonical books (for example, Ecclesiasticus, Bel and the Dragon, Susanna, First and Second Maccabees). Whether one can speak of a longer Alexandrian canon (LXX) in contrast with a shorter Palestinian canon (Hebrew Bible) is doubtful. There is nothing to suggest that the Jews in Alexandria regarded the books of the Septuagint as a closed and exclusive list and they were later to adopt the same canon as the Palestinian Jews.

The Septuagint came to have a great influence on the Christian Church. It was the Scripture of the early Christian writers of the New Testament. Subsequently, the Old Testament of the Catholic Church (cf. New Jerusalem Bible) and of the Eastern Orthodox Churches was based on the Septuagint and included the Apocrypha. The Reformed Churches, however, excluded the Apocrypha in favour of the canonical books of the Hebrew Bible.

Theological implications of the shape of the canon

The Hebrew Bible

The three-fold division of Torah, Prophets and Writings reflects the primacy of the Torah as the supreme revelation of God. In the first division, the Torah is revealed to Moses. In the second, the prophets are presented as teachers and interpreters of the Torah – applying its religious and ethical principles to Israel's national life and destiny and warning of divine judgement if Israel fails to observe the divine law. That failure and consequent judgement is the major theme of the Former Prophets (that is, the historical books, Joshua–Kings). In due course, the Hebrew kingdoms fall and the people are taken into exile. The third division ends with the books of Ezra, Nehemiah and Chronicles. Taken together, these books retell much the same story of Israel's failure and divine judgement as the earlier ones. But they continue the story further by recounting the return of the exiled people to their homeland and their reconstitution as the people of God, whose life is once again centred around and governed by the Torah. Thus, we are told that the priest Ezra brought the 'book of the law' with him from Babylon and used it as the basis for the ordering of the life of the small post-exilic community (Ezra 7). Looking at the overall shape of the Hebrew canon, it begins with the revelation of the Torah to Moses and ends with Ezra's re-ordering of the life of the community in accordance with Torah. Ezra becomes a second Moses.

The English Old Testament

By and large, this represents a more topical and chronological ordering of the books – for example, the historical books are placed together in their historical sequence. It also arguably represents a Christian ordering through the positioning of the prophetic books at the end of the canon. In this way, the law loses its centrality and the Old Testament ends by pointing beyond itself prophetically to the coming of the Messiah. Hence, the last word of the Old Testament begins 'Behold I will send you Elijah the prophet' (Malachi 4: 5), interpreted in the New Testament as a reference to John the Baptist, the forerunner of Jesus the Messiah (Matthew 11: 14).

From these differences one might be tempted to say that the shape of the Hebrew canon has its natural sequel in the emergence of Judaism – it is not without some justification that Ezra has been called the 'father of Judaism' – whereas the shape of the English Old Testament has its natural sequel in the emergence of Christianity. But that would be to set too high a premium on the significance of the differences in canonical shape. Indeed, in Malachi 4: 4, immediately before the statement about the coming of Elijah, we find the exhortation: 'Remember the law [torah] of my servant Moses'. Judaism and Christianity equally have their roots in and develop from the faith of the Hebrew Bible. At the same time, the Hebrew Bible has its own integrity and must be studied – at least in the first instance – in its own right and not simply as an extended prologue to either Judaism or Christianity.

The process of 'canonisation'

Though the canonical acceptance of a book here and there may have been settled by rabbinical pronouncement, this was the exception rather than the rule. Books were accepted as canonical on the grounds of their long use and widespread acceptance as authoritative scripture within the community at large. Accordingly, the canonisation of the Hebrew Bible should be seen as the culmination of a process of canonisation rooted within the ongoing religious life of the community – of which, indeed, there are signs within the Hebrew Bible itself.

Canonical criticism

The perception that a process of canonisation has been at work within the literary formation of the Hebrew Bible has given rise to a type of study known as 'canonical criticism'. It is most closely associated with Brevard Childs' *Introduction to the Old Testament as Scripture* (1979). Against the emphasis of historical-critical study on the historical character of the Hebrew Bible as the framework for its interpretation, canonical criticism regards the canon as setting the parameters within which the Hebrew Bible should be interpreted. Thus, in his Introduction, Childs focuses on the final, canonical form of the books and inquires after a book's 'canonical intentionality', how it functions as sacred scripture for a community of faith. The literary shape of the final form provides a key to its canonical function, while the complexities and fractures in the final form identified by historical-critical study often serve to highlight the diversity of canonical functions books may serve.

The Hebrew Bible as literature

Besides forming canonical scripture for communities of faith, the Hebrew Bible forms a compendium of the literature of ancient Israel. It reflects the activities of Israel's storytellers, historians and theologians, of its prophets, priests, wise men and scribes, during the course of its history. In this section, we will consider some aspects of the growth and formation of the literature and methods of its analysis. For some consideration of the literature as literature, see below ('The Hebrew Bible as text').

Ancient Near Eastern parallels

The literature of the Hebrew Bible belongs firmly within the context of the literature of the ancient Near East. The most relevant texts can be found in *Ancient Near Eastern Texts* (1969), edited by James B. Pritchard. Pritchard assembles texts from Egypt, Mesopotamia, Syria and Asia Minor under several headings including Myths, Epics and Legends; Legal Texts; Historical Texts; Hymns and Prayers; Didactic and Wisdom Literature; Oracles and Prophecies; Lamentations. Much of the literature of the Hebrew Bible can readily be classified under these headings.

Myth

An extract from the Babylonian story of the flood
'On Mount Nisir the ship came to a halt, allowing no motion . . . When the seventh day arrived, I sent forth and set free a dove. The dove went forth, but came back; since no resting-place for it was visible, she turned round. Then I sent forth and set free a swallow. The swallow went forth, but came back; since no resting-place for it was visible, she turned round. Then I sent forth and set free a raven. The raven went forth, and seeing that the waters had diminished, he eats, circles, caws and turns not round.' (*Ancient Near Eastern Texts*, 94–5, cf. Genesis 8: 4, 6–12)

Law

The law code of Hammurabi
'If an ox, when it was walking along the street, gored a seignior to death, that case is not subject to a claim. If a seignior's ox was a gorer and his city council made it known to him that it was a gorer, but he did not pad its horns or tie up his ox, and that ox gored to death a member of the aristocracy, he shall give one-half mina of silver. If it was a seignior's slave, he shall give one-third mina of silver.' (*ANET* 176, cf. Exodus 21: 28–32 and note the similarity in form as well as content)

Wisdom instruction

The instruction of Amenemopet
'Cast not thy heart in pursuit of riches, for there is no ignoring Fate and Fortune . . . They have made for themselves wings like geese and are flown away to the heavens.' (*ANET* 422, cf. Proverbs 23: 4–5. This section of Proverbs (22: 17–24; 34) has been thought to have been modelled on Amenemopet.)

Oral origins

The discovery and publication of texts from the ancient Near East between the latter part of the nineteenth and early part of the twentieth centuries, which for the most part pre-dated the Hebrew Bible by many centuries, led scholars to recognise that the literature of the Hebrew Bible was much older than the dates assigned to its written sources (see below) and that oral tradition was a major constituent of many books. In some measure, the literary materials of the Hebrew Bible had originated and been passed down orally before they eventually came to be written down. This is clearest in the case of the oracles of the prophets but it is doubtless also true of other materials like the didactic speeches and proverbial sayings in Proverbs or the hymns and laments in the Psalms. Many narratives, for example in the book of Genesis, probably also originated as oral compositions.

Form criticism

The particular method that investigates the oral period in the growth and formation of Israel's literature is known as form criticism. The method was first applied to the Hebrew Bible by the German scholar Hermann Gunkel (1862–1932) at the beginning of the last century. Form criticism first seeks to delimit and classify individual passages (pericope) according to their conventional literary type or genre (in German, *Gattung*): for example, folktale, saga, legend, historical writing in the case of Hebrew narratives; oracles of judgement, woe-sayings, exhortations in the case of the prophets; hymns of praise, individual laments, community laments, royal psalms in the case of the Psalter. It then seeks to identify the original setting (*Sitz im Leben*) in Israel's religious, social and political life within which the literary types arose and had their place: for example, the hymn of praise in the cult; legal sentences in the administration of justice; wisdom instruction in the wisdom schools; coronation formulas (such as Psalm 2: 7) in the ceremonial of the royal court. In this way, form criticism demonstrated that literary materials of the Hebrew Bible had an original setting within Israel's life and institutions before they were later taken up and given a 'setting in literature' in written form.

Case study: Apodictic and casuistic law

In his form critical study of Israelite law, Albrecht Alt (1966: 79–132) distinguished sharply between two different forms: apodictic law and casuistic law.

- Casuistic (or case) law is characterised by its conditional formulation and impersonal form of address. Typically, it states the general case and prescribes the penalty ('When/If a man . . . then . . .'), then elaborates subordinate circumstances which modify the general case and the penalty ('But if . . . then . . .'). For example:

> If a man steals an ox or a sheep, and kills it or sells it,
> he shall pay five oxen for an ox and four sheep for a
> sheep. He shall make restitution; if he has nothing then
> he shall be sold for his theft. If the stolen beast is found
> alive in his possession, whether it be an ox or an ass or
> a sheep, he shall pay double. (Exodus 22: 1)

- Apodictic law is characterised by its absolute, unconditional nature and by its personal form of address. It is best represented by the Decalogue, for example 'You shall not kill' (Exodus 20: 2–20//Deuteronomy 5: 6–21).

The difference in form points to a difference in setting (*Sitz im Leben*):

- Casuistic law had its setting in the secular administration of justice at the local law courts and belongs within the wider legal tradition of the ancient Near East (cf. the example from 'The law code of Hammurabi', in the box above).

- Apodictic law had its setting in the worship of Israel on periodic occasions of covenant renewal (cf. Deuteronomy 31: 10–11). This type of law was uniquely religious and Israelite in character.

The most contentious part of Alt's thesis has been the conception of apodictic law as – by definition – covenant law and unique to Israel. For example, E. Gerstenberger compared the commands and prohibitions of apodictic law with the admonitions of wisdom (cf. for example, Proverbs 1–9) and concluded that both had a common root in the moral or ethical directives of the early Israelite family or clan. As an example of such directives, he cites the reason given by the Rechabites for their abstinence from wine in Jeremiah 35: 6–7:

> We will drink no wine, for Jonadab the son of Recheb, our father,
> commanded us, 'You shall not drink wine, neither you nor
> your sons
> for ever; you shall not build a house; you shall not sow seed;
> you shall
> not plant or have a vineyard; but you shall live in tents all
> your days,
> that you may live many days in the land where you sojourn.'

Not only are the directives of Jonadab cast in the same form of commands and prohibitions as the Decalogue (though here 'you' is plural rather than singular), they also form a short 'decalogue-like' series. The passage goes on to contrast their obedience to their father's commandments with Israel's disobedience to God's commandments.

Whatever the origins of apodictic law, it became the paramount form through which the obligations of the covenant between God and Israel were expressed. A unique importance was consequently assigned to the Decalogue (cf. Exodus 20; Deuteronomy 4–5). The intimate personal form of address characteristic of the apodictic law, with its implied 'I–you' relationship, made it particularly appropriate for expressing covenant obligations.

Written sources

Only rarely do the books of the Hebrew Bible explicitly indicate the written sources upon which they are based. For example, the poem on the sun standing still in Joshua 10: 12–13 is cited as a quotation from the Book of Jashar. Or again, the book of Kings refers its readers to the 'Book of the Chronicles of the Kings of Israel/Judah' for more information on the reigns of individual kings. This is evidently a reference to state annals in which the major events of the king's reign were chronicled. It is reasonable to assume that the author of Kings has made some use of these annals. For the most part, however, the written sources that were used in the composition of the books are not mentioned and can only be hypothetically reconstructed.

Source criticism

Source criticism is the method of analysis that attempts to reconstruct these sources and to determine their date and authorship. Its earliest application was to the books of the Pentateuch (Genesis–Deuteronomy). It was held that four written sources were successively combined to produce the Pentateuch: the 'J' or Yahwistic source (so named because it uses the divine name Yahweh); the 'E' or Elohistic source (so named because it uses the term God (Hebrew, *'elohim*)); the 'D' or Deuteronomic source (so named because it is chiefly found in the book of Deuteronomy); and the 'P' or Priestly source (so named because of its interest in priestly matters). The sources were dated from the early monarchic period (J/E – tenth to ninth centuries BCE), through the late monarchic period (D – seventh century BCE) to the post-exilic period (P – fifth century BCE).

This theory of the composition of the Pentateuch is known as the new documentary hypothesis. It was given its classical exposition by the German scholar Julius Wellhausen (1844–1918) in the latter part of the nineteenth century and the basic hypothesis remained an 'assured result' of literary-historical criticism throughout most of the twentieth century. At the turn of the twenty-first century, however it has become far less 'assured' and has been considerably modified by some and totally abandoned by others. The prevailing tendency at the time of writing is to date J/E materials much closer to Deuteronomy and to replace the continuous source delimitation with the analysis of particular thematic blocks of text (for example, Patriarchal Narratives (Genesis 12–50), the Exodus from Egypt (Exodus 1–15)) in terms of (i) pre-Deuteronomic, (ii) Deuteronomic, and (iii) post-Deuteronomic or Priestly materials. This, incidentally, reflects the central importance of Deuteronomy as a more or less fixed chronological point in the formation of the Pentateuch by virtue of its identification – in some form or another – with the 'book of the law' found in the Temple, upon which the reforms of king Josiah (c. 627–609) were based (cf. 2 Kings 22–23).

The formation of books

It is already clear that, for the most part, the authors of the books of the Hebrew Bible were not authors in the modern sense of the term. They were not only writers but also collectors and editors, who preserved and adapted to their own times the traditions that had come down to them, whether in oral or already in written form.

Redaction criticism

The method which investigates the way in which the written sources were brought together and edited to produce books is called redaction criticism (redaction = edition; redactor = editor; redactional = editorial). Among the exponents of the new documentary hypothesis, redactors tended to be viewed as somewhat inept cut-and-paste merchants whose contributions merely obscured the sources. However, with a shift of interest from the analysis of sources to the formation of larger literary wholes – reflected, for example, in Gerhard Von Rad's (1966) seminal study of the formation of the Pentateuch/Hexateuch and Martin Noth's study of redaction of the books of Joshua–Kings (see below) – the figure of the redactor came to be viewed rather as a creative theologian in his own right. More especially, then, redaction criticism is concerned with the theological intentions of the redactor as expressed through the way in which he has arranged, edited and commented on his sources.

Case study: The redaction of the Former Prophets

The Deuteronomistic history
In 1943, Martin Noth (1981) presented his theory that the books of Joshua–Kings formed a unified history work written in the exilic period. Rather than revising books that had already been given their basic shape through the combining of source documents (as had previously been held), the Deuteronomistic historian had conceived and compiled the entire work drawing upon a variety of unconnected materials as his sources. He had selected and organised these sources by devising their framework (cf. the chronological/theological frameworks in Judges (3: 7ff., 10ff,; 4: 1ff., 6: 1ff., and so on) and Kings (1 Kings 14: 19–20; 21–22, 29–31; 15: 1–3, 7–8; 9–11, 23–24 and so on)), incorporating them into his work alongside his own interpretative comments (cf. especially the theological prospect in Judges 2: 11–23 and theological retrospect in 2 Kings 17: 2–23), notably in the form of speeches placed in the mouths of its major characters at key points in the story (cf. Joshua 1, 23; 1 Samuel 12; 1 Kings 8). The result is a continuous history, unified in its language and style and in its theological outlook. According to Noth, the historian also incorporated the book of Deuteronomy into his history work as the preface, providing the theological standard against which he evaluates the history of Israel (hence, the Deuteronomistic history).

Its theological purpose
Noth believed the purpose of the work was to demonstrate that the fall of the Hebrew kingdoms and the exile was fully deserved on account of the people's disobedience to God, as summed up in the theological retrospect in 2 Kings 17, and that it holds out no hope for the future. Other scholars have found a more optimistic note in the work. Thus, it has been suggested that it ends on a note of Messianic hope through the release of the exiled king Jehoiachin (2 Kings 25: 27–30; cf. the covenant with David in 2 Samuel 7); or, noting the prominence of the theme of repentance (for example, Judges; 1 Samuel 7: 3; 12: 19–25; 1 Kings 8: 46–53; 2 Kings 17: 13; 23: 5), that its purpose is to summon the exiled people to repentance and return to God.

The Hebrew Bible as history

Historical Overview of the Hebrew Bible

- *The early period*

Patriarchs	Genesis 12–50.
Exodus from Egypt	Exodus 1–15
Covenant at Sinai	Exodus 16–Numbers 9: 10
Wilderness wandering	Numbers 9: 11–Deuteronomy
Conquest of Canaan	Joshua
The era of the Judges	Judges

- *The monarchic period*

Rise of the monarchy	I Samuel 1–12
The United Kingdom	I Samuel 13–1 Kings 11//
	I Chronicles 10–2 Chronicles 9
The divided kingdoms of Israel and Judah	I Kings 12–2 Kings// 2 Chronicles 10ff.

- *The exilic period*

Exile and return	2 Kings 25; 2 Chron 36; Ezra 1–2

The question of its historicality

Almost the whole of the first half of the Hebrew Bible – from Genesis to the end of 2 Kings – gives a more or less continuous account of the history of Israel. The account begins with the story of their ancestors and ends with the fall of the Hebrew kingdoms and the deportation of the people to Babylon. Towards the end, the story of Israel is in part retold (Chronicles) and in part continued with an account of the return of the people from exile in Babylon and the establishment of a small Jewish community in Judaea – by that time a province of the Persian empire (Ezra, Nehemiah). There seems much to be said for the dictum by H. W. Robinson that 'The Old Testament is formally a history into which other forms of literature have been incorporated' (quoted in J. A. Soggin's *Introduction to the Old Testament* [ET 1976] 38). But how far is history the most appropriate term for what we find in the biblical account? How far do the narratives describe historical events? Rather than discuss this in the abstract, we will look at the biblical account of a particular event, namely the Assyrian invasion of Judah in 2 Kings 18: 13–19: 37.

Sennacherib's invasion of Judah in 701 – a case study

In 701 BCE, the Assyrians invaded Judah, captured its fortified cites and laid siege to Jerusalem. In the event, Jerusalem was spared and Hezekiah was allowed to remain on the throne. The question is, why?

In 2 Kings 18: 14–16 we are told Hezekiah surrendered and paid the crippling tribute imposed on him by the king of Assyria. Sennacherib's own account of the invasion is more detailed but says much the same thing. We might therefore reasonably conclude that this was why Jerusalem was spared.

Sennacherib's account

As to Hezekiah the Jew, he did not submit to my yoke. I laid siege to 46 of his strong cities . . . and conquered them by means of well-stamped earth-ramps and battering-rams . . . Himself I made a prisoner in Jerusalem, his royal residence, like a bird in a cage . . . Thus I reduced his country, but I still increased the tribute and the *katru*-present due to me as his overlord, which I imposed later upon him beyond the former tribute, to be delivered annually. Hezekiah himself, whom the terror-inspiring splendour of my lordship had overwhelmed and whose irregular and elite troops which he had brought into Jerusalem, his royal residence, in order to strengthen it, had deserted him, did send me, later, to Nineveh, my lordly city, together with 30 talents of gold, 800 talents of silver . . . and all kinds of valuable treasures . . . In order to deliver the tribute and to do obeisance as a slave he sent his personal messenger.

Ancient Near Eastern Texts (288)

But the account of the Assyrian invasion in 2 Kings 18: 16–19: 37 has a very different outcome. Here a defiant Hezekiah, with the support of the prophet Isaiah, refuses to surrender and prays God to deliver the city and punish the invader. The account ends with the decimation of the Assyrian camp by the 'angel of the Lord' and the subsequent death of the king at the hands of his sons in his own land.

The Taylor Prism – an Assyrian document inscribed on a hexagonal piece of stone – gives Sennacherib's own vivid account of the siege of Jerusalem.
© Copyright The British Museum.

Why, then, did Sennacherib withdraw and spare the city? Was it because Hezekiah abjectly capitulated and accepted the terms imposed upon him (18: 14–16; Sennacherib's annals) or because God miraculously intervened and decimated the Assyrian army (18: 17–19: 37)?

One way the difficulty has been resolved is by the assumption that Sennacherib campaigned twice against Judah. The campaign of 701 resulted in the surrender of Hezekiah, as described in 2 Kings 18: 14–16 and Sennacherib's annals. A second campaign, conducted some years later, was aborted by Sennacherib – perhaps because of an epidemic in the Assyrian camp – and he withdrew, leaving the city intact. The content of

2 Kings 18: 17–19: 37 would therefore relate to this campaign. That is the view argued by John Bright in his *History of Israel* (1981).

The account of Hezekiah's surrender in 2 Kings 18: 14–16 reads much like what we would expect of a sober and 'objective' piece of historical writing. Probably it is an extract from the state annals cited in 2 Kings 20: 20 – 'the Book of the Chronicles of the Kings of Judah'. On the other hand, the story of the deliverance of Jerusalem in 2 Kings 18: 17–19: 37 takes the form of a vivid and dramatic narrative, made up for the most part of direct speeches and dialogues, prayers and prophetic oracles. Interestingly enough, the account of Hezekiah's reign (2 Kings 18: 13–20: 20) recurs in Isaiah 36–39 with only some slight differences. In Isaiah, however, 18: 14–16 is conspicuous by its absence – that is, Isaiah 36: 1–2 goes directly from 18: 13 to 18: 17.

The characterisation of Sennacherib and Hezekiah in 18: 17–19: 37 is also interesting. Sennacherib is the archetype of the human pride and arrogance that dares to challenge God. Thus, he boasts that no god has been able to deliver their country out of his hands and warns Hezekiah that Judah and its God will be no exception: Hezekiah's reliance on God for deliverance is therefore futile (18: 34–35; 19: 10–13). It is for his arrogant defiance of God that he is condemned and Isaiah pronounces judgement upon him (19: 22–28). For his part, Hezekiah is portrayed as a model of faith and trust in God and his power to deliver. In Hezekiah's prayer for deliverance (19: 15–19), the issue of whether Jerusalem and Judah will fall to the Assyrians like the lands of other nations is framed in terms of the contrast between the gods of the nations who were mere wood and stone, and God as the living God, who created the heavens and the earth and to whom all the kingdoms belong. Hezekiah therefore prays to God to save the city from the hand of the Assyrians 'that all the kingdoms of the earth may know that thou, O Lord, art God alone'. Here, then, as the Assyrians besiege the city, highly fraught and profound theological issues hang in the balance.

The deliverance of Jerusalem through the decimation of the Assyrian army by 'the angel of the Lord' and the withdrawal of Sennacherib back to Nineveh to be assassinated is both the appropriate vindication of Hezekiah's faith and the appropriate punishment of Sennacherib's arrogance. One might even say that something of the kind is the only possible outcome of this narrative.

So, was Jerusalem spared because Hezekiah surrendered and accepted Sennacherib's terms or because Hezekiah displayed exemplary faith by resisting him and God miraculously intervened? That Hezekiah capitulated is not in doubt. The question is how we are to evaluate the story of Jerusalem's deliverance and its relation to his capitulation. Should we suppose that, after his initial surrender, Hezekiah thought better of it and decided to resist? Or do they relate to two different campaigns, as Bright suggests?

There is another possibility that might be considered. The fact that Jerusalem survived the Assyrian invasion at all – even at the cost of a crippling tribute – must have seemed to be something of a miracle. Its sister kingdom in the north had not been so fortunate when the Assyrians captured Samaria barely two decades earlier. It is conceivable that the story of Jerusalem's deliverance took shape in the course of later theological reflection on the survival of Jerusalem in 701.

At any rate, several things are clear: (i) the story of Jerusalem's deliverance and the defeat of the Assyrians in 18: 17–19: 37 gives expression to far-reaching theological concerns; (ii) its relationship to the capitulation of Hezekiah in 18: 14–16 is problematic; (iii) this poses problems for a historical reconstruction of the Assyrian invasion of Judah; and (iv) the interest of the story does not lie in the historicality of the event but in its theological significance.

The pre-monarchic and early monarchic periods

For the reign of Hezekiah, we have contemporary ancient Near Eastern texts that can be compared with the biblical account. Before about the middle of the ninth century, we have no contemporary extra-biblical sources that refer to the persons or events that make up the biblical account, while the biblical sources are separated from the events they purport to describe by many centuries. In addition to the lack of contemporary sources, we must also reckon with: (i) the heterogeneous literary character of the narratives themselves – ranging from the annalistic material in Kings to the more popular folktale-like stories of the ancestors in the book of Genesis – and (ii) the complexities and uncertainties surrounding the formation of the biblical accounts from possible oral origins through to final redaction. It is not surprising, therefore that the problems facing any reconstruction of the earlier part of Israel's history are much more acute and can very rapidly descend into mere speculation about what might have happened. Modern historians of Israel differ widely in their reconstructions and this should caution against too readily substituting a modern historical reconstruction for the biblical construction. Modern reconstructions are not necessarily better; they are just different and it is debatable whether they take us any closer to 'what really happened'.

No blanket generalisation can be made about historicality of the events narrated in the Hebrew Bible. It is clear that the biblical writers had some interest in providing an account of Israel's past and giving that account chronological (if somewhat schematic, cf. 1 Kings 6: 1 (480 = 12 x 40 = 12 generations)) coherence. On the other hand, it is also very clear that the primary interest of the account is not historical per se but religious and theological. The narratives about Israel's past select and shape historical data in the interests of theological interpretation.

That the resultant narrative may be judged deficient as a piece of history-writing by the canons of modern historiography is beside the point. Simply to ask 'did it actually happen?' or 'what actually happened?' scarcely begins to do justice to the narratives of the Hebrew Bible. Even if the question could be answered with any degree of certainty, would it really tell us very much?

The Hebrew Bible as theology

Its character

At its most rarefied, theology is reflective and analytic discourse about God, expressing the doctrines of the faith in the form of a coherent and unified system. There is none of this kind of theological discourse in the Hebrew Bible. The theology of the Hebrew Bible is inextricably bound up with the religious life and institutions of Israel and with the literature in which it is expressed – in narratives, hymns, didactic sermons, prophetic oracles and the like – and it is implicit rather than explicit.

Its variety

It is doubtful whether we can speak about the theology of the Hebrew Bible, if that is taken to imply a single, unified theology running through it from beginning to end, for it contains a variety of different theologies and sometimes competing theological perspectives. For example, two quite different theological points of view are found in 1 Samuel 8–12 regarding the institution of the monarchy in Israel. According to one view (cf. 9: 1–10: 16; 11), the monarchy is God's means of saving Israel from its enemies. In 10: 16, the words 'I have seen the affliction of my people, because their cry has come to me' (cf. also 10: 2) evoke the plight of Israel in bondage in Egypt (cf. Exodus 2: 23; 3: 7). Like the exodus, the institution of the monarchy is an act of divine mercy and deliverance. However, according to another view (8; 10: 17–27; 12), Israel's desire for a king is an act of rebellion and rejection of God on a par with idolatry. It is a rejection of God's kingship over Israel in favour of a human king. Thus, God tells Samuel (8: 7–8): 'Hearken to the voice of the people in all that they say to you; for they have not rejected you, but they have rejected me from being king over them. According to all the deeds which they have done to me, from the day I brought them up out of Egypt even to this day, forsaking me and serving other gods' (cf. also 10: 18; 12: 17–19).

Its traditions and themes

In the Hebrew Bible we find a range of broad theological traditions and themes articulated implicitly in a range of texts. These include, for example, creation theology centring on God's relations with the cosmos and the place of human beings within it; covenant theology centring on the relations between God and his people Israel, with its basis in the exodus deliverance and its obligations as expressed in the divine law; royal theology centring on God's covenant with the Davidic house; Zion theology centring on God's choice of Zion as his dwelling place; and priestly theology centring on such themes as sin and atonement, sacrifice and cult.

Some of these theological traditions find their foundation and/or classic expression in particular books or passages but they may also be taken up and applied in various ways and in various contexts. For example, the book of Exodus presents the foundational narrative for the covenant relation between God and Israel, while the theology of covenant receives its fullest exposition in the book of Deuteronomy. However, we also find covenant theology reapplied in different ways, both in the historical books of Joshua–Kings (cf. for example, 2 Kings 17) and in the message of some of the prophets (such as Hosea, Jeremiah).

It should be said that this is just one of the ways in which the theology of the Hebrew Bible might be explored. It implies that the most appropriate way to explore its theology is through close engagement with the text. For a variety of reasons, it could nevertheless be argued that this kind of approach falls short of what theology of the Hebrew Bible should be about – providing, at best, raw materials for theology to work with. But there is, in fact, no agreement and some very fundamental disagreements about what the nature and task of theology of the Hebrew Bible should be. We might say therefore that if the broad theological traditions and themes articulated within the text are the raw materials, they are nonetheless the touchstone against which more ambitious constructions of the theology of the Hebrew Bible must continually be tested.

The Hebrew Bible as text

Text, commentaries and exegesis

Traditionally, the kind of book that has paid the closest attention to the text of the Hebrew Bible has been the commentary. The central task of the commentator is to offer an interpretation of the text, to explain its meaning. When this is done on a verse-by-verse basis, it is called 'exegesis'. The term itself simply means 'explanation, interpretation' but is normally reserved for verse-by-verse explanation of the text. Though commentaries vary greatly in the theological stances of their authors, in their method of presentation and in the kind of discussion they include they may be generally regarded as the most direct and accessible resource for understanding and interpreting a given text. We would also expect to be given the necessary background information – literary, historical and so on – for its interpretation.

The preface to the commentary series *Hermeneia* – a heavyweight series based on the Hebrew text – describes its aim.

The series is designed to be a critical and historical commentary to the Bible . . . It will utilize the full range of philological and historical tools including textual criticism . . . the methods of the history of tradition (including genre and prosodic analysis), and the history of religion . . . In so far as possible the aim is to provide the student or scholar with full critical discussion of each problem of interpretation and with the primary data upon which the discussion is based. It is expected that the authors will struggle to lay bare the ancient meaning of a biblical work or pericope.

Preface to *Hermeneia* (1974: ix)

It might well be argued therefore that the results of textual, literary, historical and theological study of the Hebrew Bible, and their relevance for interpretation, are best exhibited and synthesised in the form of a commentary on the text.

It will be noticed that in this short passage in the box above the words 'history' or 'historical' occur no less than four times, capped by the phrase 'lay bare the ancient meaning'. Clearly, the kind of interpretation we can expect from this series of commentaries (and others like it) is one that is judged to be the product of the various historical factors believed to govern the origins and form of the given text, and one which is itself of a historical nature – the ancient meaning. Exegesis is indeed often qualified as grammatical-historical exegesis – grammatical emphasising that the words should be interpreted in their normal grammatical sense, and historical emphasising that they should also be interpreted in the sense intended by the author or in their original context.

Literary (synchronic) study of the text

The late twentieth century saw a surge of interest in literary aspects of the Hebrew Bible. This began, perhaps naturally enough, with poetic texts under the banner of rhetorical criticism. Rhetorical criticism is concerned not so much with what is being said as how it is said. It examines the various artistic and stylistic devices used in the text, such as the repetition of key words or phrases and the various symmetric balances that can be found between its parts. The tendency of rhetorical criticism is to stress the unity of texts over their dissection by source criticism and form criticism. Literary study was soon extended to Hebrew narrative. Hence, narratives came to be analysed in terms of their plots, characters, points of view, implied authors and implied readers, and the like.

One of the consequences of literary study has been to shift attention away from questions of authors and editors and the sources lying behind the text to the text itself in its final form. A text has its own literary integrity by virtue of being a text and deserves to be studied in its own right, irrespective of how, when and by whom it was created. The text might be an individual poem or narrative, a whole book or even a larger corpus, such as the Pentateuch.

Another consequence has been to shift attention away from what the text meant in its original historical context as intended by its author – its 'ancient meaning' – to what it means for the modern reader.

> Where historical criticism sought meaning in the origins or sources of biblical texts, we take the final form (itself a notion not free of problems) as our primary text. Instead of attempting to reconstruct an ancient 'history' we read these narratives as we might read modern novels or short stories, constructing a story world in which questions of human values and belief (and theology) find shape in relation to our own (and our readers') world(s) . . . Instead of seeking the one legitimate meaning, namely what the text (usually defined as the author) meant in its 'original context', we recognize that texts are multivalent and their meanings radically contextual, inescapably bound up with their interpreters.
>
> David M. Gunn and Danna Nolan Fewell,
> *Narrative in the Hebrew Bible* (1993: 9)

This is in some ways a radical view of the meaning of texts, especially when they suggest that their meanings are 'radically contextual, inescapably bound up with their interpreters'. This implies that, by themselves, texts do not have meanings, whether ancient or modern: its meaning is 'created' by the reader as they read the text. It follows that, in theory at least, a text can have as many meanings as it has readers. But if that is the case, are they all equally valid? And who is to say whether it is a valid interpretation or not? Gunn and Fewell recognise the difficulty and suggest that arbitration between valid and invalid interpretations is a function of the wider community of readers to which the individual reader belongs and with which they share the same reading conventions.

Naturally, not all those who espouse a literary approach to the final form would agree with this view of the meaning of texts. It is associated with a particular kind of literary criticism known as 'reader response criticism'. All would nonetheless agree that the question of meaning should be addressed to the final form of the text.

The difference between the newer literary approaches and the more traditional historically-orientated ones is often expressed in terms of diachronic versus synchronic study, with the line between sometimes sharply drawn. It is clear that there is more than one strategy that can be adopted in reading the Hebrew Bible and more than one context within which texts can be interpreted. They can be read and interpreted diachronically, within the historical context in which they arose, and they can read and interpreted synchronically, within the literary context in which they are now found.

It might be argued that the latter should be preferred, since it rests on the text as we now have it, while diachronic study rests on more or less hypothetical reconstructions of the growth and formation of the text. But literary study of the final form is not univocal. It too formulates its own hypothetical reconstructions as its reads and interprets the text, very often generating just as much complexity in the process. In any case, diachronic and synchronic study are not mutually exclusive and we do not have to choose between them. Both contribute to a better and richer understanding of the text.

 ## Further reading

Anderson, B. W. (1988), *The Living World of the Old Testament*, 4th ed., London: Longman. A well-illustrated, general introduction to the history of Israel and the literature of the Hebrew Bible. Ideal as a basic text book.

Barton, J. (1996), *Reading the Old Testament: Method in Biblical Study*, 2nd ed., London: Darton, Longman and Todd. A detailed study of methods, including current canonical and literary approaches alongside the more traditional ones.

Coggins, R. (2001), *Introducing the Old Testament*, 2nd ed., Oxford: Oxford

University Press. Examines a variety of key issues in the light of recent scholarly debate.

Rogerson, J. (ed.) (2001), *The Oxford Illustrated History of the Bible*, Oxford: Oxford University Press. Contains entries on the Old Testament, Hebrew Bible and various ways of interpreting the Bible.

Rogerson, J. and P. Davies (1989), *The Old Testament World*, Cambridge: Cambridge University Press.

Soggin, J. Alberto (1989), *Introduction to the Old Testament*, 3rd ed., London: SCM Press.

Questions

1. How is the Hebrew Bible different from the Old Testament? How do these differences affect the way we read and understand each one?

2. What do the following types of criticism tell us about individual books of the Hebrew Bible: form criticism, source criticism and redaction criticism?

3. How reliable do you think the Hebrew Bible is when it comes to historical facts? To what extent has theology influenced history? Do you find the suggestion that the Hebrew Bible may not be factually accurate difficult?

4. Is it possible to speak of *the* theology of the Hebrew Bible? If not, why not?

CHAPTER THREE

Introduction to the New Testament

Helen K. Bond

Introduction

What is the New Testament and how should we study it? The New Testament is a collection of twenty-seven short texts dating from the early years of the Christian movement. Although there are differences between these texts in terms of genre and theology, they all share the fundamental conviction that Jesus of Nazareth was God's Messiah, that he was crucified and that he rose from the dead on the third day.

The New Testament is much less complex than the Hebrew Bible in terms of provenance and date: all the texts were written in the Greek-speaking eastern part of the Roman Empire roughly between 50 and 150 CE. In the following chapter, we shall look at some of the main texts in chronological rather than canonical order. This arrangement will help you to appreciate the development of early Christian ideas and theology. We shall focus particularly on Paul and his letters and the gospels.

Paul and his letters

It may come as a surprise to learn that the earliest parts of the Christian Scriptures are not the gospels but the letters of Paul. Nearly a third of the New Testament bears Paul's name – though, as we shall see, he probably did not write all of the material ascribed to him.

Who was Paul?

The Acts of the Apostles tells us that Paul came from the city of Tarsus in the Roman province of Cilicia (modern Turkey). He belonged to a Jewish family of some standing and was a Roman citizen (a fact doubted by some scholars but supported by Paul's final trial before the Emperor). Paul was his Roman name; at home he would have been known by his more familiar Jewish name, Saul. A man of great passion and energy, the young Paul devoted himself to study of the Jewish Scriptures. He belonged to a group known as the Pharisees, who were well-known for their strict observance of the Jewish law, and even made his way to Jerusalem to study with Gamaliel, the most famous Pharisaic teacher of his day. The young man would undoubtedly have had a promising career in the synagogue had events not taken a surprising turn.

Paul makes his first appearance in the New Testament only a few years after Jesus's death, as a persecutor of the new Christian movement. As far as Paul was concerned, the claim that the crucified Jesus was God's Messiah (or Anointed One) was outrageous. To make matters worse, some of Jesus's followers were casting aspersions on the Mosaic law and the Jerusalem Temple. Paul the Pharisee was incensed and began to round up adherents of the new sect. It was in the course of his persecuting activities that Paul had a dramatic experience on the road to Damascus. All of a sudden he was struck with a profound sense that the messianic age foretold by the prophets in the Jewish Scriptures had been inaugurated by the death and resurrection of Jesus Christ, who was now exalted by God and would very soon return in glory. So earth-shattering was this experience that Paul withdrew into Arabia for a few years to reflect on what had happened. (The Acts of the Apostles describes events on the Damascus Road three times, 9: 1–19, 22: 4–16, 26: 9–18. Paul himself only once describes his deep sense of having been chosen and called by God, in Galatians 1: 11–17).

When next we hear of the young man from Tarsus it is as Paul the Christian missionary. He resolved to take his new faith to non-Jews (or Gentiles): while Peter led the mission to Jews, Paul became Christianity's most successful missionary to Gentiles. With incredible energy and vigour, he travelled around the cities of the eastern Mediterranean, founding churches wherever he went. Paul's letters testify to the difficulties he endured in his travels – frequent shipwrecks, beatings and imprisonments. It was perhaps during this period that he took up tent-making: having a trade meant that he could support himself financially as he went about his missionary activities.

What was distinctive about Paul's preaching was not just the fact that it was directed mainly at Gentiles but that he did not require Gentile converts first to become Jews (which would have involved keeping the Jewish law and, for men, circumcision). As far as Paul was concerned, the cross of Christ had inaugurated a radically new way for all people (Jew and Gentile) to relate to God. The Jewish law was no longer of any great significance – all that mattered was that a person had faith in Christ.

Unfortunately for Paul, not everyone agreed with him. The Jerusalem leadership, in particular, had difficulties with his views. They were happy to allow Gentiles into the church but insisted they first became Jews and kept the Jewish law. The Jerusalem leaders (consisting of Peter, John and James, the brother of Jesus) had actually known Jesus and their views were listened to and respected. Converting them to his own way of thinking would be an uphill battle for Paul. We know now that Paul's law-free gospel eventually won the day but that was far from clear in the first century, and both sides had everything to fight for.

When Paul left a church, he kept in touch through letters, some of which are preserved in the New Testament. His letters are full of advice on how Christians should live, warnings against false teachers, encouragement to stand firm in the new faith and promises that the New Age inaugurated by Christ was about to dawn. With the exception of Romans, all are written in response to a specific crisis in a particular church. Every page reflects not only Paul's intense, passionate personality but also his warmth and pastoral concern for the communities he founded. Even Paul's critics, though uncomplimentary about his physical appearance and effectiveness as a speaker, had to admit that his letters were 'weighty and powerful' (2 Corinthians 10: 9–11).

Paul's letters all date from the mid-50s CE. They provide a fascinating glimpse of both the personality of their author and the beginnings of a troubled young church trying to understand itself and its destiny.

Genuine letters of Paul

Of the thirteen letters which bear Paul's name, modern scholars believe that only seven are undisputably genuine: 1 Thessalonians, Galatians, Philippians, 1 and 2 Corinthians, Philemon and Romans. We cannot examine these in any detail but shall look at some of their main arguments and characteristics so that you can get some idea of the kind of things contained in them.

Letters in the ancient world

Twenty-one out of the twenty-seven books of the New Testament are letters. Although they may sound a little odd to us, their authors were following the standard letter-writing conventions of their day. Here is another letter from about the same time:

> 'Irenaeus to Apollinarius his dearest brother many greetings. I pray continually for your health, and I myself am well. I wish you to know that I reached land on the sixth of the month Epeiph and we unloaded our cargo on the eighteenth of the same month. I went up to Rome on the twenty-fifth of the same month and the place welcomed us as the god willed, and we are daily expecting our discharge, it so being that up till today nobody in the corn fleet has been released. Many salutations to your wife and to Serenus and to all who love you, each by name. Goodbye. Mesare 9.'
>
> From C. K. Barrett, *New Testament Background and Selected Texts* (1957: 29)

You can see that this author begins with his own name, followed by the name of the recipient and a word of greeting. He ends with a formal greeting, a final wish and the date. Paul used the basic letter formulas current in his day but Christianises them, characteristically adding a reference to his apostolic status and the words 'grace to you and peace from God our Father and the Lord Jesus Christ'.

Like most other authors in the ancient world, Paul would have dictated his words to a scribe. Sometimes he adds his signature or a few words in his own hand at the end (for example, Galatians 6: 11, Romans 16: 21–2).

Letters would have been written on rolls of papyrus and entrusted to a messenger. Receiving a letter in the first century was not the everyday occurrence it is in the modern world. A letter from Paul would have aroused great excitement in a church (and perhaps some dismay from those who opposed him). The whole community would have gathered to hear the letter read out. It would have been carefully preserved and copied, and, on occasion, lent to other Christian groups. We know that collections of Paul's letters were circulating by the end of the first century. This was the first stage of a process which eventually let to the formation of the Christian Scriptures, or New Testament.

I Thessalonians

This is generally believed to be Paul's earliest surviving letter (which makes it the oldest Christian document in existence). It is addressed to a church in the port city of Thessalonika in northern Greece.

The most striking thing about this letter is its eschatology – that is, what it says about the 'last things'. Like other Christians of his generation, Paul was convinced that Jesus's crucifixion had begun the final countdown to the end of time. Very soon Christ would descend from heaven, the dead would rise and Christ would judge the world (4: 13–18). It was important, then, that believers behaved properly and kept themselves in readiness for the end (4: 1–12). Paul reassures them that they do not have long to wait but warns them against trying to calculate when the end will be – it will come without warning, 'like a thief in the night' (5: 1–11). This sense of an imminent end pervades all Paul's letters and often lies behind his ethical instructions (for example, his urging people to stay single in 1 Corinthians 7: 8).

The Corinthian Correspondence

The Corinthian correspondence was addressed to a Christian community in the wealthy port of Corinth. Paul wrote at least four letters to Corinth: 1 Corinthians 5: 9 refers to an earlier letter (meaning that 1 Corinthians is actually the second letter) and most scholars think that 2 Corinthians is an amalgamation of at least two letters. This means that we have Paul's second letter (1 Corinthians), third letter (usually thought to be 2 Corinthians 10–13) and fourth letter (usually thought to be 2 Corinthians 1–9). This is our most extensive correspondence to any one church and provides us with a vivid glimpse of the often difficult history of a group of early Christians.

I Corinthians

Like all early Christian groups, the Corinthians were meeting in the house of a wealthy member of the church. Here the house-church seems to have met in the house of Chloe. Paul penned this letter in response to a letter from some of Chloe's servants and oral reports brought by the letter-bearers. The community seems to have been beset by serious divisions: rival cliques had developed and some were engaging in sexual misconduct, bringing law cases against one another or arguing about whether it was permissible to eat food sacrificed to idols. There were also disagreements over proper behaviour in Christian worship and the resurrection of the dead. Even the weekly eucharist had become a source of division, with wealthier members arriving early and eating all the food.

Paul addresses each of these problems in turn, urging the Corinthians to strive for unity. He tells them that they are all members of a single body and need to work together harmoniously (12: 4–31). Christians are to have faith, hope and, above all, love (13).

2 Corinthians

Things in Corinth, however, were about to take a turn for the worse. Some time later Paul visited the church and was publicly humiliated by newcomers who had gained positions of influence within the congregation. Who these people were is uncertain, though it is possible that they were Jewish Christians from Jerusalem insisting that the Corinthians keep the Jewish law. Returning to Ephesus, Paul wrote a harsh letter to Corinth (he refers to his visit and the subsequent letter in 2: 1–5 and 7: 12). Most scholars think that this letter is to be found in chapters 10–13, which are extremely sarcastic in tone. In these chapters, Paul defends his authority as an apostle, using all his considerable rhetorical skill against his opponents, accusing them of proclaiming 'another Jesus's. More than any others, these chapters show the depth of Paul's feelings and the intense emotional commitment he felt towards his communities.

Not wishing to make another painful visit, Paul sent this harsh letter with his missionary companion, Titus. Titus found Paul in Macedonia and conveyed the good news to him that the Corinthians were sorry for their behaviour and now supported him. In response, Paul wrote a joyful letter of reconciliation (quite probably 2 Corinthians 1–9).

Galatians

Exactly who the Galatians were is a matter of some debate: either they were the Celtic peoples of northern Asia Minor or, more probably, they belonged to the Roman province of Galatia in the southern coastal region of Asia Minor. Rival teachers seem to have come to Galatia, turning the believers against Paul and questioning the validity of his law-free gospel. In its place, they were persuading the Galatians that they needed to keep both the Jewish law and also some of their old pagan ways. When news of this disturbing development reached Paul, he wrote one of his most spirited and forceful letters. With hardly a pause for any of the usual greetings, he plunged into his own defence.

In the first part of the letter, Paul vigorously defends his own authority as an apostle. He makes it clear that his apostolic calling (and also his law-free gospel) came to him through a direct revelation from Jesus Christ. He had very little to do with the Jerusalem authorities at first, he maintains. But later, when he went to visit them, they recognised the validity of his Gentile mission and agreed that Gentile converts did not need to keep the Jewish law. His mission was therefore legitimated both by divine revelation and by the leaders of the church.

Paul goes on to defend his law-free gospel or, put another way, his doctrine of justification by faith (see Romans below). He brings six arguments, drawn from the Jewish Scriptures and the believers' own experiences, to argue that 'if justification were through the law, then

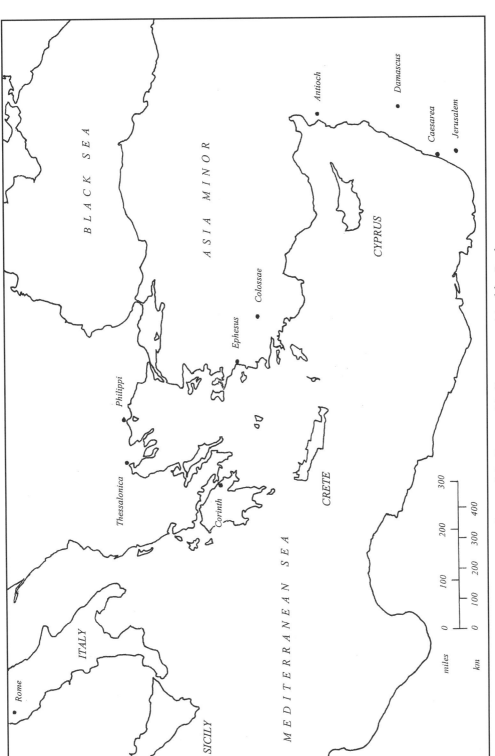

Cities of the Eastern Mediterranean visited by Paul

Christ died to no purpose' (2: 21). But a law-free gospel does not mean that people can behave as they like and the letter ends with a series of ethical injunctions.

Romans

Paul's letter to the Romans is his magnum opus: it is his longest letter and contains his most calmly reasoned presentation of his doctrine of justification through faith. It is the only letter written to a community Paul did not found and this is probably why it reads at times more like a sermon than a letter.

In Romans, Paul looks at the state of humanity. Both Jews and Gentiles are alienated from God and slaves to sin and death. The Jewish law is 'holy' and 'just' but only increases our awareness of human inadequacy. The only thing that can bring people back to God is the new relationship between God and humanity brought about through Christ's death on the cross. Through his voluntary self-sacrifice, Christ took the law's penalty for sin upon himself. All those who trust in Jesus are now liberated from the old order of sin and death. Believers are 'free in Christ', part of Christ's new creation, and receive God's grace as never before. It was God himself who initiated this process, graciously offering humans the chance to be reconciled to him.

Looked at in this way, it made no sense to Paul to require believers to keep the Jewish law: the only thing that can reconcile a person to God is faith in the saving power of Christ on the cross. To add any extra requirements would imply that the saving event of the cross was not enough. (Paul's doctrine of justification by faith has been extremely influential but it is important to remember that it is not the only view in the New Testament – Matthew 5: 19 and James 2: 24 take quite different views.)

As in Galatians, Paul ends by stressing that a law-free gospel does not mean that people have no ethical responsibilities. Quite the opposite. Christ is about to return in judgement and believers must behave correctly in both their public and private lives.

Philippians

Paul wrote this warm, friendly letter during one of his spells in prison. In the course of the letter, Paul quotes from what appears to be an early Christian hymn (2: 5–11). The hymn presents Jesus as the humbly obedient son whose death on the cross led to his heavenly exaltation and earned him 'the name above all names' before whom all creation bows.

Philemon

This is another 'imprisonment letter', written about the same time as Philippians. It is the shortest of Paul's letters and the only piece of private correspondence. Paul writes to a citizen of Colossae named Philemon and urges him to take back a runaway slave who has become a believer and to treat him 'as a dear brother'.

'Pseudonymous' letters

The majority of scholars maintain that the remaining six letters which bear Paul's name – 2 Thessalonians, Colossians, Ephesians and the Pastorals (1 and 2 Timothy and Titus) – were probably not written by the apostle. Although these disputed letters share Paul's general theological outlook, a number of factors make it unlikely that they were written by Paul.

Reasons for doubting Paul's authorship

- In places, the language and style of these letters is quite different to that of Paul. Favourite Pauline words and expressions are absent and the direct and forceful speech of Paul has given way to a more devotional tone.
- Characteristic Pauline ideas – such as justification by faith and Christ's imminent return – are absent.
- At times these letters seem to reflect the later church, well after Paul's day. The word 'church' for example is now used not for individual groups of believers (as Paul used it) but to refer to a universal institution (see Ephesians in particular). The pastorals refer to ecclesiastical offices – bishops, elders and deacons – all of which seem to reflect the more organised church of the second century. There is a concern for institutionalisation and respectability that is lacking in Paul.

In all probability, these six letters were written by disciples of Paul. The technical term for this is that they are 'pseudonymous' (written in the name of someone else). Today, this sounds quite scandalous – we think of forgeries and deceptions – but things were very different in the ancient world. Writing in the name of a famous person from the past was already a well-established feature in the Hebrew Bible (for example, the first five books claimed to have been written by Moses and the books of Daniel and Enoch were written years after the biblical characters were supposed to have lived). By putting the name of Paul to his work, an author could claim to stand within the tradition of Paul. He could interpret and defend Paul's theology for a later generation and gain credibility and authority for his views. The spirit of prophecy was still very much alive in the early church and these disciples of Paul probably honestly believed that they were conveying what Paul would have said had he been there.

We cannot know if Paul would actually have agreed with all that his later followers wrote. Sometimes their ideas are quite different, as two examples will show: 1 Timothy 2: 8–15 doesn't allow women to teach in church, while Paul himself allowed women to prophesy and to pray aloud (1 Corinthians 11: 5); and Titus 1: 6 insists church leaders be married, while Paul himself was unmarried. Of course, the situation of the church was very different and Paul might have changed his mind over time. Those who followed him certainly believed that they conveyed Paul's instructions for their own situations and the fact that so many later disciples wrote in the name of Paul shows the great esteem in which the apostle to the Gentiles was held.

Gospels

Paul (and those who wrote in his name) emphasised the death and exaltation of Jesus, but had little interest in his earthly ministry and the content of his preaching. For information on these matters, we need to turn to the gospels.

The New Testament contains four gospels: Matthew, Mark, Luke and John. But what exactly is a 'gospel'? As far as we know, the gospel was a literary category invented by the early church. Gospels are not like modern biographies – they tell us hardly anything about Jesus's appearance, his family, or his early life and influences. Instead, they are confessions of faith, declarations which show that Jesus of Nazareth was indeed the Christ, the Son of God. (The word 'gospel' comes from the Greek *euangelion*, meaning 'good news', which is of course exactly what these early Christian writers believed their message to be.)

Most scholars think that the first gospel was Mark's, written about 70 CE. This means that we have an interval of about forty years between the life of Jesus and the first report of his life. During this forty-year period, stories were circulating about Jesus in oral form. At first, they would have been in Jesus's own language, Aramaic. Then, as missionaries took the new faith to Greek-speaking territories, stories and sayings would have been translated into Greek. They would have been explained and adapted to new, urban situations. Each early Christian centre would have had its own Jesus traditions, ones the community found particularly useful in its preaching, instruction, or disputes with outsiders. You can still see a trace of these oral traditions today – if you flick through the first three gospels, you will notice that each is essentially composed of a series of short paragraphs which once circulated as oral tradition (these paragraphs are known as *pericopae*). Often these traditions can tell us as much about the early church as they do about the life and teaching of Jesus. The study of these short paragraphs and their setting in the early church – which scholars refer to as their *Sitz im Leben* – is called form criticism (see pp. 333–5 above).

Synoptic gospels

The first three gospels – Matthew, Mark and Luke – are called the 'synoptic gospels' (which simply means that they have the same viewpoint). If you looked at all three together, you would be struck by the parallels between them. Events happen in roughly the same sequence, all three often contain similar sayings and narratives, and sometimes even the vocabulary is the same.

Matthew 9: 10–15

And as he sat at table in the house, behold, many tax collectors and sinners came and sat down with Jesus and his disciples. And when the Pharisees saw this, they said to his disciples, 'Why does your teacher eat with tax collectors and sinners?' But when he heard it, he said, 'Those who are well have no need of a physician, but those who are sick. Go and learn what this means. I desire mercy, and not sacrifice. For I came not to call the righteous, but sinners.'

Then the disciples of John came to him, saying, 'Why do we and the Pharisees fast, but your disciples do not fast?' And Jesus said to them, 'Can the wedding guests mourn as long as the bridegroom is with them? The days will come when the bridegroom will be taken away from them, and then they will fast.'

Mark 2: 15–20

And as he sat at table in his house, many tax collectors and sinners were sitting with Jesus and his disciples; for there were many who followed him. And the scribes of the Pharisees, when they saw that he was eating with sinners and tax collectors, said to his disciples, 'Why does he eat with tax collectors and sinners?' And when Jesus heard it, he said to them, 'Those who are well have no need of a physician, but those who are sick; I came not to call the righteous, but sinners'.

Now John's disciples and the Pharisees were fasting; and people came and siad to him, 'Why do John's disciples and the disciples of the Pharisees fast?' And Jesus said to them, 'Can the wedding guests fast while the bridegroom is with them? As long as they have the bridegroom with them, they cannot fast. The days will come when the bridegroom will be taken away from them, and then they will fast in that day.'

> Luke 5: 29–35
>
> And Levi made him a great feast in his house; and there was a large company of tax collectors and others sitting at table with them. And the Pharisees and their scribes murmured against his disciples, saying, 'Why do you eat and drink with tax collectors and sinners?' And Jesus answered them, 'Those who are well have no need of a physician, but those who are sick; I have not come to call the righteous, but sinners to repentance.'
>
> And they said to him, 'The disciples of John fast often and offer prayers and so do the disciples of the Pharisees, but yours eat and drink.' And Jesus said to them, 'Can you make wedding guests fast while the bridegroom is with them? The days will come, when the bridegroom is taken away from them, and then they will fast in those days.'

Even in an English translation the similarities are obvious! These factors suggest there is some kind of literary dependence between all three. Analysis of this literary connection is known as source criticism (see p. 321 and Hebrew Bible parallels pp. 335–6) or, more specifically, the synoptic problem.

Synoptic problem

It used to be assumed that the shortest gospel, Mark, was an abridgement of Matthew and Luke (this is known as the Griesbach hypothesis). At the time of writing, an overwhelming majority of scholars think that Mark was written first and that Matthew and Luke used Mark as the basis for their own work. The order of all three appears to be Mark's. Where Matthew and Luke add their own material they rarely do so at the same point and always return to Mark's narrative.

Matthew contains nearly all of Mark's gospel (about 90 per cent), while Luke used about half. When all the Markan material is removed, however, there is still a large amount of material common to both Matthew and Luke. This common material often contains stories which use identical vocabulary, suggesting that both gospels used another written source. Again, you can see this for yourself by comparing Matthew 3: 7–10 with Luke 3: 7–9. This second written source is referred to as 'Q' (from the German *Quelle*, which means 'source'). Matthew and Luke therefore both used two written sources in the composition of their gospels, Mark's gospel and Q – a theory known as the 'two-document hypothesis'. It can be shown diagrammatically.

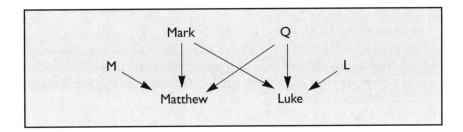

Matthew and Luke based their work on Mark's gospel, adding material from another written source, Q, and supplementing their narrative with their own special material (referred to as 'M' and 'L' in the diagram above). This special material (which may have been oral) included each gospel's distinctive birth stories and resurrection narratives.

What do we know about Q?

Q is the name given to a hypothetical written collection of teaching material common to both Matthew and Luke. It seems to have been roughly about 250 verses long and was composed of parables, instructions and prophesies of Jesus's second coming. In all probability, it did not have a passion narrative. You may be thinking that Q sounds like a rather odd document but the second-century Gospel of Thomas is also a collection of Jesus's sayings without a passion narrative. There has been a great deal of scholarly interest in Q, with some suggesting that it originated in Galilee, perhaps as early as the 50s CE.

Redaction criticism: A case study

The way in which Matthew or Luke changes his Markan source can help us to understand each evangelist's special interests. You can see this for yourself quite easily. First read Mark's account of Jesus's triumphal entry into Jerusalem (Mark 11: 1–10), then Matthew's version (Matthew 21: 1–11).

You will see that Matthew has changed Mark's single colt to two animals – a donkey and her foal. The reason for this is clear in 21: 5, where Matthew adds a quotation from the Hebrew Bible (it is actually

a mixture of Isaiah 62: 11 and Zechariah 9: 9) which appears to be referring to two animals, an ass and its foal. Matthew often adds quotations
from the Hebrew Bible to show that everything Jesus did was foretold
by the prophets. Here he has even altered Mark's narrative so that it fits
better with his quotation.

You will notice too that Matthew has altered the shout of the people.
He changes Mark's 'Blessed is the kingdom of our father David which is
coming' to 'Hosanna to the Son of David'. Matthew's version makes it
clear that Jesus is the Son of David. If you look at this gospel as a whole,
you will see that one of Matthew's favourite names for Jesus is Son of
David, so this alteration is perfectly in keeping with Matthew's interests.
Even from just ten verses we can start to piece together some of
Matthew's special concerns.

This passage also shows that, even though Matthew and Luke drew
on Mark, they were quite happy to revise and edit the earlier gospel to
conform with their own theological viewpoints. Study of the way in
which Matthew and Luke used their Markan source is called redaction
criticism (see p. 321).

The theology of Mark, Matthew and Luke-Acts

The gospels are a generation later than Paul's letters. Although they tell
the story of Jesus, they were all influenced by events of their own late
first-century setting. Each evangelist presented a picture of Jesus Christ
that both underlined Jesus's significance and spoke to the needs of his
own community. As we shall see, each presentation is quite distinctive.

Who wrote the gospels?

The gospels originally circulated anonymously. It was only in the late
second century, in the fight against heretics, that Church Fathers tried to
connect them with apostles or their disciples. Traditionally, the gospels
were written by:

- *Matthew* the tax-collector (Matthew 9: 9–13 – called Levi in Mark
  2: 14)
- John *Mark*, the companion of Peter and Paul (Philemon 24,
  Colossians 4: 10, Acts 12:12–25, 14:36–40)

> - *Luke* the physician, the companion of Paul (Colossians 4:14, Philemon 24, 2 Timothy 4:11)
> - *John* the apostle, son of Zebedee and brother of James, otherwise known as the Beloved Disciple (John 21:20–24)
>
> Modern scholars doubt the authenticity of these traditions. The people who wrote the gospels were probably leaders within their own Christian communities but we do not know who any of them were. For convenience, though, we shall continue to refer to the authors by their traditional names – Mark, Matthew, Luke and John.

Mark: The earliest gospel

Mark was written to a predominantly Gentile church around about 70 CE. Two devastating events preceded the writing of the gospel. The first was Nero's horrific persecution of Roman Christians in 64, in the course of which Peter and Paul are traditionally said to have perished (for Tacitus's description of this event see pp. 415–16). The second was the Jewish revolt against Rome which broke out in 66 and culminated with the destruction of the Temple in 70. Both these events left their imprint on Mark's gospel and explain his repeated references to suffering and persecution, and his sense that the end of all things is about to dawn. The eary church associated this gospel with Rome, though Syria or Palestine are also possibilities.

The gospel has a clear geographical arrangement. After describing Jesus's baptism by John, Mark presents Jesus's Galilean ministry. The narrative is fast-paced and breathless as Jesus goes from one Galilean village to another. What is striking about Jesus in these early chapters is his authority: he speaks forcefully and has the power to cast out demons, to control natural forces, to heal the sick – and even to raise the dead. Everywhere he goes he proclaims the nearness of the Kingdom of God and shows people – through his parables and miracles – what God's active rule will be like.

Jesus's mission is a great success and he attracts crowds wherever he goes. And yet, for all their excitement, the crowds do not really understand who Jesus is. The Markan Jesus is essentially a tragic figure. He keeps his Messianic identity secret and is misunderstood even by those closest to him, particularly his family and his disciples. Perhaps the evangelist wants to show that Jesus's messiahship can only be understood through his suffering and death.

Even during this early period, Jesus is engaged in controversy, debating the Mosaic law with Pharisees, Scribes and Herodians. The sense of

363

conflict and impending doom is heightened in the next section of the gospel, during which Jesus and his disciples make the long journey from Caesarea Philippi in the far north to Jerusalem (8: 27–10: 52). Before they set out, Jesus makes the first of three predictions in which he warns his disciples of his impending death and resurrection (8: 30–38, 9:31–32, 10: 33–34).

As they are on the way, Jesus takes the opportunity to teach his disciples about the 'way' of discipleship. Following him, Jesus declares, may well involve suffering and disciples should be prepared to follow him even to the cross. These words would have taken on added significance after Nero's persecution, when many Christians had been crucified for their faith. Their sufferings, Mark shows, were all foreseen by Jesus and are a necessary preliminary to the dawning Kingdom of God. Mark's emphasis on the dullness and stupidity of the disciples may also speak to the needs of Christians of his own day. To all who find their present suffering hard to understand, Mark shows that even Jesus's closest followers were equally baffled.

Eventually, Jesus arrives at Jerusalem, where conflict – this time with the chief priests – comes to a head. Jesus's symbolic action against the Temple (11: 15–19) and declaration that God had rejected the Jewish leaders (12: 1–12) seals his fate. In his last public discourse, the Markan Jesus predicts his imminent return as the glorified Son of Man (13) – a promise which would have comforted Mark's suffering community.

Finally, with chapters 14–16 we have arrived at Mark's passion narrative. The cross has cast its shadow over the whole gospel and now, in the passion narrative, Mark slows the story down, dwelling on every detail of Jesus's last hours: his last supper with his disciples, his agony in Gethsemane, his trials in front of Jewish authorities and Pilate, and his crucifixion. The whole passion narrative is overlaid by prophecies from the Hebrew Bible, particularly from Isaiah and the Psalms. In this way, Mark shows that Jesus's death was all part of God's divine plan from the very beginning. It is only when Jesus hangs alone on the cross that his identity is finally recognised – by a Gentile centurion who acknowledges him as the 'Son of God' (15: 39).

The gospel ends rather abruptly. In 16: 1–8 a group of women come down to the tomb; finding it empty, they run away in terror. Later scribes disliked this ending and added some resurrection appearances (16: 8b in the RSV margin, and 16: 9–20). It may well be, though, that Mark intended to end his gospel at 16: 8. Like the women, his church were bewildered and afraid and could only hope for Christ's imminent return in glory.

Matthew: A Jewish gospel

Matthew's gospel was probably written in the 80s CE, perhaps in Syria. Compared with Mark, the gospel is strikingly Jewish in tone. Matthew presents Jesus as a second Moses who, far from abolishing the Jewish law (5: 17–20), demands a higher righteousness from his followers. The evangelist frequently cites passages from the Hebrew Bible, proving that Jesus of Nazareth really was the Messiah of Jewish expectation. Clearly Matthew was writing for a group of Jewish Christians for whom adherence to the Jewish law was still important.

Yet, at the same time, this gospel has several anti-Jewish passages. Chapter 23 is a strong denunciation of scribes and Pharisees and suggests that the destruction of Jerusalem in 70 CE was proof of God's wrath towards Israel (a theme picked up in 27: 25). As far as Matthew was concerned, non-Christian Jews had forfeited their rights to God's promises by their reluctance to accept Jesus as the Messiah. For him, the church is the new Israel, the heir to God's promises. These anti-Jewish elements suggest that Matthew's Jewish Christian community had left (or was in the process of leaving) the Jewish synagogue. The pain and hostility between the two groups is still apparent in the gospel, as Matthew tries to define his own group over and against the parent religion. (We might well wish that passages such as Matthew 27: 25 were not part of the New Testament but it is important to read them in the light of their historical contexts.)

The gospel opens with an account of Jesus's birth, in which Jesus symbolically relives the history of the Jewish people (he even goes into Egypt and is brought back again by God). These opening two chapters present Jesus as the royal Son of David, born in Bethlehem, and as a second Moses, miraculously saved from an evil ruler (Herod/Pharaoh) at birth.

Even Matthew's structure reflects his Jewish background. He arranges his material into five long speeches which correspond to the five books of the Torah:

1. Sermon on the Mount (5–7)
2. Instructions to the Twelve (10)
3. Parables of the Kingdom (13)
4. Instructions to the church (18)
5. Warnings of final judgement (23–25)

Throughout the gospel, Matthew has toned down Mark's sense of an imminent end. Christ's second coming (or parousia) is still some way off and Matthew's stress on ethical instructions are to help the community in the intervening time. The gospel ends with an appearance of the risen Jesus in Galilee. As the Son of Abraham (1: 1), Jesus commands his disciples that they must 'make disciples of all nations' and promises that he will be with them always, 'to the close of the age' (28: 19–20).

Luke-Acts: Good news to the Gentiles

Luke's gospel differs from the others in that it is the first of a two-volume work – the gospel and the Acts of the Apostles. Both works were written late in the first century in a large city of the eastern empire (perhaps Antioch or Ephesus). Luke's particular concern for Christianity's mission to the Gentiles, along with his fluent, elegant Greek, suggests that the author may have been a Gentile Christian – perhaps the only Gentile Christian author in the New Testament.

The gospel charts the rise of Christianity and its spread to Jerusalem, while Acts follows the new faith to Rome, the centre of the ancient world. Writing for a Graeco-Roman audience, Luke-Acts presents Christianity as a respectable religion that can offer salvation to all people. The new faith may have begun in a lowly stable at Bethlehem but Luke ends his account with Paul preaching openly in Rome with the assurance that 'the Gentiles will listen' (Acts 28: 28).

Luke understands the history of salvation as a three-act drama. First was the time of Israel, then the time of Christ (described in the gospel) and finally the time of the church (Acts and beyond). In this scheme, Jesus stands at the centre of salvation. He is the crucial link between the Jewish biblical past and the future age of the Gentile church. Gone is the intense eschatological expectation of earlier New Testament texts. Instead, Luke concentrates on the future work of the church in the Roman world.

Luke's gospel

Both the gospel and Acts open with a formal preface addressed to Theophilus (whose name means 'lover of God'). Presumably this man was Luke's patron, or financial backer. The gospel's opening two chapters compare and contrast the birth and infancy of Jesus with that of John the Baptist. At every point, Jesus is shown to be superior to John. John represents 'old Israel' and prepares the way for Christ, who will inaugurate a new act in the drama of salvation.

Luke follows Mark's general order of a Galilean ministry followed by a journey to Jerusalem, though he makes certain additions and adaptations. He adds two large blocks of teaching material: 6: 20–8: 3 (which includes Jesus's 'sermon on the plain') and 9: 51–18: 14 (which contains some distinctively Lukan parables, such as the Good Samaritan and the Prodigal Son).

Jesus is presented as a Spirit-filled bearer of good news to the poor and oppressed (see especially Jesus's 'programme' in 4: 16–30). The gospel is particularly concerned with society's outcasts, beggars and women (who, in the first century world, were often counted as inferiors). Jesus is a model of compassion and forgiveness. Even on the cross, he dies forgiving his executioners (23: 24). For Luke, all who follow Jesus must model themselves on him.

Luke is also concerned to show that Jesus and his followers are no threat to Rome. Jesus may have died on a Roman cross but he had not done anything wrong. In the trial before Pilate, Luke makes it abundantly clear that the Roman governor finds Jesus innocent of any political activity. The man next to Jesus on the cross (23: 41) and the Roman centurion (23: 41) echo this. Luke stresses that Christianity is a peaceful and law-abiding faith.

Luke's resurrection stories all take place in and around Jerusalem. The good news has reached the centre of the Jewish world and it will be left to Acts to chart its progress to Rome.

The Acts of the Apostles

Written several decades after the events it describes, Acts presents an idealised picture of the early church. Everything is harmonious and Spirit-led – a far cry from the early struggles and disputes revealed in Paul's letters!

Acts focuses on two Christian leaders: Peter and Paul. Peter dominates the first half of the book. He represents Jewish Christianity and takes the lead in events centred in Jerusalem. The gospel ended with Jesus's promise to send the Holy Spirit, a promise which is dramatically fulfilled at Pentecost (Acts 2). Under the power of God's Spirit, the Jerusalem church grows at an astonishing rate. Following the example of Jesus, Peter and other disciples are hauled in front of Jewish leaders. Yet hardship only has the effect of promoting the church's growth. Even the death of Stephen – the first Christian martyr – and the ensuing persecution helps the church, as the new faith spreads far and wide (11: 10). Peter's last divinely guided act is to bring the first Gentile into the church, the Roman centurion Cornelius. Later, after a miraculous release from prison, Peter 'went to another place' and disappears from the story (12: 17).

The second half of Acts is dominated by Paul. His experience on the Damascus Road was described in chapter nine and now he plays the leading role in taking the new faith from Jerusalem to the Gentile world. In a series of three missionary journeys (which parallel Jesus's journey to Jerusalem in the gospel), Paul and his associates take the gospel to Asia Minor (Turkey), Syria and Greece. At the end of the first journey, Paul and Barnabas returned to Jerusalem for a conference that debated whether a Gentile believer first had to convert to Judaism. Luke presents this as an orderly, Spirit-led debate that resulted in limited rules being imposed on converts (Acts 15). (Paul's version of events in Galatians 2: 1–10 is rather different. The memory of the conference still filled Paul with anger but at least he could take comfort from the fact that no rules were imposed on his converts.)

Finally, Paul is arrested in Jerusalem on a charge of profaning the Temple and kept in Roman custody for two years. Like Jesus before him, he was tried by Jewish, Roman and Herodian rulers. Fearing he would not get a fair trial in Judaea, Paul used his Roman citizenship to appeal to the Emperor. Throughout this final narrative, Luke makes it clear that Paul (like his master) is innocent of all charges against him. We last catch sight of Paul in Rome. He is under house-arrest but free to preach without hindrance to Gentiles at the heart of the empire.

Did Luke know Paul?

Paul is clearly the hero of the second half of Acts – but had Luke ever met him? Traditionally, Luke is thought to have been a companion of Paul and Acts contains a number of 'we passages' that suggest the author was an eyewitness of some of the events. Yet there are significant differences between the Paul we know from his letters and the Paul of Acts:

- Paul fought hard for the title 'apostle'. Luke, however, rarely calls Paul an apostle, reserving the title for people who had accompanied Jesus during his ministry.
- Paul stressed his gospel's total freedom from the Jerusalem leadership. The Paul of Acts dutifully accepts the authority of the Jerusalem church and modifies his gospel in the light of their advice.
- Paul in his letters is a fiesty, passionate and independent man. The Paul of Acts is a rather bland team-player.
- Luke seems unaware of Paul's letters and his distinctive theology.

The simplest conclusion is that, although Luke held Paul in great esteem, he had no first-hand knowledge of his hero.

John's gospel

The fourth gospel is quite open about its purpose. It was written 'that you may believe that Jesus is the Christ, the Son of God, and that believing you may have life in his name' (20: 31). Like the other gospels, it was composed in the late first century, perhaps in Ephesus or even Palestine. Yet this gospel stands apart from the other three, as even a quick skim through its pages reveals.

Distinctive features of John's gospel

Style
John is fond of long discourses and sustained philosophical discussions. It

is often difficult to decide where the voice of Jesus stops and the narrator starts (for example, 3: 15). John is a master of drama and uses irony and misunderstanding to further the plot.

Timing of events
Jesus's ministry lasts no more than one year in the synoptics; in John, it lasts at least three. Jesus dies on the day of Passover in the synoptics; in John, he dies the day before Passover. The incident in the Temple takes place at the end of Jesus's ministry in the synoptics; in John, it takes place at the beginning.

Signs
The synoptics are full of miracles, while John has only seven – which he calls 'signs' – and no exorcisms at all.

Eschatology
In the synoptics, the 'Kingdom of God' is something in which believers will share at the end of the age. John, however, puts very little emphasis on the 'End'. Instead, 'eternal life' is available now through belief in Christ who is spiritually present among believers. John is often said to have 'realised eschatology'.

Jesus
John presents a picture of Jesus which is radically different from anything in the synoptics. The most striking feature of the Johannine Jesus is the stress put on his divinity and unity with the Father. Jesus is a stranger from heaven, sent by God into an often alien and hostile world. Paradoxically, Jesus's crucifixion is the supreme moment of his glorification, after which he ascends once more to heaven. John's stress on Jesus's divinity is often referred to as his 'high Christology'.

These differences have convinced most scholars that John wrote independently of the synoptic gospels.

Prologue (1: 1–18)

John's poetic prologue outlines most of the main themes of the gospel. We are introduced to the pre-existent Jesus, who takes on human flesh and brings life to humanity. We also learn that his mission will be divisive: some will reject him while others will accept his revelation and become 'children of God'.

In these opening verses, Jesus is identified as the 'Word', a term which conveys several biblical ideas. Jesus is the creative Word of God from Genesis 1 and the prophetic, revelatory Word spoken by the prophets. There are also parallels between Jesus and Wisdom, a personification of God's wisdom in the Hebrew Bible.

The Book of Signs (2–12)

The main part of the gospel falls neatly into two sections. The first section is often called the 'Book of Signs' because Jesus performs seven signs, each of which reveals his heavenly glory. The signs are:

1. Water into wine (2: 1–11)
2. Healing an official's son (2: 12a, 4: 46b–54)
3. Healing a crippled man (5: 2–9)
4. Feeding 5,000 (6: 1–15)
5. Walking on water (6: 16–25)
6. Restoring sight to a blind man (9: 1–8)
7. Raising of Lazarus (11: 1–45).

Inserted between the signs are long discourses in which Jesus openly talks about his relationship with the Father. Unlike the synoptics, where Jesus spoke about the Kingdom of God, the Johannine Jesus speaks about himself (often using the 'I am' formulas characteristic of this gospel), his unity with God and his mission.

John's gospel is very Jewish: the author often alludes to biblical passages and the whole gospel is structured around a series of Jewish feasts. Yet, like Matthew, the author can often sound extremely anti-Jewish. Both gospels reflect late first-century disputes between Jewish Christian communities and local synagogues. It is clear from John that his community has recently been expelled from the synagogue (9: 23, 34, 16: 2). This is probably the reason why John can write with such hostility about 'the Jews': although 'the Jews' are sometimes presented in a neutral way, more often they are simply part of the hostile, unbelieving world that rejects Jesus. Hostility with 'the Jews' reaches a climax in chapter eight, when Jesus tells them that their father is not Abraham as they suppose but the devil (8: 44).

Jesus's last sign is the raising of Lazarus, an act that leads directly to his death. With supreme irony, John shows that the one who gives life must now lay down his own life. And the Jewish High Priest Caiaphas prophesies more than he knows when he says that 'it is expedient for you that one man should die for the people' (11: 50).

The Book of Glory (13–20)

The hour of Jesus's glorification on the cross has now arrived. During his last evening, Jesus speaks to his disciples (13–17, often referred to as the 'Farewell Discourses'). Instead of instituting the Eucharist, Jesus washes his disciples' feet, an act of humble service. He gives them a new commandment: that they should love one another. Jesus's followers should 'abide' in him and be known by their mutual love and humility. Jesus promises that he will send them the Paraclete (variously translated as Spirit of Truth, Helper, Comforter, or Counsellor) who will support and direct the community after Jesus's death.

Finally, Jesus goes to the cross, where he will be glorified. He goes to his death perfectly in control of events (there is no agony in the garden in this gospel) and dies with the simple words 'It is finished' (19: 30). John's distinctive chronology means that Jesus dies at exactly the same time as the Passover lambs in the Temple. He is the new paschal lamb whose death 'takes away the sin of the world' (1: 29).

Originally, the gospel probably finished at the end of chapter twenty. This chapter contains resurrection appearances, describes the bestowal of the Spirit/Paraclete and ends with Thomas's climactic confession 'My Lord and My God'. Most scholars think that chapter twenty-one was probably a later addition, designed perhaps to reinstate Peter after his denial of Jesus in the High Priest's courtyard and to make sense of the death of a mysterious figure known as the Beloved Disciple.

The Beloved Disciple

This mysterious person makes an appearance only in the second part of John's gospel (13: 23, 19: 26–7, 20: 3–10, 21: 7, 20–24, and perhaps 19: 35–37). The gospel never tells us who he is, only that he had a particularly close relationship with Jesus. He is traditionally linked with John son of Zebedee, who is similarly never mentioned by name in the gospel (except at 21: 2).

The Beloved Disciple is continually presented as a model of faith and discipleship. This has led some scholars to think that he is not a real historical person at all but an ideal figure who responds perfectly to the teaching of Jesus. This is a very difficult matter to judge and scholarly opinion is divided.

One of the most interesting features about the Beloved Disciple is that he often appears in scenes along with Peter. In nearly all of these, he comes over more positively than Peter. For example, when the two disciples go to the empty tomb in 20: 3–10, Peter merely goes into the tomb while the Beloved Disciple goes in, sees and believes. It is the Beloved Disciple who lies on Jesus's breast at the last supper, and to the Beloved Disciple that Jesus entrusts his mother.

Perhaps the Beloved Disciple – who may well have been John son of Zebedee – was someone who had a particularly strong connection with the church for which John's gospel was written. Perhaps he even founded the church and passed on the traditions he had received from Jesus to the new church. Later, one or more of his disciples wrote down these traditions in the gospel. This would explain why the Beloved Discple is given such an important position in the gospel and why he is given such a prestigious title.

Historical Jesus

We have now seen that the gospels were written several decades after the life of Jesus and that they present four diverse 'Christs of faith'. For Mark, Jesus was the misunderstood Messiah; for Matthew, a second Moses; for Luke, he was a model of obedience; and for John, he was God striding over the earth. But what can we say about the real Jesus, the Jesus of history? Can we reconstruct anything of the life of a man who lived almost 2,000 years ago?

There are brief references to Jesus in early non-Christian sources, though they do not tell us much. They confirm that Jesus was a miracle-worker, that he was crucified by Pilate and that he had a following even after his death (see the box below). To say any more, we have to go back to the gospels and attempt to sift history from theology – as you might imagine, not an easy task!

References to Jesus in ancient non-Christian literature

The fullest reference to Jesus is in the work of Josephus, an aristocratic Jewish priest who was born shortly after Jesus's death. This passage must have been altered by a Christian scribe – Josephus was a Pharisaic Jew and would never have said some of the things it contains. Christian alterations, however, may be limited to the phrases I have underlined:

'About this time, there lived Jesus, a wise man, <u>if indeed one ought to call him a man.</u> For he was one who wrought surprising feats and was a teacher of such people as accept the truth gladly. He won over many Jews and many of the Greeks. <u>He was the Messiah.</u> When Pilate, upon hearing him accused by men of the highest standing amongst us, had condemned him to be crucified, those who had in the first place come to love him did now give up their affection for him. <u>On the third day he</u>

appeared to them restored to life, for the prophets of God had prophesied these and countless other marvellous things about him. And the tribe of the Christians, so called after him, has still to this day not disappeared'.

Josephus, *Antiquities of the Jews* (18: 63–64)

Christ 'had been executed in the reign of Tiberius by the procurator Pontius Pilate'

Tacitus, *Annals* (15: 44)

Claudius 'expelled the Jews from Rome [49 CE] since they were always making disturbances at the instigation of Chrestus' [Christ?].

Suetonius, *Claudius* (25: 4)

The end of the twentieth century saw an explosion of scholarly literature on the historical Jesus. Most scholars tend to rely on the synoptic pictures of Jesus, particularly for Jesus's words – the synoptics' short, pithy sayings are more likely to be authentic than John's long theological discourses. As for Jesus's deeds, events/actions that take place in all four gospels are more likely to be historical than events/actions that occur in only one source. Events that may have caused the early church some embarrassment – such as Jesus's baptism by John or his crucifixion as 'King of the Jews' – are also likely to be historical.

Modern scholars draw on their knowledge of first-century Judaism and sometimes insights from the social sciences (particularly anthropology and sociology) in an attempt to understand Jesus's context. The following is a sketch of the historical Jesus which most scholars would accept: Jesus came from Nazareth in Galilee; he was the son of a carpenter named Joseph and his wife Mary; as a young man, he was a disciple of John the Baptist, and began his own ministry after John had been killed by Herod Antipas; basing himself in the small towns and villages of Galilee, he preached the Kingdom of God, a kingdom in which ordinary social values would be reversed; he befriended people who were poor and outcast – those who were regarded as 'sinners' by most of society; reputed to be a healer and exorcist, crowds gathered wherever he went; after a ministry of a few years, he aroused opposition from the powerful Jewish leaders (perhaps because of his actions in the Temple) and met a shameful end on a Roman cross.

Beyond this, at the time of writing, scholars are as divided as ever. Did

Jesus think that he was the Messiah? Was he opposed to Jewish purity laws? Was he engaged in controversies with the Pharisees? Was he even a Pharisee himself? Did he oppose the Temple? Did he expect an imminent eschatological judgement? Did he receive any kind of burial? And what happened on Easter Sunday?

Important names connected with the most recent 'quest for the historical Jesus' are J. D. Crossan, N. T. Wright and M. Borg, J. P. Meier, P. Fredriksen and the 'Jesus Seminar'. Be warned, though, that there are as many 'historical Jesuses' as there are scholars!

Other writings

The remainder of the New Testament is made up of a sermon, a group of general letters and an apocalypse.

Hebrews, Catholic Epistles, Revelation

Hebrews is a sermon from the late first century. The anonymous author interprets the Hebrew Bible through Greek philosophy and presents Jesus as both a kingly and a priestly Messiah. Jesus was the final revelation of God's purpose and now serves in heaven as the eternal High Priest and mediator for all people.

The seven Catholic Epistles are called 'Catholic' because of their general nature. They were directed to the church as a whole (rather than a specific group of believers) and, although they use the letter format, most are more like sermons. They are all attributed to prominent members of the early Jerusalem church: two from Peter; one from James; three from John; and one from Jude (the brother of James, and so, presumably, of Jesus). Nearly all scholars, however, regard them as pseudonymous, dating from between the late first and early second centuries. Like the pseudo-Pauline letters, they reflect a later, more established church.

James (as we might expect) is strongly Jewish Christian in tone. It defines faith in terms of actions and contains what seems to be a critique of the Pauline doctrine of justification by faith (2: 24). The book of 1 Peter addresses persecuted churches in Asia Minor, reminding them of their ethical responsibilities. Jude is a defense of orthodoxy and 2 Peter attacks false teachers and longs for a return to the apocalyptic hope of earlier times.

The books of 1, 2, and 3 John tell us more about the history of the community that produced the fourth gospel. The author of 2 and 3 John identifies himself simply as 'the Elder' – this man probably wrote all three letters (though scholars doubt that he was also the author of the gospel). The letters seem to be later than the gospel.

We saw earlier that the gospel reflects a dispute between the Johannine community and the synagogue. By the time the letters were written, however, the split with the synagogue is in the past and a more pressing concern is a division within the Johannine community itself. It is clear from 1 John that some members of the church have recently withdrawn. The argument seems to be over Christ's nature. The majority of the Johannine community believed that Christ was a real man. The secessionists, however, denied Christ's humanity. The difference of opinion may well have stemmed from the high Christology of the gospel (which, as we saw, placed great emphasis on Christ's divinity).

Who were the Elder's opponents? They seem to have held a docetic view of Christ (this means that they believed that he only seemed to be human) and may well have been gnostics. Gnostics believed that salvation could only be gained through special knowledge imparted through a heavenly redeemer (*gnosis* means knowledge in Greek). They held a dualistic view of the world in which the invisible spirit world was good and pure, while the physical earthly world was corrupt. Since the divine revealer belonged to the spirit world, he could not possibly have been part of the earthly world and so only seemed human. (We know that John's gospel was widely used in gnostic circles. In fact, the first commentary on John was written by a gnostic called Heracleon at the end of the second century). The Elder's opponents probably merged with other gnostic Christians, while the Elder and his supporters eventually merged with what was becoming the mainstream church.

Revelation is the last book in the New Testament. In terms of genre, it is an apocalypse (which means that it contains the unveiling of unseen, heavenly realities). It contains all the standard elements of apocalyptic literature: visions, symbols, a dragon, beasts, seven seals and a final conflict between the forces of Good and the forces of Evil.

The apocalypse probably dates to the reign of the Emperor Domitian (81–96 CE) and was written by an unknown 'John' to the churches of Asia Minor. The author looked around him at his own, corrupt world, dominated by the Roman Empire and its imperial cult. He contrasts what he sees as an evil empire with the heavenly realm. Readers are transported to the heavenly throne room, where God is worshipped night and day. It is clear that, whatever the earthly realities, God is the supreme power in the universe. In heaven, the visionary sees the future, symbolised by beasts, apocalyptic portents and cosmic battles. John assures his readers that God is about to intervene in human affairs, evil will be destroyed and the reign of Christ will begin.

Non-canonical writings

We have now looked (in varying detail) at all the twenty-seven books that form the Christian New Testament. It is important to remember, though, that these twenty-seven texts are not the only books written by early Christians. In fact, the process of canonisation was a long and complex one. Some works – like the letter of James – took time to be accepted as canonical. Others – like the Didache (a book of early Christian instruction) – were included in early lists of recognised books but did not eventually make it into the canon.

Christian works that are not part of the canon are collectively known as the New Testament Apocrypha. This collection consists of a large number of gospels (including infancy gospels), Acts of various apostles and letters. Many of these are highly fanciful. The Gospel of Nicodemus, for example, retells the trial of Jesus and has the Roman standards bow to the ground of their own accord when Jesus enters the courtroom! Others may preserve authentic traditions. The second-century Gospel of Thomas, for example, is thought by some scholars to contain authentic words of Jesus.

Conclusion

This chapter has given an overview of the contents of the New Testament. Since Christianity is based on these texts, it is important that you appreciate the diversity of thought even from the earliest times. The New Testament contains no one theology, no one way of understanding the significance of Jesus. Paul and Matthew would not have agreed on the significance of the law; John and the author of the pastorals would not have agreed on the need for church hierarchies. What all of these texts/letters do have in common, though, is a devotion to Jesus Christ as their Lord and Saviour, and an earnest desire to work out his significance in their lives. Debates over Christ's being and purpose have continued for centuries, as the later chapters in this half of the book will make clear.

If you want to take your study of the New Testament further, the next stage is to consult some of the books below and to start to read through the texts themselves, along with commentaries. You will find that we have only skated across the surface of what is a fascinating collection of ancient texts.

Further reading

Good introductions

Drane, J. (2001), *Introduction to the New Testament*, Philadelphia: Fortress Press. A useful basic textbook with plenty of illustrations.

Dunn, J. D. G. (1990), *Unity and Diversity in the New Testament: An Enquiry into the Character of Earliest Christianity*, 2nd ed., London: SCM Press.

Elwell, W. A. and R. W. Yarbrough (1998), *Encountering the New Testament*, Grand Rapids, MI: Baker Books. A historical and theological survey.

Fredriksen, P. (1988), *From Jesus to Christ: The Origins of the New Testament Images of Jesus*, New Haven: Yale University Press.

Harris, S. L. (2000), *Understanding the Bible*, 5th ed., Mountain View, CA: Mayfield. Extremely thorough introduction.

More specific topics

Powell, M. A. (1998), *The Jesus Debate: Modern Historians Investigate the Life of Christ*, Oxford: Lion. Discusses the contributions of recent scholars on the continuing quest for the historical Jesus.

Roetzel, C. J. (1998), *The Letters of Paul: Conversations in Context*, 4th ed., Louisville: Westminster/John Knox.

Sanders, E. P. and M. Davies (1989), *Studying the Synoptic Gospels*, Philadelphia: Trinity Press International. Very useful on the synoptic problem and different ways of reading the gospels. Also has a section on the historical Jesus.

 There is a useful website at www.ntgateway.com (owned by Mark Goodacre of Birmingham University), where you will find plenty of information on a range of New Testament topics.

Questions

1. What is the significance of Paul? What was his major contribution to Christianity? Outline his concept of 'justification by faith'.

2. Imagine you are James (the leader of the Jerusalem-based Jewish Christians). Write a letter to Paul (using ancient literary conventions), arguing that new converts should keep the Jewish law.

3. What are the 'synoptic' gospels? Describe the literary relationship between them.

4. What is distinctive about (a) Mark's, (b) Matthew's and (c) Luke's view of Jesus? Why do you think Matthew and Luke needed to alter Mark's account?

5. If you were asked to reconstruct the history of the first few decades of the early church, would you put more emphasis on the Acts of the Apostles or on Paul's letters?

6. In what ways is John's gospel different from the other three?

7. Why is it so difficult to reconstruct the 'Jesus of history'?

Section Two: PRACTICAL THEOLOGY

CHAPTER ONE

What is Practical Theology?

John Swinton

- ❏ Introduction
- ❏ Understanding practical theology
- ❏ Beyond the clerical paradigm
- ❏ The church paradigm
- ❏ Practical theological method
- ❏ Conclusion
- ❏ Further reading
- ❏ Questions

Introduction

Practical theology is an emerging discipline. Its history has been one of controversy and confused identity, and its position within both church and university has often been less than clear. The intention of this chapter is to clarify some of the central issues surrounding the discipline of practical theology and to highlight the significance of its role within both church and the academy. The chapter will present an understanding of practical theology that reveals it to be a necessary theological discipline with the ability to contribute to a deeper understanding of Christian theology and tradition, as well as the ongoing praxis of the church in the world. You will be introduced to some of the principle themes and features of practical theology and will begin to explore what this might mean for the theology and praxis of the Christian community. What follows will therefore be tantalising, perhaps at times frustrating and most certainly incomplete.

There is a sense in which such uncertainty and mystery is an integral aspect of what practical theology is, as it seeks to explore the deeper levels of human living and human experience with and of God. Mystery and wonder do not always fit neatly with the human desire to categorise and systematise knowledge and experience. Nevertheless, it is hoped that your curiosity will be stimulated by this brief exploration.

Understanding practical theology

For many people reading this book, practical theology will be somewhat of an enigma. Some will assume that it is simply 'handy household hints for ministers'; hints and tips to enable ordained clergy to function effectively within their parishes. Others will assume that it is simply a vaguely theologically-oriented dimension of counselling or psychology. Either way, it might be assumed that it is unworthy of serious theological consideration; it may help us to apply our theological understandings to everyday life but it certainly does not help clarify or develop our theological understandings themselves. Such views have contributed to the Cinderella-like position practical theology occupies in the thinking of many. Considered a poor relation to the rest of the theological disciplines, it is something to be tolerated rather than considered seriously.

In order to get to the roots of what I suggest are such false beliefs, it is necessary to examine the historical context within which such understandings have developed. However, before we do that, we must first bring a little more clarity into our understanding of what practical theology is. Put simply, practical theology is critical reflection on the praxis of the church in the world done in the light of Scripture and Christian tradition and should be 'in dialogue with other sources of knowledge'. It is that dimension of theology that seeks to examine critically the actions of the church-in-the-world, in order that its practices can be understood and enabled to remain faithful to the mission of God that provides the dynamism and the goal of the theological enterprise. Practical theology is thus grounded in the life of the world in general and the life and work of the church in particular. It is this location of the theological enterprise within human experience that gives practical theology its unique theological perspective. Biblical studies begins its theological reflection with the ancient scriptural texts and seeks to work out the meaning and purpose of Christianity from that starting point; systematic and historical theologies begin their reflective tasks with the ancient historical and doctrinal documents that have been compiled and handed down by the church over the centuries. The basic text practical theology begins with is the lived experience of the contemporary Christian community as it strives to live faithfully in and for the world.

In like manner to the way in which biblical, systematic and historical theologians use such disciplines as linguistics, cultural studies, philosophy and historical studies to enlighten the meaning of their texts, practical theology draws upon other sources of knowledge – such as psychology, sociology, anthropology, cultural studies and so forth – in order to illuminate the meaning of the 'living text' of the Christian community. Whilst it seeks to remain faithful to Christian tradition and doctrine, practical theology aims to reflect not only on their historical meanings but also on their contemporary meaning in the light of the experiences of the Christian community. As such, practical theology is necessarily reflexive, contextual, imaginative, creative and transformative, seeking to explore and, at times, challenge the accepted boundaries of current theology and practice and, in so doing, develop new and innovative ways of being faithful Christians in a world of continuing change and uncertainty.

The diversity of practical theology

Such a basic understanding might be useful in terms of orienting us within the general area – in practice, tying down the specifics of practical theology can be tricky! While most would accept that some form of theological reflection on praxis lies at the heart of the practical theological task, what that actually means in terms of method and practice is diverse and open to a variety of interpretations. Various compendiums of approaches to practical theology emerged towards the end of the twentieth century, all of which contributed to our understanding of the richness, diversity, creativity and imagination that lie at the heart of the practical theological task. However, none of them reached a consensus as to the 'true' nature of practical theology. This richness is manifested in the variety of subjects explored by practical theologians and the diversity of methodologies utilised in the practical theological task, ranging from politics to pastoral care; narrative to empirical science; hermeneutics to biblical studies – all of which contribute to a rich tapestry of theological meaning within which absolute definitions of practical theology become difficult, if not impossible. All of this makes it hard for practical theology to find a place within an academic setting, where typology and systematisation are often seen as marks of academic credibility.

However, if we think for a moment about the content and focus of practical theology, such diversity is not at all surprising. Unlike other theological disciplines, the beginning point for practical theological reflection is contemporary human experience; in particular, the human encounter with God. As such, it necessarily contains an element of uncertainty, imagination and diversity. Practical theology takes seriously and incorporates fully the diversity of human experiences. Such experience is not simply illustrative material, used to illuminate a higher form of knowledge; rather, all human experiences are viewed as unique 'moments' in the drama of divine revelation.

Viewed in this way, it becomes clear that the practical theological task will be, by necessity, diverse. Rooted as it is within the complexities of human lives, cultures and ever-changing social and spiritual contexts, the 'texts' that practical theologians work with are 'living' and will always demand a spectrum of different approaches and methodologies, if only to mirror the contrasting experiences of human beings as they live out their lives amidst the complexities and uncertainties of an unpredictable world in the presence of a God who is both love and mystery.

It is true that we could interpret the diversity of practical theology as indicative of an uncertainty about what the discipline is. However, a more constructive interpretation would be that the diversity within the field of practical theology reflects and seeks to image the diversity of human experience and the magnitude and mystery of the divine.

Shifting paradigms in practical theology

Whilst there may not be a single model of practical theology, it is nonetheless possible to trace certain themes and patterns that have marked the historical and contemporary development of the discipline. Gijsbert Dingemans helpfully presents an overview of the historical development of practical theology. Dingemans highlights what he describes as four paradigm shifts that have taken place within practical theology since the eighteenth century.

> Practical theology is, as the name implies, theology in transition to the practical work of the community – to proclamation . . . The question of practical theology is how the Word of God may be served by human words. How can this Word, which has been perceived in the testimony of the Bible and of Church history and has been considered in its contemporary self-presentation, be served also through the community for the benefit of the world that surrounds it?
>
> Karl Barth, *Evangelical Theology: an Introduction* (2000: 169)

The clerical paradigm

The first paradigm he identifies is the clerical paradigm. Here, practical theology is viewed specifically as a churchly discipline that focuses on the application of theological truths, specifically to the practical context of the ordained ministry within the life of the church. This paradigm views the task of practical theology as simply to take data given to it from the other theological disciplines and apply it to the life of the church. In this model, practical theology has no independent critical role and does not participate in the process of theological critique or construction. The Christian community is viewed as the place where theology is put into action but not as a place where it is actually developed, clarified or challenged. In this paradigm, the task of practical theology is to concentrate on teaching the techniques of spiritual leadership: preaching, leading worship, stewardship, Christian education and pastoral care. Practical theology does enter into partnership with other sources of knowledge, but purely as a means of improving particular techniques, rather than as a genuine dialogue partner in the process of theological development.

The church paradigm

The second paradigm is the church paradigm. Beginning in the second half of the twentieth century, there was a movement of emphasis away from a specific focus on the pastor towards the functions of the church as a whole. The church paradigm has two dynamics – internal and external. The internal dynamic focuses on the day-to-day life within the Christian community and explores such things as discipleship, communication, pastoral care, homiletics, Christian education and so forth. The external dynamic focuses on the life of the church as it relates to the world around it. The focus here is on mission, preaching, politics, social justice and so forth. This paradigm sees the field of practical theology as focusing on the functioning of the church within the perspective of God's coming Kingdom, as it works itself out in the world. Practical theologians coming from within this paradigm would include Don Browning, Duncan Forrester and Emmanuel Lartey.

The liberation paradigm

The third paradigm is the liberation paradigm. Liberation theology finds its primary focus in the social and political aspects of the marginalised. It aims for social justice and political change that will bring about fairness and equality for the oppressed, the marginalised and all of those whom society rejects. Fundamental to this paradigm is the quest for equality and justice in the world. The theology of liberation emerged out of critical reflection on poverty and oppression within Latin America, a context where the church was seen to be totally embroiled with the oppressive political structures. It directly challenges any theological ideologies that are satisfied with simply maintaining the political and theological status quo. It is a theology of solidarity, commitment and change in the face of social and political oppression.

As with the church paradigm, liberationists understand the life of the church-in-the-world as a significant context for theological reflection and analysis. Theology is understood as critical reflection on the church's pastoral action in the world, with and for the poor. As such, according to Gustavo Gutierrez, one of the founding fathers of liberation theology, theology is seen as a secondary procedure. First comes a commitment to service; theology comes later, as critical reflection on the church's practice. Thus, the church's practice is not arrived at as a conclusion from preconceived theological premises. Theology does not lead to pastoral activity but is a reflection on it. This way of doing theology does not stop with reflecting on the world but rather tries to be part of the process through which the world is transformed. Practical theology done in this mode calls for fundamental social and political change within society and the material and spiritual emancipation of those who are oppressed by unjust social and/or religious structures.

While it has its origins in the struggles of the Latin American poor, liberation theology has been developed by a number of other groups within a Western context. Important theological works have been contributed by minority and oppressed groups, such as women, people with disabilities, those who have been abused, people with mental health problems, gays and lesbians and people of colour.

The individual paradigm

The final paradigm is the individual paradigm. This paradigm does not move from the clerical and church paradigm to the whole of society but in fact travels in the opposite direction, moving in the direction of the individual believers. It calls for attention to be paid to the lay view and insists that practical theology should focus on the needs of those who seek their own way in our complicated world full of confusing information. Here, the focus is on the individual in the pew and the person who seeks after a deeper meaning for their lives. According to Dingemans, this final paradigm is still emerging and it is too early to see how it will develop.

Conclusion: Understanding practical theology

These reflections on the paradigm changes that have taken place within practical theology over recent years helpfully captures something of the richness and diversity of the discipline and enables us to trace some significant aspects of its continuing emergence as a theological and churchly discipline. Now that we have laid down some foundational understandings, we need to begin to pick up and develop some of the themes that have been presented.

Beyond the clerical paradigm

Within the boundaries of this chapter, it is not possible to draw out the implications of each of the paradigms outlined above. We will, however, explore in some detail two paradigms that have been particularly influential in the development of practical theology within Europe and the United States: the clerical paradigm and the church paradigm. As we reflect critically on these two ways of understanding practical theology, a model of practical theology as the theology of practice will emerge that will locate it firmly within the boundaries of both the academy and the church and enable us to reflect on the place and potential of practical theology within the overall theological enterprise.

The roots of the clerical paradigm

The traditional answer to the question 'What is practical theology?' is that it is a prescriptive discipline (that is, a discipline that is viewed essentially as a means of producing tangible solutions to particular problems) that seeks primarily to apply theology to the specific needs of the church. In this paradigm, the main focus of practical theology is the fulfilment of the particular training requirements of the ordained clergy. Elaine Graham in her *Transforming Practice* points out that the historical roots of this assumption lie in the origins of the discipline within the German universities in the mid-eighteenth century. It was here that a specific form of academic syllabus emerged that has profoundly shaped the way in which divinity faculties have been structured until relatively recently. With the emergence of the theological encyclopaedia that categorised theological texts according to their major emphasis, there came a separation between those disciplines that focused on theoretical issues of faith and belief and those that focused on issues of ecclesiological practice primarily as it related to the practice of the ordained ministry. In this way, a significant split was initiated between the study of scripture, doctrine and tradition and the practical disciplines of ministry.

This movement had two effects. First, it institutionalised and legitimated the separation of theory from practice. Certain disciplines were assumed to be purely theoretical and others purely practical. Second, in fragmenting the various theological disciplines it caused particular difficulties for the identity and credibility of theology as an academic discipline. How could the various aspects of theology (biblical studies, church history, philosophical theology and practical theology) be held together in a way that maintained the professional status and academic credibility of the discipline?

Perhaps the most definitive and influential answer to this question was offered by Friedrich Schleiermacher in his monograph *A Brief Outline of Theology as a Field Study*. In this work, Schleiermacher sought to bring together the various aspects of faculty theology around the common purpose of serving the practice of the church. For Schleiermacher, the primary function of all theology was to serve the needs of the church. It was this practical aim and goal that brought unity to the fragmented theological disciplines. For him, the entire theological enterprise was designed to lead up to and into practical theology. In this sense, practical theology was seen as the 'Queen of the sciences' or, as Pannenberg has described it, 'the Crown of all theological study'. Theology, then, is primarily for the sake of maintaining and perfecting the church.

Schleiermacher likened theology to a tree, with philosophical theology forming the root, historical theology the branches, and practical theology as the crown. Practical theology took data from philosophical and historical theology and applied it to the life of the church, primarily to the training of the ministry. Practical theology was the 'queen of the sciences' in so far as it was the place where the purpose and meaning of the other theological disciplines was worked out. In this way, the academic fragmentation was overcome and the credibility of theology as a legitimate scholarly discipline was ensured.

The splitting of theory and practice

However, Schleiermacher's maintenance of theology's unity and credibility within the faculty was bought at the price of a schism between theory and practice, a split which placed practical theology in a position whereby it simply applied the basic theoretical principles of academic theology. There was no room in Schleiermacher's formulation for the experience of the church community to enter formatively into the process of theological construction. In Schleiermacher's scheme, the unity of the theological faculty was maintained by the common purpose of the various disciplines in serving the ministry of the church. Practical theology is assumed to be practical and not theoretical. Assuming that the other theological disciplines have done their work properly, there is no need for any further theological reflection. The tasks of application that are the marks of practical theology are given to it by the other theological disciplines, therefore practical theology is essentially technology.

The usefulness of the clerical paradigm

There are a number of observations one might wish to make with regard to Schleiermacher's model of practical theology as applied theology. Positively, he highlights the important point that, in a sense, all theology should be practical in so far as it is intended to enable the formation of persons and communities who will manifest a particular character and a form of living that will validate and reveal the nature of the Christian tradition and live it out in its life and practices. Faith must be rooted in historical reality and theology is, above all else, aimed at enabling faithful living and not just intellectual knowledge. Schleiermacher's focus on the ordained ministry recognised and acted upon this fundamental assertion.

The church and the Christian faith were central to Schleiermacher's understanding of theology and the practice of theological enquiry. Theology only becomes theology when it is committed enquiry into the Christian faith. Certainly, it is possible to study the church and its traditions in a critical and non-passionate manner; but it is only when the theologian commits to exploration in the name of the faith that it actually becomes theology. Any form of 'academic theology' that cuts itself off from its roots within the Christian community in a quest for 'pure knowledge' may well be legitimate as a form of academic enquiry but it is not, according to Schleiermacher, theology proper. At one level, to suggest that the life of the church community and the enabling of its faithful living was a responsible goal for all theology was not necessarily a mistaken aim in itself; however, at another level, this understanding was fundamentally flawed.

The problem with applied theology

In the theory-to-practice paradigm, theology is done either for the people or to the people . . . Neither the lived faith of the community, with all of its struggles, joys, pains, and praxis in the world, nor the historical context with its social, cultural, and political realities is taken seriously in the theological enterprise as other than points of application for the theory already assembled. If that paradigm continues, then theology will be practical only by accident rather than by design.

Thomas H. Groome, *Theology on Our Feet* (1987: 60)

The applied theology model has been deeply influential in the development of practical theology and remains popular with some today. However, the problem with the applied model of theology is that, whilst practice is given a central place, it is simply understood in terms of application and not as a potential source of theological truths. In so doing, it separates theory from practice, giving epistemological priority to detached, critical rationality and demoting human experience to the locus where theology is applied but not worked out.

Such a suggestion contains at least two erroneous assumptions. First, the theory-to-practice model makes the assumption that the primary function of the enterprise of theology is theoretical investigation that can be done without any necessary reference to the historical existence of the Christian church. This 'pure' theology can then simply be given to the practical theologian whose task it is to apply it in an appropriate manner to the life of the Christian community.

However, if we reflect a little more deeply, it becomes clear that this movement from theory to practice may not be as logical as it first appears. The reality of the human condition is that experience always precedes theory; it is only when we begin to reflect on a particular situation or experience that theory begins to emerge.

[T]heological construction does not take place in a vacuum. The theologian does not stand before God, Scripture, and the historic witness of the church like an empty slate or Lockean *tabula rasa* ready to be determined, filled up, and then plugged into a concrete practical situation ... We come to the theological task with questions shaped by the secular and religious practices in which we are implicated – sometimes uncomfortably. These practices are meaningful or theory-laden.

Don Browning, *A Fundamental Practical Theology* (1996: 6)

Even the construction of the biblical tradition took place in implicit and explicit dialogue with particular historical contexts. David Bosch, in his book *Transforming Mission*, points to the way in which the gospels were constructed within particular contexts in response to specific social circumstances. Rather than simply being uncritical diaries of the life of Jesus, he shows clearly that each of the gospels was constructed in response to the particular experiences of the gospel-writer's communities. The different emphases in the gospels – such as Luke's focus on social justice and Matthew's emphasis on the Judaic Messianic dimensions of

Jesus' life and death – reflect and seek to respond to the particular experiences of the communities within which they were living and evangelising. Thus, even the biblical texts that provide the foundation of all Christian theology use a method that includes critical theological reflection on the experience of the people of God in the world as part of the interpretative process. Practice has therefore formed an important, if often unacknowledged, part of theological construction from the very beginning.

All theologians come to the task of doing theology within a particular context and with a particular pre-history (assumptions, experiences and models of knowledge gained through their personal history and life within their specific communities) that inevitably influences the ways in which they understand and develop their theological positions.

Reuniting theory and practice

Human knowledge is always reflection on some form of action/practice. To separate theory from practice in the way the applied theology model does is to create a false dichotomy. In reality, the churches' theological understandings and actions are not formulated apart from the practice of the church and the particular social context within which it seeks to practise. Theory arises out of practice and leads back to practice. In order to develop a theory, we need to extrapolate data from experience and reflect critically upon it. The beginning point for theory construction is human experience.

If this suggestion is accurate, it is clear that all theological ideas inevitably implicitly or explicitly incorporate practice within their formulations. Part of the task of practical theology is to make explicit this contextual/experiential dimension of the theological enterprise and to enable theology to incorporate the praxis of the church community in the world as an important aspect.

Learning theology from the world

> Human beings are lovers and worshippers as well as thinkers, and all of these aspects are potential sources of theological knowledge. In fact, theological knowledge only receives its full meaning when it is worked out in practice.
>
> John Swinton, *From Bedlam to Shalom* (2000: 11)

The second assumption that underlies the applied theology model is that the primary source of authentic theological knowledge is knowledge appropriated through critical, rational thinking alone. There is a tendency within theology to give primacy to the rational and cognitive aspects of human beings. Certainly, reason and rationality are significant aspects of theology and theological construction. They are not, however, the whole. An unbalanced focus on reason and rationality risks missing out on the important fact that faith relates to something that is done and lived, as well as something that is believed. Reminding Christian faith of its holistic, embodied nature is perhaps the most powerful critique of Western ways of doing theology that has been given to us by the liberation theologians. The applied theology model does not adequately recognise the experiential dimensions of theology and the hermeneutical significance of what it means to live out theological doctrine in community. Important as the cognitive and rational aspects of theological knowledge may be, they comprise only one way of attaining knowledge of God.

Theological knowledge only receives its full meaning when it is worked out in practice. The meaning of such words as love and compassion can only be interpreted as these concepts are experienced and lived out in community. Critical, analytical thinking is only one dimension of human knowledge.

> The primary locus for theology is not the academy, nor even ecclesia, but human history as it unfolds in the world. Why? Because human history is the locus of God's activity in time and thus always the first source of God's self-disclosure at any time ... God is not only the ultimate telos but also the primary source from which all historical action, consciousness, and reflection arise ... Because the world is the arena of God's saving activity, human history must be the primary locus, the point of departure and arrival for all rational discourse about God ... Theology must arise from and return to the locus of God's universal activity – the world.
>
> Thomas H. Groome, *Theology on Our Feet* (1987: 61)

Such an approach also excludes the possibility that theological knowledge can be gained and enhanced through engagement with other forms of knowledge in the world. Although within the applied theology model there remains room for the practical theologian to co-operate and assimilate other sources of human knowledge in order to improve techniques and enhance particular forms of practice, there is no room for constructive dialogue over the nature and purpose of theological knowledge with agencies outside of the church. Truth is viewed as fixed and given, rather than dialectical and emergent. In presenting a puppeteering model of God's sovereignty, the applied theology model turns God into the divine programmer of history, thus stripping human experience of its vital dimensions of meaningful creativity, mystery and uncertainty.

Importantly, the theory-to-practice model does not take adequate cognisance of God's continuing wider mission in and to the world and the churches' place within it. While some degree of academic debate has revolved around whether the primary locus of theology in general, and practical theology in particular, should be in the church or in the world, in reality it is not located in either. In his *Theology on Our Feet*, Thomas H. Groome suggests that the theological task is located in human history as it unfolds in the world. It is here, within history, that God reveals God's self and continues to work out His transforming mission in and to the world. The world is the location that God has chosen to work out His salvific purposes. As such, it is the world that should be the location of the theological enterprise. Because the whole of the created order and human history are the locus of God's active praxis, they are also potential arenas for His self-disclosure. Theology then emerges from the world and seeks to return to the world with fresh insight, a deeper revelation and more faithful forms of praxis.

> As those primary texts arose from God's self-disclosure in history, so if we are to appropriate their revelatory possibility for our time, they must not be treated as reified revelations from outside of time. We must come, instead, to appropriate them as reflections or mirrors of the truth already present in our present reality.
>
> Thomas H. Groome, *Theology on Our Feet* (1987: 62)

The locus of theological enquiry is thus moved beyond the boundaries of the clergy, the church or academia and into the wider context of God's activity in the world. In so doing, we discover a model of 'doing theology' that views the whole of creation as a potential source of revelation. Thus, as Groome suggests, it is 'the praxis of God in history, as it is co-constituted through human praxis, that is our primary text and context for doing theology.'

This is not to suggest that we should abandon Scripture and theology and do theology in a purely contextual and experiential way. Rather, the suggestion is that we should begin to recognise the significance of God's continuing mission to the world and to allow insights and understandings that emerge from God's current activity to illuminate our theological understandings. It is in the continuing dialogue between the sacred texts and historical reality that theological truth and understanding emerges.

Thus, the theological task is not simply to reiterate dislocated theological truths. Theology is called to examine theological understandings in the light of contemporary experience, in order that their meaning within God's redemptive movement in the present can be developed and assessed. Truth is emergent and dialectical, having to be carved out within the continuing dialogue between the Christian tradition and the historical existence of church and world. By excluding this vital missiological dimension from the process of doing theology, the applied theology model of practical theology will necessarily provide a limited and limiting understanding of the task of practical theology.

Conclusion: Beyond the clerical paradigm

Whilst there are some positive things to be learned from reflection on the applied theology model, it is clear that it is inadequate in capturing the fullness of God's revelation to the world and the experience of the Christian community in living out that revelation. This being so, it is necessary to move beyond the applied theology model and explore a model of practical theology that takes seriously the lived experience of the Christian life and seeks to develop an understanding of God and human living that takes seriously the lived experience of the Christian community.

The church paradigm

In the second half of the twentieth century, there was a significant shift away from a clergy-centred understanding of practical theology towards a model that sees the functions of the church as it practices in the world as the main focus of attention for the practical theologian. This has led to major shifts in method and approach. Instead of reading Scripture and tradition with a view to applying insights to the life of the church, many practical theologians have shifted the locus of their investigations to the practice of the church-in-the-world. For these theologians, practical theology relates to theological reflection on the centrifugal and centripetal actions of religious communities. Here, the movement is from practice to theory and back to practice.

From praxis ➔ theory ➔ praxis

> As a theory of the churches' activity which includes the history of the church, practical theology will have to recognise the fundamental importance of missiology to its general theme. The mission directed to all mankind is not simply the practice which originally created the church, but also the ultimate horizon on which the whole life of the church must be understood. By its origin in mission the individual community is drawn into a history of divine election which looks towards a future in the kingdom of God; it is inserted into a Christian life-world which transcends its own particularity.
>
> Wolfhart Pannenberg, *Theology and the Philosophy of Science* (1976:438–9)

Many of the points that were highlighted previously with regard to the emergent and historical nature of theology, and the importance of human praxis as a locus for theological enquiry, are developed more fully in the work of another practical theologian who has been influential in the development of the church paradigm: James Fowler. In a number of books and articles, Fowler has outlined and developed an understanding of practical theology that will be helpful for current purposes. For Fowler, practical theology relates to theological reflection that arises out of and gives guidance to communities of faith as they seek to participate in the mission of God to the world. Practical theology arises out of and feeds back into the practice of the church-in-the-world. Like Thomas Groome, he makes the assertion that the practice of the church takes place within the overall context of its participation in the ongoing mission of God to the world.

As I point out in my book *From Bedlam to Shalom*, this missiological dimension is crucial for practical theology. It is the ongoing mission of God in the world and to the world that provides the aims, the goals, tests the methods and adds the necessary energy and vision that guides the task of practical theology.

The aim of the church is faithful praxis-in-the-world. The focus of practical theology is to ensure the faithfulness of the churches' actions. Whilst remaining a churchly discipline, in the sense that its primary focus is on the praxis of the church, practical theology is also a discipline fundamentally located in and for the world. To examine and reflect upon the praxis of the church must be understood as a task that takes place in the world and for the world in like-manner to the way in which Jesus was and remains in and for the world.

393

> The actions of Christians are celebrations of and attestations to God's reconciling work in the world which begins and ends in Jesus Christ. The relationship of these actions to non-Christians is one of both similarity and difference. The similarity is that all human actions both participate in and fall short of the purposes of God. The difference is that those who profess belief and adhere to membership of the church have been called to make explicit the celebration of God's work.
>
> A. V. Campbell in Duncan Forrester, *Theology and Practice* (1990: 16)

So the focus of practical theology is not simply the internal workings of the church community, (although it includes them) but the praxis of the church as it interacts with the praxis of God in the world. For this reason, there is a necessary critical and prophetic aspect to practical theology's reflective activity, the boundaries of which are defined by the boundaries of God's continuing mission.

This model of practical theology therefore calls theology and the church back to its roots as a fundamentally missionary church with a particular vision and a specific task to perform in the world. As a missionary church, it is crucial that it remains faithful to its missiological task and vision. One of the primary tasks of the practical theologian is to ensure that the church is challenged and enabled to achieve this task faithfully.

Practical theology is critical and constructive reflection on the praxis of the Christian community's life and work in its various dimensions. As a theological discipline, it makes its own interpretations of Scripture and tradition in the light of the contemporary practice of the church, which it then brings into dialogue with those disciplines who approach this data with different hermeneutical criteria. Because of the dialectical movement of this process, practical theology has the freedom to critique and be critiqued by traditional and accepted perspectives on Scripture and tradition. Thus, it does not simply receive theology and then merely pass it on. Rather, it has a constructive, critical and analytical part to play in the process of developing theological understandings through offering a different but legitimate perspective on the interpretation of the Christian tradition in the light of the praxis of the church in the world.

As well as this internal dialogue with Scripture, tradition and the other theological disciplines, practical theology also enters into constructive, critical dialogue with other sources of knowledge within society. In this way, as we shall see, theory and practice are drawn together to develop a type of practical wisdom; a kind of knowing that guides being and doing. Thus, theory and practice are united within this form of practical knowledge that works itself out within the continuing praxis of the church.

Understanding praxis

At the heart of practical theology and practical theological methodology lies the concept of praxis. The word praxis essentially means 'action'. However, it is a particular form of action that should not be directly equated with the word 'practice'. Whereas practice implies the simple, non-reflective performance of a task in a dispassionate, value-free manner, praxis denotes a form of action that is profoundly saturated with meaning – a form of action that is value-directed and value-laden. Praxis refers to a practical form of knowledge that generates actions through which the church community lives out its beliefs.

Praxis reveals theology in a very tangible form. In this sense actions are themselves theology and as such are open to theological reflection and critique. Thus the praxis of the church is in fact the embodiment of its theology.

John Swinton, *From Bedlam to Shalom* (2000: 11)

It is helpful to think of praxis along a bipolar continuum ranging from the more radically political Marxist/Hegelian tradition – with its focus on revolutionary social and political change – to the type of model being described here that focuses on the actions of the church and on particular communities that are shaped by and continually reflect upon particular traditions of norms and values. Praxis differs from 'practice' in that it is reflective and theory-laden – that is, it contains within it particular beliefs and understandings that guide its morals and values. Praxis is reflective because it is action that not only seeks to achieve particular ends but also reflects upon the means and the ends of such action in order to assess the validity of both in the light of its guiding vision. Praxis is theory-laden because it includes theory as a vital constituent. It is not just reflective action but reflective action laden with belief. For example, the act of giving and receiving communion is praxis. Although it may seem like a simple act, when one reflects upon it theologically, one uncovers layers of hidden meaning. It is in this process of acting and reflecting on that action that one engages in praxis. Practice would be, for example, giving soup to the poor and the homeless, a human action that is apparently neutral and value-free. However, when this practice takes place within a Christian context, and one begins to reflect upon the action in the light of the Gospel and the life, death and resurrection of Jesus, it is found to be a theory-laden act that makes a profound statement about the God who informs, shapes and guides the praxis of the church. Praxis is thus a way of being in the world and a way of critically analysing situations in the world.

Christian praxis is the place where theology becomes embodied and acted out. It is the place where actions become theology. The task of practical theology is to excavate critically such actions and reveal the hidden layers of meaning implicit within the continuing praxis of the church. In this way, the actions of the church can be tested in the light of the vision of the coming kingdom.

By taking experience and practice as the starting point for reflection, growth, transformation and theological development, a focus on ecclesial praxis enables the actions of the church to be legitimately incorporated into the reflective process that is theology.

Thus, the concept of praxis confirms the importance of theory-development (all actions are theory-laden) but shifts the overarching hermeneutical context from intellectual abstraction to active engagement with the world in the light of the Gospel. In this way, theory and practice are brought together and constructively united within the notion of praxis.

Understanding the praxis of the church

One could define the specific form praxis, which marks the actions of the church, as a dynamic human process of critical reflection carried out by the church community. Critical and constructive reflection on ecclesial praxis is the process of ongoing critical reflection on the acts of the church in the light of the Gospel and in critical dialogue with other sources of knowledge with a view to the faithful transformation of the praxis of the church-in-the-world. These sources are drawn upon not only to improve technique but also to clarify the nature of the ecclesial praxis, to uncover the meanings that lie behind and are present within the praxis of the church, and even to challenge and clarify particular understandings of theological concepts. Contrary to models of theology that suggest theology is done primarily within the faculty, a model of practical theology focusing on the praxis of the church points towards the fact that ecclesial praxis is the place where theology is done.

By focusing on critical reflection on ecclesial praxis, the practical theologian will seek to examine the meaningful acts of the church and to critically assess, challenge and seek the transformation of particular forms of praxis in the light of the mission of God and in critical dialogue with the Christian tradition and the world. The practical theologian seeks to interpret and re-interpret Scripture, tradition and praxis, in order that the contemporary praxis of both church and world can be transformed and faithful change enabled. An adequate understanding of the theological validity of Christian praxis as a form of practical knowledge allows practical theology to hold together in constructive tension theory and practice, church and world, normativity and transformation, and enables a constructive and mutual dialogue to take place between all of these elements.

Practical theological method

How, then, do we actually go about doing practical theology? Let us explore some dimensions of practical theological method, concentrating first on exploring something of the history of practical theological method and some basic ways in which practical theology is done. The particular methodology that will be the focus here is the method of mutual critical correlation. This method sees the practical theological task as bringing into dialectical conversation insights from the Christian tradition, data from other sources of knowledge (in particular, such disciplines as psychology, sociology, social anthropology and so forth) and the particular experience or situation that is the focus of inquiry.

This is not the only methodology open to the practical theologian. As one reflects on the literature, a plethora of methods emerges. For example, Stephen Pattison has aptly utilised the critical praxis theory of liberation theology to highlight the plight of people suffering from mental illness within contemporary British society. Michael Northcott has also outlined a very helpful method for doing practical theology research based on the qualitative research methods of the social sciences, whilst J. A. van der Ven has developed a complex, empirically-based form of methodology in his book *Practical Theology*. Michael H. Taylor has likewise offered a useful method for engaging in critical theological conversation at a pastoral/congregational level in his book *Learning to Care*. The practical theologian also has access to the various methodologies that have been developed more fully within the other academic disciplines such as philosophy. There are thus seen to be a number of different ways in which the task of practical theology can be facilitated. However, the method of critical correlation has been influential within the development of practical theological thinking, and as such offers a useful way into critical reflection on practical theological method.

A model of mutual critical correlation

> If we hold that theology is always assimilation of the faith, not just the abstract idea of the faith apart from its reception, then it becomes necessary to say that culture may find answers to questions raised by faith as well as to assert that faith has answers to the questions raised by culture. Theological reflection is thus seen to be a dialogical enterprise which involves listening and responding to insights from both sides of the conversation.
>
> Seward Hiltner, *Preface to Pastoral Theology* (1954: 223)

The theological method of correlation finds its origins in the thinking of Paul Tillich in his *Systematic Theology*. Tillich sought to correlate existential questions that were drawn from human experience with theological answers drawn from the Christian tradition. In this way, he hoped to achieve a degree of relevance for the Christian tradition within a rapidly secularising social context. Useful as his model is in some respects, the problem with Tillich's initial model was that it was unidirectional, allowing the Christian tradition to provide answers to temporal questions but not allowing questions and answers from culture and society to challenge understandings of the tradition. Subsequent writers, notably Seward Hiltner (*Preface to Pastoral Theology*) in the area of pastoral theology and David Tracy (*Blessed Rage of Order*), expanded Tillich's model and incorporated a dialectical element within it which enables the correlation between culture, tradition and practice to be mutually critical.

Hiltner modifies Tillich's unidirectional model to incorporate an element of dialectic and mutual conversation, believing that two-way critical reflection is necessary in order to describe effective practical theological method.

> As a generalization, it seems fair to observe that in theology the more usual temptation is to understand society and academy primarily as social realities and only peripherally as theological . . . The problem with understanding the third public, church, is usually the exact opposite. A theological understanding is almost overwhelmingly operative. A sociological understanding may be implicit but is rarely explicit. The notable

exceptions to this rule (Adams, Gustafson, Komonochak, et al) serve to highlight the need among ecclesiologists, and by extension theologians, to explicate and correlate both sociological and theological understandings of the reality of the 'church.'

David Tracy, *Blessed Rage of Order* (1975: 23)

Similarly, David Tracy in seeking to examine the true state of the church as an object of theological research, wrestles with the fact that the church is both a sociological and a theological entity, which needs a balanced and correlative approach if the focus of research is to be its true essence, rather than a perceived idea that does not reflect the truth. He argues that, in order effectively to do theology that takes seriously this dialogue, it is necessary to proceed via the method he describes as critical correlation.

This way of doing practical theology seeks to critically correlate questions and answers drawn from the Christian tradition with questions and answers thrown up by other sources of knowledge located within society and culture. In this way, tradition and contemporary theory are brought together in constructive, critical dialogue in an attempt to do justice to the spiritual, socio-historical and existential demands of Christian faith and practice. This model seeks to set up a dialogue, a critical conversation between the Christian tradition and data drawn from other sources of knowledge with a view to providing a revised theoretical basis for practice.

Tracy sees this methodological approach as central to the way in which practical theology is understood and defined. Consequently, he defines practical theology as 'the mutually critical correlation of the interpreted theory and praxis of the Christian fact and the interpreted theory and practice of the contemporary situation' (Tracy 1983: 76). The method of critical correlation has been particularly influential on the development of practical theology.

The participants in a conversation are changed, both by what they learn and by the process of conversing with other participants . . . Participation in a conversation implies a willingness to listen and be attentive to other participants . . . Conversations allow participants to discover things about their interlocutors which they never knew before; all participants end up

> seeing themselves and others from new angles and in a different light... The concept of conversation does not necessarily imply that participants end up agreeing at every point or that the identity of one over-rides the character of the others... Conversations are often difficult and demand considerable effort because participants start from very different assumptions and understandings. Considerable energy may have to be expended to try and understand the relevance or importance of another participant's contribution.
>
> Stephen Pattison, 'Some Straws for the Bricks' (1989:4–5)

The practical theological cycle

While there are a number of elaborate frameworks that have been developed to enable people to do practical theology, one of the simplest and most effective is proposed by Stephen Pattison. Pattison suggests that doing practical theology should be viewed in terms of a critical conversation. The conversation takes place between the Christian tradition, the social sciences and the particular situation or experience being addressed (or the possible hypothetical outcomes of particular understandings and practices). Such a conversation is necessarily open and 'dangerous', in so far as, like all conversations, you can never be sure what will emerge from the dialogue. Conversations can be warm and affirming but they can also be deeply challenging, frightening and even threatening.

Thus, it is in a spirit of open dialogue that genuinely seeks the truth, respects the perspectives offered by experience and by other disciplines, and is prepared to invest appropriate quantities of intellectual energy in assessing and discovering the nature of that truth that the practical theologian carries out her or his methodological task.

The pastoral cycle

The pastoral cycle is an analytical device designed to enable the practical theologian to grasp the fullness of a situation or experience and to develop innovative responses that will change, or perhaps even transform, the forms of praxis carried out by the church community in response. It is designed to enable the type of critical conversation that has been highlighted thus far and to help practical theologians to develop the type of skills of theological reflection that it has been suggested are fundamental to the practical theological task.

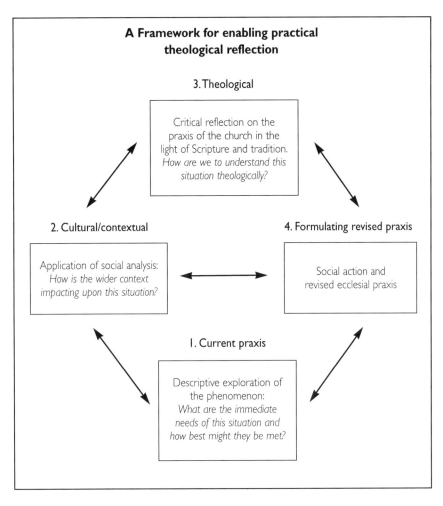

A Framework for enabling practical theological reflection

3. Theological

Critical reflection on the praxis of the church in the light of Scripture and tradition. *How are we to understand this situation theologically?*

2. Cultural/contextual

Application of social analysis: *How is the wider context impacting upon this situation?*

4. Formulating revised praxis

Social action and revised ecclesial praxis

1. Current praxis

Descriptive exploration of the phenomenon: *What are the immediate needs of this situation and how best might they be met?*

The reflective cycle illustrated in the above diagram shows how the pastoral conversation can be initiated, facilitated and brought to a constructive conclusion. A situation, experience or problem is identified within the contemporary praxis of the church or society which the practical theologian seeks to explore. The practical theologian then embarks upon a process of exploration and analytical reflection on the praxis of the church within that context in the light of the Christian tradition and in critical constructive conversation with data gathered from other sources of knowledge within contemporary society and culture. The important thing to note is that the particular questions addressed to the tradition and to the other disciplines are not abstract but are questions that have been shaped by the theologian's encounter with particular forms of ecclesial praxis-in-the-world. Thus, the unique hermeneutical principle the practical theologian brings to the analysis and interpretation of Scripture and tradition (the data from which theology is traditionally done) stems from and is intended to feed back into revised ecclesial praxis. Whilst taking full cognisance of the findings of other theological disciplines, the practical theologian has a necessary prophetic freedom to challenge established interpretations in the light of the ongoing praxis of the church, and to challenge specific forms of praxis in the light of Scripture and tradition. Having participated fully in this process of theological analysis and clarification, the practical theologian seeks to formulate a response that feeds back into and transforms ecclesial praxis. In turn, this changed situation is analysed and explored in the light of the new situation that is the result of the practical theological input. In this way, it can be seen that theory and practice are held together in critical tension by the practical theologian, with each feeding into and off of the other; each component constantly challenging, enhancing and clarifying the other The intention of this cycle is to enlighten, broaden, deepen and – if necessary – challenge both ecclesial praxis and theological understandings in the light of Christian praxis, Christian tradition and the insights that can be gained from other sources of knowledge.

Hidden agendas: The politics of counselling

It will be helpful to illustrate this process of critical theological reflection by using counselling as a case study. As we reflect on current pastoral practice, it is clear that counselling is a form of pastoral care that has become particularly popular within the Western world. Counselling is so much a part of pastoral care that there is a danger that we forget to ask critical questions of it and that we ignore the possibility that it might look different if we look at it differently. When we actually reflect critically on counselling, we find that, useful and important as it is as a form of pastoral care, our motivation for utilising it may be problematic.

Cultural context

There can be no doubt that counselling is a phenomenally popular form of caring within the Western world. In the United Kingdom, there is a multitude of training courses and some thousands of people participating in some form of counselling training. If we compare that with the amount of emphasis religious communities place on, for example, community-building courses, or the care of people with severe learning disabilities or serious mental illness, or even training for the ministry, we can see how we have come to see this particular form of caring as somehow superior to others. The question is, why?

Cultural reflection

A deeper cultural reflection reveals that counselling fits in well with a climate of individualism and a capitalist economy that seeks to commodify everything, including personal health. The idea that we can commodify a personal relationship and sell it for profit provides an interesting paradigm of contemporary approaches to health and healthcare. Whilst the difficulties surrounding the finances of pastoral counselling may be more acute within the American context, the idea of a '50-minute hour' and the professional credibility accreditation gives to a pastor fits in well with the medical model that has been so influential within Western approaches to health care. Such 'professional status' also enables ministers to find a strong sense of identity within a cultural context that is rapidly making their role less clear.

Perhaps a more important critical observation on the current emphasis on counselling is the fact that counselling is an exclusive form of caring. Roger F. Hurding, in *Roots and Shoots*, points out that a deeper reflection on the praxis of counselling suggests that many counsellors fall into the trap of offering care to what he describes as YAVIS clients – young, attractive, verbal, intelligent and successful. This tendency highlights a particular temptation in counselling to offer the most help to those who may, in fact, be in least need. This is not to suggest that so-called YAVIS clients do not have very real needs; it does, however, suggest that older, unattractive, tongue-tied, less intelligent and unsuccessful people may have less appeal to the counsellor.

Not unconnected with this observation is the fact that, while the Western world is affluent enough to be able to offer counselling and psychotherapy to all who need it, in reality such things as economics, geography, stigma and social class work towards excluding many 'ordinary' people from the possibility of receiving this form of intervention.

Quite apart from these serious difficulties, the very process of counselling poses significant problems for many people. Its emphasis on the complex use of language, coupled with the quest for insight and self-revelation, inevitably excludes many people who are not articulate and who are unable to reflect and develop the type of insight that is necessary for successful therapeutic intervention. For example, many elderly people, persons with learning disabilities and those who suffer from major mental illness can become excluded from a system of pastoral care that focuses primarily on counselling.

Theological reflection and movement towards revised forms of praxis

Having moved through the first two parts of the theological cycle, we can now begin to reflect theologically on the emphasis on counselling. Even a cursory glance at the relationships of Jesus would suggest that such exclusive practices and the commodification of the caring relationship may not be the theological norm. When we look at the relationships of Jesus, we see him becoming friends with the outcast, the stranger, those who sit on the margins of society. It is the general and open relationship of friendship that is a primary mark of Jesus's ministry and mission. Could it be that we need to redress the balance within current strategies for pastoral care by rediscovering the vital pastoral relationship of friendship? Do we need to begin to plough as much thought and as many resources into building community and developing networks of friendships that reach into our communities and bring healing and comfort to those on the margins as we currently do on specialised training in counselling and therapy? Could it be that the praxis of friendship needs to be re-introduced as a vital complementary dimension of pastoral care?

Thus, the cycle is completed and the practical theologian is able to return to the original situation with a revised form of praxis that will enable more faithful living. In this case, the conclusion is that the relationship of friendship as modelled within the life of Jesus is a form of praxis the pastoral ministry of the church needs to recover and work through in its communities, if those on the margins are to be included in its pastoral strategies.

The danger of translation

Some may question the authenticity of the use of other 'secular' sources of knowledge as central aspects of the theological enterprise. There are, of course, dangers, in particular the danger of translation – that is, simply translating theology into psychology, sociology or whatever. However, the danger of translation is not unique to practical theology: each of the theological disciplines, to a greater or lesser extent, draws on other disciplines to enable it to effectively fulfil its theological task.

Since the Encyclopaedic Movement each of the theological disciplines has used a separate methodology. Biblical studies has used the hermeneutical methods of literary criticism; church history has been subject to historical and sociological canons; and systematic theology has employed existentialist philosophy, process philosophy, Marxism or linguistic analysis.

Williams, in *The Foundations of Pastoral Studies and Practical Theology* (Ballard 1986: 43)

All of the theological disciplines are vulnerable to translation into their particular interlocutors – biblical studies into modern language study, systematic theology into historical or philosophical studies, pastoral care into psychotherapy or psychology. Certainly, selection and assessment of the validity of the sources of knowledge will be difficult, due to the fact that they are so variegated and differing in their underlying philosophies, anthropologies and metaphysical understandings. However, this simply serves to emphasise the importance of practical theological research being rigorous, critical and genuinely open to mutually critical dialogue.

It is therefore very important that the practical theologian has a firm grasp not only of Scripture, Christian tradition and the particular social context within which they are working but also of the particular disciplines he or she seeks to utilise in the service of theology, as well as the arguments and literature that seeks faithfully to bring together insights from other disciplines with Christian theology. Only when the practical theologian can be sure that she or he has a firm grasp of the particular disciplines being used, can he or she take the risk of opening his or her own perspective – in this case, the theological perspective – to challenge, critique and (hopefully) positive change. Such a method and understanding as has been proposed here demands discernment, openness, flexibility, imagination and, above all, a willingness to allow the Spirit of God to challenge entrenched philosophical and theological ideas that may be blocking a true perception of the ways in which God is working in the world today.

The tasks of practical theology

In the light of the discussion presented in this chapter, it is now possible to present a working definition of practical theology.

Practical theology is a dynamic process of reflective, critical enquiry into the praxis of the church in the world and God's purposes for humanity, carried out in the light of Christian Scripture and tradition and in critical dialogue with other sources of knowledge. As a theological discipline, its primary purpose is to ensure that churches' public proclamations and praxis-in-the-world faithfully reflect the biblical narrative that forms and inspires it and authentically addresses the contemporary context into which churches seeks to minister.

John Swinton, *From Bedlam to Shalom* (2000: 12)

From this definition, six aspects of the nature and task of practical theology can be highlighted.

(i) The focus of the practical theological task is located in the critical exploration of God's continuing mission to the world. It relates to the continuing human quest for deeper truths about God and the development and maintenance of faithful and transformative ecclesial praxis-in-the-world The fundamental aim of practical theology is to enable the church to participate faithfully in God's ongoing mission in, for and to the world. As such, it seeks to reflect critically and theologically on communities of faith as they minister to the world, and to provide reflective strategies that will enable the movement towards faithful change. It is important to bear in mind that this focus on the praxis of the church does not mean that practical theology is only interested in the inner workings of the church. All human practice is theory-laden and all theories have ultimate concerns. If this is so, then practical theology will be interested in churches' interaction with 'the practice of the world' and not just with their own internal praxis. The praxis of a church therefore includes the many ways in which a church practices in the world. As such, it encompasses the centripetal dynamics of a church's activities, such as the church's involvement in politics, social justice, healthcare and so forth.

(ii) The task of practical theology is to mediate the relation between the Christian tradition and the specific problems and challenges of the contemporary social context. It therefore moves from praxis to reflection on praxis in the light of the Christian tradition and other sources of knowledge and is aimed at feeding back into the tradition and the praxis of the church. It is an informative and transformative discipline that not only applies theology but also helps create it.

(iii) Practical theology seeks to examine the various underlying theories that underpin current forms of ecclesial praxis, as well as to contribute to the development and reshaping of new theories that are then fed back into the praxis of the church. Because Scripture, tradition and church communities are not ahistorical (that is, they do not stand outside of history), they are often implicitly or explicitly impacted by aspects of society and culture that stand at odds with the essential message of the Gospel. Part of the practical theological task is to discern such discrepancies and inconsistencies in the praxis of the church, and to point towards more authentic alternatives.

(iv) Practical theology is an interpretative discipline that offers new and challenging interpretations of Christian tradition, the specific praxis of the church and the particular challenges the church faces. In this sense, it seeks to bring the praxis of the church into the continuing process of theological formulation, clarification and construction. It takes seriously contemporary revelations of what God is doing in the present and allows this new vision to inform critically the continuing theological debate.

> Our conscious cognitive functioning constitutes a relatively limited part of our modes of knowing and relating to the physical world and to each other. We are our bodies. We have powerful emotional experiences and patterns that shape the frameworks in which we construct and interpret our experiences ... Practical theology cannot do its work with the tacit assumption that people's bodies begin with their neck and extend only upward. This means, further, that practical theology opposes docetic theologies that compartmentalise the spiritual and the physical, and that shrink the concerns of the church to the private and spiritual needs of its members.
>
> James Fowler, 'Practical Theology and Theological Education' (1985: 8)

(v) Practical theology stays close to experience. Because practical theology sees the locus of theology as the praxis of the church community as it participates with God in His mission to the world, it can never disengage or become dislocated from experience. Whilst concerned with theory as a necessary aspect of praxis, it is not focused on the development of comprehensive, theological systems that understand themselves to be concerned with the development of types of knowledge extrapolated from any form of praxis. The aim of practical theology is the enabling of personal and communal phronesis: a form of practical knowledge that combines theory and practice in the praxis of individuals and communities. This phronesis (itself the product of participation in the continuing praxis of the church) does not aim for knowledge for its own sake but for an embodied, practical knowledge that will enable a particular form of theocentric lifestyle involving a particular disposition or orientation devoted to the practical but critical living out of faith. This form of practical wisdom reveals the coming Kingdom of God in a tangible form and, as such, is vital to the continuing missiological task of the church.

Such an emphasis on embodiment is important. Most contemporary practical theologians accept as given that human beings should be understood as whole persons, if they are to be understood at all – one does not simply proclaim the Gospel with one's mind but with the whole of one's being. Practical theology is therefore a holistic discipline that sees theology as pertaining as much to embodied existence as to abstract intellectual propositions that demand particular cognitive responses.

(vi) Practical theology is fundamentally a missiological discipline that receives its purpose, its motivation and its dynamic from acknowledging and working out what it means to participate authentically in God's mission. Whilst staying close to experience, practical theology understands particular contexts within the wider overarching context of God's ongoing mission of redemption to the world. This mission provides the critical hermeneutic that guides the practical theologian in his or her task.

Conclusion

What has been developed within this chapter is an understanding of practical theology as a theology of practice, as opposed to a form of applicationist technology. As James Whyte puts it in his essay, 'New Directions in Practical Theology', practical theology is a theoretical enquiry in so far as it seeks to understand practice, to evaluate, to criticise, to look at the relationship between what is done and what is said or professed. At the same time, Whyte suggests that it is also an eminently practical discipline, not only in the sense that it seeks to understand practice but in that the understanding has the aim of guiding practice in the future, of discriminating between the possibilities – what is their relationship to faith? The aim of practical theology is therefore not simply to understand the world but also to change it. Although its locus of interest is contemporary ecclesial praxis-in-the-world, practical theology remains a definitively theological discipline and, as such, is always firmly rooted in Scripture, tradition and doctrine. However, its task is not one of pragmatic regurgitation but of critical discernment. The dominant question for practical theology is not simply 'What difference will this make in the pulpit and pew?' but rather 'Who is God and how does one know more fully God's truth?'

Practical theology is thus seen to be both dialectical and dialogical in its methodology, bringing together in mutually constructive dialogue a variety of perspectives in its quest for truth. It is also challenging and risky, in the sense that it may threaten or even strip away dearly held truths and understandings – and in exposing them, leave one vulnerable and afraid. However, practical theology is always done in the light of the revelation of the risen Christ, and it is that foundational vision of hope that will allow the practical theologian to enter into areas and face challenging possibilities that others may be unwilling or even afraid to see.

Practical theology as a credible academic discipline?

Understood in this way, practical theology is not only a transformatory discipline that seeks to enable faithful praxis within the Christian community, it is also seen to be a properly theological and genuinely academic discipline with (i) a body of tradition upon which it critically reflects in its attempts to discern the nature and truth of what has been given; (ii) a specific field of enquiry – the praxis of the church in the world; and (iii) a recognised set of methodologies that enable the practical theologian to engage in critical, systematic reflection on the historical self-understanding and contemporary praxis of a particular religious tradition in critical dialogue with secular sources of knowledge.

Understood in the ways outlined above, it is clear that practical theology is a vital theological discipline with significance for both the church and the academy. It is an important critical analytical discipline with a vital part to play in the ongoing reflective and interpretative task that is theology, and a vital contribution to make to the continuing praxis of the church community as it struggles to be and to remain faithful in a complex and fragmented world.

 ## Further reading

Ballard, Paul and John Pritchard (1996), *Practical Theology in Action*, London: SPCK. A solid, pragmatically oriented introduction to practical theology with a specific emphasis on the pastoral ministry of the church. The text utilises everyday stories to explore a variety of pastoral situations and reflect on them theologically. Contains many helpful examples of practical theology in the service of church and society.

Browning, Don (1996), *A Fundamental Practical Theology: Descriptive and Strategic Proposals*, Minneapolis: Fortress Press. A good example of practical theology in action. Browning roots his model of practical theology in Christian ethics and develops a working framework that can be utilised by practitioners and academics to analyse critically the praxis of religious communities. Very useful in terms of understanding the role of method and the ecclesial task of practical theology.

Campbell, A. V. in Duncan B. Forrester (1990), *Theology and Practice*, London: Epworth Press. A useful collection of essays tracing the development of practical theology within a British and, more specifically, a Scottish context. This text is invaluable for those who wish to understand how practical theology became what it is today.

Pattison, Stephen (1994), *Pastoral Care and Liberation Theology*, Cambridge: Cambridge University Press. A helpful model of practical theological method in action. Pattison picks up on the liberationist perspective and develops a model of practical theology for a Western context that addresses the needs of the most vulnerable within society. The book explores the predicament of people with mental health problems, utilising a liberationist perspective to reveal their oppressed state and to examine ways in which they can be liberated and drawn from the margins into the centre of society.

Pattison, Stephen and James Woodward (1999), *The Blackwell Reader in*

Pastoral and Practical Theology, London: Blackwell. This reader focuses on the theoretical background and the theological foundations of pastoral care. It provides a critical overview and introduction to the field of pastoral studies within the context of modern theology, together with a historical perspective on the development of the discipline in the modern era.

Swinton, John and David Willows (eds) (2000), *The Spiritual Dimension of Pastoral Care: Practical Theology in a Multidisciplinary Context*, London: Jessica Kingsley. A unique collection of essays by prominent practical theologians outlining the history and diversity of practical theology as an emerging theological discipline. The text provides many examples of practical theology as a multidisciplinary enterprise and explores significant issues of method and practice.

Questions

1. Why is practical theology so difficult to define?

2. In what sense is practical theology a truly 'theological' discipline?

3. What are the main problems with the applied theology model?

4. Practical theology claims to bring together theory and practice. How does it do this?

5. Is it necessary for practical theology to be as tied to the mission of the church as has been suggested? If so, why? If not, why not?

6. How does 'praxis' differ from 'practice'? What are the implications of this distinction for how we understand and carry out practical theology?

7. What are the main difficulties with the method of critical correlation and the pastoral cycle? List at least three ways in which they could be improved upon and/or constructively changed?

8. Working from the definitions of practical theology in this chapter, think through its implications for developing a theological understanding of a particular situation or context that is of interest to you.

Section Three: SYSTEMATIC THEOLOGY

An Overview of Christian History

Henry R. Sefton

- ❑ Introduction
- ❑ Christianity and Judaism
- ❑ Christianity and the Greeks
- ❑ Christianity and the Roman Empire
- ❑ Christianity and the barbarians
- ❑ East and West
- ❑ Christendom
- ❑ The Reformations of the sixteenth century
- ❑ Christianity and European imperialism
- ❑ Christianity in the twentieth century – and beyond
- ❑ Christianity and technology
- ❑ Further reading
- ❑ Questions

Introduction

The history of Christianity is a story of globalisation over twenty centuries. It is the story of how a Middle East religion became the dominant religion of Europe and then a universal religion. As long ago as 1942, William Temple spoke of this as 'the great new fact of our time' (Neill 1986: 14). Writing in 1964, Stephen Neill claimed that 'Christianity alone has succeeded in making itself a universal religion' (1986: 14). Since then, the progress of Islam in Western countries may be a challenge to this claim. The globalisation of Christianity has been achieved because of its ability to adapt over the centuries to widely different political, cultural and geographical situations. In all this, Christianity has maintained its allegiance to its founder and principal teacher, Jesus of Nazareth, to whom the title of Christ has been given.

Christianity and Judaism

Christianity has a special relationship with Judaism. It originated in a Jewish context in the land we now know as Israel-Palestine. During its early years, outsiders were unable to distinguish it from Judaism, as all its followers were devout Jews who worshipped regularly in the Temple at Jerusalem. The founder, Jesus of Nazareth, was a Jew and although he was, to some extent, critical of the Jewish Scriptures, he left no writings of his own. Thus, for some decades what is now known as the Old Testament was the only Bible of Jesus's followers.

The identity of Christianity with Judaism was more apparent than real. Jesus's followers saw him as the fulfilment of prophecies regarding a Messiah and the title Christ is the Greek translation of Messiah. This claim has been stoutly resisted by Jews then and now. Although the Jesus people observed all the required Jewish rites, they also had their own distinctive rite of the Lord's Supper, which had been instituted by Jesus himself at the last supper he shared with his closest disciples. The closeness of their fellowship was reflected in their commitment to communal ownership of property. As they increased in number, problems arose about the fair distribution of resources and this led to the appointment of seven men to supervise this. One of them, called Stephen, quickly became a prominent and controversial preacher and soon aroused the wrath of fellow members of his Jewish synagogue.

Stephen was one of the first to see that the Temple had no essential role in the furtherance of the teaching of Jesus. Seeing the Temple as transitory, he viewed that part of the Jewish law that referred to it as also transitory. He came to this conclusion because of some words spoken by Jesus but ignored by his first followers: 'I will pull down this temple, made with human hands and in three days I will build another, not made with hands.' This enraged the Jews and Stephen was stoned to death. Those who felt like Stephen had to flee Jerusalem and took refuge among the Samaritans, who shared many beliefs with the Jews but rejected the worship of the Temple. This was the first mission outside Jewry but it was to a group that was midway between Jews and Gentiles, or non-Jews.

Those followers of Jesus who were prepared to conform to the law were able, after a brief time, to continue to live undisturbed in Jerusalem; but those who shared Stephen's views went still further afield, most notably to Antioch, where the followers of Jesus were first described as Christians. To begin with, they spoke only with Jews but before long some Greeks responded to what they were saying about Jesus. Barnabas was sent by the Jerusalem fellowship to investigate this development but when he came to Antioch he was unable to do other than encourage the newcomers to remain faithful to the Lord Jesus Christ.

When they received Barnabas' report, the Jerusalem community had to decide how to treat these converts. Should they become Jews before being admitted to the Christian community? A council held in Jerusalem in 48 CE decided that this was unnecessary and so it became possible to mount a full-scale effort to reach out to the Gentiles. It was recognised that allegiance to Jesus Christ transcended ethnic differences.

Christianity and the Greeks

The dominant political power at this time was the Roman Empire but the most commonly used language was not Latin but Koine, a colloquial form of Greek. This became the medium of Christian expansion. Fortunately, there was available a Greek translation of the Old Testament known as the Septuagint and frequent reference to it is made by the Christian missionaries – we know this from their writings, which are in Greek, not Hebrew. These writings were eventually collected to form the New Testament. The Old and New Testaments comprise the Christian Bible and are regarded as the primary source of guidance about the life of Jesus and his teachings (for further details, see Chapters Two and Three of Section Three).

Among the Greek-speakers were large numbers of Jews all over the Mediterranean world. Since the Christian preachers were convinced that Jesus was the fulfilment of the Old Testament prophecies, they made their first contact with the local synagogue or worship centre of the Jews. In many cases, they met with stiff opposition from the members of the synagogue but a warm welcome from the 'God-fearers'. The God-fearers were people who were attracted by the simple worship and high standards of conduct of the Jews but comparatively few of them became proselytes or converts to Judaism. This was because they were repelled by the rituals required and the strongly nationalistic character of Judaism. Those who did become proselytes found that they were still not regarded as 'real' Jews. These God-fearers were thus thrilled to find a faith that made no distinction between Jew and Greek, that did not require circumcision and that had all the features that had attracted them to Judaism.

Despite the expansion into many cities in Asia Minor, Greece and even in Rome, the Christian communities looked to Jerusalem for leadership.

This situation was dramatically altered in 70 CE, when Jerusalem was sacked by the Romans and the Temple destroyed. Since then, Christianity has had no one local centre. There is no Christian equivalent of Mecca (to which a devout Muslim turns in prayer and to which at least one pilgrimage should be made in a lifetime). Christians do make pilgrimages but not necessarily to Jerusalem. Many places are considered to be holy but so is the whole of God's creation.

A key figure in the expansion of Christianity into the Greek-speaking world is Saul of Tarsus, first of all an opponent of the new 'way' but, after receiving a vision of the risen Christ, a courageous and eloquent exponent of the Christian message. Although by his own account a 'Hebrew of the Hebrews', Saul sees himself as an apostle to the Gentiles and takes the Gentile name of Paul. His upbringing in the Greek environment of Tarsus and his status as a Roman citizen by birth give him standing in both the Jewish and Greek-speaking worlds. His letters to various Christian communities not only gave immediate encouragement, reproof and teaching but also became a large part of the New Testament (for fuller discussion of Paul's contribution, see Chapter Three of Section Three).

Many, perhaps most, of the recipients of Paul's letters were familiar with the Jewish background of Christianity; but the next generation of Christians was largely unfamiliar with this because most of them were converts from paganism. Thus, new forms of expression had to be found to make the Christian faith intelligible to them and to interested outsiders. This was the task of the Apologists, or defenders of the faith, who came to prominence in the second century CE. One of the first and most famous of these was Justin, who, after sampling several different philosophies, became a Christian in 130 CE. In an attempt to explain the significance of Jesus, Justin used a term familiar to philosophers – Logos or Word. In his *Apology*, he speaks of the revelation of God through his Logos in the Old Testament and in the Logos made flesh in Jesus (Richardson 1953: 225–99). Justin defended his faith not only by his writings but with his life. He was put to death for refusing to sacrifice to the pagan gods in 165.

The movement from the Judaic world to the Hellenistic (or Greek-speaking) world is reflected in a change of organisation. The earlier Christian communities were patterned on the synagogue, with its corporate leadership. By the beginning of the second century, however, partly because of the passing of the original apostles and partly influenced by Greek civic organisation, there emerged in each city new leaders called bishops, who were helped by presbyters and deacons. This style of leadership is the most usual throughout the history of Christianity.

Significant dates

c. 33	Crucifixion and resurrection of Jesus
c. 35	Stephen stoned to death
46	First missionary journey of Paul
48	Council of Jerusalem
64	Christians blamed for fire of Rome
70	Jerusalem sacked by the Romans
130	Conversion of Justin Martyr

Christianity and the Roman Empire

The very existence of the Roman Empire was an important factor in the rapid expansion of Christianity over the Mediterranean world and beyond. The empire had imposed unity and peace over much of Europe and North Africa, so that travel was easier and safer than at any later time until the nineteenth century. The first Christians and their immediate successors took full advantage of this. Judaism was a lawful religion in the empire and, to begin with, the Christians were tolerated by the Roman authorities as a Jewish sect.

This toleration did not last long. In 64 CE the Christians in Rome were blamed for a great fire that may well have been started by the emperor Nero himself. To divert suspicion from himself, Nero had many of the Christians put to death in a horrifying manner as human torches. The Roman historian Tacitus records the gruesome details.

[A]n arrest was first made of all who pleaded guilty; then, upon their information, an immense multitude was convicted, not so much of the crime of firing the city, as of hatred against mankind. Mockery of every sort was added to their deaths. Covered with the skins of beasts, they were torn by dogs and perished, or were nailed to crosses, or were doomed to the flames and burnt, to serve as a nightly illumination when daylight had expired. Nero offered his gardens for the spectacle, and was exhibiting a show in the circus, while he mingled with the people in the dress of a charioteer or stood aloft on a car. Hence, even for criminals

415

> who derserve extreme and exemplary punishment, there arose a feeling of compassion; for it was not, as it seemed, for the public good, but to glut one man's cruelty, that they were being destroyed.
>
> Tacitus, *Annals* (15: 44) in C. K. Barrett (1989: 15–16)

This was the first of many localised persecutions during the first and second centuries; but it was not until the third century that Christianity was officially condemned.

Ignatius of Antioch (35–107 CE)

Ignatius is one of the 'characters' of the early Church. Although little is known about him apart from his letters, we get vivid vignettes of his personality from these. He was bishop of the church in Antioch and had been condemned to face the wild beasts in the arena at Rome. The letters were written on his way to Rome under armed guard. It is clear that he is keen to be a martyr: 'Let me be fodder for wild beasts – that is how I can get to God. I am God's wheat and I am being ground by the teeth of wild beasts to make a pure loaf for Christ.' Curiously, there is no record of the charge for which he is given this punishment.

Ignatius sees the bishop as the focus for the unity of the Church: 'Nobody must do anything that has to do with the Church without the bishop's approval.' He is the first writer to insist on the three-fold ministry of bishop, presbyter and deacon.

Ignatius has no time for those who go on observing Jewish practices, such as keeping the Sabbath (Saturday) rather than the Lord's Day (Sunday). He is equally scornful of those who assert that Jesus was not really human but only seemed to be so: 'It is not as some unbelievers say, that his Passion was a sham. It's they who are a sham!' He confronts those with mistaken views rather than arguing with them.

The Roman Empire was tolerant of the many and various religions within its bounds, provided that their adherents were willing to acknowledge the deity of the emperor and participate in his cult. A pinch of incense thrown on the altar in front of the statue of the emperor gave the worshipper freedom to practise the religion of his or her choice. Because the Christians were unable to do this, they were persecuted as disloyal subjects of the emperor. Christians were willing and ready to pray *for* the emperor but not *to* him, for this would usurp the position of God. The persecution under the emperors Decius and Valerian was short-lived but very intense and many Christians perished. However, in 261 CE the emperor Gallienus issued the first official edict of toleration of Christians.

The fourth century saw dramatic changes in the relationship of the Christians with the state. Under the emperor Diocletian, the persecution was renewed with even greater ferocity but this too did not last long. The accession to power of the emperor Constantine as a result of his victory at Milvian Bridge in 312 CE inaugurated a quite new situation in which Christianity became the official religion of the Roman Empire. Constantine attributed his victory to the intervention of the Christian God and first of all tolerated, and then favoured, Christianity. This support was not disinterested, as he saw Christianity as a means of restoring and maintaining the unity of the empire, which had been divided into eastern and western parts by Diocletian. Christianity was common to both halves and so he reasoned it must be a unifying force.

In pursuit of this aim, Constantine did not hesitate to intervene directly in the affairs of the Christian communities. This was seen most notably in his summoning of a council to settle a dispute about the relationship of Jesus to God that was causing disunity among Christians. This council met at Nicaea in 325 CE and the formulation decided there became the basis of the Nicene Creed: Jesus the Son was declared to be of one substance with the Father. This formula has stood the test of time but it was variously interpreted and the differences between eastern and western Christians became more and more marked so that, on Constantine's death in 337, the empire was again divided.

Significant dates

261 First edict of toleration of Christians
312 Battle of Milvian Bridge
325 Council of Nicaea

Christianity and the barbarians

The Greeks called all foreigners *barbaroi*. By this, they meant people who were strange or crude, especially in speech. The Romans adopted this word and they called all people who were neither Greeks nor

Romans *barbari*. On this definition, there was a good deal of Christian activity among the 'barbarians'. The independent kingdom of Armenia became the first Christian state on the conversion of its king Tiridates III about 280 CE. The size and significance of early Christianity outwith the Roman Empire was quite considerable. There were Christian minorities in south India (still represented by the Mar Thoma Church), south Arabia, the Nile valley, the Sudan, the Horn of Africa and the Caucasus, and in various parts of the Persian Empire. From the third century, there was also Christian expansion towards the north of Europe. The earliest introduction of Christianity among the Goths took place between 250 and 300 and arose out of the witness of Christian prisoners taken during raids in Asia Minor.

The son of one of these prisoners, Ulfilas, was ordained as bishop of the Gothic Christians in 341. His greatest service was the translation of the Bible into Gothic but he omitted 1 and 2 Kings, as he feared that reading about Israel's wars would make the Goths more warlike than they already were! Unknown men and women spread the Christian Gospel to other peoples, notably the Germans, so that when the Germans began to invade the empire in great numbers most of them were Christians, at least in name. Having adopted the religion of the empire, the invaders were also eager to receive its civilisation but unfortunately they were not able to manage and use that civilisation once they got control of it.

In the midst of the near chaos that ensued, Christianity did much to preserve civilisation. Christians fed the hungry, released prisoners, resisted corruption, preserved books and made new ones. They taught farming, carpentry, animal husbandry and conducted schools. This was possible because they were organised into churches based on the old Roman towns, each under the leadership of a bishop. The bishop of Rome was outstanding. But an even greater contribution was made by the monasteries.

Monasteries

Monasticism is derived from the word *monos*, alone, and the earliest monks were solitaries, like an Egyptian called Anthony (250–346 CE), who went to live by himself in the desert. This was a protest against the prevailing worldly society that had infected the Christian communities. But when communal forms of monasticism were developed, the monks played a major part in preserving civilisation. The style of life involving a balance between prayer, work and rest devised by Benedict of Nursia (480–550) for his monastery at Monte Cassino in Italy was widely

---

copied in Western Europe. A more outgoing type of monasticism was developed in Ireland by Patrick (390–460). Both types of monks kept the flame of learning alive. The Irish monks were also distinguished missionaries.

By about 1100, all of northern Europe had been converted to Christianity. There had also been significant expansion in the east, most notably to Kiev, where Christianity was proclaimed the official religion in 988, thus laying the foundation of Russian Christianity. In central Asia, there were Christians in Bactria by 550 and in 635 there was a bishop at work in the capital of T'ang China. But there were losses as well as gains. The rise of Islam in the seventh century wiped out Christianity in North Africa. In the Middle East, Christianity became and has remained the faith of minority communities.

Poor Clare Nuns.
By permission of the British Library, Cott.Dom. Axvii f.74v Poor Clare Nuns.

Significant dates

280	Armenia becomes first Christian state
285	Anthony retires to the Egyptian desert
341	Ulfilas ordained as bishop of the Gothic Christians
530	Monte Cassino abbey founded by Benedict
988	Christianisation of Kiev

East and West

At the time when Constantine adopted Christianity as the religion of the empire, there were three bishops of outstanding prestige – those of Rome, Alexandria and Antioch. The bishop of Rome came to be known as Pope, while the other two were styled patriarchs. When Constantine moved his capital to Byzantium (later called Constantinople), it was felt that its bishop should also be a patriarch and this was agreed at a council held there in 381. The Council of Chalcedon in 451 raised the bishop of Jerusalem to patriarchal status also.

There were thus four patriarchs in the eastern part of the empire but only one, the Pope of Rome, in the west. When the Muslims spread their control over the Middle East, the patriarchs of Jerusalem, Antioch and Alexandria fell under their rule and were thus eliminated as rivals to the patriarch of Constantinople. When imperial authority broke down in the west under the stress of the barbarian invasions, the Pope and the other bishops became the leaders of their communities and maintained the fabric of everyday life. With a resident emperor in Constantinople, there was no room for an ecclesiastic like the Pope of Rome.

Relationships between the Pope and the Patriarch of Constantinople have been strained right down to the twentieth century, when there was a partial reconciliation. The reasons for this have included jurisdiction and the relationship with the state: eastern Christians accorded a primacy of honour to the Pope but declined to acknowledge his jurisdiction over all Christians. In the east, supreme authority was held to reside in ecumenical councils (or councils of the whole Church) but the emperor had responsibility for the administration of spiritual as well as temporal affairs. The Pope, however, saw himself as superior to all earthly rulers and this caused conflict in many western countries during the Middle Ages.

The differences between east and west went deeper than organisation.

As we have seen, the first Christians soon adopted Greek as the medium of communication. Eastern Christians continued to do so but in the west Latin became the language of the Bible, the Church and of learning in general. The linguistic difference was reflected in styles of spirituality and attitudes to holiness.

The Greek language has a flexibility Latin does not share. For Greek Christians, worship was and is the most important area of religious experience – doctrine is secondary and open to some variety. The Latin Church came to place increasing emphasis on precision and uniformity in doctrine and in worship. Thus, Roman usages superseded the worship practices of those who used the rites of the Celts, the Spaniards and the Milanese. Similarly, doctrine became more closely defined and those who deviated were severely punished and even put to death.

Christendom

The spread of Christianity into northern and western Europe meant that there was a substantial territory in which Christianity was the basis of law and custom. It was assumed that all inhabitants were Christian and that rulers had the duty of upholding the Christian faith against error and deviation. Followers of Muhammad conquered North Africa and the Middle East and even parts of Europe, notably Spain, in the seventh and eighth centuries. This meant that Christianity, which had originated in the Middle East, was effectively European and rulers rejoiced in titles like Holy Roman Emperor, Most Christian King and Defender of the Faith.

During the eleventh and twelfth centuries, the Popes created a single sophisticated structure of Church government centralised on Rome. This was in marked contrast to the development of largely independent churches in the east, each with its own head, known as autocephalous churches. The Pope had long enjoyed a primacy of honour as the guardian of the tomb of St Peter. As such, he claimed the title of Vicar (or substitute) of Peter. Pope Gregory VII (c. 1020–1085) went further and claimed to be the Vicar of Christ, saying that, as such, his duty was to take the lead in making the world holy after making the church holy. In pursuit of this aim, he and his successors enforced the celibacy of all clergy and attempted to prevent secular rulers from appointing them.

Pope Innocent III (1160–1216)

Lothar of Segni was elected bishop of Rome in 1198 and took the name Innocent III. A lawyer rather than a theologian, he established the firm

---

control of the apostolic see of Rome over the western church and his pontificate marked the culmination of the medieval papacy. Following the example of Gregory VII, Innocent did not hesitate to intervene in secular affairs where he thought a moral issue was involved, and several kings had to submit to his will.

Innocent defied conservative opinion by recognising the possibilities in the new preaching and itinerant orders of friars founded by St Francis and St Dominic and granting them exemption from episcopal jurisdiction. On the other hand, his attempt to bring the Albigenses of southern France into line resulted in a massacre, as did his sponsorship of the Fourth Crusade.

He summoned the Fourth Lateran Council in 1215, during which the doctrine of the Eucharist was defined using the word 'transubstantiation' for the first time: bread and wine remain the same in appearance but are changed in substance into the body and blood of Christ, according to this doctrine.

In 1095, Pope Urban II proclaimed a 'crusade' or holy war of the Cross. The objective was to regain control of the lands where Jesus and his apostles had walked and a Latin Kingdom of Jerusalem was established. It was short-lived, despite subsequent crusades to save it. Later crusades attacked Muslims in Spain and Egypt. The Fourth Crusade of 1204 looted Constantinople and drove a wedge between western and eastern Christians that lasted until the twentieth century. In 1453, the Muslims captured Constantinople and Russia became the heartland of eastern Christianity. The Christian presence in Central Asia faded but the Christian communities in India and Ethiopia survived.

Significant dates

1095   First Crusade
1204   Looting of Constantinople during Fourth Crusade

Julian of Norwich (1342–1420)

In the later Middle Ages, many people found an answer to their religious needs by becoming recluses instead of joining a religious order. Julian lived as a recluse near St Julian's church in Norwich, from which she probably took her name. She experienced the first of her visions on 8 May 1373. Over the next twenty years or so, she committed her reflections to writing in *Revelations of Divine Love*. She is thus the first English woman of letters and a great teacher whose influence has been felt ever since her own time.

    She is best known for the insights she derived from a hazelnut: 'In this little thing I saw three truths. The first is that God made it; the second is that God loves it; and the third is that God sustains it.' According to Julian, 'God is as really our Mother as he is our Father.' After fifteen years' reflection, she came to this conclusion: 'You would know our Lord's meaning in this thing? Know it well. Love was his meaning ... Hold on to this and you will know and understand love more and more. But you will not know or learn anything else – ever!'

(1966: 68, 151. 211f.)

The Reformations of the sixteenth century

Partly as a result of the fall of Constantinople and the migration of Greek scholars, there was a revival of interest in Classical learning in the west. Study of the Greek language opened up the Christian Scriptures in a new way and Desiderius Erasmus (1466–1536) produced an edition of the Greek New Testament in 1516. The invention of printing meant that it was widely distributed. The progress of the various reform movements in the sixteenth century owed much to both of these developments and to the growth of self-consciously national states. There were three main categories of reform movements but only one of them challenged the concept of Christendom.

Categories of reform movements

The Catholic reformation was an attempt to consolidate and reform Christendom under the continuing control of the Pope. This reached a climax in the various sessions of the Council of Trent from 1545 to 1563.

> The magisterial reformations, which were sponsored or approved by kings and other princes, repudiated the authority of the Pope but continued the assumption that all the inhabitants of the state should follow the lead of the ruler in religious as well as secular affairs.
>
> The radical reformers wished to break the link between church and state and identified the Church with the company of true believers baptised on profession of faith. They were thus known as Anabaptists, as they did not regard infant baptism as valid and aroused such fierce opposition that they survived only in protected pockets until they migrated to North America.

The interpretation of three key concepts separated the magisterial reformers from the Catholic – grace, faith and the authority of the Scriptures. The main point of dispute centred on the word 'only'. Catholics had no difficulty with grace, faith or Scripture but were unwilling to recognise them as the only means of salvation. For them, the tradition of the Church and the intercession of the saints, and especially of the Virgin Mother of Jesus, were also necessary. This was spelled out at the Council of Trent.

It was the study of the Scriptures that led men like Huldrych Zwingli (1484–1531), Martin Luther (1483–1546) and John Calvin (1509–64) to question the authority of the Pope and the means of salvation sanctioned by him. Thus, they asserted that salvation is by grace only – that is, by divine initiative. It is achieved by faith only and not earned by human efforts. The emphasis on the authority of Scripture and the translation of the Old and New Testaments into the vernacular opened up knowledge of salvation to every believer and ended the priestly monopoly of truth. This, in turn, led to changes in worship – which ceased to be in Latin – and new forms of church government involving the laity.

> *John Knox (1513–72)*
>
> John Knox is often regarded as a Scottish reformer but even if he had not returned to his native land in 1559 he would be worthy of a place among the great Protestant reformers, for he made a significant contribution to the Reformation in England, in Frankfurt and in Geneva. In England, he became a chaplain to King Edward VI and toured the

country commending the new ideas and practices. When Queen Mary came to the throne, he ministered to the English exiles in Frankfurt and Geneva. He was a prolific pamphleteer and is remembered for his *First Blast of the Trumpet against the Monstrous Regiment* [that is, rule] *of Women*. This earned him the lasting hostility of Queen Elizabeth of England and prevented his return there.

Back in Scotland, in a series of eloquent sermons he restored the enthusiasm of those who had come to despair of achieving reformation. He contributed to the key documents of the Scottish reformation, *The Confession of Faith*, *The Book of Discipline* and *The Book of Common Order*. When he was sidelined by those who felt that he was too extreme, he wrote his own *History of the Reformation in Scotland*.

Martin Luther (1483–1546) and 'justification by faith'

Martin Luther was an anti-establishment figure and one of the authors of Protestant Christianity. One key to understanding the Reformation is that it uses a different paradigm to conceive redemption than Catholic Christianity. For Catholicism, the grace which flows from Christ's sacrifice becomes a God-given dynamic within human action. But for Luther, grace is God's decision to pardon human sin. His idea of atonement flows from his idea of what Paul meant by 'justification by faith, without the works of the law' (see Chapter Three of Section Three).

Luther conceived of 'law' as the self-reliant human effort to do good. Christ saves us in such a way that 'law' is nullified. Christ's salvific work is to negate the moral law by which humanity is condemned. Luther pictures Christ as overthrowing 'law' as earlier theologians had imagined Christ triumphing over Satan. Luther takes up Paul's statement in Galatians, that Christ became a 'curse' for us. Luther's Christ is the Accursed, the one who became sin. Sin deserves death. The crucified Christ is identified with all human sin. Therefore, the law condemns and kills him. In Christ, all sin is slain. Instead of our being punished for sin, Christ is punished. In Luther's theology, that punishment excludes the participation of believers. The technical term for the Lutheran conception of Christ's work is penal substitution: instead of our being punished for sin with death, Christ is punished.

The implementing of these reforms meant that the unity of the Western Church was permanently broken. In contrast to the East, where the various national churches remained in fellowship with each other, the reformed churches of the West, collectively known as Protestant, were no longer in communion with the churches that continued to recognise the Pope and not always with each other. But in each country and locality, the Christendom idea continued and dissent from the prevailing form of Christianity was forbidden. Toleration of religious dissent did not come until the eighteenth century.

Significant dates

1516	Erasmus's edition of Greek New Testament
1517	Luther protests in Wittenberg
1519	Zwingli protests in Zurich
1536	Calvin arrives in Geneva
1545–63	Council of Trent

Christianity and European imperialism

The relationship between Christianity and European imperialism has been intricate and, at times, difficult. Between 1492 and 1914, people of European origin gradually came to dominate the world. This had important consequences for Christianity: a religion that had come to be considered as essentially European was diffused across the world. Over the same period, numbers of active, professing Christians gradually declined in Europe itself. These two developments meant the end of Christendom as a territorial entity.

To begin with, it seemed that Christendom could be extended to include the 'new' world of Central and South America, which had been conquered by Spain. The native religions were forbidden and whole populations were forcibly baptised. The success of this was more apparent than real, however, and the brutality and greed of the conquerors did nothing to commend the Christian faith to the indigenous population. The Pope assigned the newly discovered lands to the care of Spain and Portugal. Apart from Brazil, the Portuguese area was to be to the east of a line drawn in mid-Atlantic and Spain was to have the lands to the west. Portugal was unable to imitate the tactics of Spain and failed to make headway against Islam and Hinduism in the territories it controlled, much less the hinterland on which its colonies depended.

The problems of these two empires gave rise to a new development – the emergence of missionaries who sought to commend Christianity without any coercion. Many of these missionaries were Jesuits, members of the Society of Jesus, which had been founded to promote the Catholic reformation in Europe. They did not confine their activities to the Spanish and Portuguese territories and some reached China and Japan.

As northern European nations joined the movement for expansion, it became clear that the interests of the imperial powers were political, strategic and economic rather than religious. The British East India Company actually discouraged missionary activity and assumed a posture of religious neutrality. In the heyday of European expansion, the imperial powers did give protection to the missionaries in India and sub-Saharan Africa but their policy often involved the conciliation or furtherance of Islam and other religions. The nineteenth century was a time of considerable Protestant missionary activity. In addition to evangelistic work, the missionaries contributed a great deal to educational and hospital development.

Mary Mitchell Slessor (1848–1915)

Mary Slessor has become an icon of the modern missionary movement. After working in a textile mill in Dundee, Scotland, she persuaded the United Presbyterian Church to send her to the mission station in Calabar, Nigeria. Despite her limited schooling, she proved to be a brilliant linguist and her fluency in Efik and Ibo enabled her to become an effective opponent of witchcraft, twin-killing, trial by ordeal and human sacrifice.

She constantly argued for the extension of the mission beyond the townships of Calabar and worked in Okoyong, Itu and Arochuku. In 1898, she was appointed vice-consul in Okoyong, arguably the first woman magistrate in the British Empire; and in 1905, she was appointed Vice President of the Itu Native Court, in recognition of her ability to settle disputes amicably.

She adopted several African children, mainly twins and orphans, and took them home with her to Scotland during her periods of leave. This gave her a high profile and commended her work to the Scottish public.

From the seventeenth century, thousands of Europeans settled in North America. They came from a variety of Christian backgrounds, including the radical wing of the Reformation. Baptists, Congregationalists, Mennonites and Quakers are among the modern descendants of the radical reformers. They have achieved an importance in North America that they did not have in Europe. The Methodist revival in the eighteenth century under John and Charles Wesley soon spread to America and the various British colonies. The other Protestant churches, the Roman Catholics and Orthodox are also well-represented. European settlers in South Africa, Australia and New Zealand also brought their Christian traditions with them. The Dutch Reformed Church has been very influential in South Africa and the Orthodox churches are well represented in Australia.

There was also, during the eighteenth and nineteenth centuries, a considerable amount of forced migration from Africa to America in the shape of the slave trade. Despite the harsh treatment they received from Christian slavers and masters, most of the slaves became Christian, mainly Catholic in South America and Protestant in North America. Certain indigenous belief systems crossed the Atlantic with the slaves and were combined with Catholic Christianity in the Caribbean and in South America. Voodoo in Haiti and Jamaica originates from this process.

During the eighteenth century, religious dissent became legitimate and Christian denominations proliferated. There were also intellectual challenges to Christianity in the various movements known as the Enlightenment. In answer to David Hume's scepticism, Thomas Reid developed the philosophy of Common Sense, which was popularised in America by John Witherspoon, one of the signatories of the Declaration of Independence. In the nineteenth century, the works of Karl Marx and Charles Darwin posed further challenges to received Christian thinking.

By 1900, the United States had replaced Europe as the main centre of Christian activity but its constitution ensured a separation of church and state. State churches remained in Europe but increasingly it was felt that mere membership of them did not guarantee 'real' Christianity and that individual conversion was needed for vital faith.

Christianity in the twentieth century – and beyond

During the twentieth century, the centre of gravity of Christianity moved from the northern hemisphere to the south. The development of the World Council of Churches provides an illustration of this. At its first assembly in 1948, there were 450 delegates but only 30 from Asia, Africa, Latin America and the East. There were 966 delegates at the eighth assembly in 1998, the majority of whom were not from Europe.

John R. Mott (1865–1955)

Born in Sullivan county, New York, and converted while a student at Cornell university, Mott became a world Christian who travelled two million miles in support of the YMCA and the World Student Christian Federation, of which he was the founder and first general secretary. He was known and trusted by students and church leaders in every continent and even consulted by heads of state. A Japanese Christian leader described him as 'father of the young people of the world'.

In 1910, he was the chairman of the International Missionary Conference in Edinburgh and so became the 'father of the modern ecumenical movement' that developed from that conference. In 1946, he shared the Nobel Peace Prize. Two years later, he was the first speaker at the inaugural assembly of the World Council of Churches and elected honorary president. A prolific author, he was never ordained and – despite a Methodist background – did not identify firmly with any denomination.

At the beginning of the twentieth century, it was reckoned that the Christian population of Africa was about 10 million. By the mid-1990s, it was estimated at 307 million. On the other hand, the decline in Europe became still more marked. Attempts were made in communist countries to abolish Christianity altogether but only in Albania, a largely Muslim country, did open religious activity cease. The fall of communist regimes enabled some recovery but the Church has not regained its pre-revolutionary power and it has been challenged by new religious communities from East and West.

The religious character of Europe was greatly changed during the second half of the twentieth century. Extensive immigration from India and Pakistan led to the establishment of Muslim, Hindu and Sikh communities. Thus, although most countries remained officially and nominally Christian, they became effectively multi-faith and multi-cultural.

In North America, Christianity flourished for most of the century and, especially in its conservative forms, was widely associated with traditional American cultural values. It was quietly accepted by the Inuit people of the Arctic region and less enthusiastically by the Native Americans. But towards the end of the century, Islam attracted notable converts and increased in influence.

In Latin America, despite Spanish attempts to eradicate them, indigenous religions survived and their followers often combined their rituals and beliefs with those of Catholic Christianity. During the century, there was a huge amount of urbanisation, which, in turn, created extensive social deprivation. 'Liberation theology' is an umbrella term for a movement, mainly but not exclusively within the Roman Catholic Church, that has sought to make the Christian message once more good news for the poor by placing emphasis on action – and sometimes radical action. Official church leaders have, however, been lukewarm in their support.

Protestantism made considerable inroads into what had hitherto been Catholic territory. The most successful form of Protestantism was Pentecostalism, a movement that places great emphasis on the power and the gifts of the Holy Spirit and that is institutionally flexible and adaptable.

During the 1880s, there came into currency the slogan 'The Evangelisation of the World in this Generation'; but the old religions of Asia did not collapse under the impact of Christian missionary activity and in most Asian countries Christianity remains the faith of a small but not insignificant minority. The Philippines has a Christian majority and South Korea has very large congregations of Christians and is active in missionary work. To the surprise of many, Chinese Christianity not only survived but also expanded without any assistance from Western churches. In 1950, the Christian population was estimated at well under a million; at the end of the century, estimates varied between 8 and 13 million. Many overseas Chinese also became Christians in countries like Indonesia, Singapore and Malaysia.

Christianity has had a long history in India but it is still thought of as foreign and associated with former colonial powers. Christ was honoured in much Hindu thought during the twentieth century and there was a risk of Christianity being absorbed into Hinduism. As in the early church, the socially disadvantaged have been attracted to Christianity. The establishment of the Church of South India in 1947 was a landmark in the effort to secure greater Christian unity (known as the ecumenical movement).

The strongest impact of Christianity in Asia has been upon tribal cultures with primal religions. Thus, there are significant numbers of Christians in countries like Burma, Thailand, Sumatra and Vietnam. Christians have not fared well in largely Islamic countries like Pakistan. Despite their small numbers in relation to the total population of the continent, Asian Christians – like D. T. Niles from Sri Lanka – have shown that they have much to give to Christianity as a whole.

As already noted, there was spectacular growth in sub-Saharan Africa during the twentieth century. African Christianity has had to come to terms with realities of life that are not part of recent Western experience: ancestor-worship, witchcraft, sorcery and primitive healing practices. New models of church life have been devised and new movements have developed. Some are similar to earlier patterns of Christianity but many are unique to Africa, showing the adaptability of the faith.

Daniel Thambyrajah Niles (1908–70)

A Tamil fourth-generation Christian, D. T. Niles was born at Jaffna in northern Sri Lanka. After theological study at Bangalore, he was ordained to the Methodist ministry in 1936. He came to prominence at the International Missionary Conference at Tambaram in 1938 and for the rest of his life was a well-known and trusted ecumenical leader. He founded the East Asia Christian Council and edited its *Hymnal,* to which he contributed forty-five English verse translations of Asian hymns.

He preached at the first assembly of the World Council of Churches in 1948 but made this comment about it: 'The older churches were discussing the reasons and circumstances which had led to their earlier divorce; the younger churches were only just getting married and did not wish to be asked their opinion on the subjects which had led to the quarrels between the older churches' (1972: 203f.). He preached at the fourth assembly of the WCC at Uppsala in 1968 and was elected one of its presidents.

He spoke and wrote fluently in English (over twenty books) but needed to sing Tamil lyrics to recover his spiritual balance.

During the nineteenth century, it had seemed possible for a new Christendom to be set up in the Pacific islands, for Tonga, Samoa and Fiji were converted en masse with their rulers. During the twentieth century, this was halted by colonial developments such as the importation of Indian workers to the sugar plantations of Fiji. But there was quite considerable Christian growth in Melanesia and the island of New Guinea. Sadly, the part of the island in Indonesian control was the scene of savage religious strife.

Australians and New Zealanders of European origin have shared in the general decline of European Christianity but their indigenous peoples have shown initiatives in combining Christianity with their native culture.

Olive Mary Winchester (1880–1947)

Born in Monson, Maine, a graduate in Classics at Harvard and the first woman graduate in Divinity of the University of Glasgow, Olive Winchester is thought to have been the first woman to be ordained in

Scotland. She was ordained as a minister of the newly formed Pentecostal Church of Scotland at Parkhead, Glasgow, in 1912. Five years later, a Scotswoman, Jane Brayton Sharpe, was ordained in the same church.

Other denominations were slow to follow. Vera Findlay was ordained at Partick Congregational Church, Glasgow, in 1928 but was not recognised by the Congregational Union of Scotland until the following year. Elizabeth Barr was ordained by the United Free Church of Scotland at Auchterarder in 1935 and became its first woman Moderator of General Assembly in 1960. It was not until 1969 that Catherine McConnachie was ordained by the Presbytery of Aberdeen of the Church of Scotland.

At the beginning of the twenty-first century, Christianity is more widespread, diverse and varied than at any other period in its history. Western Christianity may well have to realise that the future of the faith in human terms is with the Christians of the southern hemisphere.

Useful dates

1906	Pentecostal revival, Los Angeles
1910	Edinburgh International Missionary Conference
1947	Establishment of Church of South India
1948	First assembly of World Council of Churches, Amsterdam
1979	Churches in China opened for public worship

Christianity and technology

During the twentieth century, Christian churches made increasing use of modern technology. In the United States of America, Charles E. Fuller began an evangelistic radio ministry in the 1930s, which attained its peak in 1942, reaching over 20 million listeners to 436 radio stations. Television has given scope to tele-evangelists in many parts of the world, especially in the United States.

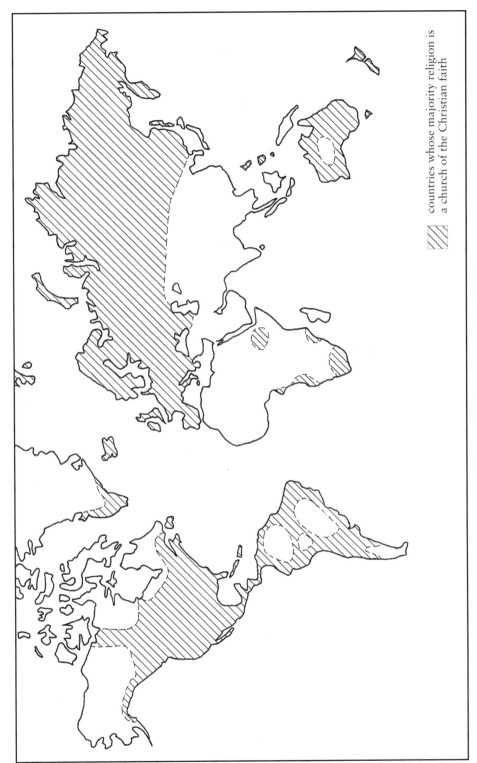

Distribution of Christian countries (2003)

countries whose majority religion is
a church of the Christian faith

John Reith, who is widely regarded as the creator of the British Broadcasting Corporation, encouraged the churches to make full use of radio and, after some hesitation, church services were broadcast. The televising of the coronation of Queen Elizabeth II, basically a Church of England service, in 1953 was another breakthrough. Since then, it has been acceptable for all kinds of services to be televised.

Commercial radio and television have also been hospitable to Christianity and some churches have paid for advertising space in both. The development of the Internet has also given scope for advertising and many churches have created their own websites.

In 1970, the Church of Scotland set up a Science, Religion and Technology Project to study the impact of new technologies on society and to provide a forum for those wishing to shape the Church's response to some of the most pressing issues of the twentieth and twenty-first centuries.

Further reading

Chidester, D. (2000), *Christianity – A Global History*, London: Penguin.
Green, V. (1998), *A New History of Christianity*, Stroud: Sutton Publishing.
Hastings, A. (1994), *The Church in Africa, 1450–1950*, Oxford: Clarendon Press.
Hastings, A. (ed.) (1999), *A World History of Christianity*, London: Cassell.
Walls, A. (1998), 'Christianity', in John R. Hinnells (ed.), *A New Handbook of Living Religions*, London: Penguin.

The following books are all lavishly illustrated

Chadwick, O. (1999), *A History of Christianity*, London: Phoenix.
Dowley, T. (ed.) (1990), *A Lion Handbook: The History of Christianity*, Oxford: Lion.
McManners, J. (ed.) (1990), *The Oxford Illustrated History of Christianity*, Oxford: Oxford University Press.

Questions

1. Very broadly, outline the movement of Christianity from Israel-Palestine to the rest of the world.

2. What was significant about the conversion of Constantine?

3. What do we mean by the term 'Christendom'?

4. What were the main points of dispute in the reformations of the sixteenth century?

5. What changes has Christianity seen over the last century?

CHAPTER TWO

Christology from the Apostolic Age to Chalcedon

Francesca Aran Murphy

Images of Christ

The post-Christian West has absorbed Christianity for two millennia. Our cultural media still project diffused images of Christ. One is the death-to-life image. Some people said that, because it is about a monster from outer space dying and returning to life, the movie *ET* was about the Resurrection. We are sometimes told that, back in the Middle Ages, most people were illiterate, so their 'Bibles' had to be the mosaics, stained-glass windows, paintings and statues in their church buildings. But today, it is said, everyone can read, so we get our knowledge of

Christ from text books. In fact, modern Christians are as much affected by images of Christ as medieval people were. We pick up pictures of Jesus from films, cartoons, comic-books and TV documentaries. We can see the ancient, medieval Russian and baroque icons of Christ by visiting a Church. We can also find generalised parables of Christ's story outside of explicitly Christian sources.

Even though tradition is not technically normative in the Protestant churches, they have deep-rooted traditions about Christ. These are expressed, for instance, in African-American gospel music and in Methodist or Lutheran hymns. These musical icons reflect particular Christian spiritualities. Theories about Christ spring from symbols the imaginations of believers have already assented to. The deepest and most lasting cognitive or 'book' definitions of Christ build on the popular faith of a community, be it the community of Benedictine monks around Anselm in the eleventh century, or a South American base-community.

A biblical story shows Christ riding a donkey into Jerusalem. A donkey is an undignified seat. Christ receives an ironic crown from one of the Roman militia who put the 'king of the Jews' to death. Paul said that those who worship this crucified man are 'fools for Christ' (1 Corinthians 4: 10; cf. 1 Corinthians 1: 27–8).

Paul imagined Christ as one who lowered himself, 'emptying' himself of divine glory (Philippians 2: 5–11). Kenotic Christologies are built on the image of the Humiliated One. Others are based on different biblical images. Athanasius saw Christ as the Immortaliser. Eastern Orthodox churches pictured him as the Cosmic Emperor. Martin Luther identified Christ as the Accursed. One reason for the complexity of Christology is the diversity of normative, biblical symbols of Christ.

Words with the suffix 'logy' are sciences. Christo-logy is the science of Christ. It is based on faith in normative guidelines, like the Bible, the creeds of the Church and tradition. In a negative sense, norms rule out some deductions. For instance, the Creeds speak of God as a Trinity, one God in three persons. So a Christology that claimed that Christ alone is God, minus the Father and the Spirit, would set itself outside Christian norms. Positively, Scripture, Creeds and tradition lay out the notions of Christ it is fertile for systematic theology to develop.

Christology has two parts. One is the 'Person of Christ'. It thinks about who Christ is. It meditates on Christ's being as Second person of the Trinity. The theology of the Person of Christ is about who he is, his identity. The second part is the 'Work of Christ'. It depicts Christ's works of salvation, which relate to humanity and the cosmos. The Work of Christ connects God to creation. In principle, one cannot separate who and what a person is from what that person does. Character and vocation go together. Historically, images of Christ's functions have impacted on ideas about his being, and vice versa. The experiential matrix of Christology is often wired to images of Christ's salvific actions. Salvific images speak to human spirituality. The theoretical matrix of Christology germinates ideas about the person of Christ, his nature or being. The task of Christology is to systematise biblical symbols. It unifies them by thinking them through and relating them to a comprehensive notion.

The Christology of the primitive Church

The disciples put their faith in Christ because of his cumulative impact on them. The New Testament is focused by an image of faith, a memory image.

> [The] evangelists did not put together their picture of Christ from individual traditions; rather they began with the overall picture of Jesus and incorporated the individual stories as illustrations of their faith. They did not want to create a mosaic but to offer a portrait of the whole.
>
> R. Schnackenburg, *Jesus in the Gospels: A Biblical Christology* (1995: 321–2)

Some of Jesus's Jewish contemporaries expected that God would soon enter history, bringing about a 'Kingdom'. Jesus claimed that the Kingdom of God was close to those who heard his own words (Matthew 17: 20). The signs of the in-breaking of the Kingdom were his miraculous healings and his power over Satanic forces. Following him was more important than keeping central religious laws, like burying one's parents (Matthew 8: 21–22; Luke 59–60).

Within Judaism, sinners were reconciled to God by offering sacrifice in the Temple. Jesus overrode this system. He offered forgiveness not just to well-intentioned people who fell below the mark but to bad people. He did this on the ground that God had made him 'something greater' than the Temple. Jesus had an apocalyptic vision of history in which he was the protagonist.

After Jesus was crucified, and no worldly kingdom emerged from the heavens, Jesus's followers grew in numbers. They believed that Jesus had been resurrected from the dead. Jewish apocalyptic expectation contained the image of a bodily resurrection of all believers. Primitive Christians believed that Jesus's resurrection was the prophetic sign that there would be a resurrection of all peoples. Their slogan was Marantha, Aramaic for 'Lord, come!'

Wisdom Christology: Christ the Logos

Jewish Wisdom writings depict a supernatural, personified Wisdom. Apocalyptic-wisdom texts from the inter-testamental period, like Enoch and the Wisdom of Solomon, describe Wisdom descending from heaven as a person.

> The Lord created me at the beginning of his work . . . Ages ago I was set up..when he marked out the foundations of the earth, then I was beside him like a master workman.
>
> Proverbs 8: 22–30

Greek philosophers called universal reason 'the Logos'. Universal reason was divine. The Jewish philosopher Philo of Alexandria (50 BC–50 AD) identified the Torah, the Word of God, with the Logos. Philo said God spoke the cosmos into existence through the Logos.

The first Christian theologians drew on Jewish literature for images of cosmic Wisdom acting in history. Paul describes Jesus as the 'image of the invisible God', in whom all things were created, in whom 'everything coheres' and who is the 'first born from the dead' (Colossians 1: 15–20). Paul pictures Christ descending from a state of glory to that of a slave (Philemon 2: 6–11). In Hebrews 1: 2–4, the writer gives a song of praise for Jesus, 'the exact representation' of the 'being' of God. In these three acclamations, Jesus is imaged as a supernatural being who descends from heaven and returns there after accomplishing salvation.

Paul tells his readers that a baptised person is 'in Christ' or 'in the Lord' (Galatians 3: 28; Romans 8: 1; Philemon 3: 8). Christians form a single body in Christ (1 Corinthians 12: 12–30). Christ is a Power whose force contains all believers. This Power instantiates a new era in history. Paul claims that 'if anyone is in Christ there is a new creation' (2 Corinthians 5: 17). It is unlikely that the writer conceived the One who incorporates the human race into himself as being simply an extraordinary human being.

John 1: 1–14 is the definitive statement of 'Wisdom' or Logos Christology. It states that the Logos/Word was God and became flesh.

The Son

In Mark's stories about Jesus's baptism and transfiguration (1: 11 and 9: 7), God the Father gives Jesus the role of Son. Jesus ascribes that role to himself in some parables (Mark 12: 6–7, the parable of the vineyard) and in relation to knowledge of the last day (even 'the Son' does not know when it will be – Mark 13: 32). As Son, Jesus has been 'sent' by the Father. The most striking synoptic saying about Jesus's Sonship is: 'All things are delivered unto me of my Father: and no man knoweth the Son, but the Father; neither knoweth any man the Father, save the Son, and he to whom the Son will reveal him' (Matthew 11: 27; Luke 10: 21 ff.).

The image of Jesus as Son was important to early believers. They remembered him as praying to God as 'Abba', Father. Paul quotes the Aramaic 'Abba', Father, when he describes how Christians pray to the Father, in the Spirit. Christians become the children of God through Jesus's filial relationship to the Father.

Paul calls Christ 'Kurios' 184 times. In the Septuagint, 'Kurios' means Lord: it is a Greek translation of Hebrew names for God. Paul says that the 'Kurios Christos', the Lord Jesus, will have the role of judge at the end of time. This is a role that hitherto was ascribed to the God of Israel. Paul also transfers some of the prophets' references to Israel's God to Jesus (Joel 2: 32–Romans 10: 13).

Mark makes Jesus's actions echo Old Testament images of divine actions. Mark's Jesus, calming the Gennesaret Sea (Mark 4: 39) is intended to recall God creating the world, overcoming chaos.

The roles and functions given to Jesus by the New Testament writers include co-creating the universe, being the agent of salvation for humanity and the cosmos, containing the new humanity in himself, and Sonship of God the Father. In this way, primitive Christians incorporated him into Jewish monolatry (worship of one God).

Logos Christology: The cosmic-historical Christ

'Soter' is Greek for saviour. The technical word for the study of the 'Work of Christ' is soteriology, the 'logy' or science of salvation. Primitive Christian soteriology was exclusive: the only story that came into it was the Judaeo-Christian one. So long as Christians were communicating with people who shared their belief that God was behind Jewish history, it worked to argue that Jesus is the Savior because he fulfils the Hebrew prophecies.

Christ as Everyman: Anakephalaiosis / recapitulation

Paul described Christ as the new Adam. Humanity begins again in him, after Adam's false start. Christ is Everyman, the representative human being, getting it right this time around. Irenaeus (130–200) also conceived of Christ as the 'second Adam'. He claimed that human history, and the physical cosmos, are renewed and 'recapitulated' in Christ. To recapitulate is to sum up. The evolution of nature and of humanity attains its full flowering in Christ.

The Greek for recapitulation is 'anakephalaiosis', which literally means 'into the head'. Irenaeus' conceived of the work of Christ as drawing the body of humanity into himself, its head. Irenaeus's Christ summarises the achievements of humanity. The examples Irenaeus gives of the historical figures who mark out the pathway to Christ are Old Testament heroes.

Inclusivism – Christ as the fulfilment of Greek wisdom

To fulfil the prophecies of a particular religion seems to answer to one local human expectation. Once they travelled beyond the Jewish social context, Christian evangelists moved to the idea that Christ fulfils deep-rooted human desires. For a Greek intellectual, the deepest human desire is to see absolute truth, beauty and goodness. Christians now presented Christ as the reality to which this human dream corresponds.

At the end of the second century, Christian apologists began to inch towards an inclusive soteriology. Justin Martyr and Clement of Alexandria argued that Christ fulfils the human quest for truth. Clement's soteriology is inclusive because it says that, beyond God's election of Israel, God has given other civilisations signposts pointing them towards Christ. Clement claims that Christ makes contact with what humanity wants to become. To be Christian is to become fully human.

Stoics called God 'ho Logos' – the Reason. Stoics also spoke of the *logoi spermatikoi*, the rational structure sown into everything in nature, like its genetic make-up. For Stoics, the human mind is the best earthly mirror of the Logos.

> Baptism is called an illumination whereby we contemplate the sacred light of salvation, that is to say, whereby we are enabled to see God.
>
> Clement of Alexandria (Bettenson 1956, 1976: 178–9)

Clement lived in Alexandria, a centre of Hellenistic philosophy. He told Alexandrian intellectuals: 'You believe in a universal rationality. The Logos in whom you believe *is* Christ. Christianity is the true philosophy. If you want the complete truth, let Christ enlighten your mind' (Bettenson 1956, 1976: 178–9).Clement conceives the person of Christ as the

Logos, reason. Baptism reminded early Christians of Christ's restoration of sight to the blind. Clement pictures the work of Christ as enlightening us, empowering us to see truth.

Apologists like Clement claimed that Christ is the archetype behind Graeco-Roman myth. They described him as the 'true Orpheus', the 'true Hercules', or the 'true Odysseus'. From the late second and third centuries, there are many pictures and statues of Christ in which Graeco-Roman figures are morphed into the image of Christ. For Clement, and those who painted the resurrected Christ as the Risen Sun, the 'true Sun-God', there is no parity between Christ and Greek wisdom or mythology. Christ includes the whole human quest for the divine because he alone contains, orders and fulfils human desire.

Christ the victor: Death identified with the Devil

In Genesis, after eating the fruit forbidden to him by God, Adam was cast out of Eden. This story responds to the human question about death. Adam's expulsion from Eden means that, through disobedience, humanity has forfeited life with God.

In the inter-testamental period, more scenes and characters were woven into the story. The 'place' to which the dead depart is the region of darkness, the lair of Satan. 'Death' owns the mortal souls of human beings because of the fall of Adam.

In the synoptics, Christ withstands the temptations of Satan and exorcises demons. Paul imagines Christ as delivering humanity from the bondage of death (Romans 8: 21) and as combating the principalities and powers (Romans 8: 38). Paul contrasts the life force of the body of Christ with the death force of the law. One theme in John's gospel is the conflict of light, and its allies, with the agents of darkness. The Book of Revelation describes the conquest of Satan. In Revelation 1: 17, Christ says 'I have died and come back to life, and I have the keys of Hades.' Christ alone was not trapped by death but escaped, carrying the key. Christians put the resurrection at the centre of their faith.

The rescue mission

Christians of the first few centuries pictured the work of Christ as a rescue mission. They conceived it on the analogy of Old Testament rescuer figures like David, Daniel and especially Jonah. A recurrent early symbol of Christ defeating a hostile power is that of Jonah struggling with the whale. The Sea-Monster stands for the cold, overwhelming, dark water of death. Early Christians pictured Christ as a hero who rescues us from death. Many Christian statuettes from the first three centuries image Jonah defeating the whale. They represent Christ defeating death and the Devil.

The Church Fathers describe the work of Christ as a combat with Satan. To fight him, Christ enters the realm of death. The Logos-Hero defeats Satan by hiding his divinity in his mortal flesh. Origen (184–254) thought that the Devil was tricked by Christ's humanity into receiving the immortal Logos into hell. Bad move for the Devil because the Logos, as immortal reason and light, vanquishes death and darkness.

Gregory of Nyssa (331–95) pictured Christ as the fish-hook on which the Devil-Sea-Monster is impaled. The 'bait' is the mortal flesh of Christ, the hook the eternal Word. There are many patristic and medieval pictures of this. A novelist or a film director tells a story by building up a sequence of images and actions. They have to use their reason to make the narrative coherent. But the core element is the story itself, not its logical explanation. Christian doctrines are built around the dramatic core of the biblical narrative. The Christ-Trickster image connects the conversion experience of liberation to a story that speaks to human hope.

Tricking the Devil might seem to make God behave immorally. So some Church fathers emphasised that God has justice on His side. The Devil took what was not rightly his, in seizing the unfallen, sinless humanity of Christ. The thief deserves to be deceived, it was suggested. The defeat of evil runs with the cosmic grain, not against it.

Does the combat conception of atonement echo the Manichaean idea of the cosmos as a battle ground of two equal forces, one good and one bad? The Church Fathers who taught a combat idea of atonement included Irenaeus, who was remorselessly hostile to Gnosticism. None of the Church Fathers thought that the Devil had a hope in hell. For them, the power of Satan extends to mortal humanity but is not comparable to that of God. But if the whole story soteriology tells is the defeat of the Devil, it echoes the dualistic notion of two gods.

Deification

Hellenistic Platonism and Stoicism were consciousness-raising schools, offering exercises in self-immortalisation. One trained for immortality by identifying oneself with that which is immortal in oneself. This is one's mind. In its reasoning, the human mind participates in the eternal Logos. Greek philosophers said that the logos in our mind is divine and immortal in and of itself. By locating one's identity in one's logos, or spiritual reason, one works out for immortality.

Athanasius (296–273) lived in Alexandria and among the monks in the Egyptian desert. Earlier Christian apologists claimed that the highest exercise of philosophy is being a Christian. Athanasius wrapped both the Alexandrian Logos Christology and the combat conception of atonement around the idea of Christ as the Immortaliser. He set out his view in *On the Incarnation of the Word*.

Athanasius could not say, like the Greeks, that the human soul is naturally divine. In Judaeo-Christian thinking, no created entity is inherently immortal. In the Bible, everything made by God depends on God's act of creation and is contingent. Athanasius argues that, when God made Adam, he gave him the gift of immortality. A gift can be lost. At the Fall, Adam lost the gift of immortality. So fallen humanity owes its life to Satan.

Christ is Everyman, identical to God as Logos and identical to human beings as man. At his crucifixion, Christ gives the Devil the death that is owed him. He dies on behalf of all. Because he is Everyman, Christ can pass on his divinity to us. Athanasius conceives the work of Christ as the deification of Christians. Salvation is conceived as being divinised by the Logos.

God became man so that man could become God.

Athanasius, *On the Incarnation of the Word*, 54

With Athanasius, Christ's work as 'death defeater' is turned into Christ the Immortaliser of believers. Thus, the image of combat between good and evil becomes a thread in a wider tapestry. The defeat of Satan is a means to Christ's ultimate mission, of restoring immortality to the human race. God's design is not undone by evil.

The Ecumenical Council of Nicaea (325)

An Ecumenical Council is one at which the universal Church is represented and which the whole Church formally agrees to. Nicaea was to be the first of these.

Arius (256–336)

Neo-Platonist teachers conceived of God as the One, out of whom lesser divine powers emanated. The higher divine powers flow out of the One, the unknowable Deity. They produce a continuum between One and the material world.

Arius's sayings

'God has originated an only Son...his perfect creature.' (*Letter to Alexandria*)

'We do not go along with those who constantly say, "Always God, always Son."' (*Letter to Eusebius*)

'There was when he was not.' (*Thalia*)

'The Son is neither unoriginated nor belongs in any way to the Unoriginated.'

Arius in J. Pelikan (1971)

Defining Christ as 'Logos' leaves the field open for interpreting what status the Logos has in relation to the divine. Does it mean he is God in the same sense as God the Father? Arius was a presbyter in Alexandria. He was a Neo-Platonist. He taught that the Father is the One, and Christ the Logos is the highest created being. For Arius, the idea that the Logos came into being clinched the matter: Christ is not identical to the One. Arius argued that, since Jesus lived and died as a human being, he could not be God in the absolute sense – for God is impassible. Moreover, to say that God is both Father and Son would introduce duality into God. Defined as the One, God does not admit of duality.

In 318, Alexander, bishop of Alexandria, ordered Arius to stop teaching that Christ is lesser than, or subordinate to, God the Father. Arius reacted by putting his views into pop songs, which were sung on the streets of Alexandria. Early in 325, Alexander excommunicated Arius. Alexander was defended by Athanasius, at this time a deacon in Alexandria.

Some bishops inclined to a subordinationist view of Christ. Eusebius, bishop of Caesaria, overturned Arius's excommunication. The bishop of Caesaria composed a splendid comparison of Christ, the created image of God, with the human Roman emperor, Constantine. Arius also found a friend in Eusebius of Nicomedia. For the subordinationists, God is the Unoriginated. Because Christ is originated, they said, he is not identical in being to God the Father.

The emperor Constantine (274–337)

In 312, the Roman emperor Constantine made an alliance with the Christian God. From a politician's perspective, religions function to give society shared moral norms and a common mythology. This is what

Constantine hoped Christianity could achieve for the Roman Empire. A decade after his conversion, he was displeased to discover that Eastern Christians were fighting in the streets and issuing mutual anathemas.

Eusebius of Caesaria was a theological advisor to the Emperor. After Eusebius revoked Arius's excommunication, Constantine exhorted the Church to call a Council to settle their differences. It will have seemed probable to Constantine, as to most observers trained in Hellenistic philosophy, that the subordinationists' Christology was the most rational, and thus the most likely to be ratified in Council.

The Creed of Nicaea (325)

Three hundred bishops, and onlookers, such as Constantine and Athanasius, gathered at Nicaea. The assembled bishops drew up a Creed intended for the acceptance of the entire Christian people. It stated that Christ the Son is God in the same way that God the Father is God.

The Creed of Nicaea

We believe in one God, the Father almighty,
maker of all things visible and invisible;
and in one Lord Jesus Christ, the Son of God,
begotten from the Father, only-begotten, that is,
from the substance of the Father,
God from God, Light from Light, true God from true God,
begotten not made,
of the same substance (homoousion) with the Father,
through whom all things came into being, things
in heaven and things on earth,
who for us men and for our salvation came down
and became incarnate, becoming man,
suffered and rose again on the third day,
ascended to the heavens,
and will come to judge the living and the dead;
and in the Holy Spirit.

T. Herbert Bindley, *The Oecumenical Documents of the Faith* (1899)

The Arian party had argued that Christ is subordinate to the Father, just as anything that is made is lesser than its creator; a table is lesser than, and different from, the carpenter who makes it. The Creed of Nicaea states that Christ is 'begotten not made'. That means that the

Father does not invent a new and different substance in Christ. The Creed uses the image of 'Light from Light' because it indicates the reproduction of the same 'substance'.

To make an unequivocal statement that Father and Son are identically God, the Creed of Nicaea used a word that is not in the Bible. This word is 'homoousios'. The Greek 'homo' means 'the same', as in 'homogenised' milk, which is the same throughout; the Greek word 'ousios' means 'being'. To say that Father and Son are 'homoousios' means that they are the same being. Father and Son exist by one and the same act of being. They are identically God.

The pro-Nicaea theologians and the subordinationists were equally well-versed in Greek philosophy. Modern Christian historians tend to consider that, with Arius, philosophical reason came first, and then he fitted the biblical testimony around it. Because ancient Christians destroyed them, we possess too few of Arius's writings to make an accurate assessment of his motivations. Arius believed his Christology was legitimated by Scripture.

In any single society, it is possible to define everyone's status with reference to their position on the social spectrum. Hellenistic Platonism conceived God and cosmos as a single spectrum, embracing the most high One, lower divine beings, the emperor, slaves and clods of earth. Subordinationists like Arius and Eusebius of Caesaria asked: where on the spectrum do we put Christ?

Athanasius: God the Creator

Philosophical reflection on the Bible's assertions about divine creation (Genesis 1, Isaiah 40: 26, 28; 42: 5; 44: 24; 45: 12, 18; 48: 13; 51: 16; Hosea 13: 4 and so on) led Athanasius to conceive the cosmos as not merely being ordered within reality by God. The cosmos was more contingent than that: it was created out of nothing and preserved in being by God. The mark of God is to be Creator. The mark of the creature is that it owes its reality and being to God's action. God is outside the created spectrum. Being God is thus an either/or matter. For Athananius, the crucial question for Christology is: is Christ creature or Creator?

Nicaea excludes the notion that there are lesser and greater levels at which Deity can be possessed. Either one is God or one is not. Since the divine Father and Son are homoousios, everything that belongs to God belongs wholly and equally to both Father and Son.

In *On the Incarnation of the Word*, Athanasius likens Christ to the Stoics' *logoi spermatikoi*, the eternal 'seeds' of reason. For Athanasius, Christ is both *logoi spermatikoi*, the universal rationality of the cosmos, and the incarnation of that rationality, in the man Jesus Christ, who lived and died under Pontius Pilate. It is as God the Logos that Christ imparts immortality to the human race. A God who 'became man so that man could become God' had to be wholly divine, wholly Creator. Athanasius said that Christ's work of deification requires that he be what he imparts – that is, God.

A new question: The relationship of divinity and humanity in Christ

The idea that Jesus was a God who only appeared to be human is called docetism, from the Greek 'dokeo', 'I appear'. A docetic image of Christ makes him a divine Superman pretending to be a human Clark Kent. Since the early second century, when it rejected the Gnostic gospels, which presented docetic images of Christ, the Church had resisted the smoke-and-mirrors 'incarnation' of docetism. Christ had to be seen as wholly God and wholly human. Humanity and divinity are marked by different activities or natures. If so, then how are God and man related within Christ?

Human nature is capable of some actions but not others. The human self, a 'minded body', is at home in the medium of time. Humans can learn, eat and sleep, enjoy friendship and weep over a friend's death. As eternal Creator, outside the spectrum in which becomings and changes occur, God does not act in these ways. God is not material: his mind is not bodied. Incorporeal being cannot hunger or thirst. As limitless power and life, God is omniscient and can overturn the laws of nature. In that case, what in Christ weeps over Lazarus? What in Christ raises Lazarus from death? How do divinity and humanity co-exist and inter-act in Christ?

From the early fifth century, the two Eastern centres of Antioch and Alexandria had different Christologies. Difference swiftly turned into theological warfare. The Antiochenes imagined the Alexandrians were repeating the errors of Apollinarius, or that they were docetists. The Alexandrians thought the Antiochenes were adoptionists, disciples of Paul of Samosata.

Paul of Samosata: Adoptionism

Paul, bishop of Samosata, became Patriarch of Antioch in 260. Paul read the synoptic account of the baptism literally. The Father's words to Jesus here recall Psalm 2: 'You are my son; today I have begotten you.' Paul suggested that the Logos entered Jesus at his baptism – that is, Jesus was not Logos as from eternity. He was adopted as Son at the baptism. Paul's Christology was condemned in 270. It was described as the heresy of adoptionism.

Apollinarius (310–90): Humanity as 'flesh'

Apollinarius was a disciple of Athanasius. He drank in the Alexandrian Logos Christology. The Stoics conceived of the human mind as a mirror-copy of the divine Logos. Everyone has a bit of 'logic' in them, in their reasoning power; through it, they imitate divine reason. If we say Christ is *the* divine Logos, why should he need a second, human back-up copy logos alongside it? Apollinarius said that Christ the divine Logos has no human mind. For a Greek intellectual, reasoning is the distinctive human power. By asserting that Christ has no human mind, Apollinarius was saying that Christ has no human nature. He is totally divine. Christ's humanity is merely the flesh that clothes his deity.

The Greek formula Apollinarius used to express his Christology was *mia phusis*: 'mia' is Greek for 'one', 'phusis' means 'nature', as in physics. Apollinarius conceived of just one 'physics', one operational system, in Christ – divinity. He called Jesus a 'celestial man'.

The Ecumenical Council of Constantinople (381)

The Council of Constantinople was held to confirm the doctrine of the Trinity, affirming that Father, Son and Spirit are co-equally God. Constantinople also condemned Apollinarius's Christology. One of the leading theologians at this Council was Gregory Nazianzus. Gregory explains why Apollinarianism was condemned. He said 'that which is not taken up is not saved' (Wace and Schaff 1974: Letter 101). The incarnate Christ must have really taken up humanness if he was to transmit deity to the human race. One does not become human by being coated with flesh. To draw humanity up into divinity, Christ had to touch it from the inside. His human nature has a saving function. It is not inert 'flesh'.

Antiochene theology: Giving a sermon

Much of the Christian theology of the first eleven centuries took the form of sermons explaining what Jesus is doing in the biblical story and drawing lessons from it. Theodore of Mopsuestia (350–428) was the wisest Antiochene theologian. Sometimes, when he was interpreting Scripture to a congregation, he wanted to stress that they should imitate Jesus. He used Jesus's behaviour as a moral lesson. When he did this, he focused on those acts of Jesus that are typically human, like learning, being obedient to God, or suffering patiently. At other times, Theodore wanted to show his hearers how Jesus acted like God, performing healing miracles and walking on the water.

Theodore taught that the God in Christ was eternally Son; but as man, Jesus was adopted into sonship. God adopted the man Jesus as son because of his moral obedience. For the Antiochenes, it was important to say that Jesus was adopted as Son after having made adult moral progress. Jesus's moral choices indicate that he exercises human moral freedom. Those fully human moral choices are the aspects of Jesus's conduct that a preacher wants his hearers to imitate.

Apollinarius's idea that Jesus's humanity is just his flesh was accepted by Alexandrian thinkers. Theodore criticised it. He said that being a good man is not achieved with our flesh alone. A complete human personality is involved in moral action – it is not just your hand that gives a beggar money. So there is more to Jesus's humanity than his flesh, said Theodore.

'Dividing the sayings'

The Antiochenes thought they would be guilty of muddled thinking if they ascribed Jesus's hunger and thirst to the infinite God in him. Conversely, they thought that if they attributed supernatural wisdom to the tiny baby Jesus, this omniscient child could not go through the normal human process of learning. Jesus's humanity and his divinity must therefore be referred to separately. They said, when Scripture depicts Jesus acting, sometimes it is referring to what his humanity does, other times to how his divinity acts. The Antiochenes ascribed the human actions to the man Jesus, the adopted son of God. They attributed the divine words and gestures to the Eternal Son, Christ the Word.

Why? Well, commanding the seas, for instance, is a display of uniquely divine power, whereas riding a donkey takes human legs and human skill. Dividing the biblical descriptions of Jesus in two sounds strange. But it is common sense to say that it is an exercise of deity to perform eschatological miracles and an exercise of humanity to weep, go fishing or eat breakfast.

The Antiochenes divided Christ's spheres of action into divine and human to preserve the fact that he is both God and man. Miracles would not be supernatural if performed by a creature. Conversely, if God is really propelling them, the human acts of Jesus would be the motions of a glove puppet; so we would have a docetic Christ who is actually divine playing at being human. The Antiochenes insisted that a double doing-activity is present in Jesus's God-manhood.

Conjunction – not union

Theodore of Mopsuestia avoided saying that Christ's humanity and divinity are united into one. Instead, he taught that, in Christ, humanity and divinity operates in conjunction. If divinity and humanity are fused into one at the Incarnation, Theodore thought, humanity is absorbed into divinity. That would give us Apollinarius's 'celestial man' Christ, all celestial and no man.

Two hypostases (substances) in Christ

The Greek philosopher Aristotle (384–322 BC) distinguished between substance and accident. A substance is the self-sufficient core of a thing, an accident is a quality that accrues to it and is dependent on the existence of its substance. If a 'table' is a substance, its particular colour is an accident. The table could do without the colour but the colour could not do without the table. The Latin 'sub-stance' means 'that which stands under': the underlying entity. The Greek word for substance is 'hypostasis'.

Theodore of Mopsuestia taught that there are in Christ two hypostases, humanity and divinity. Christ's humanity and divinity were each an independent entity. This was how Theodore tried to depict Christ's humanity and divinity as being real in themselves. What is human in Christ weeps, what is divine in him raises Lazarus. And never the twain shall meet! The danger in Antiochene Christology was that Christ could seem to be 'twins' with two independent 'halves'. What unifies the two natures?

One prosopon

The Greek word 'prosopon' means 'mask': it can also mean 'face', or 'appearance, the way one looks to others'. Theodore said that Christ has one single look, or prosopon. Because they operate in harmony, divinity and humanity in Christ present a single gestalt to the world. It is as if a movie were being projected onto a screen by two projectors producing a single image. In Theodore's theology, the prosopon is the one single image produced by Christ's two separate streams of activity.

Alexandrian Christology: Sacramental atonement

The Alexandrians' conception of deification is sacramental. For a sacramentalist, sacred things, places and persons are containers of the holy. A sacrament is a sacred element that carries the holy to people who come into physical contact with it. For the Alexandrians, Jesus's humanity is the sacrament of his divinity. It is the means by which his immortality is transmitted to us.

How could the humanity of the man Jesus do anything to anyone else's humanity? The principle is that Christ is Everyman. What happens to his humanity happens to all others. If his human nature is divinised, so is that of all believers. Christ's human nature is divinised by its unification with the Logos, said the Alexandrians.

Cyril of Alexandria (376–444)

Cyril says the flesh of Christ is real. So are the sufferings that happen to that mortal flesh. The Alexandrians were not the docetists the Antiochenes took them for. Nonetheless, the deifying Logos is more pivotal in Cyril's picture of the Incarnate Christ than is his humanity. For Cyril, it is the Logos who is the real agent in Christ. It is his reasoning, his spirituality and his morality. The humanity is passive, the Logos active. As a young, hot-headed Alexandrian, Cyril argued that Jesus's growth in wisdom (Luke 2: 52) just means the Logos is becoming more evident to others. The divine and therefore, for Cyril, unchanging and unchangeable Logos is what thinks in Christ.

In Cyril's Christology, the fusion of divinity and humanity is the means of his sacramental transmission of deity to humankind. For it to deify us, the Logos must be interwoven in Jesus's humanity. So Cyril insisted that the divine Logos and the man Jesus exist in unity. The younger Cyril argued that there is only one nature in Christ (mia phusis).

Cyril thought that, by saying there are two independent hypostases in Christ, Theodore of Mopsuestia was denying that God really became man. So long as the divinity and the humanity remain separate, God has not worked himself into the humanness in Christ, to deify it.

So who or what in Christ said 'I'? Man or Logos? Did he have two 'I's? For Cyril, there is just one 'I' in Christ: the Logos. Cyril argued for a hypostatic or substantial union. God and man in Christ are not accidentally joined, like two people tied together in a three leg race; instead, God and man become one in the Incarnation. They are unified in the Logos, the substantial core of Christ.

To express the idea that the Logos completely entered human reality, Cyril made statements like 'God was born'. Cyril also described Jesus's mother as 'Theo-Tokos', 'God-Bearer'. Mary gestated the sacred Logos within her womb (Norris 1980).

Nestorius (Patriarch of Constantinople 428–31)

By the time the Antiochene theologian Nestorius went to Constantinople, there was suspicion between Alexandria and Antioch. Nestorius's behaviour as patriarch put the torch paper to the coals. Nestorius forbid his new flock to call the mother of Jesus 'Theotokos'. For Nestorius, Mary carried the man Jesus in her womb, not the omnipresent God.

Nestorius noted that God does not become a fetus, or undergo gestation and birth – only physical creatures can do that.

Nestorius insisted that there is a conjunction of God and man in Christ but no union. For him, the idea of a union of natures in Christ meant the absorption of Jesus's humanness into his divinity.

Cyril wrote to Pope Celestine in Rome, accusing Nestorius of adoptionism. In 430, a Roman synod deposed Nestorius from the See of Constantinople. Cyril sent Nestorius several letters explaining why he was in error.

The Ecumenical Council of Ephesus (431)

John, bishop of Antioch, and his party were late to this Ecumenical Council, held up by a summer storm on the Mediterranean Sea. The papal delegates were also delayed. In their absence, Cyril of Alexandria excommunicated Nestorius (22 June). Arriving on 26 June, John of Antioch excommunicated the bishop of Alexandria. John departed. After a seasick journey, the papal delegates arrived on 10 July. They agreed that Nestorius must be excommunicated. The Council of Ephesus upheld Cyril's Second Letter to Nestorius as sound Christology. The Council states that God and man are 'hypostatically united' in Christ, and describe Mary as Theotokos.

Leo's Tome to Flavian

Eutyches of Constantinople (378–454): Monophysitism

Eutyches was an archimandrate in Constantinople. He was more Alexandrian than Cyril. Fired by the triumph of Alexandrian Christology at Ephesus, Eutyches went further. Taking the *mia phusis* formula literally, he called himself a monophysite. The one-nature in Christ is God.

Pope Leo the Great (c. 390–461)

If Christology does not say that God really became human, it denies the Incarnation. Pope Leo the Great wrote a letter attacking monophysitism. This is called Leo's Tome to Flavian. Leo sorted out the terminology. The Tome states that there are two natures in Christ – that is, a divine phusis/nature and a human phusis/nature. The two phuseis/natures exist in a single hypostasis. 'Hypostasis' can be translated as 'person' or as 'existent'. The single, existential core in Christ is the Logos. In Christ, a single existent has two natures.

The Ecumenical Council of Chalcedon (451)

For over a century, Christology had been torn between those who pointed out that there are two natures in Christ and those who insisted that the two natures are unified. It was time to call an Ecumenical Council.

The Chalcedonian formula

Following, then, the holy Fathers, we all with one voice teach that it should be confessed that our Lord Jesus Christ is one and the same Son, the Same perfect in Godhead, the same perfect in manhood, truly God and truly man, the Same [consisting] of a rational soul and a body; homoousios with the Father as to his Godhead, and the Same homoousios with us as to his manhood; in all things like unto us, sin only excepted; begotten of the Father before ages as to his Godhead, and in the last days, the Same, for us and for our salvation, of Mary the Virgin Theotokos as to his manhood;

One and the same Christ, Son, Lord, Only begotten, made known in two natures [which exist] without confusion, without change, without division, without separation; the difference of the natures having been in no wise taken away by reason of the union, but rather the properties of each being preserved, and [both] concurring into one Person (prosopon) and one hypostasis – not parted or divided into two persons (prosopa), but one and the same Son and Only begotten, the divine Logos, the Lord Jesus Christ; even as the prophets from of old [have spoken] concerning him, and as the Lord Jesus Christ himself has taught us, and as the Symbol of the Fathers has delivered to us.

T. Herbert Bindley, *The Oecumenical Documents of the Faith* (1899)

The Council of Chalcedon created a formula that uses phrases from Cyril's Second Letter to Nestorius, such as 'Theotokos'. Like Theodore of Mopsuestia, it depicts that in which the natures are united as the prosopon, the personal 'face' of Jesus Christ. It affirms that Christ does not just look unified to others. He has a single act of existence, one hypostasis, which is the divine Logos.

Two natures in one person

The Chalcedonian formula states that Christ was 'made known in two natures [which exist] without confusion, without change, without division, without separation; the difference of the natures having been in no wise taken away by reason of the union'. Some say this string of antonyms was just 'poetry'. A common interpretation is that Chalcedon was trying to please both Antiochenes and Alexandrians, so it said things everyone could agree with. The key to the Chalcedonian formula is its statement that Christ is two natures in one person.

Two 'what does' in one 'who'

Since phusis refers to what a nature does, Chalcedon is speaking of two kinds of doings present in a single being. There are two 'what does its' in Christ. In response to the question, 'what suffered on the Cross?', Chalcedonian Christology answers: the human nature. In answer to 'what walked on the water?', Chalcedon says: the divine nature. The divine and human natures operated as divine and human natures do. If you want to know 'what' acted, consider whether the action took divine operational powers or human operative capacities. Christ has two natures, two operational functions.

The next question is 'whose nature?'. The answer is: the nature of Christ. Both natures belong to the eternal Logos. For Chalcedon, hypostasis and prosopon mean existent. These terms answer 'who' questions. In answer to 'who suffered on the Cross?', Chalcedon says the divine person. In answer to any 'who' question about Christ, from 'who was born?', to 'who learned to read?' to 'who rose from the dead?', the Chalcedonian answer is: the divine Logos. Thus, it was the human nature in Jesus Christ that wept over Lazarus, for God does not have tear ducts. But these were the tears of God. Jesus's humanity did the weeping and it was God who wept.

Two 'whats' in one 'which'

Like 'who', 'which' is a useful word for nailing down particular individuals. 'Which particular existent was born of Mary?' Christ the Logos. Which unique existent taught by parables, ate fish and bread with his disciples, and appeared to Mary Magdalene on Easter morning? Christ the Logos.

If Chalcedonian Christology is asked what in Christ performed his actions, the answer can be either the divine nature or the human nature. By virtue of his humanity, Christ has the wherewithal to do things that are typical of humans, like eating breakfast and learning; by virtue of his divine nature, Christ has the wherewithal to act as God does. If it is asked to pick out which being is named by the Bible and the Creeds, the answer of Chalcedon is the Logos.

Further reading

The books in this list are ranked in order of their accessibility to under-graduate readers.

Pelikan, Jaroslav (1985), *Jesus Through the Centuries: His Place in the History of Culture*, New Haven: Yale University Press.
O'Collins, Gerald (2000), *Interpreting Jesus*, London: Cassell.
Bauckham, Richard (1988), *God Crucified: Monotheism and Christology in the New Testament*, London: Paternoster.
Macquarrie, John (1990), *Jesus Christ in Modern Thought*, London: SCM Press.

Questions

1. If you wanted to write a contemporary inclusivist Christology, what human desire would you take it from?

2. Is it primitive to conceive Christ as the hero of a rescue operation?

3. How did Athanasius use the idea of creation, a) in his idea of the person of Christ; b) in the idea of the work of Christ?

4. Which Christological ideas were excluded by Nicaea?

5. For what soteriological reason was Apollinarius condemned?

6. What were the Antiochenes' reasons for separating the divine and the human in Christ? Do they make sense?

7. What is the soteriology behind Alexandrian Christology?

8. Can there be 'two "whats" in one "who"'?

CHAPTER THREE

The Bases of Systematic Theology

Francesca Aran Murphy

Introduction

The entrance to systematic theology is knowing the doctrines and which Christian perceptions led to their formulation. Then you can begin to engage the tradition yourself. Every theologian in history has gone through this process. None of them has done it as a detached spectator. Each of them brings to their engagement in theology their own personality, which is shaped by their church, their culture and their unique calling. Different questions and motivations produce different answers. That is why the theology of Thomas Aquinas differs from Martin Luther's. The remainder of this section is written as a dialogue between nine students, each representing one typical viewpoint in modern theology. This is so you do not get the idea that systematic theology consists in answers posed by anonymous spectators with nothing at stake.

Theology is not a monologue but a dialogue amongst engaged positions, a drama. Let us introduce the cast list. In order of appearance:

- A Systematic Theology Professor
- Bob, a sceptic
- Philip, an Augustinian, interested in Benedictines
- Lara, a liberal theologian
- Fred, a Thomist, a Philosophy major, and a Catholic
- Jamaal, a liberation theologian, a Computing major, whose parents are pastors in the Episcopal-Methodist Zion Church
- Cathy, evangelical, a hard-working student, also known as 'the Boot'
- Greg, a Literature and Film major, who has a rap group, The Nihilists
- Anthony, narrative theologian, a Theology major, known as 'the Genius Kid'
- Rosie – who *is* she?

Seminar One: What is systematic theology?

A student project

The Professor asked three students to start figuring out what systematic theology is.

Theology is what theologians write about

Bob went to the Religion section in the college library. Some of the books had covers showing office workers looking like they lost their lunch packs and titles like *Is God Dead?*. He watched the Genius Kid take down a huge book. If there was a power failure in the library, they could light the place up from the top of that guy's head! He looked where Anthony had taken the book from and saw a line of identical volumes. He noted 'Karl Barth, *Church Dogmatics*'. Moving around the stacks, Bob narrowed the key areas down to Christ, the Trinity, the Church, Worship, Mary. He planned to tell the class that systematic theology is a book about one of those themes.

Personalist idea of theology

Rosie took the downtown bus to the biggest city bookstore and found the Spirituality section. There were self-help books for alcoholics, workaholics and sex-addicts. She looked at the piles of paperback biographies of Christians like Martin Luther King Jr and Henri Nouwen. She bought a book by Dallas Willard called *The Spirit of the Disciplines*, which told you how to be very ascetic, to be like Christ. She figured systematic theology comes out of the biographies of Christian believers.

A Benedictine theology

Philip travelled out of town to a Benedictine monastery. It was called Holy Trinity, and, God Almighty, was it cold. The monks were laid back. They had to be. They spent the day in the church praying; they got up in the middle of the night to chant. It sounded like they were repeating the same prayers over and again, chilling out in every sense of the word. The Abbot told him every monastery in the world was working through the same prayer books, round the Christian seasons.

The monks talked about dudes with names like Newman, Augustine and Anselm. When Philip got home, he checked them out on the Web and discovered it wasn't like the monks made it sound. Those theologians were not the contemporaries of the oldest monks in the monastery! He wrote down that systematic theology is created by people who have been praying together for thousands of years. He knew it would sound crazy to say that dead monks prayed together with live ones. But that was the way it had felt, in the monastery.

A student debate: What is systematic theology?

The students' presentations didn't line up with each other. Bob said, 'Systematic theology is information about Christian teachings.' Rosie claimed, 'Theology is ways of searching for God.' She didn't think it was in a book but in someone's life. Philip agreed that systematic theology is about living experience of God but he added that the reflection takes place within the Church.

Bob argued that theology just takes clear thinking. He thought only a nitwit would get their idea of an academic discipline from paperback self-help books and only a fundamentalist would ask a monk to define systematic theology. Anyone could pass a test on Christ by reading serious books about it. The guy who wrote *Is God Dead?* was an atheist and a systematic theologian.

Fred denied theology could be Christian if it took its starting point from non-Christians. He claimed systematic theology is the ordered body of Christian thought about God. Bob's view on it was unchristian and Rosie's ideas were disorderly. When Bob asked, 'What makes it Christian?', Fred said, 'God gives us the data-sheet and systematic theologians conceptualise the revealed information.'

Jamaal couldn't see any difference between Fred's idea of systematic theology and Bob's. He said, 'Any system that comes out of a textbook, or is theoretical, is white theology. It would be used to keep college professors in pay and it serves their interests.' The Professor winced and took her glasses off.

Is systematic theology in text books?

She asked, 'Is philosophy the content of philosophy books?' Some students who had taken Philosophy put up their hands. Cathy said, 'Yes, I got a B+ on the test by memorising the text book.' Jamaal said, 'Philosophy is like sports: you get better at it throwing the ball, not by watching it on TV.' Greg added, 'We are all philosophers, since we all ask questions about the meaning of life. We don't have to read a book about it. Philosophy is a happening, not something dead.'

The balding Genius Kid questioned the analogy between philosophical questions and theological ones. You can argue for anything in a Philosophy class. Can a theologian argue for any position? 'No!' said Cathy, Fred and Jamaal. 'Yes!' said Lara. The debate left open some questions. Does systematic theology have normative guidelines? What are its sources? Where is its starting point? The Professor told Lara and Greg to work on presentations on liberal theology.

Greg gave Fred a lift home on the back of his Harley 250. They had lived in the same shabby neighbourhood as long as they could remember. As soon as the boys were teenagers, their moms had bought their clothes from an army surplus store. Fred always looked neat in a shabby sort of way but Greg looked shabby in a neat kind of way. His mom's cooking made Fred fat; Greg's home cuisine made him slim. When Greg saw the chubby face on the spine of Fred's *Summa Theologiae*, Thomas Aquinas merged with Fred in his mind. Fred was taking Theology because it would be a helpful adjunct to the Thomistic philosophy that he loved. Greg was in the Theology class because Philosophy hadn't worked for him; it hadn't been about the meaning of anything. Greg's bedroom was packed with memorabilia from his dad's days as a minor rock musician, plus speakers, guitars, wires and drums for his own rap group. When Fred thought of The Nihilists, he uttered a private prayer of petition for his neighbour. But it bought Greg the Harley, plus the opportunity to meet women! When they hit a light, Fred told him he couldn't take his eyes off Lara. It must be love, he felt. Greg snorted. 'You've fallen in lust,' he said, shortly.

Seminar Two: Liberalism – human insight as the basis of theology

John Hick

Lara gave a power-point presentation showing the covers of Hick's books, starting from *God and the Universe of Faiths* (1973), with a starry galaxy on the front, to *The Myth of God Incarnate* (1977) and *The Myth of Christian Uniqueness* (1988), right up to *The Metaphor of God Incarnate* (1993). Using a metaphor from astronomy, Lara showed a picture of the night sky with 'God' at the centre and Buddhism, Judaism, Islam, Hinduism and Christianity circling round it. Lara said, 'There has now been a Copernican shift in our perception of reality.' Fred said, 'That was 500 years ago.' Lara's friend Cathy said, 'Attention!' Lara explained that Hick's faith journey began when he dropped the evangelical Christianity he was brought up in. In *God and the Universe of Faiths*, he presented our shift from Christ-centred theology to theo-centric theology. Believing the planets revolve around Christianity is like hanging on to a geocentric universe after Copernicus. Each planet of the great world religions revolves equally around the axis of God.

'With *The Myth of God Incarnate*, Hick recognised that talking about theocentrism was imperialistic on non-theistic religions, like Buddhism,' said Lara. 'In *The Metaphor of God Incarnate*, Hick shows that all religions are tools for achieving reality-centredness. Muhammad, Jesus, Buddha and so on mediate that goal to their followers. We use them like a sportswoman uses a retired Olympic athlete as her trainer.' She showed a new diagram:

BUDDHISTS	BUDDHAS	→→→	NIRVANA	→→	U L T	
MUSLIMS	MUHAMMAD	→→→	ALLAH	→→	I M A	
CHRISTIANS	JESUS CHRIST	→→→	TRINITY	→→	T E	
					R E	
HINDUS	GURUS AVATARS	→→→	BRAHMAN	→→	A L I T	
JEWS	PROPHETS	→→→	JAHWEH	→→	Y	

(right column reads vertically: ULTIMATE REALITY)

'Are we to take those diagrams literally?' asked Philip. 'Is the same absolute reality beyond all the religions?' 'Sure,' said Lara. 'How can you be sure?' asked Philip, 'When the picture indicates that we don't know? From that diagram, ultimate reality is ultimately unknowable even to inspired men like Jesus and Muhammad.' 'What would anyone want to look for except reality?' said Lara. 'Without being able to find it,' said Philip. 'It's beyond all the religious absolutes.' Lara argued that the minute religious people claim to have the absolute, they impose it on other religions. Hick recounts how the missionary David Livingstone said, in 1857, 'I go back to Africa to try to open a path for commerce and Christianity.' Liberal theology is pluralist about religious faith-claims, not absolutist.

Rosie asked, 'What is it that attracts you to liberalism, Lara?' Lara said, 'I don't divide the world into Christians and non-Christians. Lots of my friends aren't Christian. Hick treats religions like scientific hypotheses, instruments for drilling into reality. With that perspective, I've got common space with non-Christians. It's not that the only common space is scientific but science is the most successful rationality there has ever been. If you don't use scientific rationality, you turn religion into a private ghetto you can't talk to other people about.'

Lara added, 'Hick is doing theology scientifically. Where scientists have experimental hypotheses about facts, theologians have experiential hypotheses. The experiential hypothesis is a way of channelling our attitudes toward Ultimate Reality. All religions perform experiments, using human consciousness as material.' 'Material for what?' asked Philip. 'Transformation,' said Lara. 'The transformation of consciousness into a perfect pointer to Ultimate Reality is the goal of all religions. You can channel your transformation through Jesus, Buddha, Muhammad or a Sikh Guru.'

Greg spent a week dreading the presentation on liberal theology the Professor had so badly miscalculated in assigning to him. Maybe he should get a haircut. Sure, his Dad had spent two years in India and Greg had tried to get him to say what Indian religions are like; but all he could get out of him was that it was different from the West, even from Western Buddhism. Greg had been in mosques in Turkey and Morocco, and a Sikh Gurdwara in London, and the atmosphere was not like Fred's church, St Albert's. Not better or worse, just another solar system. The tastes, the smells, the sounds, the postures – all unique. As distinct from Christianity as the history of Ireland is from the history of Mongolia. Sure, they all had something to say. But what right did Hick have to tell every religion they were saying the same thing? He didn't even belong to one of them. Greg developed a stomach ache and sent in a sick note.

> Hick's system . . . has decided all things in advance; every form of religion is catalogued and encoded into modernity's narrative of time, space, and history. The history and particularities of the various traditions are just icing on a cake, already tasted, known, and digested. The many intractable particularities of the religions with their unique histories and traditions are drained of their power . . . Hick's pluralist project . . . mystifies, rather than illuminates, the nature of the Real . . . Agnosticism is the inevitable outcome of . . . Hick's flight from particularity, first from the particularity of the incarnation, then from the particularity of a theistic God, and then from the particularity of any religious claim, be it Christian or non-Christian.
>
> Gavin D'Costa, *The Meeting of Religions and the Trinity* (2000: 28)

Lara completed her solo presentation by saying that systematic theology is sourced to a universal human orientation. Anthony disputed that. 'It's not,' he said. 'The Christian story is unique to Christianity.' Bob said, 'It has to be because there is no orientation that is universal to the whole of humanity.' Rosie said, 'Let people in India, China, the Middle East and Africa have their different Ultimate Realities!' Lara said, 'And let them perform suttee and compulsory clictorectomies and force women to wear burkhas?' 'Look who's the imperialist now,' said Anthony. The Genius Kid added, 'So-called "pluralists" like Hick impose an artificial identical language on everyone. It's liberalism that's imperialist, imposing a single scientific order on every religion. It's an Esperanto invented by a rationalist elite. Muslims have a unique Muslim paradigm and that's their affair. Bob has a secular paradigm; he's not seeking the same transformation as Christians. I have a Christian paradigm. There is no evidence that can prove any of us right.'

Fred said, 'I wouldn't be so quick to go along with cultural relativism, if I were you. The problem with liberalism isn't the idea of common threads amongst non-Christian religions and Christians and agnostics. It's that liberalism is all common threads and no uniqueness.' Bob said, 'Doesn't liberal theology ultimately mean God is dead and we have to make the best human sense of our lives that we can? Why keep the Christian packaging?' 'What Christian packaging?' asked Cathy.

Eschatological openness

Anthony said, 'Christians who borrow Buddhist meditation techniques are treating religious practices like market commodities.' 'Not automatically,' said Jamaal. 'If Christians don't interact with Muslims and

463

Multiple incarnations

As the ancient Ptolemaic picture of the universe, with our earth at its centre, was . . . replaced . . . by the enormously expanded universe disclosed by modern astronomy, Western thinkers began to speculate about the possibility of divine incarnations on other planets . . . the idea of many incarnations is . . . viable given any . . . Chalcedonian form of Christology. For all such Christologies posit two realities, the eternal divine Son and the human nature which the Son assumes . . . this assuming could . . . occur any number of times . . . When God became incarnate as Jesus he was humanly conscious of that aspect of the divine which can be conceived in Jewish terms . . . as the personal heavenly Father . . . But incarnated as Gautama Siddhartha, the Logos was humanly conscious of that aspect of the divine . . . as the eternal reality of nirvana . . . One could proceed to interpret along analogous lines each of the other major options represented by the different world religions.

John Hick, *The Metaphor of God Incarnate* (1993: 89–91, 98)

Buddhists, they'll be the only twenty-first-century people who don't. All this talk about roots comes from fear of modernity.' *In love with the idea of modernity*, thought Fred. With a steely glint in his eye, he said, 'Hick is a Trekkie. As from the Original Series.' 'Call it Starship Enterprise if you want,' said Jamaal. 'But liberal theology sees that no one in a globalised world has a home base. Christians should know we don't get the whole story until the eschaton. We won't close in on the absolute until the end of time.' It was the end of class. The Professor went back to her office and emailed Greg: 'Present the seminar on myths and symbols or drop off the course.' But Cathy was on next.

Seminar Three: Theology based on belief alone

Theology excludes reason

Cathy had asked to present the idea that systematic theology is a matter of believing God's Word. She told the class that faith has got nothing to do with human rationality. Lara wondered whether that meant you could be a scientist and still be a Christian. 'You could,' said Cathy, 'but your faith wouldn't interact with your human knowledge.' When Fred asked if philosophy could contribute to systematic theology, Cathy answered, 'No way.' 'Philosophy is for the proud of heart,' she said coldly. 'Faith is for the humble.'

Tertullian (c. 160–220): What has Athens to do with Jerusalem?

Cathy stated that Tertullian had asked, 'What has Athens to do with Jerusalem?' Lara pointed out that it was a rhetorical question, so the answer had to be 'Nothing'. Fred said, '"Athens" stands for Greek philosophy and "Jerusalem" for the Bible.' The class asked Cathy what systematic theology would be like if it followed Tertullian's way and this evangelical student said it would be based on Bible teaching and nothing else.

Soren Kierkegaard (1813–55): Fideism

The Professor explained that Tertullian's attitude is called fideism. That word comes from the Latin 'fideo'. It literally means 'faith-ism', believing by faith alone. The greatest exponent of fideism in modern times was Kierkegaard. For Kierkegaard, Christianity is the denial of everything we rationally think. Faith can't be reasoned to from the outside, and it can't be reasoned out from the inside.

Cathy asked, rhetorically, 'Do the gospels give historical evidence that compels us to believe in Christ? Kierkegaard said "No!" You have to decide to have faith. There is no empirical proof for belief in Christ. Even if you had met Jesus in real life, you'd have seen a pauper, not a dazzling epiphany from God. Kierkegaard was right. Non-believing researchers into the gospels are bound to decide that miracles can't occur. They can't set the standard for theology, only faith can.'

Bob was in the course because Christians think up wild legitimisations of their beliefs and it was fun to question them – when they didn't roll over like porcupines. He loved to make Cathy's eyes light up with anger. He could picture her parachuting in with the 101st Airborne, crying, 'Christ and Christ crucified!' Bob remarked, 'Kierkegaard recommended Christianity on the ground that it's absurd. That makes Christian theology a no-brainer.'

Martin Kahler: The Jesus of History and the Christ of Faith

Bob said it mattered to him whether the Christian claims about Jesus could be proved to have happened, by a neutral scientist to an outside observer. 'Could they?' he asked. The Professor said, 'Martin Kahler wrote *The So-Called historical [historisch] Jesus, and the Biblical Christ of Faith* in 1896. Kahler gave the thumbs-down to the nineteenth-century "quest for the historical Jesus". He says the Jesus of history, who is pieced together by historical analysis, is our human side of the story. When you cut the Gospel into units and sources, the face of Christ disappears. The Christ of Faith could never be discovered by a secular historian. The revelation of God in Christ is the synthetic picture that emerges whole from the Gospel.'

Karl Barth (1886–1968)

Anthony was pleased with the turn the seminar had taken. He read from a huge book written by Karl Barth: 'None of the "events of revelation attested in the Bible" are 'historical' (*historisch*); i.e. apprehensible by a neutral observer or apprehended by such an observer."' 'What does historisch mean?' asked Cathy. The Professor said, 'Empirical, factual history.' Fred argued that if you distinguish empirical history and God's revelation, the objectivity of faith goes down the tubes. 'It has to be one and the same,' he said.

Fred said, 'If you refuse to say anything that makes sense to a non-believer, how can you argue them out of it? A fideist can't say that Christianity is objectively true. He can only say this is what I believe.' Jamaal denied there is such a thing as objective 'truth'. '"Truth" is an instrument the dominant class uses to impose its attitudes,' he said. Fred yelled, 'Is that true?' Then he calmed down and said, 'Fideism is zeroing out every kind of human rationality. "Athens" is equal to the secular reasoning of any time. It could be metaphysics, Biblical research, empirical science, or the idea of liberal democracy. It's unnatural not to use your mind.'

Bob said, 'If you have to be a charismatic to do it, systematic theologians should be barred from universities, places where reason is cultivated.' 'How could you even write a theology book,' asked Fred, 'if you can't reason it out?' Rosie replied that fideists feel that writing systematic theology books is not the crux of the matter. What counts is not rationalising but testifying to the faith through your life. There's nothing private about being a witness. 'If you've ever had a great teacher and then read their book, the book never comes up to the performance,' she said.

Rosie argued that one has to be a prayerful person to do theology. You can't just be very clever, you have to listen to God. Bob argued that people imagine they are listening to God, when what they are really hearing from the pulpit is the voice of the ruling class telling them they would get pie in the sky when they die. 'If we don't exercise intellectual criticism on experience,' he said, 'how do we know "God" is not just a projection of ourselves? The governing class will manipulate us to project the image of God they want us to have.'

Rosie replied that the civil rights movement was inspired to act against racial segregation. Martin Luther King called for change in the language of the Jewish prophets. Jamaal said, 'That goes back to slavery times, not just the 1960s. We know the future can be different from what society conditions us to think because experiencing the presence of Jesus shows us another place. God's justice overturns the present human social order. African-American Christians have experienced this, preached it, lived it, and that is the basis of our systematic theology.'

Seminar Four: Contrasting liberalism and fideism – myths and symbols

Liberal attitudes to mythology

Joseph Campbell (1904–87)

Greg stood up, dejectedly holding out his dad's battered copy of Campbell's *The Hero with a Thousand Faces*. Campbell had studied every religion in history and found the same story in every one. 'The myth is about salvation,' said Greg. 'Campbell names it the monomyth. There's the same hero in all religions, with an infinity of different faces. That's because the hero is the guy reading the book. He can be whatever he wants to be. Campbell is even more pluralist than Hick.'

Rudolf Bultmann (1884–1976)

Greg mumbled, 'The leading liberal of the first half of the twentieth century was a German theologian, Rudolf Bultmann. Bultmann taught that Christianity has got to demythologise Christian doctrine. That means stripping out the myths and bringing it back to experiences of personal existence.' Fred asked, 'What counts as a myth, for Bultmann?' Lara got there first, saying, 'We know from science that every event in the universe has a scientific explanation. Its only in myths that God comes in and messes with the chain of physical events.' A myth like the Exodus touches a chord if you talk about liberation and leave the parting of the Red Sea out of it.'

Jamaal said, 'What about God liberating poor people from capitalist oppression today?' Lara answered, 'That's the whole point. Liberation is a universal experience. You don't have to talk about it in mythic terms. A story that shows God acting in a special historic event, that is a myth.' Jamaal asked, 'So you leave what God does out of it?'

Hick on mythology

Lara accepted that all world religions had their myths. Liberal theologies didn't want to abolish myth. 'It just tells us not to be fixated on one particular myth, like the myth of Christian uniqueness. For Hick, a myth isn't imposed on us from outside, by a religious authority claiming contact with the "absolute". A myth is our own way of expressing our journey to the Ultimate. It's not an input, it's an output, from human consciousness.' Fred said, 'Do myths correspond to realities? Are they true?'

'The word "true" should be abolished from religions,' said Lara. 'Hick shows that a myth can't be literally true. Jesus didn't literally come down from heaven like an alien landing on earth from outer space. The Christian idea of incarnation is a myth; it expresses the way we feel about Christ, it doesn't describe Christ.' Philip asked, 'How is Hick's Christ different from Campbell's hero with infinite faces? Everyone could use the figure of Christ to express different psychological needs.'

Is God visible?

'Liberalism is weird,' said Greg. 'It acknowledges we need stories to express our hopes and fears. But the other thread is the Ultimate is unknowable and invisible. No myth comes up to it, so "Demythologise!" is what they seem to say in the end. But myths feed my imagination,' complained Greg, a Tolkien fan. '*The Lord of the Rings* is popular because it speaks to people's experience as a story.' Bob remarked that one existentialist, Kierkegaard, took Christianity back to faith experience and said 'God is unknowable to reason.' But the greatest existentialist, Friedrich Nietzsche, said 'God is dead.' '"God is invisible" and "God is dead" amount to the same,' said Bob.

Contrast of myths and symbols

Philip argued that when Kierkegaard said 'invisible', he meant not completely transparent. Great pictures are visible but their meaning isn't as clear as daylight. Rosie agreed that you don't immediately see the point of a symbol, you keep coming back to it. Scientific reasoning isn't the only kind; there's also artistic reasoning.

Philip said, 'Drawing symbols out of real things is different from using a metaphor or myth to express your own creativity. Symbols describe realities. Myths express human consciousness. A lot of science fiction is mythic. *ET* is a myth about how we'd love a friendly alien to visit us.' Rosie saw the point, and added, 'Comic-book supermen are myths. That's why they're addictive, they give us what we want. We read our fantasy selves into them.'

Philip said, 'The mythic hero is like a gnostic hero.' '*Huh?*' said Cathy. Philip said, 'What did you find when you studied the Gnostic gospels in the New Testament?' Cathy said the Gnostic 'Jesus lives' showed him as not having been a flesh and blood man, not having really died, and as not having been physically resurrected from the dead. 'No physicality, no reality,' said Cathy. 'We should stick to Bible facts, not myths.' Rosie said, 'The New Testament portraits of Christ are symbolic.'

Greg asked, 'Do you mean Christ is a symbol? A symbol of what?'

Rosie said, 'Christ isn't a symbol. Christ is a fact. But what we think and say about Christ is an attempt to symbolise his reality, in words and pictures. The Bible puts across symbolic portraits of Christ, and so do theologians. Kierkegaard's symbol for Christ was an unimpressive individual who looks like a pauper. He conceived of the historical Christ as God incognito.'

Philip added, 'Symbolic thinkers take reality input before psychological output. *The Lord of the Rings* is symbolic because it relates back to reality. Tolkien had a Christian imagination. Gandalf was a symbol for Christ and Sauron was a symbol of the Devil. Tolkien thought Christ and the Devil were real, not psychological projections. Christianity is symbolic, not mythic. It takes you where you don't want to go.' 'Mordor,' said Rosie.

She claimed that a fideist like Kierkegaard was rebelling against turning Jesus into an anonymous Everygod who fits everyone's fantasies. 'He says Christianity is absurd because it tells you to put your faith in one historical individual and no other. The scandal of the blood-stained cross doesn't fit into any bigger mythical or philosophical system.'

Jeez, thought Bob, *9.25 a.m. and we're on the scandal of the blood-stained cross*. Rosie was coming on like the Cate Blanchett character in *Lord of the Rings*. Bob couldn't stand people parading their emotions in public and turning a class into a group therapy session. He argued that if you let fideists do it, theology would be preaching, not anything a non-believer could take any interest in.

Christology

Christ is the paradox, the God-man … Christ willed to be the socially insignificant one. The fact that he descended from heaven to take upon himself the form of a servant is not an accidental something which now is to be thrust into the background and forgotten. No, every true follower of Christ must express existentially the very same thing – that insignificance and offense are inseparable from being a Christian.

Kierkegaard, *Journals and Papers*, III (in Moore 1999: 225)

Fred thought religious art was fine in churches but it has nothing to do with the rational life. He said, 'That's very lovely. But the only way to distinguish the liberals' mythic Christ and a fideist's symbolic Christ is by pointing to historical evidence.' Fred added, 'I wouldn't ask a biblical scholar to lay down what really happened in biblical history, not until

(above and opposite) Like the early Christian artists, Tolkien thought symbolically about the powers of good and evil. New Line Productions, Inc.

they can prove to me that miracles can't occur. But I'd have a rational debate with the Jesus Seminar, not just ignore them and assert my private faith. Showing them the biblical symbols isn't enough.' Bob added, 'Suppose historical research proved for certain that Christ never existed. A fideist would have to carry on believing regardless.'

G. W. F. Hegel (1770–1831): Christianity as a stepping stone to philosophy

Rosie thought Bob's hypothetical case didn't connect with Kierkegaard's life situation. She said, 'You're looking at Kierkegaard unhistorically. Kierkegaard was arguing against Hegel, who saw Christ's life as a case study for a universal philosophical truth. Hegel thought Christianity

gives us the myth, which was useful until philosophy came along and explained those truths on a higher level as a universal law. Hegel was a step ahead of Hick two hundred years ago. That's what Kierkegaard was trying to prevent.'

The acoustics of theology

Jamming without gelling

Greg asked, 'If Christianity and contemporary society can't interact, how could there be Christian rap music?' Jamaal answered, 'There isn't. That stuff is identical to rap music period. They just throw in "Jah" when it suits them. "Christian" rap music is faith and culture jamming without gelling. Satellite say they are "rappers who are also Christians, not Christian rappers". The rap and the Christianity don't gel.' 'What Kierkegaard would want,' Jamaal added, 'is for Christians to invent musical styles out of Christianity alone.' Fred saw no connection between popular music of any kind and theology. Jamaal said, 'It's unnatural to do theology without soul.'

Then the Professor threw a curve ball at the students: 'Could you be a musician if you were tone deaf?' 'Yes,' said Greg. 'Anyone who wants to can be a musician. Who is to define what "tone deaf" means? Tone deaf could mean different things in different cultures.' Jamaal had heard the Nihilists jamming. He said, 'You need sound-sensitivity to be able to hear and to play music as music, and not just as noises. Theology is like music, you have to get in touch with its soul to know what it's about.'

Philip added that, like music, theology is a kind of performance. Bob said that he didn't see any connection between music and God because you can hear music but you can't hear or see God.

Cathy agreed. You can't hear or see faith, it's within a person. The Pharisees looked for a sign. Jamaal was nettled. Maybe those frozen guys in the monastery were just repeating the same prayers, like robots. But in his church, people were free to sing, yell out or throw themselves on the floor, if the Spirit moved them that way. 'Sure you can see the Spirit acting on people,' Jamaal said.

Fred told Jamaal and Rosie that, if the source of systematic theology is what it feels like to sing in a particular church, it will be subjective. Fred said, 'I don't see what an intellectual discipline like theology has to do with music.' 'You are tone deaf,' said Rosie. Jamaal said, 'If you had ever experienced being taken out of yourself, you would know it comes from God.' Greg snorted when Fred said, 'Guess I never experienced ecstasy.' The students blamed Greg when the Professor told the class that, next week, they would have a test on the Christian canon.

Seminar Five: The Christian Canon – construct of faith or reason?

Lara and Cathy walked to their dorm together. They were both from army families; they had grown up moving from base to base. Cathy called Lara 'Army' and Lara called Cathy 'Boot'. Army's dad was logical and sharp, and to the right of Attila the Hun. Boot's dad would never make it above sergeant. He was so dumb, one year, in Carolina, he had registered Cathy in a Catholic parochial school. That was when she learned to be a Boot. It was the year she had been converted to Jesus Christ at a Pentecostal assembly. The women talked about Philip and Bob, their favourite men in the class. Lara told her friend that the test was a great opportunity to 'revise' together with Philip. 'Ask Anthony along, too,' she said, 'that wise ass will make sure you learn something useful, not about Benedictine abbeys.' 'I gotta keep him away from monks,' said Cathy. The Boot went to her room and started working.

The Christian canon is the Christian Bible

She was well prepared when she met up with Anthony and Philip at Pizza Hut to pool their resources on the canon of Christian Scripture. Cathy showed her notes on the meaning of canon to the two boys. In the eighth century BC, Homer used the word 'Kannon' to mean the strings a soldier used to tie the front of his body armour to the back. The

Greek 'Kanon' came to mean a measuring rod or rule. Canonisation is the process by which many texts are tied together and defined as the sacred Scriptures binding a religious community.

Bob worked as a waiter in the Pizza Hut. When he took their order, he told them that by the mid-first century AD, Jews like Josephus refer to the Scriptures as 'hai graphai', *the* Scriptures. Since the Jewish Scripture was there when Christianity came around, it became their 'Bible'. Philip said, 'It was because the Torah was read aloud in the Christian liturgy that it was regarded as divine revelation.' Bob asked what gave Christians the right to cannibalise the Scriptures of another religion. Anthony told him, 'They thought they could use them because they believed that Jesus Christ was the fulfilment of the Jewish law and Jewish prophecy.'

Gnosticism and docetism

Bob went to get their pizzas and the three went back to studying Cathy's notes. Christian communities heard Paul's letters in church, alongside the law and the prophets. In the early second century, the synoptic gospels were read aloud in Christian churches too. Bob came back with the drinks and pointed out that other gospels existed. Like the Gospel According to the Hebrews, the Gospel of Thomas and the Gospel According to the Egyptians. Philip said, 'Those books weren't used in the Christian liturgy.' When Bob asked, 'Why not?' Anthony said, 'It was because they don't connect the life of Jesus with the Jewish Scriptures.'

Cathy said Gnosticism pictured Christ docetically. Christians rejected the mythic or docetic idea of Jesus. So out went Gnostic biographies like the Gospel of Thomas. 'Gno' means 'I know' in Greek. Gnosticism taught that only those in the know can understand God's hidden message. Unlearned people couldn't access it. So no writing was canonised that implies that the true meaning of Jesus's life can only be grasped by smart people. Cathy added, 'Today's Gnostics are academic theologians who think only they have got the point.' Philip diplomatically suggested they better stick to what was on the test. So Cathy read on.

Marcionism: The first canon of Scripture

Dualism was another feature of Gnosticism – that's the idea that there are two divine Forces behind the universe, one good and one bad. Marcion was a dualistic Gnostic. He was teaching in Rome roughly between 137 and 144. Marcion identified the God of the Jewish Scriptures as the bad God because he created the physical cosmos and ordered the Jews to obey hundreds of moral and cultic laws. Marcion thought you had to read between the lines of Paul's letters and the synoptics because their real meaning was hidden under Jewish assumptions.

Marcion took his own antinomian and anti-physical attitudes as a test of what should be in the Bible. He was the first person to invent a canon of Christian Scripture. Marcion's canon consisted of ten Pauline letters, deleting their Jewish features, and a text that Marcion made out to be the genuine gospel behind the gospel of Luke. Marcion established a church for which this text was God's revelation. 'It may have been *a* church,' said Philip, 'but it wasn't *the* Church.'

Irenaeus: Against heresies

Philip went on, 'The primitive Christians didn't set out with an explicit theory of what should be treated as Scripture. Only systematic thinking makes the Christian community aware of the beliefs they already have. Once it started using Paul's letters and the synoptics alongside the Jewish Scriptures in the liturgy, the Christian community effectively had a new canon. But that practice was not explicitly articulated as the concept of a Bible consisting of Old and New Testaments.'

Bob came back with the pizzas and said that Christians didn't write the Bible the way that people normally put a book together. If you write a paper, and you don't have one basic driving idea, it won't gel. But the Christian Bible didn't begin that way. They were using writings by Jews and by Christians as if they were a joined up book. So what made the "canonical" version gel?'

Putting a small piece of green salad into his mouth, Anthony answered, 'The implicit idea behind their liturgy was promise and fulfilment. They made it explicit when their practice was challenged. Theologians have often been stimulated to explain Christian belief when people do something that feels weird, like Marcion calling his canon a "new Scripture."'

Cathy's notes told them that the bishop of Lyons, Irenaeus, borrowed Marcion's theory of a 'new Scripture'. But he uses it to defend a more extensive, Christian canonical Scripture. Christians didn't yet have the terms 'Old Testament' and 'New Testament'. Irenaeus speaks of the 'Old Covenant' and 'New Covenant'. These terms were stepping stones to the standard terminology because they helped Christians think about what they were doing in creating a new canon. They had to make the implicit criteria of promise and fulfilment conceptually explicit.

Canonisation implies rejection as well as acceptance of texts. Irenaeus rejects some of Marcion's 'Pauline' letters, and writings of Gnostics like Valentinus. Irenaeus lists as canonical Scripture the Old Testament, the synoptic gospels, the gospel of John, 13 Pauline letters, the pastoral epistles, 1 Peter, and 1 and 2 John. He draws on six writers who were apostles – Matthew, Peter, Paul, John, James and Jude – and on two who had apostolic backing, Luke (with Paul behind him) and Mark (backed by Peter).

Philip said that Irenaeus's argument for accepting those 'New Covenant' texts was that they had apostolic authority. Irenaeus is using the word 'apostolic' in a broad sense. Just as all the Old Testament writers have prophetic authority, so the New Covenant authors have apostolic authority. For Irenaeus, a New Covenant text has to come from an author in a position to give an accurate historical account of Jesus's life and teachings. Irenaeus claimed the apostles wrote in the power of the Holy Spirit.

Montanism

Cathy asked, 'Why didn't Irenaeus list the book of Revelation?' 'I'm coming to that,' said Philip. 'Some of Irenaeus's contemporaries believed the Holy Spirit was talking to them. Montanus was the leader of a Christian movement that hung out in the mountains of Phrygia, in northern Greece. The Montanists spoke in tongues and had visions. They were into apocalyptic texts. Irenaeus never lists the book of Revelation amongst the canonical writings because it was too hot to handle.'

Anthony deprecated Cathy's Pentecostal attitudes. He said, 'Tertullian started hanging with the Montanists. They were like happy-clappies are today. Brainless fundamentalists. Tertullian took the idea of a two-step revelation further than the orthodox Irenaeus. Tertullian claimed that Montanism was the expression of a "Third Age", the Age of the Spirit, which was the fulfilment of the New Covenant. The Montanists wrote down their visions. Christian bishops feared their flocks might not tell the difference between these writings and the Christian narrative. The Church told the happy-clappies that it was too late to add to Scripture: they said, "the canon is closed, guys . . . and girls."'

Completion of the canon

Cathy picked out of this the impression that having a canon was an excuse for being an elitist snob. But she couldn't say that with her mouth full of spinach and bacon pizza. Philip cut in and said, 'By the mid-third century, Revelation and Acts had made it to lists church leaders made of biblical texts. By the fourth century, they use the word "canonical" about the Christian Bible, and all the texts that had formed the canon had been selected.'

Cathy said, 'The reasons our canon looks like it does come from the Bible.' 'We didn't have that line of reasoning until we had the canon,' Anthony replied. Philip felt a man on a desert island couldn't recreate the canon out of a truckload of the Jewish and Christian documents that had been floating around since 1000 BC. 'You can't call an arbitrary collection of documents a line of reasoning!' said Bob, handing them the bill.

A limited canon

There was time to run after the class did their test on the canon. So they talked about the implications of what they had learned. Anthony asked, 'What would happen if someone added or subtracted books from the canon after it was "fixed" by the Church?' 'Like the Mormons,' said Greg. Rosie wondered whether Mormons could do Christian systematic theology. 'No,' said Anthony. Just as the Jewish Scriptures look different when they are called the *Old* Testament to the Christian *New* Testament, so the New Testament looks different if people think of it as leading up to a further revelation. What makes a canon a canon is its having fixed limits.

Martin Luther (1483–1546) and the reformed canon of Scripture

Cathy said, 'Luther changed the Catholic canon of Scripture. He cut out late Jewish books, like Maccabees.' Fred asserted, 'Since Protestants use a different Bible from Orthodox and Catholic Christians, we don't have one single shared norm!' Jamaal asked, 'Would you call faith in Christ a shared norm? Any doctrine should be tested against whether it builds up faith in Christ.' 'Or detracts from it,' said the Boot. 'Luther took out Catholic "canonical" books that undermine faith in Christ.'

Sources of theology

Lara didn't see why a canon was needed. The Professor said, 'The canon is important for Christianity because Christianity teaches that God speaks through the words of Scripture. The canon is a locus of revelation. That's why the Bible is a source of Christian doctrine.' She said that when we say 'systematic theology is based on faith' we mean it is grounded on God, as its sole source.

We usually describe the places where God's voice is heard as the sources of theology. 'The Bible is the only place to hear God,' said Cathy. 'Catholics add to the revelation. They believe things which are not in the Bible, like devotion to Mary.' The class broke up shortly after that.

Anthony was a rare fish, in that he was studying Theology because he wanted to be a theologian. Anthony's parents didn't loaf around the house, baking bread like Fred's mom, or getting stoned, like Greg's Dad. They were hard-working and sensible Episcopalians. So Anthony went home to a clean, airy and empty condominium. He turned off the intercom and turned on Mozart, Karl Barth's favourite composer. The Genius Kid stared at the mahogany floor while the music made patterns of numbers inside his domed head. Glancing up at the window, he saw a strange apparition. Rosie was standing on a fire hydrant, waving a sunflower! The bubbly blonde-haired girl was waving to attract his attention. Had she come round to see *him*? Then he remembered she worked in a florist and did deliveries. She was bringing the stuff for his mother's flower arranging class, at church.

Seminar Six: Systematic theology as faithful reasoning

Karl Barth's Church Dogmatics

Philip was supposed to have begun the class by talking on Augustinian theology but he phoned in to say he was stuck in a traffic jam. So the Professor got the seminar going. Nodding at Cathy, she said that Barth had entered the theological scene as a radical 'Tertullian'. His *Commentary on Romans* (1919) drives a wedge between human reason, experience and desire, and the revelation of God in Christ. Later, by studying Anselm, Barth decided there is a unique Christian reason. Now he claimed that faith creates its own kind of reason. There is a biblical logic, the revealed logic of God. 'Barth's *Church Dogmatics* demonstrates the Christian use of reason,' said the Professor.

Cathy asked, 'Why church dogmatics?' Anthony said that Augustinian theology is carried out in a community. Cathy said, 'Which church do Augustinians think you have to belong to?' 'With the Reformation,' Anthony replied, 'the idea developed that church is invisible. There is just one church, inspired by the Spirit, but it is an invisible church of believers. That's roughly the Calvinist idea. Protestants still know the Bible comes to us in church and theology happens in a community.'

Narrative theology / Postliberalism

Bob said, 'If the community is invisible, there's no way you can hang out with them.' Cathy thought a person would be better off figuring out their own theology, without conformity and group-think. The Professor asked, 'Where would that lone individual get their words for God or for acts of faith?' Anthony said that words like 'trinity' and 'baptism' come to us from our church community.

Believing the story

Lara disagreed: she said that, for liberal theology, we each have our own experiences, which are put into words – like with a religious myth – later on, when we join a community. The Professor told the class that postliberal theologians argue that is a false picture. They say there are no religious experiences until there is a verbal format for them, and that verbal format comes from our religious community. The best known postliberal theologian is the Lutheran George Lindbeck.

For Lindbeck and his disciples, theology is reflection on the narratives of Scripture, as mediated by churches. The meaning of a theological statement is how it's used in Christian contexts. One does not test theological language by its correspondence to a fact or an experience but by situating the words in the context of religious behaviour.

Cathy asked, 'Do narrative theologians deny that biblical language corresponds to the facts? Like the facts of Christ's life?' Anthony said, 'With narrative theology, understanding our faith is like picking up a story. Given the presuppositions of the story, and the characters as the plot defines them, it all makes sense. But you can't ask, like, why didn't Othello just ask Desdemona if she was fooling around? That question doesn't make sense in the context of Shakespeare's play.'

Cathy was unimpressed by this example from secular literature. She said, '*Othello* isn't supposed to be true. Irenaeus wanted to canonise the gospels whose authors had factual evidence about Christ's life. Why did an apostle have to be historically linked to Christ, if all it comes back to is believing a story?' Anthony said that canonisation was not about biographical factuality. It was about going with what people heard in church. 'Abraham, and Sarah and Joseph are paradigms for Christian living, whether they actually existed or not,' he said.

Greg asked, 'Could there be a cyber-community of Joseph Campbell fans, who live by *The Hero with a Thousand Faces*?' 'I'm not planning to make a law against it,' said Anthony pleasantly. Greg tried again. 'Campbell's books sold hundreds of thousands of copies. There is an invisible body of people who believe in Campbell's super-hero.' Anthony said, 'I told you before. Narrative theology begins from the uniqueness of the Christian story.' Rosie asked, 'What is it that makes the Christian story unique, if it's not the historical particularity of the characters?'

Fred asked if Augustinian theologians think religious language refers to anything but human behaviour. Is 'God' what Christian language points to – outside of them – or does narrative theology make the word 'God' cave in to mean Christian community?

The biography of St Augustine of Hippo (354–431)

Philip had liked Rosie's idea that theology is expressed in spiritual biographies. So he read the *Confessions* of Augustine of Hippo, the man's biography down to his conversion. He broke into the discussion on narrative theology and fought his way past a wall of rucksacks and desks angled against him into a seat.

Gasping for breath, Philip told the class that Augustine studied Greek and Roman philosophies. He didn't just read philosophy books; Augustine wanted living philosophical experience. The Roman philosopher Cicero (106–43 BC) and the Greek philosopher Plotinus (205–270) taught him to look beyond his material body to eternal truth. Augustine learned from the philosophers that, if he wanted to see the light within, he had to become a changed man. He tried to become a man of the Spirit. Sometimes he got there but he couldn't stay with it for long. Philosophy and reason were good pointers but not enough.

Christian bishops like Ambrose were telling him that Christianity is not a philosophical system; there are some parts of it you have to take on trust. But could Augustine take that leap of faith, when it meant giving up his sex life? Bob wanted to know why Augustine was so extreme: 'Why did he think Christianity meant total celibacy? It's uncool not to keep a distance on ideas.' Bob and Lara smiled at each other. Philip said, 'Augustine was a passionate person. Philosophy had been a total way of life for him. Now he wanted Christianity to take over his life.'

Understanding is the reward of faith. Therefore seek not to understand that you may believe, but believe that you may understand.

Augustine, *Homilies on the Gospel of John* (1887)

Augustine changed when he converted to Christianity. Now he felt that by making an act of faith in truths that his reason could not grasp, he got a better grasp of the ideas he had been trying to get hold of with his reason alone. Cathy asked, 'Does that mean you can think and believe at the same time?' 'Yes,' said Anthony. 'Faith tells us things we wanted to know but couldn't have learned without believing in God's revelation. Augustinian theology begins from revelation and moves from there to reasoning, always basing reasoning in faith. Once we have faith, we can think about it. Our thinking is an extension of our believing, like the leaf on the tree. Once faith starts thinking, reason is absorbed into God's revelation.'

Augustinianism and narrative theology

Cathy wondered, 'Where does Augustine connect with narrative theology?' Philip couldn't answer, since he hadn't heard of postliberalism. So Anthony explained that narrative theology is the new Augustinianism. That didn't gel with Rosie, who said, 'Augustine's biography is basic to his theology. Narrative theology is anti-experiential. The "Christian narrative" is at the back of postliberalism, not personal experiences of truths.'

Anselm of Canterbury (1033–1109): 'Faith seeking understanding'

Philip tried to get back into his presentation, saying, 'Benedictine monks would give you the same picture as Augustine. They quote Anselm: *Credo ut intelligam*, which means "I believe in order to understand."' Anthony interrupted, 'Today's Christian churches are like Benedictine monasteries were in the Dark Ages.' Jamaal could buy it: 'Theology is what makes sense in Christian life and the Christian experience of praising God,' he said. 'Call it the biblical narrative or call it faith, it's the same.'

Is narrative theology counter-cultural?

'I can't buy this at all,' said Lara. 'And it is Augustinian. Like Augustine, narrative theologians move from faith to reason. It tells you to take the patriarchal so-called "biblical narrative" as given. Liberal theologies go from experience to faith, from below to above. Augustinianism is authoritarian, top-down theology. It's reactionary. If there is any Augustinianism around now, it came up after people gave up on liberalism and voted for conservative politicians, Reagan, Thatcher and Bush.'

Anthony answered, 'I would put it differently from Lara. When our parents were in college, even back then it wasn't cool to be Christian. But it wasn't totally counter-cultural, either. Guys in the student dorm didn't think you were a freak if you went to church. There are plenty of Augustinian theologians today. Christians have got wise to the fact that they have to form their own distinct group. They can't survive outside it. Nowadays, we know our "rationality" has nothing in common with secular uses of reason.' The Professor told the students that Stanley Hauerwas describes Christians as 'resident aliens' in a society in which 'Christendom' is dead and buried.

Lara said, 'It's like the backlash against feminism. So-called "biblical logic" often excludes women's experience.' The Professor remarked that postliberal theologians are not conservative in their attitudes to politics, sexual ethics, or the culture wars. They take on board feminist critiques of Christian tradition. Hauerwas is a pacifist. Cathy said, 'In 2001, *Time* magazine called Hauerwas the greatest theologian in America.' Anthony wondered if that was more damaging to *Time* magazine or to Hauerwas. He was just indicating that he personally didn't get his ideas from popular magazines; he had a lot of respect for Hauerwas.

Fred said that narrative theology was like Augustinianism in one way. It makes the uncritical assumption that everything a theologian thinks is coming from faith and not human reason as well. Bob added, 'Its easy to imagine you have got hold of a unique faith-based idea of God, when actually your ideas are fed in from your culture.' Cathy said, 'They pick up a secular theory, like all experience is linguistic, and call that basing theology in "the biblical narrative."'

Fred said, 'That has to happen with Augustinianism because it assumes that, once a theologian gets going, his reason is worked over by God's revelation. It closes its eyes to its own reasoning processes and just takes it all as God-given.' Fred claimed that Augustinians always reproduce the secular paradigms of their own society. Contemporary Augustinians are all deep in Hegelian and Marxist sociology of knowledge. Fred was too good a debater to mention where that left feminism. Anyhow, at that moment he had a grandstand view of Lara's legs.

Seminar Seven: Systematic theology as reasoning faith

On Friday afternoon, Cathy phoned Fred and said her dad was taking them to the ocean for the weekend. Did he want to come? 'We can go scuba-diving!' said Cathy. Fred said no, he had just made a big discovery and had to follow it through. 'What's that big?' asked Cathy. 'John Searle,' said Fred. 'He's annihilated the idea that all experience is linguistic.' 'Is he one of your philosophers?' asked Cathy. 'A Catholic?' 'No, he's an agnostic,' said Fred patiently. 'I can use him to mount a rational attack on Anthony's views.' Fred would have felt more comfortable explaining this to a rational person like Lara. 'It wasn't just Anthony, it was Jamaal,' said Cathy. 'Don't give me Jamaal,' said Fred. 'For him, talking about narratives is a metaphor to put across his faith. For real narrative theology, philosophy is the bottom line. Henry Kissinger said always go after the bottom line.' Cathy's dad was calling her to help him hook up the boat to the car, so she said goodbye without asking Fred how he could have an independent agnostic philosophy tied up to his faith. Suppose it came off the back, like her dad's boat once detached from the back of the car, and terrified the Devonshire farmers as it careered down the hill?

Thomas Aquinas (1225–74)

Thomas's definition of 'faith'

Fred hadn't waited to be told to give a presentation on Aquinas's idea of systematic theology. He insisted on it. He claimed the discussion so far had been too fluid about the use of the word 'faith'. For Thomas, faith is a light that comes from God. Faith is objective. It comes to us from outside. Lara asked, 'Did he think Muslims had a faith?' Fred replied, 'You are using the word "faith" in the post-Reformation way, where it means a subjective opinion, a choice made by an individual or a group. Thomas would say the Muslim religion is not a revealed religion, that Muslim beliefs don't come about because of God illuminating their minds.'

Reason analogous in believer and non-believer

Bob said, 'So he was a crusader, he wanted to exterminate Muslims and Jews.' 'No,' said Fred, 'he wanted to argue with them; and he took over some of their own best philosophical arguments because he thought their reason was sound and strong. It was their religion he didn't accept as revealed truth.'

Fred told the class that Aquinas belonged to the Preaching Order founded by St Dominic (1170–1221). The ideal of the Dominican Friars was to pray and contemplate God in order to pass on what they learned. 'Thomas was building on Dominican spirituality when he said faith is user-friendly to reason,' Rosie observed.

Fred answered, 'For Thomas, theology is based on faith. But a Thomist realises that the reason theology uses is the same reason that Lara or anyone else uses. Reason takes its principles from faith and then works them through in a natural, human way.' Cathy didn't see the difference from Augustine, if reason is based on faith. Rosie suggested human reason and God-given faith are like the human and divine natures of Christ, interlocking but still entirely themselves.

Grace does not suppress nature, it perfects it.

Thomas Aquinas, *Summa Theologiae*, Ia, i. 8 ad 2

Fred waited for these noises off to quieten down, then, glancing at Lara, he continued, 'Once revelation has suggested a principle to human reason, you can sometimes give rational arguments for that idea that make sense to non-believers.' Jamaal asked, 'Like what?' Fred said, 'Like the existence of God and the immortality of the soul.' Lara asked, 'Could you prove to me God exists?' 'Sure,' said Fred, 'There are five ways . . .' Lara cut in, 'If you could, then I would know that God exists, I wouldn't believe it. All you need is reason, in the long run. It's detachable. You don't need faith or revelation.'

Fred came back with a speech. Thomas never forgot that God has revealed to us that He exists, and who He is. God told Moses, 'I am that I am.' When Thomas argued for God's existence, his faith had oriented him towards God's revealed character. Thomas wasn't working up to some generalised common conception of God. He knew the testimony of revelation and he knew who 'God' refers to.

But it's not like Anthony's Augustinian example, where you can't make out Othello or Desdemona unless you accept all the presuppositions of the story. Each of Thomas's proofs of God's existence ends, 'And this is what everyone calls God.' When anyone reads them, they could say to themselves, 'Hey yeah, that is what I mean by God.' They might have a pretty confused idea of God but that is where their experience was pointing them, and Thomas is spelling it out. If revelation is true to reality, and experience gives us clues about what reality is like, then faith and human thinking fit each other. Thomas's proofs point to a divine character who looks right to our reason. Thomas said some parts of systematic theology relate to ideas that we have some vague sense of, without revelation.

Most revealed truths beyond reason

But not always. Some truths can't be accepted at all, unless God enlightens our minds with faith. Most of the revealed truths systematics is based on are humanly unknowable; we only believe them on God's say-so. Cathy said, 'That would be the Trinity and the Incarnation.' Fred answered, 'Of course. No Thomist believes the central features of theology, like the Incarnation and the Trinity, can be accepted on any grounds other than God-given faith.'

Faith not a rational hypothesis

'We can't rationally know that the Trinity, Christ and the Church fit the realities. We have to believe it. A faithful mind is looking at mysteries. Reason comes up with plausible hypotheses. Having faith is not like holding a hypothesis. What we believe about the Bible or Christ doesn't conflict with the evidence but it goes way beyond it.' Rosie cut in, 'So you agree that you can't hear the "sound" of the Christian God unless you have faith.'

'Fine,' said Fred. 'But God's Word enlightens our minds. Being given faith isn't like having a prejudice, or an obsession, that can't digest questions or new information. The believer can ask rational questions about the Trinity, Christ or the Eucharist. The objectivity of faith makes it open to rational discussion in a way that private opinions and tastes are not.'

Cathy asked, 'Can't you see it all went wrong when people start taking reason as a norm for Christian theology?' Fred blew it with Lara when he replied, 'Reason is only a norm for theology because it's God-given. Our reason isn't genuinely autonomous from what faith teaches us.' Greg tried to help his buddy out, saying, 'You're a Christian philosopher, not a philosopher who is also a Christian.' 'That's right,' said Fred, disastrously, 'I'm talking about Christian reasoning.' 'You don't really believe in reason,' said Lara. 'Only someone like Bob, who uses their reason independently, does. Bob would use reason to come to any conclusion. You only come to conclusions allowed for by your church.' Then Lara asked, 'Do you have to be a Catholic to be a Thomist?' 'Yes,' said Fred, who had just decided to spend the rest of his life in a monastery on Mount Athos.

Further reading

The books in this list are ranked in order of their accessibility to undergraduate readers.

Liberation theology

Cone, James H. (1975, 1997), *God of the Oppressed*, Maryknoll, NY: Orbis.

Cone's version of liberation theology is more accessible than the Latin American versions, and he invented it first!

Liberal theology

Ruether, R. R. (1983), *Sexism and God-Talk: Toward a Feminist Theology*, Boston: Beacon.
Hick, John (1993), *The Metaphor of God Incarnate*, London: SCM Press.

Fideism

Moore, Charles E. (ed.) (1999), *Provocations: Spiritual Awakenings of Kierkegaard*, Farmington, PA: Plough. A sequence of out-takes from Kierkegaard's writings; a direct route into one of the greatest theologians of modern times.

Postliberal / narrative theology

Hauerwas, Stanley (1989), *Resident Aliens: Life in the Christian Colony*, Nashville: Abingdon.
Lindbeck, George (1984), *The Nature of Doctrine: Religion and Theology in a Postliberal Age*, Philadelphia: Westminster.

Questions

1. What would be the differences between the theology you got out of a library and the theology you got out of a monastery?

2. Does non-Christian experience reveal God?

3. Pick out three 'Christ images' from contemporary films and say whether the echo is designed or not. Are your images mythic or symbolical?

4. Does fideism make Christianity a private matter? Is it an uncritical attitude?

5. Was the Church using faith or reason when it drew up its canon?

6. How can a biography express a theology?

7. Which comes first, religious experiences or religious narratives?

8. What does 'faith' mean? How does the fideist definition of faith differ from the Thomistic one?

9. How is Thomism like and unlike liberalism?

CHAPTER FOUR

The Holy Spirit, Creeds and the Church

Francesca Aran Murphy

Seminar One: The inspiration of the Holy Spirit

What is inspiration?

Greg had to give a starter definition of inspiration. He told the class that the verb 'inspire' literally means 'to breathe into'. In Latin, *in* means 'into' and *spiro* means 'I breathe'. He added, 'Inspiration is not necessarily to do with writing. Back in 800 BC, the Greeks pictured inspiration as a godlike force. The Force could make you an inspired stage performer, an inspired basket-weaver, or an inspired seminar-presenter. But it does have a localised meaning in relation to art. Apollo and the Muses inspired musicians, poets and songwriters, who were one and the same person in those days. Inspiration is the process by which someone is empowered to sing a poem.'

Bob said, 'When it comes down to brass tacks, inspiration meant the Force puts an idea into the poet's head, right?' 'Wrong,' said Greg. 'It's connected to breathing: when Homer was feeling a poem coming on, humming to himself, he prayed to a Muse to breathe the poetry into him. And the inspiring power entered his lungs and his breath and came out in the rhythm of the song.' Jamaal said, 'You have to keep the broad sense of inspiration, even when you apply it to artists.' 'Inspiration isn't getting new concepts, it's becoming a transformed personality,' said Rosie.

Friedrich Schleiermacher (1768–1834) and the experiential idea of inspiration

Greg said, 'Biblical inspiration is exactly like Homer's inspiration.' 'No way,' replied Cathy. 'You can't talk about Homer's epics and the Bible in the same breath. How do you know Homer had a unique inspiration? We know Scripture is inspired because 2 Timothy 3:16 states that "All Scripture is given by the inspiration of God." The writer used the Greek word "theo-pneustos", God-breathed.'

'But in this day and age,' said Bob, 'We've discovered that what ancient people called divine Forces were psychological processes. When we call the Bible inspired, we have to redefine what the word means.' Lara took that as her start button. 'Liberal theology sees the inspiration of the Bible as a deep experience of the divine,' she said. Liberals have dropped the idea of inspiration as divine dictation coming down from God's megaphone to a human receiver.

> God did not just speak once upon a time to a privileged group of the world in one part of the world, making us ever after dependent on the codification of their experience. On the contrary, God is alive and with us. The Holy Spirit continues to speak, and we are mandated to continue the dialogue . . . we must reconstruct meaning for ourselves today . . . in the sparking of primal stories that spring up from our own experience, drawing upon a storehouse of cultural symbols and images.
>
> Rosemary Radford Ruether, *Sexism and God-Talk* (1983: xiv)

Schleiermacher invented liberal theology. It was Schleiermacher who showed that inspiration amounts to a pre-cognitive and pre-verbal experience of a human being. Inspiration is the experience of God, which a man or woman puts into their own words. Church words for it come a long time after the inspiration.

Philip said, 'The people who had the experience knew they did but how can we tell that the Biblical authors had any special contact with God?' Lara replied, 'You know Coleridge, who wrote "The Rhyme of the Ancient Mariner"? He believed we can tell where there's inspiration behind the Bible because those parts inspire us when we read it.'

Criticisms of experientialism

The Bible made Greg feel cold inside. He said, 'That proves there's nothing special about biblical inspiration because Rimbaud is more inspiring to me than the Book of Joshua.' Bob remarked, 'That's fine – because you have to distinguish between the biblical books that are inspirational and the parts that are not, like the Old Testament food regulations and the Israelites carrying out genocide on the Canaanites.' Greg thought, *Coleridge had to be smoking opium to find* any part *of the Bible inspiring.*

Philip asked, 'If it all comes down to a mind-blowing experience, how do we know who is inspired and who isn't?' Rosie thought an experientialist might as well say you inspire yourself. 'It reduces God out of the picture,' she said. 'Breathing, you do to yourself. Resuscitating a drowning man is something an agent does to someone else. The notion of inspiring implies an agent acting on someone else. Inspiring is into-breathing. God is breathing into the poet's body.' Greg said, 'Divine inspiration is like mouth-to-mouth resuscitation when a poet is running out of steam.'

The Holy Spirit

Philip said, 'I agree inspiration comes to us from outside, it's something an artist has done to them. But there's something inward about it, too. Learning begins on the outside, when someone says something: but the actual process goes on in me.' Philip argued that inspiration is a subjective experience event. Fred said, 'What's that?' Philip replied, 'The Spirit makes you think or do from within. That's different from running into Jesus Christ on the street in Jerusalem.'

> The special element in revelation is ... identical with what the New Testament usually calls the Holy Spirit as the subjective side of revelation.
>
> Karl Barth, *Church Dogmatics*, I/I (1975: 449)

Cathy felt that unbiblical ruminations on grammar could only get you so far. She said, 'In the Old Testament, God's Spirit is called the "ruach".

487

It's a mighty wind or breath that God manifests himself through.' 'OK,' Philip replied, 'but don't forget the manifestation always happens to a prophet.' 'Or to one of the judges, like Deborah,' said Rosie. 'It's like with the Greeks: sometimes inspiration made the Israelites write but sometimes it made them act.'

Bob said, 'I hope this Israelite ruach isn't the same as the third person of the Christian Trinity in your minds. For Israel, God's Spirit is an impersonal force. Nobody in the Hebrew Bible calls it "the Holy Spirit."' Greg felt the Old Testament ruach was God being unruly, stirring things up.

Bob asked, 'So is Jesus a Jewish prophet powered by the Spirit?' 'A prophet and some,' said Jamaal. 'The Spirit kicks off Jesus's mission when it lands on him at the baptism (Matthew 3: 16) and it's behind his being able to preach (Luke 4: 14). But John the Baptist says "I have baptised you with water, but he will baptise you with the Holy Spirit" (Mark 1: 8). No Old Testament character could hand the ruach over to other people at will; the Spirit is for God to give, not humans.' Philip added, 'Jesus breathed the Spirit on the disciples, after the resurrection (John 20: 22). He was handing it on to them.' Bob said, 'That isn't historical fact.' The Boot replied heatedly, 'Jesus's words came true! The Spirit struck the disciples at Pentecost' (Acts 2).

Bob snorted, 'We haven't got anywhere near the Christian Holy Spirit. The New Testament authors don't give the Greek word "pneuma" a capital letter, and they don't think of it as one more person in God.' Cathy replied, 'How about John 14: 16–17.' 'Huh?' said Bob. Cathy answered, 'That's where Jesus promises to send the Spirit as "another Advocate" for the disciples, after he goes.' She told the atheist student, darkly, '"No man can say that Jesus is the Lord, but by the holy *pneuma*"' (1 Corinthians 12: 3). Philip said, 'Because what the inspiration of the Spirit makes us know is Christ. Jesus, the historical fact of him, is the outward presence of God, and the Spirit is the inward manifestation. The Spirit breathes our words about Christ into us.' The class didn't blame Philip when the Professor said, 'Next week, it's heads down for a test on the Creeds.'

Seminar Two: The Christian Creeds

Biblical basis of the Trinitarian Creeds

Cathy was going to flunk the test. She sat studying her Bible, so she could crush Bob next time the Spirit came up. She found some Trinitarian language in John (15: 26; 16: 13–15). She saw that, in

Matthew, the risen Christ orders the assembled disciples to 'Go and make disciples of all nations, baptising them in the name of the Father and of the Son and of the Holy Spirit' (28: 19). Cathy was worrying that Bob would say John was 'late' and unhistorical, and that Matthew 28: 19 was a late insert, when someone shouted down the dorm corridor that Cathy had a guest. It was Philip, who knew she was home, sulking.

Philip said that late, invented, true, or whatever, Matthew 28: 19 tells us that the early Christians had a communal experience of the Trinity, when people were baptised. 'Which was adults,' said Cathy. 'And not in rituals,' she mumbled, thumbing into Paul's letters: '"because you are sons, God has sent the Spirit of the Son into our hearts, crying Abba! Father!"' (Galatians 4: 4–7). Philip said, 'That's praying in Christ, with the Spirit, to the Father. It's not spelled out like the Creeds will be but it's the basis. A first-century cat, Clement of Rome, speaks to the same triad-shaped experience: "Have we not one God, and one Christ and one Spirit of grace which has been poured upon us?". It sounds like the Baptismal Creeds.'

Cathy nodded blankly, while Philip went on: 'You can't get away from the liturgical background to statements like Paul's "Be filled with the Spirit . . . giving thanks in the name of our Lord Jesus Christ to God the Father"' (Ephesians 5: 18–20). 'They're only guessing that comes from liturgy,' said Cathy. 'I guess praise of the Son and prayer to the Father happens in liturgies,' Philip answered. 'And only in the inspiration of the Spirit, if it's genuine prayer.'

What are the Creeds for?

When Fred saw Lara going into Rosie's flat with a stack of notes on the Creeds, he followed her. Fred had never been to Rosie's. He looked around and saw a beat-up sofa with Peruvian rugs on it and posters advertising expensive coffee from South American co-operatives. Annoyed by this high-minded paraphernalia, he said, 'Save the whales and abort the babies', and shoved Rosie's arthritic cat off the sofa.

Picking up Francis, Lara told them the word 'creed' comes from the Latin 'credo', 'I believe'. Christianity has a ton of Creeds. Some people imagine systematic theology has to use them as guidelines. But why shouldn't we go on our personal reading of the Bible? Rosie said, 'Trying to say what the Bible means is like picking out constellations in the stars. The Creeds focus Christian eyes on a special way of perceiving God.' Fred said, 'A specific pattern of faith.'

He stated that the first Christian credo was 'Jesus is Lord'. When Paul wrote his letters, in the 50s and 60s AD, he urged believers to 'hold fast to the traditions [in Greek, *paradoseis*] which you have been taught' (2 Thessalonians 2: 15) and speaks of 'the pattern of doctrine' (Romans 6: 17). Lara said, 'Paul didn't write 2 Thessalonians.' Fred replied, 'Who cares? The fact is, in the 80s, Christians had a sense of identity.' The pastoral epistles refer to "the deposit" (in Greek, *paratheke*) and "the faith" (1 Timothy 6: 20; 2 Timothy 1: 14).

The second-century bishops needed a set teaching that all converts could learn before they got baptised. Irenaeus called the pattern he used in catechesis the 'Rule of Faith'. Irenaeus figured it went back to the apostles. He wrote a book called *Against Heresies*. It mentions the 'Rule of Faith' ten times. Irenaeus also refers to 'the Rule of Truth . . . which he received through baptism'. 'These early Christians thought truth matters,' said Fred.

The liturgical context of the first Credal statements

Lara said 'Converts had to confess their beliefs during the baptismal service. When a convert was plunged for the first time into the water' – she shoved Fred's head onto the table – 'the bishop asked them if they believed in the Father; at the second plunge' – she shoved Fred again – 'the bishop asked if they believed in the Son, who was Incarnate, died, and rose again; at the third plunging' – Fred now had a bruise on his forehead – 'the new Christian was asked if they believed in the Holy Spirit. Think I'd make a good bishop?' asked Lara. 'That's why the first creeds are called "interrogatory creeds". They come from the bishops' interrogating baptismal candidates about their beliefs.'

Hippolytus' *apostolic tradition*

Do you believe in the Father Almighty?

Do you believe in Jesus Christ, the son of God, who was conceived of the Holy Spirit out of the Virgin Mary, and crucified under Pontius Pilate, died [and buried] and was resurrected on the third day from death to life, and ascended into heaven and is seated at the right hand of the Father and who will come to judge the living and the dead?

Do you believe in the Holy Spirit and the Holy Church and the resurrection of the flesh?

From Stevenson (1978: 155–6)

Rosie said that the first known Credal document looks like a questionnaire. Hippolytus, bishop of Smyrna, wrote it some time between 198 and 227. People also recited a 'declaratory' creed before they were baptised. Creeds like that were called 'symbols' of the faith. In Graeco-Roman culture, a 'symbol' meant a sign that points to a reality.

The 'symbol' was the sign of the Trinity. The baptismal 'symbols' expressed Christian practice, which went on for centuries before it was conceptualised as a doctrine of the Trinity.

The Nicene Creed (325)

Lara said, 'By the early fourth century, there was a theological debate about whether the Father and the Son are both equally God. The dispute couldn't be solved by the Bible because both sides could quote the Bible to back up their case.' Fred said, 'Christians would never have got as far as the Nicene Creed if everyone had gone along with Tertullian's idea that faith excludes reason.'

An Ecumenical Council of the Church was called in 325. The bishops at Nicaea wrote a Creed using a word that is not in Scripture. They said Christ is 'homoousios' with the Father. That means 'of the same being'.

The Trinitarian Creed of Constantinople

In 381, at the second Ecumenical Council of the Church, in Constantinople, the Nicene Creed was expanded to include the fact that the Holy Spirit is God.

The Niceno Constantinopolitan Creed

We believe in one God the Father almighty,
maker of heaven and earth,
of all things visible and invisible;
and in one Lord Jesus Christ
the only-begotten Son of God,
begotten from the Father before all ages,
Light from Light, true God from true God,
begotten not made,
of the same substance (homoousion) with the Father
through whom all things came into being.
Who for us men and for our salvation came down from heaven,
and was incarnate from the Holy Spirit and the Virgin Mary,
and became man,
and was crucified for us under Pontius Pilate,
and suffered and was buried,
and rose again on the third day according to the Scriptures,
and ascended to heaven,
and sits on the right hand of the Father,

> and will come again with glory to judge the living and the dead,
> of whose kingdom there will be no end;
> And in the Holy Spirit, the Lord and the giver of life;
> who proceeds from the Father [and the Son].
> Who is worshipped and glorified together with the Father and
>   the Son,
> who spoke through the prophets;
> In one Holy Catholic and Apostolic Church
> we confess one baptism for the remission of sins;
> we look forward to the resurrection of the dead
> and the life of the world to come.
>
> T. Herbert Bindley, *The Oecumenical Documents of the Faith* (1899)

Rosie asked, 'How come a monotheistic faith ended up believing in three gods?' Fred stood up, hitting his head on an African mobile. He said, 'The opposite is what happened. Christianity was monolatrous, like Judaism. That means one-God worshipping. But Matthew 28: 19 shows the one God telling his new name: the one single name of Father, Son, Spirit, to baptise people in. They had been worshipping God as three-in-one since the early Church. When people started wondering if the Son was really God, they wrote the Nicene Creed, that says Father and Son have the same being, the being of God.

> Those who support their counting games by talking of first and second and third ought to be informed that they are importing pagan polytheism into the pure theology of Christianity.
>
> Basil of Caesaria, *On the Holy Spirit*, Chapter XVII
> (Wace and Schaff 1945)

People who didn't obey the Magisterium carried on arguing. Then the Holy Spirit came into it. Was the Spirit God as much as the Father and the Son? Basil of Caesaria pointed out that, if you think the Spirit or the Son are subordinate gods, below the Father, and you worship them at Mass, you're a polytheist, like the Greeks with Zeus plus a zillion minor gods. Basil is saying, what happened to monolatry? You have to say the Three are one God not to be a polytheist! That's why the Creed of

Constantinople says the Spirit is 'worshipped and glorified' alongside Father and Son.' 'They didn't have Mass or the Magisterium back in those days,' said Lara.

Did the Creeds alter the structure of Christian belief?

Fred said, 'After that, the Trinity was at the base of systematic theology. Nicaea and Constantinople set up norms for the interpretation of biblical references to Father, Son and Spirit.' Lara claimed that they lost the spontaneity of early Christian worship. Right at that moment, her mobile rang. Fred was disconcerted to hear Bob's voice sing out, 'Hi, honey!' Bob said, 'It was only when the Roman emperors adopted Christianity, and began influencing it, that the Church took the step of fixing its idea of God in Creeds.'

Fred grabbed the phone and said, 'The *early* baptismal creeds show Christianity was *never* a free-for-all.' 'Calm down,' said Bob, 'All I'm saying is their idea of the Trinity is copied from Greek philosophers like Plotinus.' '*In their liturgy*,' Fred yelled, '*Christians had worshipped the Father, Son and Spirit since the primitive Church.*' It was possibly the uncoolest behaviour in human history.

Seminar Three: Tradition and the Church

Does the Holy Spirit guide the Church's interpretation of Scripture?

After the test, the class talked about what the Creeds meant for theology. Bob asked, 'When the Creed of Nicaea uses language that isn't in the Bible, wasn't that adding to revelation? I thought you believed revelation is fixed, in the Bible.' 'Revelation hasn't stopped,' said Lara. 'That is why theology is open. It can keep re-inventing itself.' Jamaal agreed that God didn't hang up the phone when the last word of the Bible was written. God wouldn't hand over a book, then vanish into eternity.

Distinguishing revelation and inspiration

Fred said, 'God doesn't hang up the phone but neither does he change his number! Otherwise, we would have to keep getting a new phone book. Revelation and inspiration are different matters.' Greg said, 'It's like the phone company inspires a guy to write, and the phone book is the revelation that comes out of it.' 'Right,' said Fred, vaguely aware that Greg was pulling his leg. 'Inspiration is how the writer is stimulated, revelation is what is shown to them,' he said.

Philip added, 'Revelation is Christ in action. If what God tells us, the revelation, could expand indefinitely, theology would have no normative basis. If revelation wasn't complete, we could not have a canon of Scripture. But how the revelation is interpreted has developed and deepened. The Creeds gave people a deeper conceptualisation of Christian spirituality.'

Why should the Creeds be normative in theology?

Cathy thought it was possible for the bishops at Nicaea or Constantinople to get the story wrong. How could fallible people be incapable of misinterpreting Scripture? If we take the Ecumenical Councils as infallible, we are putting the words of human beings above the Word of God. 'I don't see why we should take the Creeds as normative,' said the Boot, firmly.

Fred replied that the discernment of a normative pattern in Scripture by Nicaea and Constantinople was not only the work of human bishops but also of the Holy Spirit. He said, 'All Christians think the only source of Christian theology is God. For Catholic and Orthodox theologians, tradition is a source of inspiration because it's led by the Holy Spirit.' Cathy asked, 'Is there a biblical basis for that belief?'

Tradition in primitive Christianity

The Professor explained that the New Testament words for tradition are 'Paradoseis' (1 Corinthians 15), meaning 'tradition', and 'Paratheke', which means 'deposit', as in 2 Timothy 1: 14: 'The deposit which was committed to you, keep by the Holy Spirit which dwells in us.' Irenaeus claimed 'the substance of the tradition' (*he dynamos tes paradises*) is the same throughout the Church. The 'Canon of Truth' holds the universal Church together. Irenaeus's notion of tradition runs together with his idea of apostolicity. The dynamism of tradition, its original impetus, comes from the inspired apostles.

Orthodox and Catholics

Philip had been studying Orthodoxy and Catholicism because he couldn't figure which church was really his. His parents had been Russian Orthodox when they emigrated from the Soviet Union but now they didn't go to church. He said that Catholic and Orthodox Christians believe tradition is a divinely inspired way of interpreting Scripture. The story of Jesus is read aloud to us by the Holy Spirit, and the Spirit put the emphasis on all the right places. The debate about tradition is a debate about the Church. To deny the Spirit is present in tradition is to deny the existence of a visible Church of God on earth. But that's what pre-Reformation Christians thought they were. When schism came about between Orthodox and Catholic Christians, in the eleventh century, each claimed to be the visible Church.

Are Ecumenical Councils sources of doctrine?

Ecumenical Councils

Seven Ecumenical Councils acknowledged by East and West

1. Nicaea I (325)
2. Constantinople I (381)
3. Ephesus (431)
4. Chalcedon (451)
5. Constantinople II (553)
6. Constantinople III (681)
7. Nicaea II (787)

Acknowledged by Roman Catholic Church

8. Constantinople IV (869–70)
9. Lateran I (1123)
10. Lateran II (1139)
11. Lateran III (1179)
12. Lateran IV (1215)
13. Lyons I (1245)
14. Lyons II (1274)
15. Vienna (1311–12)
16. Constance (1414–18)
17. Florence (1438–45)
18. Lateran V (1512–17)
19. Trent (1545–63)
20. Vatican I (1869–70)
21. Vatican II (1962–65)

The Orthodox regard only the first seven Councils as ecumenical gatherings. They think those were infallibly guided by the Holy Spirit. Roman Catholicism teaches that there have been twenty-one Ecumenical Councils and that the Spirit is also at work in the magisterial teachings of the Pope. Anglicans usually go along with the first seven Councils but they don't regard them as infallible. They figure Councils could make mistakes. Rosie said, 'You can see why theologies differ from church to church. Nothing would count as a norm for theologian unless they believed the source was God. But theologians of different churches don't agree about what is sourced back to God.'

Seminar Four: Sin, grace and the City of God

Augustine versus Pelagius (360–420)

Fred was sitting at a university computer, writing an essay on original sin. It was Augustine who put that doctrine on the map. The debate started around 410–12. A British monk named Pelagius said the fall of Adam means we get bad social conditioning. But we can deal with it. If you try hard, you can overcome your bad habits and train yourself up to perfection. You can perfect yourself, taking Christ as your role model. *Like John Hick*, thought Fred.

Augustine argued that Adam's fall put a system fault into humanity. Sinfulness is built into human nature. Fallen Adam and Eve passed on their virus – carnal desire. In the very act of procreation, every one of their descendants sends out the virus again. *It's all over with Lara anyway,* thought Fred. *It never began.* So without God's grace, humans can't do anything good at all. *Too true.* Pelagius claimed Augustine was telling people to give up responsibility for their lives to God.

Once you believe in human perfectibility, thought Fred, *political theorists become Utopian.* 'An Augustinian believes that human society on earth can never be perfectly good,' he wrote. 'It takes account of the rottenness of human beings. The Pelagian dream of perfectibility ended in the Stalinist Gulag.' At that moment, the words 'FATAL ERROR' appeared on the screen, his computer crashed and he lost everything, his notes, his essay, his A minus.

Two versions of Augustinianism

Fred went to the computer help desk. Jamaal worked there and he was in conversation with Anthony. Jamaal was saying, 'The one thing everyone knows about Augustine is that he was screwed up about the Fall, obsessed with sin and sex . . . ' 'That's not the worst of it,' Anthony asserted. 'Augustine wrote the first introspective autobiography, the *Confessions*, and ever since the Latin West has made pre-verbal private self-awareness the foundation of knowledge.' A graduate student raised her eyes from her book and asked, 'Was the *Confessions* expressing his private feelings, like Sylvia Plath?' Jamaal thought aloud: 'Why does the *Confessions* make such an issue out of stealing the apples?' 'Go ahead and tell us,' said Fred dryly. Jamaal said, 'You can't always trust classical histories as historical reporting because writers like Tacitus or Plutarch put typical speeches in their characters' mouths. Roman biographies didn't describe individuals as individuals, they were about ideal types: *the* philosopher or *the* model soldier.' Fred said, 'That's a smart point.' Jamaal continued, 'Augustine was using different conventions from those of modern romanticism or confessional poetry. His "autobiography" was a Christian version of the Roman biographies. Augustine sees himself as Adam. His teenage scrumping episode is one more Fall story, which is what happens to everyone.'

With Anthony still insisting that Augustine gave the Latin West an individualistic idea of sin and grace, Jamaal startled everyone by exclaiming, 'You can't have even heard of Augustine's *City of God*. Augustine wasn't "The Latin West". He came from Africa! The eschatology of *The City of God* synthesises ideas from a regional African debate about the Church. Augustine had the idea of sin as a social structure before Marx. Sin is built into societies. The Roman Empire was built on oppression. The egotist society is the "city of man". The "city of God" is the community of grace. Augustine knew about it by experiencing Christian community. I read that stuff back when you said narrative theology was Augustinian. *Now* you tell me you've got no time for Augustine. Make up your mind.'

Anthony thought everyone had realised that Augustinianism is a method. It's not related to personalities. Humanistic liberalism is too optimistic about human nature. A renewed Augustinian imperative entered theology when it realised humanity is sinful, especially human rationality. 'Following Barth,' said Anthony, 'the new Augustinianism recognises that God's grace deletes human nature and starts over. Theology can only be built on faith. A theology that's drawn from the human condition is drawn from our sinful desires.' *Carnal desire*, thought Fred.

Jamaal said, 'Augustine's conversion made him realise he could not achieve what he wanted, which was God, without the grace of God. Our deepest desire is for God but it is God who motorises us towards him. *It's a paradox*, thought Fred. 'We desire God because why?' asked Jamaal. 'Because God put that desire there: even in Eden, before the Fall, it was only God's grace that kept Adam in line.' 'I fully agree with you,' said Anthony, glancing at his watch. 'But Augustine's theology contained the Hellenistic virus. The task of theology is purging out its human crease.' Jamaal said, 'For Augustine, same as for Athanasius, atonement is deification. Isn't deification what the Greeks desired? When Hick says all religions seek human transformation, he means deification. Augustine's idea of divine grace is more positive about human nature than Pelagius, or modern liberalism, not less.'

Seminar Five: Church and theology

The Church is the Body of Christ

Greg never went near Fred's house around going-to-church time on

Sunday because Fred's bear of a dad had a way of *willing* him along with them. He claimed he forgot who was his son and who wasn't. But someone had to rescue Fred from the mood swings he'd been going through since he finally got the message about Bob and Lara. Greg didn't figure on Holy Days of Obligation, which could happen on Thursday. 'Howdy, son,' said the Bear, putting a fireman's lift onto Greg and hauling him into the station wagon. The old car roared to St Albert's like the Bear was driving his fire engine to a burning house. Fred said, 'I can't face another sermon on Justice and Peace.' 'Listen up to the priest,' laughed the Bear. Greg ducked so the cuff landed on Fred's newly combed head. While the priest talked, Greg studied his face. He was preaching on 'Jesus wept' and the tracks of a biking accident were written on his face. When the man reminded them that Marx had claimed 'religion is the opium of the people', Greg saw Fred take his rosary out of his pocket. The guy in the white smock was talking about the drug wars in South America, claiming the trade led to exploitation, which anyone knew. Greg thought, *Even Dad realises drug barons are not heroes.* The priest stated that religion could be opium to anyone who didn't work it through. Fred thought, *Nothing but Marxism from modern Dominicans.* Greg remembered the debates they had about sourcing theology to God or humanity. *Where was* this *sermon coming from?* The preacher said Jesus was working it through when he wept over Lazarus. Fred was fingering his rosary, wondering why Rosie wanted them to go to an arts cinema and see a Russian movie. Wouldn't she rather take in *We Were Soldiers?* Rosie and Fred went to Tarkovksy's movie, *Andrei Rublev.*

The church . . . is the community that speaks Christianese, and theology formulates the syntax and semantics of this language.

Robert W. Jenson, *Systematic Theology:* Volume I (1997: 15)

On Friday, the Professor didn't show up for class. Most people went home, delighted. But Anthony organised a seminar around the connection between church-going and systematic theology. Greg put his feet on the desk and Rosie passed around a bag of jelly babies. Anthony gave the bag to Jamaal, without taking one, and said, 'A theologian's basic language must be that of the Church. Their other loyalties must be qualified by that.' Rosie said maternally, 'You'll vanish if you never eat anything.' Lara said, 'The commitments we bring to theology are as important as what church we're in. Protestants and Catholics with the same politics talk the same language. Cathy and Fred want to legalise dope because right-wing journalists like Jonah Goldberg say so.' Anthony repeated, 'Christian theologians must speak Christianese, not Esperanto.' Greg asked, 'Tony, if preachers never talk Esperanto, how come they once in a blue moon touch base with regular people? How could a Christian touch base with himself, if his own humanity can't talk to his faith?'

Church in postliberal theology

Anthony said, 'You can't speak as if people had two sides to their head, secular and believing. The only experience available to Christians is filtered through the biblical narrative. Words like "justice" mean different things in different paradigms. Christianity is its own language.' Greg asked, inconsequentially, 'Why do Christians stop in the middle of their service and shake hands?' 'Yes, why?' said Fred. Rosie replied, 'It's to show the Church is the body of Christ.' *Does Christ think in his Body like he weeps in his humanity?*, wondered Greg.

God provides us with ongoing interpretative guidance; this is part of the mission of 'inspiration', in which the Church is enlivened by the Living Water to proclaim the word and administer the sacraments... True knowledge of God is only possible through a communally-normed reading of the biblical narratives that is made possible by the Spirit-filled Church.

David S. Cunningham, *These Three are One: The Practice of Trinitarian Theology* (1998: 83)

Bob was glad for Tony that only seven people witnessed what happened next. The Genius Kid announced, 'I want you to hear a lyric by the Anglican poet, C. H. Sisson (1981: 67). He stood up and read, from 'The Usk':

> Christ is the language which we speak to God
> And also God, so that we speak in truth;
> He in us, we in him, speaking,
> To one another, the City of God.

Bob thought, *only the Elf Queen could get an adult man to read poetry in public.* Cathy felt narrative theology is a new Pharisaism, making human traditions the base of Christian theology. Fred was not bowled over either. He said, 'Postliberalism's City of God is collective language. It's substituting group behaviour for individual experience as the base of systematics. It's just group liberalism.' Anthony answered, 'Talking Christianese is being the Church. Don't you think Church matters?' Fred said, 'Not when you define the Church as a group having Christian experiences. You need someone to tell you what Christianity is before you can define a group's experiences as Christian.'

Different churches make for different theologies

Rosie agreed that we build our language to fit our experience, not the other way around. But people in different churches still don't have the same orientation. She did flower deliveries for Episcopalians but never for Pentecostalists: 'You'd have different spiritual experiences in a building that had flowers, or icons, than you would in one that went all-out to avoid them.'

Philip said, 'Those experiences would create different theologies.' *Systematic theology is a church-based discipline*, he thought. Bob asked, 'How could what church you belong to affect your theology?' Anthony answered, 'Orthodox, Catholic and Protestant theologians articulate different sets of practices. Their social context is what they say.' Bob said, 'Sure, every church provides its own social conditioning. Train people's behaviour and you train their minds.' Jamaal replied, 'You make physical behaviour sound superficial. But we wouldn't be having a free- floating conversation if we didn't feel free to tilt our chairs and put our feet up. Physical praxis affects your thinking.' 'Our bodies are temples of the Spirit,' said Rosie.

The Church and non-Christians

Greg said, 'Once you're in your church, can you hear what outsiders have to say? Like Muslims or Buddhists?' Anthony answered, 'The idea that Christians and Buddhists and the like speak the same language is a new colonialism. Liberalism is about as pluralist as McDonalds.' 'Speak to the question, man,' said Greg. 'Can a Christian learn anything from someoone who lives by a different religious code?' Rosie said 'Yes, because your friends who are different from you can teach you how to be yourself.' Christians could learn selflessness from Buddhists, for instance.

The Church has a visible social structure, which is a sign of unity in Christ: as such it can be enriched, and it is being enriched, by the evolution of social life – not as if something were missing in the constitution which Christ gave the Church, but in order to understand this constitution

> more deeply, express it better, and adapt it more successfully to our times. The Cjurch is happy to feel that, with regard to the community it forms and each of its members, it is assisted in various ways by men of all classes and conditions ... The Church itself also recognizes that it has benefited and is still benefiting from the opposition of its enemies and persecutors.
>
> *Vatican Council II:The Conciliar and Post-Conciliar Documents,*
> Section 44 (Flannery 1975: 64)

Rosie said, 'Our feelings about justice and beauty lead on to what we say about God.' Anthony replied, 'How do you test what is Christian justice and what are secular ideas of justice?' Cathy felt the test should be whether Christ would agree with an idea. 'Christ wouldn't vote Republican,' said Jamaal. 'How do you know what Christ would do?' asked Cathy. 'You use your reason,' said Bob. 'Ask a saint,' said Rosie. 'Consult the Pope,' said Fred. 'Listen to the voice of tradition,' said Philip. 'You use your reason to decide between traditions,' said Bob.

Pre-Reformation Christians

Rosie gave Fred a kaleidoscope for his birthday. At Monday's class, he used it to put across Thomas's idea of *Sacra Doctrina*. He said that, for Aquinas, looking at a question in systematic theology was like looking into a kaleidoscope and seeing all those little bitty coloured pieces turning into patterns. The coloured pieces were writings of the Church Fathers, quotations from the Bible, Ecumenical Councils.

For Aquinas, the teachings of Ecumenical Councils like Lateran IV (1215), which taught that Jesus was present in the consecrated bread and wine, were part of Sacred Doctrine, and so a datum of faith. All inspired Church teaching is Sacred Doctrine, for Thomas. 'In short,' said Fred, 'the whole kaleidoscope of tradition.'

Bob asked, 'Did Aquinas explicitly state that we have to do theology within the Church?' 'No,' Fred admitted. 'It never occurred to him to discuss the Church. Pre-Reformation Christians just did theology in the Church, no questions asked.' Philip asked, 'Did they have no theory about tradition?' Fred replied that a few medieval theorists held that the apostles produced both a written text, Scripture, and a tradition that remained unwritten down. But there was not much explicit theorising about how the Popes or tradition were inspired to read the Scriptures. Philip said, 'Maybe they experienced their continuity with the writers of Scripture and with the past so intensely that they didn't question it.' Bob said, 'Systematic theology only gets interesting when so-called "heretics" ask questions.'

John Wycliffe (1330–1384)

> The Bible is therefore the only source of doctrine that will ensure the health of the Church and the salvation of the faithful.
>
> John Wycliffe, 'The Truth of Holy Scripture' (1377).

Fred said, 'Critics started making objections in the fourteenth century. Thomas Bradwardine (1290–1349) criticised the two-source theory. He thought Scripture is above tradition. John Wycliffe carried on the attack. He denounced papal authority and the doctrine of transubstantiation as false to Scripture. It meant, tradition isn't automatically inspired by the Spirit.'

The Reformation: Martin Luther

Cathy took up the story. At the Diet of Worms in 1518, Luther argued that Popes and Ecumenical Councils are not the only way Scripture can be infallibly interpreted. Scripture is the only source of revelation and the test of any tradition. Luther didn't think that anyone could pick up a Bible and understand it on their own steam. For Luther, a systematic theologian relies in the Spirit's guidance and it spoke to him independently of the Church.

Bob asked Cathy how Luther could know what the authors of Scripture had intended to say; there was a big time gap between him and the primitive Church. She replied that Luther experienced the presence of the Spirit so vividly that he identified himself with the characters in the Bible. There wasn't any time gap between Luther and the 'original text' because the Spirit inspired him to feel himself into the story.

The Reformed Confessions

Zwingli's Sixty-Seven Articles (1523)
The Ten Theses of Berne (1528)
The Tetrapolitan Confession (1530)
The First Confession of Basel (1534)

The First Helvetic Confession (1536; also called The Second
   Confession of Basel)
The Lausanne Articles (1536)
The Geneva Confession (1536)
The French Confession of Faith (1539)
The Scots Confession (1560)
The Second Helvetic Confession (1566)

The Lutheran Confessions

The Augsburg Confession (1530)
Apology of the Augsburg Confession (1531)
The Schmalkald Articles (1537)
The Small Catechism of Martin Luther (1529)
The Large Catechism of Martin Luther (1529)
The Formula of Concord (1577)

Philip doubted whether Protestantism was solely driven by the *sola Scriptura* principle. 'What's *sola Scriptura?*' asked Rosie. Fred said, 'The Bible alone, and don't you believe it. When Luther realised his followers were reading weird ideas out of the Bible, he wrote catechisms telling them what they were allowed to find. Protestant churches wrote Confessions or Articles of Faith.'

Protestants on Scripture and tradition

We affirm and desire to follow Scripture alone as a rule of faith and religion, without mixing with it any other thing which might be devised by the opinion of man apart from the Word of God.

Article 1 of the Geneva Confession (1538)

All those who say that the Gospel is nothing without the approbation of the Church err and slander God.

The first of Zwingli's Sixty-Seven Articles

Holy Scripture containeth all things necessary to salvation; so that whatsoever is not read therein, nor may be proved thereby, is not to be required of any man, that it should be believed as an article of the Faith, or be thought requisite or necessary to salvation.

Article VI of the Anglican Thirty-Nine Articles

Cathy said, 'The Protestant Confessions don't put themselves on a level with Scripture. They're there to remind us not to treat human traditions the way medieval Christians did.' Anthony disagreed. He said, 'The culture of Calvinism is rooted in the Westminster Confession. When Calvinists have debated theological ideas, they've tested them as much by Westminster as by Scripture.' The Boot thought, *Postliberals are bound to say Protestant culture matters more than Christ and the Bible.* But all she said was, 'True Protestants don't care about tradition. It's up to individuals to decide. But not just any individual. Individuals who read their Bible with the inspiration of the Spirit. Like Kierkegaard.'

Modern Protestant conceptions of tradition: Is the Holy Spirit still at work?

Jamaal said, 'My uncle Steve is a theology professor. You should go in his office. It's a shrine to Martin Luther King Jr. Fact is, black voices from the past are important guides to preaching the Scriptures today. The tradition isn't infallible but it gives us a longer timeline than the present moment. We look up to the leading lights of the African-American churches and we want our interpretation of God's Word to hold good by the way they preached and lived.' The Professor said, 'By the nineteenth century, most Protestant theologians were conscious of inheriting traditions.'

Fred demanded to know, 'What is the point of tradition if you can't be certain that it comes from God? Either you think the Church is human and fallible, so you have no tradition, or you believe the Church is infallibly sourced to God, and follow tradition.' Rosie whispered, 'You've got that Inquisitorial look on your face.' 'It's my Creole blood,' said Fred modestly. 'It makes me very fiery.'

Bob argued that it's more rational just to reject tradition. Today, scholars have taken the kaleidoscope apart and studied all those pieces independently. You can't put it back together again. 'Because of that,' said Bob, 'we know the biblical authors didn't intend their work to have relevance for people living thousands of years after them. A text like Exodus has the meaning its original writers intended it to have. It doesn't have another meaning for now, unless it's added on in an arbitrary way.'

Rosie growled, in a deep bassoon voice, like Louis Armstrong:

> When Israel was in Egyptland
> Let my people go
> Oppressed so hard they could not stand
> Let my people go.

Go down, Moses,
Way down in Egyptland
Tell old Pharaoh
'Let my people go!'

Jamaal said, 'The situation of slavery that Israel was in back there wasn't exactly unique in history. Black people have experienced what Israel endured back then as now, for us as well.' Fred agreed, 'The text still points a finger at our morality. Slavery was wrong then and it's wrong now.'

In black churches, the one who preaches the Word is primarily a story-teller. And thus when the black church community invites a minister as pastor, their chief question is: 'Can the Reverend tell the story?' This question . . . refers to . . . a person's ability to recite God's historical dealings with God's people from Abraham to Jesus, from St Paul to John on the island of Patmos, and to the preacher's ability to relate these biblical stories to contemporary black stories. The past and present are joined dialectically, creating a black vision of the future.

James Cone, *God of the Oppressed* (1975, 1997: 52–3)

'That and more,' said Jamaal. 'Luther was right to imagine the Bible as a living drama he could walk right into. God didn't just inspire Scripture in the past. The God who liberated Israel liberates people today. Nobody should call themselves a systematic theologian unless they can relate the story to contemporary situations of oppression – and liberation!'

Jamaal felt that Scripture is kept living by the fact that its readers are open to the guidance of the Spirit. 'But,' said Philip, 'Anyone could say the Spirit was helping them develop our picture of Scripture.' Jamaal answered, 'The Bible is God's story before it becomes our own. When Luther heard the Spirit speak to him through the Bible, he heard more than the sound of his own voice. The Spirit weaves the divine story into the tapestry of history. Otherwise, it's God out there and not "God with us". The Spirit takes hold of us and makes the biblical story the story of a particular people in their own time and place. The Spirit makes God's story our own story.'

Catholic ideas of tradition

Vatican I (1869–70)

Lara said that Catholicism is stuck with the 'Ecumenical' Council of Trent, which asserted there are two sources of revelation – Scripture and tradition. The Professor said, 'The First Vatican Council repeated Trent's "dual-source" theory of revelation.'

> This supernatural revelation, according to the faith of the universal Church, as declared by the Holy Synod of Trent is 'contained in written books and unwritten traditions which received from the mouth of Christ Himself by the apostles, or from the apostles themselves at the dictation of the Holy Spirit, have come down to us, passed on as it were from hand to hand.'
>
> Vatican I (1869–70)

Yves Congar, OP (1904–95)

But then a Catholic theologian became interested in the Greek Church Fathers, in ecumenical relations with the Orthodox and in tradition. Yves Congar grounds his idea of living tradition of the Church in biblical Trinitarian language. He says that tradition is not documents or oral information. It is a 'living subject', the Holy Spirit. God the Spirit is the source of tradition, just as God the Spirit inspires the written revelation that attests to Christ, God the Son.

Congar built his notion of tradition on two statements in John's gospel: 'As the Father has sent me, so I send you' and 'As the Father has loved me, so I have loved you' (John 15: 9). In Christian doctrine, the mutual love of Father and Son *is* the Holy Spirit. The communion of the Christian faithful *is* the shared love of Father and Son, *in* the Spirit. Tradition is a symbol of the Trinity in action and relation.

Tradition at Vatican II (1962–5)

> Sacred traditions and sacred Scripture constitute one sacred deposit of God's word committed to the Church . . . The function of authentically interpreting the Word of God, written or delivered by traditions, has been exclusively entrusted to the living teaching office of the Church, whose authority is exercised in the name of Jesus Christ . . . It is plain,

> therefore, that sacred tradition, sacred scripture and the Church's
> teaching office . . . are so interconnected and associated together that
> one cannot stand without the others, and all together, in their several
> ways, under the action of the one Holy Spirit, contribute effectively to
> the salvation of souls.
>
> *Dei Verbum*, II: 10 (Flannery 1975)

Congar was a leading figure at the Second Vatican Council, which pro-posed a unifying notion of Scripture, tradition and Church. None of these three stands without the others. Philip asked the Professor, 'Why did Congar think his view of tradition would touch base with the Orthodox?' She answered, 'Congar was trying to get away from the idea of tradition as dead words in Church documents. He said the Spirit leaves "monuments", its expressions, like the Creeds, the liturgy, the writings of the Church Fathers and the lives of the saints.' Philip said, 'For my Russian grandparents, being Christian was living in an Orthodox culture and soaking up the icons and the folk legends about the saints.' Jamaal said, 'It's cool so long as you don't bring the Pope into it.' Fred added, solemnly, 'A yogurt is alive because it has a culture; a Christian is a bacteria in the culture created by the Spirit.' 'Holy Spirit yogurt!' said Greg. Rosie felt a more biblical symbol is being inside the water of baptism, which the Spirit breathes on. 'It's like being fish in a sacred sea,' she said. 'Fred would be a whale,' said Greg, but Fred didn't hear. He was looking into Rosie's eyes. He was falling in love with God, which is where systematic theology begins. He thought he was going to faint – or throw up.

> As the question of God is implicit in all our questioning, so being in love
> with God is the basic fulfilment of our conscious intentionality.
>
> Bernard Lonergan, *Method in Theology* (1972: 105)

 ## Further reading

The books in this list are ranked in order of their accessibility to under-graduate readers.

O'Collins, Gerald (1981), *Fundamental Theology*, New York: Paulist.

Basil the Great (1980), *On the Holy Spirit*, trans. David Anderson, Crestwood, NY: St Vladimir's Seminary Press.

Congar, Yves (1983), *I Believe in the Holy Spirit*, 3 vols, New York: Seabury.

Congar, Yves (1966), *Tradition and Traditions: An Historical and Theological Essay*, trans. Michael Naseby and Thomas Rainsborough, London: Burns and Oates.

Danielou, Jean (1964, 1979), *The Christian Centuries: The First Six Hundred Years*, trans. Vincent Cronin, London: Darton, Longman and Todd.

Questions

1. Is there any difference between biblical inspiration and the inspiration of a great poet?

2. What was the relationship between Creeds and liturgy in the early Church?

3. Does the distinction between inspiration and revelation matter?

4. Does original sin affect what theology can hope to achieve?

5. How could what church you belong to affect your theology?

6. How do we test whether an idea is Christian?

7. What does it mean for liberation theology to say the Spirit is alive in tradition?

8. How and why did Roman Catholic ideas about tradition change at Vatican II?

CHAPTER FIVE

Revelation and the Trinity

Francesca Aran Murphy

Seminar One: Revelation in Scripture

Summer was nearly out. Bob picked up Lara and Cathy to sign on for the Trinity course. Bob complained, 'How come we've got a seminar on revelation in a course on the Trinity?' Cathy said, 'We have to start with biblical revelation because you can't take it literally.' 'Huh?' said Lara and Bob, surprised at this departure. The Boot had been reading modern Trinitarian theology and she was surprised at that. She said, 'Jurgen Moltmann makes the Trinity like the Greek pantheon, with three gods fooling around in heaven. And others copy him. They apply the idea of three persons in God literally. Language about God needs reflection.' Bob held up *The Onion*, a satirical magazine that showed God being interviewed after he had been slammed by a US judge for breaking the anti-monopoly laws. Cathy said, 'Moltmann is making the Trinity into three old men on a cloud, only it's not meant to be funny.' 'Theologians are not renowned for their sense of humour,' said Bob.

VOLUME 38 ISSUE 03 | AMERICA'S FINEST NEWS SOURCE™ | 31 JANUARY–6 FEBRUARY 2002

Judge Orders God To Break Up Into Smaller Deities

WASHINGTON, DC—Calling the theological giant's stranglehold on the religion industry "blatantly anti-competitive," a U.S. district judge ruled Monday that God is in violation of anti-monopoly laws and ordered Him to be broken up into several less powerful deities.

"The evidence introduced in this trial has convinced me that the deity known as God has willfully and actively thwarted competition from other deities and demigods, promoting His worship with such unfair scare tactics as threatening non-believers with eternal damnation," wrote District Judge Charles Elliot Schofield in his decision. "In the process, He has carved out for Himself an illegal monotheopoly."

The suit, brought against God by the Justice Department on behalf of a coalition of "lesser deities" and polytheistic mortals, alleged that He violated antitrust laws by claiming in the Holy Bible that He was the sole creator of the universe, and by strictly prohibiting the worship of what He termed "false idols."

"God clearly commands that there shall be no other gods before Him, and He frequently employs the phrase 'I AM the Lord' to intimidate potential deserters," prosecuting attorney Geoffrey Albert said. "God uses other questionable strongarm tactics to secure and maintain humanity's devotion, demanding, among other things, that people sanctify

their firstborn to Him and obtain circumcisions as a show of faith. There have also been documented examples of Him smiting those caught worshipping graven images."

Attorneys for God did not deny such charges. They did, however, note that God offers followers "unbeatable incentives" in return for their loyalty, including eternal salvation, protection from harm, and "fruitfulness."

"God was the first to approach the Jewish people with a 'covenant' contract that guaranteed they would be the most favored in His eyes, and He handed down standards of morality, cleanliness, and personal conduct that exceeded anything else practiced at the time," lead defense attorney Patrick Childers said. "He readily admits to being a 'jealous' God, not because He is threatened by the prospect of competition from other gods, but because He is utterly convinced of the righteousness of His cause and that He is the best choice for mortals. Many of these so-called gods could care less if somebody bears false witness or covets thy neighbor's wife. Our client, on the other hand, is truly a 'People's God.'"

In the end, however, God was unable to convince Schofield that He did not deliberately create a marketplace hostile to rival deities. God's attorneys attempted to convince the judge of His openness to rivals, pointing to His longtime participation in the "Holy Trinity," but the effort

A Deity Divided

"God has willfully and actively thwarted competition from other deities and demigods, promoting His worship with such unfair scare tactics as threatening non-believers with eternal damnation. In the process, He has carved out for Himself an illegal monotheopoly."

—Judge Charles Elliot Schofield

In compliance with Monday's decision, God must:
- Divest all holdings in churches, synagogues, and mosques
- Cede miracle-performing services to local deities
- Cease and desist strongarm tactic of smiting nonbelievers
- Allow competition from pagan gods and animistic spirits

What this means for worshippers:
- Quicker prayer-response time
- Likely reduction in yearly tithes and tributes
- Wider selection of specialized deities
- No reprisals for false-idol worship

failed when Schofield determined that Jesus Christ and the Holy Ghost are "more God subsidiaries than competitors."

To comply with federal antitrust statutes, God will be required to divide Himself into a pantheon of specialized gods, each representing a force of nature or a specific human custom, occupation, or state of mind.

"There will most likely be a sun god, a moon god, sea god, and rain god," said religion-industry watcher Catherine Bailey. "Then there will be some second-tier deities, like a god of wine, a goddess of the harvest, and perhaps a few who symbolize human love and/or blacksmithing."

Leading theologians are applauding the God breakup, saying that it will usher in a new era of greater worshipping options, increased efficiency, and more personalized

service.

"God's prayer-response system has been plagued by massive, chronic backlogs, and many prayers have gone unanswered in the process," said Gene Suozzi, a Phoenix-area Wiccan. "With polytheism, you pray to the deity specifically devoted to your concern. If you wish to have children, you pray to the fertility goddess. If you want to do well on an exam, you pray to the god of wisdom, and so on. This decentralization will result in more individualized service and swifter response times."

Other religious experts are not so confident that the breakup is for the best, pointing to the chaotic nature of polytheistic worship and noting that multiple gods demand an elaborate regimen of devotion that today's average worshipper may find arduous and inconvenient... ∅

A page from The Onion.

©Copyright 2002 Onion, Inc. All Rights Reserved. Reprinted With Permission.

What is revelation?

The Council of Trent (1545–63)

At the first class, Anthony presented the Calvinist idea of revelation. He explained that the Council of Trent drew up Roman arguments against Protestant principles, like *sola Scriptura*. Trent claimed the Spirit gave the Scriptures to the Church. 'That's right,' said Fred. 'No Church, no canonical Scripture.'

John Calvin (1509–64)

Anthony answered, 'Calvin's argument against that was that Scripture speaks for itself. You don't need the Church to tell you which is a true gospel, Matthew or Thomas, because a true gospel proclaims itself. Entering a Gnostic gospel is like going into a dark room. Reading the synoptics is broad daylight coming on you.' Fred wondered what made one experience self-evidently right and the other wrong.

Anthony said, 'According to Calvin, God would speak in propositions, rounded sentences. Calvin considered that every sentence in Scripture was revealed to its author by the Holy Spirit.' Fred cut in to point out Aquinas realised that God gives the writer the propositions that are put down in the Bible. 'For Thomas,' he said, 'revelation happens when God illuminates a prophet or apostle's mind to make them give a perfectly accurate judgement on events.'

Greg asked, 'How come sentences in the Bible? The Exodus happening was revelation before the Book of Exodus was written.' Anthony said that, for a Calvinist, history is not a revelation of God until someone has understood its divine meaning. A tourist who tripped through Egypt and saw frogs everywhere and the water drying up had a terrible holiday but he didn't get a revelation from God. For the crowd who saw Jesus crucified, knowing it happened was not divine revelation.

Propositionalists argue that it is not just the historical event but the disclosure of the true meaning of the event that is God's revelation. For propositionalists, revelation is about facts – but it is not the fact alone. God discloses himself in the Scriptural statements, which interpret Israel's history, the life of Christ and the world to come.

Criticisms of the propositional idea of revelation

Greg said, 'This is a turn-off. It's so head-orientated. What happened to the Muse breathing on the poet to make him dance?' Anthony replied, 'Calvin didn't intend to undervalue the historical events. For him, the Exodus history is a "Theatre of the Glory of God."' Fred said, 'The same for Aquinas – he thought God made the events happen.'

> How could our race betray
> The Image, and the Incarnate One unmake
> Who chose this form and fashion for our sake?
> The Word made flesh is here unmade again.
> A word made word in flourish and arrogant crook.
> See there King Calvin with his iron pen,

> And God three angry letters in a book,
> And there the logical hook
> On which the Mystery is impaled and bent
> Into an ideological instrument.
>
> Edwin Muir, 'The Incarnate One' (1960: 228)

Rosie said, 'Aquinas and Calvin are still pretty cognitive. Their view is that the biblical propositions speak more clearly than the history they're describing. Its like the Reformation idea that you shouldn't have pictures in a church because they could lead you astray. But a picture is more than a thousand words.'

Rosie argued that propositionalist churches are relics of the past when everyone is soaked in visual images, from computer games to websites to TV. Fred said, 'Sure, a church would make itself a dinosaur if it stuck with the sixteenth-century idolatry of the printed page. But it would de-humanise itself if it didn't recognise that people communicate best in words. You can show beauty in a picture but not truth. That takes words.' Fred thought the value in propositionalism is that it expresses how the Spirit speaks the truth in Scripture.

Accommodationalism

Infallibility and inerrancy

Bob said, 'The Bible can't be revealed propositional truth because scientists and historians have shown it's full of mistakes. Biblical writers assume geocentric astronomy. In Joshua 12, God makes the sun stand still to give Joshua more daytime to massacre the indigenous Palestinian people. Who, apart from fundamentalists, believes seven-day creation?'

Cathy told him he'd better learn to distinguish between Biblical inerrancy and God's infallibility. 'Fundamentalists,' said the evangelical Boot, 'put their "faith" in the inerrancy of the propositions in the Bible. That's making an idol of the Bible. But evangelicals put their faith in God's infallibility. He wouldn't say anything to mislead us about what matters.' Jamaal claimed that what concerns African-American churches is not the absolute truth of the Bible but the fact that it's a reliable guide for Christian life. Cathy said, 'That is like the evangelical principle that the Bible is revelation only when dealing with practical matters of salvation.'

The core meaning: Salvation

She told the group that the accommodationalist theory of revelation takes into account the Bible's scientific and historical defects; in revealing himself, God accommodated the mental level of the Biblical authors.

Sixteenth-Century Accommodationalists

Galileo: 'Scripture is not written to show how the heavens go, but how to get to heaven.'

Calvin: 'In Christ God, so to speak, makes himself little in order to lower himself to our capacity.'

Calvin: 'Moses addresses himself to our senses that the knowledge of God . . . that we enjoy may not glide away . . . he had respect to us rather than to the stars.'

The Jesuit Francisco Suarez: 'Although everything in Scripture has been written by the Holy Spirit, nevertheless the Spirit left it to the writer to write everything in a manner accommodated to himself, and according to his talents, education and language, although under his direction.'

From Vawter (1972)

Cathy added, 'Calvin knew that God's purpose in revealing himself in Scripture was not to give us neutral scientific information about the universe. It was to reveal the great practical truth – salvation. Calvin was trained as a lawyer. He pictured God as a rhetorician, speaking the language of his audience to win them over.' Lara felt accommodationalism shows the Bible has a surface level of meaning, which was time-conditioned, and a core, which is God's real meaning. 'What about Paul's attitude to women and gays? That's surface, not core,' said Lara.

Karl Barth's accommodationalism

Anthony said that, for Barth, 'The human conditioning that goes into the Bible and preaching is its superficial element. It's not whether the writers used the world-picture of their time, or said something we think is salvific that makes it surface or core. It's whether the Spirit is lighting it up. Barth's idea of revelation was a radicalisation of Calvin's. Barth is using the idea that the Spirit tells us when a text is inspired, minus the propositionalism.'

The Genius Kid told the class that Barth describes revelation as an explosion, not a book parachuted down from heaven. You can't take the explosion home and use it as a magic proof-kit. Only God can work the explosion. Jamaal agreed that Bible truth is not propositions on a page. Truth is the event of God acting, transforming people's lives. Anthony said, 'For Barth, God's revelation is an event, not static sentences on a page in the Bible.'

Cathy asked, 'Does Barth think the Bible is true sometimes and false other times?' Anthony said, 'Sometimes you read the Prologue to John's gospel and it means nothing. Like when you hear dead, boring preaching in church. When the Spirit doesn't speak through the Bible it doesn't matter a damn how great its historical correspondence with the facts is. But when God sends the electric Spirit through the Bible, then it comes alive and reveals Christ to us. The same biblical sentence, "The Word was made flesh" sometimes is the event of revelation and other times isn't.' Fred asked, 'Could you give me a crude idea when the Bible is revelation and when it isn't?' 'Theologians don't have crude ideas,' said Anthony, who didn't have an especially incarnational conception of theology.

The three-fold revelation

Bob said, 'All of you admit that the Bible is accommodated to us in some matters, although Fred is only going to concede that when his church lets him, Lara calls it accommodation when she decides the Bible is irrational, and Anthony and Jamaal assert it's self-evident when an event of God is happening. So accommodationalism covers every Christian position, except Scriptural inerrantists. I still don't get why we have to discuss revelation in a course on the Trinity.'

Lara said it was because Barth argues that God reveals himself in a trinitarian way. 'In triplicate?' asked Bob. Lara said, 'Barth explains the Trinity by the event of revelation. The power behind revelation is "that which reveals, the source". God the Word is Scripture and the Spirit is the preacher's proclamation: one, two, three, revealer, revelation (Word) and being revealed (Spirit).' Bob said, 'Sounds like three copies of the same divine idea of revelation.' It also sounded to him like Lara was spending too much time with the Genius Kid.

The Bible as a children's book written by God

Bob said, 'Calvin wouldn't have been an accommodationalist if Galileo hadn't been breathing down his neck. Barth knew biblical criticism would deconstruct the Bible, so he abandoned the idea of Scripture as evidence for faith. Theology backtracks, after science has shown it's false.' 'You couldn't be more wrong,' said Cathy. 'Jewish and Christian theologians have always noticed that some statements in the Bible are not literally true. God does not have a mighty arm, or a face. The Bible speaks of God in anthropomorphic ways. Those phrases are symbolic; it was God putting his point across in a way we can grasp. When he gave us the Bible, God spoke our language, like an adult writing a children's book. That's accommodation.'

The Bible as a secretary's letter OK'd by God

Bob said, 'You still think God is the author and the people who put the Bible together were hearing divine dictation they couldn't have understood. You don't seem to realise that all the biblical authors were people of their time.' Anthony replied, 'A modern Calvinist, like Nicholas Wolterstorff, pictures revelation as being like a company director telling a secretary to go away and write a letter, and giving it the OK when it's done. That allows you to take on board the individuality of the biblical writers. A secretary doesn't have to know all the company business, just enough to write that particular letter.'

Is accommodated revelation God-speak in human language, or human-speak on behalf of God?

Fred said, 'I'm going with conceiving accommodation as God speaking to us symbolically. The words in the Bible are more true than we know. They've got levels we can't appreciate.' Cathy said, 'Some children's books mean more than children realise, not less. Like the Narnia books.'

Lara replied, 'Honey, C. S. Lewis is kiddy Christianity. It's better to see accommodation as us developing our own metaphors for God. That way you make the Trinity relevant to today. Like Sally McFague in *Models of God* calling the Trinity "Mother-Lover-Friend" because that spells out the "independent, communal, reciprocal" relationship of God to the earth that is "needed today."' (1987: 183–4, 223–4) Jamaal said he'd never heard anything so much like Winnie the Pooh Christianity in his life. Bob thought, *Why can't they all grow and accept the Bible is sometimes God speaking to us and sometimes just human talk?*

Should we take biblical language about God literally?

So Bob said, 'I'm still not straight on what you think biblical language tells us about God. Fred and Cathy say when it's anthropomorphic, it's "symbolic". So what does it symbolise when God shows Moses his back? Does Christ screaming in despair on the cross symbolise something we need to know about God?'

Fred said that a Thomist rejects all notion of God changing, let alone suffering. 'What's your problem with that?' asked Bob. Fred replied, 'God is *Actus Purus*, pure activity, and pure activity does not become or change. It is eternally itself, it can't become more or less. When the Bible seems to describe God changing,' said Fred, 'it's picture-talk.'

Lara was outraged. She said, 'That's a Hellenistic idea of God, not a Christian one. Moltmann says when the Son dies on the Cross, it shows the suffering of the Son *and* the Father. When any human being is tortured to death, Moltmann says that is God dying all over again.'

515

Bob scratched his head and said, 'If propositionalism makes revelation comprehensible, what would it take to make it incomprehensible? Fred asserts the Bible is God's word through and through, and then says it's metaphorical when it describes God changing. Lara claims the Bible is our human language for God, and then takes it literally when it describes God's emotional reactions to events!'

Cathy asked, 'When Paul mentions Father, Son and Holy Ghost in one sentence, should we picture three separate people?' Bob said, 'If Moltmann takes that literally, he should be writing captions for *The Onion*! Lara could interview the Son and the Spirit demanding equal airtime with the Father.' When Bob whistled under Lara's window that night, he got hit in the eye by a well-aimed toothbrush.

Seminar Two: Modalism

Fred, Rosie and Cathy were at the bookstore, buying set texts for the Trinity course. Fred's grubby paw was intwined with Rosie's hand. 'Man,' said Cathy. 'Augustine, *The Trinity*! Heavy!' Rosie said, 'This won't connect with any religious experiences any of us ever had.' For the first time ever, the Boot felt nostalgic for her convent school. The nuns just said the Trinity is three ways of being one thing, like ice, water and steam are three modes of H_2O.

'That's a disastrous metaphor,' said Fred, guiding the girls towards the coffee shop. 'It's also heretical.' 'Here we go again,' said Rosie. 'What's the heresy this time?' 'It's called modalism,' said Fred. 'Cathy can be in different modes. Right now, you're in relaxation mode, other times in swimming mode, in your scuba gear, and sometimes working-at-McDonald's mode.' 'Wearing that vile uniform!' said Cathy. 'That's right,' said Fred, 'You look different in different settings but underneath the different behaviours and clothes, it's all one and the same Cathy. Modalists conceive the Trinity as three modes of one being, with different looks but deep down identical.'

It started because early Christian apologists like Justin Martyr were determined to prove Christ shows up in Israel's history. The problem with that way of reading the biblical history is that it tempts you to read history into God. They described Christ as the visible side of God. Whenever they found a visible manifestation of God in the Old Testament, like at the burning bush or Mount Sinai, they said that's Christ.

Sabellius: The first modalist

That bothered a third-century theologian called Sabellius. He heard Irenaeus and Justin dualising God, giving God two parts, invisible Father and visible Son. Sabellius thought the only way out was to picture the Trinity as three expressions of one God. That implies the whole Trinity does what one of them does. One of Sabellius's students, Praxeas, said the Father suffered the crucifixion. 'Alongside the Son?' asked Rosie. 'Suffering because his Son was dying?' 'Not alongside,' said Fred. 'Modalists think the Father *is* the Son; the same Cathy gets paid for working in McDonald's, even though student Cathy and scuba-diver Cathy don't look like Cathy in the baseball cap and nylon pyjamas.'

Tertullian, against Praxeas

'Sabellianism made Tertullian hot under the collar,' Fred continued. 'He said Praxeas "expelled the Holy Spirit and crucified the Father". Modalism is also called patri-passianism. That means "Father-sufferingism."' Rosie asked, 'Why did Tertullian accuse Praxeas of expelling the Spirit?' Fred said, 'Modalism merges the Three into One.'

Economy of salvation

Rosie asked, 'Isn't it important to show there is one sacred history for Jews and for Christians?' Fred said, 'The economy of salvation matters.' Rosie started teasing Fred. She said, 'It's typical of you to describe salvation history with a word like "economy". You've got an economic idea of God!' Fred replied, '"Economia" is Greek for "household management". When guys like Tertullian talked about the "economy of salvation" they meant God's household management of the cosmos. God creates the universe, then he channels it toward salvation, in the history described in the Bible.'

Does God have a history?

'Tertullian knew about the economy of salvation, all right,' said Fred. 'That's why he didn't get all the way out of modalism himself. History matters to us but thinking of God as historical gets you to modalism. If you imagine God as having a story, the Father will be the actor in the first Act, then the Son will star in Act II, and the Spirit will show up in the finale. Tertullian pictured the Trinity emerging one after another, like actors in a movie. The weird thing about modalism is it takes the three appearances literally *and* it says God is all unity, under the appearances.'

From the fourth century, theologians avoided applying the metaphor of a drama to God. It gives you a picture of God wearing new masks in different Acts. Cathy knew the Greek for a mask was 'prosopon', and Chalcedon uses that word of Christ. Fred said, 'They didn't like to speak about three prosopa in the Trinity because they thought it led to modalism.

The modalist idea of God is purely economic, totally based on what God looks like from inside creation and history. Augustine recognised that God is transcendent, above the economy of creation and salvation.

Actus Purus.' Rosie felt, if Augustine says God is outside humanity, she wasn't looking forward to *The Trinity*. Why couldn't they do something relevant to spirituality, like the *Confessions*?

Seminar Three: Augustine on the Trinity

What has the Trinity got to do with experience?

Augustine the father of individualism?

Anthony gave a presentation around Saint Augustine's *The Trinity*. He began by saying, 'Contemporary theologians, like Moltmann and Colin Gunton and Robert Jenson, despise Augustine. They recognise that the most destructive idea in Western culture is the idea of the self as a single atom. Ever since Descartes, we stopped picturing human beings socially and started conceiving the self as a self-thinking thought. The Enlightenment insisted on human autonomy and it's still with us today.'

Fred said, 'I'll start taking notes when you say something about Augustine.' 'Augustine is the reason Western Christianity promotes individualism,' Anthony answered. 'Augustine asked what the Trinity is. Instead of working from community, he looked for a Trinity inside himself. His paradigm for the Trinity is a single brain meditating on itself.' Anthony held up Gunton's *The Promise of Trinitarian Theology* and read, 'It's "in categories taken from the inner mental world" that Augustine "seeks to unpack his analogies for the threefold being of God."' (1991: 43)

The trinitarian image in humans relates to the Trinity

'Scripture' Anthony went on, 'says humans are made in the image of God. Augustine figured the image of the Trinity was his own mind. He introspected on himself and claimed his mind consisted of a triad: memory, understanding and will. He said the faculty of memory is equivalent to the Father, understanding is equivalent to the Son, and the faculty of will equals the Holy Spirit.'

Bob said, 'Like nineteenth-century faculty psychology? Could you draw a phrenological map, showing the Father in the centre of your skull, the Son over your right ear and the Spirit on the left? Is that what makes left-brained people spiritual?'

Philip had spent the last week of summer on a retreat at that Benedictine Abbey. It wasn't called Holy Trinity for nothing. When he heard Phil was taking a course on the Trinity, the Abbot got excited and made him read Augustine. So, unlike Anthony, Philip had read *The Trinity*. Philip said, 'The image of the Trinity in us isn't a phrenological map. Remembering, knowing and loving are activities, not faculties.'

Rosie interrupted: 'Did Augustine think his own mind *is* the Trinity? If the Trinity was inside his mind, was his mind God? Can we look at our selves in the mirror and see God, without looking any further?'

> This trinity of the mind is not really the image of God because the mind remembers and understands and loves itself, but because it is also able to remember and understand and love him by whom it was made. And when it does this it becomes wise. If it does not do it, then even though it remembers and understands and loves itself, it is foolish.
>
> Augustine, *The Trinity* (XIV.4.15)

Philip said, 'Anthony hasn't had time yet to get into why Augustine meditated on remembering and knowing and loving. Augustine isn't talking about finding the image of God in his head, he's describing becoming the image, by remembering, knowing and loving God. Augustine thought those activities are worth reflection because you see the Trinity through them. Reflecting on remembering, knowing and loving is not like looking in a refrigerator, a closed inner space. Your mind is a trapdoor the Trinity comes through.' Fred said, 'The Biblical creator God is forming Augustine's self-awareness, and his knowledge and love of truth. He's working from that to what God is like.'

Philip said, 'And the saving God. The image of the Trinity in us is fallen and has to be re-created. The grace of the Trinity activates the image of God in us.' Rosie asked, 'He knew the Trinity by experiencing grace?' Philip replied, 'He's talking about a lifelong journey towards God, while God re-creates the Trinity image in us.'

Do we need a communitarian model of God?

Anthony argued, 'In Eastern Orthodoxy, starting with the Cappadocians, the idea is that God is Three. In the West, from Augustine, the story is God is One, and we can bring the Threeness in later. Today, the East sets a better example because our society needs a Trinity that will heal its individualism. One that uses a society of different, interrelated people as a model. We need a communitarian model of God. We won't get it from Augustine.' Bob said, 'Is calling God communitarian supposed to be a commerical for God or for a political party? Want to sell a communitarian society? Tell people God is a community. Nice projection.' Fred figured you can't decide what our society needs then say that's what God is like.

Did Augustine put the unity of God in front of the Trinity?

Anthony said, 'Augustine had to believe God is One not Three because he proved the Trinity from introspection on one mind. The Trinity has to be an afterthought, if you start from the Oneness of God. That's why Schleiermacher put the Trinity into an appendix to *The Christian Faith*. Ask any modern Orthodox theologian, like Vladimir Lossky. He can tell you the West never really believed in the Trinity, and Augustine's to blame. It was Augustine's idea of the Trinity that led to the eleventh-century schism between the East and the West.'

Bob added, 'Philip hasn't answered Anthony's objection. Why introspection? Why isn't the human mind a trinity image when it's interacting with the world and other people?' Anthony continued the thread: 'For Augustine, it's the inner man that's real. It's an internal, non-social model of human nature and it gives rise to a non-social God.' Jamaal said, 'He didn't have to wander around looking at how society works to describe the Trinity because he pictured himself as Everyman. No one's individual experience is unique to themselves.' Fred wished he'd thought of that. He tried not to stare at the red glass bead in Jamaal's nose. Jamaal asked, 'What was Augustine trying to achieve in *The Trinity*? He believes in a triune God and he's casting around for something that is simultaneously inherently one and inherently interrelated as three. Our basic existential experience is self-presence. We're always aware of ourselves. It's inescapable. You can't sneak up outside yourself and take a look in from behind; wherever you are trying to look at yourself, there you are, aware of yourself, knowing yourself, attending to yourself. Self-awareness is the original, originating fact. Like the Father is the Origin. Augustine figured self-awareness or memory "begets" self-knowledge; that can't happen without loving attention to oneself – the Holy Spirit. The mind's eternal moment of being itself is analogous to the Trinity, the Father, the Presence or Memory, giving rise to God's self-knowing, and the Two pinned together by a willed, loving act.'

The Professor started lecturing. She said that to be real theologians, we must imagine ourselves into people of the past. A good theologian does not bend Augustine to fit a crisis that began in the eleventh century, or to meet modern concerns. Fred wasn't taking notes. He was wondering what he would look like with dreads, like Jamaal.

Augustine: Trinity as three relations

The eternal processions and the economic missions

Rosie, Fred and Philip walked home together. Rosie said, 'I thought you said Augustine's Trinity was transcendent.' Fred wisely kept silent, while Philip explained that, for Augustine, the economy of salvation is what teaches us about the Trinity. It's a fact of history that the Son and the

Spirit were sent into this world. The Trinity is the Father's eternal begetting of the Son and issuing of the Spirit; we know its shape by the historical missions of the Son and the Spirit. Fred added, '"Missio" is Latin for "I send" – the economic missions are the sendings in history. The eternal processions are the event in the transcendent God, which comes first.' Fred nodded when Rosie said, 'Eternity isn't before time. It's outside of time.'

Fred asked, 'Is it true Augustine's idea of the Trinity is the opposite of the Cappadocian Fathers? All I know is the Cappadocians were behind the Creed of Constantinople. There were still subordinationists around, saying the Son and Spirit are lesser than the Father. Basil of Caesaria said anyone who worshipped the Son or Spirit, thinking them lesser gods, was a polytheist.' Rosie remarked, 'It's still a problem for me how you can have three persons in God and not have three Gods. Whenever I see that Andrei Rublev icon, with God as three angels, I think – three Gods!'

Philip answered, 'It bothered Gregory of Nazianzus, too. What makes the problem is thinking of the Three as three substances; call it "hupostasis" in Greek and substance is a self-standing entity – which makes for three independent beings. So Gregory changes the paradigm from substance to relation. His word for relation was "schesis". So the Trinity is three relations within one being. The Father is the relationship of Fathering, the Son of being Son. Father, Son and Spirit are three ways God is related to God. There are three distinct relational activities in God – no modalism! Augustine took over that way of speaking about the Trinity from Gregory Nazianzus.'

Fred said, 'Aristotle called "relation" an "accident", something that isn't crucial to a substance. My dad's having five sons is not part of his human substance. If we were killed in a car crash, he'd be a sadder and a richer man but still a man. We'd have a human substance whatever our relationships. Plus, God is all substance and no accidents. Anything that is true of him is true of God as such.' Philip figured that Augustine would say, precisely for that reason, that within God, relation has to be an essential category, not an accidental one. It's God's eternal being to Father the Son, to be begotten as Son and to be given as the Spirit in love. For Augustine, three relationships is what God is.

Seminar Four: The trinitarian relationships

The one ocean

> Imagine a spring of water, coming up out of the ground: here we have movement, procession, a going-out-from-itself-to-itself. Such a procession

implies two relations; or, put another way, we can describe this upward movement from two different perspectives. To do this we may have to imagine ourselves as immersed in the spring itself... We can imagine ourselves floating on our backs, facing up, in the same direction as the flow of the water – looking, as it were, from the inside out. Or, we can imagine ourselves face down (bring scuba gear), against the flow – looking from the outside in. In the first case, our perspective is similar to that of the origin of the water – of where it might have come from (even though we are not located at that point and thus cannot actually see where it begins). We can call this relation *initiation*. In the other case, when we are situated 'against the flow,' we adopt the perspective of the destination of the water's movement, and become aware of its moving out beyond itself; this relation can be called *fruition*.

David Cunningham, *These Three Are One:*
The Practice of Trinitarian Theology (1988: 67–8)

Cathy asked Lara, 'Are these theologians saying God is really Three, or really One? I'm lost. It's too intangible.' Lara said, 'David Cunningham gives the best analogy. See yourself as a scuba diver swimming into a source of water. You feel that water flowing toward you and you sense it's coming from somewhere. Plus, you can feel the moving current of the water coming at you. Flip over, so you're looking away from the source, and you see the water flowing away. The origin is the Source, the movement of the water is the Word and the Spirit is the flowing-on. Like the Spirit is the inspiration of Christians in history. It's a non-gendered analogy, no male Father and Son!' Cathy said, 'Does that mean an ocean looks like three to us? Or is that ocean really One in Three? Deep down, beyond where we can dive and take pictures, is the ocean Three?'

Does God have three personalities?

Karl Barth: Three modes

[B]y preference we do not use the term 'person' but rather 'mode (or way) of being'... The statement that God is One in three ways of being, Father, Son and Holy Ghost, means... that... the one personal God, is what He is not just in one mode but... in the mode of the Father, in the mode of the Son, and in the mode of the Holy Ghost.

Karl Barth, *Church Dogmatics* (I/1 359)

Cathy had been more worried about whether to talk about God in the plural than whether to use masculine words or not. The Boot kicked off her seminar by announcing, 'Barth spelled out my problem, which is: whether the Three are male, female, or genderless, if there are three of them, why isn't Christianity tritheist? Barth said the problem is created by imagining persons. The fifth-century West laid it down that there is one substantia and three personae, persons. But today, person always conjures up a single psychological subject. Orthodox icons don't help, showing God with three faces: that makes us think – three minds, three independent subjects.'

Jamaal asked, 'What was Barth's solution?' Cathy answered, 'Dump the word "person"!' Jamaal said, 'If you take out the persons, all you have is Oneness.' Cathy answered, 'Barth said to replace persons with modes.' 'Sounds like modalism to me,' said Anthony. Cathy said, 'You can get hung up on language. Barth is certain there are three distinct orders of being in God – Father, Son and Spirit. The Trinity is one God, not a trio, like the Marx Brothers.'

PERSONS OF THE TRINITY DEMAND EQUAL AIR TIME!

Augustine: Three 'whatdoyoucallits'

'Augustine saw the problem with speaking about persons in God' Cathy continued. 'He even pointed out that Scripture doesn't say God is "three persons". He realised God is a mystery, not a puzzle we can put together. Augustine said we use the word "person" about God because it's easier than saying "three whatdoyoucallits". We don't know what the word "person" is referring to in God, it's a "whatnot", to us.'

The filioque

Schism between East and West

Anthony went to Fred's house to play chess and argue about Augustine. While Fred set up the pieces, the Genius Kid said, 'You have to admit that Augustine was to blame for the schism between the Latin West and the Eastern Orthodox.' Since he couldn't debate the filioque plus win at chess, Fred said, 'I'm sure Rosie would like to play you first.' He knew the contention between Catholics and the East was about the doctrine that the Spirit proceeds from the Son as well as the Father. The Creed of Constantinople just said the Spirit 'proceeds from the Father.' In the sixth century, the Spaniards added 'and from the Son' – *filio* (son), *que* (and). They did it as a put-down to the Arians, who always seem to be going strong, no matter what you do. When he lived in the dorm, a lapsed Catholic used to yell 'The Father is greater than I (John 14: 28)' whenever he walked past his door.

In the early ninth century, Emperor Charlemagne ordered every church in France to say the Creed with the statement that the Spirit 'proceeds from the Father and from the Son' (filioque). The Popes refused to add filioque to the Creed until 1014, when Pope Benedict VIII caved in to Emperor Henri II. In 1054, the East went into schism from Rome; they wouldn't buy the filioque.

Augustine on the filioque

> [B]y seeking for patterns of threeness apart from the economy of salvation – what actually happens in Christ and with the Spirit – Augustine introduces a tendency to draw about the being of God – what he is eternally – and his act – what he does in time.
>
> Colin Gunton, *The Promise of Trinitarian Theology* (1991: 1)

Anthony looked up from the board, and said, 'Augustine was forced into saying the Spirit proceeds from the Son, by the geometry of relationships he figured out between Father, Son and Spirit. All their relations had to be different because the style of relation is the distinguishing feature of each one of the Three. He can't say the Son and Spirit come from the Father because Son and Spirit would both be the same in relation to the Father. He adds the procession of the Spirit from the Son to give the Spirit a unique relation within the Trinity. He never looked at Scripture or the history of salvation to know the Trinity, just his own inner world and a theory about relations. Rosie said, 'Check.'

For Augustine, 'The Spirit is merely the common bond of love linking the Father with the Son.'

Jurgen Moltmann, *The Trinity and the Kingdom of God* (1981: 142)

Fred said, 'Augustine calls Father, Son and Spirit Lover, Beloved and Love. The Father loves the Son through the Spirit, and the Son loves the Father in the Spirit, so the Spirit is proceeding from both of them. The Spirit is the communication of love between the Son and the Father.' Anthony answered, 'That makes the Spirit disappear in the middle. The West devalues the Spirit.' Fred replied, 'For Augustine, the Spirit is the generosity of God, the Gift. Want something to drink?' Anthony asked for tea with a slice of lemon.

Fred went in the kitchen and whispered down his mobile to Cathy, 'What does John's gospel say on the Spirit?' She answered, 'John 20: 22, the Risen Son breathes the Spirit on the disciples.' Back with a fresh fruit loaf, Fred said, 'Augustine's base wasn't a theory about relations. He went from Scripture telling about the Spirit proceeding from the Son in the economy of salvation.' 'Check,' said Rosie.

Just as his being born means for the Son his being from the Father, so his being sent means his being known to be from him. And just as for the Holy Spirit his being the gift of God means his proceeding from the Father, so his being sent means his being known to proceed from him. Nor, by the way, can we say that the Holy Spirit does not proceed from the Son as well; it is not without point that the same Spirit is called the

---

> Spirit of the Father and of the Son [Mt 10.20, Gal 4.6]. And I cannot see what else he intended to signify when he breathed and said *Receive the Holy Spirit* [Jn 20.22] . . . it was a convenient symbolic demonstration that the Holy Spirit proceeds from the Son as well as from the Father.
>
> Augustine, *The Trinity* (IV: xx 29)

The monarchy of the Father

Fred said, 'What's wrong with saying the Spirit proceeds from the Father and the Son?' Anthony replied, 'The Orthodox object to the filioque because it undermines that the Father is Source. The Orthodox call it the monarchy of the Father; he's behind the unity of the Trinity. If you give the Son a source role, you're putting Father and Son on a level and making them indistinguishable.'

> Even supporters of the Eastern view do not contest the fact that in the *opus ad extra*, and therefore in revelation . . . the Holy Spirit is to be understood as the Spirit of both Father and Son . . . statements about the divine modes of being antecedently in themselves cannot be different in content from those that are to be made about their reality in revelation . . . He is the Spirit of both the Father and the Son not just in His work *ad extra* and upon us, but that to all eternity . . . What gives us the right to take passages like Jn 15.26, which speak of the procession of the Spirit from the Father and isolate them from many others which equally plainly call Him the Spirit of the Son? The Filioque expresses recognition of the communion between the Father and the Son. The Holy Spirit is the love which is the essence of the relation between these two modes of being of God.
>
> Karl Barth, *Church Dogmatics* (I/1 479)

'I forgot the lemon,' Fred mumbled, rushing to his room, where he put 'Augustine' through a search on his Barth CD ROM. He returned to tell Anthony, 'Barth backs up Augustine on the filioque! He says the eternal Trinity must do like the economic Trinity! You can't put a metaphysical principle like the monarchy of the Father above revelation!'

Democratic ideas of the trinitarian relationships

Anthony sipped some tea and said, 'OK, the Orthodox have a Platonic idea of the Father's monarchy. But Augustine, Barth and Aquinas were influenced as much by a Hellenistic, cultural tendency to imagine the Trinity as a hierarchy as they were by Scripture. They want the Father first, as Source, the Son second and the Spirit a poor third. Today, liberation theologians like Moltmann say all the persons of the Trinity proceed from each other. There is no one Source, back behind the others. It's less patriarchal, don't you think?' Fred replied, 'The idea of hierarchy is more biblical than modern egalitarians and collectivists imagine.' 'Like in the Magnificat?' asked Anthony (Luke 1: 46–55). 'No,' said Fred, 'like in "The Father is greater than I" (John 14: 28).' 'Checkmate,' said Rosie.

In eschatology . . . the Son is the actor: he transfers the kingdom to the Father; he subjects himself to the Father. But in eschatology the Holy Spirit is the actor equally: he glorifies the Father through the praise of all created beings who have been liberated by Christ's rule. The Father is the One who receives. He receives his kingdom from the Son; he receives his glory from the Spirit.

Jurgen Moltmann, *The Trinity and the Kingdom of God* (1981: 94)

Subsistent relations

Lara and Cathy were sitting in the cafeteria. Army said to Cathy, 'What does Fred see in Rosie? He's the only person we know who grasps Aquinas on the Trinity. There they are canoodling and what do they care that the test is on subsistent relations?' Lara and Cathy barged over to their love-stricken classmates. The Boot banged her tray down and said, 'Thomas's idea of the Trinity is totally unbiblical.'

'You're kidding,' said Fred. 'Thomas teaches that we only know there are eternal processions in God because of Scripture, like Jesus saying in John 8: 42, "I came forth from God." That tells us the procession of the Word. Thomas calls the procession of the Spirit from Father and Son the breathing out of their love.' '"Spiratio" is the Latin,' said Rosie.

[W]e *have* relationships, God *is* the relations that he has. I am someone who is a father. In God, fathering is what God, whom we call Father, is . . . In God, being uttered, conceived, enacted, understood, is what God, whom we call Word or *Logos*, is . . . God . . . is relationship without remainder, which we, most certainly, are not.

Nicholas Lash, *Believing Three Ways in the One God* (1993: 32)

Lara got to the point. 'What are subsistent relations? What's it got to do with the Trinity?' Fred answered, 'Start from the fact that God is not an object. God isn't infinity, or mind, or infinite computer memory, or any terrific noun. If we talk about God with nouns, we forget God is activity, not a static object or concept. God is one hundred per cent verb.' '*Actus Purus*,' murmured Rosie. 'All event.' Fred said, 'Thomas says, for God the action of relating is the substance. Thomas states that each person of the Trinity is "a relation . . . in the mode of subsistence." Aquinas called the three relatings in God Fathering, "Sonning" and Gifting.' Rosie said, 'Paternitas, filatio and processio. The relatings are real, the rock bottom of what God is, not added on top of a basic unitary substance. So it's not like there are three persons in God who happen to have three ways of being interrelated: the three persons *are* their relating actions.'

Lara said, 'I can't relate to this.' Cathy added, 'Fathering and Gifting aren't in Scripture and "Sonning" isn't even in the dictionary!' Fred said, 'Those are the words for the real relations in God. The names of the subsistent relations are Father, Son, Spirit.' 'Pater, Filius and Spiritus sanctus,' said Rosie. She felt using those nouns lost the verbyness of God.

Fred's reputation as the only man in town who understood subsistent relations had spread. Jamaal joined the fan club at his table and said, 'Cunningham illustrates the idea of God as Three with the image of a mother, pregnant with child, feeding the kid through her placenta. Threeness is God's very being. Not just how we picture God.' 'Even if we can't picture the Threeness,' said the Boot, wisely.

Seminar Five: Economic and immanent Trinity

The economic Trinity

Narrative theology

A story has more than one agent. In the story of God with his people, can the plurality of agents be constituted only by external relations between God and persons who are simply other than God, so that God is himself but one monadic agent of the history? Since God's *identity* is told by his story with creatures, this cannot be the case. Either God's identity would then be determined extrinsically by creatures or it would at some depth be after all immune to the gospel events. But the God of

> Exodus and Resurrection is above all free and sovereign, and if his identity is determined in his relation with others, just so those others cannot be merely extrinsic to him. We must reckon with and seek to identify a plurality of what can only be called *dramatis dei personae*, 'characters of the drama of God.'
>
> Robert W. Jenson, *Systematic Theology* (1997: 75)

Anthony introduced the seminar on the economic Trinity by depreciating the idea that, once God is revealed, our language isn't sufficient to talk about God. 'Augustine got his agnosticism about God from Greek metaphysics,' he said. 'The Esperanto God of metaphysics is beyond human knowledge. Christians know who God is from the drama of salvation. If we're speaking Christianese, we identify God as the actor in biblical history. Or actors. God is engaged in the drama of salvation up to his ears! He isn't a detached spectator of human history. Think of history as a play and we can see the plot has three divine actors – Father, Son and Spirit. Jenson says it's cool to talk about three personae, three actors, in God. His idea of God comes from the economic Trinity, not from theorising about a transcendent Trinity.'

The immanent Trinity and the economic Trinity

Cathy didn't understand the difference between economic Trinity and transcendent Trinity. Anthony said, 'The economic Trinity is the Trinity as we know it in history, like with the appearance of Christ, then the Spirit. Those two historical missions are equivalent to the transcendent processions of Son and Spirit from the Father, which is what they're always doing.'

The Professor said that in the old days, people used different words. They called the transcendent Trinity the immanent Trinity, meaning God as he is in himself, in eternity, whether or not he creates the world, or becomes incarnate, or directs the Church. Immanent Trinity meant God's own immanence to himself, God as he is inside himself, apart from his external workings on human lives.

Catholic theology and seminary teaching always used to start with the immanent Trinity. Fred cut in, 'They did that to avoid calling the immanent Trinity and the economic Trinity equivalent.' Bob asked, 'What's the matter with saying equivalent?' The Professor explained that if you say the immanent Trinity is what it is through its engagement in history, then God must be changed by our history. The Trinity wouldn't be self-contained and it wouldn't be sovereign over creation. The Trinity would change in its very being, in reaction to our actions.

529

Fred wanted to know why theologians don't start from the immanent Trinity and work down to salvation history any more. The Professor said, 'When this course began, many of you feared the Trinity was an abstract subject. In the 1950s, people felt the Trinity had got uprooted from people's religious experience, and from the concrete biblical history. Karl Rahner reminded them that "The Trinity of the economy of salvation *is* the immanent Trinity and *vice versa*."' The Professor's face took on a distant gaze.

In contemporary preaching and instruction, the most widespread presentation of the Creed is . . . as summarising the plot of a drama with three acts. First, God makes the world, then we make a mess of it which God sends his Son to clean up and, thirdly, God sends his Spirit to bring us back to him through faith and sacraments and holiness. God is not an individual with a nature. But neither is God an agent acting in three episodes . . . the scheme of one drama with three acts . . . draws us back towards . . . the oldest of all families of Trinitarian heresy, known as 'modalism.'

Nicholas Lash, *Believing Three Ways in One God* (1993: 30)

Fred thought Rahner's remark was scary. It would be OK if you read it as saying we know the immanent Trinity by the economic side. But people could interpret it to mean God becomes a Trinity by acting in history. They'd go straight back to modalism. 'Scholars read Rahner's axiom both ways,' said the Professor.

A drama in the transcendent God?

Fred thought, *We humans have a story, or a drama, but God does not.* 'Theology is not about a divine drama,' he said. Rosie didn't agree with her boyfriend. She said, 'If you imagine God as pure action, that's very dramatic.' Fred said, 'Augustine taught us not to imagine the Trinity. Thomas says the same.'

Rosie argued, 'It's like saying revelation is cognitive propositions. People who worshipped in baroque churches shouldn't have had a problem with the idea that history is a pictorial revelation of God. There is beauty in the revelation of Christ, as well as truth. And you can imagine beauty, the beauty of God.' Fred cringed.

Rosie went on, 'If there is an analogy between God and creatures, like Thomists are always saying, there's a remote analogy between the drama of human history and the eventfulness of the immanent Trinity.'

Spiritu-que?

As they walked back to Fred's house, Fred told Rosie that liberation theologians had bought into Mary's speech to Elizabeth, claiming it's about God overthrowing powerful people. Fred couldn't stand them turning the Magnificat into a socialist slogan. He said, 'We're talking about the mystery of God, not about some collectivist model of an ideal human society.' Rosie reflected for a bit, then she said, 'Moltmann is criticising Augustine for not putting the whole Trinity equally in control. The idea is that to be God is to be Power. All his egalitarianism adds is that all the persons of the Trinity have to be equally powerful. So Moltmann says they are all Source, sharing out the power.'

The Bear worshipped the ground Rosie trod upon. He uncorked a bottle of burgundy for the young people, then lumbered back to his den. Rosie felt that, if God sides with the powerless, that does tells us something about God. The Trinity in history shows us what the Trinity as transcendent God is. Fred asked, 'How could God really be powerless? God the Creator is in total command of creation.' Rosie replied, 'When Christ becomes Incarnate, he empties himself of power. Isn't Christ conceived by the Spirit, in the gospels? Isn't his preaching inspired by the Spirit? Doesn't that make him receptive to the Spirit? I'm not saying we should cut the filioque from the Creed,' she added quickly. 'But wouldn't it be broader if it also said "Spiritu-que" – the Son proceeds from the Spirit?'

Trinitarian kenosis

Hans Urs von Balthasar (1905–88)

Greg and Jamaal banged on the door. They'd been reading Russian Orthodox theology and it was doing their heads in. Fred said, 'You need red wine?' Rosie asked, 'How come you got asked to give a seminar on Russian theology?' 'We didn't,' said Greg. 'I've been made to talk on Hans Urs von Balthasar and Jamaal was helping me and we went sideways. Von Balthasar argues the gospels show a role-reversal between Son and Spirit, with the Son acting on the Spirit's prompting. His Christology turns around "kenosis": emptying. He argues all the persons of the Trinity empty themselves. The Son is receptive to being begotten, and the Spirit . . . ' Fred interrupted, 'How can the Father empty himself?' Jamaal said, 'You can picture the Father letting the Son proceed from him as emptying. Von Balthasar's dropping the Western, logocentric, power-mad idea of God.'

Sergei Bulgakov (1871–1944)

Greg helped himself to more burgundy and said, 'We're asking ourselves how a Catholic could think like this, and he quoted Sergei Bulgakov, so

531

we looked into it. Bulgakov was expelled from Russia after the Revolution and lived in the West the rest of his life.' Fred thought, *Sergei had something going for him.* Greg said, 'Bulgakov imagines the Father allowing the Son to proceed out of him as self-emptying. The Father lets the Son just be himself, be other from him. He's allowing another person to be himself. He's giving up control, giving it all away.' 'The Son abandons himself, too,' said Jamaal. The Son does not try to be someone for himself: he gives himself up to being an image of the Father. The Father and Son let themselves be known and witnessed by the Holy Spirit. So all Three Persons are passive to each other. Rosie said, 'It makes the Trinity self-emptying love, like saints let themselves be martyred.'

Fred groaned and said, 'This is *not* Thomistic! It means there is an eternal sacrifice in God.' Greg answered, 'God knew when he created the cosmos the Son would become incarnate and die. The Father's willingness to send the Son is kenotic, too. Revelation shows a Lamb that is slain from the foundations of the world. The eternal sacrifice of the Lamb belongs to the Trinitarian kenosis.' Fred had his head in his hands. He was thinking, *There is no passivity or suffering in God. God is pure activity,* Actus Purus.

In giving himself, the Father does not give something … that he *has* but all that he *is* – for in God there is only being, not having. So the Father's being passes over, without remainder, to the begotten Son; and it would be a mistake to suggest that he, the Father, *becomes* or *develops* as a result of this self-giving … This total self-giving, to which the Son and the Spirit respond by an equal self-giving, is a kind of 'death', a first, radical 'kenosis', as one might say. It is a kind of 'super-death' that is a component of all love and that forms the basis in creation for all instances of 'the good death', from self-forgetfulness in favour of the beloved right up to that highest love by which a man 'gives his life for his friends'.

Hans Urs von Balthasar, *Theo-Drama* (1998: 85)

Greg said, 'Where is this *Actus Purus* God?' Fred replied, 'God is the Act of Being creating all things. So Thomas says "God is in all things, and innermostly" – *Summa Theologiae*, Prima Pars, Question Eight, First Article.' Rosie observed, 'Saying God is "in" all things is just a metaphor. You could just as well say the world is inside the Trinity. All the suburbs and houses. And the cross.' Fred said, 'You can't just change

the metaphor without asking the leading Thomists what they think.'
Fred and Rosie split up that night. It seemed they would not be the
Jacques and Raissa Maritain of the twenty-first century after all.

Seminar Six: Revelation in history

Heilsgeschichte / salvation history

On her way to the last class of term, Cathy picked up a letter from
Philip. She was upset and showed it to Lara. Lara glanced at it casually
and passed it to Rosie. The Professor told the class that the nineteenth-
century Lutheran, J. C. K. von Hofman argued that revelation *is* history.
He called it *Heilsgeschichte*, 'saving history'. Revelation is history, so
it's anchored in something objective to believers. By calling the biblical
witness *saving* history, von Hofman kept faith with the Lutheran principle that revelation is God acting for us. For the *Heilsgeschichte* school,
revelation is not the words of Scripture but the history the words
describe. Greg said, 'They were coming back to the wider idea of inspiration. It's not an idea entering a mind. It's God provoking human
action.' 'You got it,' said the Professor. Rosie gave Greg Phil's letter.
Greg passed it to Fred, who read it and turned white as a sheet.

Wolfhart Pannenberg

Cathy said, 'They thought Christian theology needs external evidence.'
The Professor said that was the outstanding concern for Wolfhart
Pannenberg. In *Jesus God and Man*, he argued that Martin Kahler and
Karl Barth had thrown in the towel by basing theology in faith – some-
thing that can't be proved to an outsider and that is therefore subjective,
according to Pannenberg.

    Jesus God and Man argued theology has to begin from objective facts,
not from a revelation only believers have faith in. That means it must
start from the resurrection of Jesus. Bob asked, 'He thinks the resurrection is a historical fact?' 'Yes, and one that can be empirically proved,'
said the Professor. 'Pannenberg wants us to arrive at faith from an
empirical basis. That takes the notion of salvation history about as far
as it goes.' Cathy stamped on Bob's foot. Suspiciously near hers.

The liberating Bible

Jamaal said, 'Unless revelation is historical, like Pannenberg says, we
don't know that God takes the side of persons, not the side of those who
treat others like objects. He's right to put the historical resurrection at
the centre because that shows the victims are lifted up. It shows God is
at the side of the poor and that we can transcend historical circumstances through God's power. It gives us the assurance that God will help

us break through to justice on earth. The resurrection reveals that God is our liberator.' Jamaal fell silent, blushing. Fred gave him Philip's letter to chill him out.

The unity of biblical history

'That's bad,' said Greg. 'No, it's not,' said Bob. 'How do we know there is one saving history?' Lara said, 'Salvation historians want to go back to the archaic, medieval way of looking at Scripture that Fred buys.' The Professor replied, 'The salvation history school argued that God guides Israel's history to lead toward Christ. For Gerhard von Rad, Israel's history as a whole is a prophecy of Christ, not particular sentences in the Old Testament. For liberation theology, the resurrection of Jesus is *the* revelation of who God is and we should test every reading of Scripture by whether it connects to it.'

Bob said, 'The whole of human history could be saving, not just the tiny segment of it you hear of in the Christian Bible.' Fred answered, 'History can only be a unity if there is a God, and since there is, I'm OK with it. But there are thousands of streams in history, cultures and individuals going their own merry ways. The history of the world isn't one single stream of traffic going in the same direction. What I don't like about salvation history is the feeling that it turns humanity into a collective unit.'

The world is like a vast orchestra tuning up: the players play to themselves, while the audience take their seats and the conductor has not yet arrived. All the same, someone has struck an A on the piano, and a certain atmosphere is established around it; they are tuning up for some common endeavour... The choice of instruments comes from the unity that, for the moment, lies silent in the open score on the conductor's podium. In revelation, God performs a symphony, and it is impossible to say which is richer: the seamless genius of the divine composition or the polyphonous orchestra of Creation that God has prepared to play it... The unity of the composition comes from God. That is why the world was, and always will be pluralist... But the purpose of its pluralism is this; not to refuse to enter into the unity that lies in God... but symphonically to get into tune with one another and give allegiance to the transcendent unity.

Hans Urs von Balthasar, *Truth is Symphonic* (1987: 7–8)

Greg remarked that von Balthasar pictures history as a symphony with one conductor. Everyone plays their own instruments and you never know where the symphony is going. It's not like pre-recorded music; there's always something new cooking. 'You can go home if you want to,' said Jamaal. 'We're just jamming.'

Revelation as drama

Greg told the class, 'It wasn't Aquinas who turned revelation into words, instead of showing how God acted in events. It was his followers, who got fixated on only one thing he said. Some twentieth-century Catholic theologians wanted to retrieve his whole idea of revelation. They didn't want to say God dictates a series of true propositions and that's *it*. So Pierre Benoit says there are two forms of inspiration. One is dramatic, or "doing" inspiration – the kind that drove David to dance before the Ark. The other is "Scriptural inspiration" – the God-given impulsion to describe the historical events.

Alonso Schökel figured there are three forms of divine revelation. God reveals himself in creation, in history – and the top way is Scripture. The historical events the Bible depicts are revelation. For Schökel, the history is like a silent movie pointing to God with its pictorial gestures and actions. Verbal revelation is more cogent but historical revelation is, in its obscurer way, an icon that directs us to God.' 'Like *Goldrush*,' said Rosie. 'You remember Charlie Chaplin laying the table and eating his shoes.'

Greg said, 'Von Balthasar doesn't say God is three actors' – *thank God for that*, thought Fred – 'but he does picture history as a drama between God and universal humanity, inside and outside the Bible.' 'If God isn't an actor,' said Rosie, 'how can it be a drama from his side?' 'Like Barth,' said Greg, 'von Balthasar is thinking of the Trinity in history as three ways of being revelation. God the Father is the Author. Christ the Word is the Actor who perfectly represents the Author's mind. The Holy Spirit is the Director, who nudges the characters to say their lines properly. All humanity is *in Christ*, like Paul said, so we're taking part in a divine drama, following up on Christ's performance.' 'I can buy that,' said Rosie. Fred said, 'You win.' He was wondering, *Will we end up on Sky TV in our shirtsleeves ladling out porridge to famine victims in some desert?* 'Probably,' drawled Rosie, reading his mind. 'But right now, let's go check out how Philip is doing in the novitiate at Holy Trinity.' 'We'll stick with it,' said Fred. Greg said, 'We can stop off for a beer on the way back.' Cathy and Jamaal looked hopeful, so Fred said, 'Come on, everyone, we can get ten people into dad's station wagon.' Bob was up for it but Lara and Anthony had to go study.

Further reading

The books in this list are ranked in order of their accessibility to undergraduate readers.

McCabe, Herbert (1987), *God Matters*, London: Mowbray.
Jenson, Robert W. (1997), *Systematic Theology: Volume I The Triune God*, New York and Oxford: Oxford University Press.
Hill, Edmund (1985), *The Mystery of the Trinity*, London: Geoffrey Chapman.
Lash, Nicholas (1993), *Believing Three Ways in One God*, Notre Dame: University of Notre Dame Press.
Augustine (1991), *The Trinity*, trans. Edmund Hill, New York: New City Press. Read this fine modern translation and decide for yourself!
Cunningham, David S. (1988), *These Three Are One: The Practice of Trinitarian Theology*, Oxford: Blackwell.

Questions

1. What is the difference between an accommodationalism that says God wrote to our level and an accommodationalism that says God handed over to us to write?

2. What is modalism? Why did Christianity reject it as a doctrine of God?

3. Does God have a history?

4. In what way did the idea of God as creator affect Augustine's notion of the Trinity in the human mind? Did Augustine see his own mind as private?

5. What does filioque mean? Why do Catholics accept it and Orthodox Christians reject it? What reasons did Augustine have for saying the Spirit proceeds from the Son?

6. Could God be powerless? Does the 'kenotic' idea of the Trinity make rational sense?

7. What are the drawbacks and advantages of calling God three *persons*? Can we imagine the Trinity? Why do Augustine, Aquinas and Barth deny it?

Section Four: PHILOSOPHY OF RELIGION

CHAPTER ONE

The Philosophy of Religion

Derek Cross, CO

- ❏ Introduction
- ❏ Philosophy as a way of life
- ❏ The existence of God
- ❏ The problem of evil
- ❏ Miracles
- ❏ Further reading
- ❏ Questions

Introduction

This chapter introduces some questions that concern the philosopher of religion, set forth under the guise of an exchange of letters and e-mail messages between various interlocutors. Philosophy is usually expounded in a conventional treatise but throughout history philosophers have not hesitated to attempt dialogues, letters, epic poetry, or even drama. The epistolary form of this chapter allows several voices to be heard. Some of our letter-writers clearly have more expertise than others do but you will not want simply to 'believe' what any of them says. The use of letters serves as a constant reminder that writers have their crotchets and their limitations, and that a train of thought starts from a particular point of view and is often bound to a tradition. Consequently, the student is never absolved from doing her or his own thinking. The epistolary form also shows how philosophical problems can arise from and reflect on practical life. A treatise would have lacked this concreteness, in which we see the interconnectedness of philosophical inquiries and the tentative character of a thought that sometimes trails off, leaving further investigation until another day. Finally, an epistolary presentation allows for a tutorial approach to more difficult concepts and claims. One of the writers can take you by the hand and push you face-first into the steps of the argument, in something like the way a good teacher does in class or a patient friend can in a long discussion.

Philosophy as a way of life

Dear Uncle Jack,

I don't think I have written you a letter since I was small – remember those thank-you notes Mom made us write for the gifts you sent from Africa? I still have a couple of those wooden animals. Maybe I didn't appreciate them enough at the time because there were no ads on TV to tell me how much I wanted a unique hand-carved elephant from Tanzania. TV commercials! I have been thinking about technology ever since Dad told me that you do not have e-mail at your mission. It must be very medieval there in Africa. Therefore you must be just the person to help me with the course in Philosophy of Religion I am taking this term at university. We are studying all kinds of medieval topics, like proofs for the existence of God and the problem of evil.

How did you like that segue? I started writing to you out of crass self-interest, to ask for help with my Philosophy term paper, but I have just realised that I don't know very much about you and why you are spending your life on the other side of the world in such primitive surroundings. It must be connected to your philosophy. Dad told me that you were much smarter than he was. But he makes way more money!

It was Mom who suggested I write to my uncle, the priest. She thinks that my religious observance is lax. She also thinks that this has something to do with my latest boyfriend, Josh. She is right. Josh will make more money than you do, as well. He is interested in philosophy but he won't be a Philosophy professor. His favourite philosopher is some Russian lady named Ayn Rand. Rand escaped from the Communists and spent the rest of her life extolling capitalism and 'the sign of the dollar'. Josh said that if I took some Philosophy courses I would appreciate Ayn Rand more, and I would understand him better. I was very persuaded by the way he brushed aside his shock of blond hair and flashed the dimple of his smile. (Do you think I am superficial? I think my Philosophy professor does. He gave me a very unfair grade on my first paper. When Mom looked at it, she told me to write to you. You are supposed to save my faith and raise my Philosophy grade at the same time. There's a mission for you!)

Do you know anything about Ayn Rand? She hasn't figured yet in my

Philosophy class. Josh says she is brilliantly rational and that the only position for someone of reason to take is atheism. Besides being irrational, religion is altruistic. That is bad, according to Josh, because self-interest is another of those only-reasonable positions. I am not so sure about that, though. When I am in love I think I forget all about my own interests. I mean, I even take courses in Philosophy of Religion to please Mr Dimples. (I am teasing you, O Praiser of Women's Purity!) But I do think religion asks us to believe and do some crazy things. Compared to what you can learn from history or psychology or biology or physics, what religion says is pretty much nonsense.

Anyway, when I asked my professor about Ayn Rand, he smirked and said we are starting at the beginning, with the proofs for the existence of God. That was the paper he marked me down on. He is going to allow me to re-submit it. Can you help me to understand these proofs? How does this help anyone to believe?

Your loving niece,
Betsy

Philosophy is a search for first principles

Dear Betsy,

What a surprise to hear from you! You are never far from my thoughts, even though I rarely have the pleasure of seeing you and the rest of my wealthy younger brother's family face-to-face. I have heard about this 'e-mail' from one of the younger fathers. He was also appalled to find that our mission was not equipped with such a universal modern convenience. But sometimes I can get to a phone when I need to communicate quickly. Your father will know how to reach me if there is a sudden urgent development in the Philosophy of Religion – God dying, or some breaking news like that.

This is no small order you place. Your mother knows that I taught Philosophy a little before I entered the seminary. (Your Mr Joshua Dimples is right to suspect that 'philosophy butters no bread.') I also took our scholastics through the old treatise on 'natural theology' for several years before I was sent to the missions. I shall try to remember how the arguments were presented. The main issues will not have changed much; these problems are eternal. But I warn you that I am without many books and will have to develop these notions from my own unaided thought, like a real ancient Greek philosopher.

Betsy, I live in a very different world from your urban academic retreat – not that I am unhappy to meet you in your world. Just remember that your avuncular priest writes from a world full of tribal warfare, AIDS victims, disease-bearing mosquitoes and hungry lionesses. I have detached myself from contemporary conventional society. Is poverty too great a price to pay for that?

I am now preparing my own segue into the question you have put. Where is the real beginning of the Philosophy of Religion, if it is not to be found in Ayn Rand? Dear Betsy, not many 'professional' philosophers have much time for Ayn Rand. Has Josh urged *Atlas Shrugged* on you yet? Reading that brick will be a true test of your love. But, like your Josh, many have cut their philosophical teeth on Rand's books. If her gestures towards reason and querulous remarks about altruism have set you searching for bedrock reality, then even if this is not *the* beginning of Philosophy of Religion, it has become the beginning for you. This distinction, between what is first for us and what is first in itself, is of great importance for Plato and Aristotle and the way they think philosophy should be developed.

The point is that we are not in immediate possession of the principles of reason and reality. We cannot begin with some cut-and-dried subject matter and proceed unproblematically from that basis. Philosophy is a search for first principles. Everything changes in the quest for them, even the initial questions themselves.

Plato said philosophy begins when we leave the 'Cave'

Your letter raises the question of how our lives and thoughts have been shaped by modern technology, science, politics and economics. Does our modern experience serve to occlude the evidence for God and deaden any motivation we might have for pursuing the 'question of God'? Do we not need to take into account this wider human context in order to make the question live again? You know Plato's image of the cave from your Introduction to Philosophy course. Plato compares ordinary human intercourse to the babblings of those who are imprisoned in an underground cave, cut off from the beings of nature and the light of the sun.

I knew a remarkable professor – Leo Strauss – who claimed that modernity was a 'cave beneath the cave' (1964: 241). According to Strauss, we moderns are even cut off from the cave of natural human opinion and action – a horizon that must be recovered before we can attempt to escape from this cave to the real world of truth. Leo Strauss: there is another name for 'professional' philosophers to conjure with. You might try your young capitalist friend out on *Natural Right and History*. Or, more difficult, *The City and Man*. I mention that book because it concludes with these words (I quote from memory, as the ancient Greeks did): 'What is "first for us" is not the philosophic understanding of the city but that understanding which is inherent in the city as such, in the pre-philosophic city, according to which the city sees itself as subject and subservient to the divine in the ordinary understanding of the divine or looks up to it. Only by beginning at this point will we be open to the full impact of the all-important question which is coeval with philosophy although the philosophers do not frequently pronounce it – the question *quid sit deus*.' How is your Latin? It means 'what is god'?

I do mean to go through the proofs with you. But soon the bell will be ringing for vespers and our evening meal. I shall put pen to paper again tonight, after I have said compline.

Your loving uncle, a poor missionary of God,
Jack

Is philosophy about escaping cultural conditioning?

Dear Holy One,
Thank you for your letter. What you say is interesting but please don't forget that I need to re-submit my proofs of God paper! I showed your letter to Josh. He sent this e-mail in response:

```
FROM: Josh
TO: Betsy
SUBJECT: re: Philosophy of God letter
What kind of funny priest is this? Isn't he supposed
to tell you not to start sleeping with me? I thought
their job was mostly to prevent people from having sex
or from enjoying it if ever they managed it. The con-
servative ones, anyway. A lot of the liberals seem to
know where to get their own gratification. Anyway, this
guy knows about Ayn Rand. I was saving Atlas Shrugged
until after we watched the video of The Fountainhead
together. But maybe you would like to borrow my copy.
Does this guy really think there are proofs for God's
existence? Keep me posted. Where did he get the screwy
idea that my last name is Dimples? And what is vespers
and compline?
```

Uncle Jack, you know I never thought about the modern world 'warping' our perceptions and ideas of reality. Ever since we studied Egyptian mythology in the sixth grade I could see that people haven't always lived in the 'same' world we do. But I always thought ours was the normal world, the pinnacle of progress.

Anyway, is that what philosophy is about? Escaping from our intellectual conditioning? But how do we know there is anywhere else to go, once we have given up on what society tells us? I don't want to end up being a nun in some convent in the boonies or an Amish housewife, canning preserves for a bearded husband in overalls.

Your doubting niece,
Betsy

The existence of God

Augustine's Argument for God's Existence

Eternal truth in our minds

Dear Betsy,

As promised, after compline I pick up my pen and attack the proofs of God. Let's start by looking at St Augustine's argument. You will find it in the second book of his *De Libero Arbitrio* (*On the Free Choice of the Will*). Be patient and read it through first before you let criticisms well up and push it aside. We can deal with your criticisms once you have seen what is at stake in the argument. It is because it is relatively easy to be critical about this argument – I do not say to refute it – that I thought we could start here.

Augustine's dialogue with Evodius about God's existence in
De Libero Arbitrio

Step One: 'Light is not perceived by the ears nor voices by the eyes, for we do not discern these things without rational observation and thought.'
Step Two: 'We hold it as settled that there is such a thing as wisdom . . . But where do we see this? For I have no doubt at all that you see this and that it is true. Is it not one truth which we both see with our different minds common to both of us? . . . Again, take such propositions as these: Man ought to live justly . . . each man should be given his due. Don't you admit these statements are absolutely true and stable, to be shared by you and me and all who see them? . . . Can anyone claim truths of that kind as his own private truths, seeing they are unchangeably present for all to contemplate who have the capacity to contemplate them?'
Step Three: 'Do you, then, think that this truth . . . is more excellent than our minds, or equal to our minds, or inferior? If it were inferior we should not use it as a standard of judgement . . . With our minds we know not only that it *is* thus or thus, but that it *ought to be* thus or thus . . . We pass judgement on our minds in accordance with truth as our standard, while we cannot in any way pass judgement on truth . . . Hence if truth is neither inferior to nor equal to our mind it must be superior and more excellent.'
Step Four: 'There it is, truth itself. Embrace it if you can. Enjoy it. Delight in the Lord and he will grant you the petitions of your heart . . . Herein is our liberty, when we are subject to truth. And Truth is our God who liberates us from death, that is, from the condition of sin.'

Truth is changeless

St Augustine's starting point is the existence of truth in our souls. He maintains that truth has the properties of unchangeability and necessity. This is what it means to be true: the truth never alters and it does not just *happen* to be the case – it *must* be that way. Think of the truth of the Pythagorean theorem in geometry: the sum of the squares on the sides of a right triangle is equal to the square of the hypotenuse. It could not be any other way, and the proof of this theorem effectively conveys that insight to your mind (or soul, as Augustine prefers). We must try to explain the presence of unchangeable and necessary truth in our souls.

Human thinking is changeable

Now Betsy, your image is in my soul as I write. It is a memory drawn from perceptions received when I visited your family seven summers ago. (I have altered the memory somewhat in order to account for what has occurred to you in the intervening passage of time!) On my way back from the chapel, I sensed (in a couple of different ways) the garbage from our evening meal. Perhaps you want to say that truth comes to my soul from the senses. Indeed, most objects of my thought I have first sensed – elephants, lionesses, mosquito netting. But here is the difficulty: these things need not be the way they are. These things change. Little girls grow up. Animals scavenge the garbage dump. But truth, you remember, is unchanging and necessary. So truth cannot be caused by anything I can sense (a 'sensible object' Augustine would say for short, by which he does not mean a sagacious thing but a tangible one).

How does eternal truth get into our minds?

If the truth is not caused by sensible things, perhaps it comes from my own mind. But that cannot be the case either. For my mind, also, is subject to change. I no longer think what I did when I was your age. And as for your mind – I can tease, too: *femina semper mutabilis* (and that I will not translate for you!)

Truth is something above my mind. My mind does not rule it. My mind submits to it, as to an external rule. And truth is by no means confined to my mind; it is something public and shared by all who 'see' it, as we say. (Maybe it took you awhile to 'get' the Pythagorean theorem. And maybe some of your many former boyfriends were never able to 'get' your reasons for rejecting them. But in principle, we recognise truth as something shareable.) When we do manage to 'see' the truth together, we see it not in each other's minds but above our minds. You probably see where this is going. You'd better, because St Augustine concludes his proof rather abruptly. The qualities of truth – necessity, immutability, eternity – are one with the attributes of God. To affirm the existence of truth, then, is to recognise the existence of God, who alone can be its sufficient reason.

Is truth relative?

Well, are you convinced? Will you have Josh signing up for a Converts' Inquiry Class this weekend? I am fascinated by Augustine's claim but I find I have a lot of questions about it. First of all, any argument is only as good as its starting point. I wonder whether you and your friends will admit the presence of truth in your minds (or souls). Even in my youth – before e-mail, fax machines and CDs – we were plagued with relativistic suspicions. Truth with a capital 'T' did not exist, we used to say. What seemed to be true was always relative – to the times (the *Zeitgeist*, if you liked to spit out German words), to your social class, to your psychological constitution, to your sex. And if any of these things changed (pre-eminently, the times), then truth changed with them. Your parents will tell you that there have been deep changes in society's moral prescriptions during their lifetime. Even in what we used to call the 'unchanging Church' I have experienced a seismic shift in spirit and external arrangements. More radical than the various forms of relativism is the posture of generalised scepticism. Can we know anything for sure? Scepticism can be tricked out in all sorts of fancy new ways but the same nagging suspicion remains at its heart.

So Augustine's premise does pose a difficulty for us. But it also serves to alert us to what is entailed in proofs of God's existence, namely an embrace, at some level, of eternal truth. If we are sceptical or uneasy about truth with a capital 'T', we see why God finds no ready locus on our intellectual map.

Let me sow some more suspicion in order to reach my next point, Betsy. Even if you do admit eternal truths in some sense, you may not readily accept Augustine's point that their existence establishes the existence of an Eternal Mind. For Augustine, however, this followed readily from the Platonist approach to knowledge that he espoused. If you go on with your study of philosophy, you may learn about Augustine's theory of 'illumination'. What we are seeing is that it is not so easy to abstract the 'question of God' from the whole philosophical enterprise of a given thinker. Augustine's proof of God points us ineluctably to his theory of knowledge. But there I will not take you.

God is altogether off the map

You probably also have concerns about the abruptness of Augustine's conclusion. God gets thrust in, as it were, towards the very end. Augustine doesn't tell us very much about the nature of this being whose existence he claims to establish. Apart from his connection to eternal truth, what God is remains a bit of a cipher. That may not be as bad as it first seems. What do we know about the nature of God? It may be a mistake to assume that we know perfectly well what is meant by 'God' and that the only mystery is whether or not such a being exists. The philosophers we are considering take just the opposite approach: God so transcends the world that we can never form an adequate concept of God. On the other hand, we can show with sufficient certainty that he exists. If your university library has a copy of Thomas Merton's *The Seven Storey Mountain*, take a look at the beginning of Part Two, where the young Thomas Merton, a student at Columbia, buys a book called *The Spirit of Medieval Philosophy* and discovers that he has never understood what Christians mean by 'God'. What Merton encountered was the notion that God is totally unimaginable and unconceptualisable. God is altogether off the map, not just another item in the system. There is no other reality like him. (In this, God is like the aardvark. Everything is a bit like him but he is like nothing else.) Maybe Augustine's almost unarticulated breakthrough is the best way to convey this.

Your faithful purveyor of St Augustine,

Uncle Jack

In Scribner's window, I saw a book called *The Spirit of Medieval Philosophy*. I went inside, and took it off the shelf, and looked at the table of contents and at the title page which was deceptive, because it said the book was made up of a series of lectures that had been given at the University of Aberdeen. That . . . threw me off the track as to the possible identity and character of Etienne Gilson, who wrote the book. I bought it . . . and on my way home in the Long Island train, I unwrapped the package to gloat over my acquisitions. It was only then that I saw, on the first page of *The Spirit of Medieval Philosophy*, the small print which said: 'Nihil Obstat . . . Imprimatur.' The feeling of disgust and deception struck me like a knife in the pit of the stomach . . . They should have warned me that it was a Catholic book! Then I would never have bought it. As it was, I was tempted to throw the thing out the window at the houses of Woodside – to get rid of it as something dangerous and unclean . . . it was surely a real grace that, instead of getting rid of the book, I actually read it . . . The one big concept which I got out of its pages was something that was to revolutionise my whole life . . . I discovered an entirely new concept of God – a concept which showed me at once that the belief of Catholics was by no means the vague and rather superstitious hangover from an unscientific age that I had believed it to be . . . I had never had an adequate notion of what Christians meant by God. I had simply taken it for granted that the God in Whom religious people believed . . . was a noisy and dramatic and passionate character, a vague, jealous, hidden being, the objectification of all their own desires and

---

545

strivings and subjective ideals . . . The concept of God which I had always entertained, and which I had accused Christians of teaching to the world, was a concept of a being who was simply impossible. He was infinite and yet finite; perfect and imperfect; eternal and yet changing – subject to all the variations of emotion, love, sorrow, hate, revenge, that men are prey to. How could this fatuous, emotional thing be without beginning and without end, the creator of all? . . . I think one cause of my profound satisfaction with which I now read was that God had been vindicated in my own mind. There is in every intellect a natural exigency for a true concept of God: we are born with the thirst to know and to see Him, and therefore it cannot be otherwise. I know that many people are, or call themselves, 'atheists' simply because they are repelled and offended by statements about God made in imaginary and metaphorical terms which they are not able to interpret and comprehend. They refuse these concepts of God, not because they despise God, but perhaps because they demand a notion of Him more perfect than they generally find: and because ordinary, figurative concepts of God could not satisfy them, they turn away and think that there are no other: or, worse still, they refuse to listen to philosophy, on the ground that it is nothing but a web of meaningless words spun together for the justification of the same old hopeless falsehoods. What a relief it was for me, now, to discover not only that no idea of ours, let alone any image, could adequately represent God but also that we should not allow ourselves to be satisfied with any such knowledge of Him.

Thomas Merton, *The Seven Storey Mountain* (1978: 171–2, 174)

Does absolute truth require an absolute object?

Dear Uncle Jack,

Your letter explaining St Augustine's proof arrived at last. My professor was surprised that I had heard about Augustine's *De Libero Arbitrio*. I have not told him about my secret weapon. If journalists can conceal their sources, why not Philosophy students? My prof says that St Augustine's proof would not provide a suitable paper topic. Maybe Thomas Merton would appreciate its silences but it is too sketchy for an analytic term paper.

Nevertheless, Josh was intrigued by Augustine's proof. Josh does believe in absolute truths and rails about weak minds and weak wills. The virtue of selfishness is one of his absolute truths. He said he was surprised to see that Augustine is not just a mystic. He saw that

Augustine was interested in argument and that he was concerned with truth. This is Josh's main objection, which I had him write down because I am never sure that I am not missing something important about philosophical 'arguments': 'I agree with Augustine on the absolute nature of truth. What I disagree with is his inference that this requires an absolute object, namely God. In order for me to know something as eternally true, there does not have to be any eternal intelligible object.'

I don't see why Josh is so down on mystics. Something about their irrationality. Wasn't it St Augustine and his mother St Monica who had a joint vision of God? I think I remember that story from our catechism class. Anyway, what do you have to say about that?

Your studious niece,
Betsy

Why are we driven to seek a satisfying idea of God?

Dear Uncle Jack,
Either there has been a gap in your writing or the mail is clumping up. I wanted to tell you that Josh read not only the passage in Thomas Merton's book that you called to our attention but he is now reading the whole book. He says Merton is strange but cool. He had a wild life compared to American suburban teenagers today. And in the end, he became a Trappist monk. Josh says Merton became a mystic, even though he was interested in ideas. Too bad for Merton. The back cover of *The Seven Storey Mountain* has a quotation saying it is 'a twentieth-century form of *The Confessions* of St Augustine', so Josh has now got Augustine out of the library, too.

I copied out a section from Merton so I could think it over. Josh says I left out the important bits – the reason you wanted us to read it. Some difficult stuff I couldn't follow about something called 'aseity'. Anyway, I think I got the point, if not the argument for it. I also made a discovery of my own, after I got rid of all the technical language – something Josh hadn't seen. (He admitted it! It pained him. He is supposed to be the rational one.) I think it is another proof of God.

I call it the 'satisfying idea proof'. It goes like this: human beings have all kinds of ideas about God. They also have an inbuilt need to find one of these ideas satisfying. If their ideas of God are not satisfactory, they reject them, sometimes vehemently. Only a true and worthy concept of God can satisfy them. This suggests that God is more than a fiction of our minds, that he is a real being whom we are dimly aware of and cannot bear to think about in a false and misleading way.

I don't know if the 'satisfying idea proof' will satisfy my professor. Josh is just impressed that I have tried to come up with any proof at all. He says it is more subjective than rational.

Your not unsatisfied niece,
Betsy

It's hard for sinners to think theologically

Dear Betsy,

Sorry about the hiatus. I had to go into the bush for a day. To answer Josh, vespers and compline are two of the daily prayers we say, part of the 'Liturgy of the Hours', which uses the ancient psalms of David to keep us in mind of God throughout the course of the day. How easy it is for us fallen men to forget! You might also tell Josh that sin does not divide as neatly along ideological lines as he suggests. That is again tied in with the Fall. St Thomas Aquinas speaks of how the fallen human intellect is 'darkened'. That is why we need revelation in addition to philosophy. Otherwise, only very few men – and that after a very long time – would come to know the truth. So you can blame your low grade in Philosophy on the sin of Adam.

While we are talking about sin, I also take up Josh's dig about it being my job to stop his sleeping around. Well, yes – but it seems a little utopian to think he will observe the demanding bits of the Christian moral code without sharing the Christian beliefs (or their natural counterparts) that underpin it. I don't expect a great many people regulate urgent drives for pleasure without the conviction that a compensating satisfaction is somehow available. (And even then . . .) That is not a practical counsel, you understand, just an observation based on experience. St Augustine, after all, before his conversion prayed, 'Give me chastity, but not yet.'

Is God unchangeable? – one of Augustine's assumptions

I warned you that Augustine's proof would be more suggestive than demonstrative. I am surprised that none of you questioned his assumption that linked God to unchangeability. There is a school of thought – it has not quite died out, I gather – called 'process theology' that questions that link. The process theologians take their point of departure from the British philosopher, Alfred North Whitehead, a colleague of Bertrand Russell's. Josh has probably heard of Bertrand Russell. If I am not mistaken, he has read Russell's devilish little book, *Marriage and Morals*. Whitehead had an American admirer named Charles Hartshorne, who elaborated on the 'process metaphysics' he found in Whitehead's *Process and Reality*. Some of Hartshorne's students became theologians and formed the project of rewriting Christian theology to fit a god who suffers and learns and develops. I use the small 'g' for this god because such an entity is clearly finite. Remember what Merton learned from the Gilson book? That God is altogether off the map, not just another item in the system? Suppose Merton had picked up Hartshorne's book instead. Then what would he have thought?

Josh has asked a good question. Let me rephrase it this way: do the requirements of our knowledge suffice to establish the characteristics of being? That is, just because our knowledge of truth is unchanging and necessary, does this entail the existence of a real object, a being, that is also unchanging and necessary? Cannot I have unchanging and necessary knowledge of changeable beings? Again, you see that to fill out Augustine's proof we must push beyond the question of God to Augustine's doctrine of knowledge. But in the end, I am not so sure that Augustine is wrong here. How will unchanging and necessary knowledge be secured, if eternal being is unavailable as a context?

Is there a natural desire for God?

I am happy to learn of your 'satisfying idea proof'. I see how you have drawn it out of Merton's remarks. It is an argument that attempts to spell out the implications of a 'natural desire for God'. You will find something like it in St Augustine, as well. 'You have made us for yourself, O Lord, and our hearts are restless until they rest in thee' (*Confessions* I.i). That is St Augustine, Betsy. Is this a purely subjective argument? Maybe not, if you can establish that it is a natural desire we are dealing with here, a desire all members of the species share. It is possible to speak objectively about subjective matters. The crux is who is being satisfied? You with your idiosyncratic predispositions, or any member of the species as such? Josh will deny that he has a natural desire for God. But will he deny that he is aware of desire simply? If he experiences desire, how does he know the true object of that desire? 'Give me chastity, but not yet ... You have made us for yourself, O Lord, and our hearts are restless until they rest in thee.'

Out of Africa,
Uncle Jack

Anselm's argument for God's existence

The difference between being and knowledge

```
FROM: Josh
TO: Bets
SUBJECT: godproof
Your 'Satisfying Idea Proof' shows that you are learn-
ing to be rational. Now you can learn more about the
life of reason from me and the writings of Ayn Rand. I
still think your proof is too subjective, not about
objective things. I suppose it is possible to be objec-
tive about something subjective - for example, if I say
that egoism is the only rational moral code because
egoism is natural to the best men, the strong creators.
But man does not have instincts. He is a free being. I
don't think there is very much objective to say about
his subjectivity. What is important is what he does,
what he creates.
```

I like Bertrand Russell. He tried to be a rational man. *Marriage and Morals* is pretty rational but it is outdated. Russell's ideas helped get us where we are today, clearing away a lot of superstition about sex. Have you finished *Atlas Shrugged*? Later, you can read Russell's *History of Western Philosophy*.

FROM: Bets
TO: Josh
SUBJECT: re: godproof
Atlas Shrugged is a very long book. Are you sure Ayn Rand was a woman? I will keep at it, for you, dear, but I don't think I'll ever be that rational. I will happily postpone Bertrand Russell until you think I am ready for it. Isn't that the book Jeeves told Bertie Wooster was 'most unsuitable' for a gentleman?

What is all of this about being and knowledge? I can't understand what Uncle Jack is getting at here.

Buy me an ice cream cone at the coffee shop after class today?

FROM: Josh
TO: Bets
SUBJECT: Ice cream
Jeeves and Bertie never talked about Russell. Spinoza, maybe. Spinoza's *Ethics* is very rational, too. All deductive proofs like math: A = A. When you have more time for it, you'll get into *Atlas Shrugged*. It will change your life. Like me, you were meant to be a creator, not a parasite.

The relation of being and knowledge is important. In other words, how do we know reality? We want to know reality (being), not illusions. The study of knowledge is called epistemology. It was Plato who thought that, since knowledge was universal, its objects also had to be universal. He called them the Ideas. They weren't ideas in your mind or anything. Just Ideas up there. Like God, only not conscious, and there were lots of them. Aristotle's theory of knowledge got rid of Plato's Ideas. Ayn Rand has a fantastic epistemology, even better than Aristotle's.

Sorry, I have lab this afternoon. Maybe we can drop by Machiavelli's later tonight for a burger?

FROM: Bets
TO: Josh
SUBJECT: re: Steak at Machiavelli's
Machiavelli's it is, then. Luckily for the weight-watcher, they have Diet Coke. But aren't being and knowledge just different things? What is the big deal about making them fit each other? There's what is there and there's what I know. One is out there in the world, the other is in here in my mind. Maybe my knowledge in here is a copy of what is out there or something. Sometimes my mind doesn't make a good copy or picture. Just like a kid who doesn't draw very well yet. But I keep improving my pictures of reality. I don't see the problem.

What about sex? Calm down. Not that, dear. I mean, what about our various desires and the 'natural desire for God'? I like that even better than the 'satisfying idea proof'. Wait! I think I see the difference: my proof is about my *idea* of God, whereas the natural desire for God is about God directly, the being of God.

FROM: Josh
TO: Bets
SUBJECT: re: Steak at Machiavelli's
Be by your dorm a little before 9:00 tonight. We can talk about natural desire after that.

Knowing God exists and believing God exists are different acts

Dear Betsy,

I hope you have been thinking about *thinking* and *being* because this distinction is at the root of St Anselm's proof. I should tell you that the 'copy theory of knowledge' is not very successful. If you are in there making pictures, and reality is out here independent of your thought, how will you ever get outside the prison of your picturing mind to compare your pictures with the reality they supposedly depict?

St Anselm is an eleventh-century man: he lived after St Augustine, before St Thomas Aquinas. He was born in northern Italy, in Aosta, but the Middle Ages were very international and Anselm entered the Norman Abbey of Bec, later to become Archbishop of Canterbury in England.

Anselm is famous for the so-called 'ontological argument' found in his book the *Proslogion*. However, he did not call his proof an 'ontological argument'. That name and classification was given to it by the modern German philosopher, Immanuel Kant. Kant learned about the ontological argument from Descartes. In fact, neither Kant nor Descartes conceived of the argument quite the way Anselm did.

The intent of St Anselm's *Proslogion* has been variously interpreted. There was a famous Swiss Protestant theologian, Karl Barth, who thought that Anselm's *Proslogion* was a model of Protestant theology, years before Luther. Barth thought that Anselm was not attempting to prove the existence of God on the basis of reason alone but merely explicating an idea he held as a believer. In other words, Barth considered Anselm's proof to be Christian theology, not philosophy.

Your very first question was how do these proofs of God help anyone to believe? One answer to that, Betsy, is that a proof intends to produce knowledge, not belief. St Thomas says that the same thing cannot be believed and known at the same time: either knowledge exorcises mere belief, or belief is added as a supplement to the weakness of knowledge. If Anselm's proof were meant to proceed on the basis of reason alone, it would be a philosophical argument and would be addressed to and accessible to any reasonable man (or woman), whereas a theological argument presupposes the gift of faith.

The trouble is this: the *Proslogion* reads like a religious book, even addressing God in the words of prayer. On the other hand, Anselm says that after he hit upon his argument he so understood that which he formerly believed that, even if he refused to believe that God existed, he would be unable not to understand it to be true. And that sounds like a case of philosophical reason alone, 'unassisted' by revelation, as they say.

God defined as 'that than which no greater can be conceived'

And, indeed, we believe that Thou art a being than which nothing greater can be conceived. Or is there no such nature, since the fool hath said in his heart, there is no God? (Psalm xiv.1). But, at any rate, this very fool, when he hears of this being of which I speak – a being than which nothing greater can be conceived – understands what he hears, and what he understands is in his understanding; although he does not understand it to exist.

For it is one thing for an object to be in the understanding, and another to understand that the object exists. When a painter first conceives of what he will afterwards perform, he has it in his understanding, but he does not yet understand it to be, because he has not yet performed it. But after he has made the painting, he both has it in his understanding, and he understands that it exists, for he has made it.

Hence, even the fool is convinced that something exists in the understanding, at least, than which nothing greater can be conceived. For, when he hears of this, he understands it. And whatever is understood, exists in the understanding. And assuredly that, than which no greater can be conceived, cannot exist in the understanding alone. For, suppose it exists in the understanding alone: then it can be conceived to exist in reality: which is greater.

Therefore, if that, than which no greater can be conceived, exists in the understanding alone, the very being, than which nothing greater can be conceived, is one, than which a greater can be conceived. But obviously this is impossible. Hence, there is no doubt that there exists a being, than which nothing greater can be conceived, and it exists both in the understanding and in reality.

Anselm, *Proslogion*, Chapter II (1962: 7–8)

For our purposes, we shall consider the bare argument. If you are intrigued, read Anselm's *Proslogion* and decide for yourself what Anselm's project is. Here is the proof. What is this God whose existence we seek to establish? God is 'a being than which none greater can be thought'. Notice what a cunning definition it is. In fact, we cannot define God adequately (see again the passage from Merton), and it is the genius of this definition to point us beyond all limiting definitions of God. *Deus semper maior* (God is always greater) is St Ignatius Loyola's motto.

Such a being must exist. Not that men have never attempted to deny God. Your own Josh, for instance. And Josh, do not be insulted, also the 'fool' of Psalm 13, who has 'said in his heart: there is no God'. Anselm calls our attention to the biblical fool. He says that this fool who denies the existence of God nonetheless understands the meaning of 'a being than which none greater can be thought'. He must understand these words in order to deny that such a being exists. What the fool says is this: God exists only in my intellect (when I understand the meaning of 'a being than which none greater can be thought') but not in reality. Think of a purple cow. Is that something that occurs in reality? No, but the meaning exists in your mind. When something exists only in your mind, you usually say simply that it does not exist. What you mean is that it does not enjoy 'extra-mental' existence.

Now Anselm has a question for the fool. Which is greater: to exist in the intellect alone, or to exist in reality? To exist in reality, surely. Dangerous admission! What is the definition of God we are working with? 'A being than which none greater can be thought.' O fool, can you really be thinking of 'a being than which none greater can be thought' when you deny its existence? Because it is mere child's play to think of a greater being than the one you have in mind, namely this very being whose real existence you deny, only existing in reality and not in your mind alone. That existing being is the true 'being than which none greater can be thought'; unless it exists both in the intellect and in reality it cannot not be the 'being than which none greater can be thought.' QED.

Are you impressed? It may take a while to get your mind around it but the proof is very precise. Try to reduce it to a few numbered steps.

A fellow monk, Gaunilo, objected to Anselm's proof and wrote, in turn, 'On Behalf of the Fool'. In my next letter, I shall propound Gaunilo's objections and Anselm's replies.

A being than whom few more devoted to you can be thought,

Uncle Jack

A perfect island

Dear Betsy,

St Anselm's proof has always been controversial. A number of important philosophers have endorsed the proof, among them St Bonaventure, John Duns Scotus, Descartes, Leibniz, Hegel and (strangely enough) Charles Hartshorne, the process philosopher. Duns Scotus produced a very difficult version he called a 'coloratio', a 'touching up'. But an equally impressive lot have rejected the proof. Here we find St Thomas Aquinas, Locke and Kant. You will have to make up your mind about it for yourself but your final judgement is likely to be based on more than the abstract validity of the proof. It will depend on such related issues as your understanding of what it is to know.

Gaunilo's first objection: We have no such concept

To help start you off, let's look at Gaunilo's objections, his brief 'On Behalf of the Fool'. Gaunilo's first objection attacks the premise that the idea of 'a being than which a greater cannot be thought' exists in his intellect. Go back over Anselm's proof. You will see that without accepting the assertion that this idea exists in his mind, the proof cannot proceed. If there is no such idea in your mind to begin with, you cannot go on to argue that you would be thinking of an even greater being if the idea actually existed. OK? Of course, Gaunilo can't just gratuitously deny this premise without giving some reasons for his denial. Gaunilo does not, in fact, deny that it is possible to hear and repeat these words: 'a being than which a greater cannot be thought'. But they are mere words. We can form no concept of this being. St Anselm himself has admitted – a standard position, as you learned from Merton – that we cannot form a concept of God.

Anselm's reply: We can conceive of a 'more perfect' than any thing

How does Anselm meet Gaunilo's objection? You can be sure that he doesn't throw up his hands in the air and say, 'A good one! I never thought of that.' He maintains that, although God is not perfectly captured by any concept we can form, nonetheless we are able to concoct a notion sufficiently meaningful for his proof to operate upon. How? We are after the notion of the most perfect being, 'a being than which a greater is inconceivable'. What we can do is to conceive the perfections of various goods in the world. There are good hockey players, good cars, good students, and we know them when we see them. The perfections to be found in the world are limited, lesser perfections than that most perfect being that is God. Nevertheless, from these lesser perfections we can mount, as if on the rungs of a ladder, in the direction of the most perfect being. And that, according to Anselm, is all we need do. Gaunilo's fool is asking for more than is necessary in order to complete the proof.

Gaunilo's second objection: The perfect island doesn't have to exist just because I conceive it

Gaunilo has a second objection. This is the one people remember because it has a haunting image attached to it. For the purposes of this objection, Gaunilo is willing to grant that we can conceive of a being than which none greater can be thought. He now argues that, even if we should have formed such a concept successfully, there is a further objection that will still stop the proof dead in its tracks.

Gaunilo's reply: In behalf of the Fool

The fool might make this reply: This being is said to be in my understanding already, only because I understand what is said. Now could it not with equal justice be said that I have in my understanding all manner of unreal objects, having absolutely no existence in themselves, because I understand these things if one speaks of them, whatever they may be? . . .

It is said that somewhere in the ocean is an island, which, because of the . . . impossibility of discovering what does not exist, is called the lost island. And they say that this island has an inestimable wealth of all manner of riches and delicacies in greater abundance than is told of the Islands of the Blest; and that having no owner or inhabitant, it is more excellent than all other countries, which are inhabited by mankind . . .

> Now if someone should tell me that there is such an island, I should easily understand his words ... But suppose he went on to say, as if by a logical inference: 'You can no longer doubt that this island which is more excellent than all lands exists somewhere, since you have no doubt that it is in your understanding. And since it is more excellent not to be in the understanding alone, but to exist both in the understanding and in reality, for this reason it must exist. For if it does not exist, any land which really exists will be more excellent than it; and so the island understood by you to be more excellent will not be more excellent.'
>
> If a man should try to prove to me by such reasoning that this island truly exists, and that its existence can no longer be doubted, either I should believe that he was jesting, or I know not which I ought to regard as the greater fool ... For he ought to show first that the hypothetical excellence of this island exists as a real and indubitable fact, and in no wise as any unreal object, or one whose existence is uncertain, in my understanding.
>
> In Anselm, *Basic Writings* (1962: 146, 150–151)

With the concept of 'a being than which none greater can be thought' in our heads, all we have managed to do is to paint ourselves into a corner. Because once the concept is in our mind, we will never be able to get out of our mind. We cannot think our way from the thought of 'a being than which none greater can be thought' to the real existence of this being. The being we are thinking of must remain in our thought. We are very well familiar with the thought of all sorts of unreal or impossible things. Square circles? Impossible. Aragorn, son of Arathorn? Unreal. Mr Ed, the Talking Horse? Most likely, impossible again. Gaunilo comes up with the notion of the perfect island.

Wishing doesn't make it so

Stop and try to formulate the argument about the perfect island for yourself. (*Pause*.) I hope you came up with something like this: We can conceive of the perfect island. (I let you fill in the exotic details of its perfection.) This perfect island that we have conceived exists in our minds. But it must also exist in reality. Because no matter how wonderful was our conception, it would be rather an imperfect island if it did not really exist. Gaunilo offers a parody of Anselm. His point is that applying the model of Anselm's argument to any wonderful figment of our imagination would require our fantasy object really to exist. But we have all learned, by now, that wishing doesn't make it so. The world is not stocked with all the perfect entities we can imagine.

Anselm's response to Gaunilo: The argument only works for God

Anselm accepts the objection that there is a gulf between thought and reality. He knows as well as anyone else that our thought of the perfect island or the perfect tennis racquet or the perfect computer system does not entail its real existence. Anselm does not claim that we can argue ourselves from existence in thought to existence in reality – *usually*. There is one and only one case in which such a move is possible, namely when we are considering the being than which none greater can be thought. Here we are talking about a being of the utmost perfection, which our thought approaches as an asymptotic limit. (You remember asymptotes from geometry: the curve that comes closer and closer to a given line without ever quite touching it.) There is no reason to think that a perfect being of some limited kind (like an island, a tennis racquet, or a computer system) must exist. It is only when we treat of one being, the being than which none greater can be thought, that we are compelled to pass from notional to real existence. Only this concept of God necessarily involves existence.

Let us leave St Anselm's argument there. Perhaps we have a proof for God.

Your imperfect uncle,
Jack

Can a finite being conceive an infinite object?

Dear Bets,

I'm smuggling this valentine note into your philosophy of religion textbook. Isn't that more romantic than a regular old e-mail? I hope you haven't lent your book to anyone else in the meantime. I've saved a few surprises to deliver in person.

What's wrong with Anselm's argument? It keeps going in circles with the connection between thinking and being. I asked Don Malt, my friend who just started graduate school Philosophy, what the fallacy was. (A fallacy, dear Bets, is an error in argumentation.) He says the argument may show that we necessarily think 'a being than which none greater can be thought' exists but this does not mean 'a being than which none greater can be thought' exists in actuality. Another turn on the thinking/being connection. I'm satisfied with that.

Maybe because today is Valentine's Day, I have been thinking about the natural desire for God argument. I'm intrigued by the notion that you can be rational about your subjectivity, as well as about objective things. If you can believe the biographies, Ayn Rand had a little trouble with her love life. Come to think of it, Bertrand Russell did, too.

I am not convinced that any god comes out of the natural desire argument. Like Gaunilo, I have two objections. First: just because I am conscious of a strong desire for something, does that mean it must exist? Suppose I really, really want hot ice cream? It's still impossible. A = A: that's rational. Hot = Not Hot: that's absurd. How do I know God is not like hot ice cream?

My second objection is this: although I hate to admit it, I am a limited being. Isn't it odd, to say the least, that a limited being could have a natural desire for something limitless? I desire you, a flesh-and-blood woman. We are both finite objects of the same species. Wouldn't it be really wild if my natural desire were for something that surpassed the limits of my nature, like God? I think your uncle was suggesting that in loving you I was (unconsciously) loving or trying to love God. Lucky for you I don't believe that. This Valentine's card is for you alone.

Your devoted man,
Josh

If 'God' is a contradictory concept, desire for a limitless object is contradictory

FROM: Bets

TO: Josh

SUBJECT: Valentine

You see, dear one, that I am not as romantic as you are. Women aren't, you know. We love to be romanced but when I start thinking about that rationally (!) I sometimes suspect our attitude is a little materialistic and selfish. So I answer your letter with a convenient and prosaic e-mail. Finding secret letters, anyway, reminds me of concert band. Some trumpet player used to leave love notes in my flute case. Nothing would make him stop until I left some embarrassing items inside his music folder. However, as long as the rest of your surprises are sweet, I shall not send you away.

I asked Joan, our Philosophy TA, about Anselm's argument. She says it proves that if God is possible then he necessarily is. Anyway, the standing of Anselm's proof is a little more complicated than Don Malt is making it out to be. I gather some philosophers who have accepted it agree with Joan's point. Scotus's 'touch-up' Uncle Jack mentioned does something like this.

Strangely, it just occurs to me that the same issue may be involved in the natural desire argument. You say that hot ice cream is impossible, so your desire for hot ice cream can never actually be met. If God is like hot ice cream – if an infinitely perfect being is impossible – then there is nothing to correspond to Anselm's concept of a necessarily existing being or to your ravenous, infinite desire (for weird ice cream, late night burgers at Machiavelli's, or fascinating women like myself). I think I am glad that your desire is satisfied

to rest on me and not go seeking an object beyond the
heavens. I don't have to fear you will be joining
Merton or St Anselm in some God-haunted monastery. But
I know what my mother would say: 'Everything in its
proper order. Love God first, and then you can love
everything else in the right way.'

Your Valentine,
Betsy

Thomas Aquinas' five arguments for God

Thomas Aquinas starts from being, not knowledge

Dear Betsy,
St Thomas Aquinas (his dates were 1225–74) had five ways to prove the
existence of God. More than that, really, but the five ways from his
Summa Theologiae, a text designed for 'beginners' in theology, are the
Thomistic proofs usually studied in Philosophy of Religion classes. You
will find them near the beginning of the *Summa*. I refer to the book
simply as the *Summa*, even though St Thomas wrote more than one of
these *summae*. ('Summa' means something like the 'sum and substance
of'.) He also prepared a *Summa Contra Gentiles* for the use of missionary brethren among the Arabs. St Thomas wrote a great deal else in his
brief life, sometimes dictating to two different secretaries at once.

Theological beginners in the thirteenth century already had a lot of
training in logic and natural philosophy. If you were to open a copy of
the *Summa*, you would find it rough going. It has a curious literary
structure, cast in the framework of a 'disputed question', the oral
debates held periodically in the medieval university. (Those old dogmatists seemed to thrive on debates.) When you look at an article of the
Summa – as I hope you do soon – you will see that Thomas starts by
setting out a lot of objections to his thesis, then he develops the principles of his own thought and tries to establish his point, and finally he
turns back to the initial objections and responds to the difficulties they
raise in the light of his own solution of the question put. Note carefully
which part of an article you are looking at to be sure you are reading
Thomas's teaching and not a contrary objection!

You may be glad to know, Betsy, that every one of Thomas's proofs –
well, nearly every one – is more 'objective' than St Anselm's ontological
argument or our reflections on the natural desire for God.

Why five ways? Didn't he think he had accomplished his goal in the
first proof? Why prove God's existence over and over again? This question is worth thinking about in the context of the *Summa*. But it is clear
that the world offers itself to our minds under many different aspects;

why should not more than one of these lead to God? If you keep arriving at the same result after coming at it from different starting points, that is strong confirmation you are on the right track, is it not?

St Thomas's five ways start from the following facts about the world:

1. Beings in motion
2. Efficient causes
3. The existence of possible beings
4. Degrees of perfection
5. The order of the universe

One or two of these might appear on any list you tried to draw up but my bet is that you are unsure about the very meaning of some of the others. What, for example, is an 'efficient cause' or a 'possible being'? That last one has the mark of a philosopher all over it, doesn't it? I used to have a philosopher friend who, when giving directions, customarily said, 'Take a left at the third possibility' instead of 'Turn left at the third street after the light.'

How does Thomas mine these worldly phenomena in order to establish God as their necessary principle? Let us see.

Thomas's first way

It's easy enough to understand what motion is, isn't it? Oh! Oh! Do not fall into that trap, Betsy! You surely recognise motion when it occurs but it is very hard to understand or define it. Plato probably thought it could not be defined. The common-sense Aristotle, however, used words in a special way (somewhat – but only somewhat – like what we would call a 'technical vocabulary'). Aristotle's definition of motion is this: 'the actuality of a being in potency qua potential'.

I didn't quote Aristotle's definition just to dazzle you. Thomas is a disciple of Aristotle. It is true that Thomas is not a simple replica of his ancient master but he does repeat a lot of the lessons he learned from studying Aristotle's texts closely. (It was about this time – the thirteenth century – that the majority of Aristotle's works became available to the West in new Latin translations.) When he speaks about 'motion', Thomas has in mind motion pretty much as Aristotle understood it, not only motion from place to place (local motion) but any kind of change (qualitative as well as quantitative: the change in the colour of your complexion when Josh handed you the Valentine rose bouquet, the maturation of fledgling birds in the nest, or a lead ball and feather falling to the earth). What Aristotle and St Thomas are after is the cause of change.

Changes are structured

Thomas's first way

The first and more manifest way is the argument from motion. It is certain, and evident to our senses, that in the world some things are in motion. Now whatever is in motion is put in motion by another, for nothing can be in motion except it is in potentiality to that towards which it is in motion; whereas a thing moves inasmuch as it is in act. For motion is nothing else than the reduction of something from potentiality to actuality. But nothing can be reduced from potentiality to actuality, except by something in a state of actuality. Thus that which is actually hot, as fire, makes wood, which is potentially hot, to be actually hot, and thereby moves and changes it. Now it is not possible that the same thing should be at once in potentiality and actuality in the same respect, but only in different respects. For what is actually hot cannot simultaneously be potentially hot; but it is simultaneously potentially cold. It is therefore impossible that in the same respect and the same way a thing should be both mover and moved, i.e., that it should move itself. Therefore, whatever is in motion must be put into motion by another. If that by which it is put in motion be itself put in motion, then this also must needs be put in motion by another, and that by another again. But this cannot go on to infinity, because then there would be no first mover, and consequently, no other mover; seeing that subsequent movers move only inasmuch as they are put in motion by the first mover; as the staff moves only because it is put in motion by the hand. Therefore it is necessary to arrive at a first mover, put in motion by no other; and this everyone understands to be God.

Summa Theologiae, I, qu. 2, a.3

First step:

Some things in the world are in motion. We start from the perceived fact of motion or change. This is the easiest step in the proof because all we have to do is consult the world in order to verify it.

Second step:

Whatever is moved is moved by another. Changes don't just 'happen' out of the blue. Something else is responsible for these changes. Philosophers don't like to accept claims gratuitously, without some argument behind them. This claim 'whatever is moved is moved by another' has a catchy ring to it. It sounds like something Thomas thinks people would just 'know.' But he does go on to offer an argument for it anyway. The argument is a lot harder to understand than the claim that it is trying to prove. Even though it is, in some ways, the crux of the proof, the first few times through you might want to skip the argument for this second step, just assume that it is true, and go on to see how Thomas completes the first way, once the second step has been satisfactorily established.

Actuality and potentiality

Proof of the second step:

To clarify the proof of the second step of Thomas's argument, I need to return to the forbidding technical terminology introduced when I quoted Aristotle's definition of motion. The key terms are 'actuality' and 'potentiality' (or 'act' and 'potency': they are the same things). As Aristotle sees it, the world is not just all 'there' in front of us, a big objective blob of being. He says, act and potency divide all being. Take any being whatsoever and you will find running intertwined throughout it these two modes (or ways) of being: actual being and potential being.

A log of wood is just there 'objectively', as we say, in front of us. It is a real being and not a figment of the imagination. But something else is there beyond the log's objective presence. A woodworker will look at this magnificent piece of mahogany and see the fine box that it can become. He has seen the log as potency. A varsity baseball coach will look at someone on his freshman team and say, 'I could make a real hitter out of that guy.' He has seen the potentiality in a new recruit. The log is not a highly polished mahogany box and the freshman is not a varsity baseball player but they could become these things. They have in them the potentiality for change. Now you might say, 'I see. A potentiality is something that isn't there.' And you might wonder why Thomas says both potency and act run throughout all being, when what is actually there is actuality. But be careful! A potency is not a mere absence.

Think of a baby gorilla and a human baby. Babies are well stocked with potentialities, right? The human baby, let us say, is Einstein. He is potentially an ingenious physicist. It is true that if you ask him to explain the theory of relativity he will not make a much better job of it than the baby gorilla does. Neither baby is actually a physicist. Nonetheless, the baby Einstein can become an ingenious physicist and the baby gorilla cannot. Although neither baby is actually a physicist, baby Einstein is a physicist in potency. Potency is something real, even if we can't see it or touch it. Being, according to Aristotle and Thomas, is pregnant with possibilities. It is not just what is objectively there but also what can be there, given the right conditions for development.

Motion = Fulfilment of a still outstanding potential

We are training our intellectual sights on a being in motion. A being in motion, as we have said, is changing somehow. Let us say you are changing from a pale winter complexion to a charming rosy blush. Your face becomes redder and redder as the realisation of Josh's romantic gesture sinks in. Thomas would say that, as the colour of your complexion changes, you are in potency with respect to that deep rosy blush. Your face *can* blush (rather easily, as I recall); blush*ing*, you are a being in motion. Now let's put it in a general, abstract way, using Aristotelico-Thomistic terms: a being in motion is in potency with respect to that toward which it moves. When something moves or changes, it changes into something else or goes towards some other place. A being in motion must have the potential to be the thing into which it is changing or to be in the place where it is heading.

What about actuality? How does that dovetail with change or motion? Think again of baby Einstein and baby gorilla lying in their infant cribs, offering themselves for your appreciation as sweet little newborns. Their potentialities are still undeveloped, unchanged, without motion. Nothing moves unless it has the potential for change. But the bare potential isn't going to be doing any moving. Potential is something real but it isn't at all vigorous; it is merely the passive ability for change. It is the other mode of being, actuality, that takes the active role in moving. Because it is actually a ball, the baseball whips through the air, as baseballs do when thrown. Because he is actually a baby, little Einstein is eating and drinking and growing into a man who knows physics, as babies do when faced with food and drink and things to learn. Because you are actually a sensitive, red-blooded girl, your cheeks are taking on that deep pink tinge, as sweet young maids do when faced with demonstrations of their lovers' affection. A being moves insofar as it is in act.

Now let us put the two generalisations together: a being in motion is in potency with respect to that toward which it moves, whereas a being moves insofar as it is in act. This tells us that a being in motion is a being composed of both act and potency, a composite being, not a simple one. (You always liked to say that everything was 'complex': well, if it moves, a being is a complex of potency and act.) How shall we characterise the motion of this composite being? The boy Einstein is growing and learning. He is becoming the man physicist. The baseball is speeding from the pitcher's right arm towards home plate. Your cheeks are getting redder and redder. The potency each of these things had at the start of the motion is being brought to actuality.

Now we move in for the kill. (What are we trying to establish at this point? That 'whatever is moved is moved by another'. Remember?) This time let me start with the generalisation: a being cannot be brought from potency to act except by a being in act. By itself, the potential just sits there inertly waiting to be brought to actuality. The baseball with a potentiality to cross home plate doesn't spontaneously jump off the pitcher's mound. It must be propelled, moved by the force of the pitcher's throw. A kettle of water with a potential to boil does not begin to warm up without the action of something hot, an electric element or a gas flame. And if that is so, we conclude: whatever is moved (= something being brought from potency to act) is moved by another (= can only be actualised by a being already in act).

Don't animate beings move around spontaneously?

It is all so abstract you may fear you are being taken in, especially if you can easily think of a counterexample in the real world. What about animals? Don't they form a huge exception to the rule that whatever is moved is moved by another? Isn't that what it means to be an animal, to be self-moving? Yes, but being an animal also entails having organs, parts. When we say that an animal moves itself, if we look closer we shall see that one part of the animal moves another part. And so our second step remains secure.

An infinite series of movers won't produce motion

Third step:

There cannot be an infinite series of movers. For the sake of simplicity, we have been considering the case where one being (in act) moved another being (from potency to act). But it is, of course, possible that the being in act also requires to be moved from potency to act by another actual mover, and that that prior mover is moved as well, and so on and so on. The bat moves the baseball but only if the arm first moves the bat. The bat is a moved mover. It moves the ball. It is moved by the arm. Can you keep piling mover upon mover ad infinitum (making an infinite chain of movers)?

No. One being can only move (come to actualisation) in so far as it is moved (actualised) by another. If we keep pushing the line of movers back without end, we will never have anything with the actuality required to get the chain going. Everything moved will derive its motion towards a new act from its own mover, which in turn will derives its motion to actuality from yet another mover – but an ultimate source for the actuality coursing through this system is a debt that will never be paid if we stack up moved movers forever. Solve the problem by saying that there is an end. The chain of movers is not infinite. We come at last to a first mover. Each member of the chain of movers moves the next but only if there is an unmoved mover starting it all off, actualising the first moved.

Conclusion:

Therefore there is a first cause of motion, moved by nothing. This fully actual being is what we call God.

Let us leave it there for today. Putting aside Aristotle's metaphysical concepts of act and potency, which will most likely be somewhat puzzling to you, there is an obvious objection to this proof. I shall be interested to see whether you or Josh comes up with it.

A mover (but not unmoved),
Uncle Jack

FROM: Bets
TO: Josh
SUBJECT: re: new proof
I am leaving a copy of my uncle's last letter in your study carrel. Thank God (or his metaphysical stand-in) that we are finally off St Anselm's argument. Aquinas, I think I can get my imagination around. (Oops! Is that a mistake?) Maybe I will write my paper on the five ways.

The first way, I think, is taken from Aristotle. Doesn't Ayn Rand think Aristotle was very rational? Why was she an atheist, then?

I see the main point here. You can't keep pushing back movers to infinity. There must be a first mover. That is God. Fairly simple. Why don't I feel satisfied?

Is Aristotle's physics out of date? And why a first mover?

FROM: Josh
TO: Bets
SUBJECT: re: new proof
I found the letter even before I checked my e-mail. I've heard of Thomas's proofs before. Thomas knew a lot about Aristotle. Ayn Rand likes that. But he mixed in some mysticism. That is what she doesn't like. There is no argument for God that works. Aristotle did not *believe* in God. He thought he *knew* that God exists, that he had demonstrated his existence by reason. I think he was wrong. There are scientific objections to what Aristotle said. Aristotle wanted to be scientific but he didn't know as much science as we do. He would have to update his metaphysics today and take God out. That's where Ayn Rand and the other 'objectivist' philosophers can help us.

Thomas's second objection to the existence of God

It is superfluous to suppose that what can be accounted for by a few principles has been produced by many. But it seems that everything we see in the world can be accounted for by other principles, supposing God did not exist. For all natural things can be reduced to one principle, which is nature; and all voluntary things can be reduced to one principle, which is human reason, or will. Therefore there is no need to suppose God's existence.

Summa Theologiae, I, qu. 2, a.3, obj.2

I have been trying to figure out what is wrong with this argument. It reminds me of the old mythological picture of the whole universe supported by various animals, all stacked on top of a tortoise's back. There has to be a tortoise, otherwise where would the universe stand? There has to be a first unmoved mover, or how would the universe ever get moving? It's a kind of primitive picture thinking. No wonder you can get your imagination around it.

I think these are the scientific reasons against it: (i) there's nothing really wrong with a chain of causes stretching back and back in time, is there? Maybe it's always been going on this way. Why do we need to talk about God creating it all in the beginning? (ii) the principle of inertia in physics says that a body at rest will continue at rest and a body in motion will continue in motion unless acted upon by an external body. A moving body has motion and will just keep moving. The universe doesn't need a first mover to start it off.

Why is there motion?

FROM: Bets
TO: Josh
SUBJECT: re: new proof
I see what you mean about the tortoise. I remember seeing a picture of that. It's really a question of the limits of our imagination. Picture-thinking, as you say.

But about (i) the chain of causes stretching back and back in time – doesn't physics also say that there was a big bang at the beginning? Maybe the first mover is the big banger.

I don't understand about (ii). Are you saying that there just is motion in the universe and that it will stay there as long as nothing stops it? But why is there motion?

Thomas's reply to the second objection

Since nature works for a determinate end under the direction of a higher agent, whatever is done by nature must needs be traced back to God, as its first cause. So also whatever is done voluntarily must also be traced back to some higher cause other than human reason or will, since these can change and fail; for all things that are changeable and capable of defect must be traced back to an immovable and self-necessary first principle, as was shown in the body of the Article.

Summa Theologiae, I, qu. 2, a.3, ad.2

FROM: Josh
TO: Bets
SUBJECT: I remain unmoved by unmoved mover
Hang on to that idea about picture-thinking. Religion is primitive superstition. When you get rid of all remnants of mythological explanation religion and fear won't get in the way of your life.

I don't think there is a big banger, just a big bang. But that is only one theory of the beginning of the universe. If it's true, it would mean that you can't go back and back forever. But you still don't come to some perfect unmoved mover.

I don't understand your question #2. Maybe that means you are getting deeply philosophical. But maybe you are just asking a stupid question. It's always the waffle-head professors who don't know their material who chant, 'There is no such thing as a stupid question.' Of course, motion just is. We see it all around us, don't we? Matter and energy are neither created nor destroyed.

567

```
FROM: Betsy
TO: Josh
SUBJECT: re: I remain unmoved by the unmoved mover
```
I don't see why you have to be insulting if you are so
rational. I was just asking a question. I thought you
said it was good to question. I think my English prof
is a good teacher and he encourages a lot of discussion. Not everyone has it all figured out like you.

```
FROM: Josh
TO: Bets
SUBJECT: I've been moved to say sorry
```
Did I say something wrong? I didn't mean to insult you.

```
FROM: Betsy
TO: Joshua
SUBJECT: You don't understand
```
  You don't understand.

```
FROM: Josh
TO: Don Malt
SUBJECT: I think I'm blowing it again
```
  Remember that cool girl Betsy I told you about? I
showed you her uncle's letter about Anselm's argument.
I think I've done something wrong. What?

```
FROM: Don
TO: Josh
SUBJECT: Probably
```
I liked something that old priest said in one of those
letters. It was Latin. I wrote it down. *Femina semper
mutabilis*. It means women are always changeable. You
can try to be civil to her tonight and see if she's
changed her attitude towards you. Or you can join me
for a few beers at the Rat.

```
TO: Don
FROM: Josh
SUBJECT: Right
```
  You're on.

Is Aquinas denying movement could go back forever?

Dear Betsy,

I'm sorry to hear that you think Josh has been 'being a jerk lately'. But
I shall confine myself to giving advice on Philosophy papers and stay out

of your affairs of the heart. If you think he 'looks like an ass, walking around campus with his new pipe and trying to pose as a philosopher', why not take this as a cry for help? Maybe he needs a woman to advise him about his image!

Here is what I think about the two objections Josh left you with. The first one is the trap I thought you might fall into – that is, conceiving the forbidden infinite chain of movers to go back infinitely in time. Denying that an infinite chain of movers stretches out into the past is not what the argument is about. Who knows how old the universe is? (There are scientific calculations, of course, but we must remember that they are only as good as the assumptions they are based upon.) Aristotle thought the universe was eternal, so he would surely have conceded an infinite chain of movers going back in time. His point was, rather, that at this moment if something is being moved, its movement is not being conveyed through an infinite chain of movers. The causal influx of a first mover is necessary to produce any motion right now. Remember my example of the bat (the moved mover) requiring another mover (the batter) to be working at the same time in order for the bat to move the ball in turn? Take away the batter but leave the bat. The ball will never be hit. The first objection indicates that you (or Josh) are losing grip on the argument.

Aristotle's physics qualitative, modern physics quantitative

Josh's second objection is better. It is a difficult one to meet, although I think you may be getting to the point in a certain naive way. Modern physics is different from Aristotle's physics. They are after very different things. Very briefly and inadequately: modern mathematical physics aims for quantitative prediction and control over nature. Aristotle's physics was qualitatively descriptive (his 'technical terminology' was an attempt to reshape our everyday language in order to carry out this 'phenomenological' task). Aristotelian physics was intended to contribute to a philosophical understanding of all things in so far as they are moveable. Aristotle thinks it makes sense to ask what motion is and to seek its causes and principles. Modern physics wants to measure motion. A physicist may not be able to define motion but he knows what it is well enough to devise ways of measuring it. I would be far from denying that the principle of inertia poses a difficulty but to help you with your Philosophy of God paper I don't think you want me now to start giving lectures in the history of science. Stick to the naive question: 'What is motion or change?' Ask whether it requires a cause. Only a short note tonight.

Yours, doing philosophy without a pipe,
Uncle Jack

FROM: Bets
TO: Josh
SUBJECT: new sports coat
I haven't seen you for awhile, so I thought I would e-mail. I like your new tweed jacket. It makes you look very distinguished in a sporty kind of way. But I liked you better without the pipe.

I have a response to your objections to the unmoved mover, if you want to see it. My uncle says my question about your second objection is 'naive'. But he doesn't seem to think that is very bad. I wonder why not. Isn't it better to be sophisticated?

FROM: Josh
TO: Betsy
SUBJECT: old pipe
I hoped you would like the sports coat. I got some money for my birthday. Don't worry, I saved some for a celebration. I could lose the pipe. It is damn difficult to keep it lit and remember arguments at the same time.

From an ex-pipe smoker: maybe sometimes sophistication doesn't work.

FROM: Bets
TO: Josh
SUBJECT: sophistication
For you, sporty is better than sophisticated. I put the philosophy note in your study carrel. I hope you aren't going to wait too long for that celebration.

FROM: Josh
TO: Don Malt
SUBJECT: later
I've been drinking so much beer the past couple of weeks that I'm starting to get out of shape. I think I'll work out this afternoon. When I got back from the Rat last night one of my roommates said, 'He's drunk again. He always talks about sex and God when he's drunk.' I'll pass on the Rat tonight. I haven't seen Bets for awhile.
PS: I think I'll ditch the pipe. Do you want it?

Thomas's second way

Dear Betsy,

I'm glad I didn't go into a speech about that cad Josh being unworthy of you and how you should have listened to your mother. That would have driven you right back into his arms – where, come to think of it, you have ended up anyway.

Shall we move on to the second of the five ways? It gets easier. You will begin to see a common pattern in the cosmological proofs.

Thomas's second way

The second way is from the nature of the efficient cause. In the world of sense, we find there is an order of efficient causes. There is no case known (neither is it, indeed, possible) in which a thing is found to be the efficient cause of itself; for so it would be prior to itself, which is impossible. Now in efficient causes it is not possible to go on to infinity, because in all efficient causes following in order, the first is the cause of the intermediate cause, and the intermediate is the cause of the ultimate cause, whether the intermediate cause be several, or one only. Now to take away the cause is to take away the effect. Therefore, if there be no first cause among efficient causes, there will be no ultimate, nor any intermediate cause. But if in efficient causes it is possible to go on to infinity, there will be no first efficient cause, neither will there be an ultimate effect, nor any intermediate efficient causes; all of which is plainly false. Therefore it is necessary to admit a first efficient cause, to which everyone gives the name of God.

Summa Theologiae, I, qu. 2, a.3

The starting point of the second way is 'efficient causality'. When we talk about causes, we usually have in mind, as in Josh's objection to the first way, a temporal chain through which impetus is transferred from one thing to another. Think one billiard ball hitting another. For us, there is only one kind of cause, if it makes sense to speak of causes at all. (A certain brand of philosopher called 'positivist' tolerates no talk of causality.) But the Aristotelian tradition not only invoked the notion of cause in their philosophical explanation, they distinguished causes into four different sorts. The four causes are four ways of answering the question why a thing is as it is. They are: (i) formal cause; (ii) material cause; (iii) final cause; and (iv) efficient cause.

The formal cause tells you what kind of thing something is. It is the form or the determination of the thing. The formal cause of a building is the architect's blueprint. The formal cause of a cup is the shape into which it is formed to make the cup. (Let us say it is a cup made of glass. The same glass material could have been rolled out flat. Then it would have had the form of a windowpane.)

The material cause is the stuff a thing is made out of, the material taken up into the form or essence of the thing. Just as the same matter can take on different forms, so the same form can be realised in different bits of matter: the same sort of cup can be moulded out of clear glass or coloured glass or plastic or aluminium.

These first two causes are called 'intrinsic causes' because they are internal components of the thing they cause. Without the persisting co-causes of form and matter, the thing cannot continue to exist.

The other two causes are called 'extrinsic causes'. They do not exist within the thing as component parts; rather, they are external to the thing. The final cause is the purpose or goal of the thing, the reason why it exists. The final cause of a glass is to hold liquid. The final cause of your going to the mall is to shop. The final cause of a building is to serve as a market for the exchange of goods, a house to shelter a family, or a church to provide for the worship of God. The final cause can be a thing, as well. The final cause of a plant's turning is the sun drawing it towards its radiance. The final cause of the disposal of Josh's pipe was you, dear, to gain your approval.

The efficient cause of a being is its maker, the one who sets the train of events into motion, resulting in the thing of informed material. The carpenter is the efficient cause of the table. The gardener is the efficient cause of his garden. The father is the efficient cause of his offspring. The painter is the efficient cause of his painting. You get the picture.

There must be a first efficient cause

First step:

There are in the world efficient causes producing effects. How do we know this? Again, it is empirical, a matter of experience. We experience gardeners gardening, painters painting.

Second step:

Every efficient cause presupposes another. This we prove by the following consideration: every efficient cause is prior to its effect ('prior' means 'before' in some way, say in dignity or in time – the maker precedes the made). But nothing is prior to itself. Therefore nothing can be its own efficient cause.

Do you see the same pattern developing as in the first way? The first step starts from an empirical observation. The second step shows how what is given to us in experience relies upon a prior cause. Can you guess the next move? In the proof from motion it was to claim that an infinite series of moved movers was impossible. What do you suppose Thomas will say about a chain of efficiently caused efficient causes?

Third step:

There cannot be an infinite series of efficient causes. Again, the reason is because the intermediate links in this chain of causes depend on the causality of a first cause in order to be in a position to produce their own effects. None of the caused causes is able to cause unless something starts the chain of causes in the first place. You can't keep putting this off forever, or nothing will ever be caused.

Conclusion:

Therefore, there is a first efficient cause. This we call God.

Efficiently,
Uncle Jack

```
FROM: Bets
TO: Josh
SUBJECT: the second way
I left you a letter about the second way. Frankly, I
think it's a disappointment. It's almost the same as
the first way, except you can't make the objection
about the principle of inertia, since it is concerned
with 'efficient causes' and not motion. Maybe it dis-
appoints my picture- thinking. I can't picture what a
moved mover does as being very different from what an
efficient cause does.
```

```
FROM: Josh
TO: Bets
SUBJECT: re: the second way
I agree. It was sweet to see you last night. Even if
the second way disappoints, I hope the second chance
won't.
```

Dear Betsy,

You wondered whether the second way was like the first in allowing a 'horizontal' infinity of efficient causes stretching throughout time but not a 'vertical' infinity of efficient causes acting at the same time. This is correct. You can envision the efficient causes as forming a hierarchy of perfection, with the more perfect causes at the 'top'.

Thomas's third way

Ready for the third way? Thomas gives a somewhat convoluted account drawing on two fellow medieval philosophers, the Arab Avicenna and the Jew Maimonides. One could study the historical setting but I shall provide an abbreviated reconstruction of the argument. If you want to think about it 'existentially', in this proof St Thomas encounters what modern philosophers call 'nihilism' – the possibility that being is without a ground, that the world, at its core, is nothing. Too bad he didn't encounter nothingness in a thick French accent, with stinky Gauloises and a beret.

Thomas's third way

The third way is taken from possibility and necessity and runs thus. We find in nature things that are possible to be and not to be, since they are found to be generated, and to be corrupt, and consequently they are possible to be and not to be. But it is impossible for these always to exist, for that which is possible not to be at some time is not. Therefore, if everything is possible not to be, then at time there could have been nothing in existence. Now if this were true, even now there would be nothing in existence, because that which does not exist only begins to exist by something already existing. Therefore, if at one time nothing was in existence, it would have been impossible for anything to have begun to exist; and thus even now nothing would be in existence – which is absurd. Therefore, not all beings are merely possible, but there must exist something the existence of which is necessary. But every necessary thing either has its necessity caused by another, or not. Now it is impossible to go on to infinity in necessary things which have their necessity caused by another, as has been already proved in regard to efficient causes. Therefore we cannot but postulate the existence of some being having of itself its own necessity, and not receiving it from another, but rather causing in others their necessity. This all men speak of as God.

Summa Theologiae, I, qu. 2, a.3

This way starts from the existence of possible beings – that is, beings that could possibly exist or possibly not exist. Thus, we have the required starting point of a cosmological argument, namely worldly experience, although here there is a slight twist. How do we know that what we are experiencing is a 'possible' being? Things don't come wearing tags announcing their ontological status, even though you would easily admit that we do experience possible things. So Thomas gives us a little argument showing how 'possibles' are recognised.

First step:

It is possible for some beings to be or not to be. We know this because we experience genesis and corruption, the coming-into-being and passing away of certain beings: leaves and love, pipes and beer, typewriters and term papers.

Second step:

If all beings were merely possible, nothing would actually exist. To be possible means a thing does not have to be. And if all things were only possible, none of them would necessarily have to be. If any possibles actually managed to start existing, they could have done this (as a universe of possibles) only by coming to be from – nothing! But nothing comes from nothing. Therefore . . .

Third step:

The actual existence of some possible beings entails that they have been caused by a necessary being.

Fourth step:

Necessity either belongs to the necessary being in itself, or necessity is derived from yet another being. This is a somewhat puzzling tack to take. You probably thought the argument had already concluded with the discovery of a necessary being. Historians tell us that St Thomas has in mind something like the 'pure intelligences' that, according to Avicenna, emanate necessarily from the first cause and eventually generate the contingent universe. If you think there is some kind of necessary framework for the universe that is not God, this step is important to think through.

Fifth step:

Here is the expected assertion of the impossibility of an infinite regress: it is impossible that all necessary beings should derive their necessity from another being.

Sixth step:

Hence an absolutely necessary being must exist. This we call God.

Your uncle Jack,
(but not necessarily)

Distinguishing causes and causality

FROM: Josh
TO: Bets
SUBJECT: causality

I have been thinking about the first two ways of Thomas Aquinas. One thing I remember from reading Bertrand Russell's *History of Western Philosophy* is that modern philosophers have questioned this whole idea of causality. Hume points out that we cannot see any necessary connection between cause and effect. So he is very down on causal reasoning. Kant thinks Hume is a little bit extreme. Kant brings in the distinction between thinking and being again. He says we have to think of things as ordered into causes and effects but that doesn't mean they are that way in reality. According to either Hume or Kant, there is a problem with Aquinas's causal arguments to God.

FROM: Bets
TO: Josh
SUBJECT: re: causality

You are getting ahead of me here. Remember, I have just begun to study philosophy and you said I didn't have to read any history of philosophy yet. I don't really follow what you are saying about Hume and Kant. You seem to be saying that these guys don't think there are any causes. What does science discover, then?

I left the third way at your dorm. That proof makes me hope that Hume and Kant are right about causes. It has contingent beings, necessary beings, necessary beings whose necessity is caused, and a necessary being which is necessary in itself. It seems excessive.

Thomas's fourth way

Dear Betsy,

Today I am feeling acutely the contingency of my being. Some ferocious and poisonous insects have stung me numerous times around my left eye; my cheek is swollen to the size of a huge tomato and I have become unrecognisable to myself in the mirror. I write with one eye open but I hope I have not lost the light of the mind.

The next argument for God is sometimes called the argument from degrees of perfection or the 'henological argument' because it reasons from multiplicity to unity (in Greek, 'to hen'). That name may remind

576

you of the ontological argument. (In fact, after you have heard it, the argument itself may remind you of the ontological argument. I remind you, however, that St Thomas rejects Anselm's basic approach.) St Thomas drew his fourth way from the writings of St Augustine.

Thomas's fourth way

The fourth way is taken from the gradation to be found in things. Among beings there are some more and some less good, true, noble, and the like. But 'more' and 'less' are predicated of different things, according as they resemble in their different ways something which is the maximum, as a thing is said to be hotter as it more nearly resembles that which is hottest; so that there is something which is truest, something best, something noblest, and, consequently, something which is uttermost being; for those beings that are greatest in truth are greatest in being, as it is written in [Aristotle's] *Metaphysics* ii. Now the maximum in any genus is the cause of all in that genus; as fire, which is the maximum of heat, is the cause of all hot things. Therefore there must also be something which is to all beings the cause of their being, goodness, and every other perfection; and this we call God.

Summa Theologiae, I, qu. 2, a.3

First step:

We experience that some things possess more, some less of goodness, truth, nobility, perfection. My face, for example, was more lovely before it was attacked by flying stingrays. A Stradivarius instrument is finer than a cheaply produced beginner's violin. A picture by Fra Angelico is more beautiful than a comic book illustration.

Second step:

But things can be ranked 'more or less' only if they resemble some maximum by which they are measured. Without such a standard, there would be no order and measure linking these beings. Our experience is precisely that things do realise degrees of perfection. Would you group together as instances of the same basic figure all those kindergarten crayon squiggles trying to achieve circularity and the marks of a careful draughtsman using compasses and a fine pen, if you did not recognise that drawing a circle was precisely the artists' common aim? Moreover, because these properties are seen to be degrees of a common measure, they point upward: it is as if they are rungs on a ladder, and those rungs lead to the top.

Third step:

Thus, there must be some being which is best, truest, noblest, being in the highest degree. Here St Thomas follows Aristotle's claim that what possesses truth in the highest degree is the maximum being. We see his conviction that being is the source and seat of all perfections. The better, truer, nobler and so on a thing is, the more substantial being it will possess.

I hope the line of argument is clear, even if my sight is not.

Today, from the bottom rung of the ladder of beauty,

Uncle Jack

Are there degrees of being real?

Dear Uncle Jack,

Poor old sacred animal, we shall have to take you to a vet! I like the fourth way. It gives me something to imagine. I've been walking around town imagining everything I see as a rung on a ladder leading up to God. I like the idea of a world with different degrees of intensity, ordered like a musical scale.

I think I see what Thomas is getting at, even though I never thought of 'being' as having degrees before. That is what you are saying, isn't it? Not that things are just 'there' indifferently but that there are degrees of being and that the first cause of being, the source, is being in the highest degree? Wow.

But then I think: maybe a Fra Angelico is 'more beautiful' than a smudgy old comic book but I know a lot of kids who would prefer the comic book. And the reason a lot of adults choose to have a Fra Angelico painting over a comic book has nothing to do with a higher degree on the scale of beauty and goodness and perfection. Don't values depend on us, not on some 'scale of being'?

Get well soon.

From the heights of the ladder of sympathy,

Betsy

Why do we value some things more than others?

FROM: Josh
TO: Bets
SUBJECT: beauty
Bets, you are pretty close to the top of the scale of beauty – at least to me. And if all values are relative, that's what counts, isn't it?

But I partly agree with Thomas. Values are not relative. Ayn Rand shows us that you really can judge works of art. Some are better and some are worse. When you have finished with *Atlas Shrugged* (how is that coming, by the way?), I will give you a novel by Victor Hugo. Ayn Rand says Victor Hugo wrote some great novels. I am also trying to appreciate the operetta music she says is great but operettas remind me of 'chick flicks'. Sorry.

I don't follow this thing about 'degrees' of being. How can something have more or less being? I guess you have to say something like that if you believe in God, though. God is Maximum Being. Max Being: sounds like a smudgy comic book superhero to me.

FROM: Bets
TO: Josh
SUBJECT: Max Being
I have always been confused about whether values are relative or absolute. One thing I know: I don't want to impose my values on others. Maybe Ayn Rand is imposing her values on you when she says that The *Merry Widow* is great music. But then, you tolerate 'chick flicks' for some reason, don't you?

Here's the way I understand 'degrees of being'. Think of a rock. I heard that way back in the 60s or 70s or 80s it was a fad to have 'pet rocks'. Pretty stupid, if you ask me. Rocks are totally unresponsive. Most of the time I wouldn't be able to recognise my own 'pet' and I sure wouldn't get upset if it were smashed to smithereens or cracked in two. My roommate claims that she 'loves' her plants. Again, pretty dumb. How can you talk to someone who says that? But I admit that plants have more life than rocks. And bugs have more initiative than plants. Tell that to half-blind Uncle Jack! Can't we also say they have more being? I used to like catching fireflies in a mayonnaise jar. Even better than fireflies, I had a dog named Sacred Beast. (Guess who gave him to me?) S.B. was the best dog: now *there* was a pet! But you, dear one, I way prefer to S.B. He couldn't try to teach me philosophy or destroy my wavering faith in God. He never even claimed to be rational. Maybe I should have called him Brute Beast. Maybe I shall call you Brute Beast, O rational one, if you do not behave yourself.

Thomas's fifth way

Dear Betsy,
Sacred animals never know whether they are being taken to the vet or to slaughter. Hence their stubborn resistance to being led about this way and that. They try to remain tethered to the Absolute.

Yes, the fourth way does offer more food for the imagination, at least in its cosmological ramifications. You should resist trying to imagine metaphysical entities, however.

Thomas's fifth way

The fifth way is taken from the governance of the world. We see that things which lack intelligence, such as natural bodies, act for an end, and this is evident from their acting always, or nearly always, in the same way, so as to obtain the best result. Hence it is plain that not fortuitously, but designedly, do they achieve their end. Now whatever lacks intelligence cannot move toward an end, unless it be directed by some being endowed with knowledge and intelligence; as the arrow is shot to its mark by the archer. Therefore some intelligent being exists by whom all natural things are directed to their end; and this being we call God.

Summa Theologiae, I, qu. 2, a.3

The fifth way in St Thomas's *Summa* may be familiar to you from other contexts – or at least you may think so. This argument is sometimes called the 'argument from design'. Once again, we start from a perceived order in the universe. The world is not one blooming, buzzing confusion. We trust it. We take its ways for granted. We think we understand something of how it works. Of course, it is easy enough to imagine a world in which this would not be the case. Many of the complications of modern city living offer an irrational and menacing alternative to the order of nature. Think of the frustrations experienced in Kafka's novels. A lot of modern art tries to reveal chaos underlying common experience. Thomas, however, starts with the recognition of an ordered nature.

First step:

Natural bodies regularly act in the same way and achieve the same purpose. This we observe. You would be surprised if birds started acting like bees, or butterflies like porpoises.

Second step:

Natural beings attain their purpose or end neither on account of their own intelligence nor by chance. Clearly, it is not a matter of their own intelligence, since they have none. Even most of us, who do have some share of intellect, would find it difficult to replicate the intricate and highly successful workings of nature. Nor can the nearly faultless attaining of a goal be a matter of chance, which is a hit-and-miss affair.

Third step:

Therefore there must be an intelligence directing these beings to their goals. St Thomas asks us to imagine an archer, an intelligent being who directs the arrow to its target. Only an intelligence can order things to their ends. When we see nature hitting the bull's eye without an internal intelligence, this argues for the existence of a mind external to the natural system.

The fifth way is fairly easy to envisage. I leave it to you to think up some objections. If nature is so intelligently patterned, why did God put nasty stinging bugs into it?

Yours intelligently (but unconsciously) on the mend,

Uncle Jack

Does evolution rule out design? Plus, there are evils in nature

FROM: Josh
TO: Bets
SUBJECT: design
I thought this was going to come up. The universe needs an intelligent designer. Right. Betsy, the universe evolved. Darwin. The survival of the fittest. There are no goals in nature, at least not outside human intentions. Why do you want to bring in this mythical Nobodaddy to make it all come out right? And it doesn't come out right, anyway. Grow up.

Sorry about the abuse. But I couldn't help thinking of my grandmother saying, 'Now Josh, just look at how wonderful the world is. How great is the creator of all this!' Yeah. God's in his heaven and all's right with the world. Have you read the newspaper this morning? God didn't make it but his mess of a world features prominently.

Moral flaws different from design flaws

```
FROM: Bets
TO: Josh
SUBJECT: re: design
```

My Rational One, you are barking like Sacred Beast. I don't know if this argument from design works but I think I understand better than you do what it is all about. This morning's news about wars and homicides and accidents on the highway has nothing to do with the design of nature. All of that is something people do out of carelessness or malevolence. Maybe human beings aren't always so good. But this argument is about the design of nature: the migration of birds, the complexity of the ear, the healing of wounds.

In order for the argument to work, we have to accept that natural things have no in-built intelligence. What about instincts, though? And you are right: evolution, I guess. Eventually a pattern gets established, even if you suffer a period of trial and error (and extinction).

Is there a pattern in nature?

I have another argument against this, too. I was reading about Kant. He thought that our knowledge could never tell us anything about reality or being. We understand things in a systematic way because that's how our minds work. At least I think this is what he says. So there isn't really any pattern in nature, it just looks that way to us. That would destroy the argument, too.

Dear Uncle Jack,

I enclose our e-mail. This last argument persuades me when I am in a mood to believe in God. Then I like to think about how he ordered the universe. But going from an ordered universe to an intelligent orderer – I don't know. Is the universe so well-ordered? I can't answer your question about biting bugs.

By the way, we are starting a new topic in our Philosophy of Religion course. (In fact, that is how I sensed that Josh was getting off-topic in his objections to the fifth way but don't you let on to him.) Our new topic is the problem of evil. Will you extend your correspondence to help me understand this? I think that Josh likes to talk about these things and it makes even a cheap date intriguing.

Your niece,
Betsy

The problem of evil

Is an ordered universe a convenient universe?

Dear Betsy,

Since you did so well in detecting that Josh's objection about the order of the world was beside the point, I am surprised that you could not rise to my challenge of the African wasp (or whatever it was that bit me). To say that there is an intelligent order in the world of nature – does that have to mean that everything in nature will work out for my convenience? I don't think so. Remember, the argument is concerned with what philosophers call the teleology of nature – that is, with our observation that things in nature act for purposes or goals. Usually those goals are proper to the natural species in question. Some insects bite and suck blood, others sting, and so on. Their behaviour is in accordance with their design. I do not have to approve of this design. It may get in the way of my personal plans and desires. For the purposes of this proof, all I have to do is recognise the evidence that things are intelligently designed, which points to a supreme intelligence.

The problem of evil: we used to call that in seminary 'theodicy'. Theodicy is the attempt 'to justify the ways of God to man', as an English poet once said. The problem arises in a specific way with the single God of a monotheistic system; but the problem of theodicy can also be extended to other metaphysical views. Plato's *Republic* is concerned with the question, 'Is justice choiceworthy for its own sake?' One of Socrates' young interlocutors asks him to leave out all consideration of the gods when he answers this question. But it turns out that Socrates cannot neglect the gods in this instance and he registers an objection to those who retail myths saying the gods cause evil.

The 'everyday' foundation of the problem of evil is something like this: does the universe – the way all things are set up – offer any 'cosmic' support for goodness? Or is goodness just a 'value', as you were saying? 'Values' generally depend on the estimation of the evaluator but 'goods' are perceived as objective. Is the world and whatever god has made it a good thing? Or are we trapped inside a nightmare where all goes wrong inevitably?

The way this question arises in a monotheistic setting, Josh has well seen. It is fair to ask how there can be a supremely good being creating and sustaining the world, if the world is the site of so much wickedness and evil. Yes, call all the disasters reported in the daily paper to witness. Some of them are gut-wrenching. And, given more experience of the world, you will not need to draw evidence from newspapers. Some evil is traceable to the wickedness of man, some to the ignorance of man, some to the indigence and indifference of nature.

Let me sharpen the question and try to catch you on the horns of a dilemma. (That is a rare African beast with horns even more poisonous than the accursed bug who stung me.) We have been drawing on the notion of God as a perfect being. You remember that when we were looking at Anselm's argument I said some critics claimed it only established that if God is possible, then he necessarily exists. In other words, to improve the argument add another preliminary proof: (i) first prove that a being of infinite perfection is possible; (ii) then you can prove that a being of infinite perfection necessarily exists. The problem of evil, in its way, poses the same challenge. It, too, asks us to consider whether a perfect being is really possible. Perhaps the world – even its cause – is utterly shot through with imperfection, with limitation and evil, and there is no hope of ever redeeming it.

The dilemma approaches. Given the evil he has either caused or permitted to occur in the world (what exactly is the difference between these two?), any god must be either: (i) all-powerful but not entirely good; or (ii) all good but not all-powerful.

If God is not all good . . .

Why? If he is (i) all-powerful but not entirely good, there is really no 'problem' of evil. Finding evil in the world is what we should then expect. This god will have the ability to produce whatever he wants, and he wants a world in which innocent children suffer unspeakably, genocide is not unknown, friend betrays friend, only cheats and liars prosper, and the good are guaranteed nothing but grief and frustration. Such a god is monstrous. He is also imperfect. He may be all-powerful but he lacks the perfection of goodness.

If God is not all-powerful . . .

But suppose that god is (ii) good but not all-powerful. Again, it becomes easier to understand the world. Because this god is good, he is well-disposed towards his creatures. He genuinely wills their happiness and well-being. It is just that, however much he might wish it were otherwise, he does not have the power fully to effect his will. He has done the best he can and it is none too good. Perhaps we can sympathise with him in his difficulties. Such a god is also imperfect. He may be all good but he lacks the perfection of omnipotence. Just so the great and powerful Wizard of Oz owned he was 'a good man but a very bad wizard' when Toto unveiled his ruse and he proved unable to bestow his promised gifts.

A God who permits evil must be either not good or not all-powerful

All right, you say, why can't God be perfect? You know what it would take: combine the perfections of goodness and omnipotence. A perfect being will be both omnipotent and all good. That is the rub. How could a good and omnipotent God be the cause of a world in which evil is so prevalent? If he has both goodwill and the power to do something about it, why does he not eradicate evil and suffering in the world? Are we not required to do the same, in our own limited way? Isn't it wicked of God not to lift a finger in this cause? And since he created it all in the beginning, why didn't he make a better job of it?

If Josh still has his copy of the *Confessions* of St Augustine, you will find Augustine discussing the problem of evil in Book VII.

Your uncle,
Jack

FROM: Betsy
TO: Josh
SUBJECT: new problem
I think this is going to be interesting: less 'metaphysical' than the proofs of God. I can understand the logic of it. It seems to me that God can't be perfect. But if he isn't perfect, it doesn't seem he is God. Oh dear, I can see that it's going to be metaphysical, after all. The next thing you know we'll have the ladder of being back again. (Joan tells me this is called 'The Great Chain of Being'. There is even a whole book written about it.)

FROM: Josh
TO: Bets
SUBJECT: re: new problem
Right. If it isn't perfect, it isn't God. Your uncle mentioned some stuff about process theology but I think that's just a way of avoiding the issue. The universe is pretty powerful. It has all kinds of forces we can't control. But there's no reason to make up a religion about them unless it/they is/are perfect. Now you are beginning to see why religion is for fools. I must say your uncle is pretty clear about it all. Are you sure he believes in God? Sometimes I wonder.

FROM: Betsy
TO: Josh
SUBJECT: re: re: new problem
Of course he does – I think. He must have some way of resolving this. It's called the 'problem of evil'. So

there must be a 'solution of evil'. I think it has
something to do with the sin of Adam.

```
FROM: Josh
TO: Betsy
SUBJECT: re: re: re: new problem
Don't forget Eve. And the snake!
```

Distinguish a problem and a mystery

Dear Betsy,

In accord with English usage, you are right to think that a 'problem' can, in principle, be solved. But ordinary usage is neither exact nor systematic and I am afraid it will mislead if it causes you to expect a completely satisfying solution to this problem. The French philosopher Gabriel Marcel used to distinguish between 'problems' and 'mysteries'. A problem is like one of those exercises in the back of your old school maths books. The teacher has a solutions manual in which all of the problems are completely worked out; if you cannot solve the problem, there is something wrong with your understanding of maths. A mystery, on the other hand, solicits our thought. By taking thought we can become clearer about the issue involved but there is something fundamentally obscure that is never transformed into clarity, no matter how hard we think. You may regard this as a cop-out but unless you are willing to confine your thinking to a very narrow technical field, I wonder whether something like Marcel's mystery does not hold sway over many of our concerns.

Evil is an inhabitant of this realm of obscurity. Just as confronting evil in the world can give you a sick feeling in the pit of your stomach, so confronting it in thought is apt to produce a sense of puzzlement. If we allow God to be the answer to our why-questions – why there is motion, why there is efficient causality, why there are contingent beings, why there are degrees of goodness and truth, why we find intelligent design in nature, and so on – we arrive at an answer designed to be fully satisfying: a fully substantial reason. But if we try to understand the coexistence of evil with a perfect being, we are plunged into murkiness and irrationality. Evil opposes the perfect good, the perfect intelligence. One can only suppose that such a phenomenon approaches unintelligibility.

I don't want you to draw the conclusion that it is a waste of time to think about evil. Surely we can do more than stammer at its presence. Already you see that the existence of evil provides the strongest possible proof against God. Perhaps we have to live with imperfection, finitude, disharmony and evil instead. Or perhaps, as some of the ancient pagans seem to have done, we should reverence many gods rather than one God. Do you see why I say that? A plurality of gods can be involved in opposition to each another, even open hostility. The problem of conciliating the divine attributes (God's goodness and his omnipotence) then disappears. The divine realm would be inherently plural and each divine attribute, in effect, would be an independent god, distinct from the others: a father god, a mother god, a god of justice, a goddess of love, a god of learning, a goddess of beauty, and so on – all so many shining examples beckoning us in very different directions.

A lot of men and women today are prepared to settle with either finitude or a plurality of ultimate goals. They say, in effect, the world invites us to wallow around in it according to our limited and fallible lights; or the world offers us fundamental, opposing choices with no indication of how to rank them. This may be so. But the difficulty with either of these 'solutions' to the problem of imperfection and evil is that they are themselves radically mysterious. It is hard to sustain relativism or finitism as a rational choice; a fundamental plurality of worlds is radically unintelligible. Our intellect seeks unity and perfection; that is, it seeks God. Anyway we look, there is going to be mystery.

Why is there something rather than nothing?

The question is whether we will allow anything to illumine this mystery somewhat, whether we will allow the existence of an all-perfect being. Someone once said, the problem is not the existence of God: that is reasonable. The problem is the existence of the world: that is not reasonable. The finite world offers no purchase for our understanding and yet there it is, staring us in the face with an awful, wonderful, noisy, smelly insistence.

Adam and Eve

Now Betsy, one thing I am not going to do is invoke Adam (and Eve). I don't think it would get you far in your Philosophy of Religion class. Adam and Eve make their appearance in the revealed Scriptures and that is matter not for the philosopher but for the theologian. But in any case, Josh is right: what about the snake? Let's not lay all the blame at the doorstep of our first parents: already in the Garden of Eden evil is present. The problem of evil pre-dates the Fall of man, even granting all the suffering said to follow in its wake.

Let me ask you to get a little bit clearer about evil. Can you make any classifications? When we talk about evil, are we always facing the same thing? I look forward to seeing what you come up with.

A child of Adam,
Uncle Jack

Intentional evil and unintentional evil (human evils)

```
FROM: Betsy
TO: Josh
SUBJECT: mysteries and kinds
This time the atheist (Josh) was more clear-headed than
```

the muddled agnostic (Betsy). Maybe that's always the case. Anyway, my uncle says (i) no fair invoking Adam (and Eve) in a philosophy class; and (ii) moderate your expectations about how rational the 'solution' is going to be.

I like the idea that there is mystery no matter how you look at it. It resonates with my muddled and agnostic heart. (Well, muddled except when it comes to True Love, which I am now thoroughly practised in recognising.)

What do you think about the kinds of evil? It all seems pretty bad to me. I'd say there is (i) intentional evil and (ii) unintended evil. The first kind is when you dig in your heels and set out to be wicked on purpose. You throw a rock through a window and run. The second kind is when you didn't really know what was going to happen. You ran over a cat with your car because you didn't see him. It's bad enough but not quite as wicked as the first.

Distinguish physical / cosmic evils and moral evils, begun by humans

FROM: Josh
TO: Bets
SUBJECT: re: mysteries and kinds
Kind and Mysterious One, just how many times have you experienced True Love? Maybe you're not so innocent of the wooing of men but I could probably enlighten you about the scope of intentional evil. I know a guy (not me!) who runs over cats just for the fun of it.

I come at the problem more objectively. First, a lot of things wrong with the world may be no one's fault particularly: earthquakes, floods, disease, birth defects, mental illness. Second, some bad things humans are responsible for: running over cats, lying, murder, rape, tyranny, and so on. I call these categories (i) evil of cosmic origin; and (ii) evil of human origin.

I'm not into all this mystery-mongering. I like to read mystery stories because the puzzle is solved at the end. Maybe science can solve the world's problems, too, and stamp out the evil of cosmic origin, at least.

FROM: Bets
TO: Josh
SUBJECT: kinds, Kind Sir
Both of your kinds of evil are a problem for God. Why

does he cause evil of cosmic origin? Why does he allow Evil of Human Origin? I was going to say human beings introduce evil into the world because of the bad choices they make. But when I thought about evil of cosmic origin I couldn't see any way humans could be responsible for that. Maybe we are so nasty to each other because we are threatened by evil of cosmic origin. Would human beings still steal from each other if everything were available in abundance?

FROM: Josh
TO: Bets
SUBJECT: re: kinds, Kind Sir
Probably. What about sheer wickedness and stealing for the sport of it? Remember the poor cats. Do you think my friend runs over cats because he thinks there is a surplus?

Can humanity solve evil?

FROM: Bets
TO: Josh
SUBJECT: not kind, Kind Sir
All those innocent smashed cats disturb me. Maybe that's a visceral reaction to the problem of evil. It really doesn't make any sense. Mystery, anyone? It's sure not as much fun as reading Minette Walters.

   I also wonder about your brigade of scientists solving the riddle of nature. If the world isn't rational at its core, I don't think they'll get far. How do we know their tinkering won't just make things worse?

FROM: Josh
TO: Bets
SUBJECT: smashed cats
Do you want me to pound the Cat Killer for you the next time I see him? While I'm doing that, you can join a protest at Taylor Science Lab against cruelty to laboratory animals? We'll solve this problem of evil our own way!

Compatibility of God and evil

Dear Betsy,
Today I make what I can of the problem of evil. Following Augustine

and Boethius, I attempt to show only that God and evil in the world are compatible, not to work out in any detailed way how evil fits into some grand scheme.

I suggested Augustine's *Confessions* for a treatment of the issue at hand. If you look at more than the directly relevant section of Book VII (chapters 3–16), you will see that Augustine struggles with the problem of evil in the course of narrating a kind of autobiography. The *Confessions* are not so much a detailed confession of Augustine's past sins as a confession of praise to almighty God. Augustine takes some time to get around to confessing God. He has abandoned his mother's Christian faith by adolescence and joins forces with the Manichees (a now extinct group with some affinities to our New Age movement). He enters the school of rhetoric. Disappointed by the Manichees, he adopts for a time the philosophy of the Sceptics (who thought pretty much what sceptics still think: that you can't know much about anything). Finally, he discovers the Neo-Platonism of Plotinus and Porphyry. His was a passionate and questing mind.

Cosmic dualism as a solution to the problem of evil

Augustine despised the religion of his mother because he found it utterly unreasonable. Monica may well have been satisfied with simple faith but this was not the way of her son. Only after discovering the preaching of St Ambrose did Augustine come to suspect that the Christian Scriptures could convey an intelligent solution to his own problems. From the Manichees he had learned to regard God and evil as two contending substances. (It was only later that the Platonists taught him to appreciate the notion of immaterial being.) So the first solution Augustine broached to the problem of evil was dualism: two substances or two gods, one of them good and one of them evil, battle for the mastery of the world and its inhabitants. It is a real and unending struggle because they are equally matched. Dualism is a little bit like the pluralism of gods I spoke of in the last letter, although it is starker and simpler: dark versus light, good versus evil.

You remember I dismissed Adam and Eve (and the serpent) very quickly. This was not only because they properly inhabit the theological, not the philosophical, cast of characters. It was also because relying too heavily on the Devil or the fiendish will of man is a dualistic solution to the problem of evil. By making God the original cause of good and something else the spoiler, this explanation tends to give equal weight to the power of God and the power of his not-so-loyal opposition. But, of course, the God who is especially embroiled in the problem of evil is all-powerful, the One without an Other. Dualism, as Augustine came to believe, is an unsatisfactory solution to the riddle of existence.

Evil is the irrational – non-being – a privation

Now Betsy, I am afraid we are going to get 'metaphysical'. It is inevitable with these classical philosophers. I suspect you are a secret Kantian, who would like to curtail all talk about being and confine us to the realm of worldly appearances shaped by our own mind.

What is evil? We are tempted to answer this question by locating evil in some category of things. Maybe, as Augustine learned from the Manichees, it is a material substance. On the other hand, given Augustine's later spiritualistic metaphysics, maybe evil is to be traced to a malevolent spiritual entity. Augustine came to realise that the way our minds customarily proceed to answer questions sets us a trap. We tend to assume that our answer must be a kind of thing. Evil, however, is to be understood not as a being but as a negation of being, a falling off into nothingness from some positive state of being that should be present. Evil is non-being. Imagine evil as a metaphysical parasite that depends for its own life on what it sucks from a host body. Evil is parasitic upon being, which in itself is good.

Let us look at a few concrete examples to fix this notion in our minds. Having a broken leg and hobbling about on crutches with your ailing limb in a cast is an evil. (One of Josh's evils of cosmic origin, right? Philosophers usually call this physical evil.) Now in what does the evil consist? Not in anything positive. You have lost the unimpeded use of a limb a human being ought to have and that you yourself did have before you broke your leg. Evil, notice, is not just a negation. Otherwise, we should say that one of those cats Josh's malicious friend exterminates with such aplomb was already suffering from evil because he lacked the ability to do higher maths. But no one expects a cat to do higher maths. The evil is not that the cat cannot do maths but that the cat is senselessly deprived of what is owed to him, namely his cat-life. It would be clearer if we said that evil is not merely negative but privative: it negates some element required by the very nature of a thing.

What about evil of human origin, as Josh names it? (Philosophers are more likely to speak of moral evil.) Human beings are not only capable of bringing about destructive, negative outcomes; we also say that they themselves can deprive themselves and become evil. Here there is a perversion, a turning aside of the will from the order of goodness, where it would find fulfilment or happiness.

By the doctrine of evil as non-being, Augustine solves one of the questions raised by the juxtaposition of God and evil, namely how can a good God create evil? The answer is that he does not. Evil is nothing positive. God creates beings. Beings as such are good. The evil that infests them is a privation, a boring away at their essential goodness.

Uncle Jack,
somewhat deprived of sight
by what seems a very positive swelling

Calling evil 'non-being' isn't saying it's not there

FROM: Josh
TO: Bets
SUBJECT: nothing
I wasn't expecting this. As Monty Python would say, 'No one expects the Spanish Inquisition!' Solve the problem of evil by saying that evil is nothing! 'Cardinal Fang, bring out the Comfy Chair.' 'No, not the Comfy Chair!' It seems to me that evil is a twisted will, a knock on the door at night, the knout, electrodes rudely attached to your privates. This is not nothing. I don't get it. Sorry.

FROM: Bets
TO: Josh
SUBJECT: more to do about nothing
Read it again. My uncle does say, 'Evil is non-being.' But he also says, 'Evil, notice, is not just a negation.' It is, rather, 'the privation of a thing's proper development.' I highlighted these phrases on my printout. That is what we have to understand.

Difference between a nothing and a privation

FROM: Josh
TO: Bets
SUBJECT: re: more to do about nothing
Good for you, Philosopher Woman. That is what he says. I didn't bother much about following it carefully because it seemed sophistic to solve the problem by claiming that evil is non-being.

I tried to think of the difference between a mere negation and the privation of something that ought to be there. Yes, I can see it. I do not have wings but that doesn't stunt my human development. If I were an eagle, however, that would be another story. An eagle really ought to have wings. If he doesn't, it is a physical evil.

OK, but who's to say what a thing ought to have? Isn't it usually more complicated than eagles' wings?

FROM: Bets
TO: Josh
SUBJECT: privations
Thanks. I get it. There are lots of things I lack but

it is only evil if there is some reason to believe I should have had them in the first place.

We should come up with some objections for Uncle Jack. The only thing I can think of so far is that this is a pretty anaemic definition of evil. Why do we want to think of evil as a real thing?

How can we know what being should contain – and what counts as non-being?

FROM: Josh
TO: Bets
SUBJECT: re: privations
Yeah, saying that evil is nothing positive seems to dismiss it at first. That is what got me upset. But if you think about it, a privation is something real, it is just not a thing. I get pretty upset about some privations: teams losing games they should have won, women who don't show up on time (not you, dear), parking fines. Maybe this idea is strong enough to represent our sense of evil.

I did mention a problem in my last e-mail. This definition of evil presupposes that we know what properties things should have. But isn't that mostly a matter of personal opinion?

Are there fixed natures?

FROM: Joan V.
TO: Betsy Peterson
SUBJECT: the problem of evil
Betsy, while your companion Josh's formulation sounds jejune, it registers a serious issue. That is, this solution of the problem of evil presupposes the scholastic Aristotelian doctrine of fixed natures: you know what is lacking in a being because everything real has a nature that specifies its properties and attributes. But a lot of women today don't accept that idea. It is a logocentric conception, which is a bad thing. We can't really know natures but not for the reason Josh adduces, namely because we can't reach beyond personal opinion. That sounds phallogocentric to me, a typical concern of the thrusting male ego. Phallogocentrism is also bad: it is that we are inscribed in a web of signifiers, a chain that always already defers the ultimate presence it intimates.

Here is a funny consequence of the idea that God

creates only being, which is good. He has created the Devil. So the devil must be good, in so far as he is created.

Also, you have only partly let God off the hook with this argument so far. If evil has no positive being then he (sic!) is not responsible for actually creating it. But if it is so awful to have these privations of due properties, why does he (sic!) allow it?

FROM: Josh
TO: Bets
SUBJECT: another difficulty
I don't think your TA, Joan, is very rational. A rational man writes clearly so that others can understand. But what she says about the Devil being good is cool. It gave me another idea. If God is supposed to be the perfect being, and he is the only perfect being, then only God is really good. Any created being will lack God's full perfection and so be at least partly evil.

FROM: Bets
TO: Josh
SUBJECT: re: another difficulty
Silly! How can you say creation is evil just because it is not perfect? It could only be perfect if it were God, and creation was never supposed to be God. You were the one who helped me understand the bit about 'privation of a perfection due to a thing'. I can conceive of a perfect island, which has all the things an island should have. It does not become a bad island just because it lacks God's infinite perfection.

Physical evil: If creation were perfect, it would be God

Dear Betsy,

I was overjoyed at your response to my last letter. You and your friends are beginning to engage these issues capably. Maybe you are becoming philosophers.

You wanted to know whether I understood what Joan was saying. I presume you mean do I follow her when she lapses into postmodernist idiom? I have heard others fresh from the academy speak that way. If you don't understand everything she says, not to worry. Study first the classical philosophers, Plato, Aristotle, Descartes, Kant, Hegel. Don't neglect that great herald of God's death, Friedrich Nietzsche. Then, if you want, you can go on to writers who are more *à la mode*. At that point, you will be able to judge what is truly novel in their approach and what is modish jargon. Although I am too old to learn to speak post-modern, I do not imagine the major protagonists of this approach are fools. Joan quickly articulates a relativistic denial of metaphysics. I am not sure how she means this to differ from older rejections of nature, essence, substance, and so on, and I do not know how she would respond to the difficulties inherent in any form of relativism. Remember what Pascal said, 'We know too much to be sceptics, and too little to be dogmatists.'

Yes, the doctrine of evil as non-being recognises that everything that is, in so far as it is, is good. So, yes, even the Devil could not *be* unless there were something good about him. (He is said to be a rather cunning and intelligent spiritual substance.) The Devil is evil only because he has warped himself into opposing the good order of God's creation. And so with man. We never give up on our fellow creatures, as long as they draw breath. Sometimes the will swings back to good at the end. You would be surprised.

The issue of God's allowing (not creating) evil remains. You are right to take Josh to task when he labels every finite being 'evil' just because it has limits and falls short of God's perfection (and thus 'participates' in non-being). But Josh has had an insight related to the mystery we are trying to clarify. Creation is necessarily limited. Creation could only be perfect if it were a second God. But this is absurd. The absolutely perfect being has no limitations, exhibits no lacks. There could not be two such beings. They would have to differ from each other in some way. But how? If one of them possesses some perfection the other lacks, then they are not both perfect. The philosopher Leibniz speaks of the 'identity of indiscernibles'. This means that beings that are in every way the same must end up being, in fact, the same thing. Even identical twins, as you know, have their differences. God could not create another all-perfect being.

Metaphysical evil

The necessary finitude of all creation is sometimes called metaphysical evil. (You can add that to your list of evils.) It is not, as you have seen, a case of evil, strictly speaking. But it reveals that if God is going to create at all, he has to put up with imperfections and limitations. (Being perfectly wise, he will presumably direct these imperfections to the good, much as a carver incorporates into his design any defects in the wood he uses.) We see, then, how moral and physical evils are possible. If God is going to make a physical world there will be limitation, giving rise eventually to misery, suffering and other physical evils. God evidently found it better thus than not to have created any physical entities. We may not see things his way. Not having perfect intellects, it is hardly surprising if we do not. The Russian novelist Fyodor Dostoevsky creates a character in *The Brothers Karamazov* who insists that no ulterior divine purpose could be worth the suffering of a single child. What do you think of that?

Moral evil: Free will

What about moral evils? Maybe some physical evil is largely inevitable but moral evil can always be traced back to someone's free choice. Things did not have to be that way. Any occasion of lying, theft or murder might have been prevented by a contrary movement of the malefactor's will. If we can stop ourselves from doing these things, all the more could God have done so. He is supposed to be omniscient, all-knowing. Why does he not prevent at least the worst consequences of moral evil? This is surely within his power.

What happens instead seems to be this: God grants the intelligent creature the use of the free will that belongs to his nature. It is not God's intention that we should abuse this faculty but, on pain of destroying man's moral freedom, God tolerates whatever we choose, including the choice of moral evil. Just as any creation at all is going to involve giving being to possible imperfection, so the creation of beings with intellect and free choice of the will entails the possible perversion of this will. Again, given a providential God, these bad choices may be woven into a pattern beyond our immediate comprehension but they are neither impeded nor erased. Such is the lofty nature of the human estate. This is the general direction in which God's defenders have tried to approach the question of evil.

Inadequately yours,
Uncle Jack

Miracles

How could God interfere with nature?

Dear Uncle Jack,
Our final topic this term is the question of 'miracles'. You are right about philosophical questions being interrelated. I find that the topic of miracles links up to the problem of evil, at least in my mind. Say I accept the line that things have natures. (Joan insists this is very naive, that I am mesmerised by the 'metaphysics of presence'; Josh says it is the only way to think rationally.) Your solution to the problem of evil, then, is something like this: if we are going to have creation at all, we are going to have finite things with their own natures. Creation imposes a kind of obligation on God to respect those natures and the way they act, and not to go around changing the world every minute so that the outcome

always seems immediately good. That would only destroy what he has actually created (which is good but a limited good and liable to physical or moral evil). Is that more or less it? But what about miracles? Aren't they interferences with nature? Do they happen? Can they happen? Should they happen more often? Or would that wreak havoc with the solidity of God's creation?

Josh says miracles are irrational and impossible. To admit miracles, he says, would destroy the possibility of science. It would sap human initiative. He likes to make fun of a little sign we saw in an evangelical bookstore, EXPECT A MIRACLE: 'Anyone who would buy that sign needs one.' Ayn Rand does not believe in miracles. Joan says everything (and nothing) is a miracle. The 'iridescent play of signifiers' is miraculous for her. She says that miracles can be a tool of empowerment for the oppressed of the earth, such as the miraculous *tilma* of Our Lady of Guadalupe in Mexico. But she also says that miracles can be recuperated by the power structures of society and manipulated to maintain their hegemony, such as the miraculous *tilma* of Our Lady of Guadalupe.

I hope you won't claim that all of this is 'theology, not philosophy' and beyond your competence as a scholar. Didn't you study theology, too, in seminary?

Miraculously now passing PHIL 107,
Betsy

Categories of some non-existent miracles

Dear Betsy,

It doesn't hurt to be suspicious. I find the following in one of the odd books that has made its way to our library: 'The Dominican Stephen of Bourbon, in his treatise *On the Seven Gifts of the Holy Spirit*, tells how, at Villars-les-Dombes . . . the peasantry venerated, under the name of St Guinefort, a dog which had suffered an unjust death. Left alone by its masters with their child, the dog killed a snake which threatened the child's life. On their return, the parents found the baby bathed in blood and, thinking it had been attacked by the dog, threw the latter into a well where it died. But the beast's innocence was soon revealed and a devotion rapidly developed around its tomb, which became a much frequented place of pilgrimage, and scene of a large number of miracles . . . The spectacle of blood unjustly shed – even that of an animal – and of the defeat of Good by Evil provoked among the faithful a reaction of emotion and veneration which developed into a cult. The Dominican did not conceal his indignation at this abuse of the notion of martyrdom and described his various efforts to root out this impious cult; in vain, it appears . . . '

If only your Ms Joan V. seemed to believe that anything was actually the case in the world, rather than a glistening 'play of signifiers', we might know how to assess her accusation that miracles are both a

597

weapon in the revolt of the oppressed and a tool in the arsenal of the oppressors. I suspect we have seen both in the course of history but I wonder why either is philosophically relevant. I can also think of a couple of other categories of not-actually-occurring 'miracle', namely the pious fraud and the symbolic code. (For example, if you read a famous medieval compilation of saints' lives by Jacobus de Voragine, *The Golden Legend*, you will find that many of the tales are quite preposterous, until you recognise the meaning intended by the symbolism.)

Yours *sine miraculis*,
Uncle Jack

FROM: Josh
TO: Bets
SUBJECT: miracles
Guinefort the Magic Wonder Dog! It's not too difficult for a rational man to see that all miracles fall into the category of pious fraud – only they are more fraudulent than pious. If a bunch of credulous fools takes them for real, they deserve what they get – oppression and all!

Here's my go at the questions:
What is a miracle? Something so rare that it can't even happen.
Are miracles possible? Only if you are ready to believe anything.
Do miracles violate the uniformity of nature and destroy the scientific method? No, because they don't exist. If they did they would but that is why they can't.

Everything and nothing is miraculous

FROM: Joan V.
TO: Bet
SUBJECT: fw: re: miracles
I would never talk about students to other students. It would be unprofessional. Your companion Josh, of course, has never been my student, nor have you, technically, since I am only your TA. Really, Bet, he is a buffoon! I don't know what you see in him. Maybe you would like to have dinner tonight at Food for Thought and I can explain at length the ludicrousness of Ayn Rand's so-called philosophy. She did not have the conceptual armature that would have allowed her to prise apart the masculinist discourse of domination. It is bad enough that she signed onto this programme of metaphysical oppression. But when some jerky guy just out

of school latches onto Randism to prop up his flagging male ego, it is intolerable.

What Josh says about the discourse of miracles is dismissive and naive. He should read *The Golden Legend*. I have already deconstructed that charming book for a course in 'The Imago of Woman in Medieval Literature'. I shall bring the paper to dinner tonight, if you agree to meet me there. Josh should be able to see how the goddess is struggling to return in miraculous apparitions of Mary. But he can't. He is a man. Too bad.

Miracles are within us

Dear Uncle Jack,

This topic of miracles has given rise to some pretty passionate responses from my friends. My Philosophy teacher says that a 'prejudice' is a pre-judgement, a presumption you make before you begin examining evidence. I think Josh has a prejudice against miracles. I am not sure about Joan. She talks about miracles ('the discourse of miracles') but I don't know what she means. I don't believe she thinks that miracles actually happen either.

Before I started studying Philosophy of Religion, I probably would have said that miracles are real if they are in your heart. But I'm not sure what I would have meant by this. Maybe that it all depends on how you look at it. (I think this is what Joan is saying in fancier language.)

I probably also thought that the only miracle was a change of heart. You know: Jesus didn't multiply the loaves and fishes in a physical sense. He changed men's hearts so that they were willing to share their secret caches of food with one another. I don't think any of this would fly in a Philosophy class, although perhaps I would stand some chance if I termed my 'miracle as change of heart' the Moral Theory of the Miraculous.

I would like to believe in miracles. But I've never seen one and a lot of them sound pretty fishy. I guess it has to be against nature and against science to be a miracle. That's why I suspect such things do not exist. Enlighten me, O Learned One.

Puzzled,
Betsy

Miracles transgress the law of nature

Dear Betsy,

Miracles are messier than God and more ambiguous than evil. No wonder you're getting such wild responses. I should remind you that, despite the funny tale of Guinefort, significant things are at stake here. You brought up the story of Jesus's multiplication of the loaves and fishes. Throughout the Hebrew Bible and the New Testament you will find reports of similar preternatural occurrences. What are we to make of them?

No one (not even you) made much of a stab at defining miracles. Let me give you two definitions, then, to start out with. First, that of a disbeliever, the Scottish Enlightenment philosopher David Hume. Hume says a miracle is 'a transgression of a law of nature brought about by a particular volition of the Deity, or by the interposition of some invisible agent'. Second, that of a classical theologian, St Thomas Aquinas. Thomas says that a miracle is 'an effect produced by God, beyond the power of created nature'. The word itself simply means that which is wonderful or worthy of being admired.

Notice that Hume has stacked the decks by calling the miraculous a *transgression* of the law of nature. Your own intuition that 'it has to be against nature and against science to be a miracle' puts you pretty squarely in Hume's camp. We live in a culture deeply shaped by the Enlightenment project. Perhaps you agree with Hume because his thought has entered the culture and you breathed it in unconsciously from a thousand different sources.

Hume on miracles

A miracle is a violation of the laws of nature; and as a firm and unalterable experience has established these laws, the proof against a miracle, from the very nature of the fact, is as entire as any argument from experience can possibly be imagined . . . Nothing is esteemed a miracle if it ever happens in the common course of nature . . . The plain consequence is (and it is a general maxim worthy of our attention) that no testimony is sufficient to establish a miracle unless the testimony be of such a kind that its falsehood would be more miraculous than the fact which it endeavours to establish . . . There is not to be found, in all history, any miracle attested by a sufficient number of men of such unquestioned good sense, education, and learning as to secure us against all delusion in themselves; of such undoubted integrity as to place them beyond all suspicion of any design to deceive others; of such credit and reputation in the eyes of mankind as to have a great deal to lose in case of their being detected in any falsehood, and at the same time attesting facts performed in such a public manner and in so celebrated a part of the world as to render the detection unavoidable – all which circumstances are requisite to give us a full assurance in the testimony of men . . . It forms a strong presumption against all supernatural and miraculous relations that they are observed chiefly to abound among ignorant and barbarous nations; or if a civilised people has ever given

---

admission to any of them, that people will be found to have received them from ignorant and barbarous ancestors, who transmitted them with that inviolable sanction and authority which always attend received opinions.

David Hume, *An Enquiry Concerning Human Understanding* (1902: 114–16)

Hume offers us a test to apply. Appropriately enough for his general philosophical approach, it is a test that relies upon data drawn from sense experience. We recognise, first of all, the unlikelihood of miracles. If they occur at all, miracles are a rare transgression of the usual laws of nature. What could cause us to affirm that such a transgression has taken place? Not some metaphysical argument but the evidence that miracles have, in fact, occurred. Do we have such evidence? There are reports of miraculous events. Without such reports, we would be entitled to dismiss the notion out of hand. But when we begin to examine these reports, we discover this fact about them: none of them possesses a quality sufficient to induce us willingly to discard our uniform past experience. Didn't you say, Betsy, 'I've never seen [a miracle] and a lot of them sound pretty fishy'? According to Hume, the witnesses to miracles are men of 'ignorant and barbarous places and nations', just the sort who cannot be relied upon, men even willing to worship holy dogs. Hume notes, as well, that all religions claim miraculous support. Well, then, is the supporter of miracles prepared to say that all religions are equally true? So it is more rational to accept that the laws of nature hold uniformly than that ill-documented and fantastic exceptions have occurred.

```
FROM: Josh
TO: Bets
SUBJECT: Hume
This is good. I agree with Hume. I told you miracles
were not rational. The evidence is not there. I think
any modern studies supporting the miraculous can be
debunked, too.
```

Is there any 'nature' to transgress?

```
FROM: Joan V.
TO: Bet
SUBJECT: in-hume-ation of a rationalist
This seems to me very suspicious. If Hume is such a
```

great empiricist, relying on sense experience to prove
everything, then why does he start off with such a dogmatic framework about the 'laws of nature' and their
uniformity? He is a rationalist and that is not good.
Contemporary science is more postmodern: chaos theory
underlines the randomness of motion of fundamental
particles. Scientific 'laws' are only statistical
probabilities.

Laws of nature conditional

Dear Betsy,

I thought it was good to start with Hume because he is so close to
contemporary thought and your own language reminded me of the way
Hume called miracles into question. But Ms Joan V. is right, if I understand her, to suggest that Hume's presuppositions regarding what
characterises a 'law of nature' may be inadequate. I would say, further,
that Hume also makes the gratuitous assumption that miracles are
transgressions of the laws of nature. I don't know where Joan wants to
drive her observations but I would suggest we recognise that physical
laws are conditional, not absolute. A physical law describes what happens under usual conditions but if the conditions change, so will the
outcome. In particular, if we were to inject a supernatural causal agent
(God) into the equation, we can expect exceptions to the physical laws.
Hold on to Hume's empirical test, in order to keep a rein on madness,
but recognise that while the general law is not to be lightly dismissed, it
does not rule out an exception, if we have persuasive evidence in its
favour.

A miracle is 'an effect produced by God'

Now compare St Thomas's definition of a miracle with Hume's. Hume
says a miracle is 'a transgression of a law of nature brought about by a
particular volition of the Deity, or by the interposition of some invisible
agent'. Thomas Aquinas says that a miracle is 'an effect produced by
God, beyond the power of created nature'. With what does Thomas
replace the transgressive element in Hume's definition? Rather than
talking about 'breaking' the laws of nature, Thomas speaks of an effect
'beyond the power' of created nature. Nor is this a nature-surpassing
effect without an adequate cause. The effect is brought about by the
power of God, who, of course, has power and to spare. In no way is the
law of cause and effect abrogated but it is applied to a different agent in
a different context.

That might appear to be only a difference of emphasis – which it
surely is – but Thomas also gives an account of how he sees God
supplementing the causal powers of natural things. It is something we
can understand from our own experience of instruments. Consider how,

in arts and crafts or in sports, the expert practitioner is concerned about the nature and quality of his instrument. If I am a painter, I want a certain kind of paint and brush to produce one effect and another kind to produce another. In any case, I don't want some cheap brush whose bristles will split and fall out. If I am a tennis pro, I want a particular racquet produced according to the latest technology and not one of the crummy old wooden racquets we, for some reason, still have in our shed here.

Why is this? It is not that the instrument itself produces the work of art or the athletic play. Give a toddler a Stradivarius violin and he will not sound like Yehudi Menuhin. Nevertheless, without a decent instrument – without the best instrument possible – even the pro will be severely handicapped. Does the paintbrush paint the *Mona Lisa*? No. Leave it on the easel for all eternity and it will not come one stroke closer to producing this masterpiece. But Leonardo, through the instrumentality of the paintbrush, produces the portrait of this memorable smile.

In St Thomas's analysis, the instrument has, first, its own power (*virtus propria*), which the higher agent will regard when he takes up the instrument to use for his purposes. The higher agent using the instrument then imparts to the instrument an instrumental power (*virtus instrumentalis*), as he uses the proper power of the instrument to bring about an effect the instrument could never have achieved on its own. Notice, it is not that the paintbrush or the hockey stick is breaking any laws of nature when it is used as an instrument; but it does exhibit a capacity that is not native to it. Only while being taken up by a higher agent and moved by him does the instrument exert an instrumental power.

God is the principal cause of a miracle. He may work through the instrumentality of one of his creatures, which becomes, in his hands, an instrumental cause. Does the creature contribute anything to the total effect? Yes, the creature retains its proper power, and this will likely be evident somehow in the miraculous effect, as well. Does anything prevent God from acting directly or from creating anew, rather than taking up, ready-made, the instrument of his action? That could be so, as well.

What is 'nature'?

One broader question that affects the problem of miracles is our changing idea of nature. (For an orientation, read R. G. Collingwood's beautiful book, *The Idea of Nature*.)

Aristotle, with his 'metaphysical' notion of things – that there are essential identities (fixed 'kinds' of things), substances supporting different properties ('kinds' undergoing unessential modifications) and inherent powers (special 'capacities' belonging to the various 'kinds') – had one idea of nature. He said, 'nature is that which happens always or for the most part'. No one would call Aristotle a partisan of the miraculous but his understanding of nature allows for such 'higher' tinkering, as nature for Aristotle is not an ironclad 'system' of uniform laws.

The Enlightenment idea of nature, which we saw lurking behind Hume's thought, is another approach, more inimical to the idea of miraculous intervention, which it can only see as a transgression. More recent understandings in science and the philosophy of science? Well, here is something for the new generation of philosophers to examine.

My love to you.
An unworthy instrument,
Uncle Jack

FROM: Josh
TO: Bets
SUBJECT: miraculous understandings
This was an interesting letter. I see that it is more complicated than I thought. I want to read that book by R. G. Collingwood on the history of the idea of nature. I guess I always thought that past thinkers were just wrong, that we get to know more and more as society progresses and truth replaces error. But I see now that it is important to study the history of ideas and philosophy. Ayn Rand did that a little bit with Aristotle but maybe not enough. Anyway, if Joan's ideas are the most advanced on offer, in order to avoid them I think I will have to find out some way to hold back the tide of history and look for truth in the past, instead of taking the avant-garde for granted.

I see now why I wasn't very interested in the problem of miracles. I thought it was a pseudo-problem. Since there wasn't any God, there could be no miracles worked by him. There might be strange and unexplained natural happenings or hallucinations or schizophrenic episodes but no real miracles. For me, the question of God still has to be resolved. Maybe we can study it together, as you write your term paper. But I learned something from the history and the analysis connected with the prob-lem of miracles, anyway.
See you tonight?

FROM: Joan V.
TO: Bet
SUBJECT: miracle letter
The analysis of instrumental causality is new to me. I would like to deconstruct it. It sounds pretty male-

dominated, although historically women have used instruments, too. Maybe I will write a paper on the effect of the marginalisation of women's instruments on the discourse of miracles. How does the goddess fit in? Maybe we can have coffee at Alternative Grounds tomorrow after class. I should have some ideas by then.

FROM: Betsy
TO: Josh
SUBJECT: bad news
Josh, my mother just phoned with bad news. I am going home tonight. My parents got a call from Africa. There was an accident in the bush and my Uncle Jack is dead. This Thursday the order will offer a memorial Mass for him at their provincial headquarters. Will you come with me?

FROM: Josh
TO: Betsy
SUBJECT: re: bad news
I am so sorry. I never met him but I thought I knew him. The problem of God, evil and suffering, no miracle here at the end. Of course I will be with you.

Dear Betsy,

I worked with your uncle at our African missions. Please know of my sympathy and prayers at this sad time. I remembered your uncle and your family, as well, at the altar this morning.

I thought you would like to have the letter he had just started writing to you on the morning he died. You probably don't know how much he came to look forward to hearing from you and your friends. How often our conversations, of late, returned to the studies of our seminary days! Sorrowing at your loss, I think of my own Philosophy professor, one of the grand old men of our order. I was privileged to give him last rites in the community infirmary. 'Soon you must philosophise on your own,' he said. Possibile est: it is possible, dear Betsy.

Faithfully yours,
Fr Ronald Cobbingdon

Dear Betsy,
I have been looking over our entire correspondence, which fills a good part of the top drawer of my desk. I had intended to return to your question, 'How does this help anyone to believe?' The answer again is, it doesn't, directly. Faith is a gift of God and neither we nor anyone else can argue ourselves into it. But, as St Thomas used to say, '*Ama intellectum valde* – love much the intellect.' To think things through

strengthens and develops the intellect. These exercises can help us clear away false obstacles to belief, as well. They can make the God we serve less of an idol. That is what I want for you . . . [Here the letter breaks off.]

 ## Further reading

General

Davies, Brian (1993), *An Introduction to the Philosophy of Religion*, Oxford: Oxford University Press.

Augustine

Bourke, Vernon J. (1945), *Augustine's Quest of Wisdom: Life and Philosophy of the Bishop of Hippo*, Milwaukee: Bruce.
Brown, Peter (1967), *Augustine of Hippo: a Biography*, London: Faber and Faber.

Modern science and ancient cosmology

Collingwood, R. G. (1945), *The Idea of Nature*, Oxford: Clarendon.
Koyre, Alexandre (1957, 1991), *From the Closed World to the Infinite Universe*, Baltimore: Johns Hopkins University Press.

Mediaeval philosophy and scholasticism

Gilson, Etienne (1936), *The Spirit of Mediaeval Philosophy*, New York: Scribner's.
Pieper, Josef (1964), *Scholasticism: Personalities and Problems of Medieval Philosophy*, New York: Pantheon.

Anselm of Canterbury

Evans, G. R. (1989), *Anselm*, London: Chapman.

Thomas Aquinas and Thomism

Bourke, Vernon J. (1965), *Aquinas' Search for Wisdom*, Milwaukee: Bruce.
Pieper, Josef (1991), *Guide to Thomas Aquinas*, San Francisco: Ignatius Press.

The existence of God

Emonet, Pierre Marie (2000), *God Seen in the Mirror of the World: An Introduction to the Philosophy of God*, New York: Herder and Herder.

Nichols, Aidan (1991), *A Grammar of Consent: The Existence of God in Christian Tradition*, Notre Dame: Notre Dame University Press.

The problem of evil

Evans, G. R. (1982), *Augustine on Evil*, Cambridge: Cambridge University Press.

Miracles

McInerny Ralph (1986), *Miracles*, Huntingdon, IN: OSV.

Questions

Philosophy as a way of life

1. How does what we want out of life condition our approach to philosophy?

2. Is it 'rational' to be purely self-interested? What do you mean by 'rational'?

3. Would people living in different worlds have different philosophies? Or only if they lived there by choice?

4. What different sort of world does Plato think a true philosopher must want to enter?

5. What is a 'first principle'? Why do you have to decide your first principle(s) before engaging in philosophy?

The existence of God

1. What are the presuppositions of Augustine's argument for God?

2. Why can't we form a concept of God, if we can form a concept of anything else?

3. Could we be completely satisfied by any idea of God?

4. Is the 'satisfying idea proof' subjective or objective? Does it differ from a 'natural desire for God' proof?

5. What is the difference between Descartes' interpretation of Anselm's argument and Barth's interpretation?

6. What does Anselm see as the distinction between saying a perfect island must exist and God must exist? Does Anselm's argument go from thought to reality, or from reality back to thought?

7. Why is there motion? Does motion require a cause?

8. In what way does Aquinas' Third Argument for God confront the possibility of nothingness?

9. Does a scale of perfections prove the existence of God? If so, what kind of scale would it have to be?

10. Does evolution rule out design?

The problem of evil

1. Is the world basically good?

2. Would an imperfect God be God?

3. Why is the problem of evil related to monotheism?

4. How did Augustine define evil? Did he define it away? Can we know what is lacking in a thing?

5. Could a purely evil entity exist?

Miracles

1. Why were medievals more likely to believe in miracles than moderns?

2. Is there enough evidence to make any miracle possible?

3. How does our conception of 'nature' affect our view of miracles?

Select Bibliography

Albert and Thomas (1988), *Selected Writings*, ed. and trans. Simon Tugwell, New Jersey: Paulist Press.

Alt, Albrecht (1966), 'The Origins of Israelite Law', in *Essays on Old Testament History and Religion*, Oxford: Blackwell.

Anderson, B. W. T. (1988), *The Living World of the Old Testament*, 4th ed., London: Longman.

Anselm (1962), *Basic Writings*, trans. S. N. Deane, La Salle, IL: Open Court.

Aquinas, Thomas (1948), *Summa Theologiae*, trans. Fathers of the English Dominican Province, 5 vols, London: Sheed and Ward.

Aquinas, Thomas (1975), *Summa Contra Gentiles*, Books 1–4, Notre Dame: Notre Dame University Press.

Arieli-Horowitz, Dana (ed.) (1996), *Religion and the State of Israel, 1994–95*, Jerusalem: Center for Jewish Pluralism.

Asad, Talal (1993), *Genealogies of Religion*, Baltimore: Johns Hopkins University Press.

Athanasius (1971), *On the Incarnation of the Word*, 54, in *Contra Gentes and De Incarnatione*, trans. and ed. Robert W. Thomson, Oxford: Clarendon Press.

Augustine (1968), *De Libero Arbitrio*, in *The Teacher, The Free Choice of the Will and Grace and Free Will*, trans. Robert P. Russell, Washington, DC: Catholic University of America Press.

Augustine (1972), *The City of God*, trans. Henry Bettenson, London: Penguin.

Augustine (1987), *Nicene and Post-Nicene Fathers*, vol. 7, Peabody, MA: Hendrickson.

Augustine (2001), *Confessions*, trans. Philip Burton, London: Everyman's Library.

Ballard, Paul (ed.) (1986), *The Foundations of Pastoral Studies and Practical Theology*, Cardiff: Faculty of Theology, University College, Cardiff.

Balthasar, Hans Urs von (1987), *Truth is Symphonic*, trans. Graham Harrison, San Francisco: Ignatius Press.

Balthasar, Hans Urs von (1998), *Theo-Drama: Theological Dramatic Theory*, trans. Graham Harrison, vol. 5, San Francisco: Ignatius Press.

Banton, Michael (ed.) (1968), *Anthropological Approaches to the Study of Religion*, London: Tavistock.

Barbour, R. (1972), *Traditio-historical Criticism of the Gospels*, London: SPCK.

Barker, Eileen (1992), *New Religious Movements: A Practical Introduction*, London: HMSO.

Barker, Eileen (1992), 'New Religious Movements: Their Incidence and Significance', in B. Wilson and J. Cresswell (eds), *New Religious Movements: Challenge and Response*, London and New York: Routledge.

Barker, Eileen (ed.) (1982), *New Religious Movements: A Perspective for Understanding Society*, New York and Toronto: Edwin Mellen Press.

Barrett, C. K. (1989), *New Testament Background: Selected Documents*, rev. ed., San Francisco: HarperSanFrancisco.

Barth, Karl (1975), *Church Dogmatics I.I: The Doctrine of the Word of God*, trans. G. W. Bromiley, Edinburgh: T. and T. Clark.

Barth, Karl (2000), *Evangelical Theology: An Introduction*, Michigan: Eerdmans.

Barth, Lewis (ed.) (1990), *Berit Mila, in the Reform Context*, New York: UAHC.

Bartholomew I (1997), Address at the Environmental Symposium, St Barbara Greek Orthodox Church, Santa Barbara, CA, 8 November.

Basil, R. (ed.) (1988), *Not Necessarily the New Age: Critical Essays*, Buffalo, NY: Prometheus Books.

Beckford, James (1975), *The Trumpet of Prophecy: A Sociological Study of Jehovah's Witnesses*, Oxford: Blackwell.

Bendix, Reinhard (1962), *Max Weber*, Garden City: Anchor Books.

Benoit, Pierre (1965), *Inspiration and the Bible*, trans. J. Murphy-O'Connor and M. Kervene, London: Sheed and Ward.

Berger, Peter (1967), *The Sacred Canopy*, New York: Anchor Books.

Berger, Peter and Thomas Luckman (1991), *The Social Construction of Reality*, Harmondsworth: Penguin.

Bettenson, Henry (ed.) (1956, 1976), *The Early Christian Fathers: A Selection from the Writings of the Fathers from St Clement of Rome to St Athanasius*, Oxford: Oxford University Press.

Bindley, T. Herbert (ed.) (1899), *The Oecumenical Documents of the Faith*, London: Methuen.

Bloch, Maurice (1991), *From Prey into Hunter*, Cambridge: Cambridge University Press.

Bloom, William (1991), 'Introduction', in W. Bloom (ed.), *The New Age: An Anthology of Essential Writings*, London: Rider.

Blumenthal, David R. (1978), *Understanding Jewish Mysticism*, New York: KTAV.

Boas, Franz (1963), *The Mind of Primitive Man*, New York: Free Press.

Bosch, David (1991), *Transforming Mission: Paradigm Shifts in Theology of Mission*, Maryknoll, New York: Orbis Books.

Bradney, Anthony (1999), 'New Religious Movements: the legal dimension', in B. Wilson and J. Cresswell (eds), *New Religious Movements: Challenge and Response*, London and New York: Routledge.

Brierley, Peter (2000), *The Tide is Running Out: What the English Church Attendance Survey Reveals*, London: Christian Research.

Bright, John (1981), *A History of Israel*, 3rd ed., London: SCM Press.

Bruce, Steve (1997), *Religion in the Modern World: From Cathedrals to Cults*, Oxford: Oxford University Press.

Buber, Martin (1958), *I and Thou*, New York: Charles Scribner and Sons.

Bultmann, Rudolf (1955), *Essays Philosophical and Theological*, London: SCM Press.

Campbell, Joseph (1970), *Myths, Dreams and Religion*, Dallas: Spring Publications.

Campbell, Joseph (1972), *The Hero with a Thousand Faces*, Princeton: Princeton University Press.

Cantwell Smith, Wilfred (1962), *The Meaning and End of Religion*, San Francisco: Harper and Row.

Carrel, Alexis (1950), *Journey to Lourdes*, London: Hamilton Press.

Childs, Brevard (1979), *Introduction to the Old Testament as Scripture*, London: SCM Press.

Clark, Stephen M. (1992), 'Myth, metaphor, and manifestation: the negotiation of belief in a New Age community', in J. R. Lewis and J. G. Melton (eds),

Perspectives on the New Age, Albany: State University of New York Press.

Clarke, Peter B. (1999), 'Japanese New Religious Movements in Brazil: From Ethnic to "Universal" Religions', in B. Wilson and J. Cresswell (eds), *New Religious Movements: Challenge and Response*, London and New York: Routledge.

Clarke, Peter B. (ed.) (1987), *The New Evangelists: Recruitment, Methods and Aims of New Religious Movements*, London: Ethnographica.

Cohen, Hermann (1972), *Religion of Reason out of the Sources of Judaism*, New York: Frederick Unger Publishing.

Commission on the Philosophy of Conservative Judaism (1990), *Emet Ve-Emunah: Statement of Principles of Conservative Judaism*, Jewish Theological Seminary, The Rabbinical Assembly and The United Synagogue of America.

Congar, Yves (1986), *The Word and the Spirit*, London: Chapman.

Crossan, J. D. (1994), *Jesus: A Revolutionary Biography*, San Francsico: HarperSan-Francisco.

Cullmann, Oscar (1962), *Christ and Time: The Primitive Christian Conception of Time and History*, trans. Floyd Filson, rev. ed., London: SCM Press.

Cunliffe-Jones, Hubert (ed.) (1978), *A History of Christian Doctrine*, Edinburgh: T. and T. Clark.

Davie, Grace (1995), *Religion in Britain Since 1945: Believing without Belonging*, Oxford: Blackwell.

Davies, Brian (1992), *The Thought of Thomas Aquinas*, Oxford: Clarendon Press.

Davies, Brian, (ed.) (2000), *Philosophy of Religion: A Guide to the Subject*, Oxford: Oxford University Press.

D'Costa, Gavin (2000), *The Meeting of Religions and the Trinity*, Edinburgh: T. and T. Clark.

Dillistone, F. W. (1968, 1984), *The Christian Understanding of Atonement*, London: SCM Press.

Dingemans, Gijsbert D. J. (1996), 'Practical Theology in the Academy: A Contemporary Overview', *The Journal of Religion* 76: 1, 82–96.

Douglas, Mary (1984), *Purity and Danger*, London: Ark.

Douglas, Mary (1986), *Natural Symbols*, London: Routledge.

Dumont, L. (1980), 'World Renunciation in Indian Religions', in *Homo Hierarchious: The Caste System and its Implications*, London: University of Chicago Press.

Dumoulin, H. (1994), *Zen Buddhism: A History*, New York: Macmillan.

Durkheim, Emile (2001), *The Elementary Forms of the Religious Life*, Oxford: Oxford University Press.

Eliade, Mircea (1971), *The Myth of the Eternal Return*, Princeton: Princeton University Press.

Evans, G. R. (1993), *Philosophy and Theology in the Middle Ages*, London: Routledge.

Evans, J. H. (1992), *We Have Been Believers: An African-American Systematic Theology*, Minneapolis: Fortress Press.

Evans-Pritchard, E. E (1965), *Theories of Primitive Religion*, Oxford: Clarendon Press.

Evans-Pritchard, E. E. (1976), *Witchcraft, Oracles and Magic among the Azande*, Oxford: Clarendon Press.

Fackenheim, Emile (1982), *To Mend the World*, New York: Schocken.

Flannery, Austin (gen. ed.) (1975), *Vatican Council II: The Conciliar and Post-Conciliar Documents*, New York: Costello Publishing Company.

Fowler, James W. (1985), 'Practical Theology and Theological Education: Some Models and Questions', *Theology Today*, 43–58.

Fowler, James (1987), *Faith, Development, and Pastoral Care*, Philadelphia: Fortress Press.

Frazer, J. G. (1922), *The Golden Bough*, London: Macmillan.

Frei, Hans (1974), *The Eclipse of Biblical Narrative: A Study in Eighteenth and Nineteenth Century Hermeneutics*, New Haven: Yale University Press.

Gadamer, H. G. (1976), *Philosophical Hermeneutics*, trans. and ed. David E. Ling, Berkeley: University of California Press.

Gaon, Saadia (1989), *The Book of Beliefs and Opinions*, trans. Samuel Rosenblatt, New Haven: Yale University Press.

Geertz, Clifford (1968), *Islam Observed*, Chicago: University of Chicago Press.

Geertz, Clifford (1968), 'Religion as a Cultural System', in Michael Banton (ed.), *Anthropological Approaches to the Study of Religion*, London: Tavistock.

Geertz, Clifford (1973), *The Interpretation of Culture*, New York: Basic Books.

Gennep, Arnold L. van (1960), *The Rites of Passage*, Chicago: University of Chicago Press.

Gerstenberger, E. (1965), Wesen and Herkunft des 'apodiktischen Rechts', *Wissenschaftliche Monographien zum Alten und Neuen Testament*, 20.

Gilson, Etienne (1963), *The Elements of Christian Philosophy*, New York: New American Library.

Glock, Charles (1976), 'Consciousness among contemporary youth: an interpretation', in C. Glock and R. Bellah (eds), *The New Religious Consciousness*, Berkeley: University of California Press.

Glock, Charles and Robert Bellah (eds) (1976), *The New Religious Consciousness*, Berkeley: University of California Press.

Goulder, M. (ed.) (1979), *Jesus Christ and Myth*, London: SCM Press.

Graham, Elaine L. (1996) *Transforming Practice: Pastoral Theology in Uncertainty*, London: Cassell.

Grillmeier, Aloys (1965, 1975), *Christ in Christian Tradition Volume 1: From the Apostolic Age to Chalcedon (451)*, trans. John Bowden, London: Mowbray.

Groome, Thomas H. (1987), 'Theology on Our Feet: A Revisionist Pedagogy for Healing the Gap between Academia and Ecclesia', in Louis Mudge and James Poling (eds), *Formation and Reflection*, Philadelphia: Fortress Press.

Gunn, David M. and Danna Nolan Fewell (1993), *Narrative in the Hebrew Bible*, Oxford: Oxford University Press.

Gunton, Colin (1991), *The Promise of Trinitarian Theology*, Edinburgh: T. and T. Clark.

Gutierrez, Gustavo (1988), *A Theology of Liberation*, London: SCM Press.

Hanegraaff, Wouter (1996), *New Age Religion and Western Culture: Esotericism in the Mirror of Secular Thought*, Leiden: E. J. Brill.

Harlow, Jules (ed.) (1985), *Siddur Sim Shalom*, New York: RA.

Harris, Marvin (1975), *Cows, Pigs, Wars and Witches*, New York: Vintage.

Hartshorne, Charles (1965), *Anselm's Discovery: A Re-examination of the Ontological Proof of God's Existence*, La Salle, IL: Open Court.

Hartshorne, Charles (1982), *The Divine Relativity*, London: Yale University Press.

Harvey, David (1990), *The Condition of Postmodernity: An Enquiry into the Origins of Cultural Change*, Oxford: Basil Blackwell.

Harvey, Van (1966), *The Historian and the Believer*, New York: Macmillan.

Heelas, Paul (1991), 'Western Europe: self-religions', in P. Clarke and S. Sutherland (eds), *The World's Religions: The Study of Religion, Traditional and New Religions*, London: Routledge.

Heil, J. P. (1992), *The Gospel of Mark as a Model for Action*, New York: Paulist Press.

Heiler, Friedrich (1932), *Prayer*, Oxford: Oxford University Press.

Hermeneia (1974), *A Critical and Historical Commentary on the Bible*, Philadelphia: Fortress Press.

Heschel, Abraham Joshua (1955), *God in Search of Man*, New York: Harper and Row.

Hick, John (1973, 1993), *God and the Universe of Faiths*, Oxford: Oneworld.

Hick, John (1993), *The Metaphor of God Incarnate*, London: SCM Press.

Hick, John (ed.) (1977), *The Myth of God Incarnate*, London: SCM Press.

Hick, John and Paul Knitter (1988), *The Myth of Christian Uniqueness*, London: SCM Press.

Hill, Michael (1973), *A Sociology of Religion*, London: Heinemann.

Hiltner, Seward (1954), *Preface to Pastoral Theology*, New York and Nashville: Abingdon Press.

Hobsbawm, Eric (1994), *Age of Extremes: The Short Twentieth Century 1914–1991*, London: Penguin.

Hume, David (1985), *Of Miracles*, New York: Open Court.

Hume, David (1993), *Dialogues Concerning Natural Religion and the Natural History of Religion*, Oxford: Oxford University Press.

Hurding, Roger F. (1986), *Roots and Shoots*, London: Hodder and Stoughton.

Jacobus de Voragine (1969), *The Golden Legend*, New York: Arno Press.

James, William (1982), *The Varieties of Religious Experience*, Harmondsworth: Penguin.

Jenson, Robert W. (1982), *The Triune Identity: God According to the Gospel*, Philadelphia: Fortress Press.

John Paul II (1990), 'Peace with God, Peace with All of Creation', http://conservation.catholic.org/the_ecological_crisis_page_2.htm

Julian of Norwich (1966), *Revelations of Divine Love*, London: Penguin.

Jung, C. G. (1969), 'Psychology and Religion', in *The Collected Works of C. G. Jung*, vol. 2, London: Routledge and Kegan Paul.

Kahler, Martin (1988), *The So-Called Historical Jesus and the Biblical Christ of Faith*, trans. Carl Braaten, Philadelphia: Fortress Press.

Kaplan, Mordechai (1958), *Judaism Without Supernaturalism*, New York: Reconstructionist Press.

Kaplan, Mordechai (1981), *Judaism as a Civilization*, New York: JPSA.

Kluckhohn, Clyde (1967), *Navaho Witchcraft*, Boston: Beacon Press.

Kohn, Rachel (1991), 'Radical Subjectivity in "Self Religions" and the Problem of Authority', in A. W. Black (ed.), *Religion in Australia: Sociological Perspectives*, North Sydney, Australia: Allen and Unwin, pp. 132–7.

Lash, J. (1990), *The Seeker's Handbook: The Complete Guide to Spiritual Pathfinding*, New York: Harmony Books.

Leach, Edmund R. (1968), *Dialectic in Practical Religion*, Cambridge: Cambridge University Press.

Lévi-Strauss, Claude (1963), *Structural Anthropology*, New York: Basic Books.

Lévy-Bruhl, Lucien (1923), *Primitive Mentality*, London: Macmillan.

Lewis, I. M. (1971), *Ecstatic Religion*, London: Routledge.

Lonergan, Bernard (1972), *Method in Theology*, London: Darton, Longman and Todd.

Lossky, Vladimir (1982), *The Mystical Theology of the Eastern Church*, Crestwood, NY: St Vladimir's Seminary Press.

Lossky, Vladimir (1985), *In the Image and Likeness of God*, Crestwood, NY: St Vladimir's Seminary Press.

Lossky, Vladimir and Leonide Oupensky (1976), *The Meaning of Icons*, Crestwood, NY: St Vladimir's Seminary Press.

Lott, E. (1980), *Vedantic Approaches to God*, London: Macmillan.

McFague, Sally (1987), *Models of God: Theology for an Ecological, Nuclear Age*, Philadelphia: Fortress Press.

Maimonides, Moses (1956), *The Guide For The Perplexed*, trans. M. Friedländer, New York: Dover.

Malinowski, Bronislaw (1948), *Magic, Science and Religion, and Other Essays*, Boston: Beacon Press.

Maritain, Jacques (1966), *God and the Permission of Evil*, Milwaukee: Bruce Publishing.

Marx, Karl (1972 [1846]), 'The German Ideology: Part I', in Robert Tucker (ed.), *The Marx and Engels Reader*, New York: Norton.

Meier, J. P. (1991), *A Marginal Jew: Rethinking the Historical Jesus*, 2 vols, New York: Doubleday.

Melton, J. Gordon (1988), 'A History of the New Age Movement', in R. Basil (ed.),

Not Necessarily the New Age: Critical Essays, Buffalo, NY: Prometheus Books.

Melton, J. Gordon (1992), 'New Thought and New Age', in J. R. Lewis and J. G. Melton (eds), *Perspectives on the New Age*, Albany: State University of New York Press.

Melton, J. Gordon (1999), 'Anti-cultists in the United States: An Historical Perspective', in B. Wilson and J. Cresswell (eds), *New Religious Movements: Challenge and Response*, London: Routledge.

Mencher, J. (1974), 'Is the Caste System Upside Down?', *Current Anthropology, 15*.

Mendelssohn, Moses (1983), *Jerusalem*, trans. Allan Arkush, Hanover: University Press of New England.

Merton, Thomas (1978), *The Seven Storey Mountain*, London: Sheldon Press.

Middleton, John (1960), *Lugbara Religion*, London: Oxford University Press.

Moltmann, Jurgen (1981), *The Trinity and the Kingdom of God*, trans. Margaret Kohl, London: SCM Press.

Moore, Sally Falke (1967), 'Descent and Symbolic Filiation', in John Middleton, *Myth and Cosmos*, New York: Natural History Press.

Muir, Edwin (1960), *Collected Poems*, London: Faber and Faber.

Naisbitt, J. and P. Aburdene (1990), *Megatrends 2000*, New York: William Morrow and Co.

Neill, S. (1986), *A History of Christian Missions*, Harmondsworth: Pelican.

Nelson, Geoffrey K. (1969), *Spiritualism and Society*, London: Routledge and Kegan Paul.

Nichols, Aidan (1980), *The Art of God Incarnate: Theology and Image in Christian Tradition*, London: Darton, Longman and Todd.

Nichols, Aidan (1991), *The Shape of Catholic Theology*, Edinburgh: T. and T. Clark.

Niles, D. T. (1972), *A Test of Faith*, London: Epworth Press.

Norris Jr, Richard E. (ed.) (1980), *The Christological Controversy*, Philadelphia: Fortress Press.

Northcott, Michael (1991), 'Research Methods in Practical Theology', *Contact* 106: 3, 24–34.

Noth, Martin (1981), 'The Deuteronomistic History', *Journal for the Study of the Old Testament Supplement Series*, 15.

Okely, Judith (1983), *The Traveller-Gypsies*, Cambridge: Cambridge University Press.

Otto, Rudolph (1924), *The Idea of the Holy*, Oxford: Oxford University Press.

Owens, Joseph (1980), *St. Thomas Aquinas on the Existence of God*, Buffalo: State University of New York Press.

Pannenberg, Wolfthart (1968), *Jesus God and Man*, trans. Lewis L. Wilkens and Duane A. Priebe, London: SCM Press.

Pannenberg, Wolfhart (1976), *Theology and the Philosophy of Science*, London: Darton, Longman and Todd.

Parsons, Talcott (1954), *Essays in Sociological Theory*, Glencoe: Free Press.

Parsons, Talcott (1979), 'Religious Perspectives in Sociology and Social Psychology', in W. A. Lessa and E. Z. Vogt (eds), *Reader in Comparative Religion*, New York: Harper and Row.

Pattison, Stephen (1989), 'Some Straws for the Bricks: A Basic Introduction to Theological Reflection', *Contact* 99: 2, 4–5.

Pelikan, Jaroslav (1971–89), *The Christian Tradition: A History of the Development of Doctrine*, 5 vols, Chicago: Chicago University Press.

Pittinger, Norman (1969), *Alfred North Whitehead*, London: Lutterworth Press.

Plato (2000), *Republic*, trans. Tom Griffith, Cambridge: Cambridge University Press.

Porvoo Common Declaration (1992), http://www.svenskakyrkan.se/porvoo/eng/1.htm

Prestige, G. L. (1940, 1977), *Fathers and Heretics*, London: SPCK.

Pritchard, James B. (ed.) (1969), *Ancient Near Eastern Texts Relating to the Old Testament*, 3rd ed., Princeton: Princeton University Press.

614

Rad, Gerhard von (1962, 1974), *Old Testament Theology*, trans. D. M. G. Stalker, vol. I, London: SCM Press.

Rad, Gerhard von (1964), 'Interpretation of the Old Testament', in *Essays on Old Testament Hermeneutics*, trans. James Luther Mays, ed. Claus Westermann, 2nd ed., Westminster, John Knox Press.

Rad, Gerhard von (1965, 1975), *Old Testament Theology*, trans. D. M. G. Stalker, vol. II, London: SCM Press.

Rad, Gerhard von (1966), 'The Form-Critical Problem of the Hexateuch', in *The Problem of the Hexateuch and other Essays*, Edinburgh: Oliver and Boyd.

Radcliffe-Brown, A. R. (1945),'Religion and Society', *JRAI*: LXXV, 33–43.

Rahner, Karl (1997), *The Trinity*, trans. Joseph Donceel, New York: Crossroads.

Richardson, C. C. (1953), *Early Christian Fathers*, London: SCM Press.

Richardson, James T. (ed.) (1988), *Money and Power in the New Religions*, Lewiston, Queenston and Lampeter: Edwin Meller Press.

Riezler, Kurt (1940), *Physics and Reality: Lectures of Aristotle on Modern Physics*, New Haven: Yale University Press.

Rinpoche, Patrul (1994), *Words of my Perfect Teacher*, London: Altamira Publications.

Riordan, Suzanne (1992), 'Channeling: a New Revelation?', in J. R. Lewis and J. G. Melton (eds), *Perspectives on the New Age*, Albany: State University of New York Press.

Rist, John (1994), *Augustine: Christian Thought Baptized*, Cambridge: Cambridge University Press.

Robertson, Roland (ed.) (1969), *Sociology of Religion*, Harmondsworth: Penguin.

Robertson Smith, William (1894), *Religion of the Semites*, Edinburgh: A. and C. Black.

Rooden, Peter van (1996), 'Nineteenth-century Representations of Missionary Conversion and the Transformation of Western Christianity', in Peter van der Veer (ed.), *Conversion to Modernities*, London: Routledge.

Rosenzweig, Franz (1971), *The Star of Redemption*, New York: Holt, Rinehart and Winston.

Roszak, Theodore (1973), *The Making of a Counterculture: Reflections on the Technocratic Society and Its Youthful Opposition*, London: Faber and Faber.

Rubenstein, Richard (1966), *After Auschwitz*, New York: Macmillan.

Russell, Bertrand (1961), *The Basic Writings of Bertrand Russell 1903–1959*, London: Allen and Unwin.

Schleiermacher, Friedrich (1990), *A Brief Outline of Theology*, ed. Terrence N. Tice, New York: Lewiston.

Schleiermacher, Friedrich (1999), *The Christian Faith*, trans. H. R. Mackintosh and J. S. Stewart, Edinburgh: T. and T. Clark.

Schnackenburg, R. (1995), *Jesus in the Gospels: A Biblical Christology*, Westminster: John Knox Press.

Schökel, Luis Alonso (1965), *The Inspired Word: Scripture in the Light of Language and Literature*, trans. Francis Martin, New York: Herder and Herder.

Sisson, C. H. (1981), *Selected Poems*, Manchester: Carcanet Press.

Smart, N. (1971), *The Religious Experience of Mankind*, London: Fontana.

Smart, N. (1973), *The Phenomenon of Religion*, London: Macmillan.

Smith, Archie Jr (1978), 'Black Reflections on the Study of New Religious Consciousness', in J. Needleman and G. Baker (eds), *Understanding the New Religions*, New York: Seabury.

Smith, M. (1972), *Readings from the Mystics of Islam*, London: Luzac.

Söderblom, Nathan (1933), *The Living God*, London: Oxford University Press.

Sperber, Dan (1974), *Rethinking Symbolism*, Cambridge: Cambridge University Press.

Spinoza, Benedictus de (2001), *Ethics*, trans. W. H. White and A. H. Stirling, Ware: Wordsworth Editions.

Spiro, Melford E. (1968), 'Religion: Problems of Definition and Explanation', in Michael Banton (ed.), *Anthropological Approaches to the Study of Religion*, London: Tavistock.

Stevenson, J. (1978), *A New Eusebius: Documents Illustrative of the History of the Church*, London: SPCK.

Strauss, Leo (1964), *The City and Man*, Chicago: Rand McNally.

Strauss, Leo (1965), *Natural Right and History*, Chicago: Chicago University Press.

Sutcliffe, Steven (1995), 'The Authority of the Self in New Age Religiosity: The Example of the Findhorn Community', *DISKUS*, 3 (2), pp. 23–42.

Sutcliffe, Steven (1998), 'New Age', in *Britain: An Ethnographical and Historical Exploration*, PhD., The Open University.

Sutcliffe, Steven and Marion Bowman (eds) (2000), *Beyond New Age: Exploring Alternative Spirituality*, Edinburgh: Edinburgh University Press.

Swinton, John (2000), *From Bedlam to Shalom: Towards a Practical Theology of Human Nature, Interpersonal Relationships and Mental Health Care*, New York: Peter Lang.

Taylor, Michael H. (1983), *Learning to Care: Christian Reflection on Pastoral Practice*, London: SPCK.

Thomas, Keith (1983), *Religion and the Decline of Magic*, Harmondsworth: Penguin.

Thompson, Judith and Paul Heelas (1986), *The Way of the Heart: The Rajneesh Movement*, Wellingborough: The Aquarian Press.

Thrower, James (1999), *Religion: The Classical Theories*, Edinburgh: Edinburgh University Press.

Tibi, Bassam (1998), *The Challenge of Fundamentalism*, Berkeley: University of California Press.

Tipton, Steven (1984), *Getting Saved from the Sixties*, London: University of California Press.

Tracy, David (1975), *Blessed Rage of Order*, New York: Seabury.

Tracy, David (1983), 'The Foundations of Practical Theology', in Don S. Browning (ed.), *Practical Theology*, San Francisco: Harper and Row Publishers.

Troeltsch, Ernst (1931), *The Social Teachings of the Christian Churches*, trans. Olive Wyon, London: Allen and Unwin.

Turner, Victor and Edith Turner (1978), *Image and Pilgrimage in Christian Culture*, New York: Columbia University Press.

Tylor, Edward B (1871), *Primitive Culture*, London: John Murray.

Valliere, Paul (2000), *Modern Russian Theology: Bukharev, Soloviev, Bulgakov: Orthodox Theology in a New Key*, Edinburgh: T. and T. Clark.

van der Ven, J. A. (1993), *Practical Theology: An Empirical Approach*, Kampen, The Netherlands: Pharos Publishing.

Vanhoozer, K. J. (2000), 'Exegesis and Hermeneutics', in T. Desmond Alexander and Brian S. Rosner (eds), *New Dictionary of Biblical Theology*, Leicester: Inter-Varsity Press.

Vawter, Bruce (1972), *Biblical Inspiration*, London: Hutchinson.

Wace, Henry and Philip Schaff (eds) (1945), *A Library: Nicene and Post-Nicene Fathers* (Basil of Caeseria, *On the Holy Spirit*, Chapter XVII), Oxford: James Parker.

Wace, Henry and Philip Schaff (eds) (1974), *A Select Library of Nicene and Post-Nicene Fathers*, vol. 7, Michigan: Eerdmans.

Wach, Joachim (1944), *Sociology of Religion*, Chicago: University of Chicago Press.

Wallis, Roy (1976), *The Road to Total Freedom: A Sociological Analysis of Scientology*, London: Heinemann.

Walzer, R. (1962), *Greek into Arabic*, Oxford: Bruno Cassirer.

Weber, Max (1958), *The Protestant Ethic and the Spirit of Capitalism*, New York: Scribners.

Weber, Max (1922) (1966), *The Sociology of Religion*, London: Methuen.

Weber, Max (1977), 'The Social Psychology of the World Religions', in M. Weber, *From Max Weber: Essays in Sociology*, H. H. Gerth and C. Wright Mills (eds), London: Routledge and Kegan Paul.

Wesley, John (1938), *The Journal of the Rev. John Wesley*, ed. Nehemiah Curnock, 8 vols, London: Epworth Press.

Whitehead, Alfred North (1967), *Adventures of Ideas*, New York: Free Press.

Whitehead, Alfred North (1979), *Process and Reality: An Essay in Cosmology*, ed. David Ray Griffin and Donald W. Sherburne, New York: Free Press.

Whitehead, Alfred North (1999), *Religion in the Making*, New York: Fordham University.

Whitehead, Harriet (1987), *Renunciation and Reformulation: A Study of Conversion in an American Sect*, Ithaca and London: Cornell University Press.

Whyte, J. A. (1973), 'New Directions in Practical Theology', *Theology* LXXVI: No. 635.

Willard, Dallas (1991), *The Spirit of the Disciplines*, San Francisco: HarperSanFrancisco.

Williams, J. A. (1994), *The Word of Islam*, Austin: University of Texas Press.

Williams, Rowan (1987, 2001), *Arius: Heresy and Tradition*, London: SCM Press.

Wilson, Bryan (1969), *Religion in Secular Society*, Harmondsworth: Penguin.

Wilson, Bryan (1975), *Magic and the Millennium: Religious Movements of Protest Among Tribal and Third-World Peoples*, St Albans: Paladin.

Wilson, Bryan (1992), *The Social Dimensions of Sectarianism: Sects and New Religious Movements in Contemporary Society*, Oxford: Clarendon Press.

Wilson, Bryan (ed.) (1981), *The Social Impact of New Religious Movements*, New York: Rose of Sharon Press.

Wolterstorff, Nicholas (1995), *Divine Discourse: Philosophical Reflections on the Claim that God Speaks*, Cambridge: Cambridge University Press.

Wood, Matthew (2003, forthcoming), 'Kinship Identity and Nonformative Spiritual Seekership', in P. Collins and S. Coleman (eds), *Religion, Identity and Change: British Perspectives on Global Transformations*. Aldershot: Ashgate.

Wood, Matthew (2003, forthcoming), *Possession, Power and the New Age: Ambiguities of Authority in the Modern World*, Aldershot: Ashgate.

Worsley, Peter (1970), *The Trumpet Shall Sound: A Study of 'Cargo' Cults in Melanesia*, London: Paladin.

Wright, N. T. and M. Borg (1999), *The Meaning of Jesus: Two Visions*, San Francisco: HarperSanFrancisco.

Wuthnow, Robert (1976), *The Consciousness Reformation*, Berkeley: University of California Press.

Yonge, C. D. (trans.) (1993), *The Works of Philo*, Peabody, MA: Hendrickson.

York, Michael (1995), *The Emerging Network: A Sociology of the New Age and Neo-Pagan Movements*, Lanham, MD: Rowman and Littlefield.

Zizouslas, John D. (1985), *Being as Communion: Studies in Personhood and the Church*, London: Darton, Longman and Todd.

Index

Index

Index

Index

Index

Index